The politics of women's suffrage

New Historical PERSPECTIVES

New Historical Perspectives is a book series for early career scholars within the UK and the Republic of Ireland. Books in the series are overseen by an expert editorial board to ensure the highest standards of peer-reviewed scholarship. Commissioning and editing is undertaken by the Royal Historical Society, and the series is published under the imprint of the Institute of Historical Research by the University of London Press.

The series is supported by the Economic History Society and the Past and Present Society.

The politics of women's suffrage

Local, national and international dimensions

Edited by
Alexandra Hughes-Johnson and Lyndsey Jenkins

LONDON
ROYAL HISTORICAL SOCIETY
INSTITUTE OF HISTORICAL RESEARCH
UNIVERSITY OF LONDON PRESS

Published by

UNIVERSITY OF LONDON PRESS
SCHOOL OF ADVANCED STUDY
INSTITUTE OF HISTORICAL RESEARCH
Senate House, Malet Street, London WC1E 7HU

Available to download free or to purchase the hard copy edition at https://www.sas.ac.uk/publications.

ISBNs
978-1-912702-95-4 (hardback edition)
978-1-912702-96-1 (paperback edition)
978-1-912702-99-2 (epub edition)
978-1-912702-97-8 (Kindle edition)
978-1-912702-98-5 (pdf edition)

DOI 10.14296/2111.9781912702985

New Historical
PERSPECTIVES

For Professor Senia Pašeta

Contents

Foreword: the women's movement, war and the vote. Some reflections on 1918 and its aftermath*

Susan R. Grayzel

'As a woman I have no country, as a woman I want no country, as a woman my country is the whole world.'

Virginia Woolf, *Three Guineas* (1938)

I

The epigraph above comes from a text that Virginia Woolf published ten years after British women in the metropole, although not in all the territories of its extensive empire, finally received the vote on equal terms as men as the franchise finally extended across class and gender lines in 1928.[1] These words have inspired generations of women and are both meaningless (because women do live and have lived in countries, states and nations and under political regimes, whether or not they choose them) and yet speak to something that has been at the root of feminism historically. Even in the decidedly national campaigns for women's suffrage, such as those of the United Kingdom illuminated in this volume, the exclusion of women from full political rights based on their perceived biology is truly a global story. For this essay, I'm using Woolf's famous phrase as a touchstone because I want briefly to think aloud about some aspects of feminist internationalism as connected to feminist anti-militarism. I do so in order to address some of the meanings of the winning of partial suffrage for British women in 1918 as the first modern, total war came to an end. The editors, Lyndsey Jenkins and Alexandra Hughes-Johnson, have done an excellent job of stating why the chapters that follow contribute to the

* I am grateful to the editors for inviting me to participate in this exciting volume and for their feedback, as well as to Nadja Durbach, Nicky Gullace, Tammy Proctor and Michelle Tusan for their comments on earlier drafts of this essay.

[1] Virginia Woolf, *Three Guineas* (1938, rpt. Harmondworth, 1982). For crucial work on women's suffrage across the British Empire, see Ian Christopher Fletcher, Philippa Levine and Laura E. Nym Mayhall (eds.), *Women's Suffrage in the British Empire: Citizenship, Nation and Race* (London, 2000).

history of suffrage as a core aspect of Britain's political history. I can only concur and share my admiration for the compelling new research in this volume, which takes us from feminist organizing in local communities to engagement with the global movements for rights and justice, from the nineteenth century to the eve of the Second World War. I hope to offer a way to help us appreciate how they might fit into some aspects of a broader, global history of women's politics.

One thing to note at the outset is the diversity of motivating factors for women to become involved in conventional politics. The essays in this volume attest to that. The modern women's suffrage campaign brought together those concerned with the specific injustices women faced and determined to ameliorate the challenges of living life as a woman. In many cases, these issues had long motivated extra-parliamentary politics. These included, but were not limited to, the inadequacy of wages or living standards, the consequences of the double standard for what was deemed immorality, the ongoing problem of maternal and infant welfare and the inability to gain access to further education or better-paid jobs. When seeking to address what needed to be done, women ran into obstacles to achieving any of these aims because they lacked an overt political voice. For decades prior to the outbreak of the First World War, the International Council of Women (ICW) had avoided endorsing suffrage while helping to expose the subordination of women internationally. The International Women's Suffrage Alliance (IWSA), which emerged from this group in 1904, turned to the franchise as a remedy for this.[2] As women began to acquire a political voice in a few states, British women could turn to their campaigns as models, as Karen Hunt illustrates so helpfully in her essay on what the landmark suffrage victory for Finnish women could mean. We have a more robust vocabulary for understanding citizenship than restricting it solely to the political sphere. However, occupying a position without access to a ballot in a democratic regime solely on the basis of gender served to unite women, despite their differing aims, agendas and, as the early twentieth-century suffrage movement makes clear, their tactics.[3]

[2] This is nicely summed up in M. Kamester and J. Vellacott, 'Introduction' to *Militarism versus Feminism: Writings on Women and War* (London, 1987), pp. 4–6.

[3] For a useful summation of the varieties of citizenship and their meanings for women, see K. Canning and S. O. Rose, 'Introduction' to *Gender, Citizenships and Subjectivities*, ed. K. Canning and S. O. Rose (Oxford, 2002). For an overview of feminist ideas and their response to politics in Europe, see K. Offen, *European Feminisms 1700–1950: A Political History* (Stanford, Calif., 2000). For essential work on the tactics of the militant suffrage campaign, see L. E. Nym Mayhall, *The Militant Suffrage Movement: Citizenship and Resistance in Britain, 1860–1930* (Oxford, 2003).

No matter their motivation, those advocating female equality ran up against anti-suffrage discourses that tended to focus on female incapacity: the ways in which women were not qualified for participation in politics or needed to be sheltered from its corrupting influences in order to safeguard their vital roles as wives and mothers. As Sharon Crozier-De Rosa reminds us in this volume, there was a deeply emotional element to women's political organizing and the responses to it. Fear of what might happen to wives and mothers certainly motivated some anti-suffragists. But fear of what would happen to future wives and mothers if they lacked adequate provisions or redress was precisely what compelled other feminists to engage with and then to enter public political life. Women's politics then as now were intersectional, bound up with class, age, race, and sexuality, but they were also caught up in many states with their assigned roles in relation to their nation.

For instance, male participation in military action and the supposition that women were somehow naturally excluded from this formed a consistent feature of anti-women's suffrage arguments transnationally, perhaps heightened in states with military conscription. Across many geographic areas, the nation-state saw a particular role for men as warriors, for women as mothers. While warriors in modern states needed a voice in the decision making process, what mothers were thought mainly to need was protection. Yet, as sociologist Dorit Geva has pointed out, many states that implemented conscription as an obligation of male citizenship (such as France) always included an exemption for men in certain family circumstances. This meant that family roles and national roles were understood to be competing rather than complementary.[4] In the decades that witnessed the height of activism in favour of women's suffrage, some put forward arguments based less on rejecting such binary categorization about national service than on arguing that equal rights could coexist with difference, that enfranchising women could yield a reordering of priorities for the betterment of women and of the world. Nowhere was this more evident than in women-centred and feminist campaigns against militarism.

II

Feminist anti-militarism was one thread uniting activism as international campaigns for women's suffrage were being invigorated at the turn of the

[4] D. Geva, *Conscription, Family and the Modern State* (Cambridge, 2013). For more on the development of women's anti-militarism, see Offen, *European Feminisms 1700–1950: A Political History*, pp. 144–6, 247–9, 257–61. For a summation of some feminist anti-militarist arguments, see S. R. Grayzel, *Women's Identities at War: Gender, Motherhood, and Politics in Britain and France during the First World War* (Chapel Hill, N.C., 1999), ch. 5.

century and the first decades of the twentieth century. This coincided with a decidedly transnational effort to promote the curtailment of war. In 1899, the same year that the first Hague Convention convened, Austrian Berta von Suttner published the internationally acclaimed, bestselling novel *Lay Down Your Arms!*, detailing the sufferings that war placed upon wives and mothers.[5] While it would take international law a long time to recognize the status of civilians, and even longer to say anything about wartime sexual violence, the 1899 Hague Convention acknowledged, for the first time, that there should be 'undefended' places protected from the violence of modern war 'even for the purposes of reprisal'.[6] In 1905, Suttner became the first woman to win the Nobel Peace Prize in recognition of her continued work on disarmament, and two years later, a second Hague Convention resumed to promote international efforts to regulate if not curtail war.

Following the Russo-Japanese war and further tensions between the Great Powers over their imperial holdings, the Second Hague Convention occurred against a backdrop aware of the increased potential for international conflict.[7] As one of the opening speeches perhaps over-optimistically asserted, 'the whole civilized world' felt a 'sentiment of international amenity' that fostered the limiting of war's effects.[8] Such sentiments found expression in the petitions and proposals brought forward by peace societies and other extra-governmental organizations excluded from addressing the conference and partaking in its discussions. Significantly, an exception was made to such rules in order to permit delegates of the ICW to meet with the Conference's president. As the president then noted, this group 'representing as it did millions of women all over the world' deserved to be heard, and he assured them 'that the Conference wished to reduce as much as possible the suffering which war entailed upon all, and especially upon women.'[9]

[5] Bertha von Suttner is credited with persuading Albert Nobel to create the Peace Prize a few years after the publication of her novel, *Die Waffen Nieder* (1889) or *Lay Down Your Arms*, which emphasized the war-induced suffering of women and children. See D. S. Patterson, *The Search for Negotiated Peace: Women's Activism and Citizen Diplomacy in World War I* (London, 2008), p. 7; Offen, *European Feminisms 1700–1950: A Political History*, p. 247.

[6] See Articles 62 and 63 of the Hague Conventions of 1899, 'The Avalon Project at Yale Law School' <www.yale.edu/lawweb/avalon/lawofwar/hague> [accessed 20 Oct. 2018]. For an introductory overview of international law on such issues, see C. Eboe-Osuji, *International Law and Sexual Violence in Armed Conflicts* (Leiden and Boston, 2012).

[7] 'Latest News: The Second Peace Conference', *The Times*, 15 June 1907.

[8] Speech of President Nelidoff, cited in 'The Hague Conference', *The Times*, 17 June 1907.

[9] Quoted in 'The Peace Conference', *The Times*, 19 June 1907.

As a product of the last large-scale international gathering to restrict military action before the outbreak of the First World War, the Hague Conventions of 1907 affirmed the protection of particular spaces, articulating that attack 'by whatever means, of towns, villages, dwellings or buildings which are undefended is prohibited'.[10] Yet the Naval Convention of 1907 allowed for the bombardment by sea of 'military works, military or naval establishments, depots of arms or war materiel, workshops or plant[s] which could be utilized for the needs of the hostile fleet or army, and the ships of war in the harbor'.[11] In other words, one segment of the agreement protected 'undefended' locales (with their women and children) but another made anything that even potentially served a military purpose – anything that helped the army or navy – a legitimate target. This obviously had implications for internationalist feminist anti-war activism prior to 1914 that spoke out against the vulnerability of domestic spaces inhabited by women and children.[12]

Another potent strand of feminist opposition to war rooted it directly in the female, especially the maternal, body. This was articulated perhaps most forcefully at the time by South African Olive Schreiner in her 1911 *Woman and Labour*, whose publication notably occurred at the height of UK suffrage militancy, a movement also rooted in martyred bodies.[13] For Schreiner, women pay 'the first cost on all human life', producing the primal munitions of war as mothers and yet, she continues, such beliefs are not limited to 'actual' mothers; 'there is, perhaps, no woman, whether she have borne children, or be merely potentially a child-bearer' who can look at a battlefield strewn with dead and not think 'so many mother's

[10] Amendment of Article 25, Hague Convention 1907, in 'The Laws of War', at 'The Avalon Project at Yale Law School', <www.yale.edu/lawweb/avalon/lawofwar/hague04> [accessed 20 Oct. 2018] and also cited in T. D. Biddle, 'Air Power', in *The Laws of War: Constraints on Warfare in the Western World*, ed. M. Howard, G. J. Andreopoulos and M. R. Shulman (New Haven, Conn., 1994), p. 142.

[11] 'Article 1 and Article 2', 'Bombardment by Naval Forces in Time of War (Hague IX) 18 Oct. 1907' in 'The Laws of War', at 'The Avalon Project at Yale Law School', <www.yale.edu/lawweb/avalon/lawofwar/hague09> [accessed 20 Oct. 2018] and also quoted in Biddle, 'Air Power', p. 143.

[12] Such activism has been discussed briefly in Offen, *European Feminisms 1700–1950: A Political History*, and for Britain in J. Liddington, *The Long Road to Greenham: Feminism and Anti-Militarism in Britain since 1820* (London, 1989), and most fully in S. Cooper, 'The Work of Women in Nineteenth Century Continental European Peace Movements', *Peace & Change*, ix (1984), 11–28 and her *Patriotic Pacifism: Waging War in Europe 1815–1914* (New York, 1991).

[13] For a thoughtful critique of the militant suffrage use of hunger strikes and responses to force-feeding, see S. Pedersen, 'A Knife to the Heart', *London Review of Books*, xl (2018).

sons'. More significant for the discussion here is Schreiner's equation of 'munition' with flesh and particularly with the bodies of soldiers; if both men and women bear the cost of war, the battle zone imagined here is laden with male combatant, not female non-combatant, bodies.[14]

A more disturbing imagined prospect of broader, even limitless, battle zones strewn with the bodies of men, women and children came with the prospect of war in the air. A little known work by Berta von Suttner, *The Barbarization of the Sky* (published in 1912), pointed out what this could mean for women. Writing in response to the innovative documented use of military air power (in an imperial context by Italy in its war with Libya), von Suttner issued a call of action to all women.

> But to her in whose mind this terrible question of war revolves, conscience dictates plainly! Do not remain silent and hardened and resigned; do not suppress your conscientious scruples and deepest convictions with a hopeless sigh: 'It will be of no avail.' Everything avails … [and the] means would be so simple; it lies close at hand … the powers must effect a union, establish an international law which forbids throwing bombs from airships and aeroplanes, as they voiced it at the first Hague Conference.[15]

This advocacy to prevent not merely war but to curtail specific, modern modes of war-making resonated and challenged a coterie of feminists as the First World War and its introduction of the harrowing weapons of modern war unfolded.

At the outbreak of war in 1914, a conflict that transformed the political, economic, cultural and social landscape of several continents and instituted a new era of militarization, a range of British women's suffrage activists echoed prewar feminist ideas about women's roles as peacemakers and natural opponents of war. In South Wales, Women's Social and Political Union (WSPU) organizer Annie Williams declared: 'The war ought never to have been … If five years ago the men had enfranchised the women and given them a share in the government of the country it is possible that

[14] O. Schreiner, *Woman and Labour* (1911, rpt. London, 1978), p. 170. See Grayzel, *Women's Identities at War: Gender, Motherhood, and Politics in Britain and France during the First World War*; Liddington, *The Long Road to Greenham: Feminism and Anti-Militarism in Britain since 1820*; Offen, *European Feminisms 1700–1950: A Political History*; and Patterson, *The Search for Negotiated Peace: Women's Activism and Citizen Diplomacy in World War I*, among other works that have noted the prevalence of linking maternity to women's anti-war arguments during and before the war.

[15] B. von Suttner, *Die Barbarisierung der Luft* (Berlin, 1912); contemporary translation as 'Making the Air Barbarous' published in *The Chautauquan*, Mar. 1913. A new English-language translation was published in 2016 as B. von Suttner, *The Barbarization of the Sky*, trans. B. Cooper, ed. H. E. May (The Hague, 2016).

there would have been no war to-day ... emancipating women would have resulted in the attainment of a higher state of civilization.'[16] As Alexandra Hughes-Johnson reminds us in Chapter 5 in this volume, a belief that women needed to maintain their work for the vote during the war by 'continuing to realise the unity of women' and their task to uplift all humanity shows echoes of such sentiments.

The war split the women's suffrage movement internationally – as has been well documented – and it did so for both militant and non-militant suffrage campaigners in the UK. As Jo Vellacott helpfully explains, there were several kinds of feminisms operating in 1914, united in the struggle for the vote, which were broken apart by their differing attitudes to the war.[17] Many activists for female enfranchisement turned to support the national war effort of the states to which they belonged. Others began to advocate to halt the war (a more dangerous stance in many nations). Still others focused on helping the victims of war, including those suffering domestically from the immediate economic downturn caused by the war's outbreak, from the loss/absence of male breadwinners and failure of separation allowances to materialize, and from the transformation of warfare itself. Historians like Vellacott and Ryland Wallace have noted that women's suffrage campaigners created workrooms to produce socks and shirts for men in the military, sewing and knitting circles and drives to fund war-related charities. Even some women who were colonial subjects contributed to their imperial states' war efforts.[18]

Some British suffrage activists, such as Sylvia Pankhurst and her associates in the East London Federation of Suffragettes as it morphed into the Workers' Suffrage Federation, not only provided material aid, including to wives and mothers of men in the military locally, but also campaigned in favour of industrial action and against the war and conscription. Pankhurst's postwar memoir, *The Home Front: A Mirror to Life in England during the First World War*, appearing in 1932, details Pankhurst's experiences from the outbreak of war in 1914 through 1916.[19] Its war story centres on working-class

[16] *Free Press of Monmouthshire*, 12 Feb. 1915, quoted in R. Wallace, *The Women's Suffrage Movement in Wales* (Cardiff, 2009), p. 219.

[17] J. Vellacott, *Pacifists, Patriots and the Vote: The Erosion of Democratic Suffragism in Britain During the First World War* (Basingstoke, 2007).

[18] Wallace, *The Women's Suffrage Movement in Wales*, ch. 6; Vellacott, *Pacifists, Patriots and the Vote: The Erosion of Democratic Suffragism in Britain During the First World War*. I discuss some of the transnational aspects of how the war divided feminists as well as the support of some colonized women, often for strategic reasons, in *Women and the First World War* (Harlow, 2002), and more fully in the forthcoming second edition.

[19] E. S. Pankhurst, *The Home Front: A Mirror to Life in England during the First World War* (1987, rpt. London, 1932). Her suffrage memoir appeared a year earlier: E. S. Pankhurst, *The Suffragette Movement: An Intimate Account of Persons and Ideals* (1977, rpt. London, 1931).

women and their children and calls attention to the multiple levels of violence experienced both externally and internally. Like her account of being a suffragette, it blends the personal and the social, and is unstinting in its attacks on the real enemy of non-combatants, especially women at home – war itself. Building on her prior study of Pankhurst's activism, in this volume Katherine Connelly shows how much models of transnational, women-led activism to relieve the suffering of working-class women under 'ordinary' circumstances, let alone the enormous new challenges posed by a total war, contributed to new ways for Pankhurst to develop her lifelong advocacy for equity.[20]

In a variety of participant states, individual women spoke out against the war and the damage it inflicted on women as feminists, albeit usually also as a minority of voices. In March 1915, a gathering of socialist women from across Europe met in Berne to condemn the war. That April, women assembled in The Hague to call for a negotiated peace. The Hague Women's Peace Congress of 1915 gave rise to an organization, the Women's International League (later for Peace and Freedom) that would serve as a cornerstone for actions during and after the war. The UK's branch was among the largest, incorporating suffragists like Helena Swanwick, who had resigned her leadership position over the pro-war turn of the National Union of Women's Suffrage Societies (NUWSS). Despite censorship and the unpopularity of criticizing the war effort, suffragists like Catherine Marshall continued to articulate a feminism that saw itself allied with the struggle against militarism and war. In her 1915 essay 'The Future of Women in Politics', Marshall wrote that such a future depended on 'whether the women in the different nations and the different classes' advocate for 'the ideal of Right, instead of Might, of cooperation instead of conflict'. What they lacked in political or business experience, they made up for 'as mothers and heads of households' who could best determine the path to a peaceful postwar reconstruction. As Woolf would articulate later, Marshall saw women as a group apart who, having learnt the cost of supporting a status quo that had led to war, were thus poised to support greater internationalism.[21]

[20] See K. Connelly, *Sylvia Pankhurst: Suffragette, Socialist and Scourge of Empire* (London, 2013), as well as her chapter in this volume.

[21] C. Marshall, 'The future of women in politics', *Labour Year Book* (1916), reprinted in *Militarism versus Feminism: Writings on Women and War*, eds. M. Kamester and J. Vellacott (London, 1987), pp. 46–50. For more on wartime feminist anti-militarism, see Grayzel, *Women's Identities at War: Gender, Motherhood, and Politics in Britain and France during the First World War*; Liddington, *The Long Road to Greenham: Feminism and Anti-Militarism in Britain since 1820*; and Patterson, *The Search for Negotiated Peace: Women's Activism and Citizen Diplomacy in World War I*.

Across the belligerent states, criticizing the war could prove costly, as activists who spoke out were arrested and jailed. One salient exemplar – both because of her obscurity and her defence – can be seen in the trial for the crime of 'defeatism' (advocating a negotiated peace settlement) in 1917 of Parisian schoolteacher Hélène Brion. She had argued that she could not be accused of a 'political crime' when she had no 'political rights'. Moreover, she insisted, in language that echoed across national borders, that it was her feminism that made her an enemy of war: 'war is the triumph of brute force; the feminist cannot triumph except by moral force and intellectual valor'.[22]

If women's anti-war rhetoric were a product both of their exclusion from political rights and/or their identification as mothers, it evolved in reaction to the altered circumstances of the First World War. This was especially true as modern forms of warmaking brought the war's relentless violence into the metropole. Air power and chemical weapons both arrived in the spring of 1915, and feminists like Sylvia Pankhurst were among the eye-witnesses to the impact that air power made on Britain. As Pankhurst describes in *The Home Front*, her first air raid came in a burst of noise: 'I was writing at home one evening. On the silence arose an ominous grinding … growing in volume … throbbing, pulsating … filling the air with its sound … Then huge reports smote the ear, shattering, deafening, and the roar of falling masonry.' Pankhurst rallied others in the house by telling them, 'No use to worry; only a few houses will be struck among the thousands.' Her own recollections are somewhat different: 'the thought of the bombs crashing down on the densely populated city was appalling – yet for our household I had no least shade of apprehension and for myself Life had no great claim. I was only a member of the salvage corps, saving and succouring as I might amid this wreckage.' Pankhurst's account is far removed from the portrait of stoicism and calm emphasized in the newspaper reports on the arrival of air power, but Pankhurst did not judge anyone who lived through the attacks. Instead, she condemned air raid tourists, those 'well-dressed people in motors, journalists, photographers, high military officials' visiting the East End to see 'the devastation wrought by last night's air raid'. When they seem disappointed not to see more damage, Pankhurst reminds us that yet, if they had only looked a little closer, they could have seen 'miserable dwellings, far from fit for human families, poorly-dressed women of working sort, with sad, worn faces; and others, sunk lower, just covered, no

[22] H. Brion, *Déclaration lue au premier conseil de guerre* (Epône, 1918), as quoted in Grayzel, *Women's Identities at War: Gender, Motherhood, and Politics in Britain and France during the First World War*, pp. 182–3.

more in horrid rags … half-clad neglected little children – sadder these even than the havoc wrought by German bombs.'[23]

The parallels that Pankhurst evokes here between the long-term killing effects of deprivation and poverty and the new menace of aerial attack continue throughout her account of life in wartime Britain. Her insistence that it was not weaponry alone that had made things worse for those already facing poverty joins feminist anti-militarism to other struggles for equality and resources. When Pankhurst journeys to the north of England in the late autumn of 1915, arriving just after a Zeppelin raid, she finds damaged tenements and stories of orphaned children, victims who survived 'grievously dismembered' and, above all: 'Sad-eyed mothers [who] looked out forlornly from near-by doorways, their spirits long since crushed by the drab hopelessness of the slums, stunned by the new fear that even this dreariness would tumble about their ears.'[24] This is another way in which we need to reassess the arrival and legacy of this war, not just as expanding the spaces and victims of wartime violence, but also as confirming a sense that the most vulnerable were made unbearably so.

In short, the use of new industrialized techniques for waging war during the First World War literally altered the landscape of that conflict for those in the United Kingdom and helped to solidify for some activists the growing connectedness of feminist demands for women's rights and against military violence. When the war came to an end, women activists demanded to be heard during the Paris Peace Conference and, as Glenda Sluga and Mona Siegel's work has shown, women saw the international stage as one on which they could participate in new ways. Women organized a series of global protests and arranged meetings to assert their rights in 1919, and they won the ability to participate in the newly created League of Nations.[25] This gave some of the newly enfranchised a launching pad for continuing to link feminism with their advocacy for peace and justice.

Feminist anti-militarists, continuing prewar strains of feminist internationalism with their long-term roots in extra-parliamentary action,

[23] Pankhurst, *The Home Front: A Mirror to Life in England during the First World War*, pp. 191–3.

[24] Pankhurst, *The Home Front: A Mirror to Life in England during the First World War*, p. 373.

[25] G. Sluga, 'Female and national self-determination: a gender re-reading of "the apogee of nationalism"', *Nations and Nationalism*, vi (2000), 495–521; M. L. Siegel, *Peace On Our Terms: The Global Battle for Women's Rights After the First World War* (New York, 2020). Sluga reminds us that the 'international' was an 'important site of activity for women eager both to create a "feminine" political space and an alternative to the masculine space of nations' (pp. 495–6).

warned the postwar world not only of the horrors to be inflicted upon all bodies in the next conflict, but also of their consequences for domestic life. The arrival of aerial warfare provided a way for such activists to insist that all women now had a comparable experience of being exposed to danger as that of male soldiers. Several argued that the prospect of another war using the first weapons of mass destruction – chemical arms and air power – raised the stakes for the survival of humanity. This framing of disarmament as a women's issue was not new, but the context was widening.[26]

The commitment of the international feminist community to recognizing the expanded stakes and territories of modern war was evident throughout the immediate postwar meetings of the Women's International League for Peace and Freedom (WILPF). At its first postwar International Meeting in Zurich in 1919, WILPF confirmed its commitment to world disarmament, again highlighting, in the well-known words of American Jane Addams's presidential address, that 'women only benefit in a world based on justice not force'.[27] Tellingly, that justice involved asking the League of Nations to take actions that encompassed both air disarmament and the endowment of motherhood.[28] Thus did postwar feminists confront what the warfare state might bring and promote an ideal of the welfare state. At the 1921 meeting in Zurich, Addams again pointed out the underlying logic of feminist anti-militarism. War, she argued, destroyed what mothers value most: 'this world war mobilized not only armies but entire populations, the world has seen, as never before, what war means in the lives of little children in every country to the world'.[29]

In the interwar era, as states began to prepare measures to protect entire civilian populations including women and children from modern weaponry by inventing civil defence, enfranchised women mobilized in opposition, both within their nations and across borders. By the time the League of Nations was preparing seriously to take up the issues of disarmament at the start of the 1930s, feminists in groups such as WILPF were demanding

[26] See further discussion of this in S. R. Grayzel, *At Home and Under Fire: Air Raids and Culture in Britain from the Great War to the Blitz* (Cambridge, 2012). This linkage also continued into the nuclear age; see Liddington, *The Long Road to Greenham: Feminism and Anti-Militarism in Britain since 1820*.

[27] J. Addams, 'Presidential Address', in *Report of the International Congress of Women Zurich 1919* (Geneva, 1919), p. 1.

[28] *Report of the International Congress of Women Zurich 1919* (Geneva, 1919), pp. 69, 85. A more detailed account of this meeting can be found in Siegel, *Peace On Our Terms: The Global Battle for Women's Rights After the First World War.*

[29] Addams, 'Presidential Address' in *Report of Third International Congress of Women Vienna 1921* (Geneva, 1921), p. 2.

'definite and drastic measures of disarmament on land, sea and air … the abolition of air warfare … [and the] international control of civil aviation'.[30] When it became clear that a long-anticipated disarmament conference would occur the following year, Britain's branch of this international organization spent time gathering signatures to show popular support for disarmament. By July 1931, over 1 million signatures had been collected by this group and by others urging the government to take action on immediate disarmament. On the eve of the Disarmament Conference in early January of 1932, the number was close to 2 million.[31] A few days after the conference opened, a dramatic demonstration of popular support for such ideas occurred in Geneva when, on 6 February 1932, some 700 representatives of over fifteen women's international organizations, religious groups, peace societies, trade unionists, workers and students addressed the Conference's delegates. In offering these documents, the specific appeal of women was clear.

> Behind each of these eight million names stands … a human being oppressed by a great fear – the fear of the destruction of our civilization … It is not for ourselves alone that we plead, but for the generations to come. To us women, as mothers, the thought of what another great war would mean for our children is the strongest incentive impelling us to spend ourselves in the endeavour to make their lives secure from such a disastrous fate.[32]

This familiar language of a call for peace and disarmament based on women's maternal role shows the long continuity of such emotionally charged appeals. Yet there is something new in this context: a fear of the end of 'civilization', human society as such, and the task of preventing that end falling to women as citizens as well as mothers. That the Disarmament Conference tried and failed to adopt measures definitively prohibiting the use of the two most frightening modern tools of war – air power that could readily disperse chemical weapons – left a bitter legacy for feminist anti-militarists. Sylvia Pankhurst raised funds in 1936 to erect a small 'Anti-Air War Memorial' in Essex. Literally placed in a backyard, the monument

[30] General Resolution of the International Executive Committee of the Women's International League, Jan. 1931, attached to Minutes, British Section – Women's International League for Peace and Freedom, 19 Jan. 1931. British Library of Political and Economic Science (London), WILPF 1/7.

[31] See Minutes, British Section – Women's International League for Peace and Freedom, 14 July 1931 and 12 Jan. 1932. BLPES WILPF 1/7 and 1/8.

[32] M. A. Dingman, president of the Disarmament Committee of the Women's Organisations, quoted in *Vox Populi* (Geneva, 1932), p. 17. Another account of this session is found in 'Towards disarmament: campaign notes published by the National Peace Council' (London), 13 Feb. 1932.

depicts an aerial torpedo, and its inscription reads, 'To those who in 1932 upheld the right to use bombing planes/this monument is raised as a protest against war in the air.'[33] After these failures, the second half of the 1930s witnessed many of the horrors that feminist anti-militarists had been trying to stop: the return of poison gas to devastating effect in Ethiopia and the return of aerial bombing campaigns killing civilian men, women and children in Spain. Some anti-militarist feminists joined the Communist International-sponsored Women's World Committee Against War and Fascism, but fighting fascism outside of the context of war challenged a commitment to nonviolence as the decade progressed. That British women turned to such international movements is evident in Maurice J. Casey's essay on the engagement of British and Irish suffragettes with international communism. And while the form and content might be new, as Lyndsey Jenkins shows us in her chapter in this volume, the ongoing importance of class politics for working-class feminists remains crucial to the story of women's activism throughout the twentieth century. British women played a decisive role in these and other campaigns that tied feminist concerns to struggles that lay beyond the borders of the nation/national. There are many examples of interwar women responding not just as particular members of human society but also as feminists motivated by the potential destruction of domesticity, home and life that modern war threatened.

III

But here, too, is a moment when the entire story of feminist engagement with the polity and with war shifts if we widen our lens. For the destruction of home life was a fact of the First World War in more places, I would argue, than it was not. In the global context of this war, in numerous areas exposed to invasion and occupation, in the cities of the Central Powers, in the routes travelled by the millions of displaced persons in the Russian and Ottoman Empires, in the genocidal attacks on Armenians, in the famine and locust-infested lands of what would become the Middle East and across the war zones of Africa, the fundamental inseparability of the home and war fronts becomes even clearer. And this demonstrable violation of the borders between the home and war fronts did not need air power in order to be achieved.

[33] In 1925, the Geneva Anti-Gas Protocol had authorized a no-first-use of chemical arms, but activists wanted more. This is discussed in Grayzel, *At Home and Under Fire: Air Raids and Culture in Britain from the Great War to the Blitz*, as is Pankhurst's 'Anti-Air War Memorial'. For more on this, see the dossier 'Anti-Air War Memorial', Woodford Wells, Essex, National Inventory of War Memorials, Imperial War Museum.

Linking wartime service and/or sacrifice and the gaining of votes for women was more complicated where there was still no vote or a differentiated access to the vote remained. If we consider the women in the vast empires clashing during this war, we quickly realize how much we still need to learn about their experiences and about their diverse, complicated relationships to politics. Despite these limitations, a global perspective compels a different version of the connections between women's suffrage and this war. In order to understand more fully the legacy of campaigns for women's suffrage and those of the First World War in the British Empire, we need to pay attention to the women who do not figure in a history still centred on the United Kingdom.

Two examples may aid us in starting to do so. The status of women in Jamaica, for instance, clearly reveals the limits of the victory of the Representation of the People Act. Here it was only in 1919 that women over twenty-five years of age who earned at least £50 and paid £2 in taxes could vote for the Legislative Council that helped govern the colony; it was not until 1944 that women could stand for office in this body. As was the case elsewhere, possessing even this limited vote inspired different types of political activism, some concentrating on women's roles as workers and others highlighting anti-colonialism and the intersectional challenges faced by Black women.[34]

Similarly, Sumita Mukherjee's compelling recent work reminds us that the first public demands for a women's vote emerged in India in 1917 with the creation of the Women's Indian Association (WIA). This was followed by partial enfranchisement for some propertied women in Mumbai and Madras in 1921. The WIA affiliated itself to the IWSA in 1923, and key figures agitating for full voting rights for all Indian women increasingly interacted with internationalist networks during the interwar era. Yet here, too, anti-colonial nationalism could subsume feminist demands for some women. The receipt of female enfranchisement would await independence; yet, as Mukherjee explains, this resulted from active struggles amid ongoing conversations that had to acknowledge broader contexts, including the imperial, the national and the international, all of which dated to the war

[34] See L. Vassell, 'The movement for the vote for women, 1918–1919', *Jamaican Historical Review*, xviii (1993), 40–54, as discussed in H. Altink, '"We are equal to men in ability to do anything": African Jamaican women and citizenship in the interwar years', in *Women's Activism: Global Perspectives from 1890s to the Present*, ed. Francisca de Haan et al. (London, 2013), pp. 79, 82–3. Without commenting further, Jad Adams lists 1944 as the year in which Jamaican women could vote, but having voting rights in a sovereign nation was clearly something different; see J. Adams, *Women & the Vote: A World History* (Oxford, 2014), p. 438. Jamaica became an independent state in 1962.

years themselves. Such efforts included critical work by Indian women campaigners overseas and their transformative attendance at international interwar conferences. Some of these participants offered a crucial rebuttal to internationalist feminist claims: 'I have nothing against American or English sisters', argued Indian nationalist activist Madame Cama, but 'to establish internationalism in the world there must be nations first'.[35] Equal citizenship for women within some nation-states thus understandably might take precedence over advocating for a feminist agenda around disarmament, war and peace. Such activists might not be persuaded by a statement that women neither had nor wanted a country.

Looking even briefly at these examples reveals a divide between what fully enfranchised women could claim about the dangers of modern war to home life and family, deploying universalist languages of female solidarity, and what struck women without such status as priorities. This tension between feminist arguments against war and militarism, but also against fascism and imperialism (which might require violent resistance), merits further exploration as we look at the legacies of 1918 for women in Britain, its empire and elsewhere.

IV

That many, but decisively far from all, women in Europe and North America at least gained the franchise and equal political citizenship in the immediate aftermath of the First World War could be seen as recognizing a changing definition of citizenship – one that could encompass diverse aspects of women's lives and contributions to their countries, and recognize that different forms of service and sacrifice might suffice to justify full enrolment in the polity. Yet other definitions of citizenship might allow us to see how women fit into new relationships with the state, for example, via the concept of citizenship regimes.[36] Wartime and perhaps postwar citizenship vividly demonstrates how such an understanding of citizenship, which emphasizes duties over rights, flourishes in circumstances that demand individuals prioritize collective needs over their own. The differing ways in which gender affected how men and women felt and understood

[35] S. Mukherjee, *Indian Suffragettes: Female Identities and Transnational Networks* (New Delhi, 2018), Cama quote on p. 155.

[36] K. Hunt and K. Rygiel (ed.), *(En)Gendering the War on Terror: War Stories and Camouflaged Politics* (Hampshire, 2007), p. 5. See also J. Jenson and S. D. Philips, 'Regime shift: new citizenship practices in Canada', *International Journal of Canadian Studies*, iii (1996), 111–36, and the discussion of both in L. Noakes and S. R. Grayzel, 'Defending the home(land): gendering civil defence from the First World War to the "War on Terror"', in *Gender and Conflict since 1914*, ed. A. Carden-Coyne (Basingstoke, 2013).

their citizenship in the aftermath of the war is crucial for understanding what the war did and did not do to shape individuals' interactions with the polity and the state after 1918, even where they possessed a vote.

Paying attention to the female colonial subjects of Britain may help us calibrate our sense of the triumphs of 1918 (and even 1928). But we might also benefit from placing the British experience in relationship to key democratic allies, which have produced a range of contemporary and scholarly discussions precisely because the United States allowed some women similarly to gain access to the vote in the war's aftermath and France continued to exclude them. The long struggle for American women's suffrage culminating in 1920 with the passage and ratification of the Nineteenth Amendment to the Constitution did little to assist Black women and nothing to address the status of Native Americans, who were not yet considered citizens. The ability to exercise this right was limited by race and geography. However, in France, the denial of a vote to women came against a backdrop of debates in a legislature happy to recognize their sacrifices and service, but not to equate their labour and loss with reasons to give them the vote.[37]

When Britain passed the Representation of the People Act in 1918, restricting female suffrage by age, it sent a clear message that 'Votes for Women' – whether argued vociferously as necessary on the exact same terms as men or in solidarity with efforts to end property qualifications for voting – was being disregarded. As this volume helps us see, that outcome led to complex postwar legacies for activist women. Women's relationship with the postwar state thus marks a profound shift in ways that men's relationship with democratic regimes, at least, did not. Moreover, the wider European project of restoring the world shattered by the war and the internationalist project of preventing future conflict via the League of Nations offered new opportunities for women as women. If the League set out to hasten disarmament, women and feminist organizations took it as their special right to protest against the expansion of warfare via air power into their homes and daily life. A League set on defining equitable working conditions also created subcommittees to address the traffic in women. The full extent of the role played by women in reshaping the postwar world is

[37] For the United States, in a vast literature, see the recent work of E. C. Dubois, *Suffrage: Women's Long Battle for the Vote* (New York, 2020); M. S. Jones, *Vanguard: How Black Women Broke Barriers, Won the Vote and Insisted on Equality for All* (New York, 2020); L. Tetrault, *The Myth of Seneca Falls: Memory and the Women's Suffrage Movement, 1848–1898* (Chapel Hill, N.C., 2017); and see my summation of French debates in Grayzel, *Women's Identities at War: Gender, Motherhood, and Politics in Britain and France during the First World War* and C. Bard, *Les Filles de Marianne: Histoire des feminisms, 1914–1940* (Paris, 1995).

only starting to receive the attention that it merits. Some of this restoration took place on the most intimate of levels as women became caregivers for the millions of men whose health was ruined or profoundly altered by the war.[38] Some of it took place on the local level, in parishes and the new Women's Institutes, and some of it took place in, as Woolf asserted, the country that was the whole world.[39] We need all of these histories – from individual lives to collective global action – to appreciate fully what the second century after suffrage might yield.

[38] See M. Roper, 'Little Ruby's hand: young women and the emotional experience of caregiving in Britain after the First World War', in *Total War: An Emotional History*, ed. C. Langhamer, L. Noakes and C. Siebrecht (Oxford, 2020).

[39] M. Andrews, *The Acceptable Face of Feminism: The Women's Institute as Social Movement* (London, 2015); I. Sharp and M. Stibbe (ed.), *Women Activists Between War & Peace: Europe, 1918–1923* (London, 2017); H. McCarthy, *Women of the World: The Rise of the Female Diplomat* (London, 2014).

List of tables

List of contributors

Maurice J. Casey is the current Historian in Residence at EPIC The Irish Emigration Museum and the Irish Department of Foreign Affairs. He completed his DPhil at the University of Oxford in 2020, where his research explored the transnational networks of Irish radical women from 1916 to 1939. His research interests include histories of radical internationalism, the Irish Revolution and political emigration to the USSR during the interwar period.

Katherine Connelly is a historian and lecturer at the London centres of Arcadia and Lawrence universities. She is the author of *Sylvia Pankhurst: Suffragette, Socialist and Scourge of Empire* (London: Pluto Press, 2013) and edited and introduced Sylvia Pankhurst's manuscript about her tours of North America, now published as *A Suffragette in America: Reflections on Prisoners, Pickets and Political Change* (London: Pluto Press, 2019). Kate is interested in the transatlantic links of the East End suffragettes and is currently researching the life of Zelie Emerson.

Sharon Crozier-De Rosa is Associate Professor in History at the University of Wollongong, Australia. Her research is situated at the intersections of feminist activism, emotions, imperial/colonial and violence histories. Her books include *Shame and the Anti-Feminist Backlash: Britain, Ireland and Australia, 1890–1920* (2018), *Remembering Women's Activism* (co-authored with Vera Mackie, 2019) and *Sources for the History of Emotions* (co-edited with Peter Stearns and Katie Barclay, 2020). She is Deputy Editor of *Women's History Review* and is an International Federation for Research in Women's History Board Member.

Nicoletta Gullace is an Associate Professor of History at the University of New Hampshire in the United States. Her first book, *'The Blood of Our Sons:' Men, Women and the Renegotiation of British Citizenship during the First World War* (Palgrave, 2002) won the North American Conference of British Studies book prize and was selected as a Choice Outstanding Academic Title. Her current research deals with the commercialization of history in Britain and the United States through television, film, commemorative events, and merchandizing. Gullace has an ongoing research interest in suffrage culture and has frequent engagements speaking on the Edwardian Era, *Downton Abbey*, *The Crown*, and Britain's royal family in a variety of public history forums.

Alexandra Hughes-Johnson is a Research Associate at the University of Oxford and a Research Portfolio Manager at the Economic and Social Research Council, UK Research and Innovation. She completed her PhD at Royal Holloway, University of London, where her research focused on the women's suffrage movement in Wimbledon and the political career of Rose Lamartine Yates. Her research interests more broadly include women's memorialization of the British women's suffrage campaign and women's interwar political activism.

Karen Hunt is Professor Emerita of Modern British History at Keele University, UK. She has published widely on the history of women's politics in local, national and transnational settings. Suffrage has been a thread through her research from *Equivocal Feminists* (Cambridge University Press, 1996) and *Socialist Women*, co-written with June Hannam (Routledge, 2002) to 'Class and adult suffrage in Britain during the Great War' in J. Purvis & J. Hannam (eds), *The British Women's Suffrage Campaign. National & International Perspectives* (Routledge, 2021).

Beth Jenkins is a Senior Policy Manager of Children's Rights at the Welsh Government. She recently completed a British Academy Postdoctoral Fellowship at the University of Essex and has research interests in women's education, work and political cultures across nineteenth and twentieth-century Britain. Her first monograph, *Graduate Women and Work in Wales, 1872-1939: Nationhood, Networks and Community*, will be published in 2022. She is also co-editing a collection of essays titled *Gender in Modern Welsh History from 1750 to 2000.*

Lyndsey Jenkins is a Leverhulme Early Career Fellow at Queen Mary, University of London researching post-war Labour women MPs. She is a historian of women, politics, and social change. Her first book, *Lady Constance Lytton: Aristocrat, Suffragette, Martyr*, was a *Sunday Times* biography of the year and shortlisted for the Slightly Foxed/Biographer's Club Best First Biography Prize. She earned her PhD from Wolfson College, Oxford, in 2018, and the resulting monograph, *Sisters and Sisterhood: The Kenney Family, Class and Suffrage c.1890-1965* was published by Oxford University Press in 2021. She was awarded the Caroline Spurgeon Award from the British Federation of Women Graduates in 2017. She is a former civil servant and government speechwriter.

Anna Muggeridge recently completed her doctorate on women in politics and public life in the Black Country in the first half of the twentieth century, at the University of Worcester. She works as an Associate Lecturer in History at the University of Worcester and in the heritage sector, and is a Visiting Research Fellow at the Mile End Institute at Queen Mary, University of London. She is currently embarking on a new research project, which examines women's experiences with and in local government more widely.

Sarah Pedersen is Professor of Communication and Media at Robert Gordon University, Aberdeen. Her research focuses on women's engagement with the media for political purposes, including historical and contemporary source material. Her book, *The Scottish Suffragettes and the Press*, was published in 2017 by Palgrave Macmillan. The same year she was awarded funding by the Heritage Lottery Fund to produce an edition of the correspondence of Aberdeen suffragette and journalist Caroline Phillips. She was the Director of the Rise Up Quines! festival in Aberdeen in 2018 which both celebrated the centenary of (some) women achieving the Parliamentary vote and aimed to encourage women and girls to become more involved in political leadership. Her work on the Scottish suffrage campaign has been praised in a motion to the Scottish Parliament. Her book, *The Politicization of Mumsnet*, was published in 2020.

Jennifer Redmond is an Assistant Professor in the Department of History, Maynooth University. She has previously held positions in University College Dublin, Trinity College Dublin and Bryn Mawr College, USA. Her research interests lie in the social history of Irish women, migration and citizenship. Her book, *Moving Histories: Irish Women's Migration to England from Independence to Republic* (Liverpool University Press, 2018) was longlisted for Michel Déon Prize of the Royal Irish Academy and the Académie française. She is currently writing a monograph on the Irish writer, philanthropist and botanist, Charlotte Grace O'Brien.

Tania Shew is a final-year PhD candidate at the University of Manchester with a thesis entitled 'Fraternising with the enemy: sex strikes and birth strikes as tactics in the British and American women's suffrage movements, 1890-1920'. She spent a year of her PhD as a visiting doctoral fellow at Harvard University on a Fulbright scholarship. Tania has lectured at the New College of the Humanities and is currently a Scouloudi Fellow at the Institute of Historical Research. She is particularly interested in gendered intellectual history and histories of internationalism and transnationalism.

Helen Sunderland is currently a Stipendiary Lecturer in History at St Catherine's College Oxford. She recently completed her PhD at the University of Cambridge on the political socialization of schoolgirls in England between 1870 and 1914. She has published on schoolgirls' debating societies in *The Historical Journal* and her article in *Victorian Periodicals Review* on parliamentary politics and empire in the girls' periodical press won the 2018 VanArsdel prize. Her wider research interests lie in the intersections between the histories of childhood, education, gender, and political culture in modern Britain.

Acknowledgements

First and foremost, we would like to thank all the authors who have contributed chapters to this volume. It has been a pleasure and a privilege to work with them all and we thank them for their patience and hard work during a time when research and writing often felt impossible. Thanks also to Professor Susan Grayzel, Professor Nicolletta F. Gullace, Dr Zoë Thomas and Professor Selina Todd for their advice and encouragement throughout this process. We would like to thank the Women in the Humanities programme and the John Fell Fund at the University of Oxford and the Royal Historical Society for their generous financial support for the Women's Suffrage and Beyond Conference held at Oxford in 2018, at which the scholarship in this volume was first presented. We are also grateful to the Women's History Network in general, and to Professor Maggie Andrews in particular, for their efforts to showcase and champion new writing in women's history. Thanks must also go to the Royal Historical Society, Institute of Historical Research and University of London Press for commissioning and publishing this volume. Within these organisations we would particularly like to thank Jamie Bowman, Robert Davies, Lauren De'Ath, Emily Morrell, Heather Shone and Jane Winters, for their enthusiasm for the book and their guidance and assistance throughout the writing and editing process. Thanks also to Priya Kelly for her assistance with the index. We are also grateful to the anonymous peer reviewers who offered thoughtful and constructive feedback on our proposal. Finally, we would like to thank our families. Your patience, encouragement and support throughout the whole process has been extraordinary.

A very special thanks to our mentor, Professor Senia Pašeta, to whom this book is dedicated. Her guidance and support have been invaluable, not only in the process of taking this project from a call for papers for a conference to a completed volume, but in all aspects of our research and careers. We, like several successive generations of students and early career researchers at Oxford, especially scholars of women's history, owe her a great debt. Her generosity, kindness and rigour are deeply appreciated, and we are extremely grateful for her ongoing counsel and friendship.

Introduction

Alexandra Hughes-Johnson and Lyndsey Jenkins

6 February 2018 saw the largest ever gathering of women parliamentarians past and present, as they congregated in Westminster Hall in the Houses of Parliament to mark one hundred years since the Representation of the People Act had enfranchised the first British women. Joined by campaigners, professionals, young people and historians, a series of eminent politicians considered the achievements, significance and legacy of suffrage campaigners. The Prime Minister, Theresa May, for example, discussed Parliament itself as a focal point for suffrage activism, referring to the cupboard where Emily Wilding Davison hid on census night 1911, the statue to which Margery Humes had chained herself and the events of Black Friday in Parliament Square.[1] But it was seventeen-year-old Jordhi Nullatamby, a member of the Youth Parliament from Thurrock, who offered the most powerful and moving address. She spoke of the 'passionate, principled and determined' activists who had enabled women to vote for the first time, but also reminded the audience that equality had not yet been achieved, stating, 'the vision [was] not yet realised'. Instead, she suggested that the centenary celebrations should inspire women to continue campaigning and fighting for 'a better and more equal world for the women who follow us, just as those suffrage campaigners of 1918 fought to create a better world for us today'.[2]

For Nullatamby, as for many women before her, the way to create 'a better and more equal world' was through participation in politics. Yet this has frequently raised fundamental challenges for women activists. As Susan Pedersen has recently asked, 'how does one enter a world built for men, and at once inhabit it, and change it?'[3] This issue preoccupied women during

1 T. May, 'Vote 100 Speech' <www.gov.uk/government/speeches/pms-vote-100-speech-6-february-2018> [accessed 18 Jan. 2019].

2 'Jordhi Nullatamby: An honour to mark women's rights milestone alongside the Prime Minister', British Youth Council, <www.byc.org.uk/news/an-honour-to-mark-womens-rights-milestone-alongside-the-prime-minister> [accessed 29 Apr. 2021].

3 S. Pedersen, 'The women's suffrage movement in the Balfour family', *Twentieth Century British History*, xxx (2019), 299–320, at p. 320.

the long campaign for suffrage. They understood their exclusion from the formal political system as the foundation for other forms of injustice and inequality. Vast numbers of women were, of course, already active in politics. Many of these were elite women who held informal roles as wives and hostesses.[4] Increasingly, however, as the political system itself changed through the nineteenth century, women also became organizers, activists and campaigners on specific issues and within the broader context of electoral, party and class politics.[5] Nevertheless, the political structure not only excluded but also subordinated and disadvantaged women. Drawing on

[4] On elite women's involvement, see, for example, P. Jalland, *Women, Marriage and Politics, 1860–1914* (Oxford, 1986); K. D. Reynolds, *Aristocratic Women and Political Society in Victorian Britain* (Oxford, 1998); E. Chalus, *Elite Women in English Political Life* (Oxford, 2005); D. Urquhart, *The Ladies of Londonderry: Women and Political Patronage* (London, 2007). For an important, albeit unique, contrast, see J. Davey, *Mary, Countess of Derby and the Politics of Victorian Britain* (Oxford, 2019).

[5] On women's involvement in local government and politics before national enfranchisement, see P. Hollis, *Ladies Elect: Women in English Local Government 1865–1914* (Oxford, 1987); S. King, *We Might Be Trusted: Women, Welfare and Local Politics 1880–1920* (Brighton, 2006); R. Davidson, 'A local perspective: the women's movement and citizenship, Croydon 1890s–1939', *Women's History Review* (2020), 1016–33. On women and political culture, see K. Gleadle, *Borderline Citizens: Women, Gender and Political Culture in Britain 1815–1867* (Oxford, 2009); M. Smitley, *The Feminine Public Sphere: Middle-Class Women in Civic Life in Scotland, c.1870–1914* (Manchester, 2009); S. Richardson, *The Political Worlds of Women: Gender and Politics in Nineteenth Century Britain* (Abingdon, 2013); B. Griffin, *The Politics of Gender in Victorian Britain: Masculinity, Political Culture, and the Struggle for Women's Rights* (Cambridge, 2012). On specific campaigns and issues, see, for example, A. Clark, 'Queen Caroline and the sexual politics of popular culture in London, 1820', *Representations*, xxxi (1990), 47–68; C. Midgley, 'From supporting missions to petitioning Parliament: British women and the Evangelical campaign against Sati in India, 1813–1830', in *Women in British Politics, 1760–1860: The Power of the Petticoat*, ed. K. Gleadle and S. Richardson (Basingstoke, 2000), pp. 74–92; S. Morgan, 'Domestic economy and political agitation: women and the Anti-Corn Law League, 1839–1846', in *Women in British Politics, 1760–1860: The Power of the Petticoat*, ed. K. Gleadle and S. Richardson (Basingstoke, 2000), pp. 115–33. On women and political movements, see, for example, B. Taylor, *Eve and the New Jerusalem: Socialism and Feminism in the Nineteenth Century* (London, 1984); K. Gleadle, *The Early Feminists: Radical Unitarians and the Emergence of the Women's Rights Movements, 1831–51* (Basingstoke, 1995); A. Clark, *The Struggle for the Breeches: Gender and the Making of the British Working Class* (London, 1995); H. Rogers, *Women and the People: Authority, Authorship and the Radical Tradition in Nineteenth-Century England* (Aldershot, 2000); J. Hannam and K. Hunt, *Socialist Women: Britain, 1880s to 1920s* (London, 2002). Invaluable surveys of nineteenth-century women incorporating their relationship to politics include K. Gleadle, *British Women in the Nineteenth Century* (Basingstoke, 2001); A. Vickery, *Women, Privilege and Power: British Politics, 1750 to the Present* (Stanford, Calif., 2001); S. Steinbach, *Women in England 1760–1914: A Social History* (London, 2004); K. Cowman, *Women in British Politics, c.1689–1979* (Basingstoke, 2010).

a variety of justifications – philosophical, legal, economic, social, religious, cultural and nationalist – women claimed that, as women, they had both the right and the duty to participate not just in local but also in national and even international politics.[6] They frequently argued that this would not only benefit women as a group, but society as a whole. Though women felt the consequences in particular and specific ways, they recognized women's oppression as a structural, as well as an individual, experience.

The struggle for suffrage was not a straightforward demand for entry into the public sphere. Activists sought more than inclusion and incorporation into the body politic. More fundamentally, the campaign was a deliberate attempt both to utilize and reconstruct the political system as a means of transforming women's place, status and prospects in other spheres. There is, of course, an ongoing and lively debate as to how far they achieved this objective.[7] Certainly, they were not wholly successful. But it is important to understand their beliefs, priorities and strategies as well as their achievements.

The contributions in this collection examine how suffrage campaigners sought to achieve lasting structural change by navigating, interrogating, accepting, challenging and remaking the existing political system. Their

[6] See, for example, women's central role in abolitionism, articulated by C. Midgley, *Women Against Slavery: The British Campaigns* (London, 1992) and S. Stanley Holton, 'From anti-suffrage slavery to suffrage militancy: the Bright Circle, Elizabeth Cady Stanton and the British women's movement', in *Suffrage and Beyond: International Feminist Perspectives*, ed. C. Daley and M. Nolan (Auckland, 1994), pp. 213–33.

[7] Formerly pessimistic assessments, such as those found in B. Harrison, *Prudent Revolutionaries: Portraits of British Feminists Between the Wars* (Oxford, 1987) and H. L. Smith, 'British feminism in the 1920s', in *British Feminism in the Twentieth Century* (Aldershot, 1990), pp. 47–65 have, however, largely been supplanted by more optimistic conclusions, such as those found in P. Thane, 'What difference did the vote make? Women in public and private life in Britain since 1918', *Historical Journal*, lxxvi (2003), 268–85 and M. DiCenzo, '"Our freedom and its results": Measuring progress in the aftermath of suffrage', *Women's History Review*, xxiii (2014), 421–40, as well as a wider reappraisal of the extent and meaning of women's politics in the interwar period, such as H. McCarthy, 'Parties, voluntary associations and democratic politics in interwar Britain', *The Historical Journal*, l (2007), 891–912; M. Andrews, *The Acceptable Face of Feminism: The Women's Institute as a Social Movement* (London, 1997); C. Beaumont, *Housewives and Citizens: Domesticity and the Women's Movement in England, 1928–1964* (Manchester, 2013); J. Hannam and K. Hunt, 'Towards an archaeology of interwar women's politics: the local and the everyday', in J. V. Gottlieb and R. Toye (ed.), *The Aftermath of Suffrage: Women, Gender and Politics in Britain 1918–1945* (Basingstoke, 2013), pp. 124–41; Z. Thomas, 'Historical pageants, citizenship, and the performance of women's history before Second-Wave Feminism', *Twentieth Century British History*, xxviii (2017), 319–43; and C. Clay, M. DiCenzo, B. Green and F. Hackney, *Women's Periodicals and Print Culture in Britain, 1918–1939: The Interwar Period* (Edinburgh, 2018), esp. parts iv and v.

concern was with power and its unequal distribution, and the ways that women could and could not exercise control over their own lives and in wider society. This starting point, with its emphasis on political structures and power, reaffirms Karen Offen's insistence that the history of feminism is political history.[8] It might seem obvious, and even redundant, to say this in the context of suffrage history. Yet while it is vital to do justice to the social and cultural dimensions of the suffrage movement, it is important not to lose sight of the fact that this was first and foremost a political demand. As a result, it was also primarily a political movement, and, as Pedersen has noted, 'one of the most powerful consciously sex-based political movements ever'.[9]

As a political cause, it required a political solution. The enfranchisement of women could only take place through the parliamentary process. This represented the most significant and radical challenge to the constitution since 1832, seeking to fundamentally alter the terms on which politics was conducted, expanding and redefining the basis of citizenship. The suffrage campaign was not a single-issue campaign.[10] Nor was it simply a means to an end, a stepping stone on the route to other crucial reforms. Women did not aim at piecemeal change, but at systemic structural transformation. Yet they knew that in order to achieve this, they needed to operate within the political system as well as seeking to remake it. Women worked within existing structures, institutions and organizations as well as seeking to lobby and influence change from outside by creating their own networks and organizations.[11] Suffrage activists were political actors and savvy operatives who developed a far-reaching analysis of the political system from the constitutional framework to local administrative structures.[12]

[8] K. Offen, *European Feminisms, 1700–1950: A Political History* (Stanford, Calif., 2000). See also K. Offen, 'The history of feminism is political history', *Perspectives on History*, 1 May 2011 <www.historians.org/publications-and-directories/perspectives-on-history/may-2011/the-history-of-feminism-is-political-history> [accessed 1 July 2020].

[9] Pedersen, 'The women's suffrage movement in the Balfour family', p. 301.

[10] For example, Thane, 'What difference did the vote make?', pp. 268–9.

[11] S. Richardson, 'Conversations with Parliament: women and the politics of pressure in nineteenth-century England', *Parliamentary History*, xxxvii (2018), 35–51.

[12] S. Stanley Holton, *Feminism and Democracy: Women's Suffrage and Reform Politics in Britain, 1900–1918* (Cambridge, 1986); A. Clark, 'Gender, class and the constitution: franchise reform in England, 1832–1928', in *Re-Reading the Constitution: New Narratives in the Political History of England's Long Nineteenth Century*, ed. J. Vernon (Cambridge, 1996), pp. 239–53; L. E. Nym Mayall, 'Defining militancy: radical protest, the constitutional idiom, and women's suffrage in Britain, 1908–1909', *Journal of British Studies*, xxxix (2000), 340–71; J. Barnes, 'The British women's suffrage movement and the ancient constitution, 1867–1909', *Historical Research*, xci (2018), 505–27.

It is vital to understand the suffrage cause within its proper political context. Karen Offen also reminds us that 'feminist claims are primarily political claims, not philosophical claims. They never arise in – or respond to – a socio-political vacuum. They are put forward in concrete settings, and they pose explicit political demands for change.'[13] Women's suffrage was inseparable from contemporary political debates around Home Rule, demands for workers' rights, the politics of imperialism and, of course, universal male suffrage.[14] It has long been recognized, for example, that Liberal women's uneasy relationship with their party originated in the disputes over Home Rule in the 1880s, that many twentieth century suffrage activists had roots within the labour movement and that the Boer War galvanized a new generation of campaigners.[15] Many suffrage activists had clearly defined views on these issues and were working simultaneously for other objectives. Women's politics was not separate to other forms of politics. It was integral to, and constitutive of, these other political debates.

Similarly, suffrage societies did not exist separately from the political mainstream but operated within the existing political system. They often adopted the political norms and practices common to other political organizations, such as meetings, debates and resolutions. These strategies were essential in order to lobby those with political capital and power. To demonstrate their readiness for political citizenship, and to prepare others to do likewise, suffrage campaigners had a particular interest in political education, and invested a great deal in explaining political structures and practices to those who were not yet fully informed. Women developed the knowledge and skills which enabled them to operate within existing political systems, and deliberately and effectively pressed for change within the context of existing structures. They became well versed in the specificities of parliamentary procedures, of course, but also in the intricacies of party politics and electioneering. They understood local factions and interests, and the ways in which other institutions like the churches exercised political influence.

At the same time, women recognized the limitations of existing politics. They have often been rightly celebrated as pioneers of innovative

[13] Offen, *European Feminisms*, p. xv.

[14] S. Pašeta, 'New issues and old: women and politics in Ireland, 1914–1918', *Women's History Review*, xxvii (2018), 432–49; S. Pašeta, 'Feminist political thought and activism in revolutionary Ireland, c.1880–1918', *Transactions of the Royal Historical Society*, xxvii (2017), 193–209.

[15] L. E. Nym Mayhall, 'The South African war and the origins of suffrage militancy in Britain, 1899–1902', in *Women's Suffrage in the British Empire: Citizenship, Nation and Race*, ed. I. C. Fletcher, L. E. Nym Mayhall and P. Levine (Basingstoke, 2000), pp. 3–17.

campaigning, particularly when it came to incorporating artistic and creative practices.[16] However, their intentions were more far-reaching and fundamental. Women recognized that politics did not only take place in the parliamentary chamber, the town meeting or on the street corner. Rather, politics was embedded in women's everyday lives.[17] Women's activism was linked to their life experiences and negotiated in relation to their other commitments, including family obligations, friendship networks and the demands of paid work and domestic labour. As such, suffrage was inseparable from other claims around women's rights, education, work and family life.[18] Women understood these concerns as legitimate political issues.

Women therefore attempted to redefine the nature of the political itself, shifting not only how politics was conducted and how the political system functioned, but also what counted as political. They invested structures outside the conventionally political spaces – especially the home and the family – with political meaning.[19] They asserted the importance of understanding these places as political. What went on within them – including the education and welfare of children, practices of violence and abuse and the distribution of power and resources – were political concerns which could not be understood as purely private.[20] In this, they were building on the efforts of the nineteenth century women's movement, which had already recreated local politics as an acceptable and appropriate space for women. These efforts overlapped with other contemporary political concerns around poverty, housing and the health of the nation, and, as such, were instrumental in the construction of the welfare state. Their expertise and experience enabled women to assert their moral right and practical capacity to address these challenges, making common cause with other political reformers.[21]

[16] L. Tickner, *The Spectacle of Women: Imagery of the Suffrage Campaign, 1907–1914* (London, 1988); B. Green, *Spectacular Confessions: Autobiography, Performative Activism, and the Sites of Suffrage 1905–1938* (London, 1997); Z. Thomas and M. Garrett (ed.), *Suffrage and the Arts: Visual Culture, Politics and Enterprise* (London, 2018).

[17] S. Stanley Holton, 'The suffragist and the "average woman"', *Women's History Review*, i (1992), 9–24; Hannam and Hunt, 'Towards an archaeology'.

[18] For an insightful survey of these interconnections, see L. Delap, 'The "woman question" and the origins of feminism', in *The Cambridge History of Nineteenth Century Political Thought*, ed. G. Stedman Jones and G. Claeys (Cambridge, 2011), pp. 319–48.

[19] C. Dyhouse, *Feminism and the Family in England, 1880–1939* (Oxford, 1989).

[20] P. Levine, *Feminist Lives in Victorian England: Private Roles and Public Commitment* (Oxford, 1990).

[21] P. Thane, 'Women in the British Labour Party and the construction of state welfare, 1906–39', in *Mothers of a New World: Maternalist Politics and the Origins of Welfare States,*

The 2018 commemoration of the centenary of the passing of the Representation of the People Act and the 2019 Sex Disqualification (Removal) Act generated new public interest in the campaign for women's suffrage, as well as offering scholars a chance to reflect on its meaning, impact and legacy. The intense debate generated through the year, which was also linked to the ongoing centenary of the First World War, was testament to ongoing interest and debate in this particular field of women's history.[22] This book is the result of a series of papers presented at an international conference, 'Women's Suffrage and Beyond: Local National and International Contexts', held at the University of Oxford in October 2018. Convened by Alexandra Hughes-Johnson, Lyndsey Jenkins and Senia Pašeta, the conference sought to break down some of the disciplinary, geographic and periodical boundaries which have come to define but also in some instances to limit suffrage studies.

The collection consists of thirteen chapters based on papers delivered at the conference, developed from a number of different intellectual and methodological techniques. They broadly analyse three themes: how women worked within existing political structures; how they sought to advance their political demands through social and cultural structures; and how they navigated international political structures in pursuit of their goals. These themes cut across the local, the national and the transnational, as well as extending well beyond a narrow chronology. The chapters reflect ongoing debates within suffrage history, and increasing recognition of, for example, the importance of Irish and imperial politics. They also engage with other historiographical concerns and practices, such as the history of childhood and media history. Some case studies offer hints of possibilities not pursued, while others show how what was once considered radical practice became incorporated into the political mainstream. They recognize dissent and disagreement, but do not consider that either necessarily signifies political weakness. Rather, they indicate the multiplicity of perspectives among women activists who participated in the suffrage campaign, and the different priorities which women brought to the cause. Together, these chapters

ed. S. Koven and S. Michel (London, 1993), pp. 343–77; P. Thane, 'Visions of gender in the making of the British welfare state: the case of women in the British Labour Party and social policy', in *Maternity and Gender Policies: Women and the Rise of the European Welfare States, 1880s–1950s*, ed. G. Bock and P. Thane (London, 1991), pp. 93–118; J. Lewis, *Women and Social Action in Victorian and Edwardian Britain* (Aldershot, 1991).

[22] J. de Vries, 'Popular and smart: why scholarship on the women's suffrage movement in Britain still matters', *History Compass*, xi (2013), 177–88; J. Purvis, '"A glass half full"? Women's history in the UK', *Women's History Review*, xxvii (2018), 88–108, at p. 93.

are testament to the exciting and fruitful scholarship which continues to invigorate suffrage history.

Historiographical context

Early suffrage history developed as a clearly defined and demarcated field in its own right, with fixed dates for the beginning and end of the campaign: from the famous 1866 suffrage petition to the Representation of the People Acts in 1918, and occasionally 1928. Participants were often straightforwardly divided into distinct categories such as 'suffrage' and 'anti-suffrage', 'militant' and 'constitutional', 'rational' and 'irrational'.[23] This contributed to the establishment of a dominant framework from which influential narratives of the women's movement would be constructed. Historiographical attention was firmly focused on the Women's Social and Political Union (WSPU), which was frequently characterized and caricatured as an autocratic, even anti-democratic, single-issue pressure group.[24] This approach had the effect of divorcing suffrage activism from its wider political, social and economic context. It tended to marginalize suffrage, both politically and historically, and to downplay the significance of both the movement and the campaigners with it. It was all too easy for those working in other fields of history not to take suffrage seriously, seeing it as a discrete and limited movement.[25]

Neither the emergence of social history nor the subsequent development of women's history initially seriously challenged this perspective. Focused on histories 'from below' and of 'the everyday', a movement centred on parliamentary enfranchisement and apparently dominated by middle-class women seemed unpromising terrain for both social historians and women's historians. Though the emergence of new political history sought to analyse political languages and cultures, the emphasis remained largely on men's interests, efforts and lives.[26] Indeed, political history itself,

[23] These contours were reflected in the histories written by participants, such as M. G. Fawcett, *Women's Suffrage: a Short History of a Great Movement* (London, 1912); S. Pankhurst, *The Suffrage Movement: an Intimate Account of Persons and Ideals* (London, 1931); R. Strachey, *The Cause: a Short History of the Women's Movement* (London, 1928).

[24] Notoriously, in G. Dangerfield, *The Strange Death of Liberal England* (London, 1936); R. Fulford, *Votes for Women* (London, 1957); D. Mitchell, *The Fighting Pankhursts: a Study in Tenacity* (London, 1967).

[25] S. Stanley Holton, 'Challenging masculinism: personal history and microhistory in feminist studies of the women's suffrage movement', *Women's History Review*, xx (2011), 829–41; J. Purvis, 'Gendering the historiography of the suffragette movement in Edwardian Britain: some reflections', *Women's History Review*, xxii (2013), 576–90.

[26] G. Stedman Jones, *Languages of Class: Studies in English Working Class History 1832–1982* (Cambridge, 1983); P. Joyce, *Democratic Subjects: the Self and the Social in Nineteenth Century England* (Cambridge, 1994).

concerned with leaders and institutions, seemed inherently exclusionary to women.[27]

One of the first texts to insist on the wider significance of women's suffrage to political history was Sandra Stanley Holton's landmark text *Feminism and Democracy*. Here, Stanley Holton analysed the constitutional debates, institutional politics and electoral strategies of the National Union of Women's Suffrage Societies (NUWSS).[28] In doing so, she argued that division between so-called constitutionalists and militants had been greatly overstated, with both wings of the movement often working in symbiosis for women's sexual, social and economic equality.[29] Like Jill Liddington and Jill Norris's earlier ground-breaking work, *One Hand Tied Behind Us* – which highlighted the efforts of working-class 'radical suffragists', their campaigning methods, policy initiatives and connections to the labour movement – Stanley Holton rejected a focus on sensationalist militant tactics. Instead, she analysed what she termed 'democratic suffragism', and offered a new perspective on the relationship between the labour movement and the women's movement.[30] Her later work has been equally influential in its insistence that historians need to understand the everyday nature of suffrage politics, rather than focusing on leaders and full-time activists.[31]

It has taken several decades of scholarship to dismantle the barriers which had fenced suffrage history into a neat and tidy narrative. The picture which has since been painted is far richer and more nuanced, allowing for a deeper and more comprehensive understanding of the suffrage movement and its wider significance. In turn, this has facilitated a greater understanding of how suffrage politics was integrated into, and central to, other prevailing political debates, social issues and cultural norms.

A number of historiographical themes have emerged. One is an insistence on seeing the suffrage campaign as part of the political mainstream. Scholarship has demonstrated that suffrage organizations emerged from, and were recognizable within, existing political culture.[32] Campaigning

[27] J. Davey, 'Women and politics', in *The Oxford Handbook of Modern British Political History, 1800–2000*, ed. D. Brown, G. Pentland and R. Crowcroft (Oxford, 2018), pp. 417–33 offers a helpful analysis of the relationship between the fields.

[28] S. Stanley Holton, *Feminism and Democracy: Women's Suffrage and Reform Politics, 1900–1918* (Cambridge, 1986).

[29] S. Stanley Holton, *Feminism and Democracy*, p. 30.

[30] J. Liddington and J. Norris, *One Hand Tied Behind Us: The Rise of the Women's Suffrage Movement* (London, 1978).

[31] S. Stanley Holton, 'The suffragist and the "average woman"'.

[32] J. Lawrence, 'Contesting the male polity: the suffragettes and the politics of disruption in Edwardian Britain', in *Women, Privilege and Power: British Politics, 1750 to the Present*, ed.

was marked by compromise and collaboration rather than continual disagreement and division between different groups.[33] There were a myriad of organizations beyond the WSPU and the NUWSS, often rooted in professional identities, with objectives that went well beyond achievement of the franchise.[34] The struggle also incorporated campaigning beyond specific suffrage organizations, frequently involved men as well as women and was met with a concerted resistance.[35] At the same time, historians have sought to situate suffrage activism within a longer tradition of feminist campaigning, rejecting narrow chronologies which privilege WSPU activism. Careful examinations of women's activities during the First World War – rejecting simplistic assumptions that campaigning was suspended – has been integral to considering how gendered hierarchies were made and remade in wartime and postwar contexts.[36] A well-developed literature has reconsidered the legacy of suffrage. In contrast to older histories characterized by a tone of pessimism and disappointment about a supposed failure of feminism during the interwar period, more

A. Vickery (Stanford, Calif., 2001), pp. 201–26; K. Cowman, *Mrs Brown is a Man and a Brother: Women in Merseyside's Political Organisations, 1890–1920* (Liverpool, 2004).

[33] K. Cowman, *Women of the Right Spirit: Paid Organisers of the Women's Social and Political Union (WSPU) 1904–18* (Manchester, 2007).

[34] H. Kean, *Deeds not Words: the Lives of Suffragette Teachers* (London, 1990); A. Oram, *Women Teachers and Feminist Politics, 1900–1939* (Manchester, 1996); C. Eustance, 'Meanings of militancy: the ideas and practice of political resistance in the Women's Freedom League, 1907–1914', in *The Women's Suffrage Movement: New Feminist Perspectives*, ed. M. Joannou and J. Purvis (Manchester, 1998), pp. 51–64; K. Cowman, '"A party between revolution and peaceful persuasion": a fresh look at the United Suffragists', in *The Women's Suffrage Movement: New Feminist Perspectives*, ed. M. Joannou and J. Purvis (Manchester, 1998), pp. 77–89; S. S. Park, 'Doing justice to the real girl: the Women Writers' Suffrage League', in *A Suffrage Reader: Charting Directions in British Suffrage History*, ed. C. Eustance, J. Ryan, and L. Ugolini (London, 2000), pp. 90–104; T. Morton, 'Changing spaces: art, politics and identity in the home studios of the suffrage atelier', *Women's History Review*, xxi (2012), 623–37; N. Paxton, *Stage Rights! The Actresses' Franchise League, Activism and Politics 1908–1958* (Manchester, 2018).

[35] M. Boussahba-Bravard (ed.), *Suffrage Outside Suffragism: Women's Vote in Britain, 1880–1914* (Basingstoke, 2007); A. John and C. Eustance (ed.), *The Men's Share? Masculinities, Male Support, and Women's Suffrage in Britain, 1890–1920* (London, 1997); J. Bush, *Women Against the Vote: Female Anti-Suffragism in Britain* (Oxford, 2007).

[36] A. K. Smith, *Suffrage Discourse in Britain During the First World War* (Aldershot, 2005); J. Vellacott, *Pacifists, Patriots and the Vote: the Erosion of Democratic Suffragism During the First World War* (Basingstoke, 2007); N. F. Gullace, '*The Blood of Our Sons*': *Men, Women, and the Renegotiation of British Citizenship During the Great War* (Basingstoke, 2002); S. Kingsley Kent, *Making Peace: The Reconstruction of Gender in Interwar Britain* (Chichester, 1993).

recent studies insist that women's activism not only evolved into new forms but had frequent successes.[37]

Another welcome development has been the proliferation of local studies, showing that the campaign was neither focused on, nor directed from, London (or Manchester), but thrived in distinctive ways around the country.[38] Local branches were often key sites for political activism and enjoyed a considerable amount of independence and autonomy, providing space for longstanding activists and new enthusiasts to develop alliances which could transcend other existing structures, institutions, organizational allegiances and affiliations. Elizabeth Crawford's encyclopedic collections have provided an invaluable foundation for this effort.[39] Regional studies have likewise demonstrated how Irish, Scottish and Welsh campaigns were shaped by the particularities of their political cultures, particularly nationalist sentiment and movements.[40] Broader shifts towards comparative and transnational history have prompted a reappraisal of the place of

[37] J. V. Gottlieb and R. Toye, 'Introduction', in *The Aftermath of Suffrage: Women, Gender and Politics in Britain*, ed. J. V. Gottlieb and R. Toye (Basingstoke, 2013), pp. 1–18; Beaumont, *Housewives and Citizens*; C. Law, *Suffrage and Power: the Women's Movement, 1918–1928* (London, 1997); E. Breitenbach and P. Thane (ed.), *Women and Citizenship in Britain and Ireland in the Twentieth Century* (London, 2011); McCarthy, 'Parties, voluntary associations and democratic politics'; Thomas, 'Historical pageants'.

[38] B. Dobbie, *A Nest of Suffragettes in Somerset: Eagle House, Batheaston* (Bath, 1979); J. Liddington, *Rebel Girls: their Fight for the Vote* (London, 2006); K. Cowman, '"Minutes of the last meeting passed": the Huddersfield Women's Social and Political Union Minute Book January 1907–1909, a new source for suffrage history', *Twentieth Century British History*, xiii (2002), 298–315; R. Whitmore, *Alice Hawkins and the Suffragette Movement in Edwardian Leicester* (Derby, 2007); G. Barnsby, *Votes for Women: The Struggle for the Vote in the Black Country* (London, 1995); I. Dove, *'Yours in the Cause': A Brief Account of Suffragettes in Lewisham, Greenwich and Woolwich* (London, 1988); D. Neville, *To Make Their Mark: the Women's Suffrage Movement in the North East of England 1900–1914* (Newcastle, 1997); S. Quail, *Votes for Women: The Women's Fight in Portsmouth* (Portsmouth, 1983); K. Cowman, *The Militant Suffragette Movement in York* (York, 2007); A. Hughes-Johnson, 'Rose Lamartine Yates and the Wimbledon WSPU: reconfiguring suffragette history from the local to the national' (unpublished PhD thesis, Royal Holloway, University of London, 2018); J. Hannam, '"I had not been to London": women's suffrage: a view from the regions', in *Votes for Women*, ed. J. Purvis and S. Stanley Holton (London, 2002), pp. 226–45.

[39] E. Crawford, *The Women's Suffrage Movement in Britain and Ireland* (London, 2008); E. Crawford, *The Women's Suffrage Movement, A Reference Guide, 1866–1928* (London, 2003).

[40] L. Leneman, *A Guid Cause: the Women's Suffrage Movement in Scotland* (Edinburgh, 1995); U. Masson, '"Political conditions in Wales are quite different ..." Party politics and votes for women in Wales, 1912–15', *Women's History Review*, ix (2000), 369–88; K. Bohata, '"For Wales, see England?" Suffrage and the new woman in Wales', *Women's History Review*, xi (2002), 634–56; A. John, *Rocking the Boat: Welsh Women who Championed Equality 1840–1990* (Cardigan, 2018); C. Murphy, 'The religious context of the women's suffrage

the British campaign within similar struggles for women's rights and enfranchisement around the globe. Women worked across multiple international political organizations, structures, networks and cultures in a long history of transnational collaboration and cooperation which was often grounded in personal connections and friendship networks and went well beyond suffrage.[41] Other research has demonstrated the centrality of women's suffrage and demands for citizenship in broader national histories of democracy and nation-building.[42] Scholars have also explored the imperial assumptions and racial hierarchies which underpinned women's demands for enfranchisement in Britain, serving as an important reminder that women's claims were often grounded in the politics of exclusion as well as inclusion.[43]

campaign in Ireland', *Women's History Review*, vi (1997), 549–656; Breitenbach and Thane (ed.), *Women and Citizenship*; Pašeta, 'New issues and old'.

[41] K. Gleadle and Z. Thomas, 'Global feminisms, c. 1870–1930: vocabularies and concepts – a comparative approach', *Women's History Review*, xxvii (2018), 1209–24, at p. 1213; see also J. Adams, *Women and the Vote: A World History* (Oxford, 2014); H. Dampier, '"Going on with our little movement in the hum drum way which alone is possible in a land like this": Olive Schreiner and suffrage networks in Britain and South Africa, 1905–1913', *Women's History Review*, xxv (2016), 536–50; C. Daley and M. Norton (ed.), *Suffrage and Beyond: International Feminist Perspectives* (New York, 1994); I. Sulkunen, S. Nevala-Nurmi and P. Markkola (ed.), *Suffrage, Gender and Citizenship: International Perspectives on Parliamentary Reform* (Cambridge, 2009); L. Delap, *Feminisms* (London, 2020); M. Bosch and A. Kloosterman (ed.), *Politics and Friendship: Letters from the International Woman Suffrage Alliance, 1902–1942* (Columbus, O., 1990); S. Rowbotham, *Dreamers of a New Day: Women who Invented the Twentieth Century* (London, 2010); L. Delap, *The Feminist Avant-Garde: Transatlantic Encounters of the Early Twentieth Century* (Cambridge, 2007).

[42] I. Blom, 'Feminism and nationalism in the early twentieth century: a cross-cultural perspective', *Journal of Women's History*, vii (1995), 82–94; S. Stanley Holton, 'British freewomen: national identity, constitutionalism and languages of race in early suffragist histories', in *Radical Femininity: Women's Self-Representation in the Public Sphere*, ed. E. Yeo (Manchester, 1998), 149–71; D. Urquhart, *Women in Ulster Politics, 1890–1940* (Dublin, 2000); B. S. Anderson, *Joyous Greetings: The First International Women's Movement, 1830–1860* (Oxford, 2000); C. Bolt, *Sisterhood Questioned: Race, Class and Internationalism in the American and British Women's Movements, c. 1880s–1970s* (London, 2004); L. Delap, L. Ryan and T. Zackodnik, 'Self-determination, race and empire: feminist nationalists in Britain, Ireland and the United States, 1830s to World War One', *Women's Studies International Forum*, xxix (2006), 241–54; S. Pašeta, *Irish Nationalist Women, 1900–1918* (Cambridge, 2013); S. Crozier-De Rosa, 'Divided sisterhood? Nationalist feminism and feminist militancy in England and Ireland', *Contemporary British History*, xxxii (2018), 448–69.

[43] A. Burton, *Burdens of History: British Feminists, Indian Women, and Imperial Culture* (London, 1994); J. Bush, *Edwardian Ladies and Imperial Power* (London, 2000); I. Fletcher, L. E. Nym Mayhall and P. Levine (ed.), *Women's Suffrage in the British Empire: Citizenship, Nation and Race* (London, 2000); C. Midgley, *Feminism and Empire: Women Activists in*

Suffrage historiography has also been greatly enriched by methodological developments in women's history itself. The emphasis on women's cultures, artistic output, creativity and professionalism, for example, has produced a series of critical interventions.[44] The religious turn in women's history has also produced accounts of the suffrage campaign which demonstrate how far suffrage activism was informed by established religious structures and faith, as well as esoteric belief, and secular discourse.[45] This work has demonstrated how far the suffrage cause enabled women from different religious faiths – as well as freethinking and secular women – to unite in pursuit of a shared goal.[46] Other research has revisited the ongoing debate around the relationship between class and suffrage politics. Suffrage scholars increasingly recognize working-class women's participation in the suffrage movement – not as marginal figures but as significant political agents, operating within many organizations and central to shaping different campaigns.[47]

Imperial Britain, 1790–1865 (London, 2007); S. Mukherjee, *Indian Suffragettes: Female Identities and Transnational Networks* (Oxford, 2018).

[44] Tickner, *Spectacle of Women*; Thomas and Garrett (ed.), *Suffrage and the Arts*; Paxton, *Stage Rights!*

[45] S. Morgan (ed.), *Women, Religion, and Feminism in Britain, 1750–1900* (Basingstoke, 2002); C. Christensen Nelson, 'The uses of religion in the women's militant suffrage campaign in England', *The Midwest Quarterly*, li (2010), 227–42; J. de Vries, 'Sounds taken for wonders: revivalism and religious hybridity in the British women's suffrage movement', in *Material Religion in Modern Britain: The Spirit of Things*, ed. L. Matthews-Jones and T. Willem Jones (Basingstoke, 2015), pp. 101–23; L. Schwartz, *Infidel Feminism: Secularism, Religion and Women's Emancipation, England 1830–1914* (Manchester, 2013); J. de Vries, 'Transforming the pulpit: preaching and prophecy in the British Women's suffrage movement', in *Women Preachers and Prophets through Two Millenia of Christianity*, ed. B. Mayne Kienzle and P. J. Walker (London, 1998), pp. 318–34; J. de Vries, 'Challenging traditions: denominational feminism in Britain, 1910–1920', in *Borderlines: Genders and Identities in War and Peace, 1870–1930*, ed. B. Melman (London, 1998), pp. 265–285; J. Dixon, *The Divine Feminine: Theosophy and Feminism in England* (London, 2001); R. Saunders, '"A great and holy war": religious routes to women's suffrage, 1909–1914', *English Historical Review*, cxxxiv (2019), 1471–1502.

[46] K. Cowman, '"Crossing the great divide": inter-organizational suffrage relationships on Merseyside, 1895–1914', in *A Suffrage Reader: Charting Directions in British Suffrage History*, ed. C. Eustance, J. Ryan and L. Ugolini (London, 2000), pp. 37–52.

[47] Liddington and Norris, *One Hand*; M. Myall, '"No surrender!": the militancy of Mary Leigh, a working-class suffragette', in *The Women's Suffrage Movement*, ed. M. Joannou and J. Purvis (Manchester, 1988), pp. 173–87; K. Cowman, '"Crossing the great divide"'; K. Cowman, '"Incipient Toryism"? The Women's Social and Political Union and the Independent Labour Party, 1903–1914', *History Workshop Journal*, ciii (2002), 128–48; L. Jenkins, 'Annie Kenney and the politics of class in the Women's Social and Political Union', *Twentieth Century British History*, xxx (2019), 477–503; L. Schwartz, *Feminism and the Servant Problem: Domestic Labour in the Women's Suffrage Movement* (Cambridge, 2019); L. Jenkins, *Sisters and Sisterhood: The Kenney Family, Class and Suffrage, 1890–1965* (Oxford, 2021).

The edited collection has long played an important role in the methodology of suffrage history. The chapters in June Purvis and Maroula Joannou's *The Women's Suffrage Movement* offered an important re-examination of suffrage militancy, examining its creative and cultural implications, extending it beyond the WSPU and its leadership and considering its emergence from contemporary British political culture.[48] Purvis's collaboration with Sandra Stanley Holton, *Votes for Women*, highlighted new case studies on both significant and lesser-known activists, as well as seeking to shift historiographical attention beyond the WSPU and London.[49] Clare Eustance, Joan Ryan and Laura Ugolini's *Suffrage Reader* was a key text in placing suffrage within broader political, social and economic developments.[50] Collaborations were crucial in reappraising and resituating the British campaign in an imperial and global context.[51] More recent essay collections have also facilitated a thorough investigation of particular dimensions of the campaign, such as the role of men or the legacies of suffrage.[52] It is therefore appropriate and welcome that several of the publications resulting from the centenary return to this collaborative methodological approach.[53]

This text has also benefited from technological progress. Recent advances in digital history – not only online access to the 1911 census, but also improvements in the accessibility of local and international newspapers – have made it far easier for historians to identify and pursue subjects through the archives as well as opening up the possibility of large-scale data analysis.[54] In these chapters, digital approaches are deployed alongside

[48] J. Purvis and M. Joannou (ed.), *The Women's Suffrage Movement: New Feminist Perspectives* (Manchester, 1998).

[49] J. Purvis and S. Stanley Holton (ed.), *Votes for Women* (London, 1998).

[50] C. Eustance, J. Ryan and L. Ugolini, *A Suffrage Reader: Charting Directions in British Suffrage History* (London, 2000).

[51] C. Daley and M. Nolan (ed.), *Suffrage and Beyond: International Feminist Perspectives* (Auckland, 1994); I. C. Fletcher, L. E. Nym Mayhall and P. Levine (ed.), *Women's Suffrage in the British Empire: Citizenship, Nation and Race* (Basingstoke, 2000).

[52] A. John and C. Eustance (ed.), *The Men's Share? Masculinities, Male Support, and Women's Suffrage in Britain, 1890–1920* (London, 1997); M. Boussahba-Bravard (ed.), *Suffrage Outside Suffragism: Women's Vote in Britain, 1880–1914* (Basingstoke, 2007); J. V. Gottlieb and R. Toye (ed.), *The Aftermath of Suffrage: Women, Gender and Politics in Britain 1918–1945* (Basingstoke, 2013); J. V. Gottlieb (ed.), special issue of *Women's History Review*, xxiii (2014).

[53] J. Purvis and J. Hannam, 'The women's suffrage movement in Britain and Ireland: new perspectives', special edition of *Women's History Review*, xxix (2020), 911–915; J. Purvis and J. Hannam (ed.), *The British Women's Suffrage Campaign: National and International Perspectives* (Abingdon, 2020); C. Wiley and L. E. Rose, *Women's Suffrage in Word, Image, Music, Stage and Screen: The Making of a Movement* (London, 2021).

[54] J. Liddington and E. Crawford, *Vanishing for the Vote: Suffrage, Citizenship and the Battle for the Census* (Manchester, 2014); K. Gupta, *Representation of the British Suffrage Movement* (London, 2016).

more conventional uses of the historical archive, including minute books, committee papers, correspondence and lectures together with suffrage periodicals, local, national and international newspapers, suffrage plays, autobiographies and oral interviews.

Recent advances in cultural and social understandings of suffrage need to be matched with a similar focus not only on the politics of suffrage but on the political significance of suffrage. It remains a challenge for historians to insist that suffrage is central to accounts of the development of British modernization, citizenship and democracy without either replicating linear triumphalist narratives of progress or simply rewriting existing political histories with women added in. Here, as elsewhere, the contribution of feminist historians is not only to ensure that women are included in historical narratives, but to transform the narratives themselves, introducing new concerns and alternative perspectives and questioning the gendered nature of male experience in the past as the default and universal experience.

Contributions

The first set of chapters in this collection examines how women worked within existing political structures to advance their cause. Jennifer Redmond analyses how the Irish Women's Suffrage and Local Government Association and other early suffrage activists attempted to influence Irish representatives in Parliament in the latter half of the nineteenth century. Her contribution demonstrates women's firm and subtle grasp of the broader political context in which they worked, including the Irish question. She shows that women activists understood and utilized conventional political strategies, closely examining the use of petitions as a political tactic which aimed to raise public awareness and influence political decision making. She also analyses how Irish MPs themselves also contributed to the debate at a far earlier moment than is usually recognized.

The next chapter, by Lyndsey Jenkins, uses a case study of the Canning Town branch of the WSPU to examine how working-class women sought to exercise political agency through the suffrage cause. She demonstrates the dissatisfaction that unemployed women workers felt with existing political structures which failed to meet their needs, ranging from the paltry formal local welfare systems, to well-meaning but inadequate philanthropic provision, to national policy on the unemployed. While embedded in local socialist culture, the women did not seek to use the labour movement as a means to press for political change, but instead formed their own society which aimed to bring about both short- and long-term improvements in their lives. She indicates how women developed a particular kind of political practice, adopting direct action, prioritizing political education and creating an intensely sociable political culture. In highlighting these women's political capabilities and identities, the chapter illustrates the broad attraction of the suffrage cause, which many women later pursued in the better-known Adult Suffrage Society and the East London Federation of Suffragettes.

In contrast, Beth Jenkins's chapter indicates that the failure of women's suffrage societies to fully grasp the realities of the political situation impeded Welsh women's engagement with the broader national movement. While suffrage societies are often perceived as masters of communications and public relations, here their efforts were more heavy-handed, often grounded in stereotypes, and hence less effective. Jenkins argues that the relatively late and patchy emergence of suffrage societies does not mean that Welsh women lacked an interest in suffrage. Rather, building on scholarship which has asserted the importance of 'suffrage outside suffragism', she demonstrates the extent to which women actively worked for suffrage within the existing political structures, particularly Liberal and nationalist institutions, to press for change.

Anna Muggeridge's chapter likewise demonstrates that a limited local suffrage movement does not mean an absence of politicized women. Her analysis of the infant welfare movement in Walsall is a reminder that, for many women, suffrage was by no means the most pressing or relevant concern. Women in the infant welfare movement were able to further their political agenda by establishing a broad, inclusive and collaborative approach which facilitated political participation from women from a wide range of backgrounds. Reasserting the importance of the locality as a crucial site of women's political practice, her intervention not only complements the many important studies of local suffrage activity, but connects them with a broader history of women's work in local government and welfare which is often overshadowed by the historiographical focus on suffrage.

The final contribution in this section, from Alexandra Hughes-Johnson, represents the first sustained historiographical analysis of the Independent Women's Social and Political Union and the Suffragettes of the Women's Social and Political Union. The determination of these women to continue to fight for suffrage throughout the First World War was, as she argues, a striking act of political resistance against a government which sought to co-opt women into the war effort while refusing to grant them citizenship. She shows that these organizations sought to remake existing structures and networks in order to form new feminist communities. Disgruntled former members of the WSPU used the strategies and skills which they had developed within the suffrage campaign in a new political context. They tackled concerns around venereal disease and the Defence of the Realm Act while furthering debates around women's suffrage versus adult suffrage. Above all, they continued to assert the relevance of their political priorities, refusing to accept that their demands could be set aside.

The next set of chapters examines how women sought to advance their political demands through social and cultural structures beyond the conventional political arena. Sarah Pedersen demonstrates how Glaswegian suffragists sought to use the press as a means of political communication. Their relationship with the local press was fraught with difficulty. Local papers often proved hostile to militancy and sought to tar all suffrage activists with the same brush. More surprising, perhaps, is the troublesome relationship that the branch had with the editors of the *Common Cause*. This illuminates the tensions between the 'centre' and 'periphery' which is familiar to suffrage scholars from other contexts, and illustrates how they could be manifested in mutual incomprehension despite their shared goals.

In the following chapter, Sos Eltis analyses how women brought their knowledge of suffrage and class politics to literature and the arts, using their writing and performance as a campaigning tool to confront the class structure as well as the gender order. On the page and on the stage, women displayed and deployed their political knowledge as a means to create and sustain political commitment. Yet here, as elsewhere, middle-class writers and performers strove to reconcile propagandist ideals of women's solidarity with the realities of class difference and divided interests. Suffrage writers struggled to celebrate cross-class alliances while acknowledging the often complex and contested relations between class and gender.

Helen Sunderland's chapter then takes the politics of suffrage into the school. She conceptualizes the girls' school as a political community which encompassed not just teachers but also pupils and alumnae. She argues that like other all-female spaces which have long been recognized as sites for women's politicization and socialization, schools were crucial in introducing girls and young women to the suffrage debate. Girls' suffrage education occurred less through formal processes of education than in informal social activities like debating and school magazines which allowed girls a window into suffrage campaigning elsewhere. Crucially, she demonstrates that girls were not the passive recipients of ideas introduced by teachers and former students, but, drawing on new histories of childhood which assert the political capabilities and agency of children and young people, illustrates that girls had their own ideas about politics and their own strategies for contributing to debates.

Concluding this section, Tania Shew examines how some of the most radical feminist affiliates of the WSPU and Women's Freedom League (WFL) sought to explore the impact of marriage-, sex- and birth-strikes as explicit forms of political protest and as a way of securing the vote. Feminists had, of course, long been critical of the ways that marriage, domesticity and maternity restricted and confined women. Increasingly, suffrage activists believed that political equity was a prerequisite for a change in women's domestic status, explicitly linking their enfranchisement with the ongoing sexual double standard. In the immediate prewar period, as women developed new forms of militant protest, some, as Shew illustrates, sought to use their sexual power as a campaigning strategy and a way of increasing pressure on men to grant the vote. In doing so, they politicized not only the home but also the bedroom, and linked even the most intimate of relationships with the need for structural change.

The final chapters examine how women worked within international political structures to achieve their objectives. Karen Hunt's chapter uses Dora Montefiore's experience and analysis of Finnish enfranchisement as a way to analyse broader debates within the suffrage and labour movements. Frustrated by what she saw as the limited and tentative objectives of British progressive politics, Montefiore attempted to highlight the Finnish experience in her political work to demonstrate that more radical and revolutionary change – including but not limited to adult suffrage – was possible with sufficient ambition. Hunt's analysis illustrates how some women recognized that whatever contemporary activists might have liked to claim, Britain was not the 'storm centre' of an international struggle, but merely one among many stages upon which a global political debate on citizenship played out, and British campaigners could learn a great deal from developments elsewhere. Montefiore's politics illustrates a feminist internationalism which often struggled to gain a hearing when faced with the forces of nationalism, imperialism and class politics.

Pursuing the politics of suffrage in the East End of London into the later Edwardian period, Katherine Connelly places the East London Federation of Suffragettes (ELFS) in the context of a radical transatlantic dialogue. Though the ELFS is often narrowly conceived as the result of Sylvia Pankhurst's tremendous energy and particular politics, Connelly demonstrates how much it was indebted to Pankhurst's positive assessment of women's grassroots activism in settlement houses and the Women's Trade Union League that she had encountered on her lecture tours of the United States. Moreover, she shows that American women involved in these institutions assisted the ELFS' efforts to create a genuinely grassroots, bottom-up movement, embedded in the politics of the local community and their shared desire for truly democratic political practice. Her approach thus affirms the significance of positive institutional models, rather than solely individual conviction, in feminist institution-building.

In the following chapter, Sharon Crozier-De Rosa examines how activists in different parts of the British Empire attempted to put imperial politics to use in their campaigns. Considering Ireland and Australia alongside Britain, she demonstrates how both suffrage and anti-suffrage campaigners utilized the emotional dimensions of imperialism, manifesting as shame and embarrassment, anger and indignation, sympathy and solidarity, in the language and tone of their campaigns. Emotions were not only felt, but constructed and deployed in strategic and effective ways as part of political campaigns. Focusing on the emotions of nationalist and anti-colonial as well as suffrage politics, her chapter points to new ways of writing political history, in which emotions are recognized as central.

The final contribution, by Maurice J. Casey, considers the later careers of some of the most radical British and Irish suffrage activists, who sought to further revolutionary change through advancing the cause of international communism. While communist parties were often resistant to the demands of supposedly bourgeois feminist causes, many women succeeded in forging careers within satellite organizations associated with international communism, promoting a range of causes, from humanitarianism to pacifism. Some women also found employment in Moscow's revolutionary institutions. The political campaigning and administrative skills that these women had developed within suffrage activism were relevant and transferable to these organizations, enabling former activists to pursue the most fundamental structural upheaval of all: world revolution. However, Casey also demonstrates that the lack of communist interest in women's specific concerns meant a failure to attract a new generation of activists, breaking the tentative link between suffrage and communism.

The collection is bookended by two contributions which consider the political context and its implications for women's politics in 1918 and 2018. Susan R. Grayzel's foreword reflects on the myriad ways in which women's activism was remade in the crucible of, and in opposition to, new kinds of warfare, especially the destructive force of airpower. Her insistence on understanding British women's enfranchisement in relation to the ongoing denial of similar rights elsewhere in the British Empire offers a new reading of the relationship between the national and the international, the local and the global, in histories of citizenship and democracy. Finally, the afterword, by Nicoletta F. Gullace, compares the British commemorations of the suffrage centenary in 2018 with the equivalent anniversary in the United States in 2020. Gullace argues that sidelining imperialism in one case and foregrounding race in the other helps account for the outpourings of joy and muted acknowledgement on different sides of the Atlantic. A call to understand the legacies of suffrage activists in all their rich complexities, this chapter is also an important reminder that democracy itself remains a work-in-progress rather than a state which can be taken for granted.

Conclusion

Commemorations of women's enfranchisement in Britain took place against a tumultuous political and social backdrop in which women's rights were contested and attacked. In the wake of revelations against the Hollywood filmmaker Harvey Weinstein, the trials of the actor Bill Cosby and the doctor Larry Nassar and, of course, the election of Donald Trump, questions of power, exploitation and harassment were ever more present in public debate. The #MeToo and #TimesUp campaigns made many men uncomfortable, some question their behaviour and others complain that the movement had gone 'too far'. New terms for old forms of behaviour, such as 'mansplaining', 'toxic masculinity' and 'himpathy', signified women's exasperation with cultural norms which still required them to tolerate the intolerable. Significant advances in women's rights, such as the successful campaign to repeal the Eighth Amendment in Ireland, were matched by devastating losses, such as the confirmation of Brett Kavanaugh to the US Supreme Court in the face of the dignified testimony of Christine Blasey Ford. In Britain, publication of pay data by major companies demonstrated how – one hundred years after women's suffrage *and* fifty years after the Equal Pay Act, businesses were not yet paying men and women equally – a point underlined by the case of Carrie Gracie at the BBC. There were concerns about the disproportionate impact of austerity, tax and welfare policies on women, especially those with caring responsibilities, epitomized by the notorious 'rape clause' attached to eligibility for child benefit. Campaigns against period poverty and for women's pensions rights highlighted the concerns of young and older women alike. Women of colour continued to experience multiple and overlapping discrimination, with high-profile women such as anti-Brexit campaigner Gina Ford and Diane Abbott MP facing violent and racialized threats. The experience of women migrants and refugees at Yarl's Wood Immigration Centre demonstrated how the most vulnerable and marginalized women of colour are all but dehumanized in degrading conditions.

Yet the hostile political climate often seemed to invigorate and energize women activists fighting for positive change. Many activists took inspiration from the struggles of suffrage campaigners, positioning their work for women's equality as part of a feminist inheritance from these earlier struggles while also recognizing some of their limitations. While individual women were often instrumental in creating and driving particular campaigns, once again they recognized that collective action aimed at lasting structural change was the only route forward. Women did not seek to remove individual men from power, but to change the practices across entire industries. The women's marches in 2017 were aimed not only at the incoming American president but expressed broader concerns about misogyny, homophobia, racism and other forms of structural inequality. Women's feminist priorities were often interwoven with concerns about environmental degradation and climate change, the plight of migrants and refugees, the consequences of neoliberalism, the rise of far-right movements and, in the UK, Brexit. These concerns were often global, and, as a result, international structures and collaboration became even more important. Some of these, notably the internet and specifically social media, represented both major challenges and important opportunities for women, on the one hand offering places for connection and inspiration, and on the other facilitating a climate in which it became ever more difficult for women to express political opinions without facing online and offline threats.

It is too soon to determine what the legacy of the suffrage centenary will be. The limited and specific nature of government investment in the centenary hardly seemed designed to bring about significant and lasting change. Local campaigns seemed, unsurprisingly, more effective at engaging local communities, though those tied into broader efforts to promote democracy, participation and citizenship appear to promise more than those which were simply geared towards constructing a statue. Nevertheless, one important legacy may be a greater awareness and understanding of women's suffrage, especially among a generation increasingly politicized by local, national and global injustice. Another will surely be the many partnerships and relationships built between those working in the academy and those working in community and grassroots organizations to share and develop resources collaboratively.[55] But the scholarly advances made during the year will also be a crucial outcome. Some of the publications which have already emerged during and following the centenary show how the conversations which characterized that year are reshaping the debate

[55] See, for example, <https://greenwich100.com/>; <https://www.bristolmuseums.org.uk/m-shed/whats-on/votes-women-100/>; <http://dreadnoughtsouthwest.org.uk/listening-booth-tour/>; <https://www.nationaltrust.org.uk/features/women-and-power-exploring-womens-history-at-our-places> [accessed 14 Sep. 2020].

on suffrage.[56] In many cases, these are characterized by a conversation between those scholars who have defined the field for decades and the perspectives of emerging scholars.[57] We hope that this collection will also prove an important contribution to that conversation. The chapters here serve as a reminder of the power of the collective and the need for long-term commitment to structural change.

[56] Paxton, *Stage Rights!*; Mukherjee, *Indian Suffragettes*; L. Schwartz, *Feminism and the Servant Problem.*

[57] Thomas and Garrett, *Suffrage and the Arts*; Purvis and Hannam, 'The women's suffrage movement in Britain and Ireland'; Purvis and Hannam, *The British Women's Suffrage Campaign.*

I. Working within existing political structures

1. The 'success of every great movement had been largely due to the free and continuous exercise of the right to petition': Irish suffrage petitioners and parliamentarians in the nineteenth century*

*Jennifer Redmond***

Introduction

In 1870, the *Manchester National Society for Women's Suffrage Journal* reported that 'Dublin led the way' in presenting the first women's suffrage petitions to Parliament and at the last general election 'there was a greater proportion of avowed adherents of women's suffrage returned among the Irish members than in any other of the three kingdoms'.[1] Such claims might be surprising as the work of early suffragists in Ireland, as in other places, has been

* From *The Shield*, 4 Apr. 1871, p. 442.

** My sincere thanks to the editors and Professor Senia Pašeta (Oxford University) for their helpful comments. All were extremely patient and diligent, although any errors or omissions remain my own.

[1] *Manchester National Society for Women's Suffrage Journal*, i (1870), p. 14. The Manchester National Society for Women's Suffrage was established in Jan. 1867 expressly to organize petitions, but suffrage activity by Elizabeth Wolstenholme Elmy is thought to have happened from 1865. Lydia Becker became the secretary of the Society in Feb. 1867. The Manchester Society was the first of the suffrage societies in Britain to hold a public meeting in Apr. 1868 (for more, see E. Crawford, *The Women's Suffrage Movement in Britain and Ireland: A Regional Survey* (Abingdon, 2006)). The first volume of *The Women's Suffrage Journal* in 1870 (edited by Becker) listed two Irish members of the Manchester National Society for Women's Suffrage – Mr E. M. Richards of Enniscorthy and Mr John Scott of Belfast. No further information on either person could be found; neither was an elected MP for any Irish constituency between 1801 and 1922 so it is likely they were private citizens.

'The "success of every great movement had been largely due to the free and continuous exercise of the right to petition"', in *The politics of women's suffrage: local, national and international dimensions*, ed. A. Hughes-Johnson and L. Jenkins (London, 2021), pp. 25–58.

eclipsed in popular narratives by their later counterparts, the suffragettes.[2] This chapter argues for the importance of early suffrage campaigners in Ireland. This includes campaigners such as the Robertson sisters, whose contribution has become somewhat lost in the literature, and organizations like the Dublin Women's Suffrage Association (later the Irish Women's Suffrage and Local Government Association), founded in 1876 by Anna and Thomas Haslam.[3] This chapter questions the historiographical assumption that suffrage only occupied the minds of a small minority in Ireland in the long nineteenth century. It demonstrates that Irish MPs worked across party lines with likeminded politicians in different constituencies throughout the UK and could be persistent in their pursuit of legislation and submission of petitions.

The scant primary sources make tracing activities of early suffragists difficult, but this is not unusual in the realm of women's history. Carmel Quinlan and Elizabeth Crawford pioneered scholarship on the early suffragists in Ireland and identified many facts about the key individuals involved at regional and national level.[4] Scholarship has firmly established that a small number of dedicated, articulate activists in Ireland organized

[2] Key works on suffrage in Ireland focus heavily on the twentieth-century suffragettes; L. Ryan and M. Ward (ed.), *Irish Women and the Vote: Becoming Citizens* (2018 reissue, Dublin, 2007) features two out of thirteen essays on nineteenth-century suffragists; S. Crozier-De Rosa, *Shame and the Anti-Feminist Backlash: Britain, Ireland and Australia, 1890–1920* (New York, 2018) focuses on rhetoric directed towards militant suffragettes and 'Divided sisterhood? Nationalist feminism and feminist militancy in England and Ireland', *Contemporary British History*, xxxii (2018), 448–69 has a direct focus on the militants; S.-B. Watkins, *Ireland's Suffragettes: the Women Who Fought for the Vote* (Dublin, 2014); D. Gilligan, 'Anti-suffragette postcards, c. 1913', *History Ireland*, xxvi (2018), p. 41. Hanna Sheehy Skeffington, one of the founders of the militant Irish Women's Franchise League (IWFL) (in 1908), has been the subject of several monographs and features in all major accounts of the movement and modern Irish history, while Anna Haslam, founder of the Dublin Women's Suffrage Association, is the subject of just one, joint, biography, with her husband Thomas and, while known in academic circles, is not a major figure of public interest; M. Luddy, *Hanna Sheehy Skeffington: Life & Times* (Dundalk, 1995); M. Ward, *Hanna Sheehy Skeffington: A Life* (Dublin, 1997), *Hanna Sheehy Skeffington: Suffragette and Sinn Feiner* (Dublin, 2017) and *Fearless Woman: Hanna Sheehy Skeffington, Feminism and the Irish Revolution* (Dublin, 2019); C. Quinlan, *Genteel Revolutionaries: Anna and Thomas Haslam and the Irish Women's Movement* (Cork, 2005). There are numerous articles referencing Haslam, but she, and her contemporaries, have not received the same level of scholarly attention as Sheehy Skeffington and the IWFL.

[3] The association changed its name as different rights were won for women in Ireland, beginning as the Dublin Women's Suffrage Association; for clarity it will be referred to primarily as the IWSLGA here.

[4] Quinlan, *Genteel Revolutionaries*; Crawford, *The Women's Suffrage Movement in Britain and Ireland*.

petitions with high numbers of signatories, liaised with leading campaigners in Britain and successfully garnered the interest of several Irish MPs to advance their cause. This will be explored in much greater detail in this chapter, examining their frequency, where they came from and who sent them, where it is possible to identify this. The historiography to date has not focused much on the contributions of Irish MPs to the women's suffrage cause, but a detailed examination of the parliamentary record reveals more activity than previously recorded. Broadly speaking, Irish MPs did not make emphatic speeches in Parliament on women's suffrage rights, but they did produce numerous bills, form strategic alliances with likeminded MPs from different constituencies and parties and were active in forwarding petitions.

The suffragists' goal was to revolutionize their world and women's place in it, primarily through securing women's right to the franchise and expanding the societal roles they could undertake. To do so, they had to engage with both the public and their representatives at Westminster. One of their primary vehicles of protest was the petition. This 'softer' tactic has less immediacy than the militancy of the twentieth century, but was essential in building public awareness of the need for women's suffrage and was, alongside other 'soft power' techniques such as leaving literature in reading rooms and public meetings, essential to the acceptance of women's right to vote on a broader scale by the time militancy became the primary currency of activists in the twentieth century.[5] For women of the period, publicly demanding to be taken seriously as citizens was a bold act. Alongside letters to newspapers and publication of pamphlets, petitioning was an important part of political vocabulary. Hawkins has highlighted how dozens of petitions between the 1830s and 1850s 'voided or changed the outcome of constituency contests'.[6] Petitions had enormous potential as a political act and the later suffragette perception of them as useless should not colour our understanding of their meaning and weight at this time. Petitioning on suffrage coincided with the heyday of petitioning overall in the late Victorian period as a 'vehicle for popular politics'[7] because 'petitions were a crucial site of representation between people and parliament' and 'a key component of the shifting ecosystem of popular participation and

[5] This term soft power is used in the sense defined by Joseph S. Nye, Jr. as 'the ability to affect others to obtain the outcomes one wants through attraction rather than coercion or payment'; 'Public diplomacy and soft power', *The Annals of the American Academy of Political and Social Science*, dcxvi (2008), 94–109, at p. 94.

[6] A. Hawkins, *Victorian Political Culture: 'Habits of Heart and Mind'* (Oxford, 2015), p. 166.

[7] H. Miller, 'The British women's suffrage movement and the practice of petitioning, 1890–1914', *The Historical Journal* (2020), doi: 10.1017/S0018246X20000035.

representation during the long nineteenth century'.[8] Petitions also 'enabled local activity to be co-ordinated as part of national campaigns', particularly important for Irish-based activists.[9] The decline in petitioning came at the end of the nineteenth century.[10] Richardson traces the failure of the 1896 'Special Appeal' suffrage petition, which gathered 257,796 signatures, to an abandonment of petitioning as a strategy and the beginning of a move by some suffragists to militant tactics.[11]

Petitions from Irish activists have been noted in previous work but not thoroughly analysed.[12] This chapter will analyse Irish petitions more systematically, shedding new light on this tool of political campaigning. Petitions were vital to the campaign for women's rights more broadly, particularly as they were 'borderline citizens' in Gleadle's analysis, unable to access other forms of protest and decision making.[13] In the context of the time, it could also be seen as a radical act to raise a petition, as one anecdote attests. W. T. Stead, pioneer investigative journalist, observed of Anna Haslam when he heard her say she was not a militant: '"Not a militant!" he exclaimed. "Mrs Haslam, I've known you for the last forty years, and I never knew you to be anything but militant!"'.[14] Haslam never picketed or served jail time, nor did she ever heckle a politician. She was instead an activist who used the 'constitutional triptych', as Gladstone termed it, of the 'press, platform, and petition' to decry the injustices she saw for women in Victorian society.[15]

Rendall argued in 2002 that there 'is much which still remains to be recovered of the first 30 years of the campaign for women's suffrage'. This is the case when it comes to the Irish part of this story, for, as Rendall also recognized, Ireland featured regularly in contemporary political debates.

[8] R. Huzzey and H. Miller, 'Petitions, Parliament and political culture: petitioning the House of Commons, 1780–1918', *Past and Present*, ccxlviii (2020), 123–64, at pp. 123–4.

[9] Huzzey and Miller, 'Petitions, Parliament and political culture', at pp. 123–4.

[10] Huzzey and Miller, 'Petitions, Parliament and political culture', at p. 140.

[11] S. Richardson, 'The 1896 women's suffrage petition', available at <https://www.parliament.uk/business/committees/committees-a-z/commons-select/petitions-committee/petition-of-the-month/the-1896-womens-suffrage-petition-/> [accessed 6 Aug. 2020].

[12] Petitions are noted by Quinlan in *Genteel Revolutionaries*, for example, but are not systematically analysed.

[13] K. Gleadle, *Borderline Citizens: Women, Gender, and Political Culture in Britain, 1815–1867* (Oxford, 2009).

[14] As cited in F. Sheehy Skeffington, 'The pioneers of feminism in Ireland', *The Irish Citizen*, 21 Mar. 1914, p. 347.

[15] J. Thompson, *British Political Culture and the Idea of 'Public Opinion', 1867–1914* (Cambridge, 2013), p. 87.

> That recovery has to site the movement firmly within late Victorian political, social, and familial lives, and across assumed divisions between private and public worlds, as between local and parliamentary politics. Only by doing so can we understand why, in June 1868, it seemed to Priscilla McLaren that 'really this woman's question in its various aspects is, along with the Irish Church, the question of the time.'[16]

The 'question of the time' as it involved both women's place and Ireland's politics was complex and has been poorly understood by many historians of the wider movement. Pašeta has called for more attention to the confluence of both issues, for while women's suffrage was to the political fore, '*the* main political question' was Ireland,[17] an argument also highlighted by Urquhart in her treatment of Ulster women's political experiences in this period.[18]

While histories of the era have sketched a broad narrative of the main actors and their methods, there is little in-depth research on the complex interaction between activist groups in mainland Britain and Ireland in the nineteenth century.[19] Nor have there been detailed studies of the MPs from Irish constituencies who allied themselves with pioneers such as John Stuart Mill. However, letters between Mill and Thomas Haslam and the minutes and reports of the IWSLGA reveal there were activists in Ireland who attempted to push forward the agenda for women's rights, with the right to vote in national elections being their highest aspiration. There also appear to have been more supportive MPs than previously described in the literature. As they worked towards a wider public realm for women, the IWSLGA and its peers utilized the civic means available to them, and their engagement with politicians was crucial to advancing the cause.

The 'particular' case of Ireland

A note here is necessary on the wider political context and terminology deployed in this chapter. As in the rest of the United Kingdom, Members of Parliament representing Irish boroughs were not paid and were drawn from

[16] J. Rendall, 'John Stuart Mill, Liberal politics, and the movements for women's suffrage, 1865–1873', in *Women, Privilege and Power: British Politics, 1750 to the Present*, ed. A. Vickery (Stanford, Calif., 2002), pp. 168–201, at p. 201.

[17] S. Pašeta, *Suffrage and Citizenship in Ireland 1912–18: The Kehoe Lecture in Irish History 2018* (London, 2019), doi: 10.14296/119.9781912702183.

[18] D. Urquhart, *Women in Ulster Politics, 1890–1940: A History Not Yet Told* (Dublin, 2000).

[19] The exemplary publication by Elizabeth Crawford *The Women's Suffrage Movement in Britain and Ireland* most fully interrogates this history but there are still many research avenues to explore.

the middle and upper classes of society.[20] Additionally, before the Roman Catholic Relief Act 1829, all MPs were Protestant and commonly referred to as Anglo-Irish, many having deep roots in both countries, and Ireland had been governed directly from Westminster since the Act of Union in 1801.[21] There is a rather charged semantic difference, however, between using the term 'Irish MPs' and the more correct designation, 'MPs that represented Irish constituencies'.[22] For brevity, I have used the former, but the complexity of politics in Ireland means it is important to acknowledge that many of those I refer to under this term may have seen themselves as British, or as Irish Unionists, or as distinctly Irish with British affiliations, or simply as Irish. This issue of identity politics in Ireland also has geographic dimensions as Urquhart has highlighted.[23] The elision between the terms 'British' and 'Anglo-Irish' is problematic, but perhaps also emblematic of the complex identities and loyalties of those of mixed descent. Irish MPs largely represented the two major British parties until 1870 with the founding of the Home Government Association, an alliance of pro-Home Rule MPs created by Isaac Butt that would develop into the Irish Parliamentary Party under Charles Stuart Parnell.

Many Liberals in Ireland were Unionists but committed to improving Irish laws to create better conditions for the populace. Many suffragists were also Liberals, some of whom became Liberal Unionists as Irish

[20] Even Irish Parliamentary Party MPs were only supported by a stipend if they were 'unable to support themselves at Westminster without financial assistance' and this amount fluctuated depending on the party's finances. See J. McConnel, 'The view from the backbench: Irish Nationalist MPs and their work, 1910–1914', PhD thesis (Durham University, 2002), p. 269. Thanks to Dr Martin O'Donoghue for tracking down this information. While this may have made them a more socially diverse group than many other political parties, they were still an overwhelmingly middle- and upper-class party. For more, see C. C. O'Brien's *Parnell and his Party* (Oxford, 1957). My thanks to Dr Conor Mulvagh for his clarification on this point.

[21] Ireland was represented thereafter by one hundred MPs in the House of Commons, twenty-eight Irish representative peers and four bishops.

[22] A further note on the methodology deployed in this chapter is the problem of geographical electoral areas that have changed and have created a data minefield for researchers. Because constituencies have been abolished, redrawn etc., I have noted a discrepancy in how Irish MPs have been listed between the online Hansard database and work on this by B. Walker, *Parliamentary Election Results in Ireland, 1918–92* (Belfast, 1992). Tracking Irish representatives is a difficult research exercise and is made somewhat easier by the ProQuest Parliamentary Database, but it is still difficult to isolate MPs who served Irish constituencies, and many served multiple constituencies throughout the UK during their career.

[23] D. Urquhart, '"An articulate and definite cry for political freedom": the Ulster suffrage movement', *Women's History Review*, xi (2002), 273–92, at p. 273.

nationalism grew more powerful. They founded and became members of women's loyalist associations while also pursuing suffrage activities.[24] They were not too niche to be ignored in political debates; the Women's Liberal Unionist Association, for example, was mentioned by Gladstone in a Commons debate in April 1892 as an active organization that harnessed women's energies for politics.[25]

Women in Ireland in the late nineteenth century felt keenly the dual obstacles they faced in gaining attention for an issue that at best seemed farcical, and at worst a dangerous threat to wider political ambitions of men and their vision for an independent legislature for Ireland. The political clashes that defined the suffrage movement in Ireland are not unique and, as Beaumont, Clancy and Ryan have argued, 'the Irish case, therefore, bears many of the hallmarks of similar clashes elsewhere in countries which experienced the consequences of colonial rule', although many scholars debate Ireland's designation as a colony.[26] Unionist leaders seemed broadly uninterested in promoting the cause of women's suffrage, even though the Ulster Women's Unionist Council had an estimated membership of 115,000 to 200,000 organized, potential voters.[27] Unionists may also have benefited from the property qualifications, as many Irish suffragists who would have met this threshold were avowed Liberal Unionists. Whether these women overtly agitated for the vote or not, any change in voting rights for women would have primarily benefitted this key group.

Irish women 'shared the same general disabilities under English law'[28] as others in the United Kingdom and demonstrated solidarity with British counterparts by supporting women's franchise bills that did not include Ireland, such as Mill's intervention in 1867. As such, Irish campaigners had a strategic vision that covered both UK-wide ambitions and specific, local

[24] Quinlan, *Genteel Revolutionaries*, p. 132.

[25] *Cork Examiner*, 28 Apr. 1892, p. 6.

[26] C. Beaumont, M. Clancy and L. Ryan, 'Networks as "laboratories of experience": exploring the life cycle of the suffrage movement and its aftermath in Ireland 1870–1937', *Women's History Review* (2020), doi: 10.1080/09612025.2020.1745414, at p. 7.

[27] Pašeta, *Suffrage and Citizenship in Ireland*, p. 13. It must be noted, however, that the UWUC was not an explicitly feminist or pro-suffrage network – it existed to support the Ulster Unionist Council and to defend Ulster's right to remain within the United Kingdom. As Urquhart has argued, the 'women's council identified the defeat of Home Rule as their sole concern. Most strikingly this meant that the question of women's suffrage would not be discussed'; see D. Urquhart, 'Unionism, Orangeism and war', *Women's History Review*, xxvii (2018), 468–84, at p. 469.

[28] M. Cullen, 'How radical was Irish feminism between 1860 and 1920?', in *Radicals, Rebels and Establishments*, ed. P. J. Corish (Belfast, 1985), pp. 185–202, at p. 188.

rights for women in Ireland. Despite this, and notwithstanding being well networked with the main campaigners, they fail to feature in many classic accounts purporting to deal with the suffrage movement in the United Kingdom.[29] For example, the IWSLGA was among the founding members of the National Union of Women's Suffrage Societies in 1896. In one of the earliest accounts of the women's suffrage movement written, Ray Strachey notes the book deliberately ignored the 'Home Rule Agitation' of the period in an effort to have 'boundary lines' in the writing of this history.[30] As Pašeta argues, however, the 'Irish Question' was *central* to both an Irish and British perspective.[31]

The IWSLGA was keenly aware of the effect the 'Irish Question' was having on Irish society and made the decision 'owing to the present condition of political controversy in Ireland' not to have any public meetings between 1886 and 1895.[32] The 'political controversy' referred to was the introduction of the first and second Home Rule bills in 1886 and 1893, which saw a split in the Liberal Party and an intensification of political

[29] For example, the seminal book by R. J. Evans, *The Feminists: Women's Emancipation Movements in Europe, America and Australasia 1840–1920* (Abingdon, 1977) makes no reference to the Irish groups involved in the British suffrage movement, nor does H. L. Smith, *The British Women's Suffrage Campaign, 1866–1928* (London and New York, 1998), nor does M. Pugh, *The March of the Women: a Revisionist Analysis of the Campaign for Women's Suffrage, 1866–1914* (Oxford, 2000). Although sisters Eva Gore Booth and Constance Markiewicz are mentioned by Jill Liddington, the wider network of suffrage activists in Ireland is not acknowledged in *Rebel Girls: their Fight for the Vote* (London, 2006). June Purvis and Sandra Stanley Holton name Ireland in their discussion of the struggle to gain the parliamentary vote in their edited collection *Votes for Women* (Abingdon, 1999), but there is no detailed examination of the contributions of Irish activists, despite a recognition in Purvis's essay that suffrage research has been 'London-centric' – see Hannam, '"I had not been to London": women's suffrage – a view from the regions', pp. 226–45.

[30] R. Strachey, *"The Cause": A Short History of the Women's Movement in Great Britain* (London, 1928), p. 5.

[31] Pašeta, *Suffrage and Citizenship in Ireland*, p. 2. A noted exception is Sandra Stanley Holton's *Suffrage Days*, in which another perspective is offered; some viewed engagement with Irish political issues as potentially harmful to the suffrage movement. For example, the 'dark surmises' about the recently imprisoned Jessie Craigen if she was to appear on a suffrage platform resulted from her Ladies' Land League activities. The Ladies' Land League was established in New York in Oct. 1880 primarily to collect money for the Land League, which fought for tenant rights in Ireland. Craigen's negative assessment of Parnell and his breaking up of the League led to a permanent rift between her and her patron, Helen Taylor. See S. Stanley Holton, *Suffrage Days: Stories from the Women's Suffrage Movement* (Abingdon, 1996), p. 60. Note, however, this book deals with the 'Irish Question' more broadly and does not name the IWSLGA, in common with many other accounts.

[32] IWSLGA, *Report of the Executive Committee of the Dublin Women's Suffrage (and Poor Law Guardians) Association for 1896* (Dublin, 1897), p. 5.

debate on Ireland inside and outside the House of Commons. Thus, any history of the suffrage movement in Ireland must make the Irish political context abundantly clear to account for the competing political allegiances of suffrage supporters. As Pašeta has observed: 'There was no single body of feminist thought in late nineteenth – and early twentieth-century Ireland' and all were affected by the question of Irish nationalism.[33]

The early years of suffrage activity in Ireland

Existing accounts of the early suffrage movement in Ireland have pinpointed Anne Robertson as a trailblazer. She organized public meetings in Ireland from the late 1850s and later organized petitions.[34] Some literature only names her, but the evidence suggests she worked alongside her sister Catherine.[35] They both attended the first meeting of the Manchester National Society for Women's Suffrage on 14 April 1868, where Anne spoke.[36] Anne and Lydia Becker, editor of *The Women's Suffrage Journal*, became friends. Along with Helen Blackburn and Frances Power Cobbe, Robertson's work attests there was an Irish presence at the beginning of the UK suffrage movement.[37]

Anne Robertson organized a visit from Millicent Fawcett to Dublin in April 1870. Fawcett argued that the 'exclusion of women from political life is a gross and unjustifiable tyranny' and Robertson offered 'spirited support', being identified in the *Cork Examiner* as a leader in Ireland of the movement for women's rights.[38] But the *Manchester National Society for Women's Suffrage Journal* noted the attendance of 'Misses Robertson',

[33] Senia Pašeta, 'Feminist political thought and activism in revolutionary Ireland, c.1880–1918', *Transactions of the Royal Historical Society*, xxvii (2017), 193–209, at p. 193.

[34] 1858 is the date given for a meeting organized by Anne Robertson and attended by Anna Haslam in R. Cullen Owens, *Votes for Women: Irish Women's Struggle for the Vote* (Dublin, c.1975).

[35] The *Manchester National Society for Women's Suffrage Journal* records her name as 'Catharine', but the 1901 Census of Ireland records her as Catherine. In 1901, Anne and Catherine, aged 71 and 76 respectively, were living on Herbert Road in Dublin and recorded as living off 'interest of money'. It is unclear when the Robertson sisters stopped being actively involved in suffrage activities. Their return form can be accessed here: <http://www.census.nationalarchives.ie/reels/nai003695801/> [accessed 6 Aug. 2020].

[36] Crawford, *The Women's Suffrage Movement in Britain and Ireland*, p. 253.

[37] Crawford, *The Women's Suffrage Movement in Britain and Ireland*, p. 253. Blackburn was born on Valentia Island in Co. Kerry and was secretary to the National Society for Women's Suffrage from 1874; Power Cobbe was born in Dublin and was a founding member of the London National Society for Women's Suffrage in 1867.

[38] *Cork Examiner*, 20 Apr. 1870, p. 2.

indicating both women were known within suffrage circles.[39] This suggests the existence of a wider circle of supporters before the IWSLGA was established. The impression that Robertson was a solo activist may have come from Anna Haslam herself. Reflecting on Fawcett's 1870 visit, she stated it 'was got up by Miss Robertson who worked alone in the suffrage cause for some years'.[40] Undoubtedly an error in perception or recollection on Haslam's behalf, it demonstrates how easily women's contribution can be erased from history.

Newspaper reports also recorded the attendance of leading male politicians, academics and members of the upper classes, men who were key to the financial support and political advancement of women's rights.[41] The chairman, Sir Robert Kane, raised a petition afterwards, a key suffrage tactic, as will be expanded upon later.[42] A private talk by Fawcett on 'female liberty' was held separately at the house of Lord and Lady Wilde, parents of the infamous Oscar, but it is not clear if Robertson had any part in this.[43] Anne Robertson appears to have organized other meetings, in public halls and private houses, but there is little evidence of their content. Crawford notes her in 1871 as being the secretary of the Dublin Committee of the National Society for Women's Suffrage, although its records do not appear to have survived.[44] The difficulty in tracing her history has left Robertson as a marginal figure, but piecing together her archival traces indicates she may have been a more significant activist than previously thought.

Fawcett's speech seems to have been the first major public event on women's suffrage addressed by a speaker from outside of Ireland and it reveals much about the context of the movement for women's rights. She was politely introduced to the audience by Kane as 'the earnest and eloquent advocate of the social and political rights of the sex to which she belongs, and of which she is a distinguished ornament'.[45] The word

[39] *Manchester National Society for Women's Suffrage Journal*, i (1870), p. 21. The report says it is taken from the *Freeman's Journal*, 19 Apr. 1870.

[40] As quoted in the suffrage newspaper *The Irish Citizen*, 21 Mar. 1914, p. 347.

[41] Dr Mahaffy, Dr Shaw and Dr Waller from Trinity College Dublin, with Sir Joseph Napier, Sir John Gray MP and Sir Robert Kane are recorded as supporting the meeting.

[42] As stated in Crawford, *The Women's Suffrage Movement*, p. 254. As he was not an MP it is not possible to trace Kane's petition through the ProQuest database.

[43] The date for this meeting is unfortunately not recorded in the letter quoted in J. Melville, *Mother of Oscar: The Life of Jane Francesca Wilde* (London, 1994), p. 69.

[44] Crawford, *The Women's Suffrage Movement in Britain and Ireland*, p. 253.

[45] *Manchester National Society for Women's Suffrage Journal*, i (1870), p. 22.

'ornament' appears to modern eyes a rather strange designation to give a keynote speaker addressing women's fundamental political rights. Even when men supported women's suffrage, patriarchal attitudes towards women persisted.

The early activists set the tone for suffrage groups as non-party, willing to work with any politician who would help to advance their cause, and this was true throughout the United Kingdom. This sentiment is echoed in the *Manchester National Society for Women's Suffrage Journal* in its discussion of the Women's Disabilities Bill then before the House of Commons.

> For our own part, we believe that women have instincts which ally them with both parties. They will prove the truest Conservatives of all that is pure and just and ennobling in the political life of the nation. They will be the most radical of radical reformers when called upon to deal with the sources of misery, oppression, and wrong. They invite both parties to forget party considerations and unite in giving them a generous and hearty support at this juncture.[46]

This may have seemed the most strategic decision, but, in Miller's analysis, suffragists may not have been quick enough to realize the increasing strength of party discipline as the nineteenth century wore on, which made the non-party strategy 'increasingly outmoded'.[47] The importance of collaboration across party lines as outlined above calls into question this assumption for Ireland.

Irish politicians at Westminster

On 20 May 1867, Mill momentously tried to amend the Second Reform Bill to replace the word 'man' with 'person' to achieve women's suffrage. The 1867 Reform Bill did not include Ireland (only England and Wales), so any involvement by Irish activists and MPs was symbolic, a gesture reflecting ambitions to be included in future reform.[48] Almost 40% of MPs representing Ireland cast a vote on Mill's proposed amendment, as Table 1.1 illustrates, a fact that has rarely been reflected on in the historiography.[49]

[46] *Manchester National Society for Women's Suffrage Journal* (later *The Women's Suffrage Journal*), i (1870), p. 9.

[47] Miller, 'The British women's suffrage movement', p. 5.

[48] Crawford, *The Women's Suffrage Movement*, p. 253. The uneven pace of reform of women's suffrage across the UK is documented by Pašeta in *Irish Nationalist Women*, p. 17.

[49] Rendall noted that thirteen Irish MPs voted with Mill, but she did not name them all (Rendall, 'John Stuart Mill', p. 178). I have only been able to identify ten Irish MPs who voted with Mill in 1867, with nineteen voting against, as Table 1.1 demonstrates.

Table 1.1. MPs representing Irish constituencies who voted on the proposal by John Stuart Mill to amend the Reform Bill, 20 May 1867[a]

Name of MP (in alphabetical order by surname)	Political affiliation	Constituency at date of vote	Voted for or against the amendment
Hon. Hugh Annesley	Conservative	Cavan	Against
Hon. Henry Bernard	Conservative	Bandon	Against
John Blake	Liberal	Waterford Borough	For
Sir Rowland Blennerhassett	Liberal	Galway Borough	Against
Sir George Bowyer	Liberal/ Independent	Dundalk	For
Lord John Browne	Liberal	Mayo	Against
Henry Bruen	Conservative	Carlow County	Against
Hon. John Cole	Conservative	Enniskillen	Against
Mr Thomas Conolly	Conservative	Donegal	Against
Lord Dunkellin	Liberal	Galway Borough	Against
Sir John Esmonde	Liberal	Waterford Borough	Against
Samuel Getty	Conservative	Belfast	Against
Lord Claud Hamilton	Conservative	Londonderry County (Derry)	Against
Arthur Edwin Hill	Conservative	Down	Against
John King[b]	Conservative	King's County[c]	Against
Nicholas Leader	Conservative	Cork County	Against
Henry Lowry-Corry	Conservative	Tyrone	Against
Sir Joseph McKenna	Conservative	Youghal	For
John Maguire	Liberal	Cork County	For
Charles Moore	Liberal	Tipperary	For
James O'Beirne	Liberal	Cashel	For
The O'Donoghue of the Glens	Liberal	Tipperary	For
Sir James Power	Liberal	Wexford Borough	For
William Pollard-Urquhart	Liberal	Westmeath	For

(*continued*)

Table 1.1. (Cont.)

Name of MP (in alphabetical order by surname)	Political affiliation	Constituency at date of vote	Voted for or against the amendment
George Seymour	Conservative	Antrim	Against
Sir James Stronge	Conservative	Armagh County	Against
Thomas Taylor[d]	Conservative	Dublin County	Against
Crofton Vandeleur	Conservative	Clare	Against
Benjamin Whitworth	Liberal	Drogheda	For
Total number of MPs representing Ireland	**For: 10**	**Against: 19**	

[a]In addition to these names, one can observe names for which members of the same family previously represented Irish boroughs, or who went on to represent them, for example, Lord Robert Montagu voted with Mill and went on to represent Westmeath (31 Jan. 1874–31 Mar. 1880). There are other MPs associated with Ireland through the peerage who voted with Mill, but they did not represent Irish constituencies at the time. For example, Lord Naas did so, but is strangely listed in the ProQuest Parliamentary Papers database as serving only between 1847 and 1857.

[b]A J. G. King and a J. K. King are recorded as voting against Mill's amendment. John King is noted as a Conservative for King's County; there is also a James King in Herefordshire. I am not certain which is the correct middle initial for John King.

[c]This county is now known as Offaly.

[d]Colonel Taylor is noted as voting against the amendment, and I have interpreted this as Thomas Taylor who is noted in the ProQuest Parliamentary Papers Members Database as an army officer by profession.

From this analysis we can see that only one Conservative member, McKenna, voted with Mill, and he was later to become a Liberal.[50] Although the early suffragists never tied themselves to a political party, it seems in the early days this was largely a Liberal cause, both in Ireland and the wider United Kingdom. Indeed, the *Cork Examiner* (owned by Mill supporter John Maguire) uttered extreme scepticism in 1884 at apparent Conservative support for women's suffrage, accusing Conservative politicians of trying to 'overload the Franchise Bill with so many amendments as to render its carriage impossible'.[51]

[50] The ProQuest Parliamentary Papers Database notes that McKenna switched to the Liberals for his next term in office and was a Parnellite in the following election. McKenna represented Youghal, was a deputy lieutenant for the County of Cork, a magistrate for the counties of Cork and Waterford and knighted in 1867.

[51] *Cork Examiner*, 6 June 1884, p. 2.

Bowyer was the only one of the 'Irish group' to contribute to the debate.[52] He had the distinction of being interrupted by Gladstone ('No, no!') upon declaring 'as a principle that everybody was entitled, in the absence of some special disqualification, to exercise the franchise', as Gladstone himself had previously claimed.[53] Bowyer asserted women's right to vote on the same basis as men, drawing attention to the distinguished role women played in public life as monarchs, although tempering his pro-woman stance with the qualification that he 'was no advocate for strong-minded women; but he believed they might exercise the suffrage without abrogating those qualities which specially adorned their sex'.[54] He also thought voting papers, rather than a trip to the hustings, were more appropriate for women, but supported the measure on the principle that many women paid tax and thus should be able to vote.

Representatives from three of the four provinces of Ireland, and a variety of political perspectives, supported Mill. They were a small minority (14%) at this vote, but still more than double those representing Scottish seats (at just five MPs).[55] These MPs articulated a range of other concerns in their parliamentary work, and they did not all demonstrate a sustained interest in women's rights. William Pollard[56] and Benjamin Whitworth seem to have had very limited involvement with women's suffrage (though Whitworth did present eight petitions in its favour) and inevitably others left the House.[57] John Blake (Liberal) is recorded as making 367 speeches at Westminster, although he does not seem to have championed women's suffrage in any.[58] Blake, along with Bowyer, The O'Donoghue of the Glens (Daniel O'Donoghue) and Sir Joseph McKenna, are described in *Dod's* as

[52] Sir George Bowyer (1811–83) stood as both a Liberal and an Independent and represented Dundalk and Wexford during his time at Westminster. M. Stenton (ed.), *Who's Who of British Members of Parliament: a Biographical Dictionary of the House of Commons Based on Annual Volumes of Dod's Parliamentary Companion and other Sources, Volume 1* (Hemel Hempstead, 1976), p. 43.

[53] HC Deb 20 May 1866 vol 187 cc817–852.

[54] HC Deb 20 May 1866 vol 187 cc841.

[55] Rendall, 'John Stuart Mill', p. 178.

[56] Póllard Urquhart was an independent liberal who represented Westmeath, where he also served as a magistrate and deputy lieutenant. Although he forwarded fifty-six publicly sponsored petitions, none was related to women's suffrage.

[57] In 1869, James O'Beirne's election was declared void and Cashel was disenfranchised, meaning he could not be a long-term parliamentary supporter, and Sir James Power (Wexford) retired in 1868. During his three years in Parliament he made no speeches and forwarded forty-nine petitions – none related to women's suffrage.

[58] Blake (1826–87) represented Waterford and Carlow. He served as a deputy lieutenant and as a magistrate for the City of Waterford, where he was also mayor for three years (1855–7). Biographical information taken from Stenton, *Who's Who of British Members*

in favour of Home Rule, indicating that nationalism and suffrage could be harmonious.

Some MPs demonstrated an ambiguous approach to women's rights. John Maguire represented Dungarvan and Cork during his career and was proprietor and editor of the *Cork Examiner* newspaper, established in 1841.[59] Upon his death in 1872 he was acknowledged at a meeting of the Edinburgh Society for Women's Suffrage in appreciation 'of the valuable services rendered' by him on the question of women's enfranchisement, suggesting his efforts were acknowledged UK-wide.[60] This was perhaps due not just to his parliamentary work but also to his 'three-volume novel *The next generation*, which postulated what would happen if women were given basic rights'.[61] While Maguire's newspaper covered suffrage extensively, only a few articles reveal his personal beliefs. In an editorial in April 1867, Maguire chided those who derided Mill, pointing out that he had been proven correct in his thinking on many other matters. Maguire was not quite the feminist champion, however. He did not 'believe the average mental capacity of women is equal to that of men' and made clear that he did not support a radical 'woman's rights' agenda whereby the woman could become the 'father of the house' and a 'promiscuous mixing of the sexes in the House of Commons' would occur, but he could not see why unmarried women should not have the 'privilege of voting at elections'.[62]

There is, however, some evidence of sustained support from some Irish MPs. In a letter from Mill to Thomas Haslam on 17 August 1867, a number of Irish politicians are named as supportive of the cause: Maguire, Blake and Pollard-Urquhart and one other who was absent from the vote in May, Sir John Gray, who attended the 1870 suffrage meeting in Dublin.[63] In September 1867, Mill wrote that a 'good many Irish liberal members

of Parliament, p. 37. Although his parliamentary work primarily saw him involved in fisheries, he clearly had a liberal interest in social questions. He published *Defects in the Moral Treatment of Insanity in the Public Lunatic Asylums of Ireland, with Suggestions for their Remedy, and Some Observations on the English Asylums* (London, 1862) and frequently raised the issue of the mistreatment of prisoners and workhouse inmates who exhibited mental health issues.

[59] This is erroneously recorded as John Francis Meagher by Quinlan in *Genteel Revolutionaries*, p. 113.

[60] *Cork Examiner*, 10 Dec. 1872, p. 3.

[61] S. P. Jones, 'John Francis Maguire', *Dictionary of Irish Biography* database [accessed 21 Sep. 2020].

[62] *Cork Examiner*, 20 Apr. 1867, p. 2.

[63] Haslam Thomas J, Letter concerning the Women's suffrage movement in Dublin from J.S. Mill, Case III lr. Box 1, No. 25 Political, Irish Society of Friends Archive. Gray represented Kilkenny but had been born in Mayo and owned the newspaper the *Freeman's Journal*, although he had trained as a medical doctor. He was a nationalist and a supporter

of Parliament both Catholic and Protestant have already joined the Committee', suggesting there were more than I have been able to identify who offered support.[64] It is difficult to draw conclusions on why these MPs voted with Mill, but it is evidence of a small cohort of Irish MPs open to the idea of women's suffrage.

Monacelli's list of MPs who brought forward suffrage legislation in the House of Commons contains no Irish representatives.[65] This may be because they did not suggest bills solely named as suffrage bills, or bills that addressed legislation for *all* women in the United Kingdom. However, closer examination of a broader range of bills reveals that they did, in fact, attempt to secure both local and national voting rights. It is also true that Irish MPs often did not contribute to debates on franchise bills that left Irish women out. But if any of the bills proposed for Irish women had succeeded, they could have set a precedent for all women in the UK and thus are noteworthy.[66]

Campaigners knew that the pressure on politicians must be maintained, and as such their efforts to change the law had to focus on constituents as well as MPs. The issue of women's suffrage was not debated in the Commons between 1886 and 1892, so activists had to find other ways to keep the issue alive, and petitions, along with pamphlets and drawing room meetings, were a key political tool.[67]

The founding of the Dublin Women's Suffrage Association

It is not clear what happened to Anne or Catherine Robertson after the 1870s, but their early efforts were followed by the founding of the Dublin Women's Suffrage Association (DWSA; the Irish Women's Suffrage and

of O'Connell but became a more hard-line nationalist, supporting Joseph Biggar's policy of obstruction.

[64] Letter from Mill to John Elliott Cairnes, 1 Sept. 1867, from F. E. Mineka and D. N. Lindley (ed.), *John Stuart Mill, The Collected Works of John Stuart Mill, Volume XVI – The Later Letters of John Stuart Mill 1849–1873 Part III* (Toronto, 1972), available from <http://oll.libertyfund.org/titles/253#lf0223-16_head_413> [accessed 21 Sep. 2020]. No further details on who Mill is referring to are available.

[65] M. Monacelli (ed.), *Male Voices on Women's Rights: An Anthology of Nineteenth-Century British Texts* (Manchester, 2017), p. 38, footnote 177 gives a full list of MPs and their political affiliations.

[66] This in fact became a specific bone of contention for activists in the 1910s as the possibility of Irish women being granted voting rights in an Irish Home Rule settlement was mooted (and subsequently quashed).

[67] M. Luddy, 'Feminism', in *The Princeton History of Modern Ireland*, ed. R. Bourke and I. McBride (Princeton, N.J., 2016), pp. 470–89, p. 478.

Local Government Association, IWSLGA, after 1898) by Anna and Thomas Haslam in 1876, attendees at the Fawcett meeting in 1870.[68] This was the second and longest-surviving suffrage group to be initiated in Ireland.[69] Membership cost 1 shilling and though subscriber numbers remained relatively low in comparison to the later militant group, the Irish Women's Franchise League, it was well networked with British suffragists.[70] Quakers, or those connected to the community, were a large proportion of the early committee, allowing them to draw support from MPs also of the Society of Friends, such as Jonathan Pim, Liberal MP and businessman.[71] It had MPs on its committee from the beginning, and 'regular attenders' included T. W. Russell (Liberal), Maurice Brooks (Liberal), Colonel Taylor (Conservative) and William Johnston (Conservative).[72] Such men were progressive thinkers operating in an elite milieu in Ireland involved in multiple organizations interested in contemporary social problems. For example, MPs, academics, philanthropists and businessmen were members of the Statistical and Social Inquiry Society of Ireland (Pim was its sixth president); thus there were crossovers in membership of various scholarly, religious and activist groups.[73] In the case of Russell and Brooks, their wives were also involved as IWSLGA committee members, suggesting a deep connection to the cause.

[68] Anna Haslam has been described as a 'a major figure in the 19th and early 20th-century women's movement in Ireland' due to her tireless activism in the broad area of women's rights, from higher education to protesting against the sexual double standards of the Contagious Diseases Acts (CDAs) and suffrage. See M. Cullen, 'Anna Haslam's minute book', essay available from the NAI website <https://www.nationalarchives.ie/topics/DWSA/> [accessed 21 September 2020]. The social networks developed around other issues such as the CDAs were vital in sustaining and growing support for women's suffrage in Ireland.

[69] The first suffrage society in Ireland was instituted by Isabella Tod in Belfast in 1872 and included the Belfast Unionist MP William Johnston as one of its members. See Crawford, *The Women's Suffrage Movement in Britain and Ireland*, p. 254.

[70] The Irish Women's Franchise League was founded in 1908 by Hanna and Francis Sheehy Skeffington and Margaret and James Cousins, members of the IWSGLA who decided a more militant approach was needed and a distinctly Irish association was more appropriate, as opposed to founding a branch of the Women's Social and Political Union.

[71] Pim sat as a Dublin borough MP between 1865 and 1874 so was not in Parliament to offer sustained support of the suffrage movement but was important as a contact in the early years and may have been able to provide introductions. His shop in Dublin is identified in IWSLGA records as being a place they left copies of the *Women's Suffrage Journal*.

[72] C. Quinlan, 'Genteel revolutionaries: the lives of Anna and Thomas Haslam', PhD thesis (University College Cork, 1999), p. 185. Further analysis of the activities of politicians is given below. Quinlan notes Johnston as a Liberal but he was a Conservative and later a leader of Irish Unionists in Parliament.

[73] Founded in 1847, the Statistical and Social Inquiry Society of Ireland held public talks and published a journal.

MPs interested in suffrage who worked with the committee and outside of it played a key role in highlighting suffrage in this early period but have not received as much scholarly attention as those who supported or blocked suffrage bills in the twentieth century.

Although the Haslams had been officially excluded from the Society of Friends because of Thomas's religious beliefs, this did not stop positive relations between the Haslams and other Friends interested in social reform.[74] This included Alfred Webb, a Quaker publisher used by the IWSLGA, and the Haslams – and this was to prove key in the fight for suffrage. Living from 1858 in a largely Protestant Dublin suburb, Rathmines, Anna became the breadwinner in 1866 when Thomas experienced poor health. Together, they fought for women's rights and outlined their ideas for a more egalitarian society in three issues of a periodical, *The Women's Advocate*. Thomas Haslam 'identified pressure on the individual MP as being the best method of proceeding' in the May 1874 issue.[75] He believed personal entreaties to politicians from their constituents demonstrated that 'there is reality in a cause which inspires so much enthusiasm'.[76] Haslam urged for an abundance of letters from constituents to prove serious intent and the IWSLGA later pursued this as a key tactic. Haslam believed the conversion of MPs one by one would ultimately win the suffrage battle. As well as letters, he saw petitions with high numbers of signatures as crucial. To have effect, they should be forwarded consistently and persistently because while petitions 'do not wield the magical powers with which they are sometimes credited' they could still 'have their weight' and 'when the numbers swell to an aggregate of several hundred thousand, they exercise a potent influence on the public mind'.[77]

The IWSLGA held 213 committee meetings under thirty-four chairs between 1876 and 1913, figures that demonstrate persistence and a wide variety of people involved, despite the overall small numbers of official subscribers to the organization.[78] It appealed to MPs across the political

[74] Quinlan, *Genteel Revolutionaries*, p. 12.

[75] Crawford, *The Women's Suffrage Movement*, p. 255.

[76] *The Women's Advocate*, (1872), p. 6. My thanks to Dr Colin Reid for his help in accessing digitized copies of this journal.

[77] *The Women's Advocate*, (1872), p. 6.

[78] These figures are noted in the inside cover of the IWSLGA minute book which begins on 21 Feb. 1876, and these are the only years for which minutes are available, although the group continued on until 1947, when it merged with the Irish Housewives' Association (minute books available on the National Archives of Ireland (NAI) website <https://www.nationalarchives.ie/topics/DWSA/> [accessed 21 Sep. 2020]). Printed reports of their activities (available from the National Library of Ireland) only exist from 1896, and unfortunately the bequest to file the Haslams' papers with the National Library of Ireland

spectrum, engaging them as speakers and chairs for meetings and, crucially, asking them to organize and forward suffrage petitions from Irish constituencies. The IWSLGA was the most visible suffrage organization in Ireland in the late nineteenth century and was not joined by significant numbers of other groups until the early twentieth century, most notably the Irish Women's Franchise League.[79] The IWSLGA chose not to join the later Irish Women's Suffrage Federation, an umbrella body for organizations in Ireland initiated in 1911, preferring to forge its own path.[80]

The IWSLGA focused its actions in four main areas: securing support for women's suffrage from Irish politicians; conducting meetings, and occasionally larger events with key speakers addressing issues of women's rights; attempting to influence public opinion through letters to the press and the circulation of *The Women's Suffrage Journal* in reading rooms; and the collection of signatures and forwarding of petitions to Parliament. The focus here is on the lesser-researched history of its petitions and its engagement with the politicians who presented it, including a broader analysis of the activities of Irish politicians at Westminster from the 1860s until the 1890s.

Petitions

As Miller and Stuart observed, the 'suffrage campaign was, itself, founded by a petition' in 1866,[81] although thus far there have been only 'scattered references to specific petitions within the vast historiography of suffrage'.[82] Between 1866 and 1890 over 13,000 petitions were sent to Westminster in favour of women's suffrage. These were free to post and had to be handwritten and signed. They were a public form of agitation and, given the numbers of signatures, were signed by far more people than attended

does not seem to have been fulfilled. Piecing together the activities of the DWSA is laborious in the pre-1896 period – a possible reason this era has received less attention from scholars.

79 For a detailed exposition of the Irish Women's Franchise League, see Pašeta, *Irish Nationalist Women*.

80 This was likely because they were a predominantly Unionist and a wholeheartedly non-militant organization, unlike the IWFL, which quickly became the most popular suffrage group in Ireland, although other smaller groups were also non-militant. As Haslam noted in 1917, 'Many have seceded from us because we were not militant enough, from party and other reasons; but we have held on amidst all'. Anna Haslam asserted this independent line as late as 1917 in a piece published in *International Women's News*, xi (1917), p. 141.

81 H. Miller and C. Stewart, 'How 17,000 petitions helped deliver votes for women', The Conversation, 5 Feb. 2018 <https://theconversation.com/how-17-000-petitions-helped-deliver-votes-for-women-91093> [accessed 20 Aug. 2020].

82 Miller, 'The British women's suffrage movement', p. 1.

suffrage meetings.[83] This section seeks to expand our knowledge of this key tactic in the pre-1900 period as it was a major focus of campaigners inside and outside the IWSLGA.[84]

Petitions were perceived to be efficient forms of public protest and their popularity increased rapidly throughout the nineteenth century.[85] Even before the formal organization of suffragists into associations in Ireland, petitions were initiated by individuals interested in advancing the cause. Thus suffragists in Ireland were part of the widespread interest in 'petition drives' that developed 'broad popular coalitions on public issues that cut across geographical boundaries'.[86] The usual course was to forward petitions by post or through politicians, and they could be directed towards either or both houses of Parliament, the monarch or the site of local government.[87]

It has long been known that some Irish women signed the 1866 petition – including Anna Haslam – but so far little attention has been given to the petitions which were generated by Irish women themselves.[88] In addition,

[83] After 1840, petitions of up to thirty-two ounces could be posted for free if they were left open at the sides and sent without a cover; Huzzey and Miller, 'Petitions, Parliament and political culture', p. 144.

[84] Miller's ground-breaking work on suffrage and petitioning focuses on England, Scotland and Wales and does not include Irish data. Miller, 'The British women's suffrage movement'. It is beyond the scope of this chapter to analyse every petition presented from Irish politicians or constituents, but an attempt is made to exemplify their use, and this is a rich area for further research.

[85] Huzzey and Miller, 'Petitions, Parliament and political culture', p. 130.

[86] Huzzey and Miller, 'Petitions, Parliament and political culture', p. 131. Interestingly, only the mayors of London and Dublin had the right to present petitions in person, although no record of a mayor of Dublin doing so in relation to suffrage could be found.

[87] For more on the changing strategies of how petitions were directed, see Miller, 'The British women's suffrage movement'.

[88] It was signed by approximately 1,500 women and contained the signatures, it has been claimed, of twenty-five women based in Ireland. This figure seems to have been derived from the IWSLGA and Anna Haslam was herself one of the signatories, almost a decade before the association was formally founded. This fact is narrated in the IWSLGA publication *Reports of the Irishwomen's Suffrage and Local Government Association from 1896–1918* (Dublin, 1918). The figure has understandably been repeated in general histories of the period and studies of suffrage in Ireland, but it does not appear to be correct. The Houses of Parliament Vote 100 project named twenty-one women as being from Ireland, but it is possible to count twenty-four names with definite Irish addresses. There could, however, be more. There are discrepancies in the numbers due to the difficulty in identifying signatories who did not give full addresses. For example, Emma Phillips of 12 James Street or Mrs P. James of 142 Camden Street *could* be residents of Dublin's south side, or they could be from another part of the UK. This petition was organized before the founding of any formal suffrage organizations in Ireland, so no list of names can be cross-referenced to trace Irish-based

Alfred Webb, the prominent Dublin Quaker and printer, mentioned a petition from Dublin at the time of Mill's proposed amendment that 'was so poorly signed that I am ashamed to mention the number of signatures', thus suggesting a separate document, albeit a tiny show of support for Mill.[89] Mill was to observe more optimistically that 'Mr Webb is not sanguine about gaining much support in Ireland at present, but it will come in time'.[90] In 1868, petitions under the heading 'Representation of the People for the extension of the electoral franchise for women' were forwarded on behalf of the Robertsons – one by Conservative MP for Dublin County Ion Hamilton[91] on behalf of Anne and others, totalling 528 signatures (1.2% of the total 42,555 petition signatures), and one of a total of fifteen forwarded by Jonathan Pim, Liberal MP (Dublin County)[92] on behalf of Catherine and others, totalling 2,046 signatures (4.8% of the total petition signatures).[93] The record of such petitions is laconic – they were not preserved, but merely noted in printed parliamentary reports under formal titles. They made explicit demands for parliamentary franchise for women, usually based on their property qualifications.

Pim and Hamilton presented women's suffrage petitions in June 1869. Hamilton offered petitions from Dalkey (106 signatures), Booterstown (56 signatures) and Williamstown (124 signatures), while Pim presented petitions from Ballyroan (20 signatures), Cork (24 signatures), Bruree

signatories. Information on twenty-one names taken from <http://www.teach1866petition.com/app/uploads/2016/12/1866-Petition-Ireland-Worksheet.pdf> [accessed 21 Sep. 2020]. Names taken from transcribed 1866 Women's Suffrage Petition Name List, pp. 25–6, available from <https://www.parliament.uk/documents/parliamentary-archives/1866SuffragePetitionNamesWebFeb18.pdf> [accessed 21 Sep. 2020].

89 Alfred Webb, 'The propriety of conceding the elective franchise to Women', *Journal of the Statistical and Social Inquiry Society of Ireland*, iv (1867), 455–61, at p. 461.

90 Mill letter to Cairnes, 1 Sept. 1867.

91 Hamilton sat for Dublin between 1863 and 1885 and sponsored a total of 1,141 petitions during his tenure, including twenty-nine in relation to the CDAs, one in relation to the Married Women's Property Bill (15 Mar., 1869, Petition Number: 1605). He sent five petitions in total under the heading 'Representation of the People'.

92 Pim presented sixty-six petitions for the repeal of the Contagious Diseases Act between 1870 and 1873 and sixty-two petitions to alter the laws on Married Women's Property in the same period, including ones from the Robertsons in June 1868 and Mar. 1870. Interestingly, the former is also signed by Dorothea Robertson, another relation, perhaps their mother, given that Catherine's middle name is Dorothea. Pim was associated with presenting 517 public petitions throughout his career.

93 Petition number 16151 and 16152 respectively, Parliamentary Petitions for 1868, available on ProQuest UK Parliamentary Papers.

(21 signatures) and Dublin (3,164 signatures).[94] These were part of a total of 167 petitions presented on women's suffrage with 29,320 signatures, meaning the Irish proportion of signatories (3,515) was just under 12% of the total. This suggests lively support for the issue in the earliest phase of the movement.[95] In 1870, a similar petition was presented by Pim from residents of Kingstown (now Dun Laoghaire, 13 signatures), Blackrock (3 signatures), Williamstown (3 signatures), Booterstown (5 signatures) and Dublin city (129 signatures), as well as from County Longford (2 signatures) in support of women's suffrage. In total, Pim collected 155 signatures in February of that year, constituting 11% of the signatures forwarded in fifteen petitions presented in that session.[96] Unfortunately, as the petitions themselves were not kept, we cannot recover any demographic detail on the signatories of this, or any, petition unless specific names of petitioners are recorded in its title. However, the Dublin suburbs referred to are the more affluent areas of the south side, so one can speculate that they were, perhaps, of the middle and upper classes.

Early activists also rallied in support for the Women's Disabilities Removal Bill between 1870 and 1873. For example, Pim presented 106 petitions in favour of this bill, three on behalf of the Robertsons,[97] but other women's names emerge that have not come to light before: Margaret Forde of 10 Brunswick Street Dublin;[98] Mary Hatton of 17 Henry Street Dublin;[99] Lucy Fegan, Ellen Brennan, Anna Anderson, Elizabeth Whelan and Christina Coyle.[100] In the case of these individuals, it appears they forwarded petitions just with their own signature, exercising their right to

[94] Petition numbers 15731, 15732, 15733, 15734, 15735, 15736 and 15737 respectively, Parliamentary Petitions for 1869, available on ProQuest UK Parliamentary Papers.

[95] In 1861, the population of Ireland was almost 20% and in 1871 it was 17% of the overall UK population. Calculations made using 'UK population estimates 1851 to 2014 – Office for National Statistics' file available at <https://www.ons.gov.uk/file?uri=/peoplepopulationandcommunity/populationandmigration/populationestimates/adhocs/004356ukpopulationestimates1851to2014/ukpopulationestimates18512014.xls> [accessed 21 Sep. 2020].

[96] Details recorded in 'Reports of the Select Committee of the House of Commons on Public Petitions – Session 1870' in *Manchester National Society for Women's Suffrage Journal*, i (1870), p. 5.

[97] Petitions numbered 8399 (Anne), 8433 (Catherine) and 9899 (Anne).

[98] 31 Mar. 1873, Petition Number: 8400.

[99] 2 Apr. 1873, Petition Number: 8469.

[100] 25 Apr. 1872, Petition Number: 14612; 25 Apr. 1872, Petition Number: 14614; 30 Apr. 1872, 29 Apr. 1872, Petition Number: 16461; 29 Apr. 1872, Petition Number: 16462; Petition Number: 16522 respectively. No address is recorded for any of these women.

an opinion, along with those who signed the 6,406 public petitions the bill attracted. Hamilton presented fifty-eight petitions between 1870 and 1882 (most in the early 1870s) on the Women's Disabilities proposal, including one from Anne Robertson.[101] Again, other individual women living in Dublin city centre and southern suburbs appear: Emily M'Nally, Catherine M'Loughlin, Catherine Brereton, Susan Jackson and Elizabeth Ward all had city-centre addresses,[102] while Elizabeth Debitt, Eliza Langan, Mary Weston, Anne Kavanagh, Eliza Kelly, Catherine Andrews, Elizabeth Mason and Mary Keely lived in wealthy suburban areas.[103] The same date appears on many of the petitions, suggesting someone (Hamilton, Pim or perhaps one of the Robertsons, who lived near many) coordinated their creation. None are signatories of the 1866 petition. Further research is needed on these clusters of women, but their petitioning hints at an invested population of civic-minded individuals in Dublin, aware of petitioning as a legitimate form of protest for the unenfranchised. How many of these women became IWSLGA subscribers is unknown, nor can we discern if they joined other organizations, such is the fragmentary nature of the evidence. Crawford has analysed some petitions from 1870 and managed to trace names that suggest that 'women who were certainly of the "trade" class, and were possibly Catholics, were already aware of the suffrage campaign'.[104] This palimpsestic history suggests a broader and more mixed base of suffrage supporters, in Dublin at least, than the IWSLGA membership record generally indicates.

Signatories to IWSLGA petitions throw its small subscriber numbers into stark relief, for while membership was small (at a maximum it had between 700 and 800 members in 1912 after thirty-six years in existence), it regularly managed to obtain hundreds of unique signatures.[105] One of its first actions was to petition in support of the Women's Disabilities Removal Bill. At its second meeting in April 1876 it had 138 signatures, but the total finally

[101] 21 May 1874, Petition Number: 7429.

[102] 2 Apr. 1873, Petition Number: 8448; 2 Apr. 1873, Petition Number: 8449; 2 Apr. 1873, Petition Number: 8450; 10 June 1874, Petition Number: 12168; 12 June 1874, Petition Number: 12219 respectively.

[103] 4 May 1870, Petition Number: 9208; 4 May 1870, Petition Number: 9209; 4 May 1870, Petition Number: 9210; 10 June 1874, Petition Number: 12169; 10 June 1874, Petition Number: 12170; 12 June 1874, Petition Number: 12220; 19 June 1874, Petition Number: 13566; 19 June 1874, Petition Number: 13567 respectively.

[104] Crawford, *The Women's Suffrage Movement in Britain and Ireland*, p. 254. Crawford appears to have got the number of total petitions from Ireland for 1870 (she claims there were just 28) and she does not specify how she was able to identify individual names, but her insights point to some interesting avenues in need of further research.

[105] Quinlan, 'Genteel revolutionaries', PhD thesis, p. 246.

amounted to 3,741.[106] It paid for signatures to be collected, at 5 shillings per 100 signatures, a regular expense noted by the committee, although who it paid and what networks it used is sadly not recorded.[107] It is noteworthy that the committee did not undertake this activity itself. This contrasts with Anne Robertson, who claimed she spoke to 'thousands of the inhabitants of Dublin separately and individually in their own homes'.[108] However, other groups employed canvassers, a fact Pugh highlights as reflecting not just public sentiments but the resources groups had.[109]

The IWSLGA minutes do not reveal its strategy for selecting MPs to present its petitions. There is little discussion of petitions at all, suggesting their efficacy and need was accepted by all and did not require in-depth discussion. Thomas Haslam had already forcefully outlined his (and Anna's) ideas in *The Women's Advocate* two years before the establishment of the committee, arguing that 'Unless we are prepared to sign our names a hundred times within the year, should any righteous purpose seem to call for it; unless we are prepared to spend both time and money in the cause; we are not the stuff of which Reformers are made'.[110] Haslam also took for granted that MPs would help any interested citizen: 'They are bound, as honourable men, to do their duty by their constituents irrespectively of party considerations; and, unless their ears are open to such appeals, the House of Commons is not their rightful place'.[111]

Petitions from Ireland in 1866–7 in favour of the Women's Disabilities Removal Bill came from several Irish politicians as part of the 5,356 petitions forwarded with 1,650,408 total signatures.[112] A decade later, a continued commitment to petitions by Irish MPs is evident; Benjamin Whitworth, as noted above, forwarded eight petitions between March 1876 and June 1877 from Ulster constituents. Clearly this was thought to be an important issue in Ireland, despite the slow start of an organized committee outside of Belfast. The July 1877 IWSLGA meeting recorded several petitions sent in that month and the range of politicians forwarding them is noteworthy.

[106] IWSLGA, *Reports of the Executive Committee of the Dublin Women's Suffrage (and Poor Law Guardians) Association for 1896–1918* (Dublin, 1919), p. 4.

[107] IWSLGA Minutes, 29 Apr. 1879 (NAI).

[108] Crawford, *The Women's Suffrage Movement in Britain and Ireland*, p. 254.

[109] Pugh, *The March of the Women*, p. 18.

[110] *The Women's Advocate*, ii (1874), p. 8.

[111] *The Women's Advocate*, ii (1874), p. 7.

[112] Information provided on ProQuest Parliamentary Papers Database. Unfortunately, there is no way to filter the data on petitions by region in the current iteration of the database [accessed 1 Sep. 2020].

Table 1.2. Petitions in favour of the Women's Disabilities Removal Bill, July 1877.

Place	Signatures for petition and MP	Political affiliation
Inhabitants of Kingstown	126 signatures Col. Taylor	Conservative
Inhabitants of Dublin	546 signatures Mr Maurice Brooks	Home Rule
Inhabitants of Dublin	438 signatures Mr O'Shaughney (sic)[a]	Home Rule
Inhabitants of Rathmines	157 signatures Sergeant David Sherlock	Liberal/Home Rule
Inhabitants of Dublin	1 [?][b]	Home Rule/Liberal
Public Meeting	493	
Inhabitants of Dublin Women householders	132 Mr Brooks	
Inhabitants of Dublin	469 Edmund Dwyer Gray[c]	Home Rule
Professions etc. TCD	81 Edward Gibson	Conservative
Presbyterian ministers	9 Miss Tod	n/a
Total	**2,326**	

[a]This is Mr Richard O'Shaughnessy, a Home Rule MP for Limerick Borough.
[b]This could be one petition as opposed to one signature.
[c]Owner of the *Freeman's Journal* newspaper and husband of Caroline Agnes Chisholm.

Taylor is noted as presenting petitions and joining the committee, but had voted against Mill's 1867 amendment, denoting a change of mind in the decade before the DWSA's establishment. Taylor continued to forward IWSLGA petitions in 1879, 1880, 1881 and 1882.[113] William Johnston, although noted by Quinlan as attending regular committee meetings, is not recorded as forwarding any women's suffrage petitions, although he did introduce legislation, as noted below.[114]

[113] IWSLGA Minutes – handwritten notes with details of petitions appear in incomplete form after the last entry for minutes of 8 Jan. 1914. The ProQuest Parliamentary Papers Database notes Taylor as also having forwarded fifteen petitions against the CDAs, three in relation to the Married Women's Property bills in 1869 and 1881, and ten related to the Women's Disabilities Removal Bill.

[114] Information from ProQuest Parliamentary Papers Database. He is noted as forwarding twenty-four petitions against the CDAs.

Newer MPs or those absent from the momentous Mill amendment vote were nevertheless IWSLGA collaborators. O'Shaughnessy forwarded fifteen separate petitions to Parliament on the Women's Disabilities Bill (as well as six in favour of the repeal of the CDAs). Gray forwarded three petitions related to the Disabilities Bill, as well as another under the title of Parliamentary Franchise (Extension of Women) Bill. In 1879, the IWSLGA minuted that 3,191 signatures had been gathered in support of the Disabilities Bill, drawing on the same range of MPs as well as the addition of Parnell (Home Rule), Kenelm Digby (Liberal/Home Rule) and The O'Conor Don (Denis O'Connor), a Liberal who forwarded twenty-four petitions (and one protesting the CDAs).[115] Thus, despite its Unionist leanings, the IWSLGA continued to lobby and utilize politicians from across the political spectrum. For example, Parnell is not generally associated with the suffrage movement and is often regarded as a conservative force when it came to women in the public sphere due to his role in stifling the work of the Ladies' Land League. This group, including his two sisters, Anna and Fanny, invigorated the League while the male leadership were in prison and are regarded by many as feminist activists. However, records of the IWSLGA reveal that he raised two petitions for it in 1877: one with 465 signatures[116] and another with 28 signatures.[117] As Cliona Murphy observed, while Parnell could not 'be described as an ardent woman suffragist' he 'did not actively resist' the movement and recognized its 'growing significance'.[118] There is other evidence to suggest that Parnell may have been a suffragist – Ward notes that his great-aunt was an executive member of the American Women's Suffrage Association.[119] While this is speculative, it further suggests that in the nineteenth century

[115] He is not noted in the ProQuest Parliamentary Papers Database as having forwarded a petition, so it seems he gathered signatures instead.

[116] IWSLGA Minutes, 29 Apr. 1879 (NAI).

[117] ProQuest Parliamentary Papers Database biographical entry for Charles Stuart Parnell.

[118] C. Murphy, '"The tune of the stars and the stripes": the American influence on the Irish suffrage movement', in *Women Surviving: Studies in Irish Women's History in the 19th and 20th Centuries*, ed. M. Luddy and C. Murphy (Dublin, 1990), pp. 180–205, p. 185. This marks a key difference between the nineteenth and twentieth centuries in terms of political context. By the early twentieth century women's right to vote and Ireland's right to govern itself were deemed by some to be in bitter competition. Parnell's successor as leader of the Irish Parliamentary Party, John Redmond, was singled out for scorn and attacks because of his contrary position to women's right to the national vote, which was a result of his personal antipathy rather than party politics.

[119] M. Ward, 'Anna Parnell: Challenges to male authority and the telling of national myth', in *Parnell Reconsidered*, ed. P. Travers and D. McCartney (Dublin, 2013), pp. 47–60, p. 48.

campaigners could reasonably expect to be championed by politicians who stood on different sides of the Irish Question.[120]

There were other MPs, such as Thomas Russell, a Liberal/Liberal Unionist representing Tyrone who was also a committee member and forwarded ten petitions in favour of women's suffrage between 1887 and 1889, one of which specifically named the DWSA.[121] Maurice Brooks was also used by the IWSLGA until his retirement in 1885; he forwarded eleven petitions on the extension of the franchise to women, including two that specifically named the DWSA.[122] His wife, however, remained active in the suffrage cause; the 1896 report noted that Mrs M. Brooks was a committee member. MPs could also be asked to forward petitions from those not in their constituency, but perhaps known for their sympathies. Thus, Brooks forwarded women's suffrage petitions on behalf of constituents in the borough of Hyde. Similarly, the IWSLGA had petitions presented for it by politicians outside Irish boroughs, such as Jacob Bright, who is noted in the 1882 minutes as having done so.[123] Further examination of Bright's record reveals several examples of petitions from Irish constituencies, even before the founding of the DWSA. This exemplifies how activists utilized existing networks and structures to press forward its demands and indicates a connection possibly initiated by the Robertsons' links to Becker and the Manchester-based activists. The use of politicians from different boroughs throughout Britain and Ireland by constituents in each country indicates the importance of viewing the suffrage movement as a network across UK and Ireland rather than as two separate movements.

One petition from Dublin includes a rare exposition of the petition text: 'the exclusion of women, otherwise legally qualified, from voting in the election of Members of Parliament, is unjust to those excluded, contrary to the principle of true representation, and morally injurious to

[120] In a further irony, Christabel Pankhurst claimed that Parnell's radical political tactics inspired the WSPU in theirs, and yet his successors became hostile to women's enfranchisement when it threatened to scupper Irish nationalist hopes of independence in the 1910s. Pašeta, *Irish Nationalist Women*, p. 72.

[121] 1 Feb. 1887, Petition Number: 13; it is noted that this petition resulted from a meeting on 3 Dec. 1886 held in Eustace Buildings, the Friends Meeting House in Dublin city centre, chaired by Thomas Haslam.

[122] 11 June 1880, Petition Number: 947 on the Borough Franchise names Anna Haslam and the DWSA; 26 Mar. 1884, Petition Number: 3647 the DWSA and the Chair, Mr Wigham, on the Parliamentary Franchise extension to women. Usually, petitions are noted as 'Inhabitants of Dublin' or suchlike, with the occasional named person as detailed above. Brooks is listed as both a Liberal and a Home Rule MP and served the Dublin borough between 1874 and 1885. He forwarded sixty-eight petitions related to the CDAs.

[123] Bright was a well-known Liberal MP who represented Manchester South West (1886–95).

the whole community'.[124] Signed by 155 people, the main signatories were James Haughton, J.P., Anne Barbara Corbett (most likely Corlett) and C. M. B. Stoker.[125] Corlett was a member of the IWSLGA but used her position with the Queen's Institute to forward petitions in her own right too. In June 1880, Dr Robert Lyons, Liberal MP for Dublin, forwarded a petition on her behalf that used similar language.[126] This suggests a strategy of using the name of the IWSLGA *and* the names of prominent members to lend credibility to petitions.

In 1884 and 1885, Hamilton forwarded thirty-five petitions (out of a total of 1,543) for the Extension of the Parliamentary Franchise to women, including one from 'Members of the Irish Society For Women's Suffrage', with its president noted as Anne Robertson.[127] Hamilton is also minuted as forwarding petitions on behalf of the IWSLGA in 1884. This raises several questions which cannot be answered using extant sources. Why did Robertson not join the IWSLGA? Who were the members of this other society? Presumably, it was the existing Dublin Committee of the early 1870s, but why did it still exist on its own? Was there a crossover in membership between the two groups? I cannot trace any personal relationship between Robertson and the IWSLGA, but it is unlikely that in such a small circle of progressive reformers they did not know each other, and, as recorded earlier, Haslam attended a talk organized by Robertson in 1858. It appears in 1884 the two groups were duplicating their efforts and targeting the same politicians for help. This suggests either a rift between individuals in these groups, or, more positively, a buoyant cohort of interested citizens with enough members to require more than one group in Dublin.

The Reform Bill of 1884 excited much agitation from Ireland. The IWSLGA minutes of 12 March 1884 record a petition signed by the meeting on behalf of the chair, Henry Wigham, and plans to send a 'memorial to Mr Gladstone begging him to include women householders in the proposed Franchise Bill'.[128] Unfortunately, the IWSLGA's following two meetings do not mention how many petitions it raised, but do record its intention

[124] 27 Apr. 1871, Petition Number: 6959, Appendix Number: 6959 (which gives the full text).

[125] It is likely this is a misprint and it is supposed to say Corlett, Founder and Secretary of the Queen's Institute in Dublin, an educational institution for women.

[126] 8 Jun. 1880, Petition Number: 535, Appendix Number: 535 gives the full text. Lyons forwarded several other petitions in favour of women's suffrage.

[127] 1 Apr. 1884, Petition Number: 5680. The petition is recorded as arising from a meeting, the date or location of which is not recorded.

[128] IWSLGA Minute Book, 12 Mar. 1884 (NAI).

to send a petition to the House of Lords.[129] It also sent letters to fifty-four newspapers in Leinster, Munster and Connaught and at least thirty published them. It entreated support from readers for its claim, which was a 'peculiarly moderate, reasonable and seasonable one'.[130] This tactical line of pressure on both the public and politicians continued throughout the year. By October it had sent sixteen petitions to the House of Lords and twelve to the House of Commons as well as 'numerous letters' to 'various members'; this was recorded at a meeting attended by Helen Blackburn, who provided them with a 'very interesting account of the present aspect of the question in England'.[131] This phrasing denotes a certain distance between the 'present aspect' in both countries, despite their petitioning of the same Parliament. Unfortunately, 1884 was not to be the year for women's suffrage, but its activities continued and in the absence of any public meetings, petitioning and canvassing public support through letters to the newspapers were the main methods used. Fifty-eight Irish politicians are named alongside others in the 'List of parliamentary friends of women's suffrage, April, 1889' which appeared in the *Publications of the Central Committee National Society of Women's Suffrage 1889–1893*. It detailed a range of supports, from public statements, election promises by letter and signed memorandums.[132] The list included the nationalist leaders Charles Stewart Parnell and, surprisingly, John Redmond.[133] Such a guide allowed activists to identify which politicians could be counted on to highlight women's suffrage. The fact that it was presented alphabetically, rather than regionally, suggests all on the list were understood to be potential allies, no matter what constituency activists were based in. Given that Irish MPs had to travel to Westminster, they could be of use in furthering the cause in London as well as in Ireland. For example, Justin McCarthy, Irish Parliamentary Party MP, presided over a pro-suffrage meeting in Kensington in 1886 from which a petition was raised.[134]

[129] IWSLGA Minute Book, 26 June 1884 (NAI).

[130] Letter printed in *The Nation*, 19 Apr. 1884, p. 11.

[131] IWSLGA Minute Book, 27 Oct. 1884 (NAI).

[132] National Society of Women's Suffrage, *Publications of the Central Committee National Society of Women's Suffrage 1889–1893*. Available in digital form from <https://digital.library.lse.ac.uk/objects/lse:ben328xot> [accessed 21 Sep. 2020].

[133] Parnell is listed as having voted in 1878 and spoke in a debate and voted in 1879 in favour of women's suffrage; Redmond is listed as voting in 1886 and signing a memorial in 1889. National Society of Women's Suffrage, *Publications of the Central Committee National Society of Women's Suffrage 1889–1893*.

[134] The petition was titled as emanating from 'Attendants at a Drawing Room Meeting Assembled at South Kensington; Justin McCarthy, Chairman', 2 Mar. 1886, Petition

Suffrage petitions peaked in the 1870s, declined in numbers in the 1880s but became popular again in the 1890s, and the Irish experience replicates this wider UK trend.[135] Evidence on petitions is not systematically recorded in the IWSLGA minutes after 1889, which perhaps suggests a concurrence with Miller and Huzzey's findings that the 1890s saw an overall reduction in that strategy. However, petitions proposing local and national voting rights still occurred. Sir Horace Plunkett, for example, an Irish Unionist Alliance MP for South County Dublin, forwarded two petitions in June (263 signatures) and July (17 signatures) 1897 in favour of the Parliamentary Franchise (Extension of Women) Bill. The June petition emanated from a meeting presided over by Lady Margaret Dockrell, a member of the IWSLGA executive committee and an elected local government councillor from 1898, demonstrating the continued connection to Irish politicians through petitions and meetings.[136]

Irish MPs were sporadic in their support for women's suffrage in Britain, but they do seem to have been energetic at times in specifically enfranchising Irish women. For example, although Blennerhassett (Liberal) had voted against Mill's amendment, in 1880 he moved in committee a clause to the Irish Borough Franchise Bill that would extend the franchise to women, suggesting a change of mind or an acceptance of local, rather than national, voting rights for women. Suffrage bills were presented 'almost every year' after 1866, but, according to Monacelli, 'the question did not significantly reappear in the parliamentary debates until the 1884 Reform Act'.[137] Nevertheless the bills forwarded by MPs are worthy of notice for their frequency and, in the Irish case, for the commitment to keeping women's suffrage away from party lines and outside of increasing tensions about the 'Irish Question'.

The 1884 debates had some noteworthy Irish participants. Edward King Harman, Conservative MP for Dublin, drew attention to the 400,000 potentially qualified women voters in comparison to the 2 million men the bill proposed to enfranchise. He also highlighted a specifically Irish dimension to the legislation.

> The right hon. Gentleman [Gladstone] considers that the ship would be swamped by 400,000 extra votes of women; but he does not seem to fear, in the least, the enormous number of extra Irish votes he proposes to take on

---

Number: 424. McCarthy presented four petitions between 1884 and 1886 in support of women's suffrage from both Ireland and the UK.

[135] Pugh, *The March of the Women*, p. 18.

[136] Biographical entry for Horace Plunkett, ProQuest Parliamentary Papers Database.

[137] Monacelli, *Male Voices*, p. 39.

> board – a number far exceeding that which he put before us in his opening speech. Then, we are told, this is a matter which can wait. And what are the women likely to get by waiting? They have waited 17 years, during which the subject has been discussed; and now they are told that they are to wait until 2,000,000 of the common orders have been admitted to a share in the Parliamentary management of the country – 2,000,000 of the substratum of society from which the enemies, the oppressors, of women come; from which come the wife-beaters and wife-kickers, whom we see mentioned in our police reports nearly every day.

These arguments drew on the 'moral respectability' of qualified women, in comparison to the alleged 'abusers' within the lower classes who were about to be enfranchised, as well as the specific consequences of enfranchising a large proportion of Irish men. King Harman did not need to point out the majority nationalist persuasion of Irish voters in this context, but the imbrication of the Irish Question with votes for women is an element lacking in analysis in most accounts of the suffrage movement. King Harman's speech, although loaded with class bias, does highlight a key point in the debates: enfranchising new populations always contained an element of risk, so why not enfranchise respectable women who simply wanted their say?

William Johnston, the Conservative MP who founded the Belfast suffrage organization with Isabella Tod, and attended IWSLGA meetings, proved to be one of the more active MPs from Ireland, despite not forwarding any suffrage petitions. For example, Johnston introduced a bill to extend the parliamentary and municipal franchise for women in Ireland in February 1895. This bill, which had different provisions for England, Scotland and Ireland (due to the different ways women's voting rights developed), specifically stated that any person in Ireland, regardless of sex or marital status, who was a ratepayer, or who was entitled to vote at an election for guardians of the poor should receive both local and national franchise rights. This bill was drafted by MPs from different parties and parts of the United Kingdom, a collaboration which further strengthens the argument, made most strenuously by Pašeta, that any analysis of the 'British' suffrage movement must take into account the collaboration between activists inside and outside Parliament across the UK.[138] Most notably, at the same time as this bill was being proposed, Johnston and Justin McCarthy (and other nationalist politicians) vehemently disagreed on the erection of a statue of Oliver Cromwell in the grounds of Westminster. While the suffrage issue was broadly non-party, this kind of alliance by politicians divided so bitterly on the Irish Question is commendable.

[138] Pašeta, *Suffrage and Citizenship in Ireland.*

In February 1897, twenty-six Irish MPs voted in favour of the Parliamentary Suffrage Bill and seventeen against. This disappointed the IWSLGA, which thought it had at least thirty guaranteed proponents of women's suffrage among Irish MPs, with more yet to declare their sentiments. It was confident, however, that 'our Parliamentary leaders will lose no available opportunity of pushing' the bill 'if practicable, to a successful issue'. This hope was fostered again by Johnston who proposed a Dublin Corporation Bill that requested qualified women receive the municipal franchise in Dublin. This carried by 91 votes in favour to 63 against, suggesting greater political support for *local* voting rights for Irish women, undoubtedly less controversial than tackling national-level suffrage.

Conclusion

In May 1870, Lydia Becker appeared exasperated that in Parliament: 'The men get attended to first, as a matter of course and of right. If there is anything left after their wants are fully satisfied, a little of the superfluity is, as a matter of favour, bestowed on the other sex.'[139] Becker's bitter words about women as an afterthought in political life take on a more potent resonance when considered in the context of Irish women, fighting not just patriarchal notions of women's place but for attention amid the clamour for Home Rule.

Primary sources reveal a dedicated, politically savvy, well-networked bloc of middle- and upper-class activists in Ireland who attempted to push forward the agenda for women's rights, with the right to vote in national elections being their highest aspiration. While the arrival of the DWSA is a landmark in the history of suffrage activism in Ireland, it is clear from petition records there were activists long before their establishment in 1876. The existence of more than one group in Dublin suggests a larger pool of active, interested citizens than has been written about before. Nevertheless, the IWSLGA was the most visible and coordinated group and, although it had few official members, they were able to gather thousands of signatures for their cause in Ireland and consistently engaged with MPs in forwarding them to Parliament, as well as sending some directly themselves. Petitions were a consistent feature of IWSLGA endeavours, following the edict of *The Women's Advocate* that 'petitioning should be a steady, not an intermitting effort' and that 'persistent steadiness of action from one year to another is the thing most wanted'.[140] This attitude to petitioning confirms Huzzey and Miller's contention that the 'time, money and energy that campaigners invested in petitioning is testament to its central importance within

[139] *Manchester National Society for Women's Suffrage Journal*, i (1870), p. 17.

[140] *The Women's Advocate*, ii (1874), p. 6.

nineteenth-century repertoires of collective action'.[141] Unlike other groups Huzzey and Miller refer to, where petitions were married with public meetings to maximize impact, the political situation in Ireland meant the IWSLGA used them *instead* of physical meetings at times. The IWSLGA also seems to have differed from British peer petitioners in the early twentieth century as the latter moved to a focus on the 'visual spectacle' of petitions, such as posting canvassers at polling stations in a drive to gain signatures from actual rather than aspiring voters.[142]

Suffragists in Ireland enjoyed varied support from Irish MPs, an experience in common with women in the rest of the UK as members gained and lost seats, resigned or died. While this meant a core bloc of support was always lacking, it also might have sustained hope that the cause could be won as different politicians in different years offered support. There can be a tendency to downplay the achievements of early suffrage activists because they did not win the national vote in their decades of campaigning, or, as Liddington has phrased it, 'it is easy to lose sight of the quieter suffragist story'.[143] But as early scholarship on the period by Margaret MacCurtain argued, it was the 'persistent, non-militant penetration of Irish public opinion' engaged in by the IWSLGA that resulted in steady franchise gains for women.[144]

More than 16,000 petitions were presented to the Houses of Parliament asking for votes for women between 1866 and 1918. Thus, the decision to grant women the vote in 1918 did not come solely because of militant tactics of the previous decade, and Irish suffrage activists and politicians played their part in shifting public opinion. In doing so they instilled a feminist consciousness in many women as Ireland commenced its political independence which unfortunately saw a backlash against the egalitarian values aspired to by these persistent protestors.

[141] Huzzey and Miller, 'Petitions, Parliament and political culture', p. 146.

[142] Miler, 'The British women's suffrage movement', p. 22.

[143] J. Liddington, *Rebel Girls: their Fight for the Vote* (London, 2006), p. 264.

[144] M. MacCurtain, 'Women, the vote and revolution', in *Women in Irish Society: The Historical Dimension*, ed. M. MacCurtain and D. Ó Corráin (Dublin, 1978), pp. 46–57, p. 47.

2. Singing 'The Red Flag' for suffrage: class, feminism and local politics in the Canning Town branch of the Women's Social and Political Union, 1906–7*

Lyndsey Jenkins

On the evening of 29 January 1906, a group of unemployed women from West Ham met to discuss their shared plight. Minnie Baldock, who took the chair, 'explained … why they should combine together'.[1] It was duly agreed that they should send a deputation to the assistance board, articulating their demands.[2] The following week, the women met again, where they received a report from the deputation, as well as hearing how working-women in Hammersmith were benefiting from nursery provision. By the third meeting, addressed by the well-known activist Dora Montefiore, the women had resolved to stage a demonstration in favour of women's suffrage, while at the fourth meeting, where Eva Gore-Booth and Esther Roper were the speakers, they agreed to make their case in Hyde Park. During the following meeting, Emmeline Pankhurst 'made a long and good speech' and the women decided to 'form themselves into a union. A branch of the Social and Political Union was formed 34 of the women joining' (sic).[3]

These women thus founded the first branch of what is now better known as the Women's Social and Political Union (WSPU) outside

* With grateful thanks to Jenni Munro-Collins at the Stratford Archives and Heritage Centre, and Beverley Cook at the Museum of London. Thank you also to Alexandra Hughes-Johnson, Senia Pašeta, Zoë Thomas and Selina Todd for their comments on earlier versions of this piece.

[1] Canning Town Minute Book (hereafter CTMB), 29 Jan. 1906, Museum of London, 50.82/1133.

[2] An account of this meeting can also be found in 'Meeting of unemployed women', *Stratford Express*, 6 Feb. 1906.

[3] CTMB, 27 Feb. 1906.

'Singing "The Red Flag" for suffrage', in *The politics of women's suffrage: local, national and international dimensions*, ed. A. Hughes-Johnson and L. Jenkins (London, 2021), pp. 59–86.

the Pankhursts' home territory of Manchester. Through their branch, the unemployed women of West Ham not only attempted to address the difficulties that they were experiencing through lack of work, but made a case for the extension of the franchise, which they believed would make a long-term difference to their lives. These women were at the heart of WSPU activities in its first year in London and formed a prominent part of demonstrations in the capital. Members also campaigned to secure more immediate relief and support by pressurizing local authorities to take their needs seriously. Despite the urgency of their demands, meetings were often joyful occasions, characterized by songs and recitations as well as by speeches and reports, which helped to forge a shared solidarity. Yet by the following autumn membership had plummeted. In early December 1907, members were expressing 'dissatisfaction' and demanding to know 'why the branch had been neglected'.[4] The minute book ends on this plaintive note. With no further records available, it seems that the organization had collapsed before its second birthday and the promise of this energetic branch and its committed members was lost.[5]

On first reading, the history of the Canning Town branch seems to confirm many of the shortcomings of the WSPU as a political organization. Historians have often argued that the WSPU failed to engage with working-class women's needs. Many have suggested that working-class women found middle-class women's concerns irrelevant to their lives, that they perceived feminism and socialism to be incompatible and that they were unable or unwilling to participate in militancy.[6] Careful attention to the minute book of the Canning Town branch suggests that many of the criticisms levelled at the WSPU are inapplicable here. These women had their own clearly developed political agenda, linked but not limited to acquisition of the vote, which was underpinned by an explicit commitment to socialist principles. They embraced direct action, some undertaking prison sentences themselves, and celebrated others who engaged in militancy.

[4] CTMB, 5 Dec. 1907.

[5] Brief narratives of the Canning Town branch can be found in E. Crawford, *The Women's Suffrage Movement, A Reference Guide, 1866–1928* (London, 2003), pp. 94–5 and D. Atkinson, *Rise Up Women! The Remarkable Lives of the Suffragettes* (London, 2018), pp. 32–79.

[6] J. Liddington and J. Norris, *One Hand Tied Behind Us: The Rise of the Women's Suffrage Movement* (London, 1978), pp. 205–7; R. S. Neale, 'Working-class women and women's suffrage', in *Class and Ideology in the Nineteenth Century* (London, 1972); S. van Wingerden, *The Women's Suffrage Movement in Britain, 1866–1928* (Basingstoke, 1999), p. 77; M. Pugh, *The March of the Women: a Revisionist Analysis of the Campaign for Women's Suffrage, 1866–1914* (Oxford, 2002), pp. 171–223.

This chapter therefore examines the Canning Town branch on its own terms, rather than through its relationship to the national organization. It argues that the historical interest of the Canning Town branch lies in its life, not its demise, and that it has much to tell us about the ways which working-class women practised politics at the turn of the century. The women of the Canning Town branch used the opportunities offered by a woman-led organization to further their own political objectives. These women identified as workers and, as such, demanded both the right to work and the right to vote. Though a product of a thriving socialist culture, they were not afraid to challenge the gendered practice of a labour movement they thought was neglecting their interests. They embraced direct action to make immediate improvements to their own lives and to secure the vote. They took the anticipated responsibilities of citizenship seriously, and prioritized political education, determined to prepare themselves to use the vote effectively. Their efforts were grounded in an intensely sociable political culture which, by turns, expressed joy and optimism, and sorrow and sympathy. By highlighting these features, this chapter sheds new light on the nature of working-class women's political priorities and practice. It emphasizes both their political capabilities and their efforts to expand and enhance these capabilities. The significance of the Canning Town branch lies not in how we interpret its failure but in how we assess its strengths.

The recent historiographical focus on the local politics of suffrage has transformed our understanding of the suffrage campaign. Studies of the WSPU have challenged the reductive portrait of a supposedly autocratic organization run as Christabel Pankhurst's personal fiefdom. Instead, these studies have shown how much agency and autonomy local branches exercised in determining their own priorities and strategies.[7] National policy was never simply replicated in local practice. These local branches were often the initial and primary means by which women engaged with the suffrage campaign. As such, they defined both the nature of the campaign in local communities and women's experiences of it. Historians of the Labour Party have also emphasized the importance of the local context for

[7] L. Leneman, 'A truly national movement: the view from outside London', in *The Women's Suffrage Movement: New Feminist Perspectives*, ed. M. Joannou and J. Purvis (Manchester, 1998), pp. 37–50; J. Hannam, '"I had not been to London": Women's suffrage – a view from the regions', in *Votes for Women*, ed. J. Purvis and S. Stanley Holton (London, 2002), pp. 226–45; J. Hannam, '"Making areas strong for socialism and peace": Labour women and radical politics in Bristol, 1906–1939', *Radical Cultures and Local Identities*, ed. K. Cowman and I. Packer (Cambridge, 2010), pp. 71–94; A. Hughes-Johnson, 'Rose Lamartine Yates and the Wimbledon WSPU: reconfiguring suffragette history from the local to the national' (PhD thesis, Royal Holloway, University of London, 2018).

women activists.[8] Here, women both furthered their own political agenda, and helped to shape party policy.[9] Studies of local politics more generally have demonstrated how reformers sought to utilize the increasing power of municipal authorities to implement a progressive agenda.[10] These activists often included women, who frequently saw concerns around housing, health and education as particularly relevant to their own capacities, expertise and interests.[11] Male and female labour activists, and middle- and working-class women activists, thus found extensive common ground and scope for dialogue and alliances in the sphere.[12] In this chapter, detailed attention to the local dynamics of the local suffrage campaign demonstrates that it was grounded in concerns about women's unemployment and their need for paid work.

A renewed focus on working-class women's own political beliefs, motivations and demands, achieved by examining their own testimonies, has also been a transformative development in recent suffrage history.[13] Aided by digitalization, new source material continues to come to light, leading to productive reinterpretations of older material. For example, a

[8] K. Hunt, 'Making politics in local communities: Labour women in interwar Manchester', in *Labour's Grass Roots: Essays on the Activities of Local Labour Parties and Members, 1918–45*, ed. M. Worley (Aldershot, 2005), pp. 79–101.

[9] S. Ward, 'Labour activism and the political self in inter-war working-class women's politics', *Twentieth Century British History*, xxx (2019), 29–52; Hunt, 'Making politics in local communities'; J. Hannam, 'Women and Labour politics', in *The Foundations of the British Labour Party: Identities, Cultures and Perspectives, 1900–39*, ed. M. Worley (Farnham, 2009), pp. 188–90; see also D. Tanner, 'Gender, civic culture and politics in South Wales: explaining Labour municipal policy, 1918–39', in *Labour's Grass Roots*, ed. M. Worley (Aldershot, 2005), pp. 170–93; and D. Tanner, 'Labour and its membership', in *Labour's First Century*, ed. D. Tanner, P. Thane and N. Tiratsoo (Cambridge, 2000), pp. 248–80.

[10] P. Thane, 'Labour and local politics: radicalism, democracy and social reform, 1880–1914', in *Currents of Radicalism: Popular Radicalism, Organised Labour and Party Politics in Britain, 1850–1914*, ed. E. F. Biagini and A. J. Reid (Cambridge, 1991), pp. 244–70.

[11] S. King, *We Might Be Trusted: Women, Welfare and Local Politics 1880–1920* (Brighton, 2006); P. Hollis, *Ladies Elect: Women in English Local Government 1865–1914* (Oxford, 1987).

[12] A. Chadwick, *Augmenting Democracy, Political Movement and Constitutional Reform During the Rise of Labour, 1900–1924* (London, 1999).

[13] L. Schwartz, *Feminism and the Servant Problem: Class and Domestic Labour in the Women's Suffrage Movement* (Cambridge, 2019); L. Jenkins, *Sisters and Sisterhood: The Kenney Family, Class and Suffrage, c.1890–1965* (Oxford, 2021); L. Orr, '"Shall we not speak for ourselves?" Helen Crawfurd, war resistance and the Women's Peace Crusade, 1916–1918' <https://www.academia.edu/33114337/shall_we_not_speak_for_ourselves_helen_crawfurd_war_resistance_and_the_womens_peace_crusade_1916_18> [accessed 1 Feb. 2020].

wealth of scholarship has not only identified many of the working-class women who were involved in militant suffrage, but has also sensitively considered their motivations and contributions.[14] This is characteristic of a broader historiographical trend which seeks to address the relative absence of working-class women both in labour and feminist histories. Scholars increasingly insist that these histories cannot be written without placing women at their centre, and that doing so changes how we conceptualize class, gender and politics in this period.[15]

The Canning Town minute book is particularly engaging for suffrage scholars not only because it represents a detailed account of working-class women's involvement with suffrage, but because of its rarity.[16] While minute books have often been read as straightforward and detailed accounts of local organizations, historians such as Stephanie Ward and Zoë Thomas have also shown that they can be used to give richer insight into the subjective experiences, meanings and emotions of political activity.[17] The Canning Town minutes are particularly useful in this respect. While they follow the form of conventional political minutes – noting the formalities of attendance, procedures and finances – their tone, language and selection of material indicates how women were working out new forms of political identities and practice within the branch. Their words were also sometimes reported in the contemporary press. Using these means that we can understand their efforts on their own terms, rather than interpreting them through the

[14] J. Purvis, 'The prison experiences of the suffragettes in Edwardian Britain', *Women's History Review*, iv (1994), 103–33; L. Leneman, *A Guid Cause: The Women's Suffrage Movement in Scotland* (Edinburgh, 1995); J. Smart, 'Jennie Baines: suffrage and an Australian connection', in *Votes for Women*, ed. J. Purvis and S. Stanley Holton (London, 2002), pp. 246–66; L. Schwartz, 'A job like any other? Feminist responses and challenges to domestic worker organizing in Edwardian Britain', *International Labor and Working-Class History*, lxxxviii (2015), 30–48.

[15] L. Schwartz, '"What we think is needed is a union of domestics such as the miners have": the Domestic Workers' Union of Great Britain and Ireland, 1908–14', *Twentieth Century British History*, xxv (2014), 173–98; M. Davis (ed.), *Class and Gender in British Labour History: Renewing the Debate (Or Starting it?)* (Pontypool, 2011); C. Hunt, *The National Federation of Women Workers, 1906–1921* (Basingstoke, 2014).

[16] It is one of only four known to exist. For a study of another, see K. Cowman, '"Minutes of the last meeting passed": the Huddersfield Women's Social and Political Union Minute Book January 1907–1909, a new source for suffrage history', *Twentieth Century British History*, xiii (2002), 298–315.

[17] Ward, 'Labour activism and the political self'; Z. Thomas, '"I loathe the thought of suffrage sex wars being brought into it": institutional conservatism in early twentieth-century women's art organisations', in *Suffrage and the Arts: Visual Culture, Politics, and Enterprise*, ed. Z. Thomas and M. Garrett (London, 2018), pp. 23–42.

priorities of the middle-class leadership.[18] In keeping with this emphasis, this chapter replicates the spelling and grammar of the minute book, without the repeated and intrusive use of 'sic'. The minute book shows how members used the Canning Town branch of the WSPU both to experience and to reshape the practice of contemporary progressive politics.

A brief history of the Canning Town branch of the WSPU

Few areas of the country can have been the subject of such contemporary concern and historiographical scrutiny as the East End of London. In the second half of the nineteenth century, evocative and impassioned descriptions by Charles Dickens reinforced by the supposedly scientific studies of Charles Booth and the growth of the sensationalist press had helped construct a very particular image of the community in the public imagination. By the turn of the twentieth century, failures in the ship-building and weaving industries meant that skilled or well-paid work was all but impossible to find. West Ham was the first borough to implement provisions under the 1905 Unemployed Workmen's Act which set up local distress committees to reduce unemployment among 'respectable' and 'deserving' men through temporary schemes.[19] Demand, however, far outstripped supply, while there were frequent complaints in the local press about the cost to ratepayers.[20]

Concerns about unemployment were social as much as economic. Economic deprivation was understood to cause all manner of crime, deviance and vice. A 1907 investigation into the specific social problems in West Ham attributed these to the 'evil' of casual labour, which led to 'irregular earnings', 'chronic under-employment' and 'chronic poverty'.[21] Middle-class reformers – often religiously inspired – flocked to the neighbourhood to tackle the social consequences of poverty and deprivation from within. It was believed that local people were essentially passive and would be unable to improve their own lives without outside intervention.[22]

[18] The relative lack of sources has often led to a focus on the middle-class leadership of working women's organizations, for example, G. Scott, *Feminism and the Politics of Working Women: the Women's Co-operative Guild, 1880s to the Second World War* (Brighton, 1998).

[19] G. R. Boyer, 'The evolution of unemployment relief in Great Britain', *Journal of Interdisciplinary History*, xxxiv (2004), 423–9.

[20] 'Not in West Ham only, but everywhere, we are borrowing, borrowing, borrowing. We are plunging ourselves or head and ears into debt and we shall sink in it, if we do not mind'. Editorial, *Stratford Express*, 28 Apr. 1906.

[21] M. Wilson and E. Goldie Howarth, *West Ham: A Study in Social and Industrial Problems; Being the Report of the Outer London Inquiry Committee* (London, 1907), p. 401.

[22] The pioneering and essential works on this community include G. Stedman Jones, *Outcast London: A Study in the Relationship Between Classes in Victorian Society* (Oxford,

Yet the local labour movement was particularly strong and well-organized.[23] West Ham South returned Keir Hardie to Parliament in 1893 and Will Thorne in 1906, and become the first (albeit short-lived) Labour-controlled council in the country. The famous 'land grab' which founded the even shorter-lived Triangle Camp at Plaistow, involving unemployed men led by local councillor Ben Cunningham, aimed to show that unemployed men were the very opposite of idle and irresponsible.[24] Women also participated in local labour politics, as members of school boards, as Poor Law Guardians and as members of socialist organizations.[25] They had been instrumental in the 1889 strikes at Silvertown, one of the defining moments in the emergence of New Unionism, which had brought figures such as Eleanor Marx, Tom Mann and Will Thorne to national attention.[26] Despite the challenging conditions, then, the local political context was favourable to grassroots political activism.

Two women were particularly central to the Canning Town branch of the WSPU. The first was Minnie Baldock, who was either chair, secretary or speaker at almost every meeting of the organization in its first months. By the time she took the chair of the inaugural meeting, she was already a seasoned local activist.[27] Born in Poplar in 1864, her early working life was spent in a shirt factory. She was married to Harry Baldock, and the couple had two sons. They were both enthusiastic members of the local Independent Labour Party. Harry served as a local councillor and Minnie

1973); J. Walkowitz, *City of Dreadful Delight: Narratives of Sexual Danger in Victorian London* (London, 1992); E. Ross, *Love and Toil: Motherhood in Outcast London* (Oxford, 1993); S. Koven, *Slumming: Sexual and Social Politics in Victorian London* (Princeton, N.J., 2004); S. C. Williams, *Religious Belief and Popular Culture in Southwark c.1880–1939* (Oxford, 1999).

[23] M. Brodie, *The Politics of the Poor: The East End of London 1885–1914* (Oxford, 2004) has been especially important in challenging notions of political apathy and conservativism, and highlighting the rich variety of political cultures in this period.

[24] J. Field, *Working Men's Bodies: Work Camps in Britain, 1880–1940* (Manchester, 2013), pp. 87–90.

[25] D. Banks-Conney, 'Political culture and the Labour movement: a comparison between Poplar and West Ham, 1889–1914' (unpublished PhD thesis, University of Greenwich, 2005), 218; see also Thane, 'Labour and local politics'.

[26] J. Tully, *Silvertown: The Lost Story of a Strike that Shook London and Helped Launch the Modern Labor Movement* (New York, 2014), p. 163.

[27] For more details, see L. Jenkins, 'Baldock [née Rogers], (Lucy) Minnie (1864–1954), suffrage activist and campaigner', *Oxford Dictionary of National Biography*. Baldock's papers are held at the Museum of London and many of them were digitized as part of the 2018 centenary celebrations. These include her scrapbook, and can be accessed at <https://artsandculture.google.com/entity/minnie-baldock/g11f4qfb5wd?categoryid=historical-figure> [accessed 1 Mar. 2020].

was elected to the local Board of Guardians. Their immersion in local labour politics made them typical of early WSPU supporters.[28]

Another who quickly became a mainstay of the branch was Adelaide Knight. Knight's political vision and capacities were, in part, a product of a personal history marked by poverty, illness and trauma. She was born with deformed hands which limited her capacity for work, and, at the age of eight, was run over by a horse cart, necessitating a long period of recovery and a permanent limp and pain. Her father was an abusive alcoholic who beat her mother and eventually hanged himself in front of his youngest daughter. She also lost a sister to suicide. Yet she possessed significant personal resources as well. Despite her father's many shortcomings, he had invested in her education and introduced her to political debates. She also drew strength from an intense religious faith, which found expression in the temperance movement. But Knight's primary source of support was her intensely loving marriage to Donald Brown.[29] The two married in 1894, against the wishes of her sisters, who believed that, as the son of a Guyanese father, his colour was a threat to their respectability. Their marriage was marred by tragedy – they lost three children to smallpox after being misinformed about vaccination – but was intensely strong, respectful, and egalitarian. Brown took his wife's name and the division of household labour was unconventional. Knight was not, of course, unusual in supplementing her husband's income by sewing, but Donald was certainly atypical in his willingness to undertake domestic labour. He took on the heavy work of washing, which was especially difficult for Knight owing to her physical disabilities. The pair shared interests in collective solutions – trade unions, cooperative organization and socialist groups – to the problems of pervasive alcoholism and poverty in their neighbourhood.[30]

The first year of the Canning Town branch was characterized by a frenzy of activity. One of its first actions, on 19 February 1906, was to protest at the state opening of Parliament, alongside hundreds of other women from

[28] K. Cowman, *Women of the Right Spirit: Paid Organisers of the Women's Social and Political Union (WSPU) 1904–18* (Manchester, 2007), pp. 12–13.

[29] Donald Brown also had a catastrophically bleak childhood. His father murdered his mother when he was only nine, and was eventually found not guilty on grounds of insanity. Brown was raised in a workhouse and then in Greenwich Hospital, where poverty was compounded by racism.

[30] Knight and Brown's history is documented by their daughter and great-niece in W. Langton and F. Jacobsen, *Courage: An Account of the Lives of Eliza Adelaide Knight and Donald Adolphus Brown* (London, 2007). Win Langton was their youngest daughter, born after Knight's association with women's suffrage and named after three women the pair admired: Winifred Blatchford, Teresa Billington-Grieg and Florence Nightingale.

the East End in Parliament Square. The women then joined an audience of several thousand in Caxton Hall to hear Christabel Pankhurst assert that the union was formed 'solely of the women who had to work for their living' and claim their direct descendance from Chartism.[31] The meeting followed Emmeline Pankhurst to the House of Commons, but was initially refused entry, until small groups were finally allowed in.

Energized by these events, the following week the women committed to a further demonstration in May 1906. At one planning meeting, there was 'So Much Business to do that no Minutes were read'.[32] No fewer than 125 women from Canning Town took part in a thousand-strong march down the Embankment to Downing Street, where eight women led by Mrs Pankhurst met with the Prime Minister, Henry Campbell-Bannerman, only to hear that he would not help them, and that they should continue to work on converting the country. The Canning Town women joined the crowds in Trafalgar Square to hear WSPU leaders report on the disappointing discussion with the Prime Minister. A few weeks later, on 21 June, several dozen women from the branch joined Annie Kenney and around 150 others at the home of Herbert Asquith, demanding an audience. Annie Kenney, Teresa Billington, Adelaide Knight and sixty-four-year-old Jane Sparborough, a needlewoman from the neighbouring Bromley and Bow branch, were arrested.[33]

In between these large demonstrations, women held weekly meetings with invited speakers and a social element. Attendance held steady at between thirty and forty-five members at each meeting, but sixty-five women attended the social meeting at the end of April, and attendance doubled in May to between seventy-two and seventy-eight as the women planned for and reflected on their contribution to the major deputation. A few meetings attracted only sparse attendance, but many drew more than forty or fifty women, and eighty-nine turned out in November to hear Charlotte Despard. 1907 started promisingly, with nearly seventy or more attending each meeting in January. This was very much a shared and collective endeavour, which did not – at first – rely solely on particular individuals.

But a series of disruptive events rocked and weakened the branch. At the turn of the year, Dora Montefiore's supposed 'treatment' by the central

[31] *Lancashire Evening Post*, 20 Feb. 1906, p. 5. Contemporary accounts of the meeting can be found in S. Pankhurst, *The Suffragette Movement: An Intimate Account of Persons and Ideals* (London, 1931), pp. 199–200; E. Pankhurst, *My Own Story* (London, 1979), pp. 52–3.

[32] CTMB, 15 May 1906.

[33] Multiple spellings of this surname are recorded.

committee of the WSPU was the subject of intense debate. She had apparently been reprimanded for writing to a Liberal, increasingly seen by WSPU leaders as the enemy regardless of individual views. Annie Kenney promised to take her case to the committee, but it was Adelaide Knight who took a more decisive stand by drafting a resolution in support of Montefiore, which was read and agreed at the following branch meeting. Though Montefiore spoke effusively of 'the manner that the canning town branch always received her saying she was more at home with them every time she visited them', she does not appear to have visited the branch again.[34] She did maintain her relationship with Adelaide Knight, however, and her collaboration with the women in Canning Town was important in shaping her politics.[35]

Worse was to follow. A few weeks later, 'Mrs Baldock spoke a few words concerning the scandal about her self which was [illeg] all ensure members sympathise with her'.[36] Some kind of crisis had taken place, although it seems to have been overcome, and was never referred to again. However, Knight's concerns about the national leadership of the WSPU continued to deepen. In March, she reported in her capacity as liaison to the national executive committee that Canning Town women 'were to keep in the back ground' at a future demonstration 'because the central could not be responsible for any one. Mrs Knight thought it was because the branch did not pay any affiliation fee to the Central' and 'spoke of sending in her resignation'.[37] At the following meeting, she followed through on this threat, and read out her resignation letter, saying that 'the Central were not keeping their promises to the working women'.[38]

Further details of this dispute can be found in Knight's biography. Knight shared Montefiore's concerns that working-class women would inevitably lose out if the WSPU continued to press for votes on the same terms as men, linked to property. She prompted the Canning Town branch to write to Keir Hardie to secure his support for 'full and equal representation'. Emmeline and Christabel Pankhurst were scathing about this decision, essentially suggesting that the Canning Town women were too ignorant to know what they were doing. At the next executive committee meeting, Christabel reported back on Hardie's response, saying that he agreed with her that the women clearly needed educated leadership. Knight then

[34] CTMB, undated, late Dec. 1906 or early Jan. 1907.

[35] D. Montefiore, *From a Victorian to a Modern* (London, 1927), p. 63.

[36] CTMB, 20 Jan. 1907.

[37] CTMB, 19 Mar. 1907.

[38] CTMB, 26 Mar. 1907.

played her trump card. The letter had not been posted. Pankhurst was making this up. Pankhurst was able to bluster her way out of the situation, but the women back in Canning Town were horrified. Some criticized the 'lies and deception' while others were 'reluctant to accept that there had been such dishonesty and treachery', calling it a 'misunderstanding'. Those who shared Knight's outrage left along with her.[39]

The fact that these events were not recorded in the minutes may well reflect members' turmoil, as well as a desire to maintain the appearance of unity. The following week, there was a vote of confidence in Minnie Baldock, but without a full explanation. Though she evidently won the vote, the damage had been done. In May, she 'explained what was expected from the members of the WSPU she did not want women to come from what they could get in the way of Charity. But to stand by the union & abide by the rules.'[40] Clearly significant tensions remained. From then, apart from a social in September when fifty-five women attended, no meeting attracted more than thirty women. A much-discussed and anticipated excursion to Chingford involved only nine members. Minnie Baldock's presence or absence increasingly determined the success of the meeting, and her absences became ever more frequent as she was called away on business for the national branch. Meanwhile, involvement in mass direct action seems to have all but ceased in 1907. A Mrs Smith attempted to keep the women together, but the branch limped on for only a few more months. At the beginning of December, a Mrs Riley reported on a meeting of the Adult Suffrage Society she had attended, 'saying that she could see but very little difference in the two clubs'. While this entry marked the end of the WSPU, two weeks later, a group of women led by Adelaide Knight and backed by the Social Democratic Federation (SDF) founded a new branch of the Adult Suffrage Society (ASS). 'When the rich woman gets a vote, let the poor woman have one also', Knight proclaimed.[41] Soon, however, pregnancy and illness forced her resignation from both the ASS and the SDF. Though Minnie Baldock had several very successful years as a national WSPU organizer, she too eventually had to resign on the grounds of ill health.

Membership and culture

While Baldock and Knight are well known to suffrage scholars, the remainder of the membership has never previously been analysed. Yet at

[39] Langton and Jacobsen, *Courage*, pp. 118–22.

[40] CTMB, 1 May 1907.

[41] 'Adult suffrage at Canning Town', *Justice*, 28 Dec. 1907.

the back of the minute book is a list of ninety members.[42] As only their surnames and addresses are listed, comprehensive identification of all the women has proven impossible. Nevertheless, the list demonstrates that this branch attracted women from a tight-knit community. Many members lived in close proximity to one another, just a few doors apart on the same street. This may well be why the minutes never note any formal efforts at recruitment: women were able to draw on their existing networks to attract members. As well as Canning Town itself, members came from other boroughs within the locality, including Plaistow, Silvertown and Tidal Basin. Their sense of community was reflected in their ongoing concern for women experiencing particularly difficult personal circumstance. Bereavement or illness were marked with votes of sympathy and letters of condolence.[43]

Nine working-class members can be identified with near certainty in the census and, using these records, we can infer more about the branch and its members.[44] Five of the women had been born in the local area, while the others came from Birmingham, Westbury, Swansea and Frome. All were married. Indeed, only two of the branch members were listed as 'Miss', one of whom was Annie Kenney, though other unmarried women were mentioned in the minutes. These women were born between 1851 and 1877, making them aged between fifty-five and twenty-nine when the branch was founded in 1906. They were not young girls, but mature women.

None of the women had an occupation listed in the census, probably because they were married. Earlier records indicate that two of the women

[42] There are ninety-two names listed, some crossed out. Eight women – including Mrs Knight – appear on a separate page before the official list of 'members'. Mrs Knight and Mrs Baldock are listed twice, meaning there are actually ninety women recorded. Not all the members over the lifetime of the branch were listed here. Mrs Wilcox, for example, who seems to have taken over as secretary after Adelaide Knight left, does not appear.

[43] CTMB, undated, May 1906, 15 Jan. 1907, 13 Aug. 1907. For a fuller discussion of the politics of adult suffrage, see J. Hannam and K. Hunt, *Socialist Women: Britain, 1880s to 1920s* (London, 2002), pp. 105–28.

[44] These are Emily Andrews, 55 Beaumont Road, Plaistow; Charlotte Bishop, 103 Forty Acre Lane, Tidal Basin; Annie Ewers, 29 Morgan Street; Sarah Hockham, 11 Ordnance Road; Caroline Johnson, 33 Star Street; Eliza Oliver, 241 Star Lane; Emily Peters, 13 Hudsons Road; Mary Ann Smith, 20 Fox Street. All these women were living at the same address in either 1901 or 1911, and sometimes both. I have erred on the side of caution in this identification. It is likely, for example, that the Mrs Cordery listed as living in 24 Star Street may well be the Agnes Cordery listed at 67 Star Lane in 1901, and that the Mrs Riley listed in the membership corresponds to the Mrs O'Reilly named in the 1911 census. For the avoidance of doubt, though, I have analysed only those whose details correspond precisely. Adelaide Knight and Edith Kerrison are not part of this sample as they are discussed elsewhere in this chapter.

had worked as domestic servants. One, Prudence Hornblower, an active branch member who served as treasurer, had married a blacksmith relatively late in life and so more of her work history was recorded, with periods ironing for her brother in his business, as a housekeeper, and then as a forewoman in a laundry. Unsurprisingly, nearly all their husbands appear to have been employed in trades relating to the local docks, and included several who worked directly on board ships. Other roles included a house painter, wood sawyer and iron dresser. Their husbands occupied a range of positions on the social scale, from the relatively genteel assistant shopkeeper married to Emily Andrews, to Mary Ann Smith's husband, who was a manure worker.

The 1911 census indicates that many of the women's older children – girls and boys alike – were also employed. They tended to enter a greater variety of work than their parents, not necessarily related to the docks. Charlotte Bishop's three eldest daughters were employed as a shirt machinist, a bicycle tyre maker and a tailoress. Annie Ewers had one daughter making tennis balls and another making footballs. Their sons' employment perhaps hinted at a greater potential for skilled work and improved prospects. Annie Ewers' son Fred worked in a chemist and druggist wholesalers, while Eliza Oliver's son Harry was an office boy. Five also had boarders living with them, which would likely have generated more domestic work for the women, and is suggestive of the overcrowded housing which was a focus of reformers' concerns.

Large numbers of children and high rates of infant mortality characterized these women's families. Emily Andrews and Prudence Hornblower had only three children between them, all of whom lived. The remaining seven women, however, had fifty-eight children between them – an average of more than eight each – of which twenty had died by 1911. Mary Ann Smith, only thirty-seven, had twelve children by 1911, the first born when she was just seventeen. Seven had died. The statistics alone cannot illustrate how these women coped with the physical, mental and emotional toll of repeated pregnancy, childbirth and loss, but Ellen Ross's study of working-class motherhood testifies to the intense domestic burden that this involved – as well as the profound sense of grief and loss when their children died.[45]

However, the branch was by no means exclusively made up of working-class members. Other women came from wealthier backgrounds, but were

[45] Ross, *Love and Toil*, pp. 125–7 and pp. 179–90. See also Margaret MacDonald's comments on the loss of her son and how it confirmed her desire that 'we women must work for a world where little children will not needlessly die' in N. Sloane, *The Women in the Room: Labour's Forgotten History* (London, 2018), p. 160.

present in the East End by virtue of their commitment to social reform, manifested in their relationship to the settlement movement. Canning Town had long been the focus of significant efforts by reformers concerned about the effects of unemployment, poverty and overcrowding.[46] The appeal of such territory for middle-class activists, who sought to reform the community while living as part of it, has been well-documented, as has the gendered nature of their activities.[47] The Canning Town Women's Settlement, founded in 1892, complemented the work done by men at the nearby Malvern College Settlement. The settlement ran a girls' club and a women's employment office.[48] Settlement women sought to collaborate with poorer women on terms of equality and, in doing so, to transcend barriers of wealth, class and status – or, as a later statement of policy put it, 'interpret east to west; west to east'.[49] The most significant of these members was Sister Edith Kerrison, a Welsh resident at the Canning Town Women's Settlement. She had come to the area via her connection to the Mansfield House University Settlement and longstanding work as a matron at the Seaman's Hospital in Greenwich.[50] Inspired by Keir Hardie, she became a socialist and active in the ILP. The founder of Canning Town Socialist Sunday School, a member of the Board of Guardians and the first woman councillor in West Ham, Kerrison went on to serve for a decade on the Women's Labour League executive committee, and became West Ham's

[46] A Mrs Podmore gave a speech at one of the earliest meetings and in June 1907, with support from branch members, stood as a candidate for Poor Law Guardian in West Ham. CTMB, 3 Apr. 1906 and 18 June 1907. She may well have been Eleanor Podmore, estranged wife of Frank Podmore, one of the founders of the Fabian Society. However, it has not been possible to definitively establish this.

[47] See, for example, Koven, *Slumming*; M. Vicinus, *Independent Women: Work and Community for Single Women, 1850–1920* (London, 1985); K. Bradley, *Poverty, Philanthropy and the State: Charities and the Working Classes in London, 1918–79* (London, 2007); N. Scotland, *Squires in the Slums: Settlements and Missions in Late-Victorian Britain* (London, 2007). For studies which refer particularly to settlement work within this locality, see A. Harris, 'Building the Docklands settlement: gender, gentility, and the gentry in East London, 1894–1939', *Material Religion*, ix (2013), 60–84 and E. Ross, 'Slum journeys: ladies and London poverty 1860–1940', in *The Archaeology of Urban Landscapes: Explorations in Slumland*, ed. A. Mayne and T. Murray (Cambridge, 2001), pp. 11–21; I. Dove, 'Sisterhood or surveillance: the development of working girls' clubs in London, 1880–1939' (unpublished PhD thesis, University of Greenwich, 1996).

[48] Minutes of the Canning Town Settlement Executive Committee, 13 Dec. 1905, Newnham Libraries and Archives.

[49] Canning Town Women's Settlement Policy, 1927, Newnham Libraries and Archives.

[50] 'Sister Kerrison', *The Young Socialist*, iii (1903), 1.

first female alderman.[51] Another was Miss Tillyard, who was also associated with the Settlement, and had established a female-run hospital to serve local women.[52] Like Minnie Baldock, both these women were Poor Law Guardians, and they served together on a number of committees associated with relief administration.[53] The earliest efforts of this branch were also encouraged and supported – but not directed – by other women from outside the community, including Teresa Billington (later Billington-Grieg) and Dora Montefiore, who first introduced Annie Kenney to Minnie Baldock and her associates.[54]

The Canning Town branch clearly emerged out of existing personal relationships and political structures. This is an important point, because it contrasts so sharply with the narrative constructed by the WSPU. In its version, the Canning Town women were brought together under the leadership of Annie Kenney, who supposedly arrived with £2 in her pocket to 'rouse London'. This story – often repeated in *Votes for Women*, and later reiterated in autobiographical accounts – reflects the suffragettes' desire to suggest they possessed a unique ability to galvanize women who had not previously been engaged in politics.[55] However, it was evidently not true. Instead, Kenney joined a pre-existing network and community of women with longstanding interests in political and social reform. Moreover, Kenney was only one of many women mentioned in the minutes. She does not appear to have had a particularly distinctive or visible role in the organization. Minnie Baldock clearly assumed the leadership, and a number of other women – not including Kenney – took on prominent and administrative roles. The description of Kenney's arrival in a meeting in April 1906 as a 'surprise' where 'she came among us as angels do' does not suggest that she was a frequent or regular attendee.[56] Unlike Montefiore, however, she does appear on the list of members within the minute book.

The focus on the vote for women as a specific demand made the Canning Town WSPU distinct from other political groups within the community.

[51] J. Gerrard, *Radical Childhoods: Schooling and the Struggle for Social Change* (Manchester, 2014), p. 99; C. Collette, *For Labour and For Women: The Women's Labour League, 1906–1918* (Manchester, 1989), p. 198; C. Collette, *The Newer Eve: Women, Feminists and the Labour Party* (Basingstoke, 2009), p. 23; S. Ferguson, 'Labour women and the social services', in *Women in the Labour Movement*, ed. L. Middleton (London, 1977), pp. 39–40.

[52] S. Koven, *The Match Girl and the Heiress* (London, 2015), p. 67.

[53] Minutes of the Canning Town Settlement Executive Committee, 1905 and 1906.

[54] Montefiore, *Victorian to a Modern*, pp. 44, 51.

[55] See, for example, Kenney's own, rather condescending account of her move to London and the 'Poor East End women' in A. Kenney, *Memories of a Militant* (London, 1924) pp. 57–60.

[56] CTMB, 10 Apr. 1906.

Though still a very new organization, the disruptive activities of WSPU members such as Christabel Pankhurst and Annie Kenney had drawn both significant press attention and wider public sympathy. The cause of women's suffrage had become both a prominent and urgent national political issue. In this context, it appears that women who were already politically active sought to capitalize on renewed interest in politics in general, and suffrage in particular, to attract recruits. At the first meeting, Sister Kerrison said she felt 'very hopeful that women were awakening.'[57] The perception that the working classes were inclined to be apathetic and resigned to their situation was of great concern for political activists at this time, who sought to stress the merits and possibilities of organization and collective action.[58] Trade unions provided the most obvious model and structure, and many feminist activists focused on persuading women to unionize. There was, for example, a women's branch of the National Union of Gas Workers and General Labourers in Canning Town.[59] Centred around the workplace, however, they would not have been a natural choice for women who were not currently employed. The WSPU thus helped to create a context in which women's political activities were taken seriously outside the workplace. They also offered the focus of a clear and defined political objective and an institutional structure which women's efforts could be channelled through.

Two dimensions of branch culture are particularly evident in the minutes: the women's allegiance to socialism and the importance of sociability. While branch members furthered their interests in women-focused politics, they retained an explicit commitment to socialist principles. They welcomed many socialist speakers who spoke of the compatibility of their beliefs and their commitment to their demand. A Mr Wishart, for example, explained 'why he became a strict socialist and why he agreed with women suffrage' because women 'had to work just as hard in the home as well as the factory trusting that women would get the vote to be able to work hand in hand with the men and so make home more comfortable and interesting for both sexes'.[60] George Shreve, the only man present at the first meeting of the branch, was a member of the National Union of Gasworkers.[61] The branch used premises owned by the ILP, though a few

[57] 'Meeting of unemployed women', *Stratford Express*, 3 Feb. 1906.

[58] Banks-Conney, 'Political culture and the Labour movement', pp. 95–6.

[59] Tully, *Silvertown*, p. 197.

[60] CTMB, 13 Nov. 1906.

[61] Shreve interestingly stood for election as a Poor Law Guardian in the same ward as Miss Tillyard in 1906, though came only fifth out of eight candidates with 464 votes, while Tillyard was successfully elected with 1011. *Stratford Express*, 7 Apr. 1906.

months into its existence, the ILP said that as it had formed a separate entity, the women would have to pay 'a half fee that is a shilling' after a further month's grace.[62] Rousing choruses of 'The Red Flag' closed branch meetings throughout its existence, and when Adelaide Knight went to prison she scratched the lyrics into the window sill with her hairpin.[63]

As a result, the women placed particular faith in Keir Hardie to deliver their demands. They wrote to him in January 1907 to 'thank him for his noble stand for women & demanding immediate enfranchisement of women on the same terms as men'.[64] Perhaps unsurprisingly, given that he was a national political figure of real significance and long associated with their own local community, the women looked to him, rather than to the Pankhursts, to deliver their objectives. Indeed, in the light of the fact that the WSPU and the Pankhursts later became almost synonymous, it is worth noting that the Pankhursts are only mentioned in the minutes on the two occasions when they visited the branch.

Their immersion in socialist culture, however, did not necessarily mean that these women were active within formal labour organizations. Rather, they were a product of a community in which such beliefs were taken for granted. For some women, it was membership of the WSPU which acted as an entry point into labour organizations rather than vice versa. In July 1906, the women discussed joining the ILP, 'some promising to do so', and at the next meeting they reported having followed through on their decision.[65] It is worth highlighting that it is the ILP which is mentioned, rather than any other group, including a trade union or even the Women's Co-operative Guild, indicating the women's focus on politics.

Sociability, as Stephanie Ward has argued, was critical to the practice of women's politics in the interwar period. Many of the features which she identifies as important to a distinctively female culture among Labour women, particularly food, were also relevant here.[66] The first meeting explicitly designated as a 'social' noted that members 'were admitted to a very nice & substantial tea prepared by members who worked very hard indeed to make it a success. They were rewarded in this as everything went off splendid … Nuts and Oranges were shared around & everyone I am sure felt better after the fun of the evening.'[67] The sense of relief evident here

[62] CTMB, 10 Apr. 1906.

[63] Langton and Jacobsen, *Courage*, p. 111.

[64] CTMB, 29 Jan. 1907.

[65] CTMB 31 Jul. 1906 and 7 Aug. 1906.

[66] Ward, 'Labour activism and the political self', pp. 45–6.

[67] CTMB, 24 Apr. 1906.

indicates that a successful tea was key to a successful meeting. It can have been no mean feat to provide tea for sixty-five members and efforts were evidently greatly appreciated.

Singing was a consistent feature of the meetings. 'The Red Flag' was the most frequently mentioned song, but 'Old Lang Syne' (sic) was often sung too, and members regularly joined together around the piano to sing old favourites and learn new tunes. Annie Kenney stepped in to act as choir mistress on one occasion despite being a notoriously poor singer.[68] These songs were brought to larger meetings too. At the protest at the state opening of Parliament, women sang 'The Marseillaise', 'Comrades Come Rally' and 'The Red Flag', reported in one newspaper as 'Socialistic and revolutionary songs'.[69] Though some meetings were specifically designated as 'social' – and probably not coincidentally were usually the best attended – barely a meeting went without some form of shared entertainment.

Prayer was mentioned almost as frequently as song, though as the content or form of the prayer is not recorded it is difficult to reach further conclusions about the place of faith and spirituality within the branch. With some members part of the Settlement community, and the hopes invested in Keir Hardie, it is not difficult to imagine that these women were drawn to some form of Christian socialism. A belief in the divine righteousness of their cause would have provided a further source of strength, while participating in the rituals of collective worship would have strengthened the bonds of community.

This camaraderie was essential to sustain the women's commitment to the cause and the organization. Their political activity was difficult to maintain among their many other commitments. Nor was it necessarily popular, even within their local community. As Dora Montefiore recalled, other residents were 'often unintentionally cruel in their judgement. They had no notion of the idealism which inspired all of us militant women and they were only too ready with gibe and pointed finger to point out the "jail birds" or to persecute the children of these women, and annoy by rough ignorant jests the husbands.'[70] The importance of combining the explicitly political with the social was summarized by Minnie Baldock, who expressed pride in the way members 'were always good fighters & ready for work when called upon also they were to look forward to a tea in a week or two'.[71]

[68] CTMB, 6 Feb. 1907. Annie Kenney had joined the Oldham Clarion Vocal Union as a young woman but 'had the good sense not to sing'. She wanted to meet other readers of the *Clarion* newspaper and thought 'the practice would be good for me'. Kenney, *Memories*, p. 24.

[69] *Sheffield Daily Telegraph*, 20 Feb. 1906, p. 11.

[70] Montefiore, *Victorian to a Modern*, p. 52.

[71] CTMB, 8 Jan. 1907.

The projected benefits of securing the vote were abstract and there was no certain timetable for victory. In the meantime, women needed the smaller but profoundly meaningful benefits of sustenance, friendship and solidarity.

Beliefs and objectives

Within the branch records, neither the conditions of their lives nor their claims for the vote were ever discussed in terms of motherhood or any particular qualities the women shared as mothers. Indeed, children, husbands and the demands of household duties are almost entirely absent from the minutes. When children are mentioned, it is either out of concern for an individual member whose child is ill, or in the abstract, such as a discussion of education without specific reference to the needs of their own children. Only one speaker, Mrs Podmore, told the women 'not to think that they were doing their work just for themselves but for the sake of their children & others & that would give them strength to go on'.[72] Unlike many women active in the labour movement at the time, these women do not seem to have campaigned on maternity rights or nursery provision. When they heard from speakers on this issue, it was in relation to women elsewhere, and the women do not seem to have insisted that they themselves needed similar provision.[73] This lack of reference to children is a striking contrast to the maternalist rhetoric which underpinned the reforming efforts of many middle-class women.[74] When Adelaide Knight and Jane Sparborough were arrested, Emmeline Pethick-Lawrence framed their sacrifice in terms of domestic responsibilities, regretting that they had to leave behind a 'little baby' and an 'invalid husband'. 'Perhaps such devotion to the cause will really convince the British public that women – and poor women too – are really in earnest', she said.[75]

These women were not claiming the vote on the basis of their rights, capacities or duties as mothers. This was a self-consciously political space in which the domestic did not explicitly feature or shape their demands. Instead, the women defined themselves as 'unemployed'. This in itself was an important political statement. Most people – including some labour activists and socialists – saw work for women as a temporary phase or as

[72] CTMB, 3 Apr. 1906.

[73] CTMB, 6 Feb. 1906.

[74] See, for example, S. Koven, 'Borderlands: women, voluntary action and child welfare in Britain, 1840–1914', in *Mothers of a New World: Maternalist Politics and the Origins of Welfare States*, ed. S. Koven and S. Michel (London, 1993), pp. 94–135; Ross, *Love and Toil.*

[75] 'Suffragettes in court – Mrs Knight and her baby', *Stratford Express*, 7 July 1906.

a necessary evil, secondary and subordinate to their primary roles within the home. There are, for example, obvious assumptions behind the title of the Unemployed *Workmen's* Act. Men were expected to be providers, and women to be dependent. It was therefore unusual for the concept of 'unemployment' to be applied to women and certainly a radical assertion for the women themselves to claim the label.[76]

Efforts by local administrators to address unemployment primarily focused on male workers. At the Board of Guardians, no women served on the special committee appointed to 'Deal with the Question of the Unemployed' established in 1904.[77] In January 1906, the local distress committee itself advertised for prospective employers for unemployed women, but after several weeks, only three women were successfully employed. They believed, however, that the Charity Organization Society was 'making a tremendous effort'.[78] In 1906, the women of the Canning Town Settlement made several efforts to establish workrooms for unemployed women, though this was dependent on voluntary contributions which were often slow to materialize.[79] Both the Settlement and the Women's Industrial Council raised their concerns with the local distress committee in efforts to find more sustainable solutions.

Frustration at this fragmented effort and lack of urgency may well have prompted the two women who served on the Board of Guardians, Minnie Baldock and Edith Kerrison, to organize the first meeting. Here, Baldock stated that women needed 'to show the authorities it was time' to intervene, especially for single women and widows. She argued that 'women should be able to demand work in the same way as men, and that such work should be paid for at a rate that would not sweat the receivers'.[80] In a June deputation to the local distress committee, women testified to the lack of practical action to help them. All the women had registered for work, but officials had done little beyond asking them how many pawntickets they had. In a clear rejection of this insinuation that they were incapable of managing their budgets, the women stressed their ages, the length of their marriages and their contribution through the rates to implicitly underscore their

[76] K. Gleadle, *British Women in the Nineteenth Century* (Basingstoke, 2001), p. 96; Banks-Conney, 'Political culture and the Labour movement', p. 53.

[77] Board of Guardians Report, 13 Oct. 1904, Newnham Libraries and Archives.

[78] 'Women want work', *Stratford Express*, 7 Feb. 1906.

[79] Chief Worker's Report, 21 Feb. 1906, Canning Town Settlement Executive Committee Minutes.

[80] 'Meeting of unemployed women', *Stratford Express*, 3 Feb. 1906.

respectability.[81] Minnie Baldock asserted that 'it was hard upon women who were able and willing to work' to be excluded from relief efforts.[82]

Historians have shown that labour activists at this time saw work, not welfare, as the most effective solution to poverty. Work provided not only wages, but also dignity and self-respect.[83] Yet male socialists did not necessarily extend this analysis to women. Rather, they saw these attributes as forming the backbone of working-class masculinity.[84] The 'male breadwinner' model of working-class family life was championed by many of the trade unions as a means of guaranteeing jobs and higher wages for their male members, and was accepted more widely because of its resonance with middle-class ideals of separate spheres. Women workers could be perceived as victims of oppression by their male counterparts, but could also be seen as threats and rivals for work. Some men also continued to doubt women's capacity and commitment to union organization.[85] These ideas were reflected in the wider labour movement and the party, where emphasis was placed on women's domestic role.[86]

In contrast, the women of the Canning Town branch clearly believed that employment for themselves – not necessarily their male relations – would improve their situations. This was reflected by the several speakers who discussed work and working conditions for women, with an emphasis on the provisions such as fair wages and nurseries which made work possible and something more than a necessary means of subsistence.[87] This chimes with June Hannam's analysis of Labour women, who drew on a wide variety of experiences, including work, and not necessarily primarily motherhood, in their politics.[88] In positioning themselves in relation to the labour market, the women asserted their right to be taken seriously and on equal terms with men. As Adelaide Knight told her comrades when she was arrested, 'We want honest, respectable, decent conditions for the

[81] 'West Ham Distress Committee', *Stratford Express*, 30 June 1906.

[82] 'West Ham Distress Committee', *Stratford Express*, 30 June 1906.

[83] P. Thane, 'Labour and welfare', in *Labour's First Century*, ed. D. Tanner, P. Thane and N. Tiratsoo (Cambridge, 2000), pp. 80–2.

[84] E. May, 'The mosaic of Labour politics, 1900–1918', in *The Labour Party in Wales, 1900–2000*, ed. D. Tanner, C. Williams and D. Hopkin (Cardiff, 2000), p. 62.

[85] C. Hunt, 'Sex versus class in two British trade unions in the early twentieth century', *Journal of Women's History*, xxiv (2012), 86–110; Sloane, *The Women in the Room: Labour's Forgotten History*, pp. 16–20.

[86] For a useful discussion, see M. Francis, 'Labour and gender', in *Labour's First Century*, ed. D. Tanner, P. Thane and N. Tiratsoo (Cambridge, 2000), pp. 191–220.

[87] See, for example, undated meeting, early Mar. 1906, 16 Apr. 1907, 16 July 1907.

[88] Hannam, 'Women and Labour politics', pp. 180–1.

workers of both sexes, whether in work or out – for if the government won't provide work for a man or a woman, they have a duty to support him or her.' This belief in their essential equality with, rather than difference from, men was essential to her claim for the vote and transcended all her other principles.

> If they want us to obey the law, they must allow us to have a voice in the making of the laws to which our obedience is demanded. We want no charitable favours from our men – we want a recognised equality of the sexes. Equal taxation demands equal representation, and I at least am determined to continue the fight for progress even though friends, relatives, aye, even though my children, fruit of my body, and you my husband, the partner of my life, leave me.[89]

Priorities and strategies

The Canning Town women embraced direct action as a political strategy. These women saw visibility through deputations, processions and protest as being critical to furthering their cause. The numbers of women who attended the large deputations and processions always far exceeded the numbers who attended formal meetings. Questioned in court, Minnie Baldock had said 'for a number of years … they had agitated in a quiet and ladylike manner, and had done all they could to try and bring the suffrage question to the front' and would not admit that demands to see Asquith in person were 'unreasonable'.[90] The women did not use the terms 'militancy' or 'militant tactics' in the minutes, but the language of political struggle was often used by visiting speakers, who variously stressed the need for women to 'fight for this vote', to 'fight out this great fight' and to 'fight for their rights'.[91] Fighting talk was also adopted by the members. Minnie Baldock, for example, praised the members as 'good fighters' and Adelaide Knight wrote to her comrades from prison through Dora Montefiore, telling them:

> I am determined to fight on until the goal of women, Political Freedom, is reached. Tell the women of the Canning Town Branch and other branches that I would willingly serve six months or six years for that matter if I thought it would bring them the vote any quicker.

[89] Adelaide Knight to Donald Knight, 2 Aug. 1906, quoted in Langton and Jacobsen, *Courage*, p. 112.

[90] *Stratford Express*, 7 July 1906.

[91] CTMB, undated, Mar. 1906, 3 July 1906 and 16 Oct. 1906.

> But they must continue to fight while we are away. They must not let things sleep.
>
> Fight on and fight often is the motto they must keep before them.[92]

There is no suggestion that any of the women experienced either shame or hesitation in their attitude towards prison sentences. They seem to have accepted it as necessary, and were proud of the women who demonstrated their bravery in this way. Only a few members served a sentence themselves but they were supported wholeheartedly. After several comrades were arrested, a resolution was passed expressing their commitment to the women. 'The Members of the WSPU Pledging its self to stand by Mrs Knight Miss Kenney & Mrs Sparsboro in their hour of trial'.[93] Forty members of the branch presented Minnie Baldock with a petition 'to show their appreciation of the loyal, brave and noble manner in which you bore imprisonment, faced slander and criticism' in order that she had 'a lasting record of their love and admiration'.[94] A 'hearty social' with 'a beautiful recitation' and 'several labour songs' commemorated the release of Miss Steel.[95] The women also listened to the accounts of other ex-prisoners, like Marguerite Sidley, with interest.[96]

Understanding the sacrifice involved seems to have cemented the women's sense of solidarity with one another. When Annie Kenney told the women of her plans to risk arrest, 'it was rather a sad meeting for we knew & felt that some of our own members would be sent to prison'.[97] Reaction elsewhere was more mixed. Some Labour MPs, including Keir Hardie, raised questions about the sentencing of Adelaide Knight and her comrades, claiming that 'the feeling among people of all opinions … was that the sentence was unduly harsh'. The Lib-Lab member for Burnley, Fred Maddison, however, called them 'female hooligans' and said that 'no real working woman would have disgraced themselves in the way these women

[92] CTMB, 8 Jan. 1907; Adelaide Knight to Donald Knight, 2 Aug. 1906, quoted in Langton and Jacobsen, *Courage*, p. 112.

[93] CTMB, undated, but late June 1906.

[94] Nellie Martel Biographical Notes, Group A, vol. 2, Museum of London Suffragette Collections, quoted in Atkinson, *Rise Up Women!*, p. 54.

[95] CTMB, undated, late Dec. 1906 or early Jan. 1907.

[96] CTMB, 16 July 1906.

[97] CTMB, 3 July 1906.

had done'.[98] The Countess of Carlisle, meanwhile, told the Women's Liberal Federation that the women were 'making an impertinent mockery of womanhood'.[99]

The women were concerned not only about acquiring the vote, but also preparing themselves for using it, and exercising the responsibilities of citizenship. The women's desire for political education is evident throughout the minutes. They were determined to train themselves in the business of political organization, or, as Annie Kenney put it in the first meeting, 'to organise and do things in a proper way'. George Shreve suggested – somewhat patronizingly – that this meant 'taking a cue from the men', since 'with a proper method of carrying out the meetings they would soon equal the organization that men had at present'.[100] Their methods both reflected and adapted conventional political practice. Particularly in the early months, the chair rotated among different members as women tested out different skills and roles. At one social evening, a novice speaker, Miss Miller, was given the opportunity to try her hand and received warm encouragement. 'This being the first time Miss Miller had spoken in Public. A very good speech which ought to encourage those who have not yet tried.'[101] The women debated the timing of the meeting to ensure that it could best fit around women's other commitments.[102] Members who were absent owing to illness or family circumstances were remembered with sympathy within the minutes.[103]

Part of this commitment to political education involved inviting outside speakers to address the branch. Popular speakers attracted large audiences hungry for knowledge and news. The history of women's achievements was one recurring theme. For example, Sister Kerrison offered an account of Florence Nightingale, a Miss Macauley discussed women's contribution to the defence of the country, while Miss Millar simply 'gave a very interesting speech about some women in the olden times & just showed us what women can do when their minds are made up'.[104] These speeches were evidently meant to offer women a sense of legitimacy, connection to a political tradition and belief in women's capabilities, which would be more fully realized once they had acquired the vote.

[98] HC Deb 21 June 1906 vol 159 cc460–4.

[99] *Manchester Courier and Lancashire General Advertiser*, 22 June 1906, p. 7.

[100] *Stratford Express*, 10 Feb. 1906.

[101] CTMB, 24 Apr. 1906.

[102] CTMB, 12 Feb. 1906, 27 Mar. 1906.

[103] CTMB, undated but May 1906, 1 Jan. 1907, 13 Aug. 1907.

[104] CTMB, 27 Mar. 1906, 26 Feb. 1907 and 21 Aug. 1906.

More frequently, however, it was the contemporary context which provided the subject material. Some speakers offered accounts of social conditions and problems, particularly as they affected women.[105] Members provided first-hand accounts of their experiences at deputations or public meetings, and reported back on their encounters with outside bodies such as the Right to Work Committee. Others shared indirect information from newspapers. Absent members could also continue to participate and share information through letters. Letters were also used to lobby individuals and groups external to the organization.

Once informed on a particular issue, women believed they had a right to contribute to the broader public debate. Following a lecture by Harry Baldock on 'the unrest among the natives of Natal', members passed a resolution calling on the government to bring the crisis to an end and ensuring that women took part in a recommended enquiry into the situation. They determined that they would share their decision with 'the Local MP, the Local Papers, Prime Minister, Colonial Sec etc'.[106] This testifies to their self-confidence in political participation. It also indicates that their belief in their ability to contribute to government extended well beyond their local community and issues directly relating to women.

The women kept a careful eye on the development of the movement elsewhere. New branches in nearby neighbourhoods and communities – for example, in Croydon, East Ham, Bow and Bromley – were cited by name, probably because these names resonated in a more meaningful way for these women than larger but more distant cities and towns. This meant members of the Canning Town branch were able to connect their own work to a broader community outside. These developments confirmed their membership of an expanding, dynamic and successful organization, but also underscored their status as pioneers breaking new ground for others to follow. Their status as 'the first' branch was referred to several times by visiting speakers, suggesting it was a particular point of pride for members.[107]

In the end, the branch failed when this connection to a wider community weakened. Members felt not just 'neglected' by Minnie Baldock, but also isolated from events elsewhere. A lack of visitors eventually prompted the downfall of the branch. In the last few months of the minutes, few speakers are recorded beyond Minnie Baldock discussing her activities elsewhere. She reported back on her individual efforts to heckle Sidney Buxton; the women were no longer acting together, as a collective, as they had done in

[105] CTMB, 6 Feb. 1906, undated, June 1906.

[106] CTMB, undated but June 1906.

[107] CTMB, 29 Jan. 1907, 28 Apr. 1907.

the early period of the branch. Almost all the other speakers were existing members of the branch who offered their own stories of their journey to activism. While these may have been moderately interesting, they effectively told members only what they already knew. Familiar and popular faces such as Teresa Billington-Grieg and Dora Montefiore had long since departed and as the number of WSPU branches had multiplied, leading lights of the suffrage movement such as Clara Morden and Charlotte Despard had many other calls on their time. Minnie Baldock seems to have increasingly seen her own role as an ambassador and advocate for working-class women beyond the branch. Members complained that there were 'not sufficient speakers', but nor were they actually engaging in any collective action.[108] The minutes of one later meeting read simply 'Mrs Baldock away no speaker members amusing themselves with songs and the piano'.[109] But though, as has been stressed, conviviality was important to the women, it was not sufficient to sustain the branch.

Conclusion

At first sight, the history of the Canning Town branch of the Women's Social and Political Union appears to represent a failed experiment. Its decline appears to confirm longstanding narratives about the failure of the militant suffrage movement to engage and attract working-class women, limiting its effectiveness and radicalism and illustrating the difficulties of reconciling feminist and socialist principles and practice. Tensions arose not just because of Christabel Pankhurst's leadership style, but reflected more fundamental disagreements on the necessity of adult suffrage or women's suffrage.

Yet for all the difficulties outlined in this chapter, it also offers a more optimistic reading of the possibilities for working-class women's politics in this period. The women's belief in the importance of the vote went hand-in-hand with a more immediate focus on stressing their right to work, pressuring local administrative bodies and asserting their importance within the local labour market. At the same time, they clearly perceived the vote as a vital tool for bringing about longer-term positive change. Though they were visited by many outside speakers – several of whom were already, or later became, household names – these women looked to their speakers for information, not for instruction. They determined their own course of action, and were not told what to do. Reports from the WSPU national

[108] CTMB, 5 Dec. 1907.

[109] CTMB, 10 Sept. 1907.

executive were only one of many sources of information from diverse events and organizations. As such, the minutes of the Canning Town WSPU provide an important account of contemporary working-class women's political capabilities and capacities.

The Canning Town WSPU should not be seen as a brief flickering of activism which was extinguished by the clumsy mishandling by an insensitive central committee. The relative historiographical neglect of the Canning Town WSPU contrasts with the careful and detailed attention paid to the later East London Federation of Suffragettes (ELFS).[110] Yet to see the ELFS in isolation is to risk the implication that feminist politics was a later innovation in East London. This was not the case. The Canning Town branch not only grew out of pre-existing solidarity between women, but had a lasting legacy. Indeed, several members of the Canning Town WSPU, including Sarah Hockham and Prudence Hornblower, became Canning Town district leaders in the ELFS.[111] Daisy Parsons, later an important figure within the ELFS, specifically cited the inspirational example of Minnie Baldock as a formative influence on her political development.[112] It is vital that we see the continuities and traditions in women's politics at the local level as part of a richer and more comprehensive history of women's activism.

[110] R. Taylor, *In Letters of Gold: The Story of Sylvia Pankhurst and the East London Federation of the Suffragettes in Bow* (London, 1993); M. Davis, *Sylvia Pankhurst: A Life in Radical Politics* (London, 1999); R. Taylor and S. Jackson, *Voices From History: East London Suffragettes* (London, 2014); K. Connelly, 'Sylvia Pankhurst, the First World War and the struggle for democracy', *Revue Française de Civilisation Britannique*, xx (2015) <https://doi.org/10.4000/rfcb.275>; and see also her contribution in this volume.

[111] *Women's Dreadnought*, 16 May 1914, p. 4.

[112] Mary Phillips's obituary of Daisy Parsons, *Calling All Women*, 1958/9, accessed at the Women's Library, London School of Economics and Political Science.

3. Suffrage organizers, grassroots activism and the campaign in Wales*

Beth Jenkins

At the height of the suffrage campaign, Scottish suffragist Helen Fraser was one of the many paid organizers sent to regions across Britain to bolster activity and initiate local branches. In 1908, the National Union of Women's Suffrage Societies (NUWSS) despatched Fraser to Wales, where she carried out the routine work of an organizer: travelling from town to town, speaking at local meetings, raising funds and distributing suffrage propaganda.[1] In a later oral interview with historian Brian Harrison, Fraser recalled her time there.

> I had a lovely time in Wales speaking and building up their branches … [T]hey chose me to go to Wales because Wales had been difficult when they had tried other people. I got to know all the headmistresses you see and nearly all of them suffragists. They were swooped into the movement so that Wales had a very representative group of women … the most intelligent women, it got the women that were leaders.[2]

Fraser's contacts and educational networks introduced her to what she described as 'leading women' across Wales – predominantly headmistresses and middle-class women with whom she lodged and often formed lasting friendships.[3] But her recollections also hint at broader divisions in the

* I am grateful to the editors for their thoughtful comments on earlier versions of this chapter. My thanks also to Neil Evans for helpful discussions on this topic and sharing source material. Any errors or omissions are my own.

[1] Helen Moyes (*née* Fraser) originally worked as the first Scottish WSPU organizer before joining the NUWSS in 1908. L. Leneman, 'Moyes [*née* Fraser], Helen Miller (1881–1979)', *Oxford Dictionary of National Biography* (2004).

[2] Women's Library (WL), LSE: Tape 16, 8SUF/B/055, Helen Moyes [*née* Fraser] Interview with Brian Harrison, 19 Aug. 1975.

[3] WL: 8SUF/B/054-55.

'Suffrage organizers, grassroots activism and the campaign in Wales', in *The politics of women's suffrage: local, national and international dimensions,* ed. A. Hughes-Johnson and L. Jenkins (London, 2021), pp. 87–108.

campaign and of the difficulties some of her predecessors had encountered. Many of the first organizers to work in Wales hailed from middle- or upper-middle-class backgrounds and often failed to breach class boundaries with the communities to which they were sent. While social and party political divisions cut across the wider suffrage movement, in Wales this was further complicated by linguistic and cultural differences. Examining the interactions between suffrage organizers and Welsh-speaking and industrial regions in particular, this chapter highlights some of the issues suffrage societies faced in building a truly inclusive movement across Britain. It explores why certain organizers were sent to Wales and how they were received by local communities, and points to some of the different ways support for the campaign manifested at a grassroots level. In doing so, the chapter suggests that to fully contextualize women's engagement with the movement, we need to employ a much broader definition of activism which is relative to the specific socioeconomic context and local political cultures.

Organizers' testimonies and regional reports have helped to shape both contemporary perceptions and subsequent historiographical narratives of the movement in Wales: slow to develop and implanted by a middle-class leadership on 'rather stony soil', as another visiting speaker wrote.[4] This chapter examines the frequent disconnect between the intentions of organizers and their reception in local communities by analysing organizers' correspondence and suffrage papers, in tandem with local press reports and sources. The historiographical contribution of the chapter is twofold. First, it builds upon a recent body of scholarship which has challenged the interpretation that the women's movement in Wales lacked a grassroots base by exploring some of the ways support manifested outside dominant suffrage structures, as well as the economic and cultural factors which could inhibit engagement with the mainstream suffrage movement. Second, the chapter considers more broadly how historians conceptualize the relationship between centres and so-called geographical peripheries in the early twentieth-century suffrage movement: between national leadership and the regions, and between dominant local suffrage branches and their neighbouring districts.

A key question for historians of suffrage in Wales has been the extent to which there was a specifically 'Welsh' movement. While early scholarship questioned the existence of a native grassroots movement in Wales, subsequent studies have begun to revise this interpretation. Pioneering research by Kay Cook and Neil Evans and by Angela V. John provided the first surveys of Welsh women's suffrage and explored how it intersected with

[4] WL: 9/01/0690, Letter from Lady Frances Balfour to Mrs Fawcett, 13 Nov. 1909.

national identity.[5] This was followed by Ryland Wallace's comprehensive and meticulous account which charted the fortunes of the major suffrage societies across Wales and revealed no absence of agitation in even the most remote towns and villages.[6] In her nuanced analysis of Welsh women's liberalism, Ursula Masson demonstrated how support for suffrage initially flourished through other reform movements. Masson argued that although the impetus for the suffrage campaign did, to some extent, come from elsewhere, 'the conditions in its favour brought together the "outside" stimulus with elements usually considered as impeccably "national", the forces of Welsh Nonconformity'.[7] Embodied in the Cymru Fydd (Young Wales) movement, Welsh Liberal nationalism combined the causes of disestablishment, land reform, education, language and temperance in the late nineteenth century.[8] Masson highlighted that women's claims to citizenship in Wales had ideological and personnel continuities with these issues which had created fertile ground for the suffrage campaign to take hold. In particular, the Welsh Union of Women's Liberal Associations became the main early vehicle for suffrage – linking, albeit briefly, feminism and nationalism in party politics.[9]

[5] K. Cook and N. Evans, '"The petty antics of the bell-ringing boisterous band"? The women's suffrage movement in Wales, 1890–1918', in *Our Mothers' Land: Chapters in Welsh Women's History 1830–1939*, ed. A. V. John (Cardiff, 1991), pp. 159–88; A. V. John, '"Run like blazes": the suffragettes and Welshness', *Llafur*, vi (1994), 29–43, p. 30. See also U. Masson, 'The Swansea suffragettes', in *Women in Wales: A Documentary of Our Recent History, Vol. 1*, ed. L. Dee and K. Keineg (Cardiff, 1987), pp. 67–76; P. E. Jones, 'The women's suffrage movement in Caernarfonshire', *Caernarvonshire Historical Society Transactions*, xlviii (1987), 75–112.

[6] R. Wallace, *The Women's Suffrage Movement in Wales 1866–1928* (Cardiff, 2009). See also R. Wallace, '"No votes for women, no information from women": the Suffragette boycott of the 1911 Census in Wales', *Llafur*, xi (2013), 56–76; '"Gwylliaid Peisiog": Y Swffragetiaid a'r Eisteddfod Genedlaethol ['"Gwylliaid Peisiog": The Suffragettes and the National Eisteddfod]', *Llafur*, xii (2017), 38–52; '"A doughty warrior in the women's cause": Fannie Margaret Thomas of Pontycymer', *Llafur*, xii (2018), 58–87; '"A dear friend, and a loyal and devoted member of the League": Alix Minnie Clark and the women's suffrage movement in Montgomeryshire', *Montgomeryshire Collections*, cvii (2019), 207–235.

[7] U. Masson, *'For Women, for Wales and for Liberalism': Women in Liberal Politics in Wales, 1880–1914* (Cardiff, 2010), p. 16.

[8] U. Masson, '"Hand in hand with the women, forward we will go": Welsh nationalism and feminism in the 1890s', *Women's History Review*, xii (2003), 357–86; K. Bohata, 'For Wales, see England?' Suffrage and the new woman in Wales', *Women's History Review*, xi (2002), 643–56; R. Wallace, *'Organise! Organise! Organise!' A Study of Reform Agitations in Wales, 1840–1886* (Cardiff, 1991), p. 182.

[9] Masson, *'For Women, for Wales and for Liberalism'*.

More broadly, recent scholarship on the suffrage campaign in Britain and Ireland has adopted an increasingly critical approach to conceptual understandings of 'core' and 'periphery' by rejecting a one-way transmission of ideas between dominant metropolitan centres and the so-called Celtic fringe.[10] Local or regional case studies, too, have challenged top-down narratives of suffrage by showing how policy initiatives and campaign tactics could be developed in the regions before they were adopted nationally.[11] These studies have shown that for most women it was the local branch which was the key site of their campaign; as June Hannam summarized, 'local suffrage politics was not just about building support for a national movement – at particular times the local branches *were* the movement'.[12] Moreover, a local framework of analysis has proved particularly fruitful in revealing the intricate web of overlapping associations in support of the cause, and the social and friendship networks which underpinned women's activism.[13] As Myriam Boussahba-Bravard reminds us, 'suffrage outside suffragism' was an integral part of the campaign for the vote and non-suffrage associations, such as party political organizations or reforming groups, did not preclude members' support for suffrage.[14] This is particularly pertinent to the Welsh context where the relatively late development of branches of the major suffrage societies has been used by some as a metric of apathy towards the cause. However, the campaign for the vote was part of a much longer process of women's politicization and movement into public life, and a variety of party political and non-political organizations worked for

[10] S. Pašeta, *Suffrage and Citizenship in Ireland 1912–18: The Kehoe Lecture in Irish History 2018* (London, 2019), p. 4. Pašeta has shown that the Irish and British suffrage movements were deeply connected, and argued that by focusing primarily on disagreements historians risk simplifying these complex dynamics.

[11] J. Hannam, '"I had not been to London": Women's suffrage – a view from the regions', in *Votes for Women*, ed. J. Purvis and S. Stanley Holton (London, 2000), pp. 226–45; K. Cowman, *The Militant Suffrage Movement in York* (York, 2008); S. E. Peacock, *Votes for Women: The Women's Fight in Portsmouth* (Portsmouth, 1983); R. Davidson, 'A local perspective: the women's movement and citizenship, Croydon 1890s–1939', *Women's History Review*, xxix (2020), 1016–33.

[12] Hannam, '"I had not been to London"', p. 242.

[13] J. Liddington and J. Norris, *One Hand Tied Behind Us: The Rise of the Women's Suffrage Movement* (London, 1978); K. Cowman, *Mrs Brown is a Man and a Brother: Women in Merseyside's Political Organisations, 1890–1920* (Liverpool, 2004); J. Hannam, '"To make the world a better place": socialist women and women's suffrage in Bristol, 1910–20', in *Suffrage Outside Suffragism: Women's Vote in Britain, 1880–1914*, ed. M. Boussahba-Bravard (Basingstoke, 2007), pp. 157–79. See also E. Crawford, *The Women's Suffrage Movement in Britain and Ireland: A Regional Survey* (London, 2006).

[14] M. Boussahba-Bravard (ed.), *Suffrage Outside Suffragism: Women's Vote in Britain, 1880–1914* (Basingstoke, 2007), p. 13.

suffrage in Welsh communities, including Women's Liberal Association branches, temperance societies, Women's Labour League branches, Women's Cooperative Guilds and literary and debating societies.[15] Such support which manifested outside the administrative machinery of major suffrage societies is often overshadowed by the more high-profile events, but by using a broader definition of political activism we can see that support for the campaign manifested differently across communities and contexts.

Indeed, Wales, like elsewhere, was not a homogeneous entity when it came to women's suffrage. Yet limited analysis of the constituent nations in surveys of the British suffrage movement has often led to one-dimensional interpretations which mask these regional and local complexities. Working-class communities were overwhelmingly concentrated in the densely populated coalfield of the southern valleys and the slate-quarrying region of the north; both were centred around a mono-industrial economic base which afforded few opportunities for women's paid employment outside of the home. Wales's small middle and upper classes developed in the commercial centres and coastal towns of the south and north-west, whereas the Welsh-speaking heartland was predominantly rooted in the agricultural regions of the middle and north of the country. These social and cultural differences were mapped onto political differences. The Liberal Party, which had become entwined with Welsh national identity, dominated the political landscape throughout most of the suffrage campaign. By the turn of the twentieth century, this Welsh Liberal Nonconformist hegemony was also beginning to fracture under a burgeoning labour movement in the industrial and cosmopolitan south-east, areas increasingly identified with 'de-nationalising' values.[16] For suffrage organizers unfamiliar with the national context, these subtle complexities could pose significant challenges. Focusing on the reception organizers received across different communities in Wales, then, provides a lens into how the socioeconomic structure, cultural landscape and political priorities affected localities' specific engagement with the mainstream campaign.

Suffrage societies and Welsh identity: an overview

While the Women's Social and Political Union (WSPU) and Women's Freedom League (WFL) did make significant inroads throughout Wales, it was the NUWSS which had the most success across the country – particularly as suffrage branches began to replace Liberal women's associations in the years

[15] *The Wrexham Advertiser*, 5 Oct. 1895; C. Lloyd-Morgan, 'From temperance to suffrage?' in *Our Mothers' Land: Chapters in Welsh Women's History, 1830–1939*, ed. A. V. John (Cardiff, 1991), pp. 135–58, p. 149; Masson, *'For Women, for Wales and for Liberalism'*.

[16] Masson, *'For Women, for Wales and for Liberalism'*, p. 19.

preceding the war.[17] Active societies initially flourished along the relatively anglicized and affluent port cities of the south and the seaside resorts of the north-west. By 1912, the Cardiff and District society claimed the title of the largest branch outside London and, at the outbreak of the First World War, the NUWSS boasted around fifty branches in Wales.[18] The introduction of regional federations in 1909 provided alternative devolved centres of power which had financial autonomy and could challenge the national leadership over policy.[19] Pre-existing regional divisions in Wales were reflected in this new organizational structure; branches in the south joined the South Wales and Montgomeryshire Federation, while their northern counterparts were affiliated to the West Lancashire, Cheshire and North Wales Federation. The Cardiff and Bangor NUWSS branches were two of the strongest and, both situated in university towns, were largely dominated by a civic middle-class leadership. They also had close and sometimes fraught relationships with their respective neighbouring coalfield communities in the south, and the slate-quarrying villages of the north.

Welsh iconography, like that of Scottish and Irish, was co-opted by all suffrage societies to further the campaign. As Angela V. John has shown, the linking of Welsh national identity with the cause was used by both supporters and opponents of women's suffrage.[20] For the former, it was not only an expression of local or national identity but a propagandist strategy to demonstrate the spatial and cultural reach of the movement. Participants in marches and demonstrations were encouraged to don national costume, and it was not uncommon for the national anthem or Welsh hymns to be sung at meetings.[21] A specifically Welsh offshoot of the WSPU, the Cymric Suffrage Union (CSU), was founded in 1911 by a prominent London-Welsh suffrage activist, Edith Mansell Moullin.[22] The CSU made use of

[17] The WFL was the strongest presence in Swansea and Montgomery, where teachers dominated the local membership. Other branches in Cardiff, Caldicott and Aberdare were also particularly active. The first WSPU branch in Wales was established in Cardiff in 1906 and, along with the Newport branch, maintained a vibrant membership until the war. For further information, see Wallace, *The Women's Suffrage Movement in Wales*; Masson, '*For Women, for Wales and for Liberalism*', p. 170.

[18] Cardiff Central Library: National Union of Women's Suffrage, Cardiff and District Society Annual Report 1912–13; Wallace, *The Women's Suffrage Movement in Wales*, p. 157.

[19] Hannam, '"I had not been to London"', p. 229.

[20] John, 'Run like blazes'.

[21] *Votes for Women* (*VW*), 2 June 1911; 16 June 1911; 3 Nov. 1911.

[22] A. V. John, 'Moullin, Edith Ruth Mansell [*née* Thomas], 1858/9–1941', *Oxford Dictionary of National Biography* (2004). Mansell Moullin was a settlement worker, a founding member of the Anti-Sweating League and member of numerous suffrage societies.

Welsh costume, language and music and a rhetoric of Celtic liberty.[23] It also distributed Welsh handbills at concerts and lectures held in Welsh chapels in London and published material in Welsh-language newspapers.[24] Although the Union did establish several branches throughout Wales, it was predominantly London-based.[25] The symbolic use of Welshness was particularly pertinent for the national suffrage leadership because one of the leading Liberal politicians, then-Chancellor of the Exchequer David Lloyd George, was a Welshman. Lloyd George had a notoriously ambivalent stance on women's suffrage and initially opposed it. The WSPU arranged classes, taught by a Welsh inhabitant of London, Iris Davies, for its members to learn Welsh phrases so that they could heckle Lloyd George in his native tongue.[26] However, his contemporary status as a hero of Welsh cultural nationalism could also complicate the suffrage movement's engagement with Liberal strongholds within Wales.

Suffrage organizers, cultural clashes and regional centres

As the campaign gained momentum in the years preceding the First World War, full-time paid organizers were sent to regions across Britain to stimulate the formation of local branches. While the vibrancy of branch activity was dependent on and sustained by the enthusiasm of the local membership, suffrage societies recognized the deployment of organizers as the most effective and efficient way to reach sympathizers, especially during the event of a by-election. Their work entailed arranging meetings, raising funds, canvassing candidates and compiling reports on the region's activities. The reception organizers received across regions was mixed. Although Krista Cowman has pointed to the success organizers had in some regions in helping to raise local suffrage membership, other historians have

[23] Following growing frustration with the Liberal government, the CSU disbanded and regrouped in Oct. 1912 as the more militant Forward Cymric Suffrage Union, obliging members to put suffrage before other causes and oppose any government which refused votes for women. Wallace, *The Women's Suffrage Movement in Wales*, p. 62.

[24] *VW*, 18 Aug. 1911; 8 Sept. 1911; 6 Oct. 1911. It printed 5,000 copies of translated literature including Emmeline Pethick Lawrence's articles 'Does a man support his wife' and 'Who supports the children?' The articles, originally published in *Votes for Women* (21 July 1911), focused on the unpaid labour married women undertake at home and childrearing. This translation was primarily undertaken by a prominent local figure in the Union, Rev. Ivan Davies of Penrhos, Llandrillo.

[25] *VW*, 18 Aug. 1911. For an overview of the London-Welsh and suffrage, see A. V. John, '"A draft of fresh air": women's suffrage, the Welsh and London', *Transactions of the Honourable Society of Cymmrodorion*, i (1995), 81–93.

[26] Museum of London: Z6078/2, Letter from Jessie Kenney, 7 Dec. 1909.

highlighted the resentment provoked by the importation of English 'stars' to Wales, who sometimes caused more harm than good.[27] To a certain degree, the characterization of visiting campaigners as having a limited ability to empathize with some of the Welsh communities in which they worked was true. Stereotypes of Welsh women as marginal, passive and disinterested are certainly evident in some organizers' letters and reports, and this reflected broader class prejudices as well as the specificities of the Welsh context.[28] For instance, NUWSS organizer Mary Hilston lamented that 'the women are very hopeless' while working in the mining town of Blaenavon.[29] Frustrated by the limited progress she felt she was making in the town, Hilston described its inhabitants as 'naturally slow in taking things in', and reported that she had to give them 'small doses and let them filter'.[30]

Vivid descriptions of an isolated and rugged Welsh landscape were evident in many suffrage organizers' reports too – landscapes which were for some analogous to an alien and hostile cultural environment. Organizers frequently used geological metaphors to underscore the challenges they faced in gaining local trust. Hilston wrote of the 'stone wall' she met in her 'heavy task' to 'break up the ground' in North Monmouthshire.[31] Similarly, the sparsely populated 'remote little villages among the mountains' in mid and north Wales were a source of amazement for some visitors who encountered 'people who do not speak or understand English'.[32] This sense of 'otherness' also extended to attempts to recruit volunteers for campaigns;

[27] K. Cowman, *Women of the Right Spirit: Paid Organisers of the Women's Social and Political Union* (Manchester, 2007); H. Smith, *The British Women's Suffrage Campaign 1866–1928* (2nd edn, Abingdon, 2007), p. 30; J. R. DeVries, 'Popular and smart: why scholarship on the women's suffrage movement in Britain still matters', *History Compass*, xi (2013), 177–88, at p. 180.

[28] S. Crozier-De Rosa, 'Divided sisterhood? Nationalist feminism and feminist militancy in England and Ireland', *Contemporary British History*, xxxii (2018), 448–68. Sharon Crozier-De Rosa has highlighted a similar rhetoric used by the WSPU in Ireland whereby 'the more knowing, mature, rational and superior Anglo-Saxon or English core tolerated and led the more emotional, irrational, childlike and inferior Celtic peripheries', p. 450.

[29] CA: D/MAR/3/55, Catherine E. Marshall Papers: Letter from Mary Hilston to the E.F.F. Committee, 28 Apr. 1913.

[30] CA: D/MAR/3/55, Letter from Mary Hilston to Miss Mackenzie, 20 Apr. 1913.

[31] Cumbria Archive [CA]: D/MAR/3/55, Catherine E. Marshall Papers: Letter from Mary Hilston to the E.F.F. Committee, 28 Apr. 1913; D/MAR/3/55: Letter from Mary Hilston to Miss Marshall, 21 June 1913. Helen Davies, CLWS organizer, similarly wrote of the 'digging' work she had undertaken in neighbouring towns of Abertillery, Aberavenny, Blaenavon and Tredegar. *CLWS*, 1 Aug. 1914.

[32] *Common Cause* (*CC*), 22 Aug. 1912.

WSPU organizer Annie Williams, for instance, marketed the 1913 holiday campaign in the Rhondda Valley as providing 'a unique opportunity for coming into touch with the typical collier and his surroundings'.[33] Like other popular tourist towns across Britain, the western and northern coastal towns of Wales became targets for the holiday campaigns. During the summer months, organizers frequently made calls for members to notify them if they intended to spend their holiday nearby, with the promise to combine 'work and play'.[34]

The initial deployment of organizers was often based on simplistic stereotypes or a superficial perception of the region by national leaders. When later asked why she was sent to Wales, Helen Fraser replied: 'I think they thought that a good speaker was very attractive in Wales. You see, the Welsh are very eloquent … a refined flourish for oratory. And they thought that I would be good in Wales because I was a really good speaker.'[35] Other visiting campaigners tried to find shared cultural affinity with their audience. Speaking in Rhyl on behalf of the WFL, Muriel Matters reported that she had 'asked the people at headquarters to allow me to come down and take on the job because I am partly Welsh, and because I would understand your little ways, and you understand mine'.[36] The Tonypandy riots of 1910 and 1911 also contributed towards a perception of the coalfield communities as a hotbed of militancy, and the WSPU used them as evidence to argue that the Welsh understood the need for militant tactics.[37] Ahead of Pankhurst's tour of Wales in 1911, the WSPU claimed that 'the Welsh are keenly interested in matters political, and there is nothing they enjoy so thoroughly as a rousing enthusiastic meeting'.[38] The strikes were also cited by the WSPU leadership as an example of the government's hypocrisy in relation to its treatment of militant action; the miners were treated more favourably by the government and press, they argued, because of the need for their votes.[39] Reports in the suffrage press often fuelled these class and national stereotypes, even when they had little material basis. Detailing her initial caution about visiting slate-quarrying villages in north Wales in 1909, Helga Gill wrote: 'These

[33] *VW*, 19 Aug. 1910.

[34] *VW*, 23 June and 28 July 1911. This was a sentiment also echoed by the WFL; *Women's Franchise*, 24 July 1909.

[35] WL: 8SUF/B/055.

[36] *Rhyl Journal*, 13 Nov. 1909.

[37] *VW*, 26 Jan. 1912.

[38] *VW*, 30 June 1911.

[39] M. Fawcett, *Women's Suffrage: a Short History of a Great Movement* (London, 1912), p. 66; *VW*, 22 Mar. 1912.

are mining districts, and have the reputation of being terribly rough.'[40] Similar apprehension was expressed by a WSPU visiting campaigner about a meeting in the rural town of Dolgellau, 'as the large audience were almost entirely Welsh, and there appeared to be every possibility of a troublesome time'.[41] Despite their trepidation, organizers or visiting speakers were often surprised to find that they received a warm reception.[42]

Yet suffrage organizers – like their society's membership – were also a diverse group. In her study of WSPU organizers, Cowman estimates that at least 140 women from a broad range of social backgrounds worked for the society as paid agents across Britain.[43] Usually promoted from within its membership ranks, the earliest WSPU workers were drawn from the radical socialist networks which formed around the Independent Labour Party (ILP) and had some experience of agitation and propagandizing in trade unions.[44] In Wales, too, the WSPU and WFL agents appear to have been drawn from a wider range of social backgrounds than most of their NUWSS counterparts, with some hailing from the communities in which they campaigned. The selection of organizers was predominantly based on the executive committee's perceived needs of the district and their understanding of a worker's abilities.[45] NUWSS organizers were initially sent to different nations and regions from their own so that they would not get involved in partisan politics. This contrasted with the WFL policy which, following its introduction of regional organizers in May 1910, sought to appoint women already familiar with their region. Such a strategy, however, was not always successful. This was evident in the appointment of Mary McCleod Cleeves, secretary of the Swansea WFL branch and a national executive committee member, as WFL organizer for Wales. For a year, she was active in promoting the suffrage cause throughout the region, chairing meetings and helping to establish branches. But her tenure soon ended in acrimony when her fellow Swansea members claimed she was assuming too much authority – leading to her eventual resignation and defection to the WSPU. As Alexandra Hughes-Johnson notes in her chapter in this volume, McCleod Cleeves changed allegiances again in 1915 when she served on the executive committee of the Suffragettes of the WSPU, a wartime suffrage organization established in opposition to the Pankhursts'

40 *CC*, 19 Aug. 1909. See also: *CC*, 5 Sept. 1912.

41 *VW*, 27 Aug. 1909.

42 *CC*, 4 Jan. 1912.

43 Cowman, *Women of the Right Spirit*, p. 12.

44 Cowman, *Women of the Right Spirit*, p. 12.

45 Cowman, *Women of the Right Spirit*, p. 74.

patriotic feminism. Nonetheless, such regional events could determine national policy; following a full enquiry by WFL officials from London into her resignation as Welsh organizer, the national executive concluded that the relationship between branches and organizers was unsatisfactory and shortly after terminated the scheme.[46]

Following the introduction of the NUWSS Federation Scheme in 1909, the regions were given greater autonomy to choose and fund organizers. When the Cardiff and District Women's Suffrage Society (CDWSS) sought a full-time campaigner in 1912, their secretary Mabel Howell asked the national secretary, Kathleen Courtney, for 'someone not too young and not aggressive'.[47] Howell also wrote to the women's university residential halls in Wales to see whether they had any graduates suitable for the position. The qualities they sought in an organizer were clearly a reflection of the composition of the local leadership and their caution to not upset the delicate factions of their support base. Like most large branches, the CDWSS executive committee comprised a mixture of political persuasions; its president, Rose Mabel Lewis, was a Conservative, while its vice president, Millicent Mackenzie, a professor of education at the local university college, would stand as a Labour parliamentary candidate in 1918. These prominent members were also linked to major civic and educational institutions in the city. Howell, a local graduate, was to be secretary of the Cardiff WLA from 1925. Other influential committee members included Barbara Foxley, who was to be Mackenzie's successor as professor of education and a Liberal councillor in the 1920s, Mary Collin, headmistress of the city's prestigious Cardiff High School for Girls, and Ethel Hurlbatt, principal of the women's university residence, Aberdare Hall. The foundation of the university colleges in Wales and their women's halls provided important institutional spaces for visiting speakers and campaigners. Lewis, Hurlbatt and Collin all hosted NUWSS organizer Helen Fraser on her numerous visits to Cardiff – Hurlbatt in Aberdare Hall and Collin in her house attached to Cardiff High School for Girls.[48]

Organizers were often stationed in the strongest branch in the district and used this as a centre from which to reach sympathizers, especially because they were usually larger urban towns with good communication and transport links. This meant that working-class communities could be doubly marginalized by the regional civic middle-class leadership and the suffrage society leadership. Dominant regional branches, such as the

[46] Wallace, *The Women's Suffrage Movement in Wales*, pp. 108–9.

[47] CA: D/MAR/3/17, Letter from Mabel Howell to Kathleen Courtney, 13 July 1912.

[48] WL: 8SUF/B/054-55.

CDWSS, sometimes perpetuated class stereotypes of their surrounding industrial communities, reflecting pre-existing tensions between different classes and communities. Some of these tensions came to the fore when the NUWSS abandoned its non-partisan policy in 1912 and adopted the Election Fighting Fund (EFF), which gave electoral support to the Labour Party. This new stance alienated some Liberal supporters, who comprised a majority of the NUWSS membership. As a Liberal stronghold, the South Wales Federation was one of the most ardently opposed to the policy. Claiming a superior local understanding of labour politics, Mabel Howell wrote to the EFF committee: 'Cardiff is in the mining district – perhaps this accounts for the difference in one's estimate of their value as supporters'.[49]

In other instances, the greater autonomy given to regions was beneficial for breaching cultural divides. Branches in the north of Wales were affiliated to the West Lancashire, Cheshire and North Wales Federation. However, difficulties experienced by the Federation in maintaining contact with the more remote Welsh societies, as well as communicating with predominantly Welsh-language communities, prompted the formation of a Welsh Sub-Committee.[50] Established in January 1912, Charlotte Price White, secretary of the Bangor NUWSS branch, acted as the organizing secretary for the coordination of Welsh work within the Federation. A former teacher and early graduate of the University College of North Wales, Price White did much to bolster and coordinate activity in north Wales through her translation of suffrage material and sensitivity to regions' local political allegiances and cultural landscape.[51]

Welsh language, Liberalism and rural communities

Linguistic differences were a significant obstacle for all major suffrage societies in Wales, who frequently expressed the need for a Welsh-speaking organizer and understood that their campaign work in the country was significantly hampered by the lack of one.[52] At the turn of the twentieth century, nearly half of the population spoke Welsh, and in some rural and

[49] CA: D/MAR/3/17. For a detailed re-examination of the South Wales Federation's opposition to the EFF, see U. Masson, '"Political conditions in Wales are quite different…": party politics and votes for women in Wales, 1912–15', *Women's History Review*, ix (2000), 369–88.

[50] WL: 2LSW/E/09/63, National Union of Women's Suffrage Societies, West Lancashire, West Cheshire and North Wales Federation, Second Annual Report, 1912.

[51] A farmer's daughter, Charlotte Price White (*née* Bell) later became the first woman member of Caernarfonshire County Council in 1926.

[52] *VW*, 10 Sept. 1909; 22 July 1910; *CC*, 20 Oct. 1910; 3 Nov. 1910; 8 June 1911.

northern counties, such as Merionethshire, the proportion of monoglot speakers was over 50%.[53] As part of their broader strategy to engage the regions more effectively, in late 1909 the WSPU sought to address this gap by appointing Rachel Barrett as Wales's permanent organizer. Born to Welsh-speaking parents in Carmarthen and educated at University College of Wales, Aberystwyth, Barrett joined the WSPU in 1906 while working as a teacher in Penarth. During Adela Pankhurst's visit to Cardiff the following year, Barrett helped her in her work and reportedly fell into disfavour with her headmistress 'when her science mistress was reported in the local papers as drenched with flour at an open-air meeting at the Cardiff docks'.[54] She worked alongside Annie Kenney in Bristol as a volunteer before she was sent to Newport, Monmouthshire in the autumn of 1909. There she recalled carrying out the regular activities of a WSPU organizer: arranging meetings, speaking, raising funds, taking part in protests and organizing militancy.[55] Barrett's Welsh background was frequently perceived as an asset to the WSPU. During the 1910 Mid-Glamorgan by-election, the suffrage press claimed that '[i]t was fortunate that Miss Barrett, who was in charge of the campaign, is Welsh by birth, and was able to make short speeches to the people in their own language to their great delight and interest'.[56]

The support of Welsh-speaking campaigners could be a crucial factor in garnering support in communities where language barriers, rather than hostility to the message, inhibited engagement with the mainstream movement. An influential and vigorous campaigner, Barrett also addressed crowds throughout north Wales in Welsh and had a similar effect in breaching cultural divides during Pankhurst's tour of the country in 1911.[57] The spatial composition of the audience at a meeting held in the spa town of Llanwrtyd Wells reflects the initial caution felt by local residents; the front seats were filled up with tourists visiting the spa, while the body of the hall comprised Welsh miners, farmers, townspeople and their wives and daughters.[58] A report described the reception they received.

> Some of the country people have only an imperfect knowledge of 'the English'. The first words of Miss Barrett's speech from the chair spoken in Welsh carried

[53] *1901 Census of England and Wales: Languages in Wales and Monmouthshire.*

[54] Rachel Barrett Autobiography, c.1924. Cited in J. Aaron and U. Mason (eds), *The Very Salt of Life: Welsh Women's Political Writings from Chartism to Suffrage* (Dinas Powys, 2007), p. 298.

[55] Rachel Barrett Autobiography, c.1924.

[56] *VW*, 1 Apr. 1910.

[57] *VW*, 22 July 1910.

[58] *VW*, 11 Aug. 1911.

> the audience with her absolutely. In her speech, Mrs Pankhurst, who obviously enjoyed the meeting and felt herself in touch with her unsophisticated and eager listeners, dealt chiefly with matters affecting the lives or within the immediate knowledge of the simple folk of whom most of her audience was composed.[59]

Despite the patronizing tone of the report, the importance of the suffrage message being delivered through the medium of Welsh is clear. The NUWSS, too, recognized that the support of Welsh-speaking activists during their campaigns was vital to their ability to gain access to some communities. For instance, the positive reception of their Welsh caravan tour during the summer of 1909 was attributed to the presence of another University of Wales graduate and teacher from Merthyr, Magdalen Morgan, 'whose fluency in Welsh is greatly appreciated in the villages, where little or no English is spoken'.[60] At a meeting in Bala, the local press reported that Morgan, who spoke in Welsh, got a fair hearing, but attempts by her friend, Miss Edwards, to follow in English, proved abortive, with the meeting breaking up in disorder.[61]

The involvement of Welsh-speaking activists was also essential for the translation of the suffrage societies' propaganda material. Although references were scarce, there are early examples of support for women's enfranchisement in women's Welsh-language print culture, such as the periodical *Y Gymraes* (*Welshwoman*), and of literature being translated by some provincial suffrage societies in Wales from the 1870s.[62] In the early twentieth century, Welsh campaigners again highlighted the need for material to be translated and were positive about the willingness of the Welsh language press to publish it.[63] However, it was not until 1910 that the translation of propaganda material by the major suffrage societies truly gained pace. This was largely carried out by Charlotte Price White and the Bangor and District Suffrage Society, who recognized the urgent need to give people 'propaganda in their own language'.[64] Translated material included extracts from Lloyd George's speeches and pamphlets explaining

59 *VW*, 11 Aug. 1911.

60 *CC*, 26 Aug. 1909.

61 *North Wales Times*, 28 Aug. 1909; *CC*, 2 Sept. 1909; 9 Sept. 1909; 16 Sept. 1909; *Seren*, 28 Aug. 1909.

62 S. R. Williams, '"The true 'Cymraes": images of women in women's nineteenth century Welsh periodicals', in *Our Mother's Land: Chapters in Welsh Women's History 1830–1939*, ed. A. V. John (Cardiff, 1991), pp. 69–92, p. 89; Wallace, *The Women's Suffrage Movement in Wales*, p. 50.

63 WL: 9/01/0084, Letter from Josephine Davies to Miss Palliser, 20 July 1905.

64 *CC*, 4 Jan. 1912.

the Conciliation Bill. The Welsh Organization Sub-Committee of the regional NUWSS federation was particularly active in working closely with local papers and the Welsh-language press to gain coverage of suffrage news.[65] Reports consistently highlighted the warm reception that the Welsh leaflets received at local markets and in campaign work.[66] The increased coordination of translated material seemed to have been a significant factor in facilitating the engagement of Welsh-speaking communities with the suffrage movement. This was reflected in the formation of branches in 1911 in the Welsh-speaking and slate-quarrying communities of Bethesda, Tal-y-sarn and Pen-y-groes in Caernarfonshire.[67] Edith Eskrigge, NUWSS organizer for north Wales, discussing the formation of a branch in the slate-quarrying village of Bethesda in 1911, noted that: 'Bethesda will be the first society in north Wales that is composed entirely of Welsh women and it is hoped that this progressive little quarry town will prove a centre from which "The Movement" will spread to other quarry villages, hidden away among the hills.'[68]

As suffrage societies began to gain greater access to Welsh-speaking communities, the acceleration of militant tactics by the WSPU from 1911 led to an increased resistance to all suffrage organizers and speakers within some Liberal communities. Advocating the need for a more cautious and considered approach in north Wales, NUWSS organizer Edith Eskrigge reported: 'I should not be giving any idea of the situation as I found it, without saying that nine out of ten people who have expressed agreement with our aims would not have even listened to me for a minute, had I not first explained that I was "non-militant".'[69] This was further evidenced when Eskrigge visited members of the Caernarfon NUWSS branch in Lloyd George's parliamentary constituency in February 1912. Plans were discussed for a joint demonstration by the local WLA and the suffrage society in the town, but the feeling of antagonism aroused by the increase in militancy was so strong that the WLA decided not to lend its support to the event.[70] A series of highly publicized attacks on Lloyd George in Wales later that year did little to gain the sympathy of Wales's Liberal strongholds, and, as the local press secretary Miss Wortham reported back to the NUWSS

[65] This included: *Yr Aelwyd*, *Y Glorian*, *Y Rhedegydd*, *Seren Cymru*, *Golenad*, *Dydd* and *Udgorn*, and *Baner ac Amserau Cymru.*

[66] *CC*, 22 Aug. 1912.

[67] Wallace, *The Women's Suffrage Movement in Wales*, p. 157.

[68] *CC*, 4 May 1911.

[69] *CC*, 4 May 1911.

[70] WL: 2LSW/E/09/63.

executive committee, could do 'incalculable harm to suffragism in Wales'.[71] In particular, violent treatment afforded to suffragettes by local men at the National Eisteddfod in Wrexham and Lloyd George's opening of a Village Institute in his home village of Llanystumdwy attracted significant local and national press attention.[72] In the succeeding weeks, Eskrigge organized a small meeting in Mold, which was not as successful as she had anticipated, owing to the hostile feeling which had been aroused by the incident.[73] While such propagandist stunts certainly gave visibility to the cause on a national level, they did little to advance the movement in certain Welsh communities and served to alienate some sympathizers who interpreted them as an attack on their national culture.[74]

Coalfield communities, the labour movement and suffrage

Although the Liberal Party maintained parliamentary dominance throughout Wales until the war, by the turn of the century its hegemony was beginning to fracture under an emerging labour movement in the south. Historians have suggested that the low levels of working-class women's paid employment inhibited the development of a fully coordinated suffrage movement in the South Wales Valleys, in comparison to their unionized northern counterparts in the Lancashire cotton mills.[75] To a certain extent this was true. The mono-industrial structure of the coalfield afforded few opportunities for women's formal labour participation outside of the home and this had a profound effect on gendered political cultures; miner's lodges and trades and labour councils, which women had limited access to, were central to political and social life of these communities. In the years preceding the war there was, however, some degree of convergence between an emerging women's labour politics and the suffrage movement. Parallel to the decline of women's liberal associations, active branches of the Women's Labour League (WLL) flourished in Cardiff and Swansea and were soon followed by ones in Newport, Abertillery, Merthyr, Ogmore Vale and other mining towns across the coalfield.[76] Local membership of the

[71] CA: D/MAR/3/21, Letter to Miss Cummings from W. H. Wortham, Bangor, 20 June 1913.

[72] John, 'Run like blazes', pp. 30–1.

[73] WL: National Union of Women's Suffrage Societies, West Lancashire, West Cheshire and North Wales Federation, Third Annual Report, 1913.

[74] *CC*, 15 July 1909; 19 Aug. 1909.

[75] Cook and Evans, '"The petty antics of the bell-ringing boisterous band"', p. 180.

[76] N. Evans and D. Jones, '"To help forward the great work of humanity": women in the Labour Party in Wales, 1900–2000', in *The Labour Party in Wales, 1900–2000*, ed. D. Tanner,

WLLs overlapped with Women's Cooperative Guilds, eighteen branches of which were formed in Wales between 1909 and 1914.[77] These associations introduced women to public speaking, propagandizing and organizational skills which would aid their suffrage work. In some instances, suffrage activity could act as a catalyst to women's involvement in other political causes by introducing them to collective organizing. For example, following Annie Kenney's agitation in Cardiff and the South Wales Valleys in 1906, twelve of her audience at Trecynon joined the ILP and also formed a branch of the WSPU, though the latter appeared to have been short-lived.[78]

This developing women's political culture was reflected in their increased contribution to local labour newspapers.[79] In December 1911, the first 'Our women's column' appeared in the *Rhondda Socialist*, a mouthpiece for the local Rhondda ILP branches until its merger with the Merthyr-based *South Wales Worker* in 1913.[80] Anonymously authored by 'Matron', the women's column addressed issues such as pithead baths, health, education, housing, poverty, maternal and child welfare, alongside women's suffrage.[81] Similarly, an 'Our women's column' was included in the *Swansea and District Workers' Journal* (1899–1914), which was published by the Swansea ILP. Though mostly unsigned, some articles can be attributed to the secretary of the Swansea WLL, Ruth Chalk.[82] Within these pages, support for women's enfranchisement was interwoven with a wider range of demands which reflected the priorities of the local community and were concerned with improving the material basis of working-class women's day-to-day lives.

The authors of these articles were astutely aware of the material constraints many working-class women faced in participating fully in local politics. An article by 'Matron' lamented the lack of working-class leaders

---

C. Williams and D. Hopkin (Cardiff, 2000), pp. 215–40; C. Collette, *For Labour and for women: The Women's Labour League, 1906-1918* (Manchester, 1989), 204–17. Collette records at least 16 WLL branches in extistence across Wales at various points.

[77] Wallace, *The Women's Suffrage Movement in Wales*, p. 174.

[78] M. Wright, *Wales and Socialism: Political Culture and National Identity before the Great War* (Cardiff, 2016), p. 134.

[79] Aaron and Masson, *The Very Salt of Life*, pp. 215–42.

[80] Aaron and Masson, *The Very Salt of Life*, p. 165.

[81] Aaron and Masson have speculated about who 'Matron' was, suggesting either Gwen Ray, local teacher and trade union activist, or Elizabeth Andrews, who was active in the ILP and WCG and was to become Labour's women's organizer for Wales in 1919. Aaron and Masson, *The Very Salt of Life*, p. 168.

[82] Ruth Chalk was secretary of the WLL in Swansea, a member of the WCG, a frequent ILP candidate for the local council and elected to the Swansea Board of Guardians in 1913. Aaron and Masson, *The Very Salt of Life*, p. 170.

in the women's labour movement. Published in December 1912, 'Matron' wrote that '[a]ll the names of women prominent in the Labour Movement are women who have come into the movement out of sympathy, and not out of a real experience of the working woman's needs and struggles'.[83] She attributed the lack of representation of working-class women in leadership positions to the fact that they 'cannot afford to pay secretaries, agents and leaders to give their time to organization'.[84] Instead, 'Matron' argued, 'these upper-class women step in; they have money and leisure to bestow, and they do the work gratuitously'.[85] 'Matron's' criticism of the well-meaning condescension from a middle-class leadership was also confirmed, as we have seen, by the behaviour of some suffrage organizers at a time when the NUWSS and labour movement were moving closer together.[86] Also sensitive to the practical obstacles and childcare constraints inhibiting working-class women's political activism, an anonymous author of the women's column in the *Swansea and District Workers' Journal* argued that women could not fully participate in the work of the ILP 'unless the men of the movement sacrifice a little of their leisure time in order to afford their wives an opportunity of attending our meetings'.[87] For both authors, class solidarity superseded gender politics; only with the support and cooperation of working-class men, they believed, would women be able to achieve greater equality.

Despite their increasing hostility to the labour movement at national level, in 1913 the WSPU specifically began to target trade union and ILP branches in the South Wales coalfield. Annie Williams, a former teacher and Rachel Barrett's successor as Wales's WSPU organizer, led a three-week campaign in the Rhondda and Cynon valleys throughout August, addressing branches of the National Union of Railwaymen.[88] The campaign was well supported by influential figures in the community, including trade union leaders who often chaired the meetings and provided an avenue into the local political institutions.[89] The local labour press heralded the

[83] *The Rhondda Socialist*, 21 Dec. 1912. Cited in Aaron and Masson, *The Very Salt of Life*, p. 231.

[84] *The Rhondda Socialist*, 21 Dec. 1912.

[85] *The Rhondda Socialist*, 21 Dec. 1912.

[86] Masson, '"Political conditions in Wales are quite different…"'.

[87] *Swansea and District Workers' Journal*, May 1912. Cited in Aaron and Masson, *The Very Salt of Life*, pp. 237–8.

[88] *The Suffragette*, 1 Aug. 1913. Williams visited Treorchy, Ystrad, Penygraig, Tonypandy, Aberdare and Cwmaman.

[89] *The Suffragette*, 22 Aug. 1913; 29 Aug. 1913.

tour as a success and reported the conversion of many railwaymen to the cause. The *South Wales Worker*, for instance, noted the effect the tour had in swaying local opinion on women's suffrage: 'it has dawned upon the minds of hundreds of workers that to secure their emancipation without bringing along the women is hopeless.'[90] It also praised the tactics of the organizers, who it believed 'were well advised when they decided upon this line of propaganda'.[91] By the outbreak of the war, conferences of miners and railwaymen passed resolutions that women's suffrage should be one of the planks in their platform, and members of the suffrage society were co-opted onto the local Trades Council.[92]

At the same time as the WSPU began to make inroads, the constitutional suffrage movement also increasingly turned its attention to coalfield communities and focused its campaign on trade unions and labour institutions – a policy which did appear to have a positive impact. In a further attempt to widen its support base, the NUWSS began to deploy experienced working-class activists or those who had been involved in the labour movement, such as Selina Cooper and Margaret Aldersley, to South Wales.[93] Also with the aim of further building up working-class support, the Friends of Women's Suffrage scheme was adopted by the NUWSS in August 1912 to enable supporters to register as 'friends' and become adherents to the society without making any financial contribution; it recognized that for some working-class women, the cost of society membership or literature could prove prohibitive. Across Britain the scheme was received with varying degrees of warmth by district societies, but at the end of 1912 over 100 branches of the NUWSS had inaugurated the programme. When the NUWSS undertook a targeted campaign of the coalfield to coincide with the annual ILP conference in 1912, the large number of Friends of Women's Suffrage enrolled was testament to the amount of sympathy for the cause.[94]

The NUWSS's adoption of a partisan policy, a succession of targeted campaigns by the major suffrage societies, and the support provided by dominant local labour figures and institutions had a significant effect on the development of the suffrage campaign in industrial communities. When NUWSS organizer for South Wales L. F. Waring campaigned in the Rhondda Valley in the summer of 1912, she reported how the campaigners canvassed their way up the valley from Pentre, to Treorchy and Treherbert,

[90] *SWW*, 30 Aug. 1913. Also republished in *The Suffragette*, 12 Sept. 1913.

[91] *SWW*, 30 Aug. 1913.

[92] CA: D/MAR/3/57, E.F.F. Report 1914, South Wales Federation.

[93] Wallace, *The Women's Suffrage Movement in Wales*, p. 173.

[94] Wallace, *The Women's Suffrage Movement in Wales*, p. 174.

and noted, '[n]ever before have I been so well supported with helpers and workers as here in the mining district'.[95] Also outlining what she saw as a shift in the attitude of working-class women by 1913, Erie Evans, a local doctor and prominent member of the CDWSS, wrote: 'They are so much more alive to their own value and their own needs, and answering to this there is a greater sense of friendship between men and women, so that one now hardly ever meets a labouring man who expresses any fear or anger at the prospect of his wife or daughter having a vote.'[96] In a region where class solidarity could trump gender loyalties, the support of their male counterparts and dominant political institutions, such as trade unions, was crucial in advancing the movement and embedding it into community structures.

Conclusion

Focusing on the interactions between visiting campaigners and local communities, this chapter has sought to develop our understanding of some of the challenges suffrage societies faced in building a truly coordinated and inclusive movement across Britain. The reception suffrage organizers received in Wales was sometimes fraught. This could reflect specific linguistic and cultural differences, as well as broader party political and class divisions which criss-crossed the wider campaign. The targeting of national political figures and cultural events by some campaigners did little to advance the movement in Liberal Nonconformist strongholds, while the initial lack of bilingual organizers and visiting speakers posed a significant barrier for engagement between mainstream societies and Welsh-speaking communities. Similarly, the early deployment of some middle- and upper-class campaigners to the South Wales coalfield failed to break down social barriers with some working-class associations. In turn, the regular reports and letters organizers sent back to central committees could reflect the prejudices of their authors and helped to shape dominant contemporary – and sometimes historiographical – perceptions of the campaign in these regions.

But to focus solely on the social and cultural differences between organizers and local communities skews our understanding of the complex nature of the relationship between regions and national leadership, as well as the diversity of the movement across Wales. While encounters between Welsh communities and visiting organizers could – and, indeed, did – lead

[95] *CC*, 14 Nov. 1912.

[96] *CC*, 18 July 1913. See also *CC*, 7 Aug. 1914.

to cultural clashes, they could also be fruitful exchanges which informed the tactics and agendas of outside campaigners. Organizers also understood that the support of local activists was crucial for the day-to-day running of the campaign and their ability to coordinate regional activity; they provided access to community institutions, enlisted the cooperation of the local press, translated literature and shared knowledge of local political cultures. A turning point for the engagement of Welsh-speaking communities with the mainstream movement was the coordinated translation of suffrage propaganda, largely undertaken by Charlotte Price White and the Bangor NUWSS branch, and the appointment of Welsh-speaking WSPU organizer Rachel Barrett. In the southern coalfields, the development of a grassroots suffrage movement was symbiotic with an emerging women's labour politics. This was given added impetus from 1911 as the constitutional suffrage movement and labour movement moved increasingly closer together, with the former initiating new schemes to enlist working-class support and deploy more working-class speakers.

Levels of engagement with the movement are, of course, difficult to measure. But by giving greater sensitivity to the different ways women expressed their political agency, we can see how the late manifestation of suffrage branches does not necessarily represent disinterest or apathy, as some visiting campaigners suggested. It is important to move beyond simplistic stereotypes perpetuated by some organizers' reports to understand the multiple ways that support for the campaign flourished across regions, as well as the socioeconomic and cultural constraints they faced. The positive reception of Welsh-language literature or Friends of Women's Suffrage enrolments, for instance, highlights some of the practical obstacles which could inhibit engagement with the mainstream movement. Especially in communities which were isolated – both geographically and culturally – the need to gain the support of prominent community figures or to access existing political networks could be vital for garnering the support of local sympathizers. This was particularly true for rural Welsh-speaking and coalfield communities, both of which had less of a tradition of women-only organizing than their more urban and cosmopolitan neighbouring districts. In these regions, grassroots suffrage activism was embedded within, rather than in opposition to, existing community structures and organizations. Decentralizing the geographical focus of the campaign, then, highlights the complex web of party political loyalties, class interests and cultural identities which helped to shape the specific nature of the campaign across localities, regions and nations.

4. Suffrage, infant welfare and women's politics in Walsall, 1910–39*

Anna Muggeridge

By the outbreak of war in 1914, three women's suffrage organizations had been established in Walsall, a medium-sized industrial town in England. Branches of the Women's Social and Political Union (WSPU), National Union of Women's Suffrage Societies (NUWSS) and the Church League for Women's Suffrage (CLWS) were founded here in 1911, 1912 and 1913, respectively. Until then, it appears there was limited suffrage activism in the town carried out by suffrage organizations. Furthermore, even once these three branches were active, it seems that their membership was relatively small, and dominated by middle-class women. As this chapter will suggest, however, the rather limited reach of the suffrage movement in Walsall did not mean that women in the town were not politically engaged. On the contrary, a larger and somewhat more socially diverse group of women were particularly active in campaigns to improve infant welfare and reduce infant mortality rates locally. In considering both the suffrage and infant welfare movements in Walsall immediately before, and during, the First World War, this chapter offers one indication of the many other parallel, energetic and woman-led campaigns which preoccupied many activists in this period.

The chapter reflects on Karen Hunt and June Hannam's call for an 'archaeology' of women's politics, in which they argue that, by focusing on the local, historians might better understand how women's political activism developed. It was in their own neighbourhoods, communities and towns that most women tended to 'do' politics, through local organizations and campaigns.[1] This chapter, therefore, traces how certain women in Walsall 'did' politics through several local organizations working on suffrage

* I would like to express my sincere thanks to the editors of this volume for their patience, and their extremely helpful suggestions. I would also like to thank Prof. Maggie Andrews and Dr Cathy Hunt for their comments on earlier drafts.

1 K. Hunt and J. Hannam, 'Towards an archaeology of interwar women's politics: the local and the everyday', in *The Aftermath of Suffrage: Women, Gender, and Politics in Britain 1918–1945*, ed. J. Gottlieb and R. Toye (London, 2013), pp. 124–41. While their chapter focuses on the interwar years, the methodology can be applied to this earlier period.

'Suffrage, infant welfare and women's politics in Walsall, 1910–39', in *The politics of women's suffrage: local, national and international dimensions,* ed. A. Hughes-Johnson and L. Jenkins (London, 2021), pp. 109–128. License: CC BY-NC-ND 4.0.

and infant welfare in the town. There is evidence that members of Walsall's branch of the Women's Co-operative Guild (WCG) – an organization which, nationwide, campaigned for improvements to maternal welfare, among many other initiatives – sought to implement strategies which might address the town's high infant mortality rate.[2] A locally focused understanding of women's politics in contemporary Walsall must therefore embrace both the suffrage *and* infant welfare movements, pointing to the diversity of issues through which women might have become politicized at this time, and adding to research which highlights the plurality of campaigns in which the women's movement engaged, both during and beyond the suffrage campaign.[3]

This chapter largely utilizes evidence from the suffrage press and Walsall's two newspapers (the *Walsall Advertiser* and the *Walsall Observer*), as any records kept by the local WSPU, NUWSS or CLWS branches have not survived. From these sources, it is possible to ascertain that the membership of these three branches overlapped, and, from census returns, that their most visible activists were relatively affluent women. Both the suffrage and local press also provide evidence of contemporary organizations working on issues of infant welfare here: a Ladies' Health Society (LHS), Walsall's Women's Co-operative Guild and, from 1916, Walsall Child Welfare Association (WCWA). This reporting is supplemented by minutes of WCWA's meetings, which, unlike records from the LHS or WCG, have survived. These sources provide evidence for the ways both campaigns – for female enfranchisement, and for improvements to infant welfare – operated 'on the ground' in the town.

While Walsall's female activism has received relatively little attention, there is now a very extensive literature on both the suffrage and infant welfare movements in early twentieth-century Britain.[4] Although participants in the suffrage campaign differed in their tactics and approaches, all sought

[2] G. Scott, *Feminism and the Politics of Working Women* (London, 1997), ch. 4.

[3] For example, P. Thane, 'What difference did the vote make? Women in public and private life in Britain since 1918', *Historical Research*, lxxvi (2003), 268–85; C. Beaumont, *Housewives and Citizens: Domesticity and the Women's Movement in England, 1928–64* (Manchester, 2013).

[4] For good introductions, see S. Stanley Holton, *Feminism and Democracy: Women's Suffrage and Reform Politics in Britain 1900–1918* (Cambridge, 1986) or S. Stanley Holton and J. Purvis (ed.), *Votes for Women* (London, 2000) for the suffrage movement; and A. Davin, 'Imperialism and motherhood', *History Workshop*, v (1978), 9–65; E. Ross, *Love and Toil: Motherhood in Outcast London* (Oxford, 1993) and L. Marks, *Metropolitan Maternity: Maternal and Infant Welfare Services in Early Twentieth Century London* (Leiden, 1996) for the infant welfare movement.

legislative change which would allow women to vote in parliamentary elections. The infant welfare movement, meanwhile, encompassed not only the male-dominated medical profession, but also the many voluntary societies which sought to reduce infant and maternal death rates, and improve living conditions for families. The local membership of such societies was made up of what Anna Davin has termed the 'socially conscious gentry': medical professionals, teachers, local councillors and especially 'ladies whose work was voluntary'.[5] Within both movements, social class had a significant impact on how women were able to participate in, and interact with, specific organizations. The presence of working-class women in the fight for women's enfranchisement, both as suffragists and suffragettes, has been extensively detailed,[6] although the persistent class tensions within the campaign have also been acknowledged.[7] Similarly, class has long been recognized as a particularly contentious issue within the infant welfare movement. Imperialist and eugenicist ideologies informed much of the official discourse; at the turn of the twentieth century, falling birth rates and rising infant mortality rates among the working classes were felt to have a negative impact on the future maintenance of the British Empire, leading to a 'surge of concern about the bearing and rearing of children'.[8] On a more practical level, middle-class activists – often women acting in a voluntary capacity – frequently undertook to 'visit' working-class mothers, offering advice and guidance on child-rearing. Even where well-intentioned, this advice was rooted in middle-class domestic ideology, and rarely demonstrated any understanding of the lived experiences of working-class mothers, who responded with a mix of indifference and resentment towards such visitors.[9]

Until recently, relatively little consideration has been afforded to how these two contemporary campaigns were interconnected, with more attention being paid to the overlap between the anti-suffrage movement

5 Davin, 'Imperialism and motherhood', p. 12.

6 For good overviews, see J. Liddington and J. Norris, *One Hand Tied Behind Us: The Rise of the Women's Suffrage Movement* (London, 1978) for the NUWSS experience and K. Cowman, *Women of the Right Spirit: Paid Organisers of the Women's Social and Political Union (WSPU) 1904–18* (Manchester, 2007) for the WSPU.

7 Recent analysis includes: L. Schwartz, *Feminism and the Servant Problem: Class and Domestic Labour in the Women's Suffrage Movement* (Cambridge, 2019); L. Jenkins, 'Annie Kenney and the politics of class in the Women's Social and Political Union', *Twentieth Century British History*, xxx (2019), 477–503.

8 Davin, 'Imperialism and motherhood', pp. 10–12.

9 J. Lewis, *Women in England, 1870–1950: Sexual Divisions and Social Change* (London, 1984), pp. 38–40; Ross, *Love and Toil*, pp. 207–9.

and infant welfare campaigns. As Julia Bush has argued, some anti-suffrage activists felt that 'national' politics (and thus the franchise) were of limited value to women, whose energies were best expended in municipal politics, where issues related to women's and children's welfare were discussed.[10] Yet many suffrage campaigners were also deeply concerned with the problem of high infant and maternal mortality rates, and there is now an emerging scholarship on the overlap between these two movements, much of which is locally focused.[11] This chapter seeks to contribute to this scholarship through a case study of Walsall, an area where women's politics before enfranchisement has been afforded little attention.[12]

Walsall lies within the Black Country, an area synonymous with heavy industry, and was then particularly associated with the leather trade. In 1911, census returns indicate that this was Walsall's largest female employment sector; 3,727 women (and 5,789 men) worked in the trade, about a third of all employed women in Walsall.[13] There is little suggestion, however, that many of these women were unionized within either a mixed-sex or female union; indeed, a branch of the National Federation of Women Workers was not established here until 1915.[14] Politically, the constituency of Walsall returned Liberal MPs almost without exception until 1910, when Sir Richard Cooper (Unionist) was elected. Municipal politics in the town were similarly dominated by the Liberals, although Labour was gathering strength from the 1910s; two Labour councillors were elected in 1913 and 1914.[15] Slightly earlier, in 1910, Walsall elected its first female councillor, Ada Newman (Unionist). The daughter of a wealthy industrialist, Newman was one of the first women in Britain to be elected to a county borough

[10] J. Bush, *Women Against the Vote: Female Anti-Suffragism in Britain* (Oxford, 2007). As she acknowledges, the anti-suffrage movement was complex, and this was not the view of all anti-suffragists.

[11] Recent interventions include: R. Davidson, '"Dreams of Utopia": the infant welfare movement in interwar Croydon', *Women's History Review*, xxiii (2014), 239–55; A. Ronan, 'The radical responses made by women in Manchester, during the First World War, to the "special problems of child life accentuated by the war"', in *Histories, Memories and Representations of Being Young in the First World War*, ed. M. Andrews, N. Fleming and M. Morris (Basingstoke, 2020).

[12] G. Barnsby, *Votes For Women: The Struggle for the Vote in the Black Country* (Wolverhampton, 1995) is a rare exception, but offers little analysis of the wider women's movement.

[13] 12,163 Walsall women gave an occupation; see Vison of Britain <http://www.visionofbritain.org.uk/unit/10198379/cube/OCC_ORD1911_SEX> [accessed 30 June 2020].

[14] C. Hunt, *The National Federation of Women Workers, 1906–1921* (London, 2014), p. 182.

[15] 'Municipal by-election', *Walsall Advertiser* (*WA*), 9 Aug. 1913, p. 4; 'New Labour councillor', *Walsall Observer and South Staffordshire Chronicle* (*WO*), 25 Apr. 1914, p. 3.

council. Despite this, she appears not to have been active in other women's organizations in Walsall, including its suffrage societies, which began to develop around this time.[16]

Women's suffrage in Walsall

The suffrage campaign came relatively late to Walsall. In 1875, Lydia Becker chaired a meeting here, but there is no further record of any local suffrage activity until 1907, when WSPU activist Nell Kenney planned to visit the town, as part of a tour of the Midlands.[17] In 1908, a local woman, Dorothea Layton, arranged a 'WSPU-inspired meeting', but it was not until February 1911 that a WSPU branch was formally established.[18] A WSPU shop opened in Walsall's town centre in 1912, which was to prove a pivotal year for suffrage here. The failure of the third and final Conciliation Bill that year, and especially the lack of support given to the bill by Richard Cooper, Walsall's Unionist MP, appears to have galvanized local campaigners, who wrote to the *Walsall Advertiser* to express their displeasure at his decision.[19]

Their letters to the newspaper suggest Cooper had given the impression that he could not vote for a bill which might be seen as tacitly supporting WSPU militancy, although, as a Conservative backbencher, there were likely party political factors which impacted his decision not to support the Liberal government's proposal. Three letters appeared, one from George Moorcroft Wood, one from Ellen Pearman-Cooke and an open letter signed by ten local women (Dorothea Layton, Amy and Mary Cottam, Muriel Barnard, Emma and Eveline Thacker, Amy Lowry, Dorothy Hill, Nancie Cotterell and Edith Elliot).[20] The letters were measured in tone, with the signatories seeking to distance themselves from the WSPU's militancy, especially window-breaking, despite several (Layton, Barnard and Cotterell) being members of Walsall WSPU. The open letter acknowledged Cooper's 'horror at the breakers of windows and laws', but urged him to 'remember the vast number of law-abiding women who … have been working hard for years to obtain the franchise', while Pearman-Cooke went further, declaring that she did not have 'any sympathy with militant tactics'.[21] Two months

[16] P. Hollis, *Ladies Elect: Women in English Local Government, 1865–1914* (Oxford, 1987), p. 402.

[17] 'Midlands', *Votes for Women*, 1 Nov. 1907, p. 22.

[18] E. Crawford, *The Women's Suffrage Movement in Britain and Ireland: A Regional Survey* (London, 2006), p. 124.

[19] 'Correspondence', *WA*, 30 Mar. 1912, p. 9.

[20] 'Correspondence'.

[21] 'Correspondence'.

later, and likely as a consequence, a new suffrage society was established in Walsall, which formally affiliated to the NUWSS; Amy Lowry became its secretary.[22] There had been some prior attempts at organizing an NUWSS branch here – brief reference to a Walsall NUWSS branch 'having a terrible time' appears in *Common Cause* in 1909.[23] However, the branch does not seem to have taken off, and little other evidence of NUWSS activity in Walsall can be found until the 1912 branch got to work. Finally, in early 1913, the third of the town's suffrage societies, the Church League for Women's Suffrage, was established, with Pearman-Cooke serving as secretary.[24]

There was significant overlap in the membership of these three branches, with many names appearing in connection with more than one society. As Krista Cowman has demonstrated, at a local level there was often crossover in membership between different suffrage societies, facilitated by women's friendship networks, which allowed for the breaking down of 'barriers between organizations that appear impenetrable at national level',[25] while, in this volume, Alexandra Hughes-Johnson's work on the Suffragettes of the WSPU and the Independent WSPU points to the ways that women's friendship networks could span organizations.[26] This appears to have been the case in Walsall. For example, Dorothy Hill and Amy Lowry, two signatories of the open letter, were on the Walsall CLWS committee,[27] with Lowry also acting as Walsall NUWSS secretary.[28] In November 1913, the two organizations held a joint meeting in Walsall's Congregational Hall, indicating that these connections facilitated their work.[29] Dorothea Layton, meanwhile, had organized the 'WSPU-inspired meeting' in Walsall in 1908, and may have encouraged her husband, Frank, to take an interest in women's suffrage; he spoke in support of women's suffrage at Walsall WSPU's December 1912 meeting, over which Muriel Barnard, another signatory to the letter, presided.[30] Frank had earlier taken the chair at Walsall

[22] 'Another New Society', *Common Cause* (*CC*), 30 May 1912, p. 123.

[23] 'Birmingham-North Warwickshire', *CC*, 2 Dec. 1909, p. 457.

[24] 'From the branches', *Church League for Women's Suffrage* (*CLWS*), 1 Feb. 1913, p. 12. For the CLWS, see R. Saunders, '"A great and holy war": religious routes to women's suffrage, 1909–1914', *English Historical Review*, cxxxiv (2019), 1471–1502.

[25] K. Cowman, *Mrs Brown is a Man and a Brother: Women in Merseyside's Political Organisations, 1890–1920* (Liverpool, 2004), p. 97.

[26] A. Hughes-Johnson, Chapter 5 in this volume.

[27] 'Walsall', *CLWS*, 1 Mar. 1915, p. 23.

[28] Crawford, *The Women's Suffrage Movement*, p. 124.

[29] 'News from the Societies and Federations', *CC*, 14 Nov. 1913, p. 580.

[30] 'Dr Layton's View of the Government', *WA*, 14 Dec. 1912, p. 9.

NUWSS's inaugural meeting in May 1912, at which Dorothea also appears to have been present.[31]

Within Walsall, suffrage activism centred around holding meetings and, for the WSPU, fundraising through their shop. No obvious or violent acts of militancy occurred in the town. Indeed, only one Walsall WSPU member, Florence Ward (not among the signatories of the open letters, who had sought to distance themselves from violent tactics) undertook overtly militant action, significantly, outside of the town.[32] Ward participated in a window-smashing campaign in nearby Birmingham when Prime Minister Asquith spoke there in July 1913. She was arrested and imprisoned in Winson Green, where she went on hunger strike.[33] However, other local WSPU members appear to have been reluctant to publicly associate themselves with the organization even by selling its literature. A July 1913 notice in the *Suffragette* suggested that, 'the many members in Walsall who do not like, for various reasons, to sell papers on Walsall Bridge [in the town centre]' should note that 'the summer holiday is a great opportunity for doing so in a place where you are not known'; they were urged to let Walsall WSPU know where they intended to holiday, so they could be put in touch with the branch at their destination.[34]

Most suffrage activity in Walsall therefore appears to have taken more conventional forms, typically through meetings at which a speaker addressed audiences in one of the town's civic buildings. Numbers attending these meetings do not, from the evidence available, appear to have been huge. For instance, the WSPU meeting at which Frank Layton spoke in December 1912, was described as having 'a small attendance', though his speech was reported in the *Walsall Advertiser*, possibly reaching a wider audience.[35] Local NUWSS meetings similarly do not appear to have had large attendances. The May 1912 inaugural meeting resulted in the enrolment of twenty-six members, and a further 'eleven new members were obtained' following an 'at home' in Walsall's Masonic Hall in August.[36] After this point, attendance figures were rarely recorded, though an April 1913 meeting addressed by

31 'Federation Notes: West Midland', *CC*, 30 May 1912, p. 123.

32 It was not unusual for women to move outside of their locale to undertake militant action; see, for instance, K. Cowman, *The Militant Suffragette Movement in York* (York, 2007).

33 'Incidents at Birmingham', *The Suffragette*, 25 July 1913, p. 696; '"Cat and mouse" victims', *The Suffragette*, 1 Aug. 1913, p. 724.

34 'Walsall', *The Suffragette*, 11 July 1913, p. 666.

35 'Dr Layton's View of the Government'.

36 'Federation Notes: West Midlands'; 'Walsall', *CC*, 8 Aug. 1912, p. 313.

NUWSS Executive Committee member and CLWS activist Maude Royden was noted to have 'roused fresh enthusiasm, and some new members were enrolled', suggesting that membership of suffrage organizations continued to grow into and beyond 1913.[37]

As well as being relatively small, suffrage organizations in Walsall appear to have been dominated by fairly affluent women. Those who were most visible in the organizations, the signatories to the *Advertiser* letters and those who went on to take leading roles in Walsall's NUWSS, WSPU and CLWS branches, appear to have been drawn from the middle classes.[38] Of the signatories to the *Advertiser* letters, five (Barnard, Cotterell, Elliott and the two Thackers) were the wives, sisters or daughters of men who owned businesses, and George Moorcroft Wood, the lone male signatory, also gave his occupation as 'business owner'. Dorothea Layton's husband, Frank, was a GP; Lowry was the daughter of a clergyman, and the two Miss Cottams, Hill and Pearman-Cooke all stated that they lived on 'private means', usually indicating a degree of familial wealth. All twelve lived in households employing at least one, if not two, live-in domestic servants; the Laytons employed three.[39]

While those who took leading roles in these societies appear to have been middle-class, this is not to suggest that working-class women in Walsall were unsupportive of the campaign for the vote. They may, instead, have been active in the local campaign in other ways, for example, by attending meetings, but not taking on organizational roles such as branch secretary, because of the commitments this entailed. Such women rarely appear within suffrage or local press reports, rendering them less visible to the historian. Others, meanwhile, may have campaigned through women's organizations which were outside the suffrage societies themselves.[40] Evidence from other locations suggests that some working-class women, particularly within the Labour Party, were more focused on achieving universal adult suffrage, rather than a limited female franchise

[37] 'Walsall', *CC*, 11 Apr. 1913, p. 13.

[38] Based on evidence from the 1911 census. Florence Ward alone proved untraceable, though Krista Cowman has noted that she was a social worker for a Christian organization for eight years, suggesting she was unlikely to have been from a working-class background. Cowman, *Women of the Right Spirit*, p. 235.

[39] Amy Lowry could not be traced through the 1911 census, but in 1901 her household employed two servants. All other references via 1911 census returns.

[40] For the notion of 'suffrage outside suffragism', see: M. Bousshba-Bravard, 'Introduction', *Suffrage Outside Suffragism: Women's Vote in Britain, 1880–1914*, ed. M. Bousshba-Bravard (London, 2007), pp. 1–32.

tied to property.[41] The WCG took this stance, aligning itself with adult suffrage organizations like the People's Suffrage Federation (led by the WGC general secretary, Margaret Llewelyn Davies).[42] Walsall WCG had been established around the turn of the century, although because its records have not survived, it is unclear whether it participated in any local suffrage activism.[43] Certainly, any such campaigning did not reach the attention of the local or suffrage press. Similarly, local newspapers do not provide evidence of adult suffrage organizations which were active in contemporary Walsall, suggesting that any suffrage campaigning outside of Walsall's NUWSS, WSPU or CLWS branches was, at most, limited.

Furthermore, there appear to have been very few direct attempts by these three organizations to recruit working-class women. There was, for instance, no attempt to utilize the NUWSS's Friends of Women's Suffrage scheme in Walsall. This resulted from its alliance with the Labour Party from 1912, and 'aimed at attracting and demonstrating working-class support for women's suffrage'.[44] In November 1912, the Walsall WSPU arranged a 'poster parade' which 'caused much excitement among the crowds issuing from the factories', but this appears to have been a one-off, and reporting is unclear whether this 'excitement' resulted in new members.[45] Though factory work was common among women working in Walsall's leather trade, there was little tradition of women's trade unionism in the town, suggesting few had experience organizing collectively. Elsewhere in Britain, informal meetings in coffee houses or tea rooms arranged by suffrage societies proved somewhat more accessible spaces for working-class women, and helped to draw them into local branches.[46] Though the paucity of the archival record must again be acknowledged here – such informal events were less likely to

[41] P. Thane, 'Women in the Labour Party and women's suffrage', in *Suffrage Outside Suffragism: Women's Vote in Britain, 1880–1914*, ed. M. Boussahba-Bravard (London, 2007), pp. 35–51, p. 37.

[42] G. Scott, 'The Women's Co-operative Guild and suffrage', in *Suffrage Outside Suffragism: Women's Vote in Britain, 1880–1914*, ed. M. Boussahba-Bravard (London, 2007), pp. 132–55.

[43] A newspaper article from 1900 refers to Walsall Guild's anniversary: 'The Housing of the working-classes', *WA*, 17 Nov. 1900, p. 4.

[44] J. Purvis, E. Crawford and S. Stanley Holton, 'Did militancy help or hinder the granting of women's suffrage in Britain?', *Women's History Review*, xxviii (2019), 1200–34, at p. 1223.

[45] 'Walsall', *The Suffragette*, 8 Nov. 1912, p. 58.

[46] For example, in Leicester, see R. Whitmore, *Alice Hawkins: and the Suffragette Movement in Edwardian Leicester* (Derby, 2007), p. 57.

appear in local newspapers' reporting – it seems that such tactics were not used in Walsall.

It is possible that the relatively late arrival of the suffrage movement here impacted on the extent to which Walsall's suffrage societies were able to actively work with local working-class women's associations, like the WCG. As observed, organized and sustained suffrage activism does not seem to have begun here in earnest until the 1911 formation of a WSPU branch, while the NUWSS and CLWS branches were not established until 1912 and 1913. All three branches' suffrage campaigning ceased in Walsall with the outbreak of war in 1914, although, as is shortly discussed, many members redirected their energies into other work.[47] Locally, then, these groups had only a little over two years in which to build an active community. Given longer, they may have found ways to work more constructively with local working-class women's organizations, bringing them into the campaign.

The infant welfare movement in Walsall

In the prewar era, efforts to promote infant welfare in Walsall were also dominated by a limited number of middle-class women. The town had long suffered a particularly high infant mortality rate. In 1907, 154 babies out of every 1,000 born sadly died, significantly higher than the national average of 127. This worried the town council enough that councillors employed a 'lady health visitor', who, along with 'voluntary lady visitors', would advise local mothers on infant welfare.[48] These volunteers were members of Walsall's Ladies' Health Society (LHS), who also aimed to support the health visitor by delivering talks on topics such as 'home life and the care of children', 'cookery' and 'general subjects of health'.[49] The LHS's organizing committee seems to have been dominated by women from backgrounds similar to Walsall's most visible suffrage activists. The LHS president, Mrs Duignan, was the wife of a local solicitor and antiquarian; its secretary, Julia Slater, was also a solicitor's wife.[50] Both their husbands were municipal councillors, and both (per the 1911 census) employed live-in servants. As LHS records have not survived, it is unclear how many women were involved with the organization, but there does appear to have been a small amount

47 Although the war made it increasingly difficult for suffrage organizations to retain an active membership, some local branches in other places remained committed to women's suffrage during wartime, as Alexandra Hughes-Johnson's work in this volume demonstrates.

48 'Walsall Town Council', *WA*, 18 July 1908, p. 2.

49 'Walsall Ladies Health Society', *WA*, 10 Oct. 1908, p. 5.

50 'Death of Mr Duignan', *WA*, 28 Mar. 1914, p. 7; 'Death of Mrs Slater', *WO*, 26 Feb. 1916, p. 6.

of crossover with Walsall's suffrage societies. Though neither Duignan nor Slater appear connected to the suffrage movement, WSPU member Nancie Cotterell gave a talk on at least one occasion, and Frank Layton was involved with the LHS in his capacity as a GP, suggesting his wife Dorothea was at least aware of its work.[51] The LHS sought to actively engage working-class women with its talks; for example, the *Advertiser* notice of Cotterell's talk expressly highlighted that 'all working-class women [were] invited'.[52]

Despite these efforts, high infant mortality rates persisted in Walsall, but the outbreak of war spurred Walsall's Women's Co-operative Guild into action; in October 1914, it organized a conference to discuss the town's 'very high' infant mortality rate, and how it might be addressed.[53] Because Walsall WCG's records no longer survive, it is not possible to know the extent to which it had been active in the infant welfare movement locally before 1914. Nationally, however, the WCG had been campaigning for improvements to maternity care for working-class women for many years, collecting testimony from these women which gave voice to their own experiences, published as *Maternity: Letters From Working Women* in 1915.[54] These national campaigns may have spurred Walsall WCG to arrange its conference. The conference sought to draw together numerous local women's organizations to campaign collectively for improvements to infant welfare in Walsall.[55] A letter encouraging attendance at the event, signed by WCG general secretary Margaret Llewellyn Davis and WCG member and prominent Labour activist Margaret Bondfield, appeared in the *Walsall Observer*.[56]

Presiding over the conference was Mary Bradley Dewsbury, chair of Walsall WCG and already a well-known figure in local politics, having been a Poor Law guardian since 1909.[57] Walsall WCG's secretary, Mary Button, posted notice of the meeting in the local press, and guildswomen Mary Dix and Gertrude Cresswell proposed motions at the meeting. Though a full membership list of Walsall WCG does not survive, tracing these four women back through census returns offers some understanding

[51] Unfortunately, records do not indicate how well attended such events were. Cotterell, 'Walsall Ladies Health Society', *WA*, 30 Nov. 1912, p. 7; Layton, 'Walsall Ladies' Health Society', *WA*, 10 Oct. 1908, p. 5.

[52] 'Walsall Ladies Health Society', 1912.

[53] 'The care of motherhood', *CC*, 30 Oct. 1914, p. 511.

[54] M. Llewellyn Davis, *Maternity: Letters from Working-women* (London, 1915).

[55] 'Women's Co-operative Guild', *WA*, 3 Oct. 1914, p. 4.

[56] 'A plea for the mothers of the nation', *WO*, 10 Oct. 1914, p. 9.

[57] 'Public notice. Guardians' election', *WA*, 16 Mar. 1912, p. 7.

of their backgrounds. Nationally, most WCG members in this period were married housewives from the more prosperous working class, which appears broadly true here.[58] Dix was married to an engine driver and Button a warehouseman, though Dewsbury and Cresswell, married to a clerk and an elementary schoolteacher, respectively, might be considered lower-middle-class, although neither employed live-in domestic servants.[59] All had several children, with census returns indicating that Cresswell and Button had tragically lost children in infancy, which may have contributed to their personal motivations for involvement in the cause of infant welfare. Though none of the four were representative of Walsall's most impoverished women, they do appear to have been from less affluent backgrounds than many of the town's leading suffrage activists.

There is, therefore, some suggestion that the infant welfare movement locally was somewhat more socially diverse than its suffrage movement. This is also reflected in the diversity of the organizations Walsall WCG invited to participate in the conference. Alongside representatives from several other Staffordshire WCGs, delegates came from the Walsall Labour Association, the LHS ('Mrs Duignan and Mrs Slater'), Walsall NUWSS ('Miss Lowry'), 'the Ancient Order of Foresters (women's section)' and 'the NSPCC [National Society for Prevention of Cruelty to Children]', while a letter of support was read from Walsall's branch of the British Women's Temperance Association (BWTA).[60] The WCG had called the conference because, as Mary Dewsbury explained, 'it was felt that more ought to be done on behalf of expectant or nursing mothers' than the support currently provided by Walsall's 'one or two small maternity schemes'. Dewsbury acknowledged the work of the council-appointed health visitor, but noted that she 'had more to do than could ever be accomplished' and, despite the '3,200 visits' she made to local mothers in 1913, Walsall's 'infant mortality rate remained high'.[61] Small wonder; to make all 3,200 visits, she would have been required to average nearly nine appointments daily, including weekends, without a single day off.

Having outlined the problems in Walsall, the delegates planned a series of practical steps which might improve the local situation. A resolution proposed by Amy Lowry passed, urging the council to 'safeguard infant life in Walsall by extending the work for maternity in the town on the lines of the Local Government Board Scheme'; specifically, they sought to use

58 G. Scott, *Feminism and the Politics of Working Women* (London, 1997), ch. 1.

59 Schwartz, *Feminism and the Servant Problem*, pp. 22–4.

60 'Maternity centres', *WO*, 10 Oct. 1914, p. 9.

61 'Maternity centres'.

the funding this scheme offered to set up a weekly baby clinic staffed by medical professionals.[62] A second proposal from the WCG's Mary Dix and Gertrude Cresswell also passed, urging funding for the provision of 'meals for expectant and nursing mothers when medical opinion [suggests] such nourishment is necessary [for] the life and health of the child'.[63] While the health of the child was the ultimate goal here, it is notable that the support centred around providing meals for mothers in need. This was one of the WGC's proposals from *Maternity*.[64] It was further decided that a 'deputation of ladies concerned with [infant welfare] work' would seek to address the council on these proposals.[65] This deputation comprised Mary Dewsbury (representing Walsall WCG), Amy Lowry (NUWSS), Julia Slater (LHS) and Mrs Camburn (BWTA).[66] The plurality of the organizations is notable; the deputation consisted of representatives of four groups with different objects and aims, but which were able to find common ground on this issue. Some of these representatives worked with Walsall council to establish the Walsall Child Welfare Association (WCWA), which was formally inaugurated at a special meeting in Walsall Town Hall in July 1916.[67] The WCWA was partially funded by the Local Government Board Scheme grant money (as the conference had suggested), with local rates making up the shortfall, and provided a variety of support for mothers in Walsall. This included two infant welfare clinics, established in different parts of town by July 1916, for 'those who were not in a position to pay for the medical treatment that was necessary if their children were to grow up to be strong men and women'.[68] Each clinic operated twice a week, was staffed by medical professionals who gave advice and treatment and was supported by volunteers.

The establishment of the WCWA must, of course, be set within the national developments in the infant welfare movement during the First World War. That the WCG's conference was called two months after war was declared is no coincidence; Mary Dewsbury stated that although there was 'not yet much distress' in Walsall attributable to the conflict, the experience of the Boer War suggested that this would 'come later' and that, consequently, relief measures should not be organized 'at the last moment,

[62] 'Maternity centres'.

[63] 'Maternity centres'.

[64] Davin, 'Imperialism and motherhood', p. 46.

[65] 'Maternity centres'.

[66] 'Maternity centres'.

[67] 'To save child life', *WO*, 22 July 1916, p. 4. This article mentions Dewsbury and Slater; the latter had been involved until her untimely death in Jan. 1916 following a Zeppelin raid.

[68] 'To save child life'.

but should be ready to meet the strain'.[69] War likely gave renewed impetus to those working on these issues locally. Many historians have highlighted the increasing concern shown to problems of infant welfare during the war,[70] while, as Susan R. Grayzel has demonstrated, motherhood became increasingly central to women's identities during – indeed, because of – the conflict.[71] Nationwide, the number of infant welfare centres had 'more than doubled' by 1918, when 'the state took on an altogether more extensive responsibility, [passing] the 1918 Maternity and Child Welfare Act'.[72] The WCWA's formation in 1916, then, must be understood within this wider context, but locally women's organizations may have taken advantage of this greater emphasis on improving infant welfare to pursue their aims with more vigour.

The WCWA came under the council's auspices, signalling increased involvement of the state in infant welfare locally. This was approvingly noted by Mary Dewsbury at its inaugural public meeting in July 1916, where she informed delegates that a feature of the WCWA 'which commended itself to her was that it was municipal and thus carried more weight than a purely voluntary scheme'.[73] She then went on to address what she felt was one of the most pressing problems facing mothers in contemporary Walsall: provision of childcare. Though keen to assure those attending the meeting that 'she believed [that] the place of the child was with the mother at home, and the state ought to make the mother independent of work, so that she could remain at home', Dewsbury believed that the war meant that mothers 'could not stay at home for financial reasons and while they were arguing about whether the state ought to do this or that, babies were dying'.[74] Accordingly, she proposed the establishment of a nursery in Walsall, and in October 1916 one duly opened, with much of its funding coming from the council.[75] By mid 1918, over 160 such state-funded

[69] 'Maternity centres'.

[70] Davin, 'Imperialism and motherhood'; J. Winter, *The Great War and the British People* (London, 1985), pp. 141–53; D. Dwork, *War is Good for Babies and Other Young Children: a History of the Infant and Child Welfare Movement in England, 1898–1918* (London, 1987); G. DeGroot, *Blighty: British Society in the Era of the Great War* (London: 1996), pp. 214–22; A. Gregory, *The Last Great War: British Society and the First World War* (Cambridge, 2008), pp. 278–9, 285–6; Ronan, 'Radical responses'.

[71] S. Grayzel, *Women's Identities at War: Gender, Motherhood, and Politics in Britain and France During the First World War* (London, 1999).

[72] Davin, 'Imperialism and motherhood', pp. 43–4.

[73] 'To save child life'.

[74] 'To save child life'.

[75] 'A boon to working mothers', *WO*, 14 Oct. 1916, p. 5.

nurseries had opened across Britain, as increasing numbers of women undertook employment in the war industries.[76] While Walsall's nursery was largely organized by the council, the WCWA was also involved with its organization, and Mary Dewsbury chaired the WCWA's Day Nursery Sub-Committee until 1918.

Dewsbury was actively involved with the WCWA, and guildswomen Mrs Dix and Mrs Cresswell also appear to have regularly attended its committee meetings. Some of those who had been involved with Walsall's three suffrage organizations, including Amy Lowry, Nancie Cotterell and Dorothea Layton, were also active within the WCWA, suggesting a shifting of personal priorities within the wartime climate as local campaigning for the franchise largely ceased. However, the WCWA appears to have attracted far more women than those who were already active in organizations like the WCG, or the town's suffrage associations. By its first annual general meeting, in February 1917, around seventy women had attended at least one WCWA committee meeting.[77] The infant welfare movement does appear, therefore, to have engaged a somewhat larger number of women in Walsall than the number involved with the town's three suffrage organizations. For these women, especially those who had no obvious connection to the suffrage campaign, this kind of activism may have been a more acceptable form of engagement in public life than activism within suffrage groups.[78] Others may have perceived campaigns centred around infant welfare as having more relevance to their lives than the fight for enfranchisement, or perhaps felt that they had more practical experience with the former. Still others may simply have felt that there were more opportunities for active involvement in the day-to-day work that the WCWA undertook than were previously possible within Walsall's suffrage societies, where work appears to have largely been limited to attending meetings.

In addition to attending committee meetings, women were able to undertake various forms of voluntary work through the WCWA. At biweekly clinics, volunteers delivered lectures on mothercraft and helped to organize sewing parties and thrift clubs. In September 1916, a Material Aid Committee (MAC) was established, to which mothers in need could apply for temporary grants, which usually came in the form of food, milk, money

[76] H. McCarthy, *Double Lives: A History of Working Motherhood* (London, 2020), pp. 109, 125.

[77] Walsall Local History Centre, 360/68, *Walsall Child Welfare Voluntary Association General Minutes Book 1916–1924* (WCWA Minutes). Minutes date from 30 Jul. 1916; first AGM held 13 Feb. 1917.

[78] S. Koven and S. Michel, *Mothers of a New World: Maternalist Politics and the Origins of Welfare States* (London, 1993).

or coal.[79] The MAC was administered by an entirely female sub-committee of volunteers, one of whom would visit the applicant's home to assess her circumstances, before the committee decided what aid, if any, should be supplied. The MAC also arranged for sewing machines to be available for hire by local mothers, and for volunteers to make baby garments to be sold at the clinics. Significant numbers appear to have done so; 484 such garments were made by 'helpers' in the first seven months of 1917 alone.[80] Furthermore, between January and July of that year, forty-two more women signed up to be 'voluntary visitors' of mothers who had recently given birth, collectively making '427 visits' by July.[81]

The response of working-class mothers to these visits is unrecorded; neither newspaper reporting or the WCWA minutes give voice to their experiences. Nonetheless, there is a suggestion that at least some of the WCWA's services did provide local mothers with genuine support. By July 1917, only one year after the WCWA's formal inauguration, there was sufficient demand for a third clinic to open in another part of town.[82] The success of the two existing clinics likely fuelled this demand, and indicates that local mothers were engaging with their services. The practical support the WCWA offered in other ways – the nursery, or the hire of a sewing machine for those who could not otherwise afford one – likely also benefited these women. Furthermore, July 1917 also saw '232 garments' made by local mothers 'entered for the National Mothercraft Competition', held as part of National Baby Week.[83] What proportion of clinic attendees this represented is unclear; however, that 232 garments were made for the competition suggests that at least some women engaged with more than just the medical advice provided at clinics. Perhaps most telling, however, was the longevity of the WCWA. Far from being a wartime phenomenon, its work continued for many years, and women remained as volunteers in various capacities until 1950, when paid workers took over the WCWA entirely.[84]

79 WCWA Minutes, 20 Sept. 1916.

80 'Child welfare', *WO*, 21 July 1917, p. 5.

81 'Child welfare'.

82 'Child welfare'.

83 'Child welfare'. For National Baby Week, see L. Bryder, 'Mobilising mothers: the 1917 National Baby Week', *Medical History*, lxiii (2019), 2–23, at p. 8.

84 'Walsall welfare workers withdraw', *Staffordshire Advertiser*, 29 July 1950, p. 5. This was likely a response to the increased state involvement with healthcare following the introduction of the National Health Service two years earlier.

Walsall in the aftermath of enfranchisement

During the war, many, though not all, of Walsall's leading suffrage activists joined the WCWA – Ellen Pearman-Cooke, secretary to Walsall's CLWS, was not among the WCWA's members, for instance. Only the CLWS continued to meet in Walsall during the war, although its priorities seem to have shifted away from women's enfranchisement towards welfare work instead. As early as November 1914, the branch reported on its efforts to support Belgian refugees, and noted the 'useful work' Walsall CLWS members were doing through the Prince of Wales Relief Committee and the Red Cross.[85] Members of other local suffrage societies were similarly active in such welfare work; Amy Lowry, for example, acted as Walsall's Soldiers' and Sailors' Family Association's secretary,[86] while Dorothea Layton was on the organizing committee of Walsall's 'Tipperary Rooms' (a social club for women family members of servicemen).[87] Overall, however, suffrage campaigning largely vanished from public view in Walsall. The town's NUWSS remained listed in *Common Cause* – indeed, it appointed a new secretary in 1916 – but it was not reported as holding any meetings, or undertaking suffrage activism, within the suffrage or local press.[88] Similarly, Walsall WSPU remained listed in Walsall's *Red Book* (a town directory) until 1917, but did not arrange meetings.

Despite the apparent lack of wartime suffrage activism locally, the passage of the Representation of the People Act on 6 February 1918, which enfranchised women over thirty who met certain property qualifications, was swiftly celebrated through a service of thanksgiving in Walsall, arranged by the CLWS. The service was attended by 'suffragists and their friends' – perhaps a reference to local WSPU or NUWSS members – and judged to be 'deeply impressive and inspiring'.[89] Ellen Pearman-Cooke's report on proceedings for the *Church Militant* concluded by noting that 'in view now of women's additional responsibilities as electors, the Secretary hopes to join with other suffrage societies in [Walsall] to arrange meetings for the education of women in the duties of citizenship'.[90] Her language is notable in reflecting the approach of many non-partisan women's organizations

[85] 'Walsall', *CLWS*, Nov. 1914, p. 202.

[86] 'The War Relief Fund', *WO*, 9 Oct. 1915, p. 7.

[87] 'Tipperary Rooms', *WA*, 4 Dec. 1915, 5; for the 'Tipperary Rooms', see L. Nym Mayhall, *The Militant Suffrage Movement: Citizenship and Resistance in Britain, 1860–1930* (Oxford, 2003), p. 232.

[88] 'List of societies', *CC*, 29 Sept. 1916, p. 318.

[89] 'Walsall', *Church Militant*, Apr. 1918, p. 46.

[90] 'Walsall', *Church Militant*, Apr. 1918, p. 46.

which made the education of newly enfranchised women central to their aims in the interwar period.[91] However, the paucity of the archival record once again means it is not possible to know whether any local suffrage activists joined such organizations postwar.

Walsall's suffrage activists do not appear among the women who took up public office in the town after 1918 either. In contrast, two Walsall WCG members, Gertrude Cresswell and Mary Dewsbury, both active members of the Labour Party, won election to municipal office, and, significantly, maintained their interest in infant and maternal welfare as elected officials. Cresswell became Walsall's first female Labour councillor in 1925, remaining in post until her death in 1944.[92] Shortly after her initial election, Cresswell was made chair of the council's Maternity and Child Welfare Committee. She became so associated with this work that she was elected Walsall's first woman Mayor in 1934, 'largely as tribute to the work she has done in the maternity and child welfare movement'.[93] Mary Dewsbury, meanwhile, was a co-opted member of the same committee throughout the 1920s, and continued to sit on the committee after winning election to the council in 1931.[94]

Women's role in interwar local government needs to be more fully understood, but existing work suggests that women councillors could sometimes be 'pigeonholed' into taking responsibility for so-called 'women's issues', including those associated with infant and maternal welfare.[95] Cresswell and Dewsbury maintained their activism on this issue through their local government work, but do not necessarily seem to have been 'pigeonholed'. Both held numerous other, non-gendered responsibilities within municipal governance; Cresswell, for example, also sat on the council's finance, mental welfare, National Health Insurance, library and art gallery committees.[96] Both women were also local magistrates. Dewsbury, indeed, became Walsall's second woman magistrate in 1924, only five years after women became eligible for the role.[97] The plurality of issues on which

[91] Beaumont, *Housewives and Citizens*, ch. 2.

[92] 'First woman mayor', *WO*, 1 July 1944, p. 5.

[93] 'Midland installations today', *Birmingham Gazette*, 9 Nov. 1934, p. 7.

[94] 'Walsall Council elections', *WO*, 31 Oct. 1931, p. 6.

[95] J. Neville, 'Challenge, conformity and casework in interwar England: the first women councillors in Devon', *Women's History Review*, xxii (2013), 971–94; Hunt and Hannam, 'Archaeology', p. 130.

[96] 'Walsall's next mayor', *Staffordshire Advertiser*, 7 July 1934, p. 7.

[97] 'Walsall. New woman magistrate', *Staffordshire Advertiser*, 15 Nov. 1924, p. 8; A. Logan, 'In search of equal citizenship: the campaign for women magistrates in England and Wales, 1910–1939', *Women's History Review*, xvi (2007), 501–18.

they were involved perhaps suggests that infant and child welfare was one of many causes in which they remained actively interested.

Conclusion

In early twentieth-century Walsall, women were politically active within multiple organizations and campaigns. This chapter has examined their activism in local branches of suffrage societies, and in organizations involved with infant welfare. The patchiness of the archival record negates a full and complete understanding of how both movements worked locally, but it is nonetheless possible to understand how the fight for women's enfranchisement operated in Walsall through suffrage and local press reporting. Although women's suffrage societies formally arrived relatively late to the town, from 1911, three organizations were working for women's enfranchisement here. However, Walsall's three suffrage societies do not appear to have been particularly large in number, and their membership was dominated by relatively affluent women, who made little attempt to involve working-class women in the campaign locally, suggesting that Walsall's suffrage movement had somewhat limited reach.

As this chapter has demonstrated, however, suffrage was far from the only cause which attracted Walsall women in the period immediately prior to, and during, the First World War. Multiple women's organizations actively sought to improve infant and, to a lesser extent, maternal welfare through the provision of practical support for local mothers. There is some suggestion that a more socially diverse range of organizations were actively involved with these campaigns; Walsall's Women's Co-operative Guild was particularly concerned with the negative impact the war might have on the town's already high infant mortality rate, and some guildswomen went on to become involved with Walsall's Child Welfare Association, established in 1916. The WCWA drew together a significant number of women in its practical work, which appears to have facilitated a greater degree of participation in local public life than the town's suffrage movement had.

To more fully understand how women engaged in politics in this period – that is, how and through which organizations, and on which issues, they campaigned – it is necessary, as Hunt and Hannam argue, to turn to the local. This was the space in which most women, even while still unenfranchised, experienced politics.[98] In Walsall, women were actively involved with the fight for the vote alongside campaigns for improvements to infant welfare,

[98] Hunt and Hannam, 'Archaeology', p. 126.

though it was the latter which drew together a greater number of women. Refocusing on the local, therefore, helps to both highlight the diversity of the women's movement in the pre-enfranchisement era, while also developing our understanding of how women's activism actually worked, especially in areas which appear, at first glance, to have had little engagement with the suffrage campaign.

5. 'Keep your eyes on us because there is no more napping': the wartime suffrage campaigns of the Suffragettes of the WSPU and the Independent WSPU*

Alexandra Hughes-Johnson

With the outbreak of the First World War in August 1914, suffrage activists saw an end to militancy. The leadership of the Women's Social and Political Union (WSPU) elected to take what it saw as a 'patriotic' stand on the conflict and welcomed an amnesty for imprisoned suffragettes from Home Secretary Reginald McKenna on 10 August.[1] This decision to suspend activities – mirrored by parallel decisions in the NUWSS – has often been interpreted as the point at which the campaign for women's enfranchisement ground to an immediate halt.[2] However, major revisionist studies by Nicoletta F. Gullace, Angela K. Smith and June Purvis have sought to look beyond the supposed 'virtual disappearance' of suffrage activism and have offered a far more nuanced view, demonstrating the many and varied ways in which activists continued to make their case for citizenship during the war. Nevertheless, their focus has been on the strategies of WSPU, the Pankhursts' 'patriotic suffragism' and those members who remained loyal.[3]

* With sincere thanks to Dr Lyndsey Jenkins, Dr Samantha Hughes-Johnson, Professor Senia Pašeta and Dr Alex Windscheffel for their thoughtful and constructive comments on earlier versions of this piece.

1 <https://api.parliament.uk/historic-hansard/commons/1914/aug/10/release-of-prisoners#S5CV0065P0_19140810_HOC_180> [accessed 16 June 2020]. See also, <https://www.nationalarchives.ie/article/suffragettes-prison-conditions-ireland/> [accessed 16 June 2020].

2 M. Pugh, 'Politicians and the woman's vote, 1914–18', *History*, lix (1974), 358–74.

3 A. Smith, *Suffrage Discourse in Britain During the First World War* (Aldershot, 2005); N. F. Gullace, *'The Blood of Our Sons', Men, Women and the Renegotiation of British Citizenship During the Great War* (London, 2002); J. Purvis, 'The Pankhursts and the Great War', in *The*

'Keep your eyes on us because there is no more napping', in *The politics of women's suffrage: local, national and international dimensions,* ed. A. Hughes-Johnson and L. Jenkins (London, 2021), pp. 129–160.

The foundation of various wartime suffrage organizations such as the Suffragettes of the WSPU (SWSPU) and the Independent WSPU (IWSPU) – organizations that were largely made up of disgruntled former WSPU members, resentful of the Pankhursts' new direction – has received only limited scholarly attention. When mentioned in the historiography, their membership has been described as 'a very small body of extremists' and their suffrage campaigning as brief, sporadic and 'hampered by lack of funds'.[4] Suffrage societies like the United Suffragists (US) and the East London Federation of Suffragettes (ELFS) are seen to have achieved a better level of wartime organization. This has contributed to the notion that during the First World War, 'the suffragettes were sleeping' and that the majority of active suffrage campaigning was organized by the Women's Freedom League (WFL), the ELFS and the US.[5] This was not the case.[6] The IWSPU and SWSPU were among a number of suffrage societies that were able to build on their prewar connections and networks and 'keep the suffrage flag flying' while maintaining a pacifist stance to the war.[7] Their place within the wider web of wartime suffrage organizations was significant and without a comprehensive analysis of these lesser-known suffrage societies, we cannot fully comprehend the range and breadth of women's responses to and perspectives on the First World War.

This chapter demonstrates that the choice of the IWSPU and SWSPU to continue suffrage campaigning, at a time when jingoistic patriotism defined suffrage activism as working against the country's priorities, was a striking act of political resistance against a government which sought to co-opt them into defending a country, while refusing to grant them citizenship.[8] The foundation of the SWSPU and IWSPU, by disgruntled WSPU members, signalled the rebirth of the active campaign for votes

Women's Movement in Wartime: International Perspectives, 1914–1919, ed. A. Fell and I. Sharp (London, 2007); J. Purvis, 'The Women's Party of Great Britain (1917–1919): a forgotten episode in British women's political history', *Women's History Review*, xxv (2016), 638–511; Pugh, 'Politicians and the woman's vote', p. 359.

4 C. Law, *Suffrage and Power: The Women's Movement, 1918–1928* (London, 2000), p. 16; K. Cowman, *Women in British politics, c.1689–1979* (Basingstoke, 2010), p. 74.

5 Cheryl Law, for instance, refers to the Women's Freedom League, The East London Federation of Suffragettes and the United Suffragists as the 'core' or 'hardcore' of societies active during the war; see Law, *Suffrage and Power*, p. 17.

6 L. Mayhall, *The Militant Suffrage Movement: Citizenship and Resistance in Britain, 1860–1930* (New York, 2003), ch. 7.

7 'New Year's greetings', *The Suffragette News Sheet*, Jan. 1917, p. 3.

8 Mayhall, *The Militant Suffrage Movement*, p. 118.

for women.[9] This campaign was formed from within the existing structure of the old WSPU, and from 1916 developed a clear strategy influenced by the prewar campaign tactics of the WSPU, which was non-violent but still militant. While the activism was essentially constitutional, the militant mindset remained evident in the refusal to push women's political demands to one side.

Although the IWSPU and the SWSPU continued to prioritize suffrage during the war years, their campaigns intersected with women's broader social, economic and moral concerns. Despite the interests and energies of the country being absorbed by the war, this chapter shows that some suffrage activists continued to argue that women's exclusion from the public world of politics directly impacted on women's private lives. They challenged, for example, issues around the state's attempt to control women's sexuality and insisted that the vote was key to transforming women's inequalities. While the particular campaigns of the IWSPU and SWSPU are explored in detail, this chapter argues that broader collective action and collaboration was at the heart of wartime campaign strategies. Wartime suffrage societies had a shared political commitment to securing enfranchisement for women and realized that their significance and impact upon the government lay in their work as a united band of women and men.

Suffrage responses to war

When the First World War broke out in summer 1914, the women's suffrage campaign was forced to respond to a new set of political circumstances. It was far from united in its priorities and responses.[10] Broadly, organizations took one of three responses to the war. There were those who suspended or redirected activity, supporting the war effort through welfare and relief work, those who worked for peace through organizations like the Peace Crusade Bureau and those who continued to campaign for women's

[9] The notion that the violence of war would supersede militancy and essentially render it ineffective was important in this decision. This is not to say, however, that organizations didn't threaten a return to militancy in suffrage propaganda; see Mayhall, *The Militant Suffrage Movement*, p. 118. See also 'Reminding the Conference', *The Independent Suffragette*, Feb. 1917, p. 24.

[10] Gullace, *'The Blood of Our Sons'*; Smith, *Suffrage Discourse in Britain During the First World War*; J. Vellacott, *Pacifists, Patriots and the Vote: The Erosion of Democratic Suffragism During the First Word War* (London, 2007); S. Kingsley Kent, *Making Peace: The Reconstruction of Gender in Interwar Britain* (Princeton, N.J., 1993); M. Pugh, *Women and the Women's Movement in Britain, 1914–1959* (London, 1992); M. Calvini-Lefevbre, 'The Great War and the history of British feminism: debates and controversies 1914–present', *French Journal for British Studies*, i (2015), 1–15.

suffrage.[11] The NUWSS, for instance, remained committed to women's suffrage, but redirected its energies into an extensive programme of relief work, '[offering] the organization to the local authorities in whose hands relief work was placed'.[12] Although the relief work of the NUWSS was a success, it lost a number of high-profile members of its executive (including Helena Swanwick, Isabella Ford and Maude Royden) because of the organization's public stance on the war and pacifist movement.[13]

Not all suffrage organizations responded by suspending or redirecting their suffrage activism. The WFL, ELFS and US, for example, maintained that the vote remained their most important demand and therefore sought to sustain their propaganda work. The WFL – which suspended militancy in 1914 but not other forms of suffrage activity – launched new membership campaigns from 1915 to 1917 and engaged in a range of constitutional activism, including the organization of suffrage petitions, letters to MPs and deputations to Parliament.[14] The US committed to 'expressing the women's point of view and to bring about her ultimate enfranchisement by every means in our power'.[15] The ELFS declared that in order to 'secure justice for the working women of the country', it needed to 'bring pressure to bear on the government' and, unlike the other wartime suffrage societies, opted, from 1916, to support an adult suffrage agenda.[16] Moreover, as the

[11] Law, *Suffrage and Power*, pp. 13–25. It is important to note here when considering feminist responses to war that pacifism was a particularly important driving force within many wartime organizations, particularly organizations like the WFL and ELFS. When suffrage societies like the NUWSS refused to fully engage with the issue, leading members moved out of these feminist spaces, often prioritizing pacifism. J. Vellacott's *Pacifists, Patriots and the Vote* is a particularly important text for consideration here.

[12] The NUWSS officially cooperated with the Central Committee for Women's Employment and organizations like the Mayors' Committee and the Guild of Help as well as supporting initiatives like the Scottish Women's Hospitals Association and organizing Training Schools. 'Notes and comments: organisation', *The Common Cause*, 14 Aug. 1914, p. 1. For more information on NUWSS's response to war see, Vellacott, *Pacifists, Patriots and the Vote*; S. Stanley Holton, *Feminism and Democracy: Women's Suffrage and Reform Politics in Britain, 1900–1918* (Cambridge, 1986); Holton, *Feminism and Democracy*, p. 138.

[13] These women went on to 'provide inspiration and leadership for peace organizations that developed during the war', particularly the Women's International League for Peace and Freedom (WILPF); Holton, *Feminism and Democracy*, p. 138.

[14] Pugh, 'Politicians and the woman's vote', p. 361.

[15] *Votes for Women*, 11 Aug. 1914, p. 1. Quoted in Law, *Suffrage and Power*, p. 18. See also K. Cowman, 'A party between revolution and peaceful persuasion: a fresh look at the United Suffragists', in *Women's Suffrage Movement: New Feminist Perspectives*, ed. M. Joanou and J. Purvis (Manchester, 1998), pp. 77–88.

[16] *The Women's Dreadnought*, 15 Aug. 1914, p. 1. Quoted in Law, *Suffrage and Power*, p. 17.

war progressed, women within these organizations also became involved in peace and relief work, particularly centred on alleviating the effects of war on women and children.[17] This is exemplified by WFL leader and pacifist Charlotte Despard, who outlined the WFL's agenda at the beginning of the war in its newspaper, *The Vote*: 'we must by every means in our power while helping the innocent sufferers in all such times – the women and children – keep our own flag flying'.[18] Nevertheless, while the latter three organizations have been historiographically positioned as the 'hardcore' of previously militant suffrage societies, who continued suffrage work during the war, the new wartime suffrage organizations of the IWSPU and SWSPU certainly made an impact too.[19]

'Reunite without delay': the establishment of the Suffragettes of the WSPU and Independent WSPU

On 12 August 1914, WSPU members were sent a circular letter from Emmeline Pankhurst informing them of the organization's new strategy and decision to 'economise the Union's energies and financial resources by a temporary suspension of activities'.[20] Emmeline and Christabel Pankhurst argued that they 'could not be pacifists at any price' and instead offered their services to the country, calling on their members to do the same.[21] The resumption of suffrage activities and the reappearance of *The Suffragette* were to 'be announced when the time [came]'.[22] Unsurprisingly though, not all women involved in the prewar WSPU were impressed by this change in direction. The suspension of militancy and the pro-war stance taken by the Pankhursts alienated many WSPU members. Initially, WSPU women, who were 'unable to agree with the tactics' chosen by the leadership, met informally in several London locations to discuss 'the

[17] WFL leader Charlotte Despard took an openly pacifist stance to the war and, along with US founder Emmeline Pethick Lawrence, was involved in the 1915 Hague conference, established by the WILPF. With regard to relief work, the WFL founded the Woman Suffrage National Aid Corps to help women whose financial support had been impacted by the war and the ELFS established cost-price restaurants, alongside baby clinics and milk centres, to aid working-women.

[18] Charlotte Despard, 'Our president's message', *The Vote*, 7 Aug. 1914, p. 263.

[19] Law, *Suffrage and Power*, p. 17.

[20] E. Pankhurst, *Letter to WSPU Members*, Suffrage Pamphlet, The Women's Library at LSE, UDC Pamphlet Collection, UDC 396.11B.

[21] J. Purvis, *Christabel Pankhurst: A Biography* (Abingdon, 2018), p. 371.

[22] Pankhurst, *Letter to WSPU Members*, Suffrage Pamphlet.

possibility of continuing the struggle for the vote' and to rally as many members as possible, so that a large-scale event could be arranged in protest against 'the abandonment of suffrage work at this critical time in the history of women'.[23]

The first meeting took place on 22 October 1915 at Caxton Hall. While the number of women in attendance was not recorded, the venue capacity of 700 implies that space was needed for an audience in the hundreds. The meeting was arranged by Wimbledon WSPU's organizing secretary and Quaker Rose Lamartine Yates. She was joined by women from 'all over the country', including prominent activists such as WSPU organizer Dorothy Evans (recently returned from Ireland, where she had been in prison for an arson attack on Lisburn Cathedral) WSPU drum major and notorious militant Mary Leigh and WFL campaigner and pacifist Annie Cobden Sanderson.[24] The attendees met to protest against the Pankhursts' decision to no longer use the Union's name and its platform to campaign for

[23] *The Suffragette News Sheet*, 'Retrospective', Dec. 1915, p. 2.

[24] Rose Lamartine Yates was the mainstay of the Wimbledon WSPU from 1909 to 1915 and was an active speaker in Wimbledon and Surrey. She founded the Suffragettes of the WSPU and became a London County Councillor in 1919. She was also a prime mover behind the formation of the Women's Record Room. For more on Rose Lamartine Yates, see A. Hughes-Johnson, '"Here indeed one can say this life has been lived abundantly": The life and political career of Rose Lamartine Yates', *Women's History*, ii (2018), 19–26; A Hughes-Johnson, 'Rose Lamartine Yates and the Wimbledon WSPU: reconfiguring suffragette history from the local to the national' (PhD thesis, Royal Holloway University, 2018). Working for the WFL, Sanderson is described by Elizabeth Crawford as one of the WFL's 'most tireless campaigners'. She was arrested multiple times, including in Aug. 1909 when she picketed the door of 10 Downing Street. She was a pacifist during the war and, alongside her membership to the WFL, joined the Suffragettes of the WSPU in 1915. Physical education teacher and suffragette Dorothy Evans joined the WSPU in 1907. She resigned from her teaching post in 1910 to work as a WSPU organizer in the Midlands before organizing for the WSPU in Northern Ireland. In 1915 she returned to England to campaign as a pacifist and joined the Suffragettes of the WSPU. Teacher and renowned militant Mary Leigh was the drum major of the WSPU drum and fife band. In 1908, following protests that included a deputation to the House of Commons and participation in the 'rush' on the House of Commons, she spent more than six months in prison. Leigh was also one of the first suffrage activists to be force-feed while imprisoned in Winson Green. With the outbreak of war, Leigh became an ambulance driver and worked with the New Zealand Expeditionary Force hospital in Surrey. She also joined the Suffragettes of the WSPU in 1915. Biographical information from E. Crawford, *The Women's Suffrage Movement: A Reference Guide, 1866–1928* (London, 2000), pp. 208, 210, 340; L. Stanley and A. Morley, *The Life and Death of Emily Wilding Davison* (London, 1988).

women's suffrage, and also to discuss WSPU expenditure and to request an audited statement of accounts from the former WSPU leadership.[25] *The Vote* reported that the 'meeting of members and recent members of the WSPU reaffirms the unshaken faith in the women's movement and its belief that only by the attainment of the aims for which the women of the WSPU have striven and suffered can the uplifting of the human race be achieved'.[26] The women in attendance claimed these aims could only be attained 'by continuing to realise the unity of women' and by faithfully safeguarding their interests 'at the present critical time in their economic and social history'.[27] This statement suggests that despite monumental changes in the country's circumstances, the vote remained the most important demand for many women. It also indicates that the supposedly patriotic feminism embraced by the former WSPU leadership was not endorsed by those in attendance.

Attendees also sought to find out what had happened to the funds held by the national WSPU, requesting a 'properly audited Statement of Accounts and Balance Sheet' to be released by the leadership.[28] The last financial statement issued by the WSPU had been in the spring of 1914. When asked about this in December 1915, Emmeline Pankhurst explained that 'since the war had begun the WSPU's work had been diverted to new channels, and the funds contributed for suffrage work had been set aside and not touched for the purposes of the war campaigns'.[29] As her biographer, June Purvis, suggests, Pankhurst's statement to the *Weekly Dispatch* was not enough 'to silence her critics'.[30] As a consequence, and also to discuss further actions and 'the possibilities of future work', the women present at the October

[25] 'A protest meeting', *The Vote*, 5 Nov. 1915, p. 807.

[26] 'A protest meeting', *The Vote*, 5 Nov. 1915, p. 807.

[27] 'A protest meeting', *The Vote*, 5 Nov. 1915, p. 807.

[28] 'A protest meeting', *The Vote*, 5 Nov. 1915, p. 807.

[29] J. Purvis, *Emmeline Pankhurst: A Biography* (London, 2002), p. 283. Although the funds were initially put to one side during the war, June Purvis's biography of Emmeline Pankhurst reveals that by 1917 the WSPU funds had been used by Christabel Pankhurst to purchase Tower Cressey, 'a large house in Aubrey Road, Kensington'. She bought the house so that it could be turned into a nursery and adoption home for orphans. Ethel Smyth recalled being 'horrified by the unnecessary luxury, elaborate armchairs, chaises-lounges and so on with which it had been refurbished'. For further information on Tower Cressey please also see, L. Jenkins, *Sisters and Sisterhood: The Kenney Family, Class and Suffrage, c.1890–1965* (Oxford, 2021).

[30] Purvis, *Emmeline Pankhurst*, p. 283.

meeting decided to organize a 'General Conference' that was to be held at St George's Hall, Bloomsbury, in December 1915.[31]

The General Conference signalled the rebirth of the active campaign for 'votes for women' by rebellious WSPU women. It was here that attendees led by the chair of the conference, Rose Lamartine Yates, and a temporary executive of ten women, passed several resolutions that defined the organization's future policy.[32] This policy was as follows:

> Proceed to devote ourselves to suffrage work … act unitedly as a group of the WSPU for suffrage only … resume the highly important social and political work of the Union after the recent deplorable break in its activities

[31] 'Retrospective', *The Suffragette News Sheet*, Dec. 1915, p. 2.

[32] The temporary executive was: Anne Cobden Sanderson, Mrs McCleod, Gladys Schutze, Mary Leigh, Zoe Procter, Florence Haughton, Mrs F. E. Smith, Miss Tim, Mrs Best and Mrs Metge. Mrs McCleod is assumed to be the Welsh suffrage activist Mary McCleod Cleeves. Mary was the honorary secretary for the Swansea branch of the WFL that was founded in 1909. In 1910, she was a member of the WFL's National Executive and also the organizer for Wales. Zoe Procter became a WSPU member in 1911 after being taken by her sister to a WSPU meeting. In 1911, she made banners for the coronation procession and was active in the Mar. 1912 window-smashing campaign which saw her imprisoned for six weeks (here she met her life-long partner Dorothea Rock). Mrs Metge is assumed to be Irish suffragette Lillian Metge. In 1910, Metge helped to establish the Lisburn Suffrage Society. She was also the treasurer for the Northern Committee of the Irish Women's Suffrage Federation and a member of the Ulster Centre. While very little biographical information can be found on Miss Tim, Miss Best, Miss F. Haughton and Miss F. E. Smith in suffrage literature, biographical reference guides or the local, national and suffrage press, it appears that Miss F. Haughton and Miss F. E. Smith were active among a number of suffrage societies, prior to and during the war. Miss F. E. Smith is associated with the WSPU prior to 1914 as there are references to her contributing money to various WSPU funds. In Mar. 1911, for instance, Miss F. E. Smith contributed five shillings to the WSPU's £100,000 Fund (*Votes for Women*, 31 Mar. 1911, p. 418). Florence Haughton doesn't appear to have been active among suffrage organizations before the war; in 1917, she was a member of the WFL, ELFS and the SWSPU. She contributed regularly to various funds supporting the ELFS and WFL, including the Women's Dreadnought Fund and WFL National Fund in 1917. See <https://livesofthefirstworldwar.iwm.org.uk/lifestory/4957171> [accessed 29 June 2020]; *The Vote*, 2 July 1915, p. 666; *Woman's Dreadnought*, 26 May 1917, p. 412. Further biographical information from Crawford, *The Women's Suffrage Movement*, pp. 116, 574, 620. See also <https://www.acenturyofwomen.com/lilian-metge/> [accessed 29 June 2020]; D. Urquhart, 'An articulate and definite cry for political freedom': the Ulster suffrage movement', *Women's History Review*, xi (2002), 273–92; M. Ward, 'Conflicting interests: the British and Irish suffrage movements', *Feminist Review*, l (1995), 127–47; 'Retrospective', *The Suffragette News Sheet*, Dec. 1915, p. 2.

> and express our willingness to reunite on the same terms of the original membership cards.[33]

The SWSPU pledged to play no part in making any form of personal attack on the former leaders of the WSPU, in the press or otherwise. A final resolution outlined the pacifist stance of the new organization, stating that it could 'take no part of the policy of the SWSPU to recruit men for war purposes or to adopt any other form of purely militant action'.[34] All its energies were to be devoted to working for the enfranchisement of women. These resolutions were seconded by the suffragettes in attendance, who reportedly 'came from all ends of the country'.[35] The women then enrolled as new members and re-affirmed their original suffrage pledge, which was to 'endorse the objects and methods of the WSPU and hereby undertake not to support the candidate of any political party at Parliamentary elections until women have obtained the Parliamentary vote'.[36]

The conduct of the first meeting and the resolutions passed suggests that while the SWSPU did not intend to establish a suffrage organization that was completely detached from the original WSPU, the pro-war stance taken by the former WSPU leadership and the suspension of suffrage activism meant that the WSPU, as former activists had known it, no longer existed. It might have been possible for displaced and disgruntled WSPU members to move into existing organizations like the WFL, whose policies of pacifism and support for partial suffrage almost mirrored the SWSPU's. But this did not appear to be an appealing option, just as it had not been for many dissatisfied WSPU members during the prewar years. This may have been because of how women viewed the WSPU and their place within it. To the founding members of the SWSPU, the WSPU represented a cause that united women 'from within', as Lilian Metge declared in 1915.[37] For these women, it was the grassroots activists (who came from a wide range of social backgrounds, developed much of their feminism in regions and localities and had long chosen their own degree of militancy) who defined the WSPU – not the leadership.[38] 'Votes for women' was a cause to which

[33] 'Retrospective', *The Suffragette News Sheet*, Dec. 1915, p. 2.

[34] 'Report of conference', *The Suffragette News Sheet*, Dec. 1915, p. 2.

[35] 'Retrospective', *The Suffragette News Sheet*, Dec. 1915, p. 2.

[36] 'Retrospective', *The Suffragette News Sheet*, Dec. 1915, p. 2.

[37] 'The rising morn', *The Suffragette News Sheet*, Dec. 1915, p. 3.

[38] 'The rising morn', *The Suffragette News Sheet*, Dec. 1915, p. 3.

many of the individuals who were prominent in forming the SWSPU had devoted a huge part of their lives. As such, their friendship networks were vast, spanning political and geographical boundaries and conducive to developing this new organization from within its existing structure.

The use of friendship networks to build a new wartime campaign from a grassroots level can be seen in the friendship connections of the women elected to the executive committee of the SWSPU. Former WSPU activists Rose Lamartine Yates and Mary Leigh, for example, were connected for a lifetime by the loss of their close friend, Emily Wilding Davison. Leigh also spoke regularly for the Wimbledon WSPU and stayed with Lamartine Yates when recuperating from ill health. They were united in their socialist feminist outlook, support of pacifism and allegiance to the enfranchisement of women, building on that network to reach out to other like-minded women. While Lamartine Yates used the local connections that she built while organizing and speaking in Wimbledon and London to bring in London-based activists – including Florence Haughton of Winchmore Hill, Mrs F. E. Smith of Finchley, Chelsea-based Zoe Procter and prominent WFL activist Annie Cobden Sanderson, who was a regular speaker at Wimbledon WSPU meetings – these women also drew on their own networks to bring others into the SWPU. For instance, Annie Cobden Sanderson may have reached out to Mary McCleod, who, as noted in Beth Jenkins' chapter in this volume, was a former Welsh organizer and had spent time working alongside Sanderson on the WFL executive committee. Likewise, Zoe Procter and Gladys Schutze (who used the pseudonym Henrietta Leslie in her work as a novelist) were known to each other, as Procter worked as Schutze's secretary during the war.[39] Procter may have also introduced Dorothea Rock to this new organization, as the two had lived together since they had met during the March 1912 window-smashing campaign, for which they were both imprisoned. Similarly, it is plausible that Mary Leigh brought Ireland-based militants into the SWSPU, such as former Irish Women's Franchise League members Lilian Metge, Dorothy Evans and Gladys Evans. Leigh and Evans had been incarcerated in Mountjoy prison after the pair set fire to a box at the Theatre Royal, Dublin in August 1912.[40]

[39] Crawford, *The Women's Suffrage Movement*, p. 620.

[40] Metge and Evans had worked alongside each other from 1913 in Ireland. In July 1914, Metge and Evans were both arrested and imprisoned in connection to an arson attack on Lisburn Cathedral. Mary Leigh engaged in hunger and thirst strikes while in prison and was force-fed, with rumours circulating that officials were seeking to have her certified and committed to a lunatic asylum. Irish suffragettes rose in support of Leigh, with numerous articles published in the *Irish Citizen* (the official newspaper of the Irish Women's Franchise League) reflecting 'The torture in Mountjoy' and 'The duty of those outside' to rally in

In highlighting the connections of some of the members of the executive committee, it is possible to see how the SWSPU used its suffrage networks to build its movement from within an existing structure. These women were united in their desire to prioritize votes for women and take a pacifist stance to the war. Furthermore, before the war they had been devoted but not uncritical followers of the WSPU and had maintained a degree of autonomy. They defined their own political agendas and their own degrees of militancy, seeing themselves and their activism as contributing to and shaping WSPU policy and campaign tactics, rather than accepting them without question. They felt the WSPU was an organization that they had helped build. Mary Leigh, for instance, described it as 'her Union' that she had 'helped build up into power by her passion and her soul and the untellable hardships' she had undergone.[41] This state of mind was clearly shared by her fellow SWSPU members. In late December 1915, an SWSPU report declared that 'a true democracy, does not fail for its lack of leaders' as 'true growth is from within not from without'.[42] As Liz Stanley and Ann Morley have argued, WSPU women often maintained a degree of 'independence of mind and action' and as such, moved forward as they saw fit.[43] They also suggest that many women had little or no contact with the leadership. Instead, their activism was located in their own local and national feminist communities, with many only maintaining WSPU membership in order to retain involvement in an organization and network of like-minded women.[44] This evolved further in wartime, with women using existing WSPU structures to form their own feminist communities, thus uniting women who were committed to prioritizing suffrage.

The SWSPU however, was not the only new wartime suffrage organization established by building on existing networks. Four months after the establishment of the SWSPU, another wartime suffrage society was formed: the Independent WSPU. The IWSPU comprised an executive committee of the following women: former WSPU organizer Charlotte

support of Leigh and protest against her treatment. In one article, the IWFL reported that it had gathered over 1,355 signatures for a 'memorial in favour of full political treatment'. While the signatories were not all listed in the *Irish Citizen*, it is likely that fellow SWPU member and former IWFL member Lillian Metge was one of the signatories. See *The Irish Citizen*, 31 Aug. 1912, p. 113; 21 Sep. 1912, p. 137.

41 Stanley and Morley, *The Life and Death of Emily Wilding Davison*, p. 119.

42 'The rising morn', *The Suffragette News Sheet*, Dec. 1915, p. 3.

43 Stanley and Morley, *The Life and Death of Emily Wilding Davison*, p. 120.

44 Stanley and Morley, *The Life and Death of Emily Wilding Davison*, p. 154.

Marsh as organizing secretary, Dorothea Rock as assistant secretary, constitutional activist and novelist Gladys Schutze as honorary treasurer and former teacher and WSPU organizer Dorothy Evans as provincial organizer.[45] It is not apparent why another organization was formed as there was no clear difference in policy between the SWSPU and the IWSPU. All members of the IWSPU executive committee (apart from Charlotte Marsh) were SWSPU members and included in the SWSPU subscription list of March 1916. Unfortunately, this is the only subscription list that exists, so it is impossible to know if the members of the IWSPU committee left the SWSPU to form this new organization. It could be that the IWSPU was formed because of the lack of a wartime movement at both regional and local levels within the SWSPU. The structure of the IWSPU initially appeared more sophisticated than the SWSPU and less London-centric because, in addition to its committee, the IWSPU had a series of local secretaries, including Edith Rigby in Preston and Janet Barrowman in Glasgow.[46] However, local activism still remained limited within the IWSPU. Unlike the prewar period, when women's local areas were key sites for their suffrage activism, much of the IWSPU's wartime campaign work took place in

[45] Charlotte Marsh joined the WSPU in 1907 after being inspired by Preston-based activist Edith Rigby. In 1909, she became an organizer for the WSPU in Yorkshire and then later in Oxford, Portsmouth and Nottingham. While imprisoned in Winson Green, she was force-fed 139 times. After the outbreak of war, she worked as a motor mechanic and chauffeur for David Lloyd George and helped form the IWSPU in 1916. She also worked as a land girl and was active in the WILPF. Suffrage activist and novelist Gladys Schutze joined the WSPU around 1908. Although not active in violent militancy, Schutze's house became a 'safe haven' for suffragettes released under the Cat and Mouse Act. Her property, at Glebe Place, London, was also used by the WSPU as the information department following the raid on WSPU headquarters. In 1915, she was on the temporary executive of the SWSPU and in 1916 listed as treasurer for the IWSPU. It is not clear if she was a member of both organizations, or if she left the SWSPU for the IWSPU when it was formed in 1916. Dorothea Rock joined the WSPU with her sister Madeline in 1908. While Rock was particularly active in her Essex locality, speaking at various local meetings, her militancy was focused in London. In 1910, she took part in a raid on the House of Commons and in 1912 spent two months in prison after taking part in the Mar. 1912 window-smashing campaign (here she met her lifelong partner, Zoe Procter). In 1916 she joined like-minded suffragettes, including her partner Zoe Procter, on the committee of the IWSPU. Biographical information from Crawford, *The Women's Suffrage Movement*, pp. 282, 620. See also <http://www.essexrecordofficeblog.co.uk/the-smashing-rock-sisters-dorothea-and-madeleine-rock-essex-suffragettes/> [accessed 29 June 2020].

[46] As in prewar years, Edith Rigby and Janet Barrowman took on work as local secretaries but this time for the IWSPU, not the WSPU. Before the war they had both been active

London, since its membership was small and collective action in the capital was seen as the best way to advance its feminist claims.

Wartime suffrage campaigning

The formation of the SWSPU and IWSPU, at a time when a jingoistic sense of 'duty' to one's country was central to the public consciousness, was a striking form of political resistance. While these organizations did not engage in militancy, the women within them were militant in their outlook. The principle of resistance that animated their prewar militancy remained a key feature of their wartime activism and, as Laura Mayhall has argued, campaigning for women's suffrage became 'a form of resistance once the nation deemed it selfish for women to struggle for political rights during the war'.[47] Articles such as 'Patriotism before politics' appeared in August 1915 in the national newspapers, indicating, Mayhall suggests, 'the nation's new priorities'.[48] The jingoistic patriotism however, that defined suffrage campaigning as working against the national interest, did not deter the women of the SWSPU and IWSPU. Both organizations pressed forward their claims for political equality by publishing their first newsletters soon after their foundation.

The SWSPU published its first newsletter, *The Suffragette News Sheet* (*SNS*), in December 1915 and the IWSPU published its first newsletter, *The Independent Suffragette* (*IS*), in August 1916. The timing of the release of the *SNS* is particularly striking because by December 1915, rumours were already circulating regarding the potential of a franchise reform and pressure was building from within Parliament to revise voter registration requirements, so that servicemen could be enfranchised.[49] This, taken in conjunction with

in the WSPU, with Rigby particularly well known to Zoe Procter and Dorothea Rock as she had introduced Procter to the movement in 1908. Barrowman was likely active as a WSPU member from 1910 and was imprisoned for two months in 1912 for an attack on government buildings in Dundee. During the war, she was a local secretary for the IWSPU. Edith Rigby had been active in the WSPU since 1904 and was a mainstay of the Preston WSPU. Over time she became increasingly militant – in 1913 she served a nine-month sentence for setting fire to a bungalow owned by Lord Leverhulme. During the war, she was active in the IWSPU and also the Women's Land Army. Biographical information from Crawford, *The Women's Suffrage Movement*, p. 598; L. Leneman, *A Guid Cause: The Women's Suffrage Movement in Scotland* (Aberdeen, 1991).

47 Mayhall, *The Militant Suffrage Movement*, pp. 118, 127.

48 Mayhall, *The Militant Suffrage Movement*, p. 118.

49 In the autumn of 1915, Lord Willoughby de Broke was pushing to introduce a Service Vote Bill that would enfranchise servicemen over the age of twenty-one. Under current

Lord Lansdowne's announcement in the House of Lords on 4 November, of a government commitment to revise the electoral register by the end of the war, pushed the wartime women's movement forward and prompted it to show the government that it had the ability and resources to respond to the altered political circumstances.

The SWSPU and IWSPU newsletters were published monthly, ranged between three and eight pages in length and included articles, cuttings, letters, correspondence regarding suffrage work and notices that informed members of upcoming meetings and events. The *SNS* and the *IS* cost one penny and required an annual subscription and post fee of 1*s*/6*d*.[50] Although over thirteen editions of the *SNS* still exist today, only two editions of the *IS* have survived. This could be due to the fact that from the outset the IWSPU struggled to secure funds that enabled it to circulate its newspaper as widely as the SWSPU. The SWSPU, unlike the IWSPU, was able to secure support for its newspaper from other suffrage societies like the ELFS and WFL, which featured articles in their papers that encouraged their members to buy 'a LIVE paper devoted entirely to the Woman's Cause – no suffragist can go without it'.[51] Even the socialist newspaper, the *Labour Leader*, featured similar articles.[52] Given the connections of women like Mary Leigh and Annie Cobden Sanderson to the ILP, this is not surprising.

Both wartime suffrage organizations pressed members to subscribe annually to the newspapers. By March 1916, the SWSPU had over sixty annual subscriptions and was reported to have a 'splendid little band of sellers' that were 'keeping votes for women in the public mind' by selling the *SNS* across London. The IWSPU set up a 'Paper Fund' in September 1916 to enable the production of its newspaper and in February 1917, asked its members to pay monthly subscriptions earlier in the year. Both societies also faced obstacles when it came to the circulation of suffrage propaganda. During the war, the London County Council prohibited the sale of literature in parks and public spaces in London. Wartime suffrage organizations resisted this ruling by continuing to sell their literature. One

legislation, over 40% of the male population couldn't vote. See Law, *Suffrage and Power*, p. 17; Gullace, *Blood of Our Sons*, p. 7; A. Rosen, *Rise Up Women! The Militant Campaign for the Women's Social and Political Union, 1903–1914* (London, 1974), p. 257.

50 'The Suffragettes of the WSPU', *The Suffragette News Sheet*, Apr. 1916, p. 6.

51 *The Vote*, 26 May 1916, p. 7; *The Women's Dreadnought*, 20 May 1916, p. 2.

52 *The Labour Leader*, 15 June 1916, p. 8.

WFL seller was arrested in August 1917, in Brockwell Park, for defying council regulations, but the case was dismissed and never went to court.[53] However, it was not just these suffrage newspapers that were struggling with distribution during the war. *Britannia* (edited by Christabel Pankhurst) was suppressed by the government after the paper attacked the government's war policy and had to be printed in secret by 1916.[54] Regardless of the difficulties in sale and distribution, the IWSPU declared 'faith in their little paper' and was confident that its existence would make a difference to promoting votes for women and ensuring that both 'friends and enemies' would know that the women's suffrage movement 'was not dead but very much alive and will never be silent till the goal is won'.[55]

The SWSPU also challenged the notion that the fight for enfranchisement had fallen to the wayside during the war with the publication of a propaganda play script in the *SNS*. A scene in the House of Commons was presented with representatives of the SWSPU detailed as visiting the lobby of the House to remind MPs that 'you cannot as honourable men tamper with the Franchise Laws unless you include votes for women in the changes'.[56] An MP challenged the women asking, 'What? You are awake? I thought all the suffragettes had gone to sleep since the War!', to which a representative of the SWSPU told the MP – 'keep your eyes on us', because there is 'no more napping!'[57] Sustaining this form of suffrage propaganda and the use of humour as a political tactic was particularly important for smaller suffrage organizations at this time, as they were still in the process of recruiting members and establishing themselves among wartime suffrage societies.[58] Krista Cowman has argued that between 1903 and 1914, the WSPU deployed humour as 'a deliberate tactic' and 'a way of gaining suffragettes a hearing'.[59] Former members clearly believed that this tactic was effective enough to continue its use in wartime.

[53] Mayhall, *The Militant Suffrage Movement*, p. 118.

[54] Purvis, *Christabel Pankhurst*, p. 388.

[55] 'Treasurers appeal', *The Independent Suffragette*, Sep. 1916, p. 7.

[56] 'No more napping', *The Suffragette News Sheet*, Dec. 1915, p. 3.

[57] 'No more napping', *The Suffragette News Sheet*, Dec. 1915, p. 3.

[58] Cheryl Law refers to the Women's Freedom League, the East London Federation of Suffragettes and the United Suffragists as the 'core' or 'hardcore' of societies active during the war. See Law, *Suffrage and Power*, p. 17.

[59] K. Cowman, 'Doing something silly': the uses of humour by the Women's Social and Political Union, 1903–1914', *International Review of Social History, Supplement*, xv (2007), 259–74.

The SWSPU and IWSPU needed to recruit members to ensure that their presence was felt during the entirety of the war. Articles within the first editions of the newsletters addressed questions like 'why should you join us?'[60] Answers were framed around the social, economic and political difficulties that women faced in their daily lives. Inequalities, such as women's exclusion from 'well-paid occupations', 'unequal divorce laws', equal pay and women's rights over their children were emphasized, marking a continuity with prewar WSPU tactics. In one September 1916 article, the SWSPU detailed 'why the law is unjust to women'. In focusing on the fundamental unfairness of the law for women, the article explained 'women's grievances', such as 'the wife has no right to share money earned in common', and in doing so, illustrated how women's exclusion from the public world of politics directly impacted on their private lives. Again, the vote was presented as the single determining factor which would transform these inequalities.[61]

Both organizations also attempted to establish a clear set of tactics by giving women examples of 'what everyone can do' to advance the suffrage campaign.[62] The SWSPU encouraged 'all those in sympathy with what has been done to reunite without delay' and to 'strengthen the body of suffragists pressing forward their just claim to the vote' by lobbying MPs and attending open-air meetings and indoor public meetings arranged by the societies. Members were also encouraged to spread the word of the wartime suffrage movement among their existing networks. The IWSPU, for example, asked every reader to buy more copies of its newsletter and post them to friends that were likely to be interested.[63] Although these organizations encouraged members to use their personal friendship networks to grow membership, this only covered a limited proportion of potential support.[64] Therefore, from May 1916, when the SWSPU moved to new offices at the Emily Wilding Davison Lodge Rooms at 144 High Holborn, it began to extend its reach by scheduling weekly meetings. After the SWSPU move, its public campaign work appeared much more prominently in the wider suffrage press (the *Vote*, *Votes for Women* and the *Woman's Dreadnought*) than that of

[60] 'Why you should join us', *The Suffragette News Sheet*, Dec. 1915, p. 2.

[61] 'Is the law unjust to women?', *The Suffragette News Sheet*, Sep. 1916, p. 4. See also H. Kean, *Deeds Not Words* (London, 1990), p. 30.

[62] 'No more napping', *The Suffragette News Sheet*, Dec. 1915; 'What everyone can do', *The Independent Suffragette*, Sep. 1916, p. 7.

[63] 'Why you should join us', *The Suffragette News Sheet*, Dec. 1915, p. 2.

[64] K. Cowman, 'The United Suffragists', in *The Women's Suffrage Movement: New Feminist Perspectives*, ed. M. Joannou and J. Purvis (Manchester, 1998), p. 82.

the IWSPU. SWSPU meetings were advertised as taking place at least once a week, either at 3pm on a Sunday in Hyde Park or at 8pm on a Thursday in Holborn.[65]

By May 1916, rumours of a potential 'Registration Bill' being introduced by Parliament (that would expand the electorate to include servicemen) were rife.[66] Under residency requirements of the current 1884 Reform Act, many soldiers couldn't vote and this was a problem for the government.[67] While Asquith had stated in a letter to NUWSS president Millicent Fawcett in May 1916 that 'new legislation was not being contemplated', Cabinet discussions regarding franchise reform were underway, with Asquith considering the establishment of a Select Committee to consider voter registration and franchise reform.[68] Understandably, suffrage activists were cautious and refused to be caught out by a franchise reform that did not consider women. Consequently, the SWSPU's weekly meetings were coupled with public meetings in much larger indoor venues such as Essex Hall, so that the public could be 'further instructed'. Notices such as 'STOP THE PRESS! SWSPU public meeting, Votes for Women – the burning question again!' appeared in the *SNS*, and suffrage activists were urged to 'be ready to raise a loud and immediate objection to a Registration Bill which [may] not meet the claims of Women'.[69]

Though Martin Pugh has asserted that the wartime women's suffrage movement 'had no obvious strategy for success', this evidence suggests the reverse was true.[70] While the SWSPU approach was essentially non-militant, it was comparable to and clearly influenced by prewar WSPU and wartime WFL tactics. By June 1916, when the WFL was organizing petitions to Parliament and collective deputations and sustaining suffrage propaganda, the SWSPU was also now combining its meetings and sale

[65] 'SWSPU fixtures', *The Suffragette News Sheet*, May 1916, p. 6.

[66] In July 1915, the National Registration Act passed into law and paved the way for the creation of a compulsory register of men and women for war work. This was followed by pressure on the government to reform the parliamentary register and in turn consider expanding the electorate to include those serving their country during the First World War.

[67] Men serving in the war effort were particularly affected, because under the 1884 Reform Act they were required to have occupied a dwelling for a least a year preceding an election. Therefore, those who were serving abroad were effectively disenfranchised as their residences had changed to take up war work. See Law, *Suffrage and Power*, p. 17; Gullace, *Blood of Our Sons*, p. 7; Rosen, *Rise Up Women!*, p. 257.

[68] Rosen, *Rise Up Women!*, p. 258.

[69] 'There will be a registration bill', *The Suffragette News Sheet*, July 1916, p. 1.

[70] Pugh, 'Politicians and the woman's vote', p. 359.

of suffrage literature with letters and deputations to Parliament. The first deputation in which representatives of the SWSPU were present took place after the following letter was sent to all MPs:

> The Executive Committee of the SWSPU requires me [Lamartine Yates] to address you on their behalf with regard to the understood decision of the Government to bring in a Registration Bill ... My committee urges upon you the necessity of dealing with the claim of women to the Parliamentary Franchise, now that the Franchise question is being reopened ... The committee would also remind you of the many pledges given to women in the past and of the strengthening which the women's claim has received through the country's demand for their co-operation in carrying on the work of the nation ... Having regard to the numerous occasions on which, during the war you have recognised the value of women's work, my committee cannot believe other than your intention of recognising the claim of women to citizenship.[71]

It appears that rumours about the government introducing a Registration Bill (that would not only reform the parliamentary register but would likely consider the enfranchisement of men serving in the war) were particularly alarming for suffragettes. They feared that without the possession of women's points of view, any reforms that the government sought to pass would sideline women's demands for enfranchisement once more. The deputation that followed to Parliament Square on 29 May 1916 was attended by SWSPU members alongside representatives from eighteen suffrage societies. These included the WFL, the US and the Actresses Franchise League (AFL). A newspaper report described how 'a picket of women with their colours reminded Members [of Parliament] of their determination to be included in any coming Bill'.[72] What is particularly striking about this deputation, and others during 1916, is that they were regularly attended by multiple suffrage societies and not just representatives of one organization. This indicates that we should not fall foul of the myth that all suffrage campaigning stopped during the war. This is self-evidently not true. Suffrage organizations were clearly finding new ways to collaborate, while also continuing to be influenced by older suffrage campaign tactics and events that brought women from different groups together and united them under a single issue.

The collective and collaborative nature of suffrage campaigning is particularly apparent in the suffrage work of the IWSPU. The IWSPU hosted its own monthly meetings and occasional Sunday afternoon meetings in various London parks. In October 1916 it had encouraged members to

[71] 'In Parliament Square', *The Suffragette News Sheet*, June 1916, p. 2.

[72] 'In Parliament Square', *The Suffragette News Sheet*, June 1916, p. 2.

'write at once to MPs for their localities, urging them to press for a Government Bill introducing votes for women in the coming session'.[73] However, the limited size and capacity of the IWSPU meant it did not organize on a large scale, like the SWSPU. Deputations, public meetings, bazaars and other public events were usually organized in partnership with larger wartime suffrage societies. Throughout 1916 and 1917, for instance, the IWSPU collectively signed circular letters to Parliament and the Prime Minister alongside the SWSPU, WFL and US. Moreover, it attended collective demonstrations and deputations from at least September 1916 – at which time it commissioned Dr Schutze (Gladys Schutze's husband) to design and make a 'large banner in the [suffragette] colours', bearing the name of the society and 'decorated in the corners with a prison badge in white and arrows in purple'.[74] This was a clear example of how wartime organizations formed their own identities while also drawing on the inheritance of WSPU militancy and legacy.

In November and December 1916, the IWSPU was present at the same suffragette bazaars, jumble sales and fairs as several suffrage organizations including the WFL, SWSPU, AFL and US.[75] Just as in the prewar period, these events brought multiple suffrage organizations together, seeking to enlarge membership and raise money for the cause through the sale of literature, toys, crockery and homemade provisions. While these events were organized and attended by multiple societies, it is important to remember that many of the leaders of wartime suffrage societies had simultaneously been 'supporters and generous benefactors' of the WSPU.[76] It is therefore unsurprising that they collaborated, as friendship networks spanned across organizations.[77] However, these collective activities and demonstrations moved beyond friendship. They were also grounded in political strategy. Wartime suffrage societies understood that they could have a greater impact on the government and an increased chance of bringing about change if they operated collectively. Mayhall has argued that throughout the war suffrage organizations shared resources and worked together in continuing the fight for women's suffrage.[78] The SWSPU was especially closely aligned to the WFL, as these bodies worked from the same building (144 High Holborn) throughout 1916 and 1917. The fact they were working towards

[73] 'To members', *The Independent Suffragette*, Sep. 1916, p. 7.

[74] *The Independent Suffragette*, Sep. 1916, p. 6.

[75] 'Green, white and gold fair', *The Vote*, 13 Oct. 1916, p. 1207.

[76] Crawford, *The Women's Suffrage Movement*, p. 694.

[77] Crawford, *The Women's Suffrage Movement*, p. 694.

[78] Mayhall, *The Militant Suffragette*, p. 118.

the same goal, in the same set of offices, suggests that they not only shared resources, but also consulted each other and perhaps even aligned their campaign strategies to have the maximum impact. A letter from Charlotte Despard in the *SNS* exemplifies the interconnections between the SWSPU and the WFL, as she referred to 'her dear friends in the SWSPU' as 'fellow workers' and 'special comrades'.[79] Despard's use of the term 'our' when reflecting on the efforts of suffrage activists illustrates not only the collective and collaborative nature of wartime suffrage campaigning, but also women's shared political commitment to securing the vote.

Adult suffrage versus partial suffrage

Although there were a series of interconnections between suffrage organizations during the war, these societies were also often divided on the precise terms on which suffrage should be granted. While prewar debates about the merits of adult suffrage versus suffrage 'on the same terms or as it shall be granted to men' (often referred to as partial suffrage) do not appear to have been the main reason for the formation of new wartime organizations, prewar disputes on this issue were not easily resolved. The SWSPU argued that the removal of the sex barrier had to be its primary focus, being something that it considered as 'the Alpha and Omega' of its existence.[80] It insisted that societies that had yielded to the fascination of votes for all men and women were 'riding for a fall', because its demand relied on two distinct reforms: the acknowledgement of women as persons and the near doubling of the male electorate.[81] For the SWSPU, these demands were so far-reaching that they would not likely materialize in one single Act of Parliament. Like the SWSPU, the IWSPU, by 'working in the spirit of the old WSPU', sought the vote under the same partial terms.

Sylvia Pankhurst, in her history of the suffragette movement, suggested that the Workers' Suffrage Federation (WSF/formerly ELFS) tried to unite all the active suffrage societies around the demand for adult suffrage.[82] She organized numerous London meetings in 1916, first at the International Suffrage Shop and later in the year at Essex Hall, but they were unsuccessful in converting other wartime suffrage societies to adult suffrage. Pankhurst

[79] 'New Year's greetings', *The Suffragette News Sheet*, Jan. 1917, p. 3.

[80] 'Women as citizens', *The Suffragette News Sheet*, Dec. 1916, p. 2.

[81] 'Women as citizens', *The Suffragette News Sheet*, Dec. 1916, p. 2.

[82] In Mar. 1916, the East London Federation of Suffragettes changed its name to the Workers' Suffrage Federation. Alongside its humanitarian work in the East End, it also campaigned for adult suffrage, or what it later termed human suffrage. For more information, see Crawford, *The Women's Suffrage Movement*, pp. 184–5.

argued that although the idea gripped some suffragettes, with members of the US most keen to move in their direction, the 'old guard' of the WFL, IWSPU and SWSPU would not permit its old policy of partial suffrage to be dislodged.'[83]

Mayhall suggests that as militant organizations could not unite on the precise terms of any suffrage settlement – with the WFL, US, IWSPU and SWSPU maintaining support for partial suffrage – tensions arose between those organizations and the WSF.[84] Nevertheless, this did not stop the SWSPU from working alongside the WSF. In September 1916, for instance, the SWSPU and the WSF held a joint meeting in Hyde Park to discuss the hardships suffered by women during the war, focusing on the difficulty women faced 'making ends meet' due to the rise in food prices.[85] Furthermore, Stanley and Morley have noted that the *Woman's Dreadnought* reveals that the SWSPU's Rose Lamartine Yates contributed £1 a month to a variety of ELFS/WSF funds and gave pears to the ELFS food fund in 1914.[86] These examples illustrate that policy differences between organizations should not be overstated. Women were still able to work cooperatively and support each other's objectives and initiatives even if they didn't agree on specific policies or tactics. The vote could unite women and allowed them to transcend their policy, social and party political differences.

Wider concerns: National Registration Day and the Royal Commission for Venereal Disease

Although the fight for the vote dominated the strategic campaigns of wartime suffrage societies, suffragettes remained active in the broader crusade for improving the social, moral and economic inequalities that directly affected women's lives. One of the first campaigns that the SWSPU joined was the opposition to National Registration Day on 15 August 1915. National Registration Day required 'all individuals between the ages of fifteen and sixty-five' to sign a national register which would be used by the government to compile a list of those suitable for war work and national service.[87] Some

[83] Pankhurst, *The Suffragette Movement*, p. 599. For more on Sylvia Pankhurst see K. Connelly, *Sylvia Pankhurst, Suffragette, Socialist and Scourge of Empire*, (London, 2013).

[84] Mayhall, *The Militant Suffragette*, p. 119.

[85] 'SWSPU meetings and fixtures', *The Suffragette News Sheet*, Sep. 1916, p. 6.

[86] Stanley and Morley, *The Life and Death of Emily Wilding Davison*, p. 182.

[87] The National Registration Act 1915 was passed by Parliament on 15 July 1915. It paved the way for the creation of a compulsory register of men and women for war work a month later, on 15 Aug. See also <http://www.legislation.gov.uk/ukpga/Geo5/5-6/60/contents/enacted> [accessed 1 Aug. 2020]; Mayhall, *The Militant Suffrage Movement*, p. 132.

suffragettes opposed the compulsory nature of the register, believing that it would pressure women into a wartime employment market. For some feminists, this was yet another opportunity to increase the exploitation of women in the workplace.[88] While the Pankhursts encouraged everyone to register, other organizations (like the ELFS) actively protested against this and staged a demonstration, arguing that 'no register be passed without safeguards, that parliament implement legislation forbidding sweated labour, that women receive equal pay for equal work and that women be enfranchised immediately'.[89] Although the SWSPU was not officially formed until December 1915, its future members were actively involved in resisting registration. Musician, singer and SWSPU member Alice Heale, for instance, was arrested and appeared at the South London police court in August 1915 after refusing to fill in a registration form supplied by the municipality. In the March 1916 edition of the *SNS*, the former WSPU activist and contributor to *Votes for Women* recalled her protest against National Registration. On her form, Heale declared the following:

> No Vote No Register: I refuse, without the safeguard of the vote, to help the government in any way to build up the lost trade of the country, I refuse without the safeguard of the vote to help in any way to compile a register of women which can and may be used for forced immigration schemes ... I refuse to take part in any underhand plot to force men against their will to give their lives to the defence of the country.[90]

Although wartime suffrage organizations chose not to engage in violent forms of militancy, this protest was reminiscent of the 1911 census boycott, with 'No Vote No Census' replaced by 'No Vote No Register' – illustrating how women continued to assert their political and economic rights even in this changing context.[91] It appears however, that the lack of a vote was not Heale's only reason for refusing to provide information to her municipality.

[88] Law, *Suffrage and Power*, pp. 24–6.

[89] Mayhall, *The Militant Suffrage Movement*, p. 132. The WFL was more ambivalent towards the question, because after WFL branches took a referendum on the issue, 'there was no majority in support of resistance. Members were therefore told to take action on their own behalf but that the WFL would not officially support them'.

[90] 'No vote, no register', *The Suffragette News Sheet*, Mar. 1916, p. 3.

[91] For more information on the 1911 census boycott, see J. Liddington and E. Crawford, '"Women do not count, neither shall they be counted": suffrage, citizenship and the battle for the 1911 census', *History Workshop Journal*, lxxi (2011), 98–127. J. Liddington and E. Crawford, *Vanishing for the Vote: Suffrage Citizenship and the Battle for the Census* (Manchester, 2014).

She also objected to forced male conscription and she was far from alone in this objection.[92] As Jo Vellacott has shown, by December 1915, male conscription was 'imminent' and by the time Heale's article was published in March 1916, the Military Service Act had been introduced. As a result, some women who had initially retained their original wartime commitment to women's suffrage redirected their efforts to resisting these policies. Former NUWSS member Catherine Marshall, for example, sought to combine her feminism and pacifism by focusing her energies into the No Conscription Fellowship.[93] While the SWSPU did not lobby against male conscription, it opposed it in its newspaper.[94] Moreover, Rose Lamartine Yates also opened the top floor of the old Wimbledon WSPU shop and offered it as a place conscientious objectors could visit for help and legal advice from her husband Tom, who was a solicitor.[95]

Resistance to the National Registration Act and male conscription were not the only campaigns opposed by wartime suffrage societies. The SWSPU also strenuously resisted the attempt to regulate women's sexuality and curtail their rights through the Royal Commission on Venereal Disease (Royal Commission) and the Criminal Law Amendment Bill (CLAB). The SWSPU opposed the findings of the final report of the Royal Commission released on 2 March 1916. The Royal Commission had been established in 1913, following mounting pressure by the medical profession and some feminist and social purity campaigners for an inquiry which would consider the reasons for the prevalence of venereal disease (VD) and specific measures for prevention. The Royal Commission had already caused controversy within feminist circles before the war, with Millicent Fawcett commenting on the absence of women as commissioners and witnesses.[96] In 1916, the

[92] 'No vote, no register', *The Suffragette News Sheet*, Dec. 1915, p. 3.

[93] Marshall became the honorary secretary of the NCF by July 1916. For more information, see Vellacott, *Pacifists, Patriots and the Vote*, pp. 125–6. See also J. Vellacott, 'Marshall, Catherine, Elizabeth (1818–1961)', *Oxford Dictionary of National Biography.*

[94] 'Report of conference', *The Suffragette News Sheet*, Dec. 1915, p. 2.

[95] P. Lamartine-Yates, *Paul Lamartine-Yates' Autobiography*, The John Innes Society, Rose Lamartine-Yates Collection, 1875–1954, Vol. 1. The lower floor of the old WSPU shop and office was opened by Lamartine Yates and other Wimbledon WSPU members in 1915 as a cost-price restaurant and produced in just one year over 40,000 meals for people in the local area. For further information, see Hughes-Johnson, 'The life and political career of Rose Lamartine Yates'.

[96] Millicent Fawcett, who was invited to sit on the Commission by Asquith but declined the invitation because of her suffrage work, was particularly outraged at the omission of Dr Helen Wilson (secretary and president of the Association for Moral and Social Hygiene and president of the Sheffield Women's Suffrage Society) from the Commission. Also, out of the eighty-five witnesses, only eight were women. For further information on this, see D. Evans,

Royal Commission's final report concluded that VD was essentially an urban phenomenon, with the number of persons infected with syphilis being more than 10% of the population in large cities. Consequently, VD was declared 'a major threat to public health'.[97]

Some women, including leading suffragist and National Council for Combating Venereal Disease (NCCVD) member Maude Royden, saw the report as 'a great step forward' in terms of its endorsement of treatment over punishment. The SWSPU suggested that 'every woman should make a point of studying' the report and welcomed its educational recommendations on the consequences of sexual promiscuity for 'the big schoolboys'. They also described it as 'sorry reading' and highlighted its limitations.[98] One of the main issues was that although the report advocated medical treatment and moral instruction, it failed to consider alternative preventative strategies involving physical hygiene, self-disinfection and condoms. This, in their view, essentially shifted the moral and physical burden of the disease onto the 'wretched victim – driven to prostitution by the starvation of a wage that man took care should alone be within her reach' (sic).[99] The SWSPU's central concern however, was the impact of the report on the family. It stated that the report condoned vice, 'penalis[ed] motherhood' and protected men, leaving families (and particularly wives) open to the dangers of infection. In a series of articles, it repeatedly used the example of the infection of a wife by her seemingly 'respectable' husband.[100]

The findings of the Royal Commission on Venereal Disease and the publication of the report took on new significance in the wartime context. In October 1914, local authorities in Plymouth, fearful of the risk of infection for soldiers and sailors, had already attempted to introduce restrictions that the WFL, ELFS, Catholic Women's Suffrage Society and British Dominions Woman Suffrage Union had compared to those introduced under the CD Acts. This was followed by a Cardiff decree which set a curfew for 'a certain class of women who should not be allowed outdoors between 7pm and

---

'Tackling the "hideous scourge": the creation of venereal disease treatment centres in early twentieth century Britain', *The Social History of Medicine*, v (1992), p. 417.

[97] Evans. 'Tackling the "hideous scourge"', p. 417.

[98] 'The Royal Commission on Venereal Disease: no tinkering with the devastating evil', *The Suffragette News Sheet*, July 1916, pp. 4–5. See also S. R. Grayzel, *Women's Identities at War: Gender, Motherhood and Politics in Britain and France during the First World War* (London, 1999), p. 148.

[99] 'Compulsory notification of venereal disease: the case for and the case against', *The Suffragette News Sheet*, Dec. 1916, p. 2.

[100] 'The penalising of motherhood', *The Suffragette News Sheet*, Apr. 1916, pp. 3–4.

8pm'.[101] While women's suffrage societies had already organized in opposition to these perceived infringements on women's rights, the announcement of a pending Criminal Law Amendment Bill (introduced in 1917 in response to the Royal Commission's report) and its recommendation for compulsory notification of VD, pushed suffragettes to further action.[102]

The speed at which the CLAB was proposed, following the Royal Commission, highlights the urgency felt by the government to deal with VD and 'protect' soldiers and sailors who were seen as highly valuable assets in the present crisis. While the bill's proposal to raise the age of consent for women was welcomed by many feminists, Susan R. Grayzel has noted that feminist organizations rose in opposition to compulsory notification and also to 'the infamous Clause 3', that targeted girls under the age of nineteen found guilty of 'loitering' or behaving in 'a riotous or indecent manner'.[103] The SWSPU's position on compulsory registration was complex. The 'official position' of the SWSPU was to oppose the proposed CLAB and object against compulsory notification and detention of women.[104] Nevertheless, the SWSPU prided itself on being a 'democratic organization' and, because of that, it stated that it was perfectly acceptable for 'women [to] voice individual opinions' on the issue, but that those opinions had 'no authority to speak for their sisters'.[105] The organization offered its members the opportunity to read articles published in the *SNS* by SWSPU member Juliette Heale and NCCVD representative Maude Royden, on the 'case against' and the 'case for' compulsory notification. This was a markedly different approach to the renowned autocratic style of the WSPU leaders during the prewar period.

In November 1916, representatives from the leadership of both the SWSPU and IWSPU attended an emergency conference of women's organizations that was coordinated by the WFL, to discuss the pending CLAB. Rose Lamartine Yates represented the SWSPU and Dorothea Rock the IWSPU. They also signed a manifesto, along with fifteen other suffrage organizations, that laid out their objection to the bill. *The Manifesto of Organised Women*, the main purpose of which was to 'strenuously oppose'

[101] Mayhall, *The Militant Suffrage Movement*, p. 127.

[102] Compulsory notification is the idea that that every doctor is bound by law to register a patient with venereal disease.

[103] Grayzel, *Women's Identities at War*, pp. 149–50.

[104] 'Compulsory notification of venereal disease: the case for and the case against', *The Suffragette News Sheet*, Dec. 1916, p. 2.

[105] 'The Manifesto of Organised Women', *The Suffragette News Sheet*, Dec. 1916, p. 3.

the immediate introduction of compulsory notification and compulsory treatment, was published in the suffrage journals and sold to the national press.[106] Publication was followed by a deputation of sixteen women's societies to the Home Secretary on 4 December 1916.[107] Essentially, feminist organizations felt that while legislators claimed men and women would be subject to the same laws and treatment, it was women's sexuality that was being regulated and women who would be blamed. This is exemplified in an *SNS* report in December 1916, where the SWSPU argued that this legislation would 'invariably let the male partner escape by penalising the female'.[108] The deputation to the Home Secretary sought to connect this sexual double standard to women's suffrage by suggesting that 'the only true remedy for this situation' was the enfranchisement of women. The vote was the only thing that could combat 'this social evil' and achieve 'a high moral standard for men and women.'[109]

This direct association of sexual morality and the vote however, is not surprising considering members' former association with the WSPU. WSPU leader Christabel Pankhurst ardently believed that because legislation was 'made and administered by men', without the consultation of women, men were protected and therefore male immorality and the sexual exploitation of women was encouraged.[110] The only solution to (in her words) 'the real cure of the great plague' was 'votes for women', as the vote would 'give women more self-reliance and a stronger economic position'.[111] Paula Bartley has suggested that this relationship between sexual morality and the vote has 'enjoyed a long history in the annals of women's suffrage' and that throughout the campaign for women's enfranchisement, campaigners placed women's franchise within the wider context of sexual politics.[112] Although it is apparent that suffrage societies engaged in wider campaigns for women's equality during the First World War, the vote remained their most pressing priority as it was seen as the key to their full emancipation.

[106] 'The Manifesto of Organised Women', *The Suffragette News Sheet*, Dec. 1916, p. 3.

[107] 'Deputation to home secretary', *The Suffragette News Sheet*, Jan. 1916, p. 3.

[108] 'Compulsory notification of venereal disease: the case for and the case against', *The Suffragette News Sheet*, Dec. 1916, p. 3.

[109] 'Deputation to home secretary', *The Suffragette News Sheet*, Dec. 1916, p. 3.

[110] C. Pankhurst, *The Great Scourge and How To End It*, 1913. The Women's Library, 616.951 PAN.

[111] Pankhurst, *The Great Scourge*.

[112] P. Bartley, *Votes for Women: 1860–1928* (Tunbridge Wells, 2008), pp. 185–6.

The Speaker's Conference and the Representation of the People Act

October 1916 marked a turning point for wartime suffrage societies because the Prime Minister established a Parliamentary Conference on Electoral Reform.[113] Speaker James William Lowther presided over the conference, overseeing discussions about types of electoral reform that should be recommended to Parliament. The SWSPU and IWSPU increased their campaigning efforts accordingly. From October 1916 to January 1917 the suffrage press was littered with reports of suffrage propaganda sales, meetings and discussions regarding the Speaker's Conference. In November 1916, the SWSPU's Rose Lamartine Yates sent a telegram to the Speaker of the House asking for a 'prompt solution to their question' on women's enfranchisement.[114] Likewise, in February 1917, the IWSPU's Charlotte Marsh wrote a letter to the Electoral Reform Committee urging it to include a recommendation for women's suffrage. She also suggested that the Committee remind the House of Commons of the militant 'truce' made by suffragettes before the war and the consequences of violent militancy should MPs ignore women again.[115] By December 1916, the SWSPU and IWSPU were among several societies present at a picket at the House of Commons, 'every Wednesday and Thursday during the sittings of the Conference on Electoral Reform'.[116] The same prominent women from leading suffrage societies also attended 'a private conference of working towards women's suffrage' in December 1916.[117]

By the end of 1916, a strategic and well organized campaign was clearly in place to lobby on the issue of women's suffrage and all efforts were being made to secure a recommendation for women's enfranchisement in the Report of the Speaker's Conference. In December 1916, Rose Lamartine Yates encouraged readers of the *SNS* to maintain their campaigning efforts and pushed for members of the House to 'have no fear' in including women in politics. In her front-page article, she appealed to men and women alike, stating

[113] Pankhurst, *The Suffragette Movement*, p. 600. Lowther chose 32 MPs and Peers to be members and attempted to represent all parties and interests. He included 'approximately 17 women's suffrage supporters and 10 anti-suffragists'. See <https://www.parliament.uk/1917speakersconference> [accessed 4 June 2019].

[114] 'Our message to the Speaker', *The Suffragette News Sheet*, Nov. 1916, p. 4.

[115] 'Reminding the Conference', *The Independent Suffragette*, Feb. 1917, p. 24.

[116] 'Picketing the House', *The Suffragette News Sheet*, Dec. 1916, p. 4.

[117] 'Our message to the Speaker', *The Suffragette News Sheet*, Nov. 1916, p. 4. Interestingly, the tactic of picketing the government during wartime was also embraced by American suffragettes in the National Women's Party. Led by Alice Paul, they too controversially continued suffrage activism during the war but were arrested for 'obstructing traffic'. See E. Carol Dubois, *Suffrage: Women's Long Battle for the Vote* (New York, 2020), p. 227.

'women have never failed him in his need, why fear her in politics … let him have the courage to resist no longer women's full enfranchisement'.[118] This notion of having no fear was replaced with 'hope' in the January edition of the *SNS*. In the 'New Year's Greetings', members from other suffrage societies wrote to the SWSPU.[119] Former WSPU activist Edith Mansell Moullin wrote to encourage members to 'hope on, work on with hearts full of love'.[120] Mrs Despard wrote with 'hope [that 1917] would see the recall of women to their true place in the State'.[121] This wish was to some extent granted by the end of January 1917, when the Report of the Speaker's Conference was published recommending a form of women's suffrage.[122]

The recommendation in the Report was as follows:

> A majority of the Conference was also of the opinion that if Parliament should decide to accept the principle, the most practical form would be to confer the vote in the terms of the following resolution – 33) Any woman on the Local Government Register who has attained a specified age and the wife of any man who is on that Register if she has attained that age, shall be entitled to be registered and to vote as a parliamentary elector. Various ages were discussed, of which 30 and 35 received most favour.[123]

The proposal was a huge compromise for suffrage societies, many of whom had campaigned for the enfranchisement of women on the same terms as men. However, it was a compromise that suffrage societies like the SWSPU and the IWSPU were willing to accept, as it was believed that it would enfranchise about 6 million women.[124] The SWSPU labelled the recommendation as 'The women's victory'.[125] Nevertheless, it admitted its dissatisfaction with the fact that the resolution had 'no legislative value'.[126] The SWSPU argued that it would not be a victory until the proposal

[118] 'Have no fear', *The Suffragette News Sheet*, Dec. 1916, p. 1.

[119] 'New Year's greetings', *The Suffragette News Sheet*, Jan. 1917, p. 3.

[120] 'New Year's greetings', *The Suffragette News Sheet*, Jan. 1917, p. 3.

[121] 'New Year's greetings', *The Suffragette News Sheet*, Jan. 1917, p. 3.

[122] For more detail on the Speaker's Conference Report, see M. Takayanagi, 'Votes for women and the Speaker's Conference on Electoral Reform 1916–17', The History of Parliament Blog <https://thehistoryofparliament.wordpress.com/2017/01/18/votes-for-women-and-the-speakers-conference-on-electoral-reform-1916-17/> [accessed 25 Nov. 2020].

[123] David Lloyd George, *The Recommendation on Women's Suffrage in the Speaker's Conference Report*. 29 Jan. 1917, Parliamentary Archives, LG/F/166/5/1.

[124] In reality, 8.4 million women were enfranchised. Takayanagi, 'Votes for women and the Speaker's Conference'.

[125] 'The women's victory', *The Suffragette News Sheet*, Feb. 1917, p. 1.

[126] 'The women's victory', *The Suffragette News Sheet*, Feb. 1917, p. 1.

was approved by Parliament and received Royal Assent. Likewise, the February edition of the *IS* reminded its readers not to be 'bought off by promises and the appearance of their fulfilment'.[127] Both organizations felt so strongly that the recommendations shouldn't be taken for granted and should be passed into law as soon as possible, that Charlotte Marsh wrote to all members of the Electoral Reform Conference, urging them to press the House of Commons to give the recommendation its 'fullest consideration'.[128] Rose Lamartine Yates, along with leaders of other suffrage societies, wrote to the Prime Minister to ask whether he would 'receive a deputation on the immediate need of the enfranchisement of women'.[129] When no reply was received by either organization, the IWSPU sent a deputation to Downing Street and was promised an interview with the Prime Minister. The SWSPU recognized the important pressure applied by the IWSPU during this deputation and congratulated the society, writing in its newspaper, 'Bravo IWSPU – direct methods always prove effective!'[130] Both organizations were also represented in the March 1917 deputation of women workers to the Prime Minister, presided over by Millicent Fawcett.[131]

Further analysis of the IWSPU and SWSPU's reaction to the recommendation of the Speaker's Conference and their continued work to ensure its passage into law is unfortunately impeded by the lack of sources. After February 1917, no more editions of the *SNS* or the *IS* were published. As noted earlier, the front page of the February *SNS* declared a 'women's victory' in relation to the Speaker's Conference on Electoral Reform. This could imply that the suggestion for women's suffrage to be included in the Electoral Reform Bill meant that the SWSPU, like the US, felt that its work was complete. Cowman's research into the US has argued that the recommendations of the Speaker's Conference and the passage of the bill into law in 1918, 'removed the US's *raison d'etre*'.[132] While this could also be the case for the IWSPU and SWSPU, no statements appeared in the February editions of the *SNS* or the *IS*, insinuating that their activism would stop or that their newspapers would cease printing. *The Vote* suggests that the SWSPU remained active until at least October 1917, and the IWSPU until as late as November 1919. It could simply be the case that the

[127] 'The political outlook', *The Independent Suffragette*, Feb. 1917, p. 21.

[128] 'Reminding the Conference', *The Independent Suffragette*, Feb. 1917, p. 24.

[129] 'Deputations to the prime minister', *The Suffragette News Sheet*, Feb. 1917, p. 4.

[130] 'Deputations to the prime minister', *The Suffragette News Sheet*, Feb. 1917, p. 4.

[131] 'Deputations to the prime minister', *The Suffragette News Sheet*, Feb. 1917, p. 4.

[132] Cowman, 'A fresh look at the United Suffragists', p. 85.

later editions of the newspaper have been lost to history or that the costs of running the paper became prohibitive during the later stages of the war.[133]

Conclusion

On 6 February 1918, the hopes and dreams of the SWSPU and the IWSPU were to some extent realized when the Representation of the People Act received Royal Assent and enfranchised over 8 million women. While the wartime suffrage campaigns of these two organizations only lasted between two and four years, this chapter has illustrated that their contributions to the wartime campaign for women's suffrage were significant. By highlighting the efforts of these wartime suffrage organizations, this chapter rejects the notion that suffrage politics disappeared during the First World War and that the vote was a reward for women's war work. Instead, it illustrates that the SWSPU and the IWSPU were among a large number of suffrage societies that refused to suspend the campaign for the vote during wartime, ensuring that women's suffrage continued to feature in the political discussions that preceded the Representation of the People Bill.

These newly formed organizations were able to build on their prewar suffrage activities and connections by constructing a wartime movement from within their existing WSPU structure and feminist community. They united disillusioned WSPU activists and sought to revive their movement by forming societies that continued to campaign for women's social, economic and moral rights, while remaining focused on the franchise. Their campaigning, whether as lone organizations or in association with other suffrage societies, was strategic, organized and influenced by the prewar tactics of the WSPU and WFL, which emphasized that women's exclusion from politics directly impacted on women's everyday lives. For the SWSPU and IWSPU, the vote remained the most important way to challenge women's inequality and it was through the collaborative work and the persistent political agitation of several wartime suffrage societies that the women's suffrage movement maintained momentum. The wartime suffrage movement, including the SWSPU and IWSPU, did not just have a shared political commitment to women's enfranchisement. They also understood that they could have a greater impact on the government as a collective band of women who worked together to 'keep the suffrage flag flying'.[134]

[133] Only one copy of the newspaper exists, as far I am aware, and it is housed in the Emily Wilding Davison Collection at the Women's Library at LSE. There are no copies or even references to the paper in any of Rose Lamartine Yates's collections.

[134] Law, *Suffrage and Power*, p. 17.

Nina Boyle, WFL member and chief of the Women's Police Volunteers, recognized the contribution of organizations like the SWSPU and the IWSPU to maintaining the suffrage movement in wartime. She wrote that 'the fact that so many of the smaller groups of suffragists have kept the suffrage flag flying and have held together and kept their little journals published gives hope and heart and help to us all'.[135] This poignant statement reminds us that while more prominent suffrage societies like the WFL carried the campaign for enfranchisement into the war years (maintaining strategy, organization and momentum), we must not overlook the crucial role, contribution and impact of small, newly formed wartime suffrage societies like the IWSPU and SWSPU.

[135] 'New Year's greetings', *The Suffragette News Sheet*, Jan. 1917, p. 3.

II. Working through social and cultural structures

6. English girls' schools and women's suffrage

Helen Sunderland

The girls' secondary school was an important site for the women's suffrage debate in late Victorian and Edwardian England. While it is well known that many women teachers were active in the campaign, previous studies have focused on their suffrage politics outside the classroom.[1] Teachers' suffrage activism within the school itself has been largely neglected. Further, based on an assumption that political engagement is intrinsically adult, schoolgirls' interactions with the suffrage question have been especially overlooked. In contrast, female university students' involvement in the suffrage movement is relatively well understood, but it is unlikely that these young women entered higher education entirely disengaged from politics.[2] Indeed, the campaign for the parliamentary vote not only mobilized large numbers of adult women – on both sides of the debate – but also captivated a younger audience. By integrating the histories of childhood, education and politics, this chapter argues that schoolgirls, teachers and a growing alumnae community of 'old girls' engaged with the discourses and divisions of the women's suffrage movement in their everyday lives at school.

All-female, residential institutions have long been recognized as spaces for women's politicization and community.[3] Bringing together educated, likeminded women, the middle-class girls' day school played a similar role

[1] H. Kean, *Challenging the State? the Socialist and Feminist Educational Experience, 1900–1930* (London, 1990); H. Kean, *Deeds Not Words: the Lives of Suffragette Teachers* (London, 1990); D. M. Copelman, *London's Women Teachers: Gender, Class and Feminism, 1870–1930* (London, 1996); A. Oram, *Women Teachers and Feminist Politics, 1900–39* (Manchester, 1996); A. Oram, 'Women teachers and the suffrage campaign: arguments for professional equality', in *Votes for Women*, ed. J. Purvis and S. Stanley Holton (London and New York, 2000), pp. 203–25.

[2] On university students and suffrage, see C. Dyhouse, *No Distinction of Sex? Women in British Universities, 1870–1939* (London, 1995), pp. 217–21.

[3] M. Vicinus, *Independent Women: Work and Community for Single Women, 1850–1920* (London, 1985); K. B. Beauman, *Women and the Settlement Movement* (London, 1996).

'English girls' schools and women's suffrage', in *The politics of women's suffrage: local, national and international dimensions,* ed. A. Hughes-Johnson and L. Jenkins (London, 2021), pp. 163–190.

and nurtured women teachers' suffragist politics. Teachers and old girls used the school building and magazine as a venue and organ for sharing their political opinions. Colleagues and pupils, past and present, provided a ready audience. However, schoolgirls were far from passive recipients of adult suffragism. Through debating, writing and even joking about aspects of the campaign for the parliamentary vote, schoolgirls themselves contributed to the suffrage debate.

Hilda Kean, Dina Copelman and Alison Oram have compellingly demonstrated the important connections between women teachers' professional and feminist identities at the turn of the twentieth century. Their studies illuminate women teachers' political activity beyond the classroom, in trade unions and feminist, socialist and suffrage organizations.[4] However, this analytical focus overlooks how the school itself might provide a site for teachers' political expression, reflecting a general trend in histories of girls' education to marginalize political experiences at school.[5] Where the politicizing potential of the educational setting has been considered, schoolgirls are largely conceptualized in passive terms. Julia Bush and Gillian Sutherland highlight contemporary fears about suffragist teachers corrupting supposedly impressionable schoolgirls, giving important insights into the perceived reach of the suffrage debate into everyday spaces like schools.[6] Carol Dyhouse notes a couple of examples where teachers encouraged girls to show their support for women's suffrage more openly.[7] Nevertheless, the links between the participation of teachers, old girls and schoolgirls in the suffrage debate have yet to be considered fully. Building on a growing literature that positions children and young people as

[4] Kean, *Challenging the State?*; Kean, *Deeds Not Words*; Copelman, *London's Women Teachers*; Oram, *Women Teachers*; Oram, 'Women teachers'.

[5] S. Fletcher, *Feminists and Bureaucrats: a Study in the Development of Girls' Education in the Nineteenth Century* (Cambridge, 1980); C. Dyhouse, *Girls Growing Up in Late Victorian and Edwardian England* (London, 1981); *Lessons for Life: the Schooling of Girls and Women, 1850–1950*, ed. F. Hunt (Oxford, 1987); J. S. Pedersen, *The Reform of Girls' Secondary and Higher Education in Victorian England: a Study of Elites and Educational Change* (New York, 1987); J. Purvis, *Hard Lessons: the Lives and Education of Working-Class Women in Nineteenth-Century England* (Cambridge, 1989); M. Gomersall, *Working-Class Girls in Nineteenth-Century England: Life, Work and Schooling* (Basingstoke, 1997).

[6] J. Bush, *Women Against the Vote: Female Anti-Suffragism in Britain* (Oxford, 2007), pp. 232–7; G. Sutherland, *In Search of the New Woman: Middle-Class Women and Work in Britain, 1870–1914* (Cambridge, 2015), p. 128.

[7] C. Dyhouse, *Girl Trouble: Panic and Progress in the History of Young Women* (London, 2013), pp. 63–4. Dyhouse referenced the experiences of Vera Brittain and Winifred Starbuck, discussed later in this chapter.

political actors, this chapter restores girls' own contributions to the vibrant, intergenerational political culture of the girls' school.[8]

Some historians have explored the interplay of youth and suffragism. Jill Liddington convincingly showed how criticism of 'baby suffragette' Dora Thewlis, who was arrested aged sixteen at a suffrage protest in 1907, centred on conflicting constructions of her age. Thewlis was criticized both for her childishness and precocious behaviour, refracted through gendered and sexualized terms.[9] Indeed, age could be used to delegitimize suffragist commitment. As Kean observed, women teachers who supported the cause were often stereotyped as young and, therefore, immature, naïve and impulsive.[10] Looking across the school community sheds new light on how age shaped suffrage activity; childhood and adolescence offered girls different routes to engage with the suffrage question, while adulthood brought its own opportunities and challenges for the participation of alumnae and teachers in the movement.

This chapter focuses primarily on the educational communities of feepaying girls' day secondary schools in London, Nottingham, Manchester and Blackburn. In the capital, this includes the prestigious North London Collegiate School and City of London School for Girls, two Girls' Public Day School Company (GPDSC) schools in Notting Hill and Wimbledon and Central Foundation Girls' School in Spital Square which, with cheaper fees, attracted lower-middle-class families.[11] Manchester High School for Girls, Blackburn High School for Girls and Nottingham Girls' High School (another GPDSC institution) offer insights into schoolgirl experiences in

[8] K. P. Kallio and J. Häkli, 'Tracing children's politics', *Political Geography*, xxx (2011), 99–109; B. E. Wood, 'Crafted within liminal spaces: young people's everyday politics', *Political Geography*, xxxi (2012), 337–46; T. Skelton, 'Young people, children, politics and space: a decade of youthful political geography scholarship 2003–13', *Space and Polity*, xvii (2013), 123–36.

[9] J. Liddington, *Rebel Girls: Their Fight for the Vote* (London, 2006), pp. 112–34.

[10] Kean, *Deeds not Words*, p. 14.

[11] North London Collegiate School Archive (school magazines and prospectuses available via the school's digital archive <nlcsarchives.daisy.websds.net> [accessed 28 May 2020]); London Metropolitan Archives, City of London, City of London School for Girls, *The Magazine of the City of London School for Girls*, CLA/054/B/02/003–004; Notting Hill and Ealing High School Digital Archives <nhehsarchives.net> [accessed 28 May 2020]; Wimbledon High School Digital Archives <wimbledonhighschool.daisy.websds.net> [accessed 28 May 2020]; Central Foundation Girls' School Historical Archive Resources <central.towerhamlets.sch.uk/page/?title=CFGS+Historical+Archive+Resources&pid=26> [accessed 28 May 2020].

other urban contexts.[12] Alongside school magazines and old girls' association newsletters from these institutions, the chapter also draws on periodicals aimed at elementary school teachers and autobiographical accounts of school life. This range of sources enables an exploration of how age and class influenced schoolgirls' engagement with the suffrage question. The younger elementary school leaving age, which rose in this period from ten to thirteen, meant that working-class schoolgirls engaged with women's suffrage on different terms to their middle-class adolescent peers. Using the different resources available to them, girls' school teachers encouraged older, middle-class pupils to tackle the subject intellectually in debates or creative writing for the school magazine. Meanwhile, in elementary schools, attempts were made to guide younger, working-class girls' interactions with suffrage more closely, through scripted dramatic performance.

There is an expansive literature on the importance of women's periodicals to building and sustaining the women's movement.[13] This chapter reinstates the girls' school magazine and wider educational press into this story. School magazines are especially rich sources for educational experience that have received renewed interest from historians in recent years. Catherine Sloan expertly demonstrated the value of the genre for studying scholars' participation in and contributions to educational and literary cultures.[14] Sara Delamont noted that women's suffrage is rarely mentioned in official girls' school histories and Stephanie Spencer's study of the GPDSC Sutton High School magazines showed that some publications remained silent on the issue of women's suffrage.[15] However, in other institutions where headmistresses were more willing to engage openly with issues affecting women in public life, school magazines provide a fascinating window onto how teachers, old girls and pupils engaged with the suffrage debate.

[12] Manchester High School for Girls Archive; Nottingham Girls' High School Archives; Lancashire Archives, Blackburn Girls' High School, Old Girls' Association newsletters, SMBz/9/acc7536/box 3.

[13] M. DiCenzo with L. Delap and L. Ryan, *Feminist Media History: Suffrage, Periodicals and the Public Sphere* (Basingstoke, 2011); B. Green, *Feminist Periodicals and Daily Life: Women and Modernity in British Culture* (Basingstoke, 2017); *Women's Periodicals and Print Culture in Britain, 1918–1939: the Interwar Period*, ed. C. Clay, M. DiCenzo, B. Green and F. Hackney (Edinburgh, 2018).

[14] C. Sloan, 'The school magazine in Victorian England' (unpublished DPhil thesis, University of Oxford, 2019).

[15] S. Delamont, 'Distant dangers and forgotten standards: pollution control strategies in the British girls' school, 1860–1920', *Women's History Review*, ii (1993), 233–51; S. Spencer, 'Advice and ambition in a girls' public day school: the case of Sutton high school, 1884–1924', *Women's History Review*, ix (2000), 75–94, at p. 83.

The first half of this chapter demonstrates how teachers used subtle strategies – such as school magazines and old girls' associations – to celebrate women's suffrage activism at school while avoiding the reputational risks of participating more openly in suffrage work. It then considers how teachers encouraged schoolgirls' engagement with the suffrage question through debating societies and suffrage plays. The final section shows how girls themselves took the initiative, approaching suffrage through subversive humour and expressing opinions at both extremes of the debate more easily than adults could in the school context. The chapter therefore offers a new perspective on the suffrage activism of teachers and alumnae, highlights schoolgirls' active participation in the debate and argues that their shared experience of women's suffrage is key to understanding the girls' school as an intergenerational political community.

The girls' school nurtured women teachers' and old girls' suffragist politics, both on site and through the textual spaces of school publications. By bringing together educated, professional women, girls' schools provided opportunities for political discussion. As Oram argued, recruitment among teachers was an important way to bring more women into the suffrage movement.[16] Women elementary teachers, especially, linked their suffrage activism to the inequalities they faced in the workplace, like the marriage bar and equal pay.[17] With the latter, at least, less of an issue among the all-female workforce of middle-class girls' schools, it is important to consider what alternative narratives these women constructed about their suffrage work. The disconnect between their professional standing as teachers and their unenfranchised status as women no doubt contributed.[18] However, conceptualizing the girls' school as a community where teachers, old girls and current pupils engaged with the suffrage question together suggests that teachers not only framed their suffragism against professional struggles but around the unique opportunities that the educational setting offered.

The all-female school environment could foster mutual encouragement and solidarity between colleagues, providing a route to collective action for a shared cause like women's suffrage. In November 1884, for example, the headmistress and twenty assistant mistresses at the Girls' Public Day School Company school in Dulwich delivered a petition to Parliament

[16] Oram, 'Women teachers', p. 208.

[17] Oram, *Women Teachers*, p. 1; Oram, 'Women teachers', pp. 203–4.

[18] Kean, *Deeds Not Words*, pp. 6, 29; Oram, *Women Teachers*, p. 7.

demanding the inclusion of women householders in the Reform Bill.[19] As the leading signatory, the support of headmistress Mary Jemima Alger was decisive. Other headmistresses similarly encouraged their staff to engage with suffrage work. At North London Collegiate School, Sophie Bryant, who joined the teaching staff in 1875 and became headmistress twenty years later, went to considerable lengths to share her suffragist politics with her colleagues. As one example, in 1904, she invited Emily Davies, a leading figure in the women's movement, to open a discussion on women's suffrage at a staff meeting.[20] Bryant made the most of her political contacts to raise the profile of women's suffrage among mistresses at North London Collegiate School.

Old girls also benefited politically from their school connections. In the late nineteenth century, numerous old girls' associations were formed as the first generation of pupils left the newly established high schools. These provided an ongoing social focus for former pupils, a space for them to pursue shared – and suitably 'feminine' – interests and continue some of the extracurricular activities of their school days. However, young middle-class women were also keen to maintain links to their school for other reasons. Sarah Richardson has pointed to the 'informal political networks' that radical dissenting schools offered middle-class pupils in the late eighteenth and early nineteenth centuries.[21] A similar phenomenon can be identified in girls' schools a century later. As an all-female space, the school could legitimize activities that were deemed inappropriate for women in other contexts. This included opportunities to discuss political issues, including women's suffrage. As early as 1888, for example, Old North Londoners addressed the question of women's political rights formally for the first time. Miss Balgarnie – referring, perhaps, to the suffragist Florence Balgarnie – spoke on the matter. Following a short discussion, attendees voted almost unanimously for headmistress Frances Mary Buss to sign a women's suffrage petition on behalf of the group.[22] In the same way that teachers agitated collectively for women's suffrage, associations of likeminded alumnae could make tangible contributions to the cause.

Suffragist teachers recognized the potential of old girls' associations for the women's movement. Educated women who had attended schools

[19] Parliamentary Archives, A Petition of the Mistresses of Dulwich High School, 3 Nov. 1884, HL/PO/6/11A. The signatures of two men associated with the school are also included.

[20] E. M. Hill, 'The chronicle: miscellaneous', *Our Magazine* (*OM*), xxix (Nov. 1904), p. 83.

[21] S. Richardson, *The Political Worlds of Women: Gender and Politics in Nineteenth Century Britain* (New York, 2013), p. 31.

[22] S. G. T., 'The old pupils' meeting', *OM*, xiii (Nov. 1888), pp. 120–1.

that celebrated women's civic duty were prime recruitment targets. Headmistresses sometimes made direct appeals to old girls. In 1900, the retiring headmistress of Notting Hill High School, Harriet Morant Jones, used her final speech to the old girls' association to promote women's suffrage and urge former pupils still seeking useful occupation to volunteer for the cause.[23] On other occasions, old girls took the initiative and raised the question of women's suffrage with their peers. For example, a group of Nottingham Girls' High School alumnae selected universal suffrage for women as a subject for a debate at their old girls' association, the Whetstone of Wit, in 1887.[24]

As the women's suffrage campaign grew, so did the scope of school-based suffrage activity. A meeting was held at Notting Hill High School in November 1910 'to promote discussion on the burning question of Woman Suffrage'.[25] With the permission of the headmistress, Agnes S. Paul, sixth-formers attended alongside teachers and old girls, suggesting that engaging the eldest and most intellectually mature pupils with the suffrage debate was acceptable to both staff and parents. Despite attempts to foster a balanced discussion, the organizers were unable to find a former pupil to speak against suffrage for a formal debate. Representatives from various women's suffrage societies even sold literature to those who remained undecided.[26] The school seemed comfortable publicizing its suffragist stance; the meeting was reported in some detail in the school magazine, reflecting a wider appetite in educational circles for news and information about the women's suffrage campaign.

School magazines for current and former pupils played a key role in publicizing teachers' and old girls' suffrage activities within school communities. For example, North London Collegiate School's *Our Magazine* regularly published details of Sophie Bryant's political work after she became headmistress in 1895. Despite occasional references to other teachers' political endeavours – like second mistress Sara Burstall's 1897 lecture series on 'Elementary Politics' given to the Oxford Women's Liberal Federation[27] – Bryant's contributions received the most attention in *Our Magazine*. Given her reputation for public political activity, this is

[23] 'Old girls' association', *The Notting Hill High School Magazine* (*NHHSM*), xvii (1901), p. 29.

[24] 'Analysis of debates', *Tenth Annual Report of the Whetstone of Wit Society* (Dec. 1887), pp. 36–7.

[25] 'A meeting to discuss woman suffrage', *NHHSM*, xxvii (1911), pp. 11–12.

[26] 'A meeting to discuss woman suffrage', p. 12.

[27] 'The chronicle: miscellaneous', *OM*, xxii (Nov. 1897), p. 106.

unsurprising.[28] Eleanor Hill (born Eleanor Margaret Childs in 1861), old girl, former teacher, school governor and long-serving editor of the school magazine between 1894 and 1923, shared short, factual updates on Bryant's political activities with its readership of staff and current and former pupils. We can assume that the attention given to women's suffrage in these updates owed much to Hill's own suffragist convictions; Hill was a member of the Hampstead Local Committee of the Central Society for Women's Suffrage, as *Our Magazine* noted in February 1907.[29] Between 1905 and 1909, readers could learn about Bryant signing women's suffrage petitions, being invited to speak at suffrage meetings, leading processions and serving as president of the local women's suffrage committee in Hampstead.[30] Similar reports continued in the following years, as the magazine turned its attention towards Bryant's longstanding support for Irish Home Rule.[31] Funded primarily through its subscribers, *Our Magazine* was an important mechanism for publicizing Bryant's political work to an audience with connections to the school. Although old girls made up the majority of subscriptions – nearly 60% in 1890 – repeated efforts were made to increase readership among girls at the school.[32] A reduced subscription rate for current girls was introduced in 1907 and the school's prospectus repeatedly advertised the publication.[33] Underlying these school magazine reports, then, was an implicit assertion that readers – including current and old girls – had the right to know about their headmistress's political activities. Perhaps it was hoped they would share Bryant's suffragist beliefs.

Like school magazines, old girls' association newsletters also provided opportunities for teachers and former pupils to promote the cause. At Nottingham Girls' High School, we can see this information sharing

[28] S. A. Burstall, *Retrospect and Prospect: Sixty Years of Women's Education* (London, 1933), pp. 129–30; N. Watson, *And Their Works do Follow Them: the Story of North London Collegiate School, 1850–2000* (London, 2000), p. 50.

[29] E. M. Hill, 'The chronicle: concerning old pupils', *OM*, xxxii (Feb. 1907), p. 19.

[30] E. M. Hill, 'The chronicle: the head mistress', *OM*, xxx (June 1905), p. 45; E. M. Hill, 'The chronicle: the head mistress', *OM*, xxxii (Feb. 1907), p. 14; E. M. Hill, 'The chronicle: the head mistress', *OM*, xxxiii (Nov. 1908), p. 90; E. M. Hill, 'The chronicle: the head mistress', *OM*, xxxiv (Feb. 1909), p. 13.

[31] E. M. Hill, 'School chronicle: the head mistress', *OM*, xxxvii (July 1912), p. 58; E. M. Hill, 'School chronicle: the head mistress', *OM*, xxxvii (Dec. 1912), p. 91; E. M. H., 'School chronicle: the head mistress', *OM*, xxxviii (Mar. 1913), p. 15.

[32] 'Editorial jottings', *OM*, xv (Mar. 1890), p. 3.

[33] E. M. Hill, 'The chronicle: "Our Magazine"', *OM*, xxxiii (Feb. 1908), p. 13; *Prospectus, North-London Collegiate and Camden Schools for Girls*, Jan. 1892, p. 5; *Prospectus for the Session 1906–7 of The North London Collegiate School*, p. 20.

process in action. One contributor to the March 1897 hand-made volume of the *Whetstone of Wit*, produced by Nottingham's old girls, presented an intellectual case for women's suffrage in a handwritten plea that ran to seven pages.[34] Following established practice, the volume was then circulated between association members, who offered feedback on the contributions. One reviewer especially welcomed the article on the suffrage question – 'one that ought to be taken up by W. W. Members'.[35] Over the years, associations became more explicit in their recruitment efforts. In 1909, the *Newsletter of the Blackburn High School Old Girls' Association* printed a lengthy article on 'Women and the suffrage' detailing the history and principles of the movement and seeking support for its constitutional side from readers. This included arguments that enfranchisement would bring material improvements to women's lives, like equal pay, and the contributions women could make to political life.[36] In 1911, the school's headmistress, Margaret Gardner, used her regular newsletter entry to implore her former pupils to be ready for full citizenship which would soon be given to women.[37]

As well as publicizing potential further education and employment options, old girls' networks exposed current schoolgirls and alumnae to ideas about women's suffrage. The small number of pupils who progressed to higher education kept in touch with their schools through 'college letters' – a regular feature of girls' school magazines in the late nineteenth and early twentieth centuries, where students wrote back about their experiences at university.[38] These students encountered a wealth of opportunities to engage with the suffrage debate and the university political scene featured strongly in their correspondence. Between 1890 and 1912, college letters referencing women's suffrage were published in the school magazines or old girls' association newsletters of Blackburn High School for Girls, Central Foundation Girls' School, North London Collegiate School, Notting Hill High School and Wimbledon High School.[39] These were sent

[34] Lady Jane, 'Women's suffrage', *Whetstone of Wit*, xi (1897), pp. 17–23.

[35] 'Criticisms', *Whetstone of Wit*, xi (1897), p. 84.

[36] K. E., 'Women and the suffrage', *Newsletter of the Blackburn High School Old Girls' Association* (*NBHSOGA*) (Nov. 1909), pp. 38–43.

[37] M. E. Gardner, 'From Miss Gardner', *NBHSOGA* (Nov. 1911), pp. 3–4.

[38] N. J. Humble, '"Ambassadors must represent the best": the Benenden School Magazine, 1927–87', *Journal of Educational Administration and History*, xxi (1989), 17–27, at p. 25; Dyhouse, *Girl Trouble*, p. 49.

[39] E.g., H. Sharles (sic), 'Reminiscences of a year at Newnham', *NBHSOGA* (Nov. 1912), pp. 31–4; L. Powell, 'An Aberystwyth letter', *Central Foundation Girls' School Magazine*

from former pupils at a range of higher education institutions, including women's colleges at Oxford and Cambridge, Royal Holloway and Bedford Colleges, the University College of Wales, Aberystwyth and London School of Medicine. Correspondents described women's suffrage debates, suffrage societies and fundraising. Through their letters, alumnae celebrated the political activities available to them at university and encouraged teacher, old girl and schoolgirl readers to follow their suffrage work with interest.

Girls' school magazines acted as communication channels for the suffrage movement in other ways. They gave regular updates on former pupils, including changes of address, employment, educational achievements, marriages and the births of children. Occasionally, magazines recorded old girls' work for the suffrage movement. Between 1906 and 1914, Manchester High School for Girls, Notting Hill High School and North London Collegiate School each referenced former pupils' involvement with constitutional women's suffrage societies.[40] The proliferation of examples from the latter in part reflected the editor's own suffragist views, as discussed earlier. Old girls took on roles such as secretary, chairman and treasurer of local branches of the National Union of Women's Suffrage Societies (NUWSS), the Church League for Women's Suffrage and various university suffrage societies. Although a large number of alumnae went into teaching, the lack of references to membership of the Women Teachers' Franchise Union, founded in 1912, can be explained by the relatively small proportion who chose to work in elementary schools, where – in a mixed-gender setting – issues of professional equality like equal pay were more pressing. Nevertheless, the references to suffrage society membership that

(*CFGSM*) (1901), pp. 23–4; An Old North Londoner, 'College letters: Bedford College', *OM*, xix (Mar. 1894), p. 31; 'Girton College, Cambridge', *NHHSM*, vi (1890), p. 15; G. M. Macaskie, 'College letters: the London School of Medicine', *NHHSM*, xxii (1906), p. 8; M. Williams, 'College letters: Royal Holloway College', *NHHSM*, xxiii (1907), pp. 8–9; D. Sulman, 'College letters: Somerville College, Oxford', *NHHSM*, xxvi (1910), pp. 6–7; D. Apperson, M. E. Holland, H. Townsend and E. M. Woodhouse, 'Newnham letter', *The Wimbledon High School Magazine* (*WHSM*), xxii (1911), pp. 8–9.

40 'News of old girls', *The Magazine of the Manchester High School*, xiv (June 1912), p. 21; 'List of members of old girls' association in 1905', *NHHSM*, xxii (1906), p. 30; E. M. Hill, 'The chronicle: concerning old pupils', *OM*, xxxiv (Feb. 1909), p. 19; E. M. Hill, 'The chronicle: concerning old pupils', *OM*, xxxiv (July 1909), p. 68; E. M. Hill, 'The chronicle: concerning old pupils', *OM*, xxxiv (Nov. 1909), p. 106; E. M. Hill, 'The chronicle: concerning old pupils', *OM*, xxxv (Dec. 1910), p. 120; E. M. Hill, 'The chronicle: concerning old pupils', *OM*, xxxvi (Mar. 1911), p. 16; E. M. Hill, 'The chronicle: concerning old pupils', *OM*, xxxvi (July 1911), pp. 64–5; E. M. Hill, 'Concerning old pupils', *OM*, xxxviii (Mar. 1913), pp. 9, 11; E. M. Hill, 'Concerning old pupils', *OM*, xxxviii (July 1913), pp. 45, 49; E. M. Hill, 'Concerning old pupils', *OM*, xxxviii (Dec. 1913), p. 85; E. M. Hill, 'Concerning old pupils', *OM*, xxxix (Apr. 1914), p. 8.

can be identified demonstrate that school magazines had the potential to play an important role facilitating contact between women active in the movement. They offered a valuable communication tool for maintaining links across the suffragist community and enabling others to get involved.

School magazines sometimes gave lengthy accounts of old girls' campaigning for the parliamentary vote. These glamorized suffrage work, presenting it as an exciting part of independent, adult life that was attainable for other alumnae and would be for current pupils in the future. The Blackburn High School old girls' association was keen to publicize its members' suffragist work, like Leila Williamson's comic account of her fact-finding mission for a local suffrage organization in 1909.[41] North London Collegiate School had plenty of examples to draw on. In 1913, readers of *Our Magazine* were informed that old girl and artist Jessie Mothersole had written a poem for the suffrage-themed supplement to the *Labour Leader*.[42] Later that year, the magazine reported Gladys Misick's key organizational role in the Women's Suffrage Pilgrimage, marching with a group from Cornwall and Devon.[43] However, it was Margaret Robertson who dominated *Our Magazine* reports of Old North Londoners' suffrage campaigning. From 1908, when she gave up teaching to devote her energies to organizational work for the NUWSS, readers could follow her involvement with the movement in detail. In doing so, she joined a wider group of teachers turned full-time suffrage activists that has more typically been associated with militancy.[44] Robertson worked as a by-election organizer and later as head of the Election Fighting Fund. She sold suffrage literature, wrote articles and pamphlets, gave speeches and spoke in numerous debates.[45] The school magazine acknowledged that it was hard to keep track of all her work for the cause: 'It is impossible, owing to the variety and extent of *Miss Margaret Robertson's* activities, merely to mention half of what she does for the cause of Woman Suffrage'.[46] In

[41] L. Williamson, 'The individual file', *NBHSOGA* (Nov. 1909), pp. 22–5.

[42] E. M. Hill, 'Concerning old pupils', *OM*, xxxviii (Mar. 1913), p. 9.

[43] E. M. Hill, 'Concerning old pupils', *OM*, xxxviii (July 1913), p. 49.

[44] K. Cowman, *Women of the Right Spirit: Paid Organisers of the Women's Social and Political Union (WSPU), 1904–18* (Manchester, 2007), pp. 14–16.

[45] E. M. Hill, 'The chronicle: concerning old pupils', *OM*, xxxiii (June 1908), p. 59; E. M. Hill, 'The chronicle: concerning old pupils', *OM*, xxxiv (Nov. 1909), p. 106; E. M. Hill, 'The chronicle: concerning old pupils', *OM*, xxxvi (Mar. 1911), p. 16; E. M. Hill, 'Concerning old pupils', *OM*, xxxvii (July 1912), p. 53; E. M. Hill, 'Concerning old pupils', *OM*, xxxvii (Dec. 1912), p. 82; E. M. Hill, 'Concerning old pupils', *OM*, xxxviii (Mar. 1913), p. 9; E. M. Hill, 'Concerning old pupils', *OM*, xxxviii (Dec. 1913), p. 85.

[46] E. M. Hill, 'Concerning old pupils', *OM*, xxxvii (July 1912), p. 53.

these articles, *Our Magazine* celebrated the outstanding contributions of individual alumnae. Old girls like Robertson were depicted as role models for others to emulate and their example was mobilized to inspire others to action.

The school also celebrated the involvement of teachers, governors and old girls in women's suffrage processions. Here the narrative shifted from individual effort to collective strength; it was the scale of North London Collegiate School's participation that was most important. In 1908 and 1911, *Our Magazine* articles listed the names of marchers associated with the school – sixty-two at the first and thirty-five at the second.[47] The numbers were not designed to surprise readers but to normalize active involvement in the suffrage campaign. Indeed, in the 1911 article, forty-nine-year-old editor Eleanor Hill wrote, '[a]mong the 40,000 women who walked in the great suffrage procession of June 17th, there were naturally many representatives of the N.L.C.S.G.'.[48] Joining mass demonstrations and marching in demand of the parliamentary franchise was presented as a *natural* response – both characteristic and fitting – for Old North Londoners to the suffrage question.

Although some teachers and old girls were involved in the militant campaign, most girls' school magazines only recorded constitutional suffrage activities.[49] Of course, divisions between militant and constitutional suffragism were complex; definitions of militancy were fluid and individuals could be members of multiple organizations simultaneously.[50] However, teachers were keen to maintain this division as far as possible, as it allowed them to emphasize schools' interactions with the more palatable, constitutional side of the movement. Reflecting her own allegiance to constitutional suffragism, Eleanor Hill, editor of *Our Magazine*, was keen to remind readers when mentioning former pupils' work with the NUWSS that the organization

[47] E. M. Hill, 'The chronicle: concerning old pupils', *OM*, xxxiii (Nov. 1908), pp. 97–8; E. M. Hill, 'The chronicle: concerning old pupils', *OM*, xxxvi (July 1911), p. 64.

[48] 'The chronicle: concerning old pupils', *OM*, xxxvi (July 1911), p. 64.

[49] For teachers' suffrage militancy see Oram, 'Women teachers', p. 208; J. Purvis, '"Deeds, not words": daily life in the Women's Social and Political Union in Edwardian Britain', in *Votes for Women*, ed. J. Purvis and S. Stanley Holton (London and New York, 2000), pp. 135–58, at pp. 140–1; Cowman, *Women of the Right Spirit*, p. 155.

[50] S. Stanley Holton, *Feminism and Democracy: Women's Suffrage and Reform Politics in Britain, 1900–1918* (Cambridge, 1986), pp. 29–52; K. Cowman, '"Crossing the great divide": inter-organizational suffrage relationships on Merseyside, 1895–1914', in *A Suffrage Reader: Charting Directions in British Suffrage History*, ed. C. Eustance, J. Ryan and L. Ugolini (London and New York, 2000), pp. 37–52.

was non-militant.[51] On the few occasions that Hill acknowledged old girls' involvement with militant suffrage, the activities mentioned remained firmly within the bounds of the law. Participation in militant suffrage organizations was reframed in constitutional terms. For example, Dorothy Evans led a contingent of 400 Women's Social and Political Union (WSPU) members from Birmingham in the 1911 Coronation Procession, Amy Hicks and Edith How Martyn wrote articles for the official organ of the Women's Freedom League (WFL) and How Martyn participated in a deputation of representatives from various suffrage organizations to the Prime Minister.[52] References to their militant activity, including arrests, imprisonment and hunger strikes by Evans and Hicks, were avoided.

Across all the schools in this chapter, constitutional suffragism was by far the favoured approach; indeed, for most it was the only legitimate tactic. Although details of former pupil and suffragette Myra Sadd Brown's activism were published by North London Collegiate School's magazine in her obituary in 1938, at the time the magazine remained silent on her militancy in the WSPU, WFL and Tax Resistance League, including her arrest, imprisonment and hunger strike in 1912.[53] In her 1911 history of Manchester High School for Girls, headmistress Sara Burstall could present a more balanced view. She listed three old girls – Alice Cooke, Alice Crompton and Mary Tout – with positions of responsibility in the North of England Society for Women's Suffrage and Scottish Federation of Women's Suffrage Societies. However, she also acknowledged the work of Christabel and Adela Pankhurst for the WSPU, who along with their sister Sylvia had studied at the school from 1893.[54]

Equally, there are far fewer recorded instances in school magazines of old girls engaging in anti-suffrage activities. Only two references have been found to former pupils working actively on the anti-suffrage side of the debate, both from Notting Hill High School, which still had difficulties recruiting anti-suffragist speakers for its 1910 meeting, as highlighted earlier. Jeanie Ross, who left the school around 1892, was recorded in the school magazine as the honorary treasurer of the Kensington branch of the Women's National

[51] E. M. Hill, 'Concerning old pupils', *OM*, xxxvii (July 1912), p. 52; E. M. Hill, 'Concerning old pupils', *OM*, xxxviii (Dec. 1913), p. 85.

[52] E. M. Hill, 'The chronicle: concerning old pupils', *OM*, xxxvi (July 1911), p. 65; E. M. Hill, 'The chronicle: concerning old pupils', *OM*, xxxv (July 1910), p. 74; E. M. Hill, 'The chronicle: concerning old pupils', *OM*, xxxvi (Dec. 1911), p. 96.

[53] E. M. Hill, 'Concerning old pupils', *N.L.C.S. Magazine*, lx (July 1938), pp. 496–7.

[54] S. A. Burstall, *The Story of the Manchester High School for Girls, 1871–1911* (Manchester, 1911), appendix ii, pp. 199–201.

Anti-Suffrage League in 1910.[55] Three years later, Henrietta Stevenson, who first appeared in the old girls' association membership list in 1886, was noted as vice-president of the Kensington Anti-Suffrage Society.[56] These examples suggest that anti-suffragism attracted an older generation of alumnae. Bush has demonstrated the considerable scale of women's involvement in the anti-suffrage movement, so it is unlikely that these women's experiences were unique. As she observed, anti-suffrage women were less inclined to publicize their position.[57] They might be particularly reluctant to do so in publications that lauded suffragist alumnae. As with old girls' suffrage militancy, editorial views probably clouded the picture school magazines gave of old girls' contributions to the anti-suffrage cause.

While many women teachers were keen advocates of women's suffrage, carving a path of acceptable public activism required careful negotiation of professional duty and political principle. For example, Sara Burstall, headmistress of Manchester High School for Girls from 1898, described herself in her autobiography as an avowed suffragist, but 'had never felt able to do anything of a public character'.[58] The headmistress of a leading middle-class girls' school, she explained, 'could not in honour set an example of breaking the law'.[59] Aware of the risk of reputational damage, Burstall had to choose the nature of her involvement wisely. She recalled with pride that it was at its 1908 meeting hosted at her school that the Headmistresses' Conference passed a resolution in support of women's suffrage, leading to a petition to the Prime Minister.[60] Teachers' associations provided opportunities for collective action; individual protest was more problematic. Burstall took part in the 1913 suffrage pilgrimage between Manchester and Stockport but felt unable to join the income tax boycott.[61] Although many of the women who refused to pay tax were, like Burstall, educated and financially independent career women, for a headmistress responsible for maintaining an institution's reputation, this proved a step too far.[62] Women teachers' suffrage activism was shaped by their specific

[55] 'List of members of old girls' association in 1909', *NHHSM*, xxvi (1910), p. 30.

[56] 'List of members of old girls' association in 1912', *NHHSM*, xxix (1913), p. 27.

[57] Bush, *Women Against the Vote*, pp. 2–3.

[58] Burstall, *Retrospect and Prospect*, p. 203.

[59] Burstall, *Retrospect and Prospect*, p. 204.

[60] Burstall, *Retrospect and Prospect*, pp. 204–5.

[61] Burstall, *Retrospect and Prospect*, pp. 203–5.

[62] H. Frances, '"Pay the piper, call the tune!": the Women's Tax Resistance League', in *The Women's Suffrage Movement: New Feminist Perspectives*, ed. M. Joannou and J. Purvis (Manchester, 1998), pp. 65–76, at p. 74.

personal and school contexts; what was possible for some, perhaps those more junior or with less of a public profile than Burstall, remained beyond others' reach.

It was even more controversial for women teachers to encourage current schoolgirls to engage with the suffrage campaign. Suffragist teachers were mindful that they had to tread carefully, but this did not necessarily mean concealing their views entirely – at least among older pupils. Vera Brittain appreciated the encouragement of her 'ardent though always discreet feminist' teacher, Miss Heath Jones, who introduced her to books on the women's movement and even accompanied her and other senior girls to a constitutional suffrage meeting.[63] As the experience of sixteen-year-old Mary Brinton (later Baroness Stocks) suggests, teachers were more willing to show their suffragist views to a sympathetic audience. Brinton won the tacit approval of her teachers at St Paul's Girls' School after taking part in the 1907 Mud March with relatives. Although unsure how her teachers would react to this 'public exploit', she later noted in her autobiography: 'I need not have worried. All the mistresses were suffragists'.[64] Brinton was from an unusually politically active household, with relatives dividing their allegiance between the WSPU and NUWSS. Suffragist teachers could be more open about their political opinions around adolescent schoolgirls when a supportive family was concerned.

However, in most institutions, teachers who instigated pupils' active involvement with the movement crossed a line – or were, at least, perceived to do so by a critical and hostile press. Accusations of pro-suffrage bias in schools surfaced multiple times in the Edwardian press. Sutherland and Oram observed that women teachers were widely perceived to support women's suffrage in this period.[65] As Bush explained, this sparked numerous controversies over the influence feminist teachers were feared to have on schoolgirls.[66] With the women's suffrage movement gaining ground, the press latched onto allegations about women teachers supposedly exploiting their position to recruit for the cause. In June 1907, for example, *The London Teacher and London Schools Review* reported a case where an assistant mistress distributed 'Votes for Women' leaflets outside the school gates.[67] Three years

[63] V. Brittain, *Testament of Youth: an Autobiographical Study of the Years 1900–1925* (London, 1933), pp. 38–9.

[64] M. D. Stocks, *My Commonplace Book* (London, 1970), pp. 72–4.

[65] Sutherland, *In Search of the New Woman*, p. 128; Oram, 'Women teachers', p. 208.

[66] Bush, *Women Against the Vote*, pp. 232, 236–7.

[67] 'Specially for mistresses: conduct', *The London Teacher and London Schools Review*, xxiv (June 1907), p. 146.

later, an article in the *Girl's Own Paper and Woman's Magazine* criticized cases of teachers allegedly bringing politics into the classroom, including a mathematics mistress at a large secondary school in South London who, as 'an ardent worker for Women's Suffrage', devoted part of her lessons to the 'controversial' subject.[68]

Despite the sensationalized reporting of such scandals, they were probably isolated examples. Certainly, some elementary teachers were warned by local education authorities that their militant suffragism would incur serious consequences for their professional futures.[69] Indeed, the leading Irish suffragist Hanna Sheehy Skeffington was fired from her teaching post in 1912 because of her militant activity.[70] But teachers' politics did not always translate straightforwardly to the classroom. Spencer highlighted one example where the headmistress of Sutton High School, herself a local councillor, discouraged the old girls' society from promoting candidates in a local election.[71] Educational periodicals were also keen to reiterate the need for political neutrality within the classroom and it appears that many teachers took this seriously. *The Schoolmaster* aimed to reassure its readers in January 1912 by reprinting a testimony from suffragist Lady Chance, which first appeared in the *Standard*. Chance was an NUWSS member who lived near a large girls' school, where, she claimed, though the staff are 'strong Suffragists', 'no such thing as propaganda work is allowed in the school'.[72] *The Teacher's World* concurred in December 1913 when it suggested that the press's accusations of teachers 'preaching Woman Suffrage doctrines among the girls' were probably unfounded.[73] As Dyhouse observed, though many women teachers were feminists, most were careful to keep their views away from the attention of the education authorities.[74] The press outcry that was triggered by moments when these opinions entered the classroom – whether inadvertently or intentionally – shows how the charged issue of women's

[68] 'Some pitfalls of the modern teacher', *Girl's Own Paper and Woman's Magazine*, xxxi (Mar. 1910), pp. 359–60.

[69] This was the message given to two assistant mistresses arrested and imprisoned at a suffrage demonstration outside the House of Commons in 1907. 'Specially for mistresses: teacher suffragettes', *The London Teacher and London Schools Review*, xxiv (June 1907), p. 146.

[70] L. Levenson and J. H. Natterstad, *Hanna Sheehy-Skeffington: Irish Feminist* (Syracuse, N.Y., 1986), pp. 42–3.

[71] Spencer, 'Advice and ambition', pp. 81–2.

[72] 'The women's world', *The Schoolmaster*, lxxxi (6 Jan. 1912), p. 21.

[73] 'The week's causerie: suffrage propaganda', *The Teacher's World*, x (17 Dec. 1913), p. 280.

[74] Dyhouse, *Girl Trouble*, pp. 62–3.

suffrage crystallized around another contentious subject: the relative authority of teachers and parents in a new educational domain.

This did not mean that women's suffrage was absent from schoolgirls' educational experiences. While overt attempts to proselytize for the cause in the classroom were vilified, teachers used subtle strategies to introduce schoolgirls to the suffrage question, offering them constructive ways to engage in suffrage politics through debating societies in middle-class secondary schools and suffrage plays in elementary schools. These extra-curricular activities enabled teachers to familiarize their pupils with the intellectual arguments and satirical tropes surrounding the suffrage debate, as well as channel their own opinions on the subject.

From the 1880s, school debating societies gave middle-class adolescent girls a unique forum to engage with politics. Here, schoolgirls debated a wide range of supposedly 'masculine' political issues, from fiscal policy to constitutional reform, foreign affairs and the British Empire.[75] Women's suffrage was another popular topic. Schoolgirls debated women's suffrage thirteen times across six schools between 1900 and 1912, with most discussions taking place between 1904 and 1909.[76] Schoolgirls' debates on women's suffrage were concentrated in the mid-Edwardian years, as support for the constitutional suffrage movement gathered pace but before the campaign of militant violence began. This increase in suffrage debates in the early twentieth century reflected both schoolgirls' growing interest in the subject and teachers' encouragement. Teachers were able to lend their support for girls' intellectual engagement with women's suffrage as the formal, controlled setting of a debate gave opportunities for both sides of the issue to be aired.

[75] For a more detailed discussion of schoolgirl debating, see H. Sunderland, 'Politics in schoolgirl debating cultures in England, 1886–1914', *The Historical Journal*, lxiii (2020), 935–57.

[76] *North London Collegiate School Debating Society Minutes Book, 1900–1909* (Midsummer term 1900); H. Macdonald, 'Report of debating society', *WHSM*, xvi (1905), pp. 25–6; D. Fish, 'The debating club', *Nottingham Girls' High School Magazine* (*NGHSM*), xii (1905), p. 19; M. Bailhache, 'Debating society', *OM*, xxxi (Feb. 1906), pp. 30–1; D. Chick, 'The debating society', *NHHSM*, xxii (1906), p. 33; E. J. G. Kirkwood, 'The literary and debating society', *The Magazine of the City of London School for Girls* (*MCLSG*), xi (Mar. 1907), pp. 4–5; W. Todd, 'Form notes: form IVB', *CFGSM*, i (Apr. 1907), p. 277; N. Hearn, 'Debating society', *NHHSM*, xxiv (1908), p. 31; M. E. Lewis, 'The debate club', *WHSM*, xix (1908), p. 41; C. Birnberg, 'Form notes: form VB', *CFGSM*, i (July 1908), pp. 373–4; M. Parsley, 'Debating society', *OM*, xxxiv (Nov. 1909), pp. 120–2; R. C. Allen, 'Form notices: VB', *MCLSG*, xv (Mar. 1911), p. 6; H. M. Browning, 'The debating society', *NGHSM*, xx (1913), p. 26.

It only became acceptable for schoolgirls to debate women's suffrage once it was well established within mainstream political debate. The debating society at Notting Hill High School was the first to address women's suffrage explicitly, in 1892.[77] However, middle-class schoolboys held similar debates much earlier. In 1875, debaters at Manchester Grammar School rejected a motion for increasing women's political rights by a large majority.[78] By contrast, two years later, sixth-formers at City of London School voted narrowly to extend electoral rights to women.[79] Debating was more prolific in boys' schools, where a well-established public school debating culture trained schoolboy orators first for the debating chambers of the Oxford and Cambridge Unions, and ultimately Parliament.[80] Women's suffrage was arguably more contentious for schoolgirls to tackle because it represented a direct challenge to the political status quo. Debate organizers in girls' schools had to approach the subject more cautiously than their counterparts in boys' schools.

Surviving reports of debates published in school magazines allow us to reconstruct the content of some discussions. Schoolgirls' arguments for and against giving women the vote varied but followed the key themes of the national campaign. Adolescent girls were familiar with suffragist and anti-suffragist discourse and added their voices to the wider debate. Like their adult counterparts, schoolgirl supporters of women's suffrage preferred logical arguments to sentimental appeal.[81] They referred to 'no taxation without representation', the precedent already set by local government at home and women's enfranchisement overseas and women's moral right to vote. Suffragist debaters at Central Foundation Girls' School also insisted that 'women *should not* be classed with paupers and lunatics'.[82] Conversely, opponents emphasized the fundamental differences between the sexes and the damage enfranchisement would inflict on women's moral standing and domestic duties. Others argued that women were already amply represented in local government and recompensed as taxpayers by public services. Disapproval of the militant suffrage campaign featured prominently.

[77] 'Notting Hill High School debating society', *NHHSM*, ix (1893), p. 40.

[78] Manchester Grammar School Archives, 'The union', *Ulula*, xiv (1875), pp. 201–2.

[79] London Metropolitan Archives, City of London, S. L. Lee, 'Sixth form discussion society', *The City of London School Magazine*, i (Oct. 1877), pp. 256–7, CLA/053/03/01/001.

[80] J. S. Meisel, *Public Speech and the Culture of Public Life in the Age of Gladstone* (New York, 2002), pp. 11–49.

[81] J. E. Lewis, 'Introduction', in *Before the Vote was Won: Arguments For and Against Women's Suffrage*, ed. J. E. Lewis (New York and London, 1987), pp. 1–10, at p. 4.

[82] Birnberg, 'Form notes: form VB', p. 374.

Sometimes debates focused solely on this issue. In December 1910, fifth-formers at the City of London School for Girls agreed 'That the methods of the militant party of the Women's Suffrage movement should be censured'. In her brief report to the school magazine, form member Ruby Allen suggested that the outcome was inevitable: 'Of course, the meeting was in favour of the last motion, which was discussed with great excitement.'[83]

Women's suffrage proved popular debating material and girls embraced the subject enthusiastically, as some debating society reports commented.[84] At North London Collegiate School, women's suffrage debates drew a large audience. Fifty-one people voted in the November 1905 discussion and 126 in July 1909.[85] On this second occasion, the presence of the pioneering women's educational reformer and constitutional suffragist Emily Davies as a guest speaker no doubt prompted the unusually high turnout. Her attendance points to the school's exceptionalism and the prominent position of its teachers within the women's movement. However, reflecting her broader pedagogical views on the value of political education, it is important that headmistress Sophie Bryant used these connections to enable pupils to hear from prominent suffragists, in a similar way to their teachers who, as previously highlighted, had met Davies at a staff meeting five years earlier.[86]

It was sometimes assumed that schoolgirls' debating and suffragism went hand in hand. Some teachers connected girls' debating skills with their aptitude and motivation for suffrage work. In her autobiography, Sara Burstall recalled her involvement in a short-lived debating society as a sixth-former at North London Collegiate School in the late 1870s. Debating at school, she noted, 'has trained women speakers from that day to this, some of whom did fine work for the suffrage movement'.[87] School debating was seen as valuable preparation for future work for the campaign.

However, it should not be presumed that secondary schoolgirls were predisposed to support women's suffrage, despite their educational privilege. Whereas anti-suffrage sentiment among old girls and teachers is difficult to identify in the sources, schoolgirl debaters voiced their opposition more openly. Sarah Wiggins has eloquently argued that women university students

[83] Allen, 'Form notices: VB', p. 6.

[84] 'Notting Hill High School debating society', p. 40; Lewis, 'The debate club', p. 41.

[85] Bailhache, 'Debating society', pp. 30–1; Parsley, 'Debating society', p. 122.

[86] For an overview of Bryant's thoughts on political education, see S. Bryant, *Moral and Religious Education* (London, 1920), pp. 91–100.

[87] Burstall, *Retrospect and Prospect*, p. 57.

used debating to develop and display a 'collegiate political identity'.[88] This was not unique to the higher education context. A similar process took place among schoolgirls, who used debates about women's suffrage to construct a collective political viewpoint, on either side of the suffrage question. In 1907, Winifred Todd described the anti-suffrage sentiment of her fourth-form classmates following the defeat of a women's suffrage motion. 'The majority was against it', she wrote, 'which shows that the "Suffragettes" cannot be well represented in our Form.'[89] Of course, Todd's allusion to suffragettes overlooked the diversity of the suffrage movement. More importantly, though, it suggested that the school would be an inappropriate venue for schoolgirls to display militant suffrage sympathies. The report of the North London Collegiate School suffrage debate in November 1905 is particularly revealing on this question of collective political opinion. Following the narrow defeat of a motion to introduce women's suffrage, by twenty-seven votes to twenty-four, the society's schoolgirl secretary appeared particularly keen to explain the outcome. Betraying her own suffragist sympathies, she credited 'the persuasive force of a flow of brilliant, though illogical eloquence, from the pen of the opposer'.[90] As the results show, debaters held diverse views on the matter. However, the secretary's uncharacteristically detailed reasoning for the defeat suggests she expected North Londoners to support women's suffrage.

How should we interpret schoolgirl debates that rejected the cause? Of the girls' schools in this chapter, Central Foundation had by far the most well-developed 'civics' curriculum, the subject which taught pupils how Britain was governed. The school's course was publicized as a model of best practice for other institutions to emulate in *Public Schools for Girls* (1911).[91] However, two debates on women's suffrage at the school in 1907 and 1908 resulted in anti-suffragist victories.[92] As the outcomes of these debates suggest, schoolgirls did not necessarily connect their own political education with the broader question of women's right to vote. There are a few caveats here. It is impossible to know whether debaters' arguments accurately reflected their personal opinions. Voters might have

[88] S. Wiggins, 'Gendered spaces and political identity: debating societies in English women's colleges, 1890–1914', *Women's History Review*, xviii (2009), 737–52.

[89] Todd, 'Form notes: form IVB', p. 277.

[90] Bailhache, 'Debating society', p. 31.

[91] E. H. Major, 'History', in *Public Schools for Girls: A Series of Papers on their History, Aims, and Schemes of Study by Members of the Association of Head Mistresses*, ed. S. A. Burstall and M. A. Douglas (London, 1911), pp. 85–96, at p. 93.

[92] Todd, 'Form notes: form IVB', p. 277; Birnberg, 'Form notes: form VB', pp. 373–4.

been motivated by genuine conviction or voted for the best speakers or simply to support their friends. But these examples are an important reminder that schoolgirls' political activity may not be as subversive as it seems. The irony was not lost on sixteen-year-old Daisy Adina Green, who wrote a report on the fifth forms' joint 1908 women's suffrage debate for the school magazine. She noted wryly that, although the motion was narrowly defeated, 'most people seemed disposed to use their vote if they had one'.[93]

Middle-class girls were not the only targets of teachers' efforts to politicize school experience. In elementary schools, teachers could encourage their working-class pupils to engage with women's suffrage through dramatic performance, as educational periodicals advised them on how to co-opt the suffrage play genre into school entertainments.[94] Dramatic performances are an important example of how education operates on and through children's bodies, contributing to a growing scholarship on embodied educational experiences.[95] They also evidence how pupils interacted with suffrage humour. In 1885, for example, the educational journal *The Teachers' Aid* published a script for a debate on women's social and political rights in its regular feature on school entertainments.[96] Although originally scripted for fourteen *children*, the objectification and othering of women in the debate's content suggests that it was designed for male speakers. A later article summarizing various entertainment debates confirmed that it was intended for a *schoolboy* cast.[97] This was characteristic of the periodical's political entertainment debates that prioritized male over female voices. However, in this case, it perpetuated the view among an elementary school audience that women's political rights should be discussed and determined by men. The debate considered arguments on both sides and, somewhat surprisingly, concluded in favour of the suffragists. The claim that the debate would 'bring down the house' does, though, cast doubt on whether this outcome was meant to be taken seriously.[98]

93 D. A. Green, 'Form notes: form VA', *CFGSM*, i (July 1908), p. 374.

94 On suffrage theatre, see K. Cockin, 'Women's suffrage drama', in *The Women's Suffrage Movement: New Feminist Perspectives*, ed. M. Joannou and J. Purvis (Manchester, 1998), pp. 127–39; N. Paxton, *Stage Rights! The Actresses' Franchise League, Activism and Politics 1908–58* (Manchester, 2018).

95 M. Gleason, 'Metaphor, materiality, and method: the central role of embodiment in the history of education', *Paedagogica Historica*, liv (2018), 4–19.

96 'Debate for children's entertainment', *The Teachers' Aid*, i (19 Dec. 1885), pp. 279–80.

97 'School entertainments', *The Teachers' Aid*, xxi (30 Nov. 1895), p. 193.

98 'School entertainments', p. 193.

By 1909, the focus of the journal's suffrage-themed entertainments had turned to the militant campaign. In the following examples, schoolgirls embodied a recurring trope in anti-suffrage imagery of children dressed as militants.[99] In one dialogue, a schoolgirl dressed as a suffragette was midway to a local 'suffragette lecture' when a schoolboy soldier – embodying the threat of enlistment that could come with the vote – helped her see the error of her ways.[100] Another article that year gave instructions for a school performance of a song entitled 'The Suffragettes'.[101] This drew on a more sinister theme in anti-suffrage propaganda: violent and sexualized encounters between suffragettes and policemen.[102] Ten infant schoolgirls, each wearing a large letter spelling out 'Christabel', would march across the stage, carrying banners of white, green and purple, and shouting 'Votes for Women'. When a policeman appeared mid-performance, one 'suffragette' would wave a 'dog-whip' in self-defence. A choreographed 'scuffle' with the policeman would then ensue, with the skit finishing with 'the Law … triumphant'.[103] It is particularly shocking that dark humour that hinted at the often sexual violence inflicted by policemen on suffragettes was brought into the school. Nor can it be explained away by the young age – and sexual innocence – of the schoolgirl performers. The script was deemed 'suitable for infants' but, if 'elaborated would form a capital item for older children'. Provided that the suffragette cause remained the target of the joke, even the most sinister aspects of suffragette satire were fair game in school entertainments.

The Teachers' Aid was written primarily for elementary school teachers. It is unclear how many teachers took up these performance suggestions, but the longevity of entertainment articles in the magazine indicates a perceived demand. Articles on suffrage performances encouraged preadolescent, working-class girls to briefly become 'suffragettes' for entertainment. Militant suffragism was only allowed into schools in its least threatening form, as an object of derision. However, these spectacles relied on a careful balancing act. The gulf between childhood innocence and suffragette violence was what made the sketches entertaining, but this could never entirely allay fears that, through embodying suffragettes, young

[99] L. Tickner, *The Spectacle of Women: Imagery of the Suffrage Campaign, 1907–14* (London, 1987), p. 34.

[100] 'Dialogue: votes for women', *The Teachers' Aid*, xlviii (10 Apr. 1909), p. 41.

[101] 'Entertainment item: the suffragettes', *The Teachers' Aid*, xlvii (13 Mar. 1909), p. 570.

[102] Tickner, *Spectacle of Women*, p. 201.

[103] 'Entertainment item: the suffragettes', p. 570.

and supposedly impressionable working-class girls might sympathize with their cause.

Schoolgirls' experiences of women's suffrage were not limited to formal, teacher-sanctioned activities like debating and school plays. Instead, girls engaged with the subject on their own terms. It was the militant side of the movement that captured their interest. Although, as discussed earlier, it was believed inappropriate for teachers to do so, a handful of schoolgirls expressed their militancy in the classroom. The experience of Winifred Starbuck and her private school classmates who, shortly before the First World War, decorated their classroom with WSPU colours and photographs of the Pankhursts, with the tacit approval of their militant suffragist teachers, was exceptional. After the headmistress and four other teachers were dismissed because of their militancy, the school descended into rebellion, with several girls deploying militant tactics against school property.[104] It was exceedingly rare for schoolgirls to adopt militant violence, but they could engage with militant suffragism at school in other ways. With comic poems and fancy dress, girls brought the concept of militancy into school. Beyond the debating platform and appropriating some of the tropes of elementary school suffrage plays, it was the suffragettes who appealed most to schoolgirls, as objects of curiosity, admiration and often ridicule.

It is well known that the suffragettes were targets of Edwardian humour. As Krista Cowman has observed, 'satirizing the suffragette' was widespread in both print and popular culture.[105] Schoolgirls contributed to this corpus of suffragette humour with their own jokes about the militant movement. Schoolgirls invoked suffragette humour in their literary efforts, as two poems published in the school magazines of North London Collegiate and Wimbledon High Schools in 1908 demonstrate. In February, fifteen-year-old North Londoner Dorothy Harbottle had her poem – 'A Suffragette to the Cabinet Ministers' – published in *Our Magazine*.

[104] Winifred Starbuck was interviewed for BBC *Woman's Hour* on 6 Jan. 1958. 'A Term of Disorder: a schoolgirl's view of the suffragette campaign, from Winifred Starbuck', *Woman's Hour* [radio programme, online] Pres. Marjorie Anderson. BBC, UK, 14.00, 06/01/1958, BBC Radio 4. 6.02mins <https://www.bbc.co.uk/archive/womans-hour--a-term-of-disorder/zvjxkmn> [accessed 28 May 2020]. See also Dyhouse, *Girl Trouble*, pp. 63–4.

[105] K. Cowman, '"Doing something silly": the uses of humour by the Women's Social and Political Union, 1903–1914', *International Review of Social History*, lii (2007), 259–74, at pp. 261–6.

THEY call me a suffragette,
And I know the reason why,
Tho' we've not got votes as yet,
We're determined still to try.

Though deaf Mr. Birrell may be,
And others as utterly blind,
In time you'll *have* to see
We *never* change our mind.

We stick through thick and thin
To railing, knocker and bell,
And if you won't hear us within,
To you from the street we'll yell.

That unless you vote for our cause,
Innumerable will be the fights,
Like limpets we'll cling to your doors,
For we *will* have Women's Rights.[106]

Portraying the desperation of the suffragettes in a comic way, the poem appears to undermine the seriousness of the militant movement. Admittedly, a more positive portrayal of militant suffragism would hardly have been appropriate for publication in the school magazine. Nevertheless, Harbottle focused her criticism on the methods rather than the principles of the suffragettes. The reference to the Liberal Cabinet member Augustine Birrell, a frequent suffragette target despite his pro-suffragist stance, also suggests she had more than a cursory knowledge of militant activity.[107] Schoolgirls' suffragette humour did not simply repeat adult attitudes but drew creatively on their own knowledge and opinions about the subject. Here, Harbottle participated in a suffragist literary culture that harnessed poetry's subversive potential to communicate her albeit veiled support for the cause.[108]

Lower-third-former Fay Mitchell's poem, 'Ten Little Suffragettes', published two months later in *Wimbledon High School Magazine*, was more explicit in its criticism of militancy.[109] Although Mitchell would have been

[106] D. Harbottle, 'A suffragette to the Cabinet ministers', *OM*, xxxiii (Feb. 1908), pp. 10–11. Reprinted with the kind permission of North London Collegiate School Archive.

[107] M. Pugh, *The March of the Women: A Revisionist Analysis of the Campaign for Women's Suffrage, 1866–1914* (Oxford and New York, 2000), p. 190.

[108] D. Tyler-Bennett, 'Suffrage and poetry: radical women's voices', in *The Women's Suffrage Movement: New Feminist Perspectives*, ed. M. Joannou and J. Purvis (Manchester, 1998), pp. 117–26.

[109] F. Mitchell, 'Ten little suffragettes', *WHSM*, xix (1908), p. 19.

too young to participate in the debate on women's suffrage at the school earlier that year, poetry offered an age-inclusive route for her to express her views. Following the standard format of the well-known racist verse, the poem counted down in rhyming couplets from ten suffragettes to none. One by one, the suffragettes lost interest in the cause, changed their mind, or were imprisoned; four met a nastier end. Some causes of their demise – one suffragette 'talked herself to death' at a debate and another got tired of waiting for the vote – suggest that the poem could be interpreted more broadly as anti-suffragist. It was not unusual for girls to adapt well-known literary motifs in their compositions. Five years later, a similar poem – 'Ten Little Schoolgirls' – appeared in the school's magazine.[110] Mitchell added her voice to a growing chorus of suffragette jokes that reworked the same tropes. Indeed, a different version of 'Ten Little Suffragettes' circulated in a couple of local London newspapers in 1910.[111] Interestingly, in this case, Mitchell seems to have got there first. Krista Cowman has shown how the WSPU used humour as a 'political tactic' to rebut critics, deal with the emotional demands of campaigning and raise publicity for the cause.[112] The use of suffragette humour was a calculated move for schoolgirls too. They deployed an irreverent stance towards the militant movement to make their engagement with it acceptable in the school context.

Fancy dress offered girls another outlet for their suffragette humour. From the late Victorian period, fancy dress was an increasingly popular pastime that was adopted by some schools with enthusiasm. Rebecca Mitchell has noted that the late Victorian fancy-dress ball featured 'abstract costumes that directly engaged with issues of their day'.[113] Schoolgirls' dressing up choices could also represent current events in sartorial form. At Myra Lodge, one of the North London Collegiate School boarding houses, a costume dance in October 1912 featured ten-year-old Francie Buss – the great-niece of the school's founder Frances Mary Buss – dressed as 'a militant suffragette'.[114] Incidentally, this was not the only politically themed costume; another

[110] R. Sharp, 'Ten little schoolgirls', *The Wimbledon Hill School Magazine*, xxiv (1913), pp. 14–15. Facing competition from the new secondary schools created following the 1902 Education Act, the Council of the Girls' Public Day School Trust changed the name of five of its schools. Wimbledon High School was renamed Wimbledon Hill School in Aug. 1911.

[111] 'The world of women', *Kilburn Times*, 9 Dec. 1910, p. 2; 'The world of women', *Shoreditch Observer*, 10 Dec. 1910, p. 6.

[112] Cowman, '"Doing something silly"', pp. 261, 269–74.

[113] R. N. Mitchell, 'The Victorian fancy dress ball, 1870–1900', *Fashion Theory*, xxi (2017), 291–315, at p. 293.

[114] E. M. Hill, 'School chronicle: Myra Lodge', *OM*, xxxvii (Dec. 1912), p. 94.

guest came dressed as the equally topical subject of 'The Insurance Act'. Unlike the eighteenth-century masquerade, Victorian fancy dress allowed the wearer to blend their own identity with that of their costume. As Celia Marshik observed, costumes were a way 'to enhance, but not disguise, their everyday appearance and persona'.[115] Francie Buss's suffragette costume can therefore be read in two ways. It both mocked militant suffragism and allowed a controversial subject to be aired within the school context. Its genius lay in exploiting the same ambiguity in the suffragette school entertainments; the comic dissonance between a young schoolgirl and a violent adult suffragette always contained the possibility of sympathy and identification with the cause.

One example from a Lancashire elementary school suggests that militant suffragism could provide girls with symbolism and resources to deploy, albeit playfully, in their struggles against school authority. The autobiography of Bessie Blackburn, who was born in Blackburn, Lancashire, in 1902, includes a fascinating example of a suffrage-inspired school strike in 1914.[116] Bessie and her classmates were angry that the neighbouring boys' school's half-holiday (arranged so teachers could watch a local football game) was not extended to them. They responded with 'a pretend strike at playtime' – a tactic with which girls from a highly unionized and politicized community were probably familiar. Impersonating the suffragettes, the girls marched around the playground holding strike notices and singing 'Votes for Women'. Of course, this was lower-key than other school strikes, such as the mass, nationwide walkouts of 1889 and 1911 against grievances like corporal punishment, excessive homework and long school hours.[117] However, it suggests the remarkable extent to which this form of political activism could permeate schoolchildren's culture and imaginary play. The schoolgirls seized upon a small instance of gender inequality to protest the much larger issue of women's suffrage.

This chapter has demonstrated how the girls' school community offered physical and textual spaces for teachers, old girls and current schoolgirls to participate in the women's suffrage debate. At the hyperlocal level of individual institutions, the considerable reach and intergenerational dimensions of the

[115] C. Marshik, *At the Mercy of their Clothes: Modernism, the Middlebrow, and British Garment Culture* (New York, 2016), p. 105.

[116] E. K. Blackburn, *When I was a Little Girl: A Bunch of Childhood Memories 1907–1916*, 3rd edn (Burnley, 1982), pp. 55–6.

[117] D. Marson, *Children's Strikes in 1911* (Oxford, 1973); S. Cunningham and M. Lavalette, *School's Out! The Hidden History of Britain's School Student Strikes* (London, 2016).

suffrage question become clear. The key arguments for and against women's suffrage that were voiced on the platform and in Parliament echoed around the school debating chamber. Both the pro-suffragist messages of campaign literature and the popular press's satirical takes on militant suffragism could be found in the pages of school magazines. Women's suffrage slogans – voiced with varying levels of conviction – can be traced into the classrooms, corridors and playgrounds of girls' schools.

At school, teachers and old girls found supportive networks to spark and nurture their commitment to women's suffrage. This led, at times, to material contributions to the cause, including parliamentary petitions and new recruits. Suffragist teachers and alumnae exploited the growing networking role that the school and its publications offered as a key means of communication to promote their views. In doing so, they had to navigate shifting boundaries of acceptable public engagement with the suffrage movement, reputational risk and personal principle. Within the school community, constitutional suffragism remained the only legitimate form of suffrage activism. School magazines celebrated teachers' and old girls' tireless work for the NUWSS but avoided allusions to the militant work of those involved in the WFL and WSPU.

Reframing the educational context as a site for suffrage activity shows that interest in the campaign reached a wide age range. Although constrained by boundaries of respectability, teachers used diverse strategies to bring suffrage into schoolgirls' educational experiences. Once women's suffrage had become established in mainstream political discourse, teachers encouraged middle-class adolescent schoolgirls to tackle the subject in their debating societies. Appropriating many of the main arguments on both sides, girls embraced the suffrage question enthusiastically, demonstrating a clear grasp of the national debate. Whereas teachers and old girls were less likely to share their anti-suffrage views with the school community, schoolgirls could express them more freely in the debating chamber.

Outside these debates, it was the militant movement that most interested schoolgirls. Educational journals encouraged elementary teachers to use suffrage plays at school, where preadolescent working-class girls embodied suffragette satire. Schoolgirl 'suffragettes' were intended to delegitimize militancy, but there was always the possibility that performers might subvert teachers' efforts by sympathizing with their characters. Indeed, schoolgirls were never passive recipients of adults' ideas about suffrage; they could engage with the issue on their own terms, in extreme cases by co-opting the symbolism, tools and language of militancy to protest school authority. More often, girls used suffragette humour in their writing and imaginary play, participating in a popular culture that satirized the militant movement. Middle-class schoolgirls caricatured the suffragettes in their poetry and performed militancy in fancy-dress parties. Schoolgirls therefore responded to the examples of their teachers' and old girls' suffragism in their own ways, using subversive humour, expressing anti-suffrage opinions and even on occasion being more militant than their teachers.

7. 'A mistake to raise any controversial question at the present time': the careful relationship of Glasgow's suffragists with the press, 1902–18

Sarah Pedersen

This chapter investigates how a constitutional suffrage organization navigated two distinct and problematic relationships – with the suffrage press and with local newspapers. It demonstrates that not all suffrage campaigners strode confidently into the public sphere of press debate, and that there were clear risks as well as benefits in doing so. Such an investigation moves the discussion beyond the publicity-seeking agenda of the militant campaign and focuses instead on the constitutional suffragists. It also offers new insight into the somewhat difficult relations between the Scottish constitutional suffragists and London headquarters of the National Union of Women's Suffrage Societies (NUWSS).

Discussion of the women's suffrage campaign and its relationship with the press has tended to focus on newspaper coverage of militant organizations, with their headline-grabbing stunts aimed at raising the profile of 'the cause'.[1] The newspapers gave the suffragettes publicity while the suffragettes offered exciting and controversial stories that sold newspapers. The suffragettes also made full use of newspaper correspondence columns, which allowed them

[1] J. Chapman, 'The argument of the broken pane: suffragette consumerism and newspapers', *Media History*, xxi (2015), 238–51; K. Cowman, '"Doing something silly": the uses of humour by the Women's Social and Political Union, 1903–1914', *International Review of Social History*, lii (2007), 259–74; K. E. Kelly, 'Seeing through spectacles: the woman suffrage movement and London newspapers, 1906–13', *European Journal of Women's Studies*, xi (2004), 327–53; J. Mercer, 'Making the news: votes for women and the mainstream press', *Media History*, x (2004), 187–99; R. Nessheim, *Press, Politics and Votes for Women, 1910–1918* (Oslo, 1997); S. Pedersen, *The Scottish Suffragettes and the Press* (Basingstoke, 2017).

'A mistake to raise any controversial question at the present time', in *The politics of women's suffrage: local, national and international dimensions*, ed. A. Hughes-Johnson and L. Jenkins (London, 2021), pp. 191–212.

to present their arguments in some detail, even in anti-suffrage newspapers.[2] However, the constitutional suffragists also worked to publicize their policies and events through the press, and, as time wore on, also attempted to distinguish themselves in the public eye from their militant sisters.[3]

This chapter utilizes the minutes and public correspondence of the Executive Committee of the non-militant Glasgow and West of Scotland Association for Women's Suffrage (GWSAWS), and its correspondence to suffrage and Scottish newspapers, to explore the changing relationship of this organization with the press. A 1906 letter of protest from the GWSAWS Executive Committee against militant suffrage activities in Glasgow provoked somewhat of a backlash in the local press, resulting in the women of the Glasgow Association becoming more wary of entering into press debate. This set something of a pattern for several years, as recognized by researchers who have described the Association as being 'obstinate and insular' and 'curiously uncooperative'.[4] However, with the advent of the First World War, GWSAWS adopted a more confident approach to the press, reflecting the general higher-profile engagement of women civic leaders throughout the country who were 'doing their bit' for the war effort.

The minutes of the Executive Committee detail both a growing realization of the need to heighten the public profile of suffragists in Glasgow and a reluctance to engage too closely with the local press, particularly after the arrival of the Women's Social and Political Union (WSPU) in the city after 1906. Most of the members who *were* happy to engage in correspondence with the local press had left GWSAWS to join the Glasgow branch of the WSPU by the end of 1907. The first honorary secretary of GWSAWS, Nellie M. Hunter, stands out as one of the few members of the Committee happy to engage in press correspondence under her own name during the prewar years. She finally resigned from GWSAWS in disgust in 1917, after the cautious press committee submitted a letter to the *Glasgow Herald* under a *nom de plume* rather than the name of the Association itself.

The chapter also explores the sometimes-difficult relationship between local and national organizations, particularly between a Scottish organization uncomfortable with a London-based leadership. The NUWSS, based in

[2] Pedersen, *The Scottish Suffragettes and the Press.*

[3] M. DiCenzo, 'Unity and dissent: official organs of the suffrage campaign', in *Feminist Media History: Suffrage, Periodicals and the Public Sphere*, ed. M. DiCenzo, L. Delap and L. Ryan (Basingstoke, 2011), pp. 76–119.

[4] M. K. Smitley, '"Woman's mission": the temperance and women's suffrage movements in Scotland, c. 1870–1914' (unpublished doctoral thesis, University of Glasgow, 2002), p. 224; E. King, 'The Scottish women's suffrage movement', in *Out of Bounds: Women in Scottish Society 1800–1945*, ed. E. Breitenbach and E. Gordon (Edinburgh, 1992), p. 136.

London, was the umbrella group for constitutional suffrage societies and had affiliated branches all over the country. The GWSAWS affiliated to the NUWSS in 1903, but, as we shall see, there were tensions in the relationship. While the GWSAWS Executive Committee was more open to sending reports and letters to constitutional suffrage publications such as *Suffrage Record* and *Common Cause*, the relationship between these London-based publications and Glasgow was not always straightforward, and tended to reflect the wider problematic relationship between GWSAWS and NUWSS headquarters.

While the GWSAWS sought newspaper promotion of its meetings and fundraising campaigns, there was more reluctance to enter into debate in the press, with either anti-suffragists or suffragettes. In addition, the editors of Glaswegian newspapers might refuse to cover suffragist meetings or even mock them. This resulted in a diminished profile for GWSAWS and a loss of members, and their subscriptions, to the militant organizations in the city.

The Glasgow and West of Scotland Association for Women's Suffrage

The GWSAWS was re-founded in 1902 by some of the leading women in civic life in the city.[5] An earlier association had been established in 1870 (an Edinburgh National Society for Women's Suffrage was founded in 1867), but lapsed in the succeeding decades. Membership of GWSAWS came primarily from the educated middle classes, with many prominent members also associated with the local Liberal Party – the first meeting of the new association in 1902 was held at the home of Jessie Turnbull Thomson, referred to in the minutes as Mrs Greig, a former president of the Glasgow Women's Liberal Association.[6] Invitations to send representatives to join the committee of the new society were extended to local temperance associations. King also noted the overlap in membership between GWSAWS and the Scottish Council for Women's Trades (SCWT).[7] The Suffrage Association even met at the offices of the SCWT in Renfield Street from 1902 to 1909. GWSAWS had gained 200 members by the end of its first year, and by 1911 had supported the formation of four other suffrage societies in the west of Scotland. It affiliated to the NUWSS in 1903, 'feeling that union is strength', but also instigated the formation of a Scottish Federation of Women's Suffrage Societies.[8] By 1914, there were

5 *Common Cause*, 12 Oct. 1911, p. 9.

6 E. Crawford, *The Women's Suffrage Movement: A Reference Guide 1866–1928* (London, 1999), p. 246.

7 E. King, *The Hidden History of Glasgow's Women* (Edinburgh, 1993), p. 91.

8 King, *Glasgow's Women*, p. 91.

sixty-three suffragist societies in Scotland, with a membership of 7,370.[9] The Federation's chairman was Andrew Ballantyne, who worked for the Railway Servants' Union and Scottish Trades Union Congress. From 1905, he was also manager of the Glasgow Public House Trust.[10] The Public House Trust movement was established to promote the 'disinterested' management of pubs and represented the 'moderate wing' of the temperance movement.[11] For the first seven years of its existence, GWSAWS business was conducted from the home of honorary secretary Nellie M. Hunter (*née* Galbraith). In April 1911, however, an office was taken at 202 Hope Street, making it 'the centre of the Constitutional Women's Suffrage movement in Glasgow'.[12]

The minutes of the Executive Committee of GWSAWS are held at Glasgow's Mitchell Library and date from 1902 to 1933. Elspeth King has provided a number of useful introductions to the collection, and she, Sandra Stanley Holton and Leah Leneman used the Association's minutes to inform their early and valuable surveys of the Glasgow, Scottish and UK suffrage movements, particularly the movements of members between suffragist and suffragette organizations.[13] Megan Smitley and Annmarie Hughes used the minutes to identify interconnections between the Scottish suffrage and temperance movements and explore the fraught relations between the GWSAWS and the Independent Labour Party (ILP) after the war.[14] Nonetheless, the minutes of the GWSAWS continue to be a rich source for further study of the constitutional suffrage campaign in Glasgow, and this chapter investigates the light they cast on the relationship between the Executive Committee of GWSAWS and the suffrage and non-suffrage press. This expands on earlier work on the relationship between the press and suffrage organizations in Scotland, which has demonstrated how suffrage campaigners used Scottish newspapers – particularly correspondence

[9] L. Leneman, *A Guid Cause: the Women's Suffrage Movement in Scotland* (Edinburgh, 1995), p. 189.

[10] Smitley, 'Woman's mission', p. 219.

[11] D. W. Gutzke, 'Progressivism and the history of the public house, 1850–1950', *Cultural and Social History*, iv (2007), 235–59.

[12] *Common Cause*, 12 Oct. 1911, p. 9.

[13] S. Stanley Holton, *Feminism and Democracy: Women's Suffrage and Reform Politics in Britain, 1900–1918* (Cambridge, 2003); E. King, *The Scottish Women's Suffrage Movement* (Glasgow, 1978); King, 'The Scottish women's suffrage movement'; King, *Glasgow's Women*; L. Leneman, *A Guid Cause.*

[14] Smitley, 'Woman's mission'; A. Hughes, 'Fragmented feminists? the influence of class and political identity in relations between the Glasgow and West of Scotland suffrage society and the independent labour party in the West of Scotland, c. 1919–1932', *Women's History Review*, xiv (2005), 7–32.

columns – to communicate their arguments to the general public from the 1860s onwards. However, it is clear that it was the arrival of the WSPU in Scotland in 1906 that stimulated greater press coverage of the demand for votes for women, especially as militancy arrived in the country in the last few years before the outbreak of war.[15]

The oxygen of publicity

From the establishment of their campaign in the 1860s, suffragists had embarked on a press strategy that included placing letters, articles and reports in as many newspapers as possible in order to shift public opinion on the subject of women's suffrage.[16] Scottish leaders such as Priscilla Bright Maclaren, signatory of the 1866 suffrage petition and first president of the Edinburgh National Society for Women's Suffrage, were keen correspondents to the press. On Maclaren's death in 1906, *The Scotsman* acknowledged her frequent use of its correspondence pages, describing her as 'a ready and pungent writer'.[17] Following Maclaren's example, Jessie Methven, honorary secretary of the Edinburgh Society, was another frequent letter-writer, using letters to the editor to publicize the missionary work of the Edinburgh society throughout Scotland. She was particularly quick to write letters of praise to newspapers such as the *Dundee Advertiser* that covered the meetings of new constitutional suffrage societies as they were established.[18] It should be noted, in light of what will be discussed below, that Jessie Methven left the Edinburgh Society to join the WSPU in 1906 after the death of Priscilla Bright Maclaren. Elizabeth Crawford noted that, after Bright Maclaren's death, many of the Edinburgh Society's members flocked to the city's newly established WSPU branch.[19] However, even before this, Methven was expressing sympathy for the suffragettes' impatience with the slow and steady tactics of the suffragists. For example, in a letter to the *Glasgow Herald* in May 1906 she commented that 'it was not to be wondered at if at last some impatient spirits have not been able to restrain themselves'.[20]

While the leaders of the Edinburgh Society were writing to local and national newspapers on the subject of women's suffrage, what of their

[15] Pedersen, *The Scottish Suffragettes and the Press.*

[16] DiCenzo, 'Unity and dissent' p. 83.

[17] *The Scotsman*, 'The late Mrs Priscilla Maclaren', 6 Nov. 1906, p. 4.

[18] Pedersen, *The Scottish Suffragettes and the Press*, pp. 37–40.

[19] E. Crawford, *The Women's Suffrage Movement in Britain and Ireland* (London, 2016), p. 234.

[20] *Glasgow Herald*, 'Letters to the editor', 1 May 1906, p. 3.

counterparts in Glasgow? The GWSAWS used newspapers to advertise its public meetings, and there was some coverage of these meetings by the local press. However, there seems to have been less of an appetite among the Glasgow women to engage in debate on the subject of women's suffrage in newspaper correspondence columns before the advent of the WSPU in the city. The usual policy of Scottish newspapers at this time was publication of all letters received, as long as the correspondent supplied a name and address to the editor. The lack of correspondence from the Glasgow suffragists suggests that they chose not to write to the newspapers. Correspondents could even choose to use a pen name in print, removing another barrier to publication. Anonymity offered the opportunity of offering an opinion on a contentious issue without revealing one's identity, a step which might invite criticism or even attacks. An investigation of Aberdeen newspapers of the same period shows that, with the arrival of militant suffragism, there was an increase in both the discussion of women's suffrage in newspaper correspondence and the use of pen names to cover the identities of the letter-writers.[21]

Reports of the meetings of GWSAWS that were published in local newspapers tended to be short summaries of events, perhaps noting speakers and the titles of their papers, or the wording of the motion in favour of women's suffrage supported by the meeting. They were very similar in style to reports of meetings of other societies, such as branches of the Young Scots or the Women's Liberal Association, and were probably submitted by secretaries of the branches themselves. The names of speakers and chairs of the meetings make it clear that they came from the civic leadership of Glasgow, connected to the council, charities, the Church or university, which helps to explain the mostly respectful, albeit abbreviated, way meetings were usually covered in the press.

One of these meetings, addressed by Nellie M. Hunter, caused the first rift between GWSAWS and the local press. By this time the Association had hired Mary Phillips[22] to work as a paid organizer, and it was she who wrote to the *Paisley and Renfrewshire Gazette* in January 1905, complaining about its report of a local meeting. Instead of a clear representation of the meeting, she complained, the newspaper had 'contented [itself] with a mere farcical misrepresentation of the subject'.[23]

[21] S. Pedersen, 'What's in a name? The revealing use of noms de plume in women's correspondence to daily newspapers in Edwardian Scotland', *Media History*, x (2004), 175–85.

[22] Phillips later worked as an organizer for the WSPU from 1907.

[23] *Paisley and Renfrewshire Gazette*, 'Correspondence', 21 Jan. 1905, p. 5.

One can understand Phillips' unhappiness. The *Gazette*'s report started with a short poem.

> The wife has left the kids unwashed.
> She's off to her society,
> Where female votes as antidotes,
> Are offered in variety:
> Her manly clo'es and 'suffrage shows',
> To other virtues blind me;
> So I'm off the scene with the 9.15 –
> And the wife I'll leave behind me.[24]

The report also commented on the appearance of the suffragists: '[T]hey are rather severe looking than otherwise, but I suppose those women who had a right to insist on rights would be minding the baby or something else of that kind'.[25] Phillips used her letter to the *Gazette* to repeat some of the arguments presented at the meeting. However, the editor merely commented under her letter: 'The meeting referred to, turned out to be such a paltry affair that it was not worth a serious report, but our correspondent is here granted the "little space" she asks, to re-state the views last week addressed to empty benches – Ed'.[26]

The minutes of the GWSAWS Executive Committee frequently mention the need to promote meetings and disseminate information about the activities of the wider NUWSS. In December 1903, it was agreed to ask 'the Editors of the Herald, the Citizen, the Daily Record and the News to receive a deputation from the Association',[27] while advertisements were to be inserted into the press to encourage those interested in setting up local societies to contact either the Glasgow or Edinburgh Associations.[28] Communication with the press might also be more targeted, such as the decision in January 1905 to instruct the secretary 'to write to the Lab Leader, Clarion, Reynold's Newspaper, New Age, the Scottish Co-operator and the Co-operative News' to protest against the Labour party's support of an adult suffrage bill rather than one focused on women's suffrage.[29] The majority of these minutes placed the responsibility for communicating with the press on Nellie M. Hunter.

[24] *Paisley and Renfrewshire Gazette*, 'Town talk', 14 Jan. 1905, p. 5.

[25] *Paisley and Renfrewshire Gazette*, 'Town talk', 14 Jan. 1905, p. 5.

[26] *Paisley and Renfrewshire Gazette*, 'Correspondence', 21 Jan. 1905, p. 5.

[27] Minute Book 1902–1905, 23 Dec. 1903.

[28] Minute Book 1902–1905, 16 Mar. 1905.

[29] Minute Book 1902–1905, 31 Jan. 1905.

On 15 January 1906, the Prime Minister of the newly elected Liberal government, Sir Henry Campbell-Bannerman, visited Glasgow to speak at St Andrew's Halls. His speech was interrupted by a woman shouting, 'What about women's suffrage?' She was removed from the building and Sir Henry passed the incident off with a joke.[30] Mortification at such an event occurring in Glasgow led the Executive Committee to immediately submit letters disowning such militancy to the *Glasgow Herald* and *The Scotsman*.

> Sir – On behalf of the Glasgow and West of Scotland Association for Women's Suffrage, allow me to say that, in common with the general public, we deeply deplore the unseemly interruptions by some women suffragists at Sir Henry Campbell-Bannerman's meeting tonight. Strongly as we feel the justice of our demands, we equally feel that those are not the methods by which we would seek to have them conceded, and we desire to dissociate ourselves from all such discourteous behaviour.
>
> Nellie M. Hunter, Secretary.[31]

An immediate response to this letter came from Elizabeth Pollok, honorary secretary of the newly formed Glasgow WSPU. This is the earliest mention of a branch of the WSPU in the city. Elizabeth Crawford notes that one had been established by at least March 1906, but this letter suggests that the date can be moved to the start of the year.[32] Pollok wrote to the *Herald* to mock the 'hasty meeting' of Glasgow suffragists that had led to the letter and compared them unfavourably to the 'noble Glasgow women' who were willing to make sacrifices for reform, 'which they consider of immediate necessity for the economic and social welfare of themselves and their more helpless sisters'.[33] This was not merely a difference of opinion over tactics between suffragists and suffragettes, but also reflected wider divisions. As has been noted, many of the leaders of the Glasgow suffragists were associated with the Liberal Party. Indeed, the minutes of the Executive Committee frequently note a desire for Lady Aberdeen, president of the Women's Liberal Federation, to agree to accept the presidency of GWSAWS.[34] Elizabeth Pollok, in contrast, was

30 *Aberdeen Daily Journal*, 'The Premier in Glasgow', 16 Jan. 1906, p. 6.

31 *The Scotsman*, 'Letters to the editor', 17 Jan. 1906, p. 10.

32 Pedersen, *Scottish Suffragettes*, pp. 48–9.

33 *Glasgow Herald*, 'Letters to the editor', 18 Jan. 1906, p. 12.

34 Although she continued to turn them down, citing her heavy workload.

a member of the Independent Labour Party (ILP). The Glasgow WSPU enjoyed strong support from the ILP, and in particularly from Tom Johnston, editor of the new radical publication *Forward*. Hence Elizabeth Pollok's attack in her letter on 'Lady Aberdeen and the West of Scotland Women Suffragists' who could 'afford to wait' for suffrage reform, unlike 'the women factory workers, seamstresses and the unfortunate employees in the sweated trades'.[35]

The action of the Glaswegian suffragists in attempting to disassociate themselves from the suffragettes was not only attacked by Pollok. For several days after the meeting at St Andrew's Halls, the correspondence columns of Glasgow newspapers were filled with letters either denouncing or supporting the suffragettes' disruption of Campbell-Bannerman's meeting. Several of these letters referred to the suffragists' condemnation of militancy. 'J.S.H.' suggested that Mrs Hunter's letter was written 'in too great haste',[36] while 'Non-Suffragist' stated that she could 'hardly understand the attitude of those organizations which profess to make it [suffrage] a leading object, in repudiating and apologising for their sisters', asking 'Are we to be "ladylike" when "feminine serfdom" is in the question?'[37] On the other hand, 'Juden' stated, 'I quite agree with the secretary of the Glasgow branch of that association in her disapproval of the action of those women who both in London and in Glasgow, quite needlessly excited the animosity of many in the audiences by their irrelevant outcries.'[38]

It is clear that the experience of being attacked in the press dismayed the women of the Glasgow Association, and made them much more wary of engaging in such newspaper debate. Apart from 'Juden', quoted above, most of the letters to the press that mentioned the GWSAWS condemned their letter. In May 1906, the Executive Committee was asked by NUWSS headquarters to circulate to the local press another letter condemning suffragettes who had made a disturbance in the gallery of the House of Commons. The minutes noted that 'it was decided to take no further steps as already it had been pointed out in the Press that our Association was in no way connected with them'.[39] Thus the Glaswegian suffragists both

[35] *Glasgow Herald*, 'Letters to the editor', 18 Jan. 1906, p. 12.

[36] *Glasgow Herald*, 'Letters to the editor', 22 Jan. 1906, p. 11.

[37] *Glasgow Herald*, 'Letters to the editor', 19 Jan. 1906, p. 14.

[38] *Glasgow Herald*, 'Letters to the editor', 22 Jan. 1906, p. 11.

[39] Suffrage Executive Committee Minute Book Dec. 1905 onwards, Mitchell Library 891036/1/2, 8 May 1906.

asserted their independence of action against headquarters, and also stepped away from engaging in more correspondence with the local newspapers, particularly in relation to another WSPU outrage.

Nonetheless, individual members of the Executive Committee did continue to engage in newspaper correspondence. Margaret Irwin, Mary Phillips and Dr Marion Gilchrist all had letters published in the *Glasgow Herald* in March 1907, under their own names, in reference to an attempt to gather Glaswegian signatures on a national anti-suffrage petition.[40] Irwin was the secretary of the SCWT. She had been a leading campaigner for the establishment of a Scottish Trade Union Congress and was elected its first secretary in 1897. Marion Gilchrist was the first female graduate from the University of Glasgow and the city's first woman doctor, while Phillips was GWSAWS's paid organizer and, after leaving the Association and joining the WSPU, would become one of the longest-serving suffragette prisoners. These letters served the dual purpose of presenting arguments for granting women the parliamentary vote, and also promoting a meeting organized by GWSAWS that week. Later in the same month another committee member, Eve Baker, wrote to the *Herald* to refute a suggestion by another correspondent that the Conservatives supported women's suffrage because they believed women to be 'naturally and incurably stupid, silly or both'.[41] Thus it seems that some members of the Executive Committee were still willing to step into the public sphere via the press, but as individuals rather than representatives of GWSAWS.

However, all four of these women had resigned from the Executive Committee by the end of 1907 to join the militant WSPU. Their resignations were driven by a frustration at the ineffectualness of constitutional tactics, the lack of direct action undertaken by GWSAWS and unhappiness at the refusal of others in the Executive Committee to engage with the WSPU, objecting in particular to the Executive Committee's refusal to invite Teresa Billington, a militant, to address the Association. Their letters to the Glasgow press can therefore be seen as signs of their increasing attraction to the tactics of the militants. Unlike their compatriots on the Executive Committee, they saw the value of raising the question of women's suffrage in newspaper correspondence, and were confident enough in their own positions to step into the public sphere of newspaper debate. Their move to the WSPU also demonstrates the draw of Billington – an excellent and witty public speaker – who had

40 *Glasgow Herald*, 'Letters to the editor', 9 Mar. 1907, p. 11; 11 Mar. 1907, p. 11.

41 *Glasgow Herald*, 'Letters to the editor', 18 Mar. 1907, p. 10.

transformed the fortunes of the Scottish suffrage campaign on her arrival in the country in 1906.

The remaining members of the Executive Committee continued to be wary of engaging too readily in newspaper correspondence. In October 1909, a proposal to send a letter to the press outlining a NUWSS resolution condemning the use of violence in political propaganda occasioned 'a long discussion'. It was finally passed, but the suggestion moved by Miss Young and seconded by Miss Lamont '"[t]hat we make a statement of our own policy and send it frequently to the press without referring to violent methods" was lost by 3 votes to 11'.[42]

Mrs Taylor was appointed GWSAWS's first press secretary in 1912 in response to a request from the wider Scottish Federation for someone to monitor the Glasgow newspapers. However, it is evident that she did not feel up to the full task, and at first the job was shared between members of the committee, with each undertaking 'to be responsible for all notices and letters appearing in the papers, cutting them out and sending them on to the Secretary'.[43] Mrs Taylor was invited to a national meeting of press secretaries in September that year in Manchester, although there is no indication that she attended. There are several references in the minutes of the difficulty and expense of travelling to England for meetings. It was later agreed that she could hire Durrant's Press Cuttings Agency to cover the newspapers under her supervision, which suggests that the amateur approach of individual committee members had been found to be insufficient.

There was some reluctance among the Committee to take on the role of press secretary, which appears to have been an unpaid honorary role. Apart from paid organizers, the majority of work undertaken for the suffrage cause in Scotland was voluntary and taken on by women who were already involved in many other causes and organizations. This was not unusual across the UK, especially within local branches. Mrs Taylor did not hold the role for very long and her apparent successor, Miss Brownlees, is only mentioned in the minutes as press secretary when she resigned from the role in 1914. To a certain extent, the role was covered by the Scottish Federation's able press secretary, Miss Stuart Paterson, who was also a member of the GWSAWS Executive Committee. In 1913, the Committee gave her permission to carry on her role as Federation press secretary in its Glasgow offices, perhaps hoping that her presence would absolve it of the need for its own separate

42 Suffrage Executive Committee Minute Book Dec. 1905 onwards, 20 Oct. 1909.

43 Suffrage Executive Committee Minute Book Dec. 1910–1915, 31 Jan. 1912.

official. Miss Stuart Paterson was a key speaker for the Glasgow Association at by-elections and brought a more professional approach to the role of press secretary. She was also more comfortable with dealing with the press, giving statements, for example, on the occasion of Mrs Pankhurst's arrest when she tried to speak at a WSPU meeting in Glasgow in 1914.[44] A report in *Common Cause* in 1913 praised her for tackling the press work 'with much energy' and noted that, of the 115 papers on her list for supervision, '54 are reported as favourable, including those of Glasgow, and only 19 as definitely Anti-Suffragist'.[45]

It was Miss Stuart Paterson who suggested that GWSAWS needed to appoint both a press secretary and a committee to support her, 'which would considerably lighten the Press Secretary's work'.[46] However, despite Committee members helpfully suggesting the names of other women to fill the role of press secretary, none was appointed. It was finally agreed to appoint a press committee, to be convened by Miss Stuart Paterson, and including the erstwhile press secretaries Mrs Taylor and Miss Brownlees, among others.

As mentioned earlier, the Executive Committee of GWSAWS has been characterized by researchers as 'obstinate and insular' and 'curiously uncooperative'. This is certainly true of its dealings with the mainstream press. There was little appetite among the majority of Committee members to enter into press debate about the suffrage question, and many of those who were willing to do so soon lost patience with this attitude and moved to the new WSPU branch in the city. The press was mostly to be used to publicize public meetings and other events. In this, the women of the Glasgow suffragist association were not dissimilar to other suffragists in Scotland during the first years of the twentieth century. In Aberdeen, the new WSPU branch poured scorn on the lack of public engagement undertaken by the older suffragist branch – which was also intertwined with the Liberal Women's Federation. Similarly, the most active press correspondent among the Edinburgh suffragists, Jessie Methven, soon moved to the WSPU on the arrival of Teresa Billington in Scotland in 1906. For many Scottish suffragists, engagement with the mainstream press for reasons other than publicizing meetings and

44 *The Scotsman*, 'The Constitutional Suffragists and Mrs Pankhurst', 10 Mar. 1914, p. 6.

45 *Common Cause*, 'Press department', 2 May 1913, p. 59.

46 Suffrage Executive Committee Minute Book Dec. 1910–1915, 16 Mar. 1914. For more on the pro- and anti-suffrage positions of the Scottish press, see Pedersen, *The Scottish Suffragettes and the Press.*

other events could open them to attack, and a cautious approach was therefore taken.

Relations with the suffrage press

In comparison to its uneasy relations with the local press, the Executive Committee was more confident in its dealings with the suffrage press. It demonstrated independence in setting its own agenda and was confident in disagreeing with the London-based suffrage press, an attitude which is indicative of the wider relationship between the centre and the Scottish 'periphery' in the constitutional suffrage campaign. The suffrage press had been established because of a perceived 'boycott' of the women's suffrage issue by the mainstream press – Helena Swanwick described the lack of mainstream coverage of the suffrage issue as 'extreme and grotesque' censorship.[47] From 1907 onwards, the number of 'official organs' also reflected the reality of a growing but factionalized suffrage movement.[48]

It was part of the role of the honorary secretary to write to suffrage newspapers such as *Women's Suffrage Record* (1903–6), *Women's Franchise* (1907–11) and *Common Cause* (1909–20) with updates on the work of GWSAWS. The relationship here was a reciprocal one; the suffrage periodicals covered the news of societies throughout the country and those societies were expected to encourage members to buy copies of the publication and to sell them at meetings and other events. The minute books of the Committee frequently noted requests from the editors of these periodicals to encourage sales. For example, in March 1909, 'The Secretary reported that Mrs Swanwick was anxious to get local newsagents to stock the Common Cause and it was agreed after receipt of the first copy to do what was possible in this direction.'[49] The Executive Committee agreed to send a copy of the first edition to each subscriber in March 1909, but by September a request for further help in making the *Common Cause* better known was met with the response that nothing further could be undertaken at present, as it had already distributed 600 copies.[50]

The *Common Cause* had been established by the NUWSS as a replacement for *Women's Franchise*, the editor of which refused to exclude reports of the

[47] DiCenzo, 'Unity and dissent', p. 76.

[48] DiCenzo, 'Unity and dissent', p. 77. Suffrage publications included *Common Cause*, *Conservative and Unionist Women's Franchise Review*, *Women's Suffrage Record*, *The Suffragette* (later *Britannia*), *The Suffragist*, *The Vote*, *Votes for Women* and *Women's Franchise*.

[49] Suffrage Executive Committee Minute Book Dec. 1905 onwards, 31 Mar. 1909.

[50] Suffrage Executive Committee Minute Book Dec. 1905 onwards, 1 Sept. 1909.

activities of the militant Women's Freedom League.[51] *Women's Franchise* was published by John E. Francis, owner of the Athenaeum Press and a member of the Men's League for Women's Suffrage.[52] The Executive Committee minutes for 10 February 1909 noted the receipt of a letter from *Women's Franchise* 'announcing that the NU [National Union] had decided not to send any further news to that journal and inviting local societies to send news. It was agreed to do so'.[53] This spirit of independence, if not rebellion, was typical of the temper of GWSAWS when dealing with NUWSS headquarters. While the Association had affiliated with the NUWSS in 1903, this had not been a whole-hearted commitment and Glasgow suffragists would have preferred to establish a Scottish federation of suffrage societies if they could have persuaded the Edinburgh Society. A Scottish federation was finally formed in 1909, under the umbrella of the NUWSS, and chaired by Andrew Ballantyne.[54] The minutes of the Executive Committee bear testimony to a fraught relationship with London headquarters, which was seen as being too far away and unsympathetic to the Scottish view of matters. Smith notes that the Scottish suffragists campaigned under the slogan 'ye mauna tramp on the Scottish thistle' and worked to resist the imposition of an English cultural identity upon the Scottish movement.[55] In particular, the strong links between Scottish suffragists and the Liberal Party meant great unhappiness at the NUWSS's electoral alliance with the Labour Party in 1912.

The decision by the Executive Committee to continue to send news to *Women's Franchise* in spite of national policy to the contrary was typical of this uneasy relationship with London. It immediately responded with a report about campaigning in the Glasgow Central Division by-election written by Nellie M. Hunter.[56] This report explained the decision of the committee to do propaganda work only during the by-election since the only candidate who declared himself to be in favour of women's suffrage, sitting Unionist MP Charles Scott Dickson, would not commit to any active support. Advice had been sought from NUWSS headquarters after a meeting with Scott Dickson, but no response was received. When headquarters belatedly

[51] Crawford, *The Women's Suffrage Movement*, p. 458.

[52] Crawford, *The Women's Suffrage Movement*, p. 461.

[53] Suffrage Executive Committee Minute Book Dec. 1905 onwards, 10 Feb. 1909.

[54] Crawford, *The Women's Suffrage Movement*, p. 621.

[55] H. Smith, *The British Women's Suffrage Campaign, 1866–1928* (Basingstoke, 2014), pp. 30–1.

[56] *Women's Franchise*, 'National Union of Women's Suffrage Societies', 25 Mar. 1909, p. 479.

sent orders that Glasgow suffragists should campaign for Scott Dickson, the Executive Committee declined to do so. A letter was then received from London headquarters demanding to know 'on whose authority the Glasgow Secretary had sent the report to *Women's Franchise* that the NU would do propaganda work only'.[57] 'The Secretary was instructed to send in reply a history of the bye-election' – presumably to point out that the advice of headquarters had been sought but, when no timely response was received, GWSAWS had decided to act (or not act) on its own initiative.

The editorial staff of *Common Cause* continued to appeal to Glasgow for support. In May 1910, a meeting was arranged between the Committee and Miss Walshe of *Common Cause*, who was in Glasgow for a week, and this seems to have led to a better understanding between the two groups and more coverage of Glasgow news. In September 1910, Nellie M. Hunter wrote to the journal to announce that Glasgow Town Council had unanimously agreed to petition Parliament in favour of the Conciliation Bill. The motion had been brought by Councillor Pratt, a member of the Executive Committee of GWSAWS. Hunter ended her letter, 'I am under the impression, but am, of course, open to correction, that this is the first time a Corporation has taken action in the matter.'[58] The Editor responded, 'We welcome with great pleasure this recognition of the value of women as citizens by men who have had the opportunity of observing their work on the Council of a great city like Glasgow.'[59]

Smitley's work on representations of 'Scotch' women in late nineteenth-century suffrage periodicals suggests that Scotswomen who wrote to such journals posited a special role for Scotland in the campaign by asserting a progressive political heritage.[60] This is evident in several of Hunter's letters to the *Common Cause*, which either reported on the leadership shown on the suffrage issue in Glasgow or explained differences between Scottish and English law. Hunter's next letter to the *Common Cause*, however, was much more critical in tone. She wrote in response to a cartoon published in the journal of 15 June 1911, entitled 'The March of England's Women':

> I am somewhat short-sighted, and on looking at the cartoon of 'Common Cause' for June 15th my first thought was: There is something wrong with my glasses to-day. So I polished them well, but still saw the same word. My second

[57] Suffrage Executive Committee Minute Book Dec. 1905 onwards, 10 Mar. 1909.

[58] *Common Cause*, 'Correspondence', 1 Sept. 1910, p. 345.

[59] *Common Cause*, 'Correspondence', 1 Sept. 1910, p. 345.

[60] M. Smitley, 'Feminist Anglo-Saxonism? Representations of "Scotch" women in the English women's press in the late nineteenth century', *Cultural and Social History*, iv (2007), 341–59, at p. 342.

> thought was: Oh, they've sent me some stupid provincial weekly instead of our 'Common Cause,' and I looked at the heading again to make sure, and there read 'The Common Cause, the organ of the National Union of Women's Suffrage.' Well, I have hitherto been under the impression that the Union was National, but when its official organ designates the March of the Women 'the March of England's Women,' some of us have been rudely awakened and have realised the fact that though we may have had the temerity to include ourselves among the nation's women the N.U.W.S.S. denies our right to any such position.[61]

As Smitley has pointed out, while Scottish women and Scottish affairs were not wholly absent from the suffrage press, they tended to be marginal to the overall reporting, and the periodicals were primarily addressed to an English audience.[62] Hunter's letter was followed by an apology from the editor stating that it had received other letters on the subject and 'can only abjectly apologise for the legend which was most certainly not intended as an insult to any Celt or Australian'.[63]

Smitley also suggested a tendency among English feminists to perceive Edinburgh as representative of the whole of Scottish feminism, perhaps because of the dominance of London in England.[64] As she noted, this narrow focus on the capital was not replicated in Scotland in many areas of charitable and political work, with Glasgow organizations being equals with their eastern sisters. Hunter's emphasis on the leadership shown by Glasgow must therefore be seen in light of the tendency of English suffragists to ignore Glasgow in favour of Edinburgh. For example, when the Scottish Federation was formed in 1909, the minutes of the Executive Committee noted that the National Union 'was under the impression that the Scottish Federation had been initiated and organized by the Edinburgh Society' despite the fact that the primary movers had been members of GWSAWS.[65] Hunter's emphasis on Glaswegian exceptionalism continued into the war years. In May 1916, she responded to a *Common Cause* article praising Bristol for appointing the first woman detective to its police force, claiming 'that honour is really due to Glasgow', a worker with the National Vigilance Association of Scotland having been appointed to the detective force of Glasgow the previous September.[66]

[61] *Common Cause*, 'Correspondence', 29 June 1911, p. 217.

[62] Smitley, 'Feminist Anglo-Saxonism?', p. 344.

[63] *Common Cause*, 'Correspondence', 29 June 1911, p. 217.

[64] Smitley, 'Feminist Anglo-Saxonism?', p. 344.

[65] Smitley, 'Woman's mission', p. 245.

[66] *Common Cause*, 'Correspondence', 5 May 1916, p. 49.

On the outbreak of war in August 1914, GWSAWS suspended its campaign for the vote and instead focused on establishing an organization to provide work for unemployed women, the Exchange for Voluntary Workers, and supporting the work of the Scottish Women's Hospitals. While the headquarters of the Scottish Women's Hospitals was in Edinburgh, there was also a committee in Glasgow and several members of the Executive Committee were heavily involved in the administration of the Hospitals, with Nellie M. Hunter eventually becoming Chairman (sic) of the organization. A statement on the suspension of the suffrage campaign was sent to the local press in August 1914, and from then on correspondence to the press focused on fundraising for various schemes associated with the war effort. In December 1914, the Executive Committee 'agreed on Miss Stuart Paterson's suggestion that a letter be sent to the Editors in Glasgow thanking them for the space given in their papers to the important work done by the Suffrage societies'.[67] A separate minute book for the Exchange for Voluntary Workers also agreed that a good way of advertising the Exchange was through 'a letter sent to the Editor of the Glasgow Herald, signed by well-known people'.[68] There is a notable increase in confidence in dealings with the press on matters relating to the war emergency, reflected in both minute books and the increase in correspondence to newspapers. As I have argued elsewhere, newspaper correspondence from women's voluntary organizations associated with war work allowed women to demonstrate their contributions to the war effort and to assert themselves in the public sphere with confidence and legitimacy.[69] At the same time, the campaign for women's enfranchisement was continued throughout the war in Scotland by other organizations, in particular branches of the Women's Freedom League and the Northern Men's Federation for Women's Suffrage.[70]

The establishment of the Speaker's Conference on electoral reform in 1916 led the National Union to write to GWSAWS in November suggesting that 'leading articles, paragraphs or letters to the editor dealing with women's work and its political significance should be inserted in the press, also that Editors should be interviewed'.[71] It was agreed that the secretary should approach the editors of Glasgow newspapers to interview them about the possibility of pro-suffrage material being inserted in their

[67] Suffrage Executive Committee Minute Book Dec. 1910–1915, 17 Dec. 1914.

[68] Exchange for Voluntary Workers (National Emergency) Minute Book, Mitchell Library 891036/5, 24 Aug. 1914.

[69] S. Pedersen, 'A surfeit of socks? The impact of the First World War on women correspondents to daily newspapers', *Scottish Economic and Social History*, xxii (2002), 50–72.

[70] S. Pedersen, 'Suffragettes and the Scottish press during the First World War', *Women's History Review*, xxxvii (2018), 534–50.

[71] Suffrage Executive Committee Minute Book 1915–1920, 6 Nov. 1916.

papers. The National Union also supplied a memorandum that it had drawn up on the subject of women's work and offered copies at a shilling each. However, it was pointed out by the Executive Committee that the memorandum only dealt with England.[72]

The minutes of 20 November 1916 dutifully recorded the outcome of the interviews with newspaper editors, which were not particularly positive. Mr Bruce of the *Glasgow Herald* considered that the work women were doing spoke for itself and it would be a mistake to raise such a controversial question as women's suffrage at the present time. Mr Letham of the *Daily Record* could not see his way to inserting any paragraphs on the subject, but offered to publish a letter in reply to anti-suffrage letters. The same offer was made by Mr Graham of the *Glasgow Evening Times*, while Mr Smith of the *News* stated that his newspaper was definitely anti-suffrage in its views.

A letter signed by representatives of the National League for Opposing Woman Suffrage had been recently published in newspapers throughout the country.[73] It was signed by, among others, Lords Curzon and Cromer, Rudyard Kipling, Beatrice Chamberlain, Margaret Macmillan, Gladys Pott and Flora Fardell, and argued that the present government had no moral right to consider an extension of the parliamentary franchise to women and that it should not be considered until after a general election, to be conducted on the usual terms. On the motion of Nellie M. Hunter, seconded by Mrs Taylor, it was agreed that a letter should be sent to all Glasgow newspapers in response. A small committee, including Mrs Hunter, Andrew Ballantyne and Frances Melville, was established to produce such a letter and the product of this committee, signed by the officials of the Association, was published in newspapers such as the *Daily Record* and *Glasgow Herald* at the end of the month.

The letter emphasized that it was not at their prompting that the question of women's enfranchisement had been raised once more, 'but that it is entirely due to the proposals made in some quarters to alter the basis of the Parliamentary franchise. Should this be attempted, we cannot possibly stand aside.'[74] The letter concluded, 'We take our stand now, as we have done in the past, on the ground that women should have the vote as a simple matter of justice. The work the women of the country are doing we hold to be merely additional evidence of their willingness and ability to share the responsibilities of nation and empire.'[75]

[72] Suffrage Executive Committee Minute Book 1915–1920, 6 Nov. 1916.

[73] For example, in *The Scotsman* on 18 Nov. 1916.

[74] *Glasgow Herald*, 'Letters to the editor', 27 Nov. 1916, p. 5.

[75] *Glasgow Herald*, 'Letters to the editor', 27 Nov. 1916, p. 5.

An answer to this letter was published in the *Herald*, signed W. M. Cheshire. Cheshire objected to women being distracted from their domestic and maternal duties by politics and party warfare. Cheshire was not from Glasgow and similar letters were sent by him to newspapers throughout the UK during the later war years. The one published in the *Hastings and St Leonards Observer* in May 1917 gives his address as N6 London. A discussion recorded in the minutes on 4 December 1916 indicates the Executive Committee did not feel it was its responsibility to answer his letter to the *Herald*. Since the president of the Association, Colonel Denny, was referenced in Cheshire's letter, it was suggested that it would be better if he was asked to answer it.[76] Eventually, a letter was published in the *Herald* on 19 December, some weeks after Cheshire's letter, written by some members of the press sub-committee. While engaging with Cheshire's points, and presenting statistics and other arguments to present the case for women's suffrage, the letter was not signed by either Colonel Denny or the members of the press sub-committee. Instead, it was signed 'O.F.Q.'.[77]

The decision not to officially sign the letter angered Nellie M. Hunter. At the next Executive Committee meeting on 8 January 1917, she stated that she had not been present when this letter had been drawn up and asked why it had not been signed officially. Frances Melville 'replied that the Press Committee had considered it wisest to answer this individual letter by a nom de plume'.[78] This was clearly not sufficient explanation for Mrs Hunter, who raised the matter again at the following month's meeting. She demanded to know which members of the press committee had been present when it was decided to make the letter to the *Herald* anonymous and whether the decision was unanimous. In her opinion, 'the Press Committee had been appointed to answer letters on behalf of the Executive Committee, and … it was not competent for it to do so anonymously without the sanction of the Committee'.[79] Mrs Hunter 'considered that it was neither competent nor wise to sign the letter anonymously, and that a letter carried far more weight if signed on behalf of the society'. Her motion that it was not competent for a sub-committee to act in this way was defeated by seven votes to six. In comparison, a further motion moved by Miss Morris that such things should be left to the discretion of the press committee was carried by ten

[76] Suffrage Executive Committee Minute Book 1915–1920, 4 Dec. 1916.

[77] *Glasgow Herald*, 'Letters to the editor', 19 Dec. 1916, p. 3.

[78] Suffrage Executive Committee Minute Book 1915–1920, 8 Jan. 1917.

[79] Suffrage Executive Committee Minute Book 1915–1920, 12 Feb. 1917.

votes to two. 'Mrs Hunter asked that her name be withdrawn from the Press Committee.'[80]

It was not unusual for correspondents to the press on the subject of women's suffrage to use pseudonyms. However, it was usually individual women who sought the cloak of anonymity rather than official associations affiliated to the NUWSS. The choice of the press sub-committee to hide behind a pen name was in direct contrast to Mrs Hunter's willingness to correspond with the newspapers as both an individual and a representative of GWSAWS. Like others before her, she felt unable to continue her association with the Executive Committee and left to continue her work for women and the war effort elsewhere. She not only left the press committee in anger at its choice to use a *nom de plume*; she also left GWSAWS itself. She continued to correspond with the Scottish press and *Common Cause* as chair of the Scottish Women's Hospitals, and was later awarded the Order of St Sava IV from Serbia and the Royal Red Cross. Hunter also continued her work with the National Vigilance Association of Scotland, and in 1920 was one of the first women to be appointed a Justice of the Peace for Glasgow.[81]

While the press sub-committee continued to report to the Executive Committee, after the departure of Nellie M. Hunter much of its work now focused on recommending newspapers for subscription for the office on Hope Street rather than further correspondence with the newspapers. Indeed, there is a clear indication that it considered communication with Scottish newspapers to be the responsibility of NUWSS headquarters in London. On several occasions the Executive Committee sent letters to headquarters querying whether the *Herald* was included in its list of national newspapers and insinuating that the dearth of suffragist news in this paper was related to a lack of action on the behalf of headquarters. There seems to have been little consideration as to whether GWSAWS itself could do more to achieve such coverage. In February 1918, advertisements were taken out in the *Herald* and *Daily Record* indicating that information for new women voters could be found at GWSAWS headquarters in Hope Street. However, even this motion was not passed without the proviso that London headquarters should be telegraphed for further information before printing the advertisement.[82]

80 Suffrage Executive Committee Minute Book 1915–1920, 12 Feb. 1917.

81 *The Scotsman*, 'The late Mrs J. T. Hunter, Glasgow', 23 Mar. 1933, p. 7.

82 Suffrage Executive Committee Minute Book 1915–1920, 11 Feb. 1918.

Conclusion

The minute books of the Executive Committee of GWSAWS demonstrate how the majority of its members were reluctant to embrace the possibilities of public debate offered by local newspapers, despite increasing pressure from NUWSS headquarters to raise its profile in order to better deal with the eye-catching actions of the militants and the increasing activity of the anti-suffrage campaign. And they were right to be wary. The Association's reprimand of WSPU disruption in 1906 caused an upsetting backlash, which meant that it was several years before GWSAWS returned to the newspaper correspondence columns. Of those Executive Committee members who were willing to expose themselves and their opinions in newspaper correspondence columns, only Nellie M. Hunter remained a member of the Committee by the end of 1907, with the other members who were confident enough to correspond with the newspapers attracted by the enthusiasm and public engagement of the WSPU. Their move to the militant organization was echoed in Edinburgh by the erstwhile honorary secretary of the Edinburgh Society, Jessie Methven. The Scottish constitutional suffragists' slow and steady approach to reform was contrasted unfavourably to the direct action and publicity of the militants, leading to a haemorrhage of members to the WSPU in the years after 1906, particularly in Glasgow, Edinburgh and Aberdeen. However, it must be noted that, outside the major cities, it was NUWSS-affiliated rather than WSPU societies that continued to be established.

The Glasgow suffragists showed more enthusiasm for coverage of their activities in the suffrage press, although again their contributions were frequently penned by Hunter. These periodicals, however, brought their own issues. Pressure to sell more copies, in order to promote and financially support the NUWSS, was pushed back by Glaswegian suffragists who felt they had done enough and who queried the relevance of the periodicals to their own situation. It is clear that the English-centric coverage of the nineteenth-century suffrage campaign identified by Smitley was continued by the new publications of the twentieth century. The relationship with the suffrage press reflected the sometimes prickly relationship of GWSAWS with NUWSS headquarters, with the Glasgow suffragists both wishing to assert their independence and the difference between England and Scotland while at the same time complaining that the National Union and suffrage press did not do enough to acknowledge Scottish achievements. Nonetheless, in comparison to the biting contempt that might be shown by Glaswegian newspapers, editors of the suffrage press were always ready to apologize when challenged.

The press committee of GWSAWS was finally wound down in December 1918, when it was decided that its work could now be carried on by other committees. Its disappearance marked the transformation of the Association into the Glasgow Women Citizens' Association with a focus on women's active citizenship.[83] Breitenbach and Wright suggest that, after the achievement of partial suffrage, many women's organizations were treated more respectfully by the press, with a level of coverage that made them highly visible to their contemporaries.[84] Links might be made here with the more respectful coverage given to the Association's war work during the emergency. Since the minutes of the Executive Committee continue until 1933, further work should be undertaken to investigate this new relationship between the Association and the press.

[83] E. Breitenbach, and V. Wright, 'Women as active citizens: Glasgow and Edinburgh c. 1918–1939', *Women's History Review*, xxiii (2014), 401–20.

[84] Breitenbach and Wright, 'Women as active citizens', p. 413.

8. 'The weakest link': suffrage writing, class interests and the isolated woman of leisure

Sos Eltis

'All women were appealed to. Class barriers were broken down; political distinctions swept away; religious differences forgotten. All women were as one.'[1] Annie Kenney's 1924 memoir offered an idealized vision of equality and unity in the women's suffrage movement, but this has been qualified and challenged by a succession of recent scholars.[2] The recognition that working-class women played a significant and active role in the suffrage campaign, including within the leadership of the Women's Social and Political Union, has revealed not the erasure of class distinctions but rather a history of careful negotiation and tactical deployment.[3] As studies have shown, while cross-class solidarity and a concern for the plight of the most destitute and exploited women in society were a prominent part of the campaign's image, the lived experience and active agency of working-class women were often elided, and they were reduced to passivity and helpless victimhood.[4] Seamstress Hannah Mitchell proudly recalled that 'there was a unity of purpose in the suffrage movement, which made social distinction seem of little importance'; but, as she famously noted, for working women

[1] A. Kenney, *Memories of a Militant* (London, 1924), p. 298.

[2] See R. S. Neale, 'Working-class women and women's suffrage', in *Class and Ideology in the Nineteenth Century* (London, 1972), pp. 143–68; J. Liddington and J. Norris, *One Hand Tied Behind Us: The Rise of the Women's Suffrage Movement* (London, 2000); M. Pugh, *The March of the Women: a Revisionist Analysis of the Campaign for Women's Suffrage, 1866–1914* (Oxford, 2002).

[3] See L. Jenkins, 'Annie Kenney and the politics of class in the Women's Social and Political Union', *Twentieth Century British History*, xxx (2019), 477–503.

[4] See K. Hunealt, *Working Women and Visual Culture, Britain 1880–1914* (Aldershot, 2002); L. Schwartz, *Feminism and the Servant Problem: Class and Domestic Labour in the Women's Suffrage Movement* (Cambridge, 2019).

'The weakest link', in *The politics of women's suffrage: local, national and international dimensions,* ed. A. Hughes-Johnson and L. Jenkins (London, 2021), pp. 213–236. License: CC BY-NC-ND 4.0.

with families to care for, suffrage campaigning could only be done 'with one hand tied behind us', producing a strain that eventually led Mitchell to a nervous breakdown and serious illness, through which some of her richer colleagues supported her while others turned aside.[5]

As has been well documented by scholars such as Lisa Tickner, Julie Holledge, Sheila Stowell, Naomi Paxton, Maroula Joannou, Katharine Cockin and Sowon Park, literature and dramatic performances were a valuable resource for the suffrage campaign.[6] The year 1908 saw the formation of the Women Writers' Suffrage League (WWSL) and the Actresses' Franchise League (AFL), 'To work for Votes for Women on the same terms as they are, or may be, granted to men', by disseminating propaganda literature, staging performances and raising funds. The WWSL declared itself 'entirely independent of any other suffrage league' and at the same time 'formed with the intention of assisting every other suffrage society', and its membership was, as Park has noted, remarkably inclusive in terms of gender, literary genre and political persuasion.[7] The AFL similarly aimed to 'assist all other leagues whenever possible', thus requiring a tactful navigation of political and policy differences.[8]

Qualifications for membership of the WWSL involved an annual payment of *2s 6d* and the requirement that members had received payment for a book, article, story, poem or play, thus enabling them to claim the status of professional workers. Given the limits to state education, however, the League's membership was inevitably drawn from the middle and upper classes. The AFL's membership was potentially far broader. As Tracy Davis notes, after a huge increase in middle-class entry to the profession in the later decades of the nineteenth century, 'performers' incomes spanned the highest upper middle-class salary and the lowest working-class wage, and

5 H. Mitchell, *The Hard Way Up: the Autobiography of Hannah Mitchell, Suffragette and Rebel*, ed. G. Mitchell with a preface by G. E. Evans (London, 1968), pp. 159, 130, 167–70.

6 L. Tickner, *The Spectacle of Women: Imagery of the Suffrage Campaign, 1907–1914* (London, 1987); J. Holledge, *Innocent Flowers: Women in Victorian Theatre* (London, 1981); S. Stowell, *A Stage of their Own: Feminist Playwrights of the Suffrage Era* (Manchester, 1992); N. Paxton, *Stage Rights! The Actresses' Franchise League, Activism and Politics, 1908–1958* (Manchester, 2019); M. Joannou, 'Suffragette fiction and the fictions of suffrage', in *The Women's Suffrage Movement: New Feminist Perspectives*, ed. M. Joannou and J. Purvis (Manchester, 1998), pp. 101–17; K. Cockin, G. Norquay and S. S. Park, *Women's Suffrage Literature*, 5 vols. (London, 2007).

7 WWSL leaflet, reproduced in E. Robins, *Way Stations* (London, 1913), p. 106; S. Sowon Park, 'The first professional: the Women Writers' Suffrage League', *Modern Languages Quarterly*, lvii (1997), p. 189.

8 A.J.R. (ed.), *The Suffrage Annual and Women's Who's Who 1913* (London, 1913), p. 11.

were earned in work places that ranged in status from patent theatres to penny saloons'.[9] The AFL responded vigorously to these disparities, campaigning to improve actresses' working conditions and wages. Leading members of the WWSL and the AFL, such as Elizabeth Robins, Cicely Hamilton, Inez Bensusan and Gertrude Jennings, came from comfortable middle-class professional backgrounds, but their working lives as theatremakers, including in touring companies, took them far beyond the shelter of their class origins, bringing them in contact with women from a wide range of social backgrounds and giving them first-hand experience of the precarity and hardship of the majority of working women's lives.

Committed to using their professional skills to recruit, educate and entertain on behalf of the suffrage cause, members of the WWSL and the AFL were therefore called upon to support the message of cross-class female solidarity – particularly important when some advocates of adult suffrage warned against enfranchising women on the same terms as men, on the grounds that adding propertied women to the electoral rolls could exacerbate the sufferings of working women who had 'more to fear from propertied women than from unpropertied men'.[10] Any impulse towards idealized visions of cross-class unity was simultaneously tempered by a call from Elizabeth Robins, president of the WWSL, for writers to take this opportunity to escape the constraints of male editors and publishers, and to describe life 'fearlessly from the woman's standpoint', to look clearly at the 'Real Girl' and to 'report her faithfully'.[11] These complex dynamics can be traced in a range of suffrage dramas, sketches and novels, as writers sought to meet the potentially conflicting requirements of propaganda and verisimilitude, while negotiating the literary conventions, class perspectives and consumer expectations inherent in each medium. By comparing short-form dramas with the longer-form literature of the four-act play and the novel, this chapter reveals how a number of suffrage writers did not simply promote the key suffrage message of cross-class unity but carefully calibrated their writing to cater to the particular sensibilities of bourgeois and aristocratic consumers and to assuage potential class anxieties. Analysis of the fiction of leading anti-suffragist Mary Augusta (Mrs Humphry) Ward offers a further challenge to suffragist claims to an exclusive interest

[9] T. C. Davis, *Actresses as Working Women: their Social Identity in Victorian Culture* (London and New York, 1991), p. 3.

[10] Editorial, *New Age: an Independent Socialist Review of Politics, Literature, and Art*, ed. A. R. Orage and H. Jackson, 23 May 1907, p. 50.

[11] E. Robins, 'The women writers', an address to the WWSL, 23 May 1911, *Way Stations*, pp. 235–6.

in women's social and economic deprivation in contrast to the supposed self-interest and snobbery of the 'antis'.

Short plays and sketches were a central part of the suffrage campaign's arsenal, performed as fundraisers at theatres and as entertainment at outdoor meetings, rallies, 'At Homes' and exhibitions. In these plays compassion for the suffering of exploited working-class women was repeatedly represented as the inspiration for more privileged women's conversion to the cause. Gertrude Vaughan's *The Woman with a Pack* (first performed at the Portman Rooms, Baker Street, on 8 December 1911 by the Actresses' Franchise League) staged the awakening of a female graduate through a series of visionary and symbolic tableaux. Comedy, however, was by far the most common mode, as in Joan Dugdale's *10, Clowning Street* (1913) in which the Prime Minister's plan to distract women from suffrage activities by a scheme of National Service backfires. The PM's three anti-suffragist daughters lead the way by working as a laundress, shopkeeper and parlour maid, but return outraged by their first-hand knowledge of women's employment conditions, angrily demanding the vote – and, in the maid's case, further enlightened as to the 'humbug' of Labour concerns for the 'downtrodden classes' after slaving from 5am till midnight in the house of a Labour MP.[12]

The capacity for compassion, or indeed the most basic interest in working-class lives, commonly marked out the difference between suffragists and anti-suffragists in such plays. Antis were depicted as snobbish, complacent, self-centred and ignorant. In Evelyn Glover's popular skit *A Chat with Mrs Chicky* (1909), for example, Mrs Houlbrook sits lecturing the eponymous charwoman about the dangers of female suffrage, while Mrs Chicky cleans efficiently around her, calmly dismantling the middle-class woman's arguments with her superior knowledge of man-made law, having been made aware of its absurdities by 'knockin' up against it'.[13] Mrs Chicky proudly recalls an encounter with anti-suffragists: ' "We've h'always got on very well without women 'avin' the vote" says one. "Yus' I calls back, *you* may 'ave but what price us?" '[14] In another one-act play by Evelyn Glover, *Miss Appleyard's Awakening* (1911), Miss Appleyard marks herself out from her fellow anti-suffragist by recognizing that her

[12] J. S. Dugdale, *10, Clowning Street* in *Votes for Women*, vii (1913), p. 186. First performed in 1913 for the Men's Political Union for Enfranchisement.

[13] E. Glover, *A Chat with Mrs Chicky*, in D. Spender and C. Hayman (ed.), *How the Vote Was Won, and Other Suffragette Plays* (London, 1985), p. 107. First performed at Rehearsal Theatre, London, 20 Feb. 1912.

[14] E. Glover, *A Chat with Mrs Chicky*, p. 112.

employees have a right to their own political views, after agreeing to sign an anti-suffrage petition.

> MRS CRABTREE: Thank you very much. And I hope you'll allow your servants to do the same?
> MISS APPLEYARD: My servants?
> MRS CRABTREE: Well it swells a list of signatures so beautifully – especially if a large staff is kept. Lady Carter's signed to the boot boy!
> MISS APPLEYARD: I'm afraid I don't keep a boot boy and I have only two servants. I've never really asked them their views on the Suffrage.
> MRS CRABTREE: Their views? I didn't ask my servants their views. I merely sent the petition to the kitchen for signatures.[15]

Mrs Crabtree unwittingly converts her colleague to the suffrage cause by revealing the gross misogyny that underlies opposition to women's enfranchisement. Miss Appleyard determines to find out more about the cause and calls for her maid, whose political affiliations are first signalled to the audience at the beginning of the play as she hums Ethel Smyth's suffrage anthem 'March of the Women' while laying the table.

> MISS APPLEYARD: Morton, some papers came by post this morning – printed papers from a Suffrage Society. I put them in the waste-paper basket. I suppose they'll have been thrown away by now?
> MORTON: No, 'm, they've not. Cook and me have got them in the kitchen.
> MISS APPLEYARD: I'd rather like to look at them.
> MORTON: I'll bring them, 'm. If you'll excuse my saying, Cook and me think there's a deal of sound common sense in this Suffrage business.
> MISS APPLEYARD: D' you know, Morton, I'm beginning to think it's quite possible that you may be right![16]

Newly awakened to her servants' political autonomy, the employer's education is brought up from the kitchen.

Such sketches provided an opportunity for suffragists to bond together in laughter, rather than necessarily being designed to convert opponents.

[15] E. Glover, *Miss Appleyard's Awakening*, in D. Spender and C. Hayman, *How the Vote Was Won, and Other Suffragette Plays* (London, 1985), p. 119. Published by the AFL in 1911. Notably the leading anti-suffragist Mary Ward brought her servants en masse from her country home to fill the gallery and hear her speak at an anti-suffrage rally at the Queen's Hall in London in Mar. 1909. See D. Ward, 'Diary', 26 Mar. 1909, in J. Sutherland, *Mrs Humphry Ward: Eminent Victorian, Pre-eminent Edwardian* (Oxford, 1990), p. 303.

[16] E. Glover, *Miss Appleyard's Awakening*, p. 124.

Logically, the idiocy and ignorance of privileged anti-suffragist women would hardly have made a convincing argument for extending the franchise to encompass precisely such propertied women. The short-form play conveniently allowed writers to stage significant or entertaining incidents without following through their further implications. How Miss Appleyard will interact with her cook and her maid now they have become fellow suffragists, reading the same papers and attending the same meetings, lies conveniently outside the borders of *Miss Appleyard's Awakening*. The relation between suffragists and their employees could be contentious; as a heated exchange of letters between employers and domestic workers in *Common Cause* over six months from August 1911 attested, many suffragists could be blind to the long hours and low wages suffered by their servants.[17] There was a reason, as Laura Schwarz has shown, why domestic servants were the workers least likely to be depicted in suffrage propaganda, despite being by far the most common employment for women; suffragist mistresses did not necessarily appreciate independence in their female employees.[18] While airing the issues and facts that underpinned suffrage arguments, performances did not necessarily aspire to realism. For example, Christopher St John and Cicely Hamilton's *Pot and Kettle* (1909), in which an anti-suffragist loses her temper with an aristocratic suffragette interrupting a political meeting and punches her, was advertised in a programme as based on 'an incident which occurred at a Meeting held by the Anti-suffrage League at Queen's Hall, London, in March 1909'.[19] The play turns on a comic reversal; the anti-suffragist Marjorie has been drawn into politics for the opportunities it offers to mix with the aristocratic leaders of the movement, but instead her social ambitions are fulfilled when the woman she assaulted, Lady Susan Pengarvon, proves to be a 'ripping good sort' and invites her assailant to tea despite a black eye.[20]

[17] See Schwartz, *Feminism and the Servant Problem*, pp. 87–8, and passim.

[18] Domestic service accounted for over a quarter of all women workers in the first decade of the twentieth century. The 1911 census recorded about 1.3 million women in private service in England and Wales and about 135,052 in Scotland; Schwartz, *Feminism and the Servant Problem*, p. 5.

[19] Play programme, Edith Craig Archive at the National Trust's Ellen Terry Memorial Museum, Kent, quoted in K. Cockin, 'Women's suffrage drama', in *The Women's Suffrage Movement: New Feminist Perspectives*, ed. M. Joannou and J. Purvis (Manchester, 1998), p. 137.

[20] C. Hamilton and C. St John [Christabel Marshall], *Pot and Kettle*, in *The Methuen Book of Suffrage Plays*, ed. N. Paxton (London, 2013), p. 64. Performed at the Scala Theatre, London, 12 Nov. 1909.

Simple character types and broad humour similarly characterize the style of Cicely Hamilton and Christopher St John's *How the Vote Was Won* (1909), one of the most popular suffrage plays, which offers a comic vision of victory achieved through cross-class solidarity. Expanded from a pamphlet with cartoon illustrations, the play repurposed archetypes – an overworked governess, a golf-playing New Woman novelist, a wealthy business owner, a music-hall singer and a boarding-house landlady – to new effect, as they all join a national strike and come to live with their nearest male relative, anti-suffragist Horace Cole.[21] Each of them wage-earning and self-supporting, the women embrace each other's acquaintance as members of the same family – metaphorically as well as literally – and welcome Horace's forced conversion (and energetic mansplaining) as he leaves to join a march of desperate men demanding that the government grant women the vote.

These sketches staged working women refusing to be overlooked or silenced and embracing suffrage on the basis of their own lived experience, but their voices were largely the creation of middle-class women; *A Chat with Mrs Chicky*, for example, was written by Evelyn Glover, who was born into an upper-middle-class family, and the charwoman was first played by Inez Bensusan, playwright, suffragette, head of the AFL's play department and daughter of a wealthy Australian businessman. When Bensusan played Mrs Chicky at the Rehearsal Theatre in 1912, *The Vote* congratulated her on the 'absolute fidelity' of her performance, but it also indicated that she chose to play 'the over-worked, under-fed, char-woman with a "code id 'er dose," but with a magnificent spirit of independence'.[22] The head cold was an addition to Glover's script, and while it perhaps emphasized the hardship of Mrs Chicky's life, it also introduced an element of potentially reductive humour to the role. Designed to be playable in makeshift conditions with minimal props and set, these plays did not aspire to naturalistic verisimilitude; they alluded to the off-stage reality of working women's lives without claiming to bring those lives on stage.

Where sketches and one-act plays were made available to working-class suffragists – tickets for exhibition performances cost 1*s* but plays were often performed free of charge at rallies and meetings – novels and full-length

[21] L. Whitelaw, *The Life and Rebellious Times of Cicely Hamilton: Actress, Writer, Suffragist* (London, 1990), p. 83. First performed at an AFL matinee at the Royalty Theatre, 13 Apr. 1909.

[22] 'Propaganda plays', *The Vote*, 2 Mar. 1912, p. 226.

plays were necessarily more limited in their reach, being confined to those with the money and leisure to access them.[23] Where short plays were often extravagantly comic, fantastical or visionary, suffrage novels tended to advertise their verisimilitude; so, for example, Constance Maud prefaced *No Surrender* (1911) with a disclaimer as to any reference to specific individuals or historical events, but then added that her fictional characters 'move among events that are historically real and true, and there is not a statement touching prison and law-court experiences, or present laws regarding women in this country, related here, for which chapter and verse cannot be given'.[24] Alliances and friendships across the class divide remained a central element in the pro-suffrage message of such works, but the greater space to explore issues in more depth and the requirements of realism to engage with the complexities and tensions within such relations produced a notably different vision of social relations – as did the more privileged status of their readers and audiences.

American actress, playwright and novelist Elizabeth Robins was the first woman to write a play as a deliberate contribution to the suffrage campaign. *Votes for Women!* opened at the Court Theatre, London, on 9 April 1907, and Robins divided half her profits between the WSPU and the NUWSS. Subtitled 'A Dramatic Tract in Three Acts', it was a drama of suffrage conversion, including a scene set in Trafalgar Square that made the audience proxy attendees at a suffrage rally. A member of the NUWSS, Robins converted to militancy in the course of her research for the play, joining the WSPU committee at the invitation of Mrs Pankhurst.[25] She was a founding member of the WWSL and the AFL with fellow writers and theatre professionals such as Cecily Hamilton, Bessie Hatton, Winifred Mayo and Inez Bensusan, who together campaigned for improved working conditions and equal pay for women, and produced a host of works that

[23] Tickets for the Court Theatre, where Robins's *Votes for Women!* was performed, ranged from 10*s* 6*d* in the stalls to a half-crown in the pit, or a few gallery seats at 1*s*, with the further barrier that the first run of eight performances were matinees staged during working hours. The script was advertised in *The Suffragette* at 1*s*. Gertrude Colmore's novel *Suffragette Sally* was on sale in *The Suffragette* at 4*s* 6*d*; Elizabeth Robins's *The Convert* was published by Methuen in its Popular Novels series at 6*s*. For comparison, Hannah Mitchell was paid 4*s* a week, plus board and lodging, as a domestic servant, and then 8*s* a week as a dressmaker's assistant, from which she paid her brother 2*s* a week rent.

[24] C. Maud, 'Preface', in *No Surrender* (London, 2011; first published 1911).

[25] On Robins's research for the play and her lifelong activism, see A. V. John, *Elizabeth Robins: Staging a Life* (London and New York, 1995), and J. Gates, *Elizabeth Robins, 1862–1952* (Tuscaloosa, Ala., 1994).

not only promoted the suffrage cause but also challenged the sexual double standard, legal inequalities and economic injustice.[26]

A message of cross-class solidarity is central to *Votes for Women!*, in which Vida Levering, a suffrage activist, encounters a former lover, the rising Conservative MP Geoffrey Stonor, and recruits him to the cause. Vida's sexual past is not, as in so many 'fallen woman' plays, a key to her moral character, but a spur to her politicization as she determines to improve other women's financial and social situations and so 'move that rock of offence' – women's economic and sexual vulnerability – on which she herself stumbled.[27] Women's shared interests are a theme of the Trafalgar Square speeches, from a Working Woman (notably not given a name beyond her class designation) who declares that '*Every* child is our child', to Vida's declaration that a servant girl jailed for the death of a baby fathered by her employer will only secure justice when she faces a jury of '*her* peers' – in other words, women who can understand the trials of childbirth and post-partum mania.[28]

As Maroula Joannou has noted, the play was written at a moment when cross-class solidarity was key to the suffrage movement's political positioning, yet, despite the shared interests that Joannou notes, the play's texture is actually one of constant disagreements and tensions.[29] Allegiances are formed between women, but they are tactical alliances, not personal bonds. The first act takes place at a country-house weekend party, common to so many Edwardian West End plays, but the action, more unusually, consists of women arguing over suffrage tactics, protests in the Commons and funding for women's refuges. Solidarity, even within the closed circle of the upper classes, must overcome ideological and personal differences. The personal is subordinate to the political; Stonor's fresh-faced fiancée is enthralled by Vida – an emotional bond which Vida calmly exploits to leverage Stonor's cooperation. Eschewing sentimentality, Robins represented women's shared interests as essentially political rather than emotional, rooted in a cross-class recognition of sexual, economic and legal vulnerability.

While unsure of securing a producer for her play, Robins wrote a novelized version, *The Convert* (1907), taking her narrative back to Vida's

[26] For further details, see Paxton, *Stage Rights!*

[27] E. Robins, *Votes for Women!*, in J. Chothia (ed.), *The New Woman and Other Emancipated Woman Plays* (Oxford, 1998), p. 207.

[28] E. Robins, *Votes for Women!*, II, pp. 171, 184. Robins's papers include 26 pages of typed notes detailing eight suffrage meetings on which she drew; see John, *Elizabeth Robins*, pp. 144–9.

[29] M. Joannou, '"Hilda, harnessed to a purpose": Elizabeth Robins, Ibsen, and the vote', *Comparative Drama*, xliv (2010), pp. 179–200, 253–4.

first encounters with the suffrage campaign and tracing her slow conversion from a class-based to a gender-based identity. Prompted by disdainful curiosity, Vida attends a suffrage rally together with her sister in outlandishly dowdy clothes, disguised as a 'Woman of the People'.[30] Bemused and disgusted by the lower-class speakers, the sisters are simply bored by a working-class woman: 'having no key either to her pathos or her power, [they] saw nothing but "low cockney effrontery"'.[31] A lower-middle-class speaker sporting an extravagant hat strikes them as 'excruciatingly genteel' and her flowery rhetoric is 'torturing' to their 'fastidious feminine sense'.[32] The speaker's crude performance of gentility serves as an uncomfortable reminder that class superiority is a matter of costume and manners; stripped of such theatrical props, Vida and her sister are disconcerted at the 'coolly watchful, slightly contemptuous stare' of two policemen – 'a way no policeman had ever looked at either of them before'.[33] A gulf of disdain divides the upper-class women from the speakers, whose power to move the crowd remains incomprehensible to them. Robins and the play's director, Harley Granville Barker, produced this dynamic of class distance in the Court Theatre staging of the Trafalgar Square rally by placing the sceptical Stonor, his hostess Lady John and his adoring fiancée Jean between the suffrage speakers and the audience. Doubly distanced by the heckling crowd and the amused indifference of the upper-class thrill-seekers, the working-class speakers deliver their appeals to the audience across a visible class divide.

The Convert charts Vida's growing awareness and questioning of the gender conditioning that accompanies her social position. She struggles to shake off her instinctive desire to please men like Lord Borrodaile, who, given a choice between women progressing to suffrage and higher education or reverting back, impulsively exclaims, 'Back. Yes, back to the harem.'[34] The greatest shock to Vida's class loyalties, however, comes from a suffragette who dismisses aristocratic women as 'sexless' – these 'curled darlings of society' have 'no sex-pride', declares the seasoned campaigner, who notoriously carries a dog-whip to ward off indecent assaults when she

[30] E. Robins, *The Convert* (London, 1980; first published 1907), p. 74.

[31] Robins, *The Convert*, p. 83.

[32] Robins, *The Convert*, p. 87.

[33] Robins, *The Convert*, p. 74. For further analysis of this moment, see L. Winkiel, 'Suffrage burlesque: modernist performance in Elizabeth Robins's *The Convert*', *Modernist Fiction Studies*, l (2004), 570–94.

[34] Robins, *The Convert*, p. 147.

is thrown out of political meetings.[35] Vida describes her political conversion as 'seeing beyond my usual range', a new 'view of life'.[36] This new perspective reveals her former class-based instincts as those of a 'geisha' whose only role was to please the men around her; released from her class conditioning, Vida can begin to develop the sympathies that constitute sex-pride.[37] The novel's narrative perspective mirrors Vida's enlightenment, shifting from her initial bourgeois perspective in which lower-class women are incomprehensible and absurd to a defamiliarized view of upper-class women as complicit in their own and other women's exploitation.

While Vida is awakened to her class conditioning amid the democratic jostle of suffrage meetings, her maid Gorringe experiences only 'genteel horror' at 'the proximity to her mistress of these canaille'.[38] Vida attempts to make light of 'the affront to seemliness' she feels at her servant seeing her pushed and shoved aside; as the narrator comments, 'Under circumstances like these the observant are reminded that no section of the modern community is so scornfully aristocratic as our servants.'[39] In Maud's *No Surrender*, a butler is depicted as similarly protective of class distinctions, deriving a sense of his own social status from the eminence of his employers; it is therefore necessary to smuggle members of the Men's League for Women's Suffrage into the household under the guise of footmen in order to deliver a petition to Cabinet ministers dining there. The notion that servants were less democratically minded than their employers was perhaps a more comfortable notion for a middle- and upper-class readership than the contrary position.

For all Vida's glowing description of the movement as 'Women, the poorest and the most ignorant (except of hardship), working shoulder to shoulder with women of substance and position', both novel and play make

[35] Robins, *The Convert*, p. 161.

[36] Robins, *The Convert*, p. 144.

[37] Robins, *The Convert*, p. 24.

[38] Robins, *The Convert*, pp. 97–8.

[39] Robins, *The Convert*, p. 98. Robins's actual relationship with her domestic employees was more democratic; her Danish housekeeper heard Mrs Pankhurst speak in Brighton in 1912, went on to college and translated Elizabeth Robins's suffrage essays into Danish, eventually became principal of a Danish labour college and spent some time at Ruskin College, Oxford. She corresponded with her former employer for decades, maintaining that she was 'one of those who gets others growing'; quoted in A. V John, 'Radical reflections? Elizabeth Robins: the making of suffragette history and the representation of working-class women', in *The Duty of Discontent: Essays for Dorothy Thompson*, ed. O. Ashton, R. Fyson and S. Roberts (London, 1995), p. 199.

clear the differences that temper cross-class solidarity.[40] When Geoffrey Stonor determines to espouse female suffrage as just the 'political dynamite' that his career needs, his decision is framed in both play and novel as a moment of intense self-absorption and isolation. Oblivious to his fiancée's distress at discovering his past involvement with Vida, Stonor muses that, 'After all, women are much more Conservative *naturally* than men, aren't they?' He believes that civilization itself will be in danger if only women of the lower classes, 'inoculated with the Socialist virus', have political training when the vote is eventually granted.[41] If Vida's conversion is motivated by cross-class sympathy and a concern for the most vulnerable women in society, Stonor's conversion is motivated by the interests of class, party and personal ambition. Class divisions and divergent interests remain robustly apparent in Robins's vision of the suffrage campaign, though Vida Levering has begun to see beyond them.

The most famous act of cross-class solidarity in the suffrage campaign took place in 1910, when Lady Constance Lytton disguised herself as a seamstress in order to expose the differential prison treatment accorded to working-class suffragettes. Lytton, the most prominent aristocratic member of the WSPU, was arrested in her own persona in 1909, her heart condition was carefully diagnosed and she was confined to the prison's sickbay; a year later, disguised as 'Jane Warton', her heart condition was overlooked and she was force-fed eight times before serious illness and suspicions of her identity led to her release. Praise for Lytton's self-sacrifice was unanimous across the full spectrum of suffrage organizations. The authorities' reluctance to inflict force-feeding on a member of the aristocracy exposed force-feeding as a torture, designed to punish women and intimidate them into abandoning militant tactics – not the 'special medical treatment' the government claimed.[42] In her memoir *Prisons and Prisoners: Some Personal Experiences*, 'by Constance Lytton and Jane Warton, Spinster' (1914), Lytton, like Robins, was to condemn the aristocratic woman of leisure as 'the weakest link in

[40] Robins, *The Convert*, p. 171.

[41] Robins, *The Convert*, p. 276. See Robins, *Votes for Women!*, III, p. 189. Notably Stonor's comments on the danger posed to civilization by working women's enfranchisement were only added after the licensing copy was submitted, suggesting they were incorporated from *The Convert*. See E. Robins, *Votes for Women!*, Lord Chamberlain's Plays Collection, British Library, 1907/6, Act III.

[42] 'Questions in the House', *Votes for Women*, 8 Oct. 1909, p. 20. See also 'Suffragist women prisoners', *Home Office Papers and Memoranda 1889–1910* (London, 1910), appendix E in C. Lytton, *Prisons and Prisoners, Some Personal Experiences*, ed. J. Haslam (Peterborough, Ont., 2008). For further details, see L. Jenkins, *Lady Constance Lytton: Aristocrat, Suffragette, Martyr* (London, 2015).

the chain of womanhood. Isolated and detached, she has but little sense of kinship with other women', uncritical of the constraints and limitations imposed on their lives because a 'maiming subserviency' has become their ideal.[43]

Lytton's self-sacrifice was fictionalized in two novels structured around cross-class allegiances and friendships in the suffrage movement: Gertrude Colmore's *Suffragette Sally* (1911) and Constance Maud's *No Surrender* (1911). Both novels contain multiple narrative strands, tracing the interwoven lives of working-class, middle-class and upper-class activists. These novels are designed to showcase the cross-class solidarity of the movement, but, aspiring to offer a truthful portrait of contemporary events and aware of the sensibilities of their readership, the resultant narratives also acknowledge class tensions and the limitations of empathy and imagination. Colmore, like Robins and Lytton, was a member of the WSPU, and Maud was a member of the Women's Freedom League and dedicated her novel to Charlotte Despard. The allegiances in their novels underline the potential benefits to working-class women that even partial female enfranchisement could bring.

Lady Geraldine Hill is a fictional incarnation of Constance Lytton in Colmore's *Suffragette Sally*. A concern for the less privileged drives Geraldine's activism and gives 'force to her words, the ring of conviction to her voice', enabling her to recruit Sally Simmonds, a maid-of-all-work, to the cause, and to inspire her middle-class friend Edith Carstairs to make the step from constitutional to militant suffragism.[44] Where Elizabeth Robins and Constance Lytton took full aim at the cushioned and useless lives of the upper classes among whom they mixed, Colmore instead questioned how far class distinctions apply to women. Informing her husband that she is determined to engage in militant activism, Lady Hill dismisses his appeal to her social standing: 'What is my position? what is it, after all? Lower, politically, than the meanest man's on the Duke's estate. Yet I am to be held back by it from doing anything towards attaining the position of

[43] *Prisons and Prisoners: Some Personal Experiences*, by Constance Lytton and Jane Warton, Spinster (New York, 1914), p. 40. For further analysis of the class dynamics in Lytton's memoir, see S. Eltis, 'A class act: Constance Lytton and the political, literary and dramatic dynamics of suffrage prison writings', *Feminist Modernist Studies*, ii (2019), 1–20; M. Myall, '"Only be ye strong and very courageous": the militant suffragism of Lady Constance Lytton', *Women's History Review*, vii (1998), 61–84; S. Thomas, 'Scenes in the writing of "Constance Lytton and Jane Warton, Spinster": contextualising a cross-class dresser', *Women's History Review*, xii (2003), 51–71.

[44] G. Colmore, *Suffragette Sally*, ed. A. Lee (Peterborough, Ont., 2008; first published London, 1911), p. 68.

a citizen!'[45] Edith is awakened to the realities of class distinction in men's eyes when she appeals to male voters to sign her NUWSS petition and discovers that a woman seeking political rights is treated 'with manners so different from the manners of the drawing-room and the tennis-court!'[46] Class status is merely a veneer, *Suffragette Sally* informs its socially privileged readership; women need not fear a loss of caste from their political activism, for in truth they never had it. Hearing an anti-suffragist speaker explain that men's electoral rights depend on qualifications of class, but women's are ineluctably a matter of sex alone, Edith finds herself dwelling on the question, 'If a woman has no class, how can she be *declassé*?'[47]

Despite giving her name to the novel, Sally's primary role in the book is as an adoring follower of Lady Hill, whose suffrage speech she responds to instinctively while she 'could not recall the words, the meaning of many of which was naught to her', experiencing it instead as a 'song of freedom' that awakens a fluttering bird within her.[48] As she becomes a speaker herself, the narrative notes her earthy wit and repartee without recording her actual words, locating her political voice sufficiently far from the reader as to be virtually inaudible. Colmore's account of Sally's treatment in prison mirrors the brutal treatment of working-class suffragettes Selina Martin and Leslie Hall – force-fed, mercilessly beaten, thrown handcuffed into a cold punishment cell, kicked down the stairs and left to fall on her face with her hands locked behind her.[49] A single woman with no family to support, and living more comfortably on a salary from the suffrage society than she did as a maid-of-all-work, Sally does not face the greater hurdle to working-class suffrage involvement described by Hannah Mitchell in her autobiography: running a household, tending to children and facing not only public disapproval but domestic unhappiness.[50] But Sally's lifetime of hard work and poor diet and her brutal prison treatment mean she pays with her life for her activism. She remains a somewhat childlike recruit to the cause, however, referring to the internal injuries sustained from being kicked by a policeman as 'the toothache'.[51] Far from setting aside class differences, Sally's deference makes an impulsive kiss from Lady Hill her

[45] Colmore, *Suffragette Sally*, p. 103.

[46] Colmore, *Suffragette Sally*, p. 56.

[47] Colmore, *Suffragette Sally*, p. 153.

[48] Colmore, *Suffragette Sally*, p. 50.

[49] Colmore, *Suffragette Sally*, pp. 232–45; for Martin and Hall's treatment, see G. Sigerson, *Custodia Honesta* (London, 1913), pp. 5–6.

[50] Mitchell, *The Hard Way Up*, pp. 112, 130, 149.

[51] Colmore, *Suffragette Sally*, p. 262.

greatest moment of pride: 'That she, Sally, the erstwhile "general", should be kissed by *the* lady of all ladies, was a bliss of which she had never dreamed. It made prison worth while, apart from the Cause; it was compensation, consecration, and reward.'[52]

Colmore not only eschewed Lytton's scathing criticism of the leisured class to which she belonged, she significantly revised her source material to elevate her version of Constance Lytton to a Christ-like role. She closely mirrored Lytton's accounts of her prison experience, including the near-fatal weakness to which Lytton almost succumbed after being repeatedly force-fed and left in a freezing cell, and from which she was revived by the thought of the oppressed and destitute women for whom she must continue to fight. In numerous speeches to suffrage audiences and in her memoirs, Lytton also recounted being almost overwhelmed by bitterness at the cruelty of some prison wardresses and doctors, a feeling which was only dispelled by the light falling upon the crossbars of her cell window, reminding her of the three crosses of Calvary: 'One for the Lord Christ who died for sinners, and one for the sinner who was kind, and one for the sinner who had not yet learnt to be kind.'[53] Behind the third cross Lytton pictured all the hateful institutions and blind officialdom within and beyond the prison, and reminded herself that it was for such as these that Christ died. In *Suffragette Sally*, by contrast, after parallel musings on Lady Hill's part, the narrative shifts to focus on the cruellest of the prison doctors, noting that:

> Now between this man and [Lady Hill] … a cross was reared, raising them both; ay, even though he knew not, this man, that he was raised; knew not that by the forgiveness of the woman, whom, as a working woman, he despised he was brought a little nearer to the glory that waits, far onward on the upward path of evolution, for every living soul.[54]

Lytton humbly reminds herself of Christ's ordinance; Colmore's aristocrat, like Christ, raises the sinner.

Suffragette Sally was greeted by *The Observer* as 'propaganda, pure and simple', a copy of which 'might be placed with advantage in the hands of every broad-minded Anti-Suffragist'.[55] If so, its target readership was one to whom class distinctions remained important. An episode in which Sally

[52] Colmore, *Suffragette Sally*, p. 263.

[53] 'A speech by Lady Constance Lytton. Delivered at the Queen's Hall, January 31, 1910', *Votes for Women*, 4 Feb. 1910, p. 292.

[54] Colmore, *Suffragette Sally*, p. 259.

[55] 'New novels', *The Observer*, June 1911, p. 5; 'Suffragette Sally', *The Bookman*, xl (1911), p. 144.

encounters Edith and her mother while selling suffrage papers on the street demonstrates the fine line the novel treads between celebrating cross-class friendships and tactfully marking their limits. Edith shocks her mother by greeting this 'common-looking woman' and telling her they are on their way to have tea with Lady Hill. Left alone, Sally warms herself with the thought that, 'She was helping her dear ladyship more by standing there in the cold than if she were to go and share her tea.'[56] Sally's adoring dedication quietly elides the fact she was never invited. Not for Sally the intimate friendships that Annie Kenney enjoyed with her middle- and upper-class WSPU colleagues, the Pankhursts and Pethick-Lawrences – such proximity might be celebrated by Kenney in her memoir, but it was less likely to be attractive to the novel's well-heeled readers.[57] Colmore's fictional tale of cross-class solidarity was carefully targeted to flatter and reassure a privileged readership.

Constance Maud's novel *No Surrender* is similarly structured around a growing friendship between mill-worker Jenny Clegg and Mary O'Neil, niece of the mill owner, Sir Godfrey Walker. Sympathies and concerns for the most deprived women are presented as the primary inspiration for suffragists throughout the novel. In a chapter titled 'The Canterbury Tales', imprisoned suffragettes each recount their conversion, variously motivated by compassion, principles of social justice and the determination to save other women from the sufferings they themselves endured. A central plot strand establishes shared interests between working men and the women's movement. Joe Hopton, a trade union leader, is firmly opposed to women's enfranchisement and has forged an alliance with the Liberal Party, unaware of the contempt in which Sir Godfrey, a Liberal MP, holds his workers, whose political opinions he believes he has a right to dictate. Joe learns where working-class interests really lie when his young sister is seduced and abandoned by her employer, and in desperation she attempts suicide, thereby killing her baby. She is sentenced to death by the magistrate (part of a recurring pattern in the novel of male judges favouring men's interests and feelings over those of the women they abuse), and Joe is rebuffed by his Liberal allies when he seeks their help; as he comments bitterly, 'They've no time to waste on a poor workin' girl. Why, a girl don't count as much as one o' their horses or dogs – not by a long shot.'[58] It is the suffragists who raise a petition for clemency and ensure the girl's sentence is commuted, proving their genuine commitment to helping the most vulnerable in society.

[56] Colmore, *Suffragette Sally*, p. 93.

[57] See Kenney, *Memories*, chs. 5, 13, 15.

[58] Maud, *No Surrender*, p. 252.

Mary O'Neill's disguise as a working-class woman and her consequent force-feeding remain a relatively minor detail in *No Surrender*, which climaxes with the 1911 suffrage march through London, uniting women of all classes, together with the Men's League, led by Joe Hopton carrying a banner of John Stuart Mill. Jenny, unlike Colmore's Sally, is an articulate and autonomous political agent, a committed socialist from the start. But class deference nonetheless guides her relationship with Mary; when both friends are imprisoned and set to scrub their cells,

> For herself, Jenny minded nothing, but for her beloved Miss O'Neill she felt each hardship acutely, and longed to be able, Monte-Cristo fashion, to creep through some crevice in the wall and do her scrubbing for her.[59]

Given the *Academy* reviewer's objection to the 'bludgeon-like argument … delivered by Lancashire mill-hands in very broad dialect' in this 'extremely aggressive volume', Colmore was evidently wise to include such conciliatory details to flatter her upper-class readers.[60]

Like Colmore, Constance Maud negotiated class sensibilities with strategic tact, as exemplified by the careful nuancing of the image of suffrage women as an army united across class differences. The metaphor is first used when Mary offers a holiday to Jenny's brother, who has been injured in an industrial accident. Jenny demurs, and Mary responds:

> Aren't we women all bound together in a common cause to make the world a little better and happier – working shoulder to shoulder, like soldiers in a regiment? What would you think of the man who refused to share a flask of water or a loaf of bread with his comrade on the battlefield when his own happened to be empty? Why, we'd call him a surly fellow not to take as freely as he'd give. Now don't you be a surly fellow, Jenny![61]

And the offer is gratefully accepted. The image recurs when Jack Wilmot, the son of an upper-class suffragist, falls in love with Jenny and proposes marriage. Jenny declines, explaining that she may have left the mill, but she has not left 'my own people or my own class. I am one with them … I suffer with them – I feel as they do, Mr. Wilmot, and not as you do.'[62] Jack insists that he feels with the workers, not his own class, but Jenny is adamant.

59 Maud, *No Surrender*, p. 257.

60 'No Surrender', *Academy*, 17 Feb. 1912, p. 211.

61 Maud, *No Surrender*, p. 55.

62 Maud, *No Surrender*, p. 171.

> 'You'd have to begin from your cradle,' she explained, 'fed on our food, speaking our speech – trained in the mill – beginnin' as a half-timer at eight year old, rising at five o'clock o'the cold winter's morn, and hurryin' out in the dark through the snow, fearin' to hear the clock strike six 'fore you get to mill.'
>
> He followed her every word with his quick sympathy and artist's ready imagination: 'I can picture it,' he assured her, 'it is not necessary to have lived through it.'
>
> 'Oh yes, it is,' said Jenny. 'It's only what we've lived through as we can feel – that's what shapes our thoughts and shapes our souls. You must work in your class, God knows you're needed there, and I must work in mine.'
>
> 'But we are fighting in the same army – under the same banner, little Jenny – for the same goal.'
>
> 'Aye, but in different regiments, with different work and different weapons and different training.'[63]

Jenny's response serves as a reassurance for the upper-class reader that unfortunate marriages will not result from campaigning alongside lower-class women. But Jenny's response to Jack's faith in the power of his artist's imagination also deliberately marks out the limits to representation – both artistic and political. Nothing can replace direct experience and the knowledge that is born of it. The crucial limits to imaginative empathy and art's ability to communicate lived experience mark not only the constraints of the novel but also the essential need for individual enfranchisement as the only true form of political representation; no gender or class can fully represent another's interests.

This issue of representation became particularly problematic in suffrage fiction when it came to the most abject members of society. A central plank of the suffrage argument was the need for qualified women to secure the vote in order to speak on behalf of the poorest women, those doubly deprived by gender and class; but to assert the ability of privileged women to imagine the lives and needs of the most deprived also risked undermining the principle of self-representation. In *Suffragette Sally*, Edith's friend Rachel explains how, as a middle-class young woman, she was left destitute and forced to work for starvation wages among the poorest women, and it is for their sake that she believes in militant tactics, because they cannot afford to wait patiently for constitutional methods to take effect. These are the women who most need the vote, but who 'don't

[63] Maud, *No Surrender*, p. 172.

know that they need it; who are so crushed, so broken, so near the level of animals that they don't even desire it; because they desire nothing, are capable of desiring nothing, beyond food, sleep – just, and nothing more than just – what an animal desires.'[64] Living beyond the borders of the text, these women's lives can only be communicated in negatives – a distance that raises questions both about Rachel's confidence in filling the blank of their needs and desires, and the precise mechanism whereby those needs are to be met by the vote.

Elizabeth Robins was less convinced than Colmore of the ability or right of more privileged women to access the lives of the most socially deprived. In *The Convert*, a campaign leader stops a less experienced speaker going into detail about the lives of the women she has encountered in a homeless shelter. As the leader explains to Vida, 'We sometimes make a passing reference – just to set men thinking, and there leave it. But it always makes them furious, of course. It does no good. Either people know and just accept it, or else they won't believe, and it only gets them on the raw.'[65] Based on the real-life activist Mary Higgs, who disguised herself as a tramp to visit a homeless shelter and recorded her experiences in *Three Nights in Women's Lodging Houses* (1905), Robins's activist pays the same price for her experiences as Higgs did: three months serious illness. Inspired by the leader's example, Vida too takes a 'pilgrimage' in the 'Underworld', as she later tells an aristocratic house party.

> 'I put on an old gown and a tawdry hat –' She turned suddenly to her hostess. 'You'll never know how many things are hidden from a woman in good clothes. The bold free look of a man at a woman he believes to be destitute – you must *feel* that look on you before you can understand – a good half of history.'[66]

Vida's experiences, like those of the suffrage leader, lie discreetly outside the boundaries of the novel. Her masquerade serves to highlight rather than bridge the gap between classes. 'You needn't suppose', objects an aristocratic houseguest, 'that those wretched creatures feel it as we would'. To which Vida responds, 'The girls who need shelter and work aren't *all* serving-maids.'[67]

64 Colmore, *Suffragette Sally*, p. 167.

65 Robins, *The Convert*, p. 200.

66 Robins, *The Convert*, p. 224. Higgs's account offered a markedly distanced and middle-class perspective on the lives of homeless women, blaming their destitution on weakened bonds of marriage among the working classes, aspirations to economic independence, inadequate moral teaching and the influence of sentimental literature. See M. Higgs, *Three Nights in Women's Lodging Houses* (Manchester, 1905).

67 Robins, *The Convert*, p. 225.

Vida does not challenge the notion that a serving maid feels differently; her cross-class masquerade gives her knowledge of 'that look' but she does not presume to have experienced how 'those wretched creatures feel'. Vida Levering speaks *for* the abject, but she does not presume to speak *as*.

A concern for the most vulnerable women in society was not, of course, unique to suffrage campaigners. The first organized female opposition to women's enfranchisement, the 1889 'Appeal Against Female Suffrage' penned by Mary Ward and signed by over 1,500 women, declared that, 'The care of the sick and the insane; the treatment of the poor; the education of children' were matters in which women 'have made good their claim to larger and more extended powers', but crucially argued that women's activism should be confined to the local not the national or international arenas.[68] The Appeal concluded both that 'the emancipating process' had reached the limits fixed by the physical constitution and occupations of women, and that 'certain injustices of the law towards women', especially among working women, could safely be entrusted to the current constitutional machinery given the 'new spirit of justice and sympathy among men'.[69] Campaigns to improve conditions for working women brought together supporters and opponents of suffrage. The National Union for Women Workers, for example, was formed in 1895 to advance women's work through collective organization and political influence, and included both Millicent Fawcett and leading anti-suffragist Mary Ward among its members – until the passing of a special pro-suffrage motion in 1912 prompted Ward to resign.

Mary Ward, a founder and president of the Women's National Anti-Suffrage League, was both a tireless campaigner against women's enfranchisement and an energetic and effective social activist, who founded children's play-centres and in 1899 established the first Invalid Children's School.[70] A proponent of the 'Forward Policy' for women, Ward campaigned to expand women's role on school boards, as Poor Law guardians, in local elections and even to have seats reserved on county and borough councils.[71] Cross-class sympathies were at the heart of her political mission, but crucially within a clearly hierarchical social structure. A prolific novelist, Ward, like so many suffrage writers, used her fiction as a platform for her views. In

[68] 'An appeal against female suffrage', *Nineteenth Century*, cxlviii (1889), p. 782.

[69] 'An appeal against female suffrage', *Nineteenth Century*, cxlviii (1889), pp. 782, 784–5.

[70] For further details, see B. Sutton-Ramspeck, *Raising the Dust: The Literary Housekeeping of Mary Ward, Sarah Grand, and Charlotte Perkins Gilman* (Athens, O., 2004) and J. Sutherland, *Mrs Humphry Ward: Eminent Victorian, Pre-eminent Edwardian* (Oxford, 1990).

[71] For further details, see J. Bush, 'British women's anti-suffragism and the Forward Policy, 1908–14', *Women's History Review*, xi (2002), 431–54.

her 1894 novel *Marcella*, for example, the idealistic young heroine espouses Fabian socialism and exhausts herself as a rent-collector and a nurse in the East End until she embraces her position as a member of the landowning classes, improving her tenants' lives through good management and the introduction of a carefully measured minimum wage, which raises living standards while preserving the wealth of the estate. Ward depicts Marcella's aspiration to solidarity with the working classes as naive and misplaced; attempting to comfort the wife of a poacher hung for murder, she does not realize that her presence is 'a burden and constraint', isolating the widow from the 'homelier speech and simpler consolations' of her community.[72]

Ward launched her most direct fictional attack on militant suffragism in *Delia Blanchflower* (1916), whose eponymous heroine is a motherless girl drawn into the movement by her fierce governess, Gertrude Marvell. After her father's death, Delia devotes her energies and money to the suffrage cause, in the company of a disparate collection of female malcontents, each motivated by personal resentments and injuries, and bound together in their hatred of men. A dressmaker, excited by her unwonted access to Maumsey Abbey, the Blanchflowers' ancestral home, muses rhapsodically on Delia's involvement in 'The Daughters of Revolt': 'The Movement was indeed wonderful! How it broke down class barriers, and knit all women together!'[73] In the eyes of Delia's guardian, Mark Winnington, however, this supposed class solidarity is no more than Gertrude's dereliction of her duties as a paid companion, leaving Delia unchaperoned while she pursues her suffrage activities and then requisitioning Delia's flat with scant regard to its owner.

Like Marcella, Delia must be educated by her guardian to understand her responsibilities as the owner of Maumsey Abbey, learning to focus her energies on giving informed help to the cottagers on her estate rather than concerning herself with the more distant plight of sweated women. Symbolically, Gertrude's militant arson attack on the ancient estate of a local Cabinet minister results not only in the destruction of part of England's heritage but also the accidental death of the caretaker's invalid daughter, a child whom Mark had enrolled in his newly established school for handicapped children. The novel sets up a direct conflict between personal duties and political activism when Delia chooses to nurse the maid who has been with her since childhood rather than obeying Gertrude's demand that she attend militant meetings in London. But it is Mark's example,

[72] M. A. Ward, *Marcella*, ed. B. Sutton-Ramspeck and N. B. Meller (Peterborough, Ont., 2002), p. 300.

[73] H. Ward, *Delia Blanchflower* (London, 1916), p. 140.

above all, that converts Delia to a more parochial and hierarchical model of philanthropy.

> And what frankly amazed her was Winnington's place in this world of labouring folk. He had given it ten years of service; not charity, but simply the service of the good citizen; moved by a secret, impelling motive, which Delia had yet to learn. And how they rewarded him! She walked beside a natural ruler, and felt her heart presently big with the pride of it.[74]

In Ward's depiction, cross-class alliances, however well intended, are self-deceiving and disruptive; the key to social improvement lies in deference, service and duty.

Mark echoes Ward's own views as he muses on the travails of working-class women and then on the men, 'marred and worn like them, only more deeply, more tragically'.[75] The answer, Mark determines, is not the vote, which has done so little to alleviate the men's suffering. The parliamentary vote, underpinned by male power, rules the Empire, while women and men together must take on responsibility for the 'national house-keeping' of England.[76] But Ward allows a plethora of voices into her novel, including that of Miss Dempsey, a long-term suffragist who has devoted her life to 'rescue' work, and who 'loved those whom no one else would love – the meanest and feeblest of the outcast race'.[77] Despite desiring the vote, she is, alongside older fellow suffragists, willing to wait as long as it takes to be granted the franchise peaceably. To Mary Ward there was nothing utopian about Annie Kenney's vision of a movement that transcended class barriers. Class distinctions and gender roles were intrinsically linked in her vision of social structure, and the most vulnerable must depend upon the leadership of men and women within their particular spheres. The traditional heterosexual romance plot enabled Ward to validate both gender and class structures; the marriage of Delia Blanchflower and Mark Winnington confirms the chivalrous landowner's place as a natural leader, the propertied man whose knowledge and sensitivity enable him to represent the interests of every section of the community.

[74] Ward, *Delia Blanchflower*, p. 266.

[75] Ward, *Delia Blanchflower*, p. 339.

[76] B. Sutton-Ramspeck, 'Shot out of the canon: Mary Ward and the claims of conflicting feminisms', in *Victorian Women Writers and the Woman Question*, ed. N. D. Thompson (Cambridge, 1999), p. 212. Ward herself called women's civic duties the 'enlarged housekeeping of the nation'; quoted in 'The anti-suffrage demonstration', *The Times*, 14 July 1910, p. 9.

[77] Ward, *Delia Blanchflower*, p. 165.

Gender and class structures were inherently entwined, as both suffragists and anti-suffragists recognized. To grant the vote to women would be, as Robins wrote to her sister-in-law in 1908, 'a pulling out of the chief cornerstones of privilege. Ibsen saw that years ago.'[78] There was a significant difference between compassion for society's vulnerable – which both suffragists and anti-suffragists expressed – and aspirations to greater social equality. Mary Ward's novels offered a counterpoint to the ignorant, self-interested anti-suffragists depicted in plays such as Glover's *A Chat with Mrs Chicky* and *Miss Appleyard's Awakening*, while the Anti-Suffrage League was keen to emphasize the social commitment of its members; a series of profiles of aristocratic leaders of the movement in *The Anti-Suffrage Review*, for example, repeatedly highlighted the women's philanthropic activities – even when such activism was limited to the opening of an extensive art collection to weekly public viewings.[79] Both suffragists and antis claimed to be more urgently concerned with the sufferings of the poor than their political opponents, but, crucially, the anti-suffragists insisted that women must accept, like Ward's Marcella and Delia Blanchflower, that their service could most effectively be delivered through established structures and hierarchies.

Suffrage writers, by contrast, faced the more considerable challenge of envisioning the dismantling of gender structures and the conjoined hierarchies of class without offending or alienating middle- and upper-class audiences and readers. The multi-stranded plots of *Suffragette Sally* and *No Surrender* sought an innovative egalitarian form to represent the interconnected lives and interests of their diverse cast of women.[80] But Colmore and Maud showed more respect for class distinctions and hierarchies than the utopian vision of cross-class unity in plays such as *How the Vote Was Won* might suggest. Where Constance Lytton and Elizabeth Robins were robust and unsparing in their critiques of the parasitism of the aristocratic women of leisure in whose circles they moved, middle-class writers such as Maud and Colmore were more conciliatory, constructing fictions that bound women together in cross-class friendships while carefully preserving a class deference that Lytton firmly repudiated. For suffragist writers, harnessing the truth-telling claims of realism to propagandist effect

[78] Robins to M. Dreier Robins, 1 Aug. 1908, quoted in John, 'Radical reflections?', p. 207.

[79] *The Anti-Suffrage Review*, Apr. 1910–Dec. 1911; see, especially, profile of Lady Glenconner of Glen, July 1911, p. 1.

[80] For the relation between suffrage fiction, romance and innovations in form, see J. Eldridge Miller, *Rebel Women: Feminism, Modernism and the Edwardian Novel* (London, 1994), ch. 4, and S. S. Park, 'Suffrage fiction: a political discourse in the marketplace', *English Literature in Transition, 1880–1920*, xxxix (1996), 450–61.

also meant acknowledging and negotiating the tensions between different class interests and sensibilities; visions of perfect solidarity remained the province of the utopian and the comic. Vitally, it was when suffrage writers acknowledged the limits of representation – the poverty and suffering that lay beyond the margins of their texts and performances – that they achieved the fine balance between highlighting the deprivation that blighted working-class lives and laying claim to a right or ability to represent them.

9. Militancy in the marital sphere: sex strikes, marriage strikes and birth strikes as militant suffrage tactics, 1911–14

Tania Shew

As the women's suffrage movement in Britain entered its fifth decade, ongoing discussions about tactical efficacy gained momentum. During the final ten years of their protracted campaigns, suffrage organizations significantly altered and augmented their existing efforts, resulting in the advent of several notable acts of protest which have shaped the legacy and memory of the movement. To cite just a few examples, in 1908, members of the Women's Social and Political Union (WSPU) engaged in window-breaking for the first time; in July 1909, Marion Wallace Dunlop became the first imprisoned suffragette to undertake a hunger strike; in October 1909, the Women's Tax Resistance League was formed; in April 1911, many women conducted a census boycott and, in June 1913, Emily Wilding Davison disrupted the Epsom Derby, resulting in her death.[1] As part of this wider context of rapidly expanding and evolving political practices, a passionate minority of women's suffrage campaigners looked to a set of tactics during these years which have, by contrast, almost entirely avoided both scholarly and popular attention. These tactics were sex,

1 'Women's suffrage timeline', *British Library Blog*, 6 Feb. 2018 <https://www.bl.uk/votes-for-women/articles/womens-suffrage-timeline> [accessed 18 Aug. 2020]; C. Eustance, 'Meanings of militancy: the ideas and practices of political resistance in the Women's Freedom League, 1907–1914' and H. Frances, '"Pay the Piper, call the tune!": the Women's Tax Resistance League', in *The Women's Suffrage Movement: New Feminist Perspectives*, ed. M. Joannou and J. Purvis (Manchester, 1998); H. Frances, '"Dare to be free!": The Women's Freedom League and its legacy', in *Votes for Women*, ed. J. Purvis and S. Stanley Holton (London, 2000); L. E. Mayhall, *The Militant Suffrage Movement: Citizenship and Resistance in Britain, 1860–1930* (Oxford, 2003), pp. 3, 45; J. Liddington, *Vanishing for the Vote: Suffrage, Citizenship and the Battle for the Census* (Manchester, 2014).

'Militancy in the marital sphere', in *The politics of women's suffrage: local, national and international dimensions,* ed. A. Hughes-Johnson and L. Jenkins (London, 2021), pp. 237–260.

marriage and birth strikes.[2] As the campaign for women's enfranchisement continued, particularly radical members of the WSPU and the Women's Freedom League (WFL) asked whether they could win political rights by leveraging men's desires that women perform sexual acts, domestic chores and, most significantly, maternal duties.

This chapter identifies three instances in which these tactics were explored extensively: a pair of books written by WSPU member Lucy Re-Bartlett in 1911 and 1912 respectively; a letter published in *The Freewoman* journal by WSPU supporter Coralie Boord in January 1912; and the WFL's annual conference of March 1914.[3] Combinations of sex-striking, marriage-striking and birth-striking were discussed interchangeably on all three occasions. This chapter disentangles the three kinds of strikes being considered, analyses how suffrage campaigners thought these varying tactics might prove effective, why they might have been favoured in place of more traditional acts of protest and which interpretations suffrage activists placed on winning citizenship on these terms.[4]

The flurry of proposed birth strikes, as distinct from sex or marriage strikes, among socialist-feminist campaigners in continental Europe in the years leading up to, and during, the First World War provides important context here.[5] Birth-strike debates enjoyed a particular moment of engagement in Germany in this period which exceeded the levels of public discussion these tactics received within the British suffrage movement. The socialist German doctor Alfred Bernstein wrote a pamphlet on birth-striking in 1913 which sold over 30,000 copies in less than a year.[6] In the

[2] Lucy Bland makes a passing reference to the debates in *Banishing the Beast: Feminism, Sex and Morality* (London, 2001; first published 1995), p. 247.

[3] L. Re-Bartlett, *The Coming Order* (London, 1911); L. Re-Bartlett, *Sex and Sanctity* (London, 1912); C. M. Boord, 'To the editors', *The Freewoman*, 4 Jan. 1912; LSE, Add. MS 2WFL/2/07.

[4] Since the historical subjects in this chapter largely did not leave behind a recorded self-identification with the term suffragette or suffragist, I will refer to them all as 'suffrage campaigners' or 'suffrage activists'.

[5] R. P. Neuman, 'Working class birth control in Wilhelmine Germany', *Comparative Studies in Society and History*, xx (1978), 412–14; J. M. Winter, 'Socialism, social democracy, and population questions in Western Europe: 1870–1950', *Population and Development Review*, xiv (1988), 135; A. McLaren, 'Reproduction and revolution: Paul Robin and Neo-Malthusianism in France', in *Malthus, Medicine and Morality: 'Malthusianism' after 1798*, ed. B. Dolan (Atlanta, Ga., 2000), p. 178; J. Brown, *Birth Strike: The Hidden Fight over Women's Work* (Ebook edition; Oakland, Calif., 2019), pp. 127–9.

[6] English title 'How do we promote a culture of a declining birth rate?'. Original: *Wie fördern wir den kulturellen Rückgang der Geburten?* For details of the pamphlet's publication and sales, see D. Nelles, 'Anarchosyndikalismus und Sexualreformbewegung in der

pamphlet, Bernstein suggested that working-class women 'organize a birth strike' in 'demand' of their 'human rights'.[7] He believed that women could leverage power by refusing to supply the German Empire with workers or cannon fodder.[8] Although still not widely studied, the debates between Bernstein and his contemporaries have received historiographical attention which equivalent discussions held by British suffrage campaigners have not.[9] While less prominent, the British debates require discrete analysis as they were distinct from the broader European birth-strike movement in two key ways. First, the German debates largely isolated the tactic of birth-striking, whereas the British debates closely entangled birth-striking with the related tactics of sex- and marriage-striking. British suffrage campaigners considered whether to support a birth strike via contraception, which was predicted to prove the most popular (therefore posing the biggest threat to the economy and national security), or advocate politicized celibacy, which was expected to induce more suffering in individual men. Second, in the German context, birth-striking was favoured in place of more established socialist protest methods because it was envisaged as a peaceful, 'bloodless' tactic which could be performed by 'quiet, decent' women, exhibiting 'passivity'.[10] By contrast, in the British context, sex-, marriage- and birth-striking were explicitly conceptualized as a form of militancy.

As far as surviving sources indicate, none of these strikes was enacted on a mass scale in either country, partially explaining why they have escaped extensive academic analysis in Anglophone scholarship. However, the discourse around these potential tactics is revealing in terms of furthering

Weimarer Republik'. Written for the workshop Free Love and the Labour Movement at the International Institute of Social History in Amsterdam, 6 Oct. 2000, p. 2.

[7] In original German: 'Sozialistische Frauen, fordert eure menschenrechte! Gewährt man sie euch nicht, dann organisiert den Geburtenstreik'. Bernstein, 'How do we promote a culture of a declining birth rate?', p. 5.

[8] Bernstein, 'How do we promote a culture of a declining birth rate?', p. 5.

[9] Scholarship in English: Neuman, 'Working class birth control in Wilhelmine Germany', 412–44; Brown, *Birth Strike*, pp. 127–9. Selected scholarship in German: K. H. Roth, 'Kontroversen um Geburtenkontrolle am Vorabend des Ersten Weltkriegs: Eine Dokumentation zur Berliner "Gebärstreikdebatte" von 1913', *Autonomie*, ix (1978), 78–103; Nelles, 'Anarchosyndikalismus und Sexualreformbewegung in der Weimarer Republik', p. 2; A. Bergmann, 'Am Vorabend einer neuen Sexualmoral? Die Debatte um den »Gebärstreik« im Jahr 1913', *Indes*, ii (2013), 2191–9.

[10] Bernstein uses the German word 'unblutige', which translates as bloodless, in 'How do we promote a culture of a declining birth rate?', p. 5; 'Advocates "birth strike"', *The Bemidji Daily Pioneer*, 28 July 1913, p. 4; 'Advocates "birth strike"', *The Madison Daily Leader*, 29 July 1913, p. 1; A. Harrison, 'The state and the family', *The English Review*, Jan. 1914, pp. 278, 283; S. Foy, 'If parents went on strike', *The Daily Citizen*, 18 Feb. 1914, p. 4.

our understanding of how the issues of sexuality and motherhood were expressed within the militant suffrage movement in Britain. As pioneering scholarship from the 1980s and 1990s demonstrated, nineteenth- and early twentieth-century feminists articulated women's enfranchisement as a means of ending the sexual double standard and its many manifestations such as legalized rape in marriage, expectations of unlimited maternity and prostitution.[11] In a trend this chapter bucks, previous historians have prioritized the writings of suffrage campaigners who predicted that political representation would need to precipitate cultural sexual equality. The most striking example of this approach was posited by Susan Kingsley Kent. She claimed that suffrage activists believed that 'a sexual identity that rendered women sexual objects could be altered *only* by a political identity that gave them citizenship', deeming 'civic equality' the 'requisite precondition' to dismantling sexual double standards.[12] Sandra Holton concurred that from the 1890s onwards, suffrage campaigners increasingly saw the vote as 'the key' for ushering in political and sexual liberation via 'a single measure'.[13] Outlining the arguments from Christabel Pankhurst's famous treatise on sexuality, *The Great Scourge and How to End It*, Margaret Jackson similarly emphasized the significance that Pankhurst accorded enfranchisement in her campaign to end prostitution.[14] In *The Great Scourge*, Pankhurst expressed her famous mantra 'Votes for Women, Chastity for Men', which bears some resemblance to the suggestions made by the women explored in this paper. What set Pankhurst apart from the sex-, marriage- and birth-strike advocates, however, was her implication that 'Votes for Women, Chastity for Men' was a two-part process in which enfranchisement legislation would have to precede attempts to bring about widespread male chastity.[15]

In two key ways, sex-, marriage- and birth-strike debates allow us to build on this historiography by demonstrating the range of perspectives that existed among suffrage campaigners on the relationship between the vote and sexual double standards. First, rather than subscribing to the idea that

[11] S. Kingsley-Kent, *Sex and Suffrage in Britain, 1860–1914* (Princeton, N.J., 1987), pp. 3, 13, 89, 91, 93, 210; Bland, *Banishing the Beast*, pp. xiii–xiv, 244–5; S. Stanley Holton, *Suffrage Days: Stories from the Women's Suffrage Movement* (London, 1996), p. 77; M. Jackson, *The Real Facts of Life: Feminism and the Politics of Sexuality c.1850–1940* (Ebook edition, 2005; first published London, 1994), pp. 1–3.

[12] Emphasis my own. Kingsley-Kent, *Sex and Suffrage*, p. 210.

[13] Holton, *Suffrage Days*, p. 77.

[14] Jackson, *The Real Facts of Life*, p. 48. Lucy Bland made a similar argument, although not specifically relating to *The Great Scourge*, in *Banishing the Beast*, p. 244–5.

[15] C. Pankhurst, *The Great Scourge and How to End It* (London, 1913), pp. viii, 21–3, 36–7.

enfranchisement was an essential precondition to widespread sexual and marital liberation, strike advocates asserted that women, inversely, already had some (militant) power in the private realm that could be exploited to win the vote.[16] Key figures in this chapter focused on the means of striking as much as the ends of enfranchisement. They theorized that enduring the sacrifice of sex-, marriage- and, in particular, birth-strikes would strengthen women spiritually and psychologically, thus also rendering them more capable of fighting for additional social and cultural reforms once enfranchised.[17] Second, the strike advocates gendered these proposed protests in surprising ways. While the most famous examples of suffrage militancy subverted gender norms by challenging women's exclusions from public spaces, sex-, marriage- and birth-strike advocates contrastingly claimed that women could demonstrate traditionally masculine attributes of strength, force and even violence in the ways they negotiated their roles within the home.[18]

These proposed strikes highlight less prominent suffrage campaigners as tactical pioneers and indicate new ways of thinking about how and why women wanted to achieve political rights. Holton described her history of lesser-known suffragists as 'a shake of the kaleidoscope' causing 'different aspects of the historical pattern' to 'move to the fore', and an analysis of sex, marriage and birth strikes performs this same function.[19] This chapter first introduces sex-, marriage- and birth-striking as three distinct yet connected tactics; second, it explores how these strikes were intended to demonstrate a gendering of militancy; finally, it examines the effects undergoing a sex, marriage or birth strike were believed to have on suffrage campaigners themselves.

[16] Boord, 'To the editors', p. 130; Re-Bartlett, *Sex and Sanctity*, pp. 25–6; LSE, Add. MS 2WFL/2/07, p. 61.

[17] Boord, 'To the editors', pp. 130–1; Re-Bartlett, *Sex and Sanctity*, pp. 31, 42, 74.

[18] E. Pankhurst, *My Own Story* (London, 2015; first published London, 1914), pp. 16–17, 68–70, 118; L. Tickner, *The Spectacle of Women: Imagery of the Suffrage Campaign, 1907–14* (London, 1987), pp. ix–x, 55–7; M. Vicinus, *Independent Women: Work and Community for Single Women, 1850–1920* (Chicago, Ill., 1985), pp. 252–5; Mayhall, *The Militant Suffrage Movement*, p. 7; K. Cockin, 'Cicely Hamilton's Warriors: dramatic reinventions of militancy in the British women's suffrage movement', *Women's History Review*, xiv (2005), 527–8, 535; D. Cohler, *Citizen, Invert, Queer: Lesbianism and the War in Early Twentieth-Century Britain* (Minneapolis, Minn., 2010), especially chap. 2, 'Public women, social inversion: the women's suffrage debates', pp. 52–4, and J. Purvis, E. Crawford and S. Stanley Holton, 'Did militancy help or hinder the granting of women's suffrage in Britain?', *Women's History Review*, xxviii (2019), 1200–34.

[19] Holton, *Suffrage Days*, p. 1.

The three tactics: sex-, marriage- and birth-striking

Surviving records indicated that sex-, marriage- and birth-strike propositions within the British suffrage movement were pioneered by the campaign's foot-soldiers between the years 1910 and 1914.[20] There were different opinions on how the distinctive elements of these strikes should be prioritized. Some suffrage campaigners focused their discussions on depriving the nation of children, potentially by any means necessary (birth-striking); others advocated that a refusal to have children be achieved via abstention from sexual relations specifically, rather than through the adoption of contraceptive practices (sex-striking); and still others suggested that women abstain from sex, motherhood and any other domestic duties by rejecting the entire institution of marriage (marriage-striking). As a refusal to have sex necessarily resulted in a refusal to bear children, and as a refusal to marry often (although, of course, not always) involved the rejection of sex and motherhood, these strikes were, to a significant extent, discussed interchangeably. Reflecting a common feminist view, the strike advocates implied that marriage and motherhood, in their current forms, were part of one coherent system that accorded men liberties denied to women.[21] Unlike the most dominant feminist discourse, however, sex-, marriage- and birth-strike propositions were predicated on a belief that women could exploit men's reliance on this system to engender female enfranchisement.

In her 1911 book *The Coming Order*, WSPU member Lucy Re-Bartlett began formulating her ideas on using celibacy to bring about political equality.[22] Although she never held a leadership position within the British suffrage movement, Re-Bartlett enjoyed an illustrious international career as a writer and philosopher.[23] Born in Scotland, then moving to Italy after graduating from university, Re-Bartlett was the first woman to serve on the

[20] I have found one significant recorded instance prior to this. The Malthusian League's newspaper reported in Dec. 1907 that Emmeline Pankhurst, 'speaking at Swansea a few months back', had stated that 'if she had her way, women would refuse to be mothers until they were treated as citizens'. C. V. Drysdale, 'The dawn of recognition', *The Malthusian*, Dec. 1907, p. 92. Emmeline Pankhurst conducted a well-publicized tour of Wales in 1906, which may be what *The Malthusian* editors were referring to, but there is no further evidence of Pankhurst's reported birth-strike advocation specifically. K. Cook and N. Evans, '"The petty antics of the bell-ringing boisterous band"? The women's suffrage movement in Wales, 1890–1918', in *Our Mothers' Land, Chapters in Welsh Women's History 1830–1939*, ed. A. John (Cardiff, 1991), p. 166.

[21] Boord, 'To the editors', p. 130; C. M. Boord, 'Why do we discuss sex?', *The Freewoman*, 14 Mar. 1912, p. 331; Re-Bartlett, *Sex and Sanctity*, pp. 49–50.

[22] Re-Bartlett, *The Coming Order*, p. 7.

[23] I. Margesson, 'Obituary – Mrs. Re-Bartlett', *Common Cause*, 12 May 1922, p. 119.

Italian Royal Commission, influencing policy on juvenile offenders.[24] She married Emilio Re in Rome in 1910, demonstrating her feminist credentials by adopting a double-barrelled surname.[25] Re-Bartlett also represented the Theosophical Society at a sex education conference in 1908 and travelled to India to study theosophy with renowned English feminist Annie Besant.[26] Re-Bartlett's subscription to this belief system influenced her interest in sex-, marriage- and birth-striking as a spiritually and politically transformative process.[27] Laying the foundations for her later more detailed meditation on sex-striking, Re-Bartlett suggested in *The Coming Order* that women cultivate 'purity' from 'sensuality' and 'vanity', predicting that 'in this spirit the woman of to-day will gain her Vote'.[28] She substantially expanded upon these ideas in her 1912 sequel, *Sex and Sanctity*, which was translated into French and Italian.[29] Re-Bartlett maintained that women were boycotting marriage and motherhood in response to their lack of political rights, the sexual exploitation of women and children and the majority of men's indifference regarding these issues: 'In the hearts of many women to-day is a rising cry, somewhat like this … "I will know no man, and bear no child, until this apathy be broken through – these wrongs be righted!" … It is the "silent strike" and it is going on all over the world.'[30]

The same year as *Sex and Sanctity* was published, 'housewife' and suffrage supporter Coralie Boord attempted to influence the uptake of sex-, marriage- and birth-striking within the WSPU.[31] Although very little information about Boord has survived, we know that she was a regular contributor to the feminist periodical *The Freewoman*, a donor to the WSPU and that she claimed to 'slightly know' leading WSPU member Annie

[24] Margesson, 'Obituary – Mrs. Re-Bartlett', p. 119.

[25] Margesson, 'Obituary – Mrs. Re-Bartlett', p. 119.

[26] C. Spurgeon, 'The International Moral Education Congress', *The Vāhan*, Nov. 1908, p. 31; L. Hall, *Outspoken Women: An Anthology of Women's Writing on Sex, 1870–1969* (Abingdon, 2005), p. 320.

[27] J. Dixon, *Divine Feminine: Theosophy and Feminism in England* (Baltimore, Md., 2001), pp. 12–13. Influenced by her theosophical beliefs, Re-Bartlett held a strong disregard for contraception. While she explicitly advocated that women refuse to 'bear' children, I therefore assume she intended that this be achieved via abstinence. As a result, I generally refer to her proposals as a 'sex and marriage strike', except when she most explicitly discussed the implications of foregoing motherhood. Re-Bartlett, *The Coming Order*, pp. 52–4.

[28] Re-Bartlett, *The Coming Order*, p. 7.

[29] Margesson, 'Obituary – Mrs. Re-Bartlett', p. 119.

[30] Re-Bartlett, *Sex and Sanctity*, pp. 25–6.

[31] Boord, 'To the editors', p. 130.

Kenney.[32] She was 39 in 1912, managing an upper-middle-class household as the wife of the younger brother of a baronet, and was the mother of their three small children.[33] In her letters to *The Freewoman* in 1911 and 1912, she depicted a complicated but largely positive relationship with her domestic life and demonstrated a penchant for sexual humour.[34] In one notable example, arguing against claims that the paper had generated entirely new opportunities for sexual exploration, Boord joked of the 'sex-love' she had 'wrung from life, in spite of obstacles (and, craving your pardon, before the advent of THE FREEWOMAN!)'.[35] She added 'I think very highly of THE FREEWOMAN, but my sense of proportion (*i.e.,* humour) forbids my admitting that the first opportunity for men and women in the whole wide world to study these questions properly and openly arose about three months ago!'[36]

In January 1912, Boord wrote a letter to *The Freewoman* on sex-, marriage- and birth-striking. She was responding to an article by the Neo-Malthusian Charles Vickery Drysdale, on 'The Freewoman and the Birth rate', in which he had proposed a birth strike in aid of women's enfranchisement.[37] This article had been commissioned by the journal's editor, 'disillusioned' suffragette Dora Marsden.[38] Boord announced that she had made a similar but more elaborate suggestion than Drysdale's to the leading militant suffrage organization.

> When militancy was resumed by the W.S.P.U. a few weeks ago I wrote to Miss Annie Kenney … sending her a cheque for the use of the W.S.P.U., and

[32] Boord, 'To the editors', p. 130; C. M. Boord, 'Facilities for scientific study in sex', *The Freewoman*, 28 Mar. 1912, p. 376; C. M. Boord, 'A correction', *The Freewoman*, 18 Apr. 1912, p. 439; Boord, 'Why do we discuss sex?', p. 331.

[33] 'Orcombe Lodge, Battery Rd, Exmouth', 1911 census.

[34] C. M. Boord, 'Divorce', *The Freewoman*, 1 Feb. 1912, p. 213; Boord, 'Facilities for scientific study in sex', p. 376.

[35] C. M. Boord, 'A reply', *The Freewoman*, 4 Apr. 1912, p. 398.

[36] Boord, 'Facilities for scientific study in sex', p. 376.

[37] C. V. Drysdale, 'The freewoman and the birth rate II', *The Freewoman*, 21 Dec. 1911, p. 89.

[38] Marsden commissioned the article in a letter to Drysdale. Princeton Special Collections, 'Dora Marsden papers', Additional MS. C02832. Marsden had cut ties with the militant suffragette movement partly due to her perceived expectations that rank-and-file activists make sacrifices to the leadership. For more about this dispute, see L. Delap, 'Individualism and introspection: the framing of feminism in the *Freewoman*', in *Feminist Media History: Suffrage, Periodicals and the Public Sphere*, ed. M. Dicenzo, L. Delap and L. Ryan (Basingstoke, 2011), p. 160, and C. Franklin, 'Marketing Edwardian feminism: Dora Marsden, *Votes for Women* and *The Freewoman*', *Women's History Review*, xi (2002), 633–5.

> I ventured to suggest that the time had come when … every member of the W.S.P.U., and other Feminists who were engaged to be married, should refuse to marry, and every married member should refuse to 'live with' or bear children to her husband until the Franchise was won.[39]

These tactics were, of course, not adopted as WSPU policy. As Boord wrote indignantly, her 'money was gratefully acknowledged' and yet her 'suggestion was not even referred to' and the existing tactic of 'window-breaking methods began again'.[40]

Calls for birth strikes and, to a lesser extent, sex and marriage strikes were taken more seriously within the WFL. At its 1914 annual conference, Nina Boyle, the head of the organization's Political and Militant Department, proposed that:

> A definite threat be made, embodied in letters directed to the Prime Minister, the Archbishop of Canterbury, and other authorities, that should women's suffrage be denied beyond a certain date, a campaign to assist working women to limit the birth rate be commenced.[41]

WFL delegate Margaret Huntsman, described as being actively involved with the organization to a 'Herculean' degree, claimed that her unnamed local WFL branch had 'at least twenty' members 'ready' to start disseminating birth control information with the purpose of encouraging a politicized birth strike.[42] The motion was met with some fatigue by less enthusiastic attendees. One member commented that propositions to encourage women to limit the birth rate were an annual occurrence at WFL meetings. The WFL's representative for Hampstead complained that such proposals happened even more frequently than this, stating 'this is hardly annual. It is always coming up, and it has always been rejected.'[43] An article in *The Malthusian* reports that Charles Vickery Drysdale had given a talk to the WFL on birth-striking in aid of enfranchisement just a few weeks before this conference.[44] Although the birth-strike motion was, once again, rebuffed after a vote at the 1914 annual conference, the Hampstead

[39] C. M. Boord, 'To the editors', *The Freewoman*, 4 Jan. 1912, p. 130.

[40] Boord, 'To the editors', p. 130.

[41] LSE, Add. MS 2WFL/2/07, p. 61.

[42] LSE, Add. MS 2WFL/2/07, p. 63. 'Margaret Huntsman', *Vote*, 21 Feb. 1913, p. 278.

[43] LSE, Add. MS 2WFL/2/07, p. 70. The relationship between birth control and women's suffrage was reportedly discussed at earlier WFL meetings. 'Women's Freedom League', *The Malthusian*, 15 Mar. 1914, p. 21; 'Emancipation and motherhood', *The Malthusian*, 15 Aug. 1911, p. 64.

[44] 'Women's Freedom League', *The Malthusian*, 15 Mar. 1914, p. 21.

delegate's comment is an indicator that birth-strike discussions happened more frequently among British suffrage supporters than is recognized within surviving sources.

One significant motivation for advocating a combination of sex, marriage and birth strikes was to render calls to politicize the domestic sphere accessible to women with different martial statuses. Lucy Re-Bartlett claimed that her 'silent strike', which involved a refusal to 'know' men or 'bear' children, was being enacted by 'women both married and single'.[45] Although she did not elaborate further, with this description she was presumably suggesting that single women reject marriage and married women attempt to boycott the marital bed or even home. Coralie Boord explicitly distinguished between married and unmarried women, advocating that 'feminists who were engaged to be married' should 'refuse to marry', while married feminists should 'refuse to "live with"' or 'bear children' for their husbands.[46] The idea that these tactics might be more widely accessible than established political practices, or appeal to previously alienated women, seems to have been part of the strikes' general appeal. Re-Bartlett repeatedly claimed that sex-, marriage- and birth-striking was taking place 'all over the world', including among women in countries without an organized suffrage movement.[47] Huntsman, from the WFL, was similarly interested in the strikes as a form of protest which could be organized with 'ease', predicting that, once initiated, a birth strike would 'spread itself'.[48]

Re-Bartlett, Boord and the WFL representatives did not, however, consider sex-, marriage- and birth-striking a homogeneous strategy; they ascribed varying value to the three different incarnations of these tactics. In Britain, as in Europe, interest in birth-striking was often predicated on perceived government fears around the economic and military consequences of depleted populations.[49] This was especially the case among the WFL members and Coralie Boord, which can partly be explained by them both responding to influences from Drysdale, the well-known Neo-Malthusian, who was himself informed about the German birth-strike movement.[50]

[45] Re-Bartlett, *Sex and Sanctity*, pp. 25–6.

[46] Boord, 'To the editors', p. 130.

[47] She did not cite any evidence for this, however. Re-Bartlett, *Sex and Sanctity*, pp. 23, 25–6, 33, 45.

[48] LSE, Add. MS 2WFL/2/07, p. 61.

[49] Bernstein, 'How do we promote a culture of a declining birth rate?', pp. 4–5.

[50] Drysdale's wife, Bessie, was a WFL member. *The Malthusian*, which Drysdale helped edit, had previously published on the German birth-strike movement. 'Socialism and family limitation', *The Malthusian*, 15 Dec. 1913, pp. 98–9.

Huntsman implied interest in the large-scale military and economic implications of birth-striking when she claimed, 'the real force here rests with women; if you refuse to have children, the country is powerless'.[51] Boord similarly devoted more attention to restricting the birth rate than to the implications of other forms of domestic striking. While still heavily championing the tactic, she anticipated that refusing to have children could, in fact, prove too effective. Boord posited that an unintended consequence of the birth strike could be that it delivered women's enfranchisement only for the nation to be 'swallowed by a bigger, coarser, less civilized Power, as France will probably be swallowed by Germany'.[52]

Other campaigners evaluated the different types of strike through a moral or religious lens and birth-striking fared less well on these terms. At the 1914 conference, the delegates of the WFL expanded their birth-strike discussion, debating whether a limited birth rate should be achieved via contraception or via abstinence and, therefore, a sex strike.[53] At least three members articulated an objection to birth-striking via contraception due to concerns about the moral implications of these practices.[54] WFL National Executive member Alice Schofield Coates advocated a sex strike based on her objection to sanctioning 'unlimited sexual license'.[55] She concluded that 'the only right way to' restrict the birth rate 'is to limit all sexual relations with men'.[56] The group's president, Charlotte Despard, was also among those worried about the effects of promoting contraception. Despard proposed that suffrage supporters 'stop marriages as much as possible … Get women to give us a pledge that they will not marry' until 'the rights of citizenship are conceded to us'.[57] As a Catholic-turned-theosophist, it is highly likely that Despard held a theological objection to contraception and envisaged sex and marriage strikes as both a vehicle to enfranchisement and a means of ushering in her desired reformed sexual moral codes.[58]

A final consideration which suffrage campaigners used to compare sex-, marriage- and birth-striking was individual women's likely preferences and

[51] LSE, Add. MS 2WFL/2/07, p. 63.

[52] Boord, 'To the editors', p. 130.

[53] LSE, Add. MS 2WFL/2/07, pp. 68–9.

[54] LSE, Add. MS 2WFL/2/07, pp. 67–9.

[55] LSE, Add. MS 2WFL/2/07, p. 67.

[56] LSE, Add. MS 2WFL/2/07, p. 67.

[57] LSE, Add. MS 2WFL/2/07, pp. 68–9.

[58] E. Clark, 'Catholics and the campaign for women's suffrage in England', *Church History*, lxxiii (2004), 646–8; Dixon, *Divine Feminine*, pp. 245–61.

capacity for agency. When considering this theme, the strike advocates upheld the premise that the domestic realm was a sphere in which women possessed at least some existing power. Re-Bartlett suggested that abstention from the legal marriage contract was the optimum form of strike because it placed women in the best bargaining position. She claimed that 'the girl still free' had more power over potential suitors than a wife had over her husband, as the wife would have 'forfeited her title in a certain way'.[59] Schofield Coates, although a champion of the sex strike, expressed apprehension that celibacy would prove less popular with most women than the uptake of birth control. However, she did not elaborate on whether she thought women's reluctance to commit to abstinence would be due to simple preference or more substantial barriers.[60] Despard was relatively forthcoming when she assessed women's agency to carry out the different types of strike. Citing the fear that using birth control to achieve the strike would make it harder for women to find 'excuses' for avoiding unwanted sexual activity with their husbands, Despard worried that birth-striking left women more vulnerable to abuse than marriage-striking, which she saw as a viable option.[61] Despard warned her comrades, 'we must not use a threat which we are not able to carry out'.[62] As Despard's concerns remind us, not all women had the agency to enact each form of strike. Many would not have had the economic independence needed to reject marriage and no Edwardian women had the legal right to refuse sexual relations once married.[63] These hurdles generally form a surprising and conspicuous absence in these sources. An unnamed WFL representative for Middlesbrough came closest to raising issues of inhibited agency when she demanded that the group put 'all questions of mock modesty on one side' so they could discuss the fact that 'there are two persons to be consulted and who have to agree in this matter'.[64] The other WFL members did not, however, choose to extensively discuss the Middlesbrough representative's concerns.

Even if the strikes were always an elusive dream in practice, the process of imagining sex, marriage and birth strikes as a source of untapped power seems to have inspired WFL members, who turned to the theme repeatedly

[59] Re-Bartlett, *Sex and Sanctity*, p. 53.

[60] LSE, Add. MS 2WFL/2/07, p. 67.

[61] LSE, Add. MS 2WFL/2/07, pp. 68–9.

[62] LSE, Add. MS 2WFL/2/07, pp. 68–9.

[63] Kent, *Sex and Suffrage*, pp. 87–8.

[64] LSE, Add. MS 2WFL/2/07, p. 64.

during the final decade of the suffrage campaign.[65] Re-Bartlett perhaps obfuscated themes of women's legal and economic barriers due to her belief that sex and marriage strikes were already in existence. The word 'silent' in Re-Bartlett's phrase the 'silent strike' referred to her conviction that many of the increasing numbers of unmarried or childless women in Edwardian England were choosing to distance themselves from men as part of a feminist impetus, even if they were not fully conscious of these motives themselves.[66] Re-Bartlett seems to have seen herself less as prescribing a new tactic, and more as giving a name to an existing power which women were yet to fully realize they possessed.

Striking, militancy and gender

Part of the imagined power behind sex, marriage and birth strikes lay in their being perceived as militant tactics. Acts of suffrage militancy were often intended to blur gender distinctions and Re-Bartlett, Boord and members of the WFL's 1914 conference rhetorically engaged in this endeavour. The most extensively studied form of gendering suffrage militancy involved suffragettes embodying masculinity by carrying out protests in the public sphere traditionally enacted by men, such as marching on Parliament or newspaper-selling. Suffragettes would simultaneously feminize these acts by performing them to a moderated degree or by wearing overtly feminine dress.[67] For example, in her 1914 memoir, Emmeline Pankhurst drew parallels between the WSPU and disenfranchised nineteenth-century farm labourers, implying that suffragettes carried out similar tactics to these previous generations of (predominantly male) rights campaigners with relatively less violence or more patience.[68] She intended these analogies to uphold a claim that women were deserving of citizenship. Suffragettes were carrying out protests which had previously resulted in men being rewarded with extended voting rights and were doing so with relative political maturity.[69] Sex, marriage and birth strikes reveal a corresponding, and previously overlooked, attempt to equip traditionally feminine spaces with

[65] LSE, Add. MS 2WFL/2/07; 'Women's Freedom League', *The Malthusian*, 15 Mar. 1914, p. 21.

[66] Re-Bartlett, *Sex and Sanctity*, pp. 25–6.

[67] Cohler, *Citizen, Invert, Queer*, pp. 52–4; Pankhurst, *My Own Story*, pp. 16–17, 68–70, 118; Tickner, *The Spectacle of Women*; Cockin, 'Cicely Hamilton's warriors', p. 535; Mayhall, *The Militant Suffrage Movement*, p. 56; Purvis, 'Did militancy help or hinder the granting of women's suffrage in Britain?', p. 1202.

[68] Pankhurst, *My Own Story*, pp. 16–17, 68.

[69] Pankhurst, *My Own Story*, p. 118. See also Cohler, *Citizen, Invert, Queer*, pp. 52–4.

'masculine' force, power and even violence. By contrast, these proposed strikes were intended to demonstrate that women had means of cultivating power which had not previously been employed by male activists.

The sex-, marriage- and birth-strike advocates described their proposed tactics as a form of suffrage militancy and, in the case of Boord and Huntsman, explicitly attributed this militancy to their conviction that these practices had been freshly devised by women and would take place within a private setting. Conceiving of these strikes as militant adds to the arguments of historians of suffrage militancy, most notably Sandra Holton, Laura Mayhall and Krista Cowman, who have encouraged consideration of militant suffragism as an evolving and complex continuum of approaches to politics rather than as a discrete set of tactics.[70] Invoking militant language, Boord referred to sex, marriage and birth strikes as 'women's weapons'.[71] She suggested that the militant potential of the strikes arose from them taking place within a traditionally feminine sphere. Boord ascribed power to sex, marriage and birth strikes precisely because they would implicate 'quiet home lives', a space which was not usually politicized.[72] When prescribing these strikes, she used explicitly gendered language, asking, 'one wonders when Feminists will learn to be feminine' and use 'women's forces?'[73] Boord's rationale for describing these tactics as simultaneously forceful and feminine was that, in refusing to become wives or mothers, women would be causing a kind of social disruption not previously imagined by male activists. She critiqued existing militant tactics, most specifically window-breaking, as a mere replica of 'men's ideas and methods' and therefore, conversely, as an example of women behaving 'weakly' and 'meekly'.[74]

The WFL delegate Margaret Huntsman ascribed militant power to birth-striking on similar terms. Huntsman believed that this tactic would

[70] S. Stanley Holton, *Feminism and Democracy: Women's Suffrage and Reform Politics in Britain 1900–1918* (Cambridge, 1986), pp. 4, 29–52; Mayhall, *The Militant Suffrage Movement*, pp. 3–8; K. Cowman, '"A party between revolution and peaceful persuasion": a fresh look at the United Suffragists', in *The Women's Suffrage Movement: New Feminist Perspectives*, ed. M. Joannou and J. Purvis (Manchester, 1998), pp. 78–80, 86. They challenged earlier historians who constructed a sharp divide between militants and constitutionalists, depicting suffrage militancy as a discernible set of, largely illegal, tactics associated with the WSPU specifically. See G. Dangerfield, *The Strange Death of Liberal England* (1935, rpt. New York, 1961), p. 147; A. Rosen, *Rise Up Women! The Militant Campaign of the Women's Social and Political Union, 1903–1914* (1974, rpt. Abingdon, 2013), pp. xviii–xix.

[71] Boord, 'To the editors', p. 130.

[72] Boord, 'To the editors', p. 131.

[73] Emphasis my own. Boord, 'To the editors', p. 130.

[74] Boord, 'To the editors', p. 130.

be so powerful that the mere 'threat' of it could usher in political equality for women.[75] She suggested this threat was partly predicated on a 'fear of the unknown' as birth-striking had not been enacted before.[76] Huntsman predicted that Members of Parliament would be alarmed by the sense that they 'would never be able to tell how far it spreads' as the intrinsically private nature of the strike would mean it was 'a difficult thing to check'.[77] In making this proposal, Huntsman joined a wider tradition of women's suffrage campaigners who constructed arguments for enfranchisement based on the distinct 'national service' that women demonstrated as mothers.[78] Desires for enfranchisement on these terms were often articulated as a *plea* that women be rewarded with political rights in recognition of their social contributions within the home.[79] By formulating her proposition for a strike, Huntsman expressed similar ideas but in the traditionally militant rhetorical style of a *threat*, warning that if women were not given the vote they would take this 'national service' away.

Instead of devoting attention to the men in Parliament directly, when considering the militant potential of sex and marriage strikes, Re-Bartlett emphasized the impact these tactics might have on the jilted fiancés and abandoned husbands who made up the electorate.[80] Making her understanding of these tactics as a form of militancy explicitly clear, Re-Bartlett dubbed the 'silent strikers' a 'body of private militants'.[81] She gendered this militancy by suggesting that these strikes would be a representation of 'womanhood' and 'motherhood'.[82] Like Boord, Re-Bartlett politicized 'feminine' decisions concerning marriage and motherhood by assigning them traditionally masculine attributes of strength and 'forcefulness'.[83] Re-Bartlett's endeavour to gender militancy in this way was likely informed by her theosophical connections. One strand of feminist-theosophical literature emphasized associations between masculinity and force and femininity and passivity, while encouraging male and female

[75] LSE, Add. MS 2WFL/2/07, p. 63.

[76] LSE, Add. MS 2WFL/2/07, p. 63.

[77] LSE, Add. MS 2WFL/2/07, p. 63.

[78] Kent, *Sex and Suffrage*, p. 95; Mayhall, *The Militant Suffrage Movement*, p. 100.

[79] Kent, *Sex and Suffrage*, p. 95.

[80] Re-Bartlett, *Sex and Sanctity*, pp. 44, 48–9.

[81] Re-Bartlett, *Sex and Sanctity*, p. 31.

[82] Re-Bartlett, *Sex and Sanctity*, p. 24.

[83] Re-Bartlett, *Sex and Sanctity*, pp. 29, 31, 44–5, 74.

followers to embody both sets of attributes.[84] Re-Bartlett's development of a political tactic which combined a rescinding of action (and therefore, arguably, inherent passivity) with imagery of destruction would have served these ends.

Taking these ideas to their extreme, Re-Bartlett made the surprising claim that sex and marriage strikes would constitute a form of 'violence'.[85] She considered sex and marriage strikes to be comparable to the destruction of property, writing that '"window-breaking" is only as one wave breaking from a great sea'.[86] The sex and marriage strikes, in her analogy, were another wave forming from this same body of water.[87] Anticipating opposition from critics outside the women's rights movement who might deem her calls for celibacy excessively harsh, Re-Bartlett acknowledged that her proposed tactics would not be easy for any party to endure.[88] She nevertheless justified her interest in sex-striking by commenting that 'we are told that the kingdom of heaven must be taken with "violence" and in no field is that more true than in the love of man and woman'.[89] Re-Bartlett continued, 'there must always be a period of violence' when existing norms dictating relationships between men and women are 'cut suffering and bleeding away' as 'woman fights desperately with herself and with man'.[90] Developing her military metaphor, she dubbed celibate women 'warrior maids'.[91] Re-Bartlett's use of inverted commas when she first employed the word 'violence' in relation to domestic strikes confirms that she almost certainly viewed these strikes as an instance of allegorical or, possibly, what we might now term 'structural violence' rather than literal violence. However, she nevertheless believed that this violence would have a material effect on victims. She implied that denying men the emotional and physical joys of love, sex and marriage would cause them the 'pain of denial'.[92] For Re-Bartlett, this pain had important spiritual significance. She elaborated by invoking the *Divine Comedy*, maintaining that just as Beatrice inspired Dante to face hell-fire and ultimately reach salvation, women embarking on sex and marriage

[84] Dixon, *Divine Feminine*, pp. 251–2.

[85] Re-Bartlett, *Sex and Sanctity*, p. 44.

[86] Re-Bartlett, *Sex and Sanctity*, p. 26. For other comparisons between sex and marriage strikes and window-breaking, see pp. 25, 45, 31–2.

[87] Re-Bartlett, *Sex and Sanctity*, p. 26.

[88] Re-Bartlett, *Sex and Sanctity*, p. 44.

[89] Re-Bartlett, *Sex and Sanctity*, p. 44.

[90] Re-Bartlett, *Sex and Sanctity*, p. 44.

[91] Re-Bartlett, *Sex and Sanctity*, p. 45.

[92] Re-Bartlett, *Sex and Sanctity*, pp. 50, 53.

strikes would force non-feminist men to face 'depths of pain, and long-drawn penitence' and ultimately develop deeper empathy.[93] As Christabel Pankhurst noted in *The Great Scourge*, feminist calls to end prostitution were often met with cries that denying men sexual outlets would constitute 'injury' to their health.[94] Re-Bartlett's writing capitalized on these fears.

The idea that a sex and marriage strike would provoke more individual male suffering than a birth strike involving contraception seems to be an additional key reason why Re-Bartlett advocated the former tactics.[95] With her definition of the sex and marriage strikes as violent, Re-Bartlett reimagined power relations within the sexual sphere. Feminists commonly pointed to men's acts of sexual violence as evidence of their aggression within the perceived 'sex war'.[96] Typically, suffragettes proposed that women fight male oppression with acts of militant protest such as public demonstrations or the destruction of property, which would secure their most powerful weapon, the vote.[97] Re-Bartlett alternatively asserted women's control over male sexual temperance as a militant weapon within this war, as well as a desired outcome. However, blurring boundaries between passivity and forcefulness and masculinity and femininity once again, she was keen to assert that this weapon would be employed out of love, prompting men to undertake a spiritual journey and enabling them to become respectful husbands.[98]

Deciding on whether all men, or just the most egregious offenders, should be the targets of militancy was a hot topic within suffrage discourse.[99] Feminists engaging with these debates sometimes operated at opposite ends of this spectrum, either seeing all bystanders as fair game or only wishing to target the handful of politicians most forcefully standing in the way of women's enfranchisement.[100] Re-Bartlett, and in particular Boord, occupied a middle ground, wanting to target a significant proportion of the male population, but noting that men who already supported feminist

[93] In this instance Re-Bartlett referred to sex and marriage-strikers as the women who choose to 'stand afar off' from men. Re-Bartlett, *Sex and Sanctity*, pp. 48–9, 53.

[94] Pankhurst, *The Great Scourge*, pp. 6, 24.

[95] Re-Bartlett, *Sex and Sanctity*, p. 50.

[96] Kent, *Sex and Suffrage*, pp. 157–8.

[97] Kent, *Sex and Suffrage*, pp. 172–5.

[98] Re-Bartlett, *Sex and Sanctity*, pp. 44–5, 49.

[99] Eustance, 'Meanings of militancy', pp. 54–5; L. E. Mayhall, 'Defining militancy: radical protest, the constitutional idiom, and women's suffrage in Britain, 1908–1909', *Journal of British Studies*, xxxix (2000), p. 367.

[100] Eustance, 'Meanings of militancy', p. 55.

demands should be exempted.[101] Presumably, one of the benefits of sex, marriage and birth strikes, in contrast to other militant tactics, was the precision with which the male targets could be chosen. In Boord's case, the decision to explicitly exempt the wives of feminist-sympathizing men was perhaps driven by a personal motivation as, fortunately for her, Boord's own husband, Alexander Boord, was an ally to the cause.[102] He wrote his own letter to *The Freewoman* a few editions after hers, demonstrating his feminist sympathies and signing the letter from only 'the happy husband of Coralie M. Boord'.[103] Re-Bartlett, however, believed that, for most women, separatism was a significant component of the journey to both female enfranchisement and much wider social reform. Emphasizing the extent to which she envisaged an emotional and spiritual connection between sex-strikers and other militant suffrage activists, Re-Bartlett claimed that a sense of not being able to tolerate men until they shared women's outrage at female subjugation was 'the essence of women's militancy today'.[104]

Sex and birth strikes as women's sacrifice

Those suffragettes conceptualizing sex, marriage and birth strikes as militant did not only do so because of the effect they thought this tactic would have on men, but also due to the impact they thought it would have on themselves. Arguably, sex and marriage strikes undermined feminist endeavours to dismantle sexual double standards as the tactics could be seen to suggest that men would 'suffer' from a lack of sexual companionship in a way women would not. However, Boord and Re-Bartlett countered this implication by asserting that the strikes would, indeed, involve an emotional, and possibly physical, sacrifice for the women carrying them out.[105] Self-sacrifice was a central theme within militant suffragette rhetoric. The leadership of the WSPU was well-known for reappropriating traditional expectations that women subjugate their own desires to those of their husbands.[106] Many

[101] Re-Bartlett, *Sex and Sanctity*, p. 52; Boord, 'To the editors', p. 130.

[102] Marriage records of Coralie Hoskier and Alexander Edgar Boord, *Civil Registration Marriage Index, 1837–1915*.

[103] The happy husband of Coralie M. Boord, 'A conundrum', *The Freewoman*, 22 Feb. 1912, p. 272.

[104] Re-Bartlett, *Sex and Sanctity*, p. 26.

[105] Boord, 'To the editors', p. 130; Re-Bartlett, *Sex and Sanctity*, pp. 26, 67.

[106] Vicinus, *Independent Women*, pp. 252, 255, 263; G. L. Gullickson, 'When death became thinkable: self-sacrifice in the Women's Social and Political Union', *Journal of Social History*, li (2017), pp. 367, 370, 374; L. Jenkins, *Lady Constance Lytton: Aristocrat, Suffragette, Martyr* (London, 2018), pp. 109, 143; M. Jones, *The Last Great Quest: Captain Scott's Antarctic Sacrifice* (2003, rpt. ebook, Oxford, 2004), pp. 233–6.

militant suffragettes believed that their comrades should alternatively make sacrifices for the women's movement by devoting their lives to the cause, risking arrest, imprisonment and even torture.[107] Boord and Re-Bartlett engaged with this same enterprise, suggesting that self-sacrifice would bestow sex-, marriage- and birth-strikers with additional power.

Boord believed that enduring sex, marriage and, in particular, birth strikes would be an additional feminist avenue through which suffragettes could channel their willingness to make sacrifices. She was responding to Drysdale, who characterized a birth strike as non-sacrificial on the grounds that having fewer children would constitute a liberation for women.[108] He asserted that a hindrance to the implementation of birth-striking would be 'the idea of self-sacrifice', claiming that this expectation 'has always been drilled into women', making 'it difficult to convince them' to look after 'their own self-interest'.[109] Drysdale's stance reflected the editorial line of *The Freewoman*, which entirely rejected notions of female sacrifice, instead arguing that 'freedom' from such traditionally gendered expectations was superior feminist praxis.[110] In her response to Drysdale, Boord called this thesis into question; 'Alas!', she wrote, 'I fear' Drysdale 'flatters' militant suffragettes.[111] She claimed that the reason why suffragettes had 'not yet adopted' a sex, marriage or birth strike 'to obtain their liberty' was 'because they are not self-sacrificing *enough*, not big enough yet to face this very real ordeal'.[112] Implying that a sex, marriage and birth strike might constitute a more arduous act of martyrdom than conventional militant protests, she asserted that the former 'would be no "sham fight" '.[113] Referencing the well-publicized clashes between the WSPU and the police that took place in 1910 and 1911, Boord claimed that the archetypal suffragette was willing to 'face martyrdom in the open – standing shoulder to shoulder', but was not 'yet ready silently to plunge the sword – no blare of trumpets to cheer her – into her own quiet home life'.[114] Boord implied that militancy in the marital

[107] Vicinus, *Independent Women*, pp. 252, 255, 263; Gullickson, 'When death became thinkable', pp. 367, 370, 374; Jenkins, *Lady Constance Lytton*, pp. 109, 143; Jones, *The Last Great Quest*, pp. 233–6.

[108] Drysdale, 'Freewoman and the birth rate II', p. 89.

[109] Drysdale, 'Freewoman and the birth rate II', p. 89.

[110] Boord, 'To the editors', pp. 130–1; L. Delap, 'The superwoman: theories of gender and genius in Edwardian Britain', *The Historical Journal*, xlvii (2004), 101–26, at p. 122.

[111] Boord, 'To the editors', p. 130.

[112] Boord, 'To the editors', p. 130.

[113] Boord, 'To the editors', p. 130.

[114] Boord, 'To the editors', pp. 130–1.

sphere would demonstrate greater bravery than more traditional protests because domestic harmony was, in her contemporary world, one of the few joys extended to many women. 'To some life has been so little sweet', Boord observed, 'they have not yet the strength – for the sake of posterity – to make it *all* bitter'.[115]

Similarly to Boord, Re-Bartlett countered assumptions that sex, marriage and birth strikes might reinforce double standards when she confirmed that the strikes were not a symptom of lack of sexual desire.[116] Re-Bartlett sought to engender a culture where male and female sexual enjoyment was predicated on a spiritual 'passion' for conceiving children and thereby creating new life.[117] She nevertheless assured her readers that her calls for celibacy were intended as 'a temporary protest – an appeal', and did not represent 'the weakening of sex attraction' on the part of women.[118] Emphasizing the difficulty this protest would pose for women, Re-Bartlett asserted that the strikers were so committed to their feminist refusal to marry and have children that they were prepared to endure 'loneliness,' social 'opposition' and 'pain'.[119] Re-Bartlett was aware that encouraging women to make sacrifices could nevertheless be seen as reinforcing patriarchal expectations among some members of her feminist readership. She addressed this concern by asserting a distinction between conventional gendered sacrifice and the sacrifice behind the sex and marriage strike. Re-Bartlett saw traditional feminine sacrifice as being motivated by a sense of 'duty' and therefore oppressive, while she contrastingly characterized politicized celibacy as driven by a 'greater *love*' for both other women and men, and therefore spiritually empowering.[120]

For both Boord and Re-Bartlett the spiritual implications of this greater love were significant to the strikes' imagined power.[121] Using provocative language, Boord predicted that by sacrificing the joys to be found within the home, women could cause 'motherhood' to 'slay itself only to rise purified from its ashes'.[122] She focused on foregoing motherhood, rather than foregoing sex or companionship, as a site for sacrifice possibly for this very

[115] Boord, 'To the editors', p. 131.

[116] Re-Bartlett, *Sex and Sanctity*, p. 26.

[117] Re-Bartlett, *The Coming Order*, pp. 52–3.

[118] Re-Bartlett, *Sex and Sanctity*, pp. 26, 67.

[119] Re-Bartlett, *Sex and Sanctity*, p. 42.

[120] Re-Bartlett, *Sex and Sanctity*, pp. 51, 74.

[121] For more on the relationship between spirituality and sacrifice in the suffrage movement, see Vicinus, *Independent Women*, p. 252.

[122] Boord, 'To the editors', p. 131.

reason. Boord's vision of sacrifice here rested on the notion that selflessness was inherent to the maternal role. She suggested that a birth strike would be purifying because it would usher in a greater motherhood through women prioritizing creating a more equal society for all future generations over becoming a mother to their own, biological, offspring.[123] By referring to motherhood as being 'purified' by this process, Boord suggested that birth-striking would enable women to develop on a spiritual level.[124]

For Re-Bartlett, the cleansing potential of sacrifice was especially key to how sex and marriage strikes derived their power. Re-Bartlett maintained that enfranchisement unaccompanied by such spiritual growth would be significantly less meaningful.[125] The crux of Re-Bartlett's argument was that the 'spirit' behind militant activism – shared by window-breakers and sex- and marriage-strikers alike – was more significant than any individual 'manifestation' of militancy.[126] She maintained that this spirit was partly demonstrated by 'the enormous power of the woman militant to suffer and to sacrifice themselves for an impersonal cause'.[127] Re-Bartlett's interest in this spiritual process was intimately linked to her theosophical beliefs. She championed these strikes because she believed that foregoing marriage and motherhood, in causing women to 'suffer', would develop their 'souls', 'personalities' and 'psyches'.[128] This claim combined the theosophical-feminist tenets that political and spiritual progress needed to be brought about simultaneously and that sexual self-control could be conducive to spiritual development.[129] While the influence of theosophy on suffrage campaigners and Edwardian sexual commentators has been extensively mapped, Re-Bartlett's writings provide an especially clear illustration of how the sexual, spiritual and political implications of theosophy could be coherently amalgamated. Her theory of striking lends support to historian Joy Dixon's contention that it is 'anachronistic' to construct a dichotomy between spiritual and political motivations within a first-wave feminist context.[130] As men were cleansed of their privilege, Re-Bartlett

[123] Boord, 'To the editors', p. 131.

[124] Boord, 'To the editors', p. 131.

[125] Re-Bartlett, *Sex and Sanctity*, p. 31.

[126] Re-Bartlett, *Sex and Sanctity*, pp. 24–6.

[127] Re-Bartlett, *Sex and Sanctity*, pp. 22–3.

[128] Re-Bartlett, *Sex and Sanctity*, pp. 9, 10, 12, 23, 44.

[129] Dixon, *Divine Feminine*, pp. 12–13, 153–5, 247–8. See also J. Dixon, 'Sexology and the occult: sexuality and subjectivity in theosophy's new age', *Journal of the History of Sexuality*, vii (1997), 409–33, at p. 432.

[130] Dixon, *Divine Feminine*, pp. 246, 26–7.

theorized, women would be similarly cleansed of their subservience and become emotionally and spiritually robust enough to achieve all their political demands.[131]

Without this robustness, Re-Bartlett believed, enfranchisement would not be as empowering for women as some others hoped. While Christabel Pankhurst, arguably the dominant voice within the so-called 'sex war' debates, had claimed that enfranchisement would automatically enable women to 'feel greater respect for themselves', Re-Bartlett believed that the specific tactics that led to political rights would be essential in determining the impact of enfranchisement on women's sense of self.[132] In this belief, Re-Bartlett provides an illustration of the pervious relationship between suffragism and suffrage-scepticism for some campaigners. She suggested that only by enduring hardships through militant activism, including participating in the 'silent strike', would women develop the strength to carry on fighting for further reforms pertaining to marriage and sexuality once enfranchised. Underlining her belief in the importance of these additional reforms, Re-Bartlett wrote: 'the suffragists have told us … that it is towards social purity and the protection of women and child life that their forces will be principally turned when the vote is gained'. She problematized this: 'we all know what forces of resistance will oppose them when they attack only one of these questions'.[133] Winning the vote through arduous militant tactics, Re-Bartlett therefore concluded, would be 'the only thing which can give real value to suffrage'.[134] She went on: 'new laws will help, the vote will help but *only* with this force behind them. And where do we find this force today? Only in the militant', by which she was including 'that still larger body of private militants whom the world does not always know'.[135]

Conclusion

Between 1911 and 1914, some affiliates of the WSPU and WFL considered the impact of politicizing women's choices to marry, have sex and become mothers. As Re-Bartlett described, these women and their ideas did not receive wide publicity, either at the time or in subsequent scholarship, but their writings embellish our understanding of the complex relationship between sexuality, motherhood and suffrage. Reflecting on the different

[131] Re-Bartlett, *Sex and Sanctity*, pp. 26, 31, 33, 45.

[132] Pankhurst, *The Great Scourge and How to End It*, p. viii.

[133] Re-Bartlett, *Sex and Sanctity*, p. 31.

[134] Re-Bartlett, *Sex and Sanctity*, p. 31.

[135] Emphasis my own. Re-Bartlett, *Sex and Sanctity*, p. 31; see also pp. 40–1.

implications of women's roles as spouses, sexual partners and parents, Re-Bartlett, Boord and members of the WFL's 1914 conference considered whether they wanted to target the military and economy with a mass birth strike and/or make individual men pay a higher price by refusing all sexual and romantic contact, simultaneously requiring a significant sacrifice from women themselves. While all the strike advocates discussed here campaigned for votes for women, and expressed their hope that the vote would be accompanied by broader changes to sexual culture, they also shared a belief that women had existing power to provoke both cultural and political shifts through their choices within the private sphere. In the case of Boord, and in particular Re-Bartlett, these strikes were considered to be of utmost importance. They advanced that unless the vote were won via specific tactics, and unless women undertook an accompanying spiritual journey, political representation would not prove transformative. Boord, Re-Bartlett and the WFL delegates found new ways to subvert gender norms, suggesting that women could demonstrate force, threatening behaviour and even a form of structural violence by using contraceptive methods, moving out of the family home or rejecting a proposal. As such, they provide further evidence of the diverse and complicated ways suffrage campaigners demonstrated militancy. For most strike advocates, perhaps the most powerful aspect of their proposed tactics was that they believed that no man had thought of them before.

III. Navigating international structures

10. 'East Side Londoners': Sylvia Pankhurst's lecture tours of North America and the East London Federation of Suffragettes*

Katherine Connelly

The certainty of others, the life, love, sight, hearing of others.

Walt Whitman, 'Crossing Brooklyn Ferry' (1856)

Sylvia Pankhurst's transatlantic lecture tours, from 5 January to 12 April 1911 and again from 11 January to 3 April 1912, were the most sustained, high-profile campaigning that she had yet been involved in. Lecturing on the militant suffragette campaign in which she was an active participant, Pankhurst travelled extensively, speaking 'once, twice or thrice a day', often to audiences of thousands, across nineteen American states, Washington, DC and parts of Canada.[1]

The tours traversed a dramatic change in her approach to the dominant militant suffrage organization, the Women's Social and Political Union (WSPU), led primarily by her mother and older sister Emmeline and Christabel Pankhurst and, up to the autumn of 1912, Emmeline and Frederick Pethick-Lawrence. Whereas previously Sylvia Pankhurst had striven to maintain a degree of independence from the organization, after her return from her 1912 tour she threw herself wholeheartedly into its work in an attempt to redirect it towards collective, working-class activism. From the autumn of 1912, Pankhurst began establishing WSPU branches

* With thanks to Morgan Daniels, Alexandra Hughes-Johnson, Lyndsey Jenkins and Senia Pašeta for comments on the draft, to Vicky Iglikowski-Broad at the National Archives and Katie Vogel at Henry Street Settlement for archival advice and to Eric Anderson for showing me around Haskell College and sharing his expertise in its history with me.

[1] E. S. Pankhurst, *The Suffragette Movement: An Intimate Account of Persons and Ideals* (London, 1977), p. 347.

'East Side Londoners', in *The politics of women's suffrage: local, national and international dimensions*, ed. A. Hughes-Johnson and L. Jenkins (London, 2021), pp. 263–284.

composed of working women in East London; within months, she led a federation of six branches that defied the WSPU leadership by establishing close relationships with the labour movement.[2]

In January 1914, shortly after Pankhurst appeared on a platform alongside the socialist trade unionist James Connolly in solidarity with locked-out workers in Dublin, the WSPU leaders decisively rejected the independent and socialistic approach of the East London groups, and instructed them to form a separate organization. In its subsequent existence as the East London Federation of Suffragettes (ELFS), this organization developed innovative campaigning tactics and further differentiated itself from the WSPU by opposing British involvement in the First World War and advocating adult suffrage. Later, accompanied by a variety of name changes, it became a tributary of the international communist movement. Pankhurst's actions in 1912, then, set in train a series of developments that impacted profoundly on Britain's feminist and socialist movements.

It was in the midst of her campaigning efforts in East London that Pankhurst wrote eight chapters of a book that she did not complete about America.[3] This chapter explores that manuscript alongside some of Pankhurst's previously uncited journalism from this period, her correspondence and American archives connected to her tours, to show that Pankhurst's transatlantic experiences provided formative and enduring influences upon the character of the ELFS. In particular, this chapter contends that Pankhurst was inspired by a network of female social reformers around the New York and Chicago branches of the Women's Trade Union League (hereafter NYWTUL and CWTUL), and in the female-run settlement houses at Henry Street in New York and Hull House in Chicago. Settlement houses and the WTUL were ventures that originated in Britain. It was, however, in their reformulation by radical American women that Pankhurst drew inspiration, modifying them to fit her own campaigning needs. While Pankhurst's creation of the ELFS has been seen primarily as the result of a schism in the British suffragette movement, the contextualization offered in this chapter shows that it was also part of a wider transatlantic dialogue about social change in which reformers shared and adapted ideas and models of organization.

The extent of these influences have not previously been recognized, hindered by the lack of a comprehensive account of Pankhurst's transatlantic tours that was only recently provided with the publication of my edition

[2] Pankhurst, *Suffragette Movement*, p. 438.

[3] See my introduction to E. S. Pankhurst, *A Suffragette in America: Reflections on Pickets, Prisoners and Political Change*, ed. K. Connelly (London, 2019), p. 7.

of her American manuscript.[4] This chapter therefore marks a departure from the historiography of the suffragette movement that has tended to regard Pankhurst's actions in 1912 as the inevitable result of longstanding disagreements with the WSPU leadership, thereby emphasizing Pankhurst's role at the expense of other activists.[5] While biographical studies posited connections between Pankhurst's American experiences and the foundation of the ELFS, speculating that the tours enhanced her self-confidence and prompted a deeper engagement with socialist ideas, they similarly situated her 1912 shift towards collective, working-class suffrage activism in a framework that foregrounded Pankhurst's individual intellectual development.[6] Thus, biographical studies by Barbara Winslow and Les Garner both identified that Pankhurst's American manuscript asserted the importance of independent representation for working-class women and men, particularly in her response to the Milwaukee socialist administration's top-down approach to reform. In Garner's formulation, Pankhurst's critique 'reflected her growing belief in socialism from below ... a belief she was soon to develop in the East End'.[7] Valuable as these insights are, and to which my own work is indebted, they nevertheless insufficiently explain how an increased self-confidence and socialist analysis resulted in Pankhurst's commitment to working more intensely *inside* the suffrage movement, nor can they account for the practical decisions she subsequently took.

Winslow's conclusion, that Pankhurst necessarily envisaged an alternative to top-down models of reform as 'her vision of women's emancipation came from the power of working women themselves, organizing and rebuilding their workplaces, homes and communities on their own terms', provides the starting point for this chapter.[8] First, it shows that Pankhurst's

[4] Pankhurst, *Suffragette in America.* P. G. Harrison, *Connecting Links: The British and American Woman Suffrage Movements, 1900–1914* (Westport, Conn.; London, 2000) contains primary research into Sylvia Pankhurst's tours, although the parameters of her study militate against a more comprehensive treatment. C. Bolt, 'America and the Pankhursts', in *Votes for Women: The Struggle for Suffrage Revisited*, ed. J. H. Baker (Oxford; New York, 2002), pp. 143–58 predominantly focuses on Emmeline Pankhurst.

[5] For example, M. Pugh, *The March of the Women: A Revisionist Analysis of the Campaign for Women's Suffrage, 1866–1914* (Oxford, 2000), p. 215.

[6] L. Garner, 'Suffragism and socialism: Sylvia Pankhurst 1903–1914', in *Sylvia Pankhurst: From Artist to Anti-Fascist*, ed. I. Bullock and R. Pankhurst (Basingstoke, 1992), pp. 58–85, at pp. 70–1; B. Winslow, *Sylvia Pankhurst: Sexual Politics and Political Activism* (London, 1996), pp. 18–25; K. Connelly, *Sylvia Pankhurst: Suffragette, Socialist and Scourge of Empire* (London, 2013), pp. 39–44.

[7] Garner, 'Suffragism and socialism', p. 71.

[8] Winslow, *Sylvia Pankhurst*, p. 24.

writings identified emancipatory potential in practical examples of 'female institution building' in America.[9] The following sections demonstrate how these institutions and the women involved in them influenced Pankhurst's efforts to build her female institution in East London. The second section shows that the ELFS directly emulated women's community organizing in the Chicago labour movement. The third section demonstrates that the ELFS was modelled on, and in part financed by women connected to, New York's Henry Street Settlement. In so doing, this chapter examines Pankhurst's reliance on what historian Blanche Wiesen Cook has identified as the long-overlooked female networks of love, support and friendship that sustained the social work and activism of many reformers, including many of those Pankhurst met in the settlement houses and WTUL.[10] It therefore argues that the ELFS was far from being a lone endeavour, solely attributable to Pankhurst's enduring or strengthened convictions. Not only were the tactics and culture of the ELFS developed in reaction to what Pankhurst judged to be flawed, top-down models of social change; they were also positively inspired by women's networks of solidarity in the American labour movement and drew upon their practical experience to implement change in the British suffragette movement. The internationalism of Pankhurst's organization, so apparent after the outbreak of the First World War and in its approach to the Russian Revolution, had been an essential component from the beginning.

Organizational models: the WTUL and settlement houses

In the first edition of the ELFS's newspaper, Sylvia Pankhurst alluded to the WSPU leadership when she wrote '[s]ome people tell us that it is neither specially important that working-women should agitate for the Vote, nor specially important that they should have it'.[11] Pankhurst had grown increasingly uneasy at the WSPU leadership's redefining of militancy as acts of sacrifice undergone by wealthy women on behalf of poorer women; on one of her transatlantic tours Emmeline Pankhurst boasted that 'the privileged women, the honoured women are doing the hardest and most

[9] On 'female institution building', see E. Freedman, 'Separatism as strategy: female institution building and American feminism, 1870–1930', *Feminist Studies*, v (1979), 512–29.

[10] B. W. Cook, 'Female support networks and political activism', in *A Heritage of Her Own: Toward a New Social History of American Women*, ed. N. F. Cott and E. H. Pleck (New York, 1979), pp. 412–44.

[11] 'The East London Federation of the Suffragettes', *Woman's Dreadnought*, 8 Mar. 1914, p. 3.

unpleasant work' in the militant movement.[12] Sylvia Pankhurst's insinuation that the WSPU also disregarded the importance of the working women's franchise referred to the abandonment of its longstanding insistence on women's enfranchisement 'on the same terms as it is or may be granted to men' to extend pragmatic support to the 1910 Conciliation Bill, which proposed to enfranchise around a million propertied women.

Before 1912, Pankhurst felt that state repression of the suffragettes inhibited her from publicly voicing her disagreements: 'I would rather have died at the stake than say one word against the actions of those who were in the throes of the fight.'[13] That changed after her return from her second transatlantic lecture tour in 1912. Within a month of her return, she argued that winning working-class women's inclusion in the franchise 'can only be rendered at all secure by a great working class women's suffrage movement' – something she endeavoured to create later that year in East London.[14] Her change of approach, however, was not prompted by any lessening of state repression, rather by its intensification. In March 1912, the WSPU launched a mass window-smashing campaign in response to the government's effective sabotage of the Conciliation Bill; Emmeline Pankhurst and the Pethick-Lawrences were charged with conspiracy and Christabel Pankhurst fled into exile. Sylvia Pankhurst later explained that these developments convinced her to dedicate herself to advancing an alternative strategy for the WSPU: 'I determined that on my return home I would give all my time as a voluntary worker in the active movement, doing whatever I saw required to be done which would not be attempted without my intervention.'[15] What occasioned Pankhurst's more interventionist approach in 1912 were her American lecturing fees, which allowed her to volunteer her time, and her conviction that she had distinctive, practical ideas to impart that allowed her to avoid simply negative criticism of her fellow activists.[16] Like the funds, some of Pankhurst's practical ideas can be traced to America.

In its first meeting after its expulsion from the WSPU, the ELFS stated that the difference between the two organizations was 'that they [the WSPU] were working from the top down & we from the bottom up'.[17] As

[12] Quoted in E. C. DuBois, 'Harriot Stanton Blatch and the transformation of class relations among woman suffragists' in *Gender, Class, Race, and Reform in the Progressive Era*, ed. N. Frankel and N. S. Dye (Lexington, Ky., 1991), p. 174.

[13] Pankhurst, *Suffragette Movement*, p. 316.

[14] E. S. Pankhurst, 'The woman's vote', *Pioneer*, 11 May 1912, p. 6.

[15] Pankhurst, *Suffragette Movement*, p. 383.

[16] On the funds, see Pankhurst, *Suffragette Movement*, p. 383.

[17] Minute book [ELFS], 27 Jan. 1914.

noted earlier, Pankhurst's adoption of a more confrontational approach to the 'top-down' WSPU was preceded by her critique of top-down attitudes to social reform she observed in America. Pankhurst's criticisms were developed in dialogue with sympathetic socialists. Her complaint in the fifth chapter of her American manuscript that Milwaukee's socialist administration emphasized efficiency instead of improving workers' material conditions was first contained in a letter to Keir Hardie, the former Labour Party leader and Labour MP with whom Pankhurst was romantically involved.[18] This letter also formed the basis for Pankhurst's second chapter, about a laundry in Milwaukee that was run according to the supposedly progressive principles of Taylorism but which Pankhurst judged inhuman: 'the workers were absolutely silent – they seemed just a part of the machinery'.[19] The sixth chapter, concerning the treatment of young Native Americans at Haskell College, first appeared as an article for Hardie's socialist newspaper the *Pioneer* under the pseudonym 'S' (perhaps to conceal her authorship from the WSPU).[20] Pankhurst was similarly critical of this ostensibly enlightened institution's inhuman treatment of those subject to its regulations. She observed that Haskell aimed to annihilate its students' cultural heritage, with its harmony with the natural world, training them instead to serve the needs of contemporary capitalist production.[21] Drawing on the Arts and Crafts-influenced socialist critique of modern industry, Pankhurst wrote that she regretted seeing students' work that was 'embroidered with floral patterns, exactly like those which are designed, in the least possible time, by the jaded sweated factory wage slaves, who cannot pause to observe real flowers'.[22]

Although Pankhurst's socialist critiques of top-down notions of progress have been the focus of discussions of her American writings, they did not necessarily point towards new openings in her political practice. These discussions have overlooked the way Pankhurst contrasted critical observations with examples of institutions that she judged more positively,

[18] See Connelly, introduction to ch. 5, in Pankhurst, *Suffragette in America*, p. 106.

[19] E. S. Pankhurst to J. K. Hardie, 5 Feb. 1912, p. 17, Estelle Sylvia Pankhurst Papers, 9, International Institute of Social History.

[20] S., 'A Red Indian College', *Pioneer*, 14 Oct. 1911, p. 8.

[21] On this as the declared ethos of Haskell, see M. Vučković, *Voices from Haskell: Indian Students between Two Worlds, 1884–1928* (Lawrence, Kans., 2008), pp. 11–29.

[22] E. S. Pankhurst, untitled typescript on America [Chronicle of two visits to Canada and the United States, based on letters to J. Keir Hardie], Estelle Sylvia Pankhurst Papers, 117, International Institute of Social History, ch. 6, p. 6.

such as the WTUL branches she encountered in New York and Chicago. If Pankhurst's American writings were in part working through the problems she identified in the WSPU, then these positive examples suggested alternative approaches to reform that she might emulate.

The WTUL, an organization that helped to unionize women workers, originated in Britain with Emma Paterson's creation of its forerunner the Women's Protective and Provident League in 1874. Pankhurst, however, expressed her particular admiration for branches of the American organization. In America, Pankhurst was able to collaborate with WTUL activists who were not divided from the women's suffrage movement in the way that labour activists in Britain were by the existence of the property qualification, a factor that predisposed them to support adult suffrage as opposed to women's suffrage.

Pankhurst's transatlantic tours coincided with a wave of industrial unrest that began in late 1909 in the sweatshops of New York City, primarily led by and composed of immigrant women, and spread across American cities up until 1915. Pankhurst made significant contact with this movement and witnessed the WTUL's contribution to it in New York and Chicago. In January 1911, Pankhurst arrived in Chicago towards the end of a four-month-long strike of around 40,000 garment workers that had been met with a level of violence characteristic of the reaction elsewhere; pickets were arrested, imprisoned and beaten by thugs hired by their employers; two strikers were shot dead by the police.[23] On 21 January, two CWTUL members, Zelie Emerson – who was later to play an important role in the ELFS – and Olive Sullivan, took Pankhurst to view the cells in which arrested garment workers had been held.[24] Later that day, Pankhurst wrote to the *Chicago Tribune* denouncing the conditions in the cells, drawing parallels with the treatment of British suffragettes and paying tribute to the CWTUL.

> Happily, their trade union organizations have been able to come to their aid and bail them out within a short time, but it must be remembered that the people being on strike were practically penniless and had no money of their own, and therefore had others not come to their assistance they would have been obliged to continue suffering this terrible form of confinement.[25]

[23] P. S. Foner, *Women and the American Labor Movement: from Colonial Times to the Eve of World War I* (New York, 1979), p. 353.

[24] 'City jail shocking to Miss Pankhurst', *Inter Ocean*, 22 Jan. 1911, p. 7.

[25] 'Sylvia Pankhurst, suffraget [*sic*] chief, assails Harrison Street Station', *Chicago Tribune*, 22 Jan. 1911, p. 7.

Similarly, after speaking with striking laundry workers in New York in January 1912, Pankhurst praised, in another pseudonymous *Pioneer* article, the 'energetic members' of the NYWTUL and its president Mary Dreier for organizing this majority-female workforce.[26] Pankhurst reproduced this article as the first chapter in her American book, immediately preceding the chapter on the Milwaukee laundry. Whereas the workers in Milwaukee seemed atomized and dehumanized, Pankhurst signalled the emancipatory potential of workers' collective organization in New York by noting that the strike had overcome the racial and sexual divisions fostered by the laundry bosses through unequal pay. She described a meeting at which a white, American-born woman and a Black man, both recently released from prison for picketing, spoke alongside an Italian immigrant. The Italian worker drew a parallel between their experiences and those of the suffragettes: 'as a stimulus and encouragement to all present, [he] called upon them to remember the hundreds of British women who have suffered violence and imprisonment in the cause of their Enfranchisement'.[27] Pankhurst's writing on Chicago and New York praised examples of woman-led activism, in which middle-class women such as Emerson and Dreier are presented as contributing to a predominantly female workforce discovering its humanity and undertaking acts of militancy comparable to the suffragettes' experiences of police violence and imprisonment. In so doing, Pankhurst highlighted the CWTUL and NYWTUL as positive examples of ways that middle-class women could support, rather than substitute for, a working-class women's militant movement – something she sought to implement in Britain in 1912.[28]

Pankhurst also endorsed the women-led settlement houses in Chicago and New York to which the WTULs were closely connected. As with the WTUL, Pankhurst had already encountered settlement houses in England where they originated; in her childhood, she visited Manchester's Ancoats Brotherhood.[29] The first settlement house, Toynbee Hall, was established in 1884 in East London, less than three miles from Pankhurst's first East London headquarters. However, it was with two American settlement houses that Pankhurst and her organization forged connections. The socially

[26] S., 'The laundry workers' strike in New York', *Pioneer*, 10 Feb. 1912, p. 7. This article incorrectly records Dreier's name as Brien.

[27] Pankhurst, [Chronicle] ch. 1, p. 6.

[28] Although significant class tensions emerged in the WTUL, Pankhurst neither commented on nor was likely to have witnessed this to any great extent while on tour. Indeed, the CWTUL showed greater commitment to the garment workers' strike than did the United Garment Workers Union.

[29] Pankhurst, *Suffragette Movement*, p. 124.

radical qualities that Pankhurst praised in them were far less apparent in English settlements. These latter were established on the principle that the educated elite could elevate the lives of the urban poor through settling in their communities and providing a superior cultural example, while women's settlements tended to be organizationally separate and deprived of the professional status of their male counterparts.[30] By contrast, women played a more central role in the American settlement movement, where its houses were more likely to be mixed-sex.[31] Pankhurst was a guest at Hull House and Henry Street, both of which were founded and run by women: Jane Addams and Lillian D. Wald, respectively. The expertise their residents gained through their implantation in working-class communities served as a platform to both provide and demand social services for their neighbourhoods, including sanitary reform, factory inspections, medical assistance, playgrounds, clubs, lectures and classes. Pankhurst valued the way in which American settlements connected direct knowledge of working people's lives to the reforms they championed; in her critique of the Milwaukee socialist administration's much-vaunted Bureau of Efficiency and Economy, Pankhurst noted that the only member with 'any knowledge of working lives' was from the Milwaukee University settlement.[32] Moreover, at female-dominated institutions like Hull House and Henry Street, the residents' understanding of social problems and the evidence-based solutions they proposed ensured that they functioned as a powerful argument for women's enfranchisement.[33] Speaking in Lima, Ohio in 1912, Pankhurst challenged her audience: 'Can you not see that a woman with the mind of Jane Addams could have great weight in legislative matters?'[34]

Pankhurst also admired the cultural work of Henry Street Settlement. In its visitors' book, which was only rediscovered in 2019, she invoked their shared cultural values: 'I believe that to make and to do beautiful things will bring us the greatest joy that we can win. Let us strive to give all that

[30] On the radicalism of American settlements in this period, see A. F. Davis, *Spearheads for Reform: the Social Settlement and the Progressive Movement, 1890–1914* (New Brunswick, N.J., 1984).

On differences between English and American settlements, see R. C. Reinders, 'Toynbee Hall and the American settlement movement', *Social Service Review*, lvi (1982), 39–54; on the status of women's settlements in England, see M. Vicinus, *Independent Women: Work and Community for Single Women 1850–1920* (London, 1985), ch. 6.

[31] Reinders, 'Toynbee Hall', p. 45.

[32] Pankhurst to Hardie, 5 Feb. 1912, p. 55A.

[33] M. Vicinus, *Independent Women*, p. 213.

[34] 'Welcomed warmly was suffragist speaker by Limaites', *The Lima News*, 27 Feb. 1912, p. 4.

opportunity.'[35] This was likely, at least in part, a reference to the emergent Neighbourhood Playhouse, a cultural project run by Alice and Irene Lewisohn initially from the gymnasium of Henry Street Settlement for children living in the local tenements. Pankhurst, who was the Lewisohns' guest when she stayed in New York in 1912, was profoundly affected by their work.

> I lost my heart to the lovely Lewisohn sisters, expending their wealth and talents for the creation of a school of dance and drama for the young people of New York's East Side at Henry Street Settlement.[36]

The Lewisohns recognized rich, cultural traditions in the immigrant communities of New York's Lower East Side and helped working-class children to rediscover this heritage. In Alice Lewisohn's words: 'Although the children of the neighborhood had inherited an old culture from their ancestors, in the city practically no contact remained with its source – nature.'[37] The Lewisohns, who, like Pankhurst, were influenced by the ideals of the Arts and Crafts movement, thus began devising performances around the change of the seasons that drew on the stories and rituals of the local immigrant communities as well as from other international folk cultures.[38]

It was almost certainly the Lewisohns' production of *Sleeping Beauty: A Midwinter Myth* that Pankhurst recalled in the third chapter of her American manuscript.[39] Pankhurst described 'a band of little figures, short skirted and with flowery garlands round their waists … playing on reedy pipes and set to dancing, … their firm bare legs and sandaled feet prancing most vigorously'.[40] Here, then, was the antithesis of the destruction of indigenous culture, replaced by artificial flowers, at Haskell. Pankhurst's appreciation of *Sleeping Beauty*, like her appraisal of the WTUL, lay in its direct involvement of working-class people in a project that contrasted with the inhuman, machine-like character of contemporary capitalism and unleashed instead expressions of natural, shared humanity.

[35] Lillian D. Wald's visitors' book [undated]. On its discovery: <https://www.nytimes.com/2019/08/23/nyregion/henry-street-settlement-lillian-wald.html> [accessed 24 Feb. 2020].

[36] Pankhurst, *Suffragette Movement*, p. 349.

[37] A. L. Crowley, *The Neighborhood Playhouse: Leaves from a Theatre Scrapbook* (New York, 1959), p. 16.

[38] L. J. Tomko, *Dancing Class: Gender, Ethnicity, and Social Divides in American Dance, 1890–1920* (Bloomington, Ind., 1999), pp. 79–103.

[39] For a detailed explanation, see Connelly, introduction to ch. 3, Pankhurst, *Suffragette in America*, pp. 84–8.

[40] Pankhurst, [Chronicle] ch. 3, p. 4.

> As they danced on, it seemed to me that we were all whelmed by a flood of love and joy and radiance, and that cleansed of pain and sin, and throwing off social wrongs and false standards of life, we might begin to be brothers and sisters from that hour.[41]

Pankhurst's writings on the WTULs and settlements celebrated their foregrounding of working-class experience and activity in the struggle for reform. These positive examples suggested models that Pankhurst might emulate in her endeavour to create a militant working-class campaign. That she did so is underlined by the connections between the organization that she founded and those she admired in America.

Emerson and the CWTUL

The Chicago labour organizer Zelie Emerson embodies the most direct link between Pankhurst's transatlantic tours and the ELFS. A year after meeting Pankhurst in Chicago, with whom she formed a friendship and later possibly a romantic relationship, Emerson travelled to London to assist her efforts inside, and subsequently outside, the WSPU.[42] Assessments of Emerson have been shaped by Pankhurst's memoirs, written in the knowledge that Emerson's life had been put at severe risk by her participation in the suffragette struggle. Emerson tried to take her own life after weeks of forcible feeding in 1913; the following year Pankhurst persuaded her to leave for America after police fractured her skull. Exuding guilt 'for being the cause' of Emerson's suffering, Pankhurst's memoirs poignantly recalled Emerson on arrival as 'that merry little American, whose youthful desire for adventure had brought her across the Atlantic to join the movement'.[43] However, a close reading of Pankhurst's references to Emerson and examination of Emerson's activism prior to the suffragette movement reveal the extent to which the ELFS benefited from her organizing experience from its inception.

The 'youthful' Emerson was born in 1883 (only a year after Pankhurst) to an extremely wealthy family in Jackson, Michigan.[44] Interested in social reform, in July 1910, Emerson became a resident at Chicago's Northwestern University settlement and joined the CWTUL. In the Chicago garment

[41] Pankhurst, [Chronicle] ch. 3, p. 6.

[42] On Pankhurst and Emerson's relationship, see Winslow, *Sylvia Pankhurst*, p. 34; S. Harrison, *Sylvia Pankhurst: A Crusading Life, 1882–1960* (London, 2003), pp. 161–2.

[43] Pankhurst, *Suffragette Movement*, pp. 446, 395.

[44] Emerson's income was rumoured to be $10,000 a year; 'Girl of wealth scrubs floors', *Muncie Evening Press*, 30 Jan. 1912, p. 5.

workers' strike, the CWTUL identified particular pressures on women, as food providers and rent payers, and mobilized in the community to ensure that these pressures would not undermine the industrial struggle. One history of the CWTUL has shown that the work of its Rent and Relief Committees 'most directly represents the WTUL's concern with community issues'.[45] Emerson was centrally involved in both. She was the 'chairman' of the Rent Committee, which effectively coordinated a rent strike for the duration of the industrial action.[46] She was also a co-director of the relief effort that included supplying daily milk for thousands of babies, medical services, clothes and coal, and a series of commissary stores that secured donations and bulk purchases of food for families who bought tickets.[47] Additionally, Emerson ran a lunchroom for single workers: 'where a cup of coffee and two cheese or ham sandwiches were given at cost to 200 single men and girls'.[48] After the strike, Emerson and three other CWTUL members went to Muscatine, Iowa 'to plan the restaurant arrangements on a sound basis' for striking button workers.[49] Emerson later co-authored a paper on the Chicago relief efforts, which she termed 'co-operative philanthropy', thereby distinguishing them from charity. The commissary stores, she asserted, represented 'a permanent addition to organized labour's equipment' – a way for women's organizations to support industrial action by working women.[50]

At some point, probably in March 1912, Emerson decided to assist the British suffragettes. In March 1913, in an interview apparently given from prison, Emerson explained that her connection with the suffragettes began when 'I heard Sylvia Pankhurst speak in Detroit two years ago and she and I became fast friends'.[51] Pankhurst had spoken in Detroit, Michigan in March 1911, two months after she and Emerson first met in Chicago. The following year, Pankhurst returned to Detroit and on 28 February lectured

[45] C. A. Hyman, 'Labor organizing and female-institution building: the Chicago Women's Trade Union League, 1904–24', in *Women, Work and Protest: A Century of US Women's Labor History*, ed. R. Milkman (Boston, Mass.; London, 1985), pp. 22–41, at p. 26.

[46] Women's Trade Union League of Chicago, *Official Report of the Strike Committee: Chicago Garment Workers' Strike, Oct 29-February 18 1911* (Chicago, Ill., 1911), p. 1.

[47] CWTUL, *Report*, pp. 20, 35; Z. P. Emerson and K. Coman, 'Co-operative philanthropy: administration of relief during the strike of the Chicago garment workers', *The Survey*, 4 Mar. 1911, pp. 942–8, at pp. 947, 946, 945–6; 'Merry Christmas in sight for strikers', *Inter Ocean*, 22 Dec. 1910, p. 12.

[48] Emerson and Coman, 'Co-operative philanthropy', p. 945.

[49] 'Buttons – pearl buttons', *Life and Labour*, May 1911, pp. 143–5, at p. 144.

[50] Emerson and Coman, 'Co-operative philanthropy', p. 942.

[51] 'American suffraget, starving herself in English prison tells Shepherd what a "hunger strike" means!', *Evansville Press*, 5 Mar. 1913, p. 3. The reporter's claim of an interview with

nearby in Jackson, Emerson's home city. It seems likely that Emerson was involved in this arrangement. Moreover, Emerson's mother, a prominent suffragist in Jackson, would certainly have known about her daughter's friend's lecture.[52] Pankhurst was in Detroit at the beginning of March when she received news of the WSPU's window-smashing campaign, which provoked outrage and the cancellation of some lectures.[53] It is therefore noticeable that CWTUL activists were among the few who pledged greater support for Pankhurst at this time. Miles Franklin, co-editor of the WTUL's Chicago-based *Life and Labour* publication, recalled:

> when Sylvia Pankhurst had to abandon her lecturing tour when the news of a violent eruption of window smashing was cabled over, a few of us with the office of 'Life and Labor' and The Women's Trade Union League as a starting point, tried to get up a 'fair play' meeting for her, but as with Sodom and Gomorrah, there were not enough of us to save the situation.[54]

Franklin and her CWTUL colleague Mary Anderson personally demonstrated their support by joining the WSPU.[55] Thus, at the very moment of intensified state repression in Britain, which Pankhurst attributed to her resolution to dedicate herself to transforming the WSPU, Pankhurst was in dialogue with women in the Chicago labour movement.[56] Perhaps Emerson, her future collaborator, was among them – certainly, her close acquaintances were.[57]

If Emerson was among those in contact with Pankhurst at this time, it would explain why a few months later she travelled to Britain to campaign with the WSPU. She appears to have primarily worked with Pankhurst in her efforts to redirect the WSPU towards collective action accessible to working-class people. When Pankhurst organized a demonstration in Hyde Park on 14 July 1912, Emerson was among those who worked alongside

Emerson in prison is highly implausible; it is far more likely this account came from one of the letters she smuggled out of Holloway. See Pankhurst, *Suffragette Movement*, p. 446.

52 Local newspapers recorded Mrs Emerson's suffragist sympathies, one describing her as 'president of the Suffragist Association of Jackson'; 'Zelie Emerson, seeking knowledge through experience, scrubs floors', *Evening Sun*, 3 Feb. 1912, p. 4.

53 Connelly, introduction, Pankhurst, *Suffragette in America*, pp. 32–3.

54 S. M. F. [Stella Miles Franklin], 'Mrs. Pankhurst in the United States', *Life and Labour*, Dec. 1913, pp. 364–6, at p. 365.

55 S. M. F., 'Mrs. Pankhurst', p. 365.

56 Pankhurst, *Suffragette Movement*, p. 383.

57 Emerson was evidently close to Franklin; in the early summer of 1911, they were both sleeping on the floor of a resident's flat at Hull House. See J. Roe, *Her Brilliant Career: The Life of Stella Miles Franklin* (Cambridge, Mass.; London, 2009), p. 146.

her all night producing banners.[58] Further, after Pankhurst effectively took control of the Crewe and Nantwich by-election campaign away from the WSPU organizer, she gave Emerson responsibility for Nantwich. The campaign Pankhurst and Emerson organized included a demonstration and emphasized the issue of women's sweated labour in the textile industry.[59]

After a brief return to America to campaign for women's suffrage in the referendum in Michigan, Emerson arrived back in Britain to help Pankhurst found the East London branches of the WSPU in the autumn of 1912; according to Pankhurst, Emerson helped her choose a site for its first headquarters on the Bow Road.[60] Emerson was appointed honorary organizer in East London, 'to keep all the others going', and, after the WSPU terminated the East London campaign's funding in early 1913, she suggested the location for their new premises, telling Pankhurst: 'Come to the Roman Road; all the people go there!'[61] Although very new to the area, this comment testifies to Emerson's confidence and experience of organizing in a working-class community.

In 1913, the East London suffragettes began agitating for a rent strike to increase pressure on the government to grant women's suffrage. Although rent strikes were hardly exclusive to the American labour movement, and had recently accompanied industrial action in East London's Limehouse during the 1911 dock strike, it was Chicago that the ELFS cited as its prototype.

> A couple of years ago the garment workers of Chicago, in America, were obliged to strike against rent, as well as against sweated employment, because they could not pay. There were many thousands of strikers, and only one family was evicted.[62]

58 E. S. Pankhurst, 'Hyde Park demonstration', *Votes for Women*, 19 July 1912, p. 686.

59 'Crewe by-election', *Votes for Women*, 26 July 1912, p. 705; E. S. Pankhurst, 'We kept the Liberal out!', *Votes for Women*, 2 Aug. 1912, p. 719.

60 Pankhurst, *Suffragette Movement*, p. 417. This was in Oct. 1912, although some newspaper accounts maintained that Emerson campaigned in the unsuccessful referendum until Nov.; see 'Jackson girl is jailed in London for beating "cop"', *Detroit Free Press*, 15 Feb. 1913, p. 2.

61 Pankhurst, *Suffragette Movement*, pp. 439, 438.

62 'No Vote! No Rent!' leaflet [1913], ESP Papers, 231, IISH; reiterated in 'No vote! No rent!', *Woman's Dreadnought*, 8 Mar. 1914, p. 8; '"No vote, no rent!"', *Woman's Dreadnought*, 18 July 1914, p. 70. The figures were likely from Emerson. Three months into the Chicago strike, 'Miss Emerson said that only one case of eviction for non-payment of rent has come under her notice so far'; 'Says starvation confronts strikers', *Inter Ocean*, 12 Dec. 1910, p. 3. By the strike's end, Emerson slightly revised: 'There were only four actual evictions in the course of the four months the strike lasted, and two of these could have been prevented

The rent strike appeared to counter the WSPU leadership's strategy by enabling working-class women to seize the initiative through protest that relied upon collective, community-based solidarity. The WSPU leaders evidently identified the rent strike as a tactic that was the preserve of working-class communities. After the East London suffragettes' expulsion, the ELFS's minute book noted that the WSPU

> had no objection to the No Vote No Rent strike, but said it was impossible to work it through their organization because their people are widely scattered & because it is only in working class homes that the woman pays the rent.[63]

One of the tactical innovations, then, that distinguished the East London suffragettes from the WSPU, and contributed to their forming an independent organization, had been inspired by Pankhurst's contact with, and Emerson's involvement in, the American labour movement.

The outbreak of war, which brought acute social distress to East London, forced the ELFS to abandon plans for the rent strike. In its subsequent turn towards welfare provision, the ELFS was not dissimilar to other suffragist groups which also established relief schemes around the same time.[64] While Pankhurst had a diverse range of examples to draw inspiration from, the combination and character of the ELFS's welfare services bear resemblance to those Emerson oversaw in Chicago three years earlier. Thus, the ELFS established daily milk distribution for babies, medical services and what it termed cost-price restaurants: '[T]he name should be a slogan against profiteering, and would carry no stigma of charity.'[65] Food, bought in bulk or donated, was distributed to those who purchased meal tickets (and discreetly provided free to the very poorest). It might be said that in her desire to avoid charity and preference for collective solidarity, Pankhurst turned to the methods of 'co-operative philanthropy' pioneered by her collaborator. Moreover, Emerson, who had evidently followed the progress of these schemes from America, returned shortly after the outbreak of the war to help expand the ELFS's relief efforts, which suggests that, though having been persuaded to desist from suffrage campaigning, she nevertheless felt she could be of assistance

if the advice of the committee had been taken'. Emerson and Coman, 'Co-operative philanthropy', p. 946.

[63] Minute book of the Council of the East London Federation, 27 Jan. 1914, ESP Papers, 206, IISH.

[64] For some examples, see the chapter in this volume by A. Hughes-Johnson.

[65] E. S. Pankhurst, *The Home Front: A Mirror to Life in England During the First World War* (London, 1987), pp. 22, 43.

in these kinds of endeavours. Pankhurst remembered that Emerson 'was stirring me up to do something for our old Bow Road district. Presently she was ladling out soup in Tryphena Place, Bow Common Lane, an unsavoury neighbourhood'.[66] Emerson also organized a clinic and milk centre in Bethnal Green. Emerson was, therefore, directly involved in shaping the ELFS's relief efforts, which so closely resembled those she had directed in the Chicago garment workers' strike.

When Emerson's political experience is accounted for, it changes the reading of her impact on the ELFS from the thrill-seeking adventurer that Pankhurst remembered to one confident of imparting practical advice. From establishing organizing centres, to the idea of a rent strike and relief distribution, Emerson's experience helped Pankhurst to envisage and establish a community-based campaign that assisted working-class women's agitation for political change.

The Lewisohns and Henry Street Settlement

The ELFS was politically and structurally distinct from the WSPU and more closely resembled the settlement houses that Pankhurst admired at Hull House and Henry Street. These female-run settlements eschewed the traditional domestic family structure; instead, they fused public and private realms by establishing communal households among their residents, who were also the settlements' workers. The ELFS, with its combined living quarters and headquarters embedded in a working-class neighbourhood, can be seen to emulate a similar kind of household. Politically, Hull House and Henry Street were involved in a wide range of democratic and progressive campaigns. Addams and Wald were founding members of the WTUL and were involved in the women's peace movement during the First World War. Addams was president of the Women's International League for Peace and Freedom, while Pankhurst, representing the ELFS, was elected to the British section's executive of the Women's International League. By this point, then, Pankhurst was evidently politically closer to Henry Street and Hull House, institutions that supported labour organizations and were aligned with the peace movement, than she was to the WSPU, which was urging women's participation in a more vigorous prosecution of the war. Testimony from one Henry Street resident and the long-term, substantial financial support the ELFS received from the Lewisohn sisters, who were connected to Henry Street, suggest that this settlement house in particular functioned as a model for the nascent ELFS.

[66] Pankhurst, *Home Front*, p. 44.

In some ways, the campaign Pankhurst initiated in the autumn of 1912 appeared to differ little from the WSPU's strategy for organizing in a new district. She held street meetings and opened a suffrage shop to draw in members of the public.[67] In November 1912, the local MP George Lansbury resigned in order to contest his seat on the issue of women's suffrage, propelling the area into a by-election, which was another of the established ways that the WSPU 'worked up' a district.[68] However, the character of the East London organization changed as the influence of the WSPU headquarters diminished. When the WSPU withdrew its financial support shortly after the by-election, Pankhurst signalled her independent commitment to a longer-term engagement with the area by leaving her Kensington home and moving in with Jessie and James Payne, two suffrage supporters living on Bow's Old Ford Road. After its expulsion from the WSPU, the ELFS became increasingly structurally distinctive and began instead to resemble a settlement house.

In the spring of 1914, Pankhurst acquired a house attached to two halls (formerly a school and a factory), again on the Old Ford Road. Moving into the premises with the Paynes and her suffragette friend Norah Smyth, Pankhurst created a female-dominated household where the division of labour allowed her more time for activism.[69] Like a settlement house, the residents' living space was politically and physically connected to their public role. The attached halls – the larger dubbed the 'Women's Hall' – were used for a broader range of activities than a WSPU shop; even before the First World War, the ELFS had established a number of schemes that looked like a smaller-scale version of Hull House or Henry Street. There was a choir, a lending library, lectures on a variety of topics including sex education, concerts, a Christmas Savings Club and a Junior Suffragettes' Club for girls aged fourteen to eighteen.[70] Pankhurst also envisaged ELFS nurseries, which would finally be established after the outbreak of war.[71] In

[67] On the WSPU's shops, see K. Cowman, *Women of the Right Spirit: Paid Organisers of the Women's Social and Political Union (WSPU) 1904–18* (Manchester; New York, 2007), pp. 84–5.

[68] Cowman, *Women*, pp. 40–5. While it was WSPU policy to work solely for the defeat of the governing (Liberal) party, in this by-election the WSPU actively supported Lansbury.

[69] Jessie Payne, for example, took care of the cooking; see Pankhurst, *Suffragette Movement*, p. 479.

[70] Pankhurst, *Suffragette Movement*, p. 542; East London Federation of the Suffragettes, *First Annual Report* (London, 1915), p. 11, LSE Digital Library <https://digital.library.lse.ac.uk/objects/lse:duz875laz> [accessed 24 Feb. 2020]; 'Sylvia, what is she?', *T.P.'s Weekly*, 4 July 1914, p. 14.

[71] 'Sylvia', *T.P.'s Weekly*, 4 July 1914, p. 14.

contrast with a shop, there was greater potential for the local community itself to determine the use of the Women's Hall, which in turn strengthened their connections to the ELFS. The 'place became a hive of activity and the first house of call for everyone in distress', especially for workers taking industrial action.

> Strikes, especially of women, and some of them only lasting a few days, were breaking out on all sides of us. All day our hall was often requisitioned for strike meetings; we were appealed to for speakers and help in every sort of way.[72]

Moreover, that the welfare schemes Pankhurst established during the war were prompted by people turning to the ELFS shows how intimately linked it had become to the local community.[73]

Pankhurst informed at least one visitor that the ELFS was specifically influenced by Henry Street Settlement. Lavinia Dock was a longstanding Henry Street resident who met Pankhurst on the day she arrived in America in 1911.[74] In March 1914, Dock visited Pankhurst and Emerson in East London while they were making plans for the Women's Hall. Dock identified similarities with Henry Street, describing Pankhurst's venture to a friend through the New York topography of her own settlement house: 'She is deeply and abidingly in love with these East Side Londoners'. Dock continued:

> Sylvia has the settlement idea in her mind. She was deeply impressed with our settlement, especially, and she is planning a settlement life down there for herself. [...] Then, after the vote is won, she looks forward to settlement life, a return to her art, but always keeping a political center as a main purpose.[75]

These comments indicate that Pankhurst anticipated the development of the ELFS into a settlement like Henry Street that integrated artistic projects within its community work. In particular, the influence of the Lewisohns, whose Neighbourhood Playhouse she admired, can be detected in the ELFS.

In January 1916, the ELFS organized a 'Spring Pageant' for 900 children, which bore considerable resemblance to the *Sleeping Beauty* that Pankhurst had witnessed in New York. Like that other wintertime performance heralding the spring, this pageant was performed by young people from the local working-class 'East Side' community and invoked the natural world of flowers and trees with similar use of dance, costumes and instruments.

72 Pankhurst, *Suffragette Movement*, pp. 542, 543.

73 ELFS, *First Annual Report*, p. 17.

74 Pankhurst, *Suffragette Movement*, p. 347.

75 'Suffragette in settlement life', *Democrat and Chronicle*, 17 Apr. 1914, p. 24.

George Lansbury's daughter Violet, bedecked in a garland of primroses, played the Spirit of Spring, there was a Rose, a Lily, a Sunflower and, to Pankhurst's eye, 'the central loveliness of it all' was sixteen-year-old Junior Suffragette and factory worker Rose Pengelly as the Spirit of the Woods; '[p]laying upon Pan's reeds, she danced with unimagined grace, artless, untaught – a vision of youth's loveliness, the denizen of a slum!'[76] Like the New York *Sleeping Beauty*, spring represented advancing comradeship and equality; the children held banners proclaiming 'Peace' and 'Plenty'.

For their part, the Lewisohns directly contributed to the ELFS's cultural life when, during a visit to London, they performed a concert at the Women's Hall on the evening of 31 July 1914.[77] They evidently identified with the ELFS as they extended it considerable support – something that has not previously been acknowledged. In November 1914, the ELFS's newspaper, the *Woman's Dreadnought*, listed 'The Misses Lewisohn' as contributing £40 – far more than any other donor (most of whom were only able to contribute in shillings). They were the largest donors in September 1916 and February 1919, donating £20 on each occasion; in 1922, two years before the *Dreadnought* folded, they contributed £5.[78] These were transformative sums of money; to put their £40 donation in 1914 into perspective, in that year women workers at Morton's factory in East London were earning an average of 10 shillings a week, and went on strike when they were replaced by younger women paid 7 shillings.[79] Thus, the Lewisohns' first donation was equivalent to nineteen months' wages of some of the better-paid women in East London. Pankhurst's connection to the Lewisohns, forged on her lecture tours, therefore proved vital to the ELFS's existence.

Much like her encounter with the CWTUL, it was Henry Street's resonance with Pankhurst's pre-existing political (and artistic) sympathies that allowed it to function as a model for her efforts to reshape the suffragette movement.

[76] 'New Year festivities', *Woman's Dreadnought*, 15 Jan. 1916, p. 406; Pankhurst, *Home Front*, p. 275.

[77] For Alice Lewisohn's account of the ELFS, see A. L. Crowley, *The Neighborhood Playhouse: Leaves from a Theatre Scrapbook* (New York, 1959), p. 38. An advertisement for the gathering in the Women's Hall with 'entertainment by Alice Irene (sic) Lewisohn, of Henry-street Settlement, New York' appeared in the *Daily Herald*, 31 July 1914, p. 2. Further details of the concert have been lost; it was later remembered as the meeting at which Pankhurst, about to depart for Dublin, promised to return if Britain declared war – as it would four days later. See Pankhurst, *Home Front*, p. 12; Pankhurst, *Suffragette Movement*, p. 590.

[78] 'Gratefully acknowledged', *Woman's Dreadnought*, 7 Nov. 1914, p. 135; 23 Sept. 1916, p. 554; *Workers' Dreadnought*, 8 Feb. 1919, p. 1120; 21 Jan. 1922, p. 6.

[79] Wages at Morton's cited in 'The strike at Morton's', *Woman's Dreadnought*, 21 Mar. 1914, p. 3.

Henry Street, and the Lewisohns in particular, provided Pankhurst with longstanding inspirational and material support that helped ensure the existence of the ELFS and shaped its distinctive character.

Recontextualizing 1912

It is commonplace to describe Pankhurst as an internationalist and invoke her longstanding opposition to imperialism and support for self-determination.[80] This chapter has suggested that her internationalism extended to an identification of common interests across national boundaries, enabling detailed engagement with and willingness to import ideas from social movements abroad. A more well-known example is the ELFS's People's Army, which emulated James Connolly's Citizen Army in Dublin, with which it had political affinity.[81] Something similar took place in Pankhurst's transatlantic tours. In America, her political convictions were not substantially altered; instead, she found them reinforced by women connected to the labour movement and drew practical conclusions.

Pankhurst admired the WTUL branches and settlement houses because they seemed to embody and assert the value of direct experience from below in social reform. In her American manuscript she reflected that the representation of working-class experience was the democratic antidote to top-down, paternalistic conceptions of reform as well as to unfettered capitalism.

> With the more perfect application of the representative idea, and the consequent development of the view that all forms of labour must receive due representation, one may look forward to the time when the garbage collectors, the scrub women, and the other city employees, will be powerfully represented by those who will be able to speak for them with direct knowledge of their lives and work[.][82]

Socialism from below? Perhaps, but the emphasis on representation 'by those who will be able to speak for them', even on the basis of a (vaguely defined) 'direct knowledge', hardly provides a cast-iron safeguard against accusations of misrepresentation and paternalism. Four years after writing this passage, Pankhurst would find practical resolution of the contradictions between her emphasis on first-hand experience and the separation implied by representative democracy in the direct democracy of the Russian soviets.

[80] Most prominently in Ireland, Russia, India and Ethiopia.

[81] Pankhurst, *Suffragette Movement*, pp. 504–5.

[82] Pankhurst, [Chronicle] ch. 5, p. 18.

Once again, the development of Pankhurst's thought was occasioned by working-class action in an international context, which she applied to her theoretical and practical approach to social change.

Pankhurst sought to democratize the struggle for women's suffrage by placing working-class women at its centre. This chapter suggests that we need to reappraise suffrage history in much the same way. The ELFS was profoundly shaped by Pankhurst's encounters with the WTUL and two American settlement houses, which provided inspirational models of organizing that suited a women's campaign based in a working-class community. The ELFS's tactical innovations drew upon Emerson's experience of labour organizing, while the Lewisohns, who likely inspired aspects of the ELFS's cultural life, provided vital funding. If Pankhurst's divergence from the WSPU is understood in this context, it reveals that it was a result of more than her own individually strengthened convictions or self-confidence. Rather, the ELFS is revealed as a product of the distilled and collected experiences of a group of women who organized together, supported and learnt from each other in their struggles for political and social change.

11. Suffrage internationalism in practice: Dora Montefiore and the lessons of Finnish women's enfranchisement

Karen Hunt

During the centenary year of some women getting the vote, a partial and frequently partisan narrative dominated the public celebrations and often the academic ones too. In the sea of purple, white and green, a more nuanced history of the women's campaign for enfranchisement in Britain was lost. This chapter addresses a number of aspects of suffrage history that we still hear too little about: the contested nature of the demand for votes for women among suffragists; the campaign for adult suffrage; the importance of tensions around class within the struggle for women's enfranchisement; and the ways in which suffrage politics were made across national boundaries, often deploying the experience of women in one campaign in the politics of another.

To tease out these issues, this chapter focuses on the first European country to give women the vote, exploring how the lessons drawn from Finnish women's victory were put to work in suffrage campaigns elsewhere. It centres on the nature and impact of one British suffragist's narration of the Finnish success. For Dora Montefiore the most important aspect of the Finns' achievement was that they had won the vote for all women over twenty-four, irrespective of their social class. This was full adult suffrage; it contrasted with the demand of the main suffragist societies in Britain which, by seeking equality with men on the basis of a property franchise, were only asking for the vote for some women.[1]

The implementation of female suffrage in Finland was exceptionally early, rapid and almost unnoticed by contemporaries, according to its

[1] For British adult suffrage campaign, see K. Hunt, *Equivocal Feminists: the Social Democratic Federation and the Woman Question, 1884–1911* (Cambridge, 1996), ch. 6; J. Hannam and K. Hunt, *Socialist Women. Britain 1880s to 1920s* (London, 2002), ch. 5; S. Stanley Holton, *Feminism and Democracy: Women's Suffrage and Reform Politics in Britain, 1900–18* (Cambridge, 1986), ch. 3.

'Suffrage internationalism in practice', in *The politics of women's suffrage: local, national and international dimensions,* ed. A. Hughes-Johnson and L. Jenkins (London, 2021), pp. 285–308.

principal historian Irma Sulkunen.[2] This was largely because of the particular circumstances of the Finns, where demands for democratic reforms sat at the heart of their nationalist struggle for liberation from the Russian Empire. In 1905, after its defeat in the war against Japan, a weakened Russia was faced by revolution at home and disturbances across its empire. Soon Finland was engulfed in revolutionary ferment with a general strike gripping the country from 1 November.[3] Transport was halted and all factories and shops were closed while the streets were full of men and women from across the social classes, with even servants joining the strike.[4] The crowds called for the abolition of the semi-feudal Finnish Diet based on four estates for which only about 7% of the population were qualified to vote, and for a new National Assembly elected by universal adult suffrage. *The Times* described the strike as 'national, complete, pacific, orderly, and triumphant'; certainly by the fourth day of the strike Tsar Nicholas II agreed to the strikers' demand for full adult suffrage and to drop his 'Russification' programme, thus giving the country greater autonomy.[5] The Finns had taken their opportunity.

What was remarkable about the Finnish example was the virtual unanimity among all the popular movements that the call should be for universal and equal suffrage, which necessarily included women. Only the small bourgeois women's movement continued to make the lesser demand for limited women's suffrage based on a property franchise. The number of women involved in the separatist women's associations was under 2,000, whereas those organized in the workers' movement (the Social Democratic Party and trade unions) was greater by a factor of ten.[6] Moreover, women were active participants in the various mixed-sex social movements such as the largely working-class temperance movement, which fed into the nationalist resistance, so that there was broad recognition of

[2] I. Sulkunen, 'Suffrage, nation and political mobilisation – the Finnish case in an international context', in *Suffrage, Gender and Citizenship: International Perspectives on Parliamentary Reforms*, ed. I. Sulkunen, S.-J. Nevali-Nurmi and P. Markkola (Newcastle upon Tyne, 2009), p. 84. See also J. Adams, *Women and the Vote: a World History* (Oxford, 2014), pp. 177–83.

[3] I. Sulkunen, 'The General Strike and women's suffrage' <http://www.helsinki.fi/sukupuolentutkimus/aanioikeus/en/articles/strike.htm> [accessed 13 Feb. 2020].

[4] For a witness account of the Finnish general strike, see W. T. Stead, 'The revolution in Finland', *The Times*, 11 Nov. 1905, p. 15, which includes references to the participation of servant girls.

[5] *The Times*, 15 Aug. 1906, p. 6.

[6] Sulkunen, 'Suffrage, nation and political mobilisation', p. 89.

the commonality of interests between different unenfranchised groups. The significance of the women workers' movement was recognized by the appointment of two of its representatives to the General Strike Committee, while their determination to achieve full civil rights was reflected in the large meetings and processions of women workers held in support of suffrage in sixty-three localities during December 1905.[7] When Finland's new parliament convened for the first time in March 1907, there was a remarkable number of working women among the nineteen female MPs, including a former servant, seamstresses and teachers.[8] In Finland, class was not as divisive an issue as it was in many other suffrage struggles. There was also a tradition of men and women working together in Finland's social movements with differences submerged in the more pressing nationalist cause.

One English woman was particularly keen to understand how Finnish women had achieved what decades of campaigning in Britain had failed to deliver. In 1906, Dora Montefiore travelled to Finland to discover the answers for herself. She was already a longstanding suffragist. International travel and networking were important features of her suffrage politics as she explored how best to frame the demand for full female suffrage and the most effective tactics to use.[9] For her, Finland showed that adult suffrage was the only way to enfranchise working-class women and that collaboration between the increasingly polarized labour and women's movements was essential to achieving this goal. In the polemical world of women's suffrage, this was not what many suffragists or socialists wanted to hear. Each caricatured the other as only representing the interests of middle-class women or the working-class respectively; as the frequent debates on the Woman Question in the socialist press put it, it was 'Sex versus Class'.[10] The group that seemed to get squeezed out was working-class women, who were asked to choose between their loyalties to their class or their sex. The problem in Britain was the property franchise. As one working-class socialist woman argued in 1906:

[7] M. Lähteenmäki, 'Women workers and the suffrage issue' <http://www.helsinki.fi/sukupuolentutkimus/aanioikeus/en/articles/workers.htm> [accessed 13 Feb. 2020].

[8] For their photograph and individual profiles, see A. Korppi-Tommola, 'The first women Members of Parliament in Finland, 1907–1908' <http://www.helsinki.fi/sukupuolentutkimus/aanioikeus/en/articles/first.htm> [accessed 13 Feb. 2020].

[9] See K. Hunt, "Whirl'd through the world': the role of travel in the making of Dora Montefiore, 1851–1933', *Österreiche Zeitschrift für Geschichtswissenschaften*, xxii (2011), 41–63.

[10] See Hunt, *Equivocal Feminists*, ch. 2.

> Given the vote the propertied women would not be likely to agitate for adult suffrage, their superior education has made them more class-conscious than the working class are and they would, therefore, look after their class interests. Let us then be satisfied with nothing less than the vote for every adult.[11]

If one's priority was how to ensure a fully democratic franchise that included all working-class women, then Finland seemed to be an inspiring achievement. So, at least, it seemed to one English suffragist in the summer of 1906.

Dora Montefiore (1851–1933) was an English suffragist, socialist and later communist.[12] By the time she became politically active she, like a number of her generation of British suffragists, such as Emmeline Pankhurst and Charlotte Despard, was a widow from a middle-class background. And like both of them (albeit in different ways) her suffragism was bound up with her socialism. Montefiore's participation in the struggle for economic and social justice was driven by her political commitment to working-class emancipation rather than by her own class position. She described socialism as the 'demand for the social, economic and political freedom of every human being' and criticized those who 'try to stir up a sex-war instead of preaching class-war'.[13] By 1912, a New Zealand socialist newspaper said of her, 'We rank our comrade among the world's leading useful women workers of the working-class movement.'[14] Her organizational affiliations changed over time but give some sense of her location across the key issues of the day. Her suffragism had begun in the early 1890s in Australia as a founding member of the Womanhood League of New South Wales.[15] On her return to England she channelled her energies through various women's suffrage pressure groups, such as the Union of Practical Suffragists and the Hammersmith Suffrage Society, as well as becoming an early member of the Women's Social and Political Union (WSPU). In 1907, she transferred her loyalties to the Adult Suffrage Society (ASS). At the same time she

[11] R. Scott, 'Votes for Women', *Justice*, 8 Dec. 1906, p. 2.

[12] For Dora Montefiore, see 'Montefiore [*née* Fuller], Dora Frances Barrow', *Oxford Dictionary of National Biography* <https://doi.org/10.1093/ref:odnb/39456> [accessed 9 Mar. 2021] and her autobiography, D. B. Montefiore, *From a Victorian to a Modern* (London, 1927).

[13] D. B. Montefiore, 'Why I am opposed to female suffrage', *Social Democrat*, Apr. 1909; D. B. Montefiore, *Some Words to Socialist Women* (London, 1908), p. 13.

[14] 'In our opinion', *Maoriland Worker*, 12 Jan. 1912, p. 1.

[15] For Montefiore's suffragism, see K. Hunt, 'Journeying through suffrage: the politics of Dora Montefiore', in *A Suffrage Reader: Charting Directions in British Suffrage History*, ed. C. Eustance, J. Ryan and L. Ugolini (London, 2000), pp. 162–76.

developed her commitment to socialism as a leading member of the Marxist Social Democratic Federation/British Socialist Party from about 1900 to 1912, re-joining in 1916. Finally, she was a founding member of the Communist Party of Great Britain in 1920, elected as the only woman member of its first executive. In both strands of her politics, which she refused to see as separate, she was an energetic although often dissident activist in both national and international organizations. Though based in England, she spent key periods of her life travelling, networking and making her politics outside Britain. This chapter focuses on one example of her particular way of doing politics. It explores Montefiore's narration of the victory of Finnish women and how she deployed her visit to Finland in her subsequent suffrage activism, nationally and internationally.

Dora Montefiore visits Finland

Dora Montefiore's announcement in the summer of 1906 that she was going to visit Finland was news because she had just completed a dramatic act of militancy: Fort Montefiore. The six-week siege by bailiffs of her home in Hammersmith following her stand of 'No Taxation without Representation' had reverberated around the world.[16] This was the latest episode in her increasingly militant suffrage activism which, later that year, would result in her imprisonment in Holloway.

In 1906, there were few countries where women had achieved enfranchisement (only New Zealand, Australia and now Finland) and, in the increasingly combative suffrage politics of Britain, these examples were deployed by all sides within the debate.[17] However, unlike the examples from within the British Empire, Finland was not a country of which many in Britain had intimate knowledge and up to this point had rarely figured within the rhetoric of the suffrage debate. Yet Montefiore had already referred to Finland on one of the occasions when she addressed the crowd from Fort Montefiore. She taunted the government with the up-to-the-minute jibe that '[t]hey were even behind Finland where women had been enfranchised'.[18]

[16] Fort Montefiore was reported across the world, for example, 'Fort Montefiore', *Pall Mall Gazette*, 25 May 1906, p. 8; 'English women fight for the right to vote', *Reading Eagle* (USA), 6 July 1906, p. 12; 'The women suffrage movement', *Otago Daily Times* (NZ), 25 June 1906, p. 2.

[17] See R. Dalziel, 'Presenting the enfranchisement of New Zealand women abroad', in *Suffrage and Beyond: International Feminist Perspectives*, ed. C. Daley and M. Nolan (Auckland, 1994), pp. 42–64.

[18] 'The siege on the Mall', *West London Observer*, 1 June 1906, p. 2.

On 1 August 1906, Montefiore began her journey to Finland via Copenhagen, where she attended the International Woman Suffrage Alliance (IWSA) congress.[19] Here would be an opportunity to meet Finnish suffragists. This was not her first international conference. For some time she had been exploring whether the International Council of Women and/or the IWSA would provide an opportunity to publicize her particular reading of British women's politics and allow her to connect with the experiences of women activists from other countries.[20] Initially she was optimistic that women's transnational organizations would provide a promising additional political space where women would learn from one another.

In 1906, Montefiore was a fraternal delegate to the IWSA from the already-militant WSPU.[21] She had also represented it at the 1904 congress in Berlin, but now her credentials were challenged by other British delegates.[22] Montefiore was a 'fraternal' delegate because the congress only recognized the constitutionalist National Union of Women's Suffrage Societies (NUWSS) as the sole voice of British suffragists. From its formation, the IWSA had decided that only one organization could represent each country. Montefiore questioned how representative this so-called 'National' society was, as it 'did not represent the thousands and tens of thousands of working women who sympathise with, and work actively in, the Women's Social and Political Union, under the battle-cry of "Votes for Women"!'[23] At this point on her suffrage journey, Montefiore believed that the best way to achieve her democratic goal of the enfranchisement of all working-class women was to argue for women to qualify for the vote on the same terms as men (a limited franchise based on property) as a stepping stone to full adult

[19] For Montefiore and the Copenhagen congress, see K. Hunt, 'Transnationalism in practice: the effect of Dora Montefiore's international travel on women's politics in Britain before World War 1', in *Crossing Boundaries: Women's Organizing in Europe and the Americas, 1880s–1940s*, ed. P. Jonsson, S. Neunsinger and J. Sangster (Uppsala, 2007), pp. 81–2.

[20] For Montefiore's internationalism and its context see, K. Hunt, '"The immense meaning of it all": The challenges of internationalism for British socialist women before the First World War', *Socialist History*, xvii (2000), 22–42. For the IWC and the IWSA, see L. J. Rupp, *Worlds of Women: The Making of an International Women's Movement* (Princeton, N.J., 1997).

[21] Montefiore was appointed by the Central Committee of the WSPU as its delegate on 12 July 1906 (Montefiore, *From a Victorian*, p. 84).

[22] 'The Women's Congress in Berlin', *New Age*, 30 June 1904, pp. 363–4.

[23] D. B. Montefiore, 'Women in Scandinavia: the Women's Congress', *Forward*, 20 Oct. 1906.

suffrage.[24] Before she went to Finland, like many British suffragists, she believed that adult suffrage was not an achievable demand in itself. Finland was to change her mind.

Montefiore was finally allowed to speak to the IWSA after the intervention of its president, Carrie Chapman Catt. In her speech, Montefiore defended the new militancy in which she was playing a highly visible part. She described the WSPU as 'a movement of working women led by Socialist women of intellect and culture, bringing to downtrodden women the gospel of their rights as human beings'.[25] This representation was already at variance with that of the WSPU leadership, whose antipathy towards a socialist analysis of suffrage became more explicit from the summer of 1906, when Christabel Pankhurst unilaterally introduced a policy of opposing Labour as well as Liberal candidates at by-elections.[26] Even before Montefiore reached Finland, it was becoming clear that her days in the WSPU were numbered. Her Finnish experiences would demonstrate to her that a stepping stone of limited suffrage was not required to achieve full adult suffrage.

After a brief visit to Stockholm, where she spoke at the Folkets Hus (headquarters of the Swedish labour movement) on 'Women's Suffrage', Montefiore sailed to Helsingfors (Helsinki) in Finland, arriving on 2 September. Now, she said, 'the real object of my journey began – to find out how the Finnish women had gained their political emancipation'.[27] This involved a close study of Finnish, Swedish and Russian history, as well as participation in the fast-moving events around her as the Finns moved to implement their new democratic constitution. She attended the final meeting of the Diet's Chamber of Nobles before it was dissolved – as she noted, 'closing in one country of Europe the feudal epoch'.[28] When she got to know fellow socialist Miina Sillanpää and some of the other working women's leaders, they helped her to understand more fully the reasons for the success of the Finnish women. In particular, Montefiore was struck by the crucial role of the mobilization of domestic servants, of whom Sillanpää was the organizer, and who, at the eleventh hour, joined in the general strike. This, according to Montefiore, gave the signal to include women

[24] See, for example, D. B. Montefiore, 'Woman suffrage resolution', *New Age*, 14 Apr. 1904, p. 235.

[25] 'Women's interests: the International Conference of Woman Suffragists', *New Age*, 16 Aug. 1906, p. 522.

[26] S. Stanley Holton, 'Women and the vote', in *Women's History: Britain 1850–1945*, ed. J. Purvis (London, 1995), p. 291.

[27] Montefiore, *From a Victorian*, p. 87.

[28] Montefiore, *From a Victorian*, p. 88.

in the franchise reform, which was then won 'by a stroke of the pen' of the Tsar.[29] While in Finland, Montefiore also benefited from the help of feminists who had attended the IWSA congress in Copenhagen the month before, such as Baroness Alexandra Gripenberg and Annie Furuhjelm – 'all of whom', she later wrote, 'helped to make my visit to Finland a very happy spot in my memory'.[30] Soon Montefiore's busy visit to Finland was over. She sailed for England, arriving in Hull on 16 September.

While she was away, Montefiore's trip to Finland had caused contention back in England. It had allowed some to poke fun. The *West London Observer* commented: 'It is believed that Mr Asquith would gladly subscribe to a small fund to send the rest of the suffragettes with her, in the hope that their investigations would be prolonged out there – that, in fact, they would never Finnish.'[31] Fort Montefiore had made Dora Montefiore a recognizable public figure as a suffrage activist. This in turn made some of her socialist comrades uncomfortable. When Montefiore announced she was going to Finland, Herbert Burrows (a fellow member of the SDF) publicly criticized her for using her foreign trips to misrepresent British suffrage politics to an international audience: 'If Mrs Montefiore cannot really work for it she might at least leave off talking about "solidarity" of the workers. I hope the Finnish women will teach her what real suffrage means.'[32] Here, from one of the SDF's leading pamphleteers on the Woman Question, was a reminder of the Party's view that the *only* acceptable socialist position on the franchise was adult suffrage and even that was not a political priority.[33] Dora Montefiore's by now longstanding and increasingly notorious activism for women's suffrage was what rankled with Burrows, particularly when it was her version of suffragism which reached international audiences.

Writing in the pages of *Justice*, Montefiore replied to Burrows from Helsingfors. She took the opportunity to give her reading of the state of international suffragism and her place within it. At the IWSA, she said, there were women from almost every European state, from America and 'from our various colonies'.

> I venture to say that every one of these delegates (with the exception, perhaps, of the half dozen sent by the so-called English 'national' Suffrage Society)

[29] Montefiore, *From a Victorian*, p. 89.

[30] Montefiore, *From a Victorian*, p. 90. The British press spelled Finnish names in a range of ways. I have adopted the Finnish spelling in the text while replicating the original spelling in quotations.

[31] 'Enfranchisement of women', *West London Observer*, 31 Aug. 1906, p. 6.

[32] H. Burrows, 'The "votes for women" fraud', *Justice*, 1 Sept. 1906, p. 6.

[33] See Hunt, *Equivocal Feminists*, ch. 6.

> were Adult Suffragists, as I myself am; but, as each country possessed its own, more or less complicated franchise basis, so each country provided a different problem for the women working therein for their emancipation; and in each country this problem resolved itself into a question of tactics.[34]

She said it was these tactics which were discussed in public meetings of the congress and more privately among the socialist group of delegates. Montefiore then went on to explain how women had recently achieved adult suffrage in Finland. She structured her narration of the Finnish victory to make a point to her domestic audience.

> Those six days of darkness, of lack of most of the necessaries of life and civilization, brought both Liberals and Conservatives to their knees, and the three parties coalesced for the time in a general demand for Adult Suffrage. Other factors that made for victory were the complete organization of the workers (including domestic servants) in the ranks of Social Democracy, and the self-abnegation of the nobility, who voluntarily renounced their privileges as hereditary legislators. As we cannot at present hope in England for the apparition of either of these most desirable factors; and – as far as I know – Comrade Burrows has not yet begun to organize for a general strike, I and my friends shall continue our campaign of 'Votes for Women' in the hope that by educating the women to demand the vote we may obtain it before long for all women.[35]

At this point Montefiore underlined how widespread adult suffragism was outside Britain and that the issue was how to achieve it. It was debates about tactics within individual nations that had been central to her discussions with other suffragists at the IWSA and which she then reflected upon when she met a range of activists in Finland.

Telling the story of Finnish women's enfranchisement

Having investigated the Finnish achievement for herself, Montefiore's reflections about Finland were now to feature in her propaganda work. Speaking on her return to England with Mrs Pankhurst and Flora Drummond at a WSPU meeting in Bury, Montefiore used her Finnish experience to justify militancy and her belief that the ultimate goal of suffrage activism was adult suffrage. She argued that recent events in Finland showed that people who were outside the Constitution could not work by constitutional methods; that it was only by getting the sex disability removed that adult suffrage could be achieved; and that women's

34 D. B. Montefiore, 'Votes for women', *Justice*, 15 Sept. 1906, p. 6.

35 D. B. Montefiore, 'Votes for women', *Justice*, 15 Sept. 1906, p. 6.

enfranchisement had not resulted in the dominance of women in public life (an anxiety of anti-suffragists).[36]

Montefiore now gave lectures on Finland to suffragist and to socialist audiences as well as writing a number of articles. One lesson she drew was 'the very large and important share taken by women in the work of the country … and the way women have stood by men, and shown their solidarity with men in the various political causes through which Finland has recently passed'.[37] She told one audience that people had the wrong impression of Finland as a bleak and half-civilized country and people, with the Finns having obtained Home Rule from Russia and universal suffrage. In this talk for Hammersmith Independent Labour Party (ILP) on 'Socialism in Scandinavia', she argued that understanding how working people in other countries had made real advances could itself be the spur to domestic political action.[38] At the close of 1906, she reviewed the year's suffrage politics in England for the progressive journal *New Age*. She saw the success of Finnish women as an inspiring example.

> Could not the working women of England make use of the stream they have already set running in their direction, and uniting with it the great tide of democratic demand for equality of opportunity, force universal Adult Suffrage in the place of manhood suffrage, and thus range themselves side by side with the freed women of Finland?[39]

The most important lesson she drew at this point was that adult suffrage was an achievable demand within Britain.

Dora Montefiore was to continue to deploy her Finnish experiences and networks in her suffrage politics in Britain and beyond. Much of what she was now to argue was challenging for her audiences, but her message was seen to have more authority because she had actually travelled to Finland to see for herself how the Finns had made this breakthrough. As a middle-class woman of private means, she had the resources (money, time and personal networks) to do this. Crucially, she also had the curiosity and growing international reputation to make these journeys possible. Indeed, political travel was to become an increasingly important feature of her propaganda work from this Scandinavian journey onwards.[40] What is clear is that

[36] 'Mrs Pankhurst at Bury', *Manchester Guardian*, 19 Sept. 1906, p. 5.

[37] D. B. Montefiore, 'First impressions of Finland', *The Race Builder*, Oct. 1906, p. 325. This article was also discussed in 'Women's interests', *New Age*, 11 Oct. 1906.

[38] 'Lecture on Finland', *West London Observer*, 14 Dec. 1906, p. 2.

[39] D. B. Montefiore, 'Votes for women in 1906', *New Age*, 3 Jan. 1907.

[40] See Hunt, '"Whirl'd through the world"'.

without meeting key actors and exploring for herself the nature of Finnish politics she would not have been able to make the case that she did on her return.[41]

New friendships with Finnish socialist women were forged during this visit, which influenced the way in which Montefiore narrated the achievement of women's suffrage in Finland as well as how she put this example to work in her subsequent suffrage politics. This was apparent in 1910, when she told a New York audience how much she had learnt from meeting Miina Sillanpää in Finland. Sillanpää was clearly very different to the middle-class Montefiore. Having started her working life as a domestic servant when she was ten years old, she later became an organizer of other servants. She eventually became one of the first Social Democrat women to be elected to the Finnish parliament. Meeting Sillanpää gave Montefiore a personal connection with the successful Finnish suffragists and provided yet more evidence that suffragism did not have to have a middle-class face and could particularly benefit working-class women.[42]

The fact that the full democratic demand had been won without the kind of compromises which featured in the mainstream demand for women's enfranchisement in Britain was important to Montefiore's representation of the Finnish victory. But so too was the crucial role of a labour movement in which, as she had learnt from Sillanpää, even women servants were organized (not an area of work which many in the British labour movement saw as fruitful).[43] Yet, she later recalled that what had seemed such a persuasive and hopeful achievement to her as a socialist woman who supported adult suffrage was not always heard in this way by her audiences at home and abroad.[44]

Many did not understand the ways in which class impacted on British suffrage politics. All the main suffrage societies made the same demand; women should be enfranchised on the same terms as existed for men. In Britain, men only qualified for the vote on the basis of the value of the accommodation they occupied. As a result, in the Edwardian period about 40% of adult men did not qualify to vote. The property franchise meant that the British voting system was divided by class as well as gender. There

[41] For further discussion on how Montefiore put her Finnish experiences into play in her suffrage politics, see Hunt, 'Transnationalism in practice', esp. pp. 85–94.

[42] D. B. Montefiore, 'A word for Finland', *New York Call*, 21 June 1910.

[43] For attempts to organize domestic servants, see L. Schwartz, '"What we think is needed is a union of domestics such as the miners have": The Domestic Workers' Union of Great Britain and Ireland 1908–14', *Twentieth Century British History*, xxv (2014), 173–98. Dora Montefiore worked closely with Grace Neal (DWU organizer) in the Dublin Lockout, 1913.

[44] Montefiore, *From a Victorian*, p. 89.

was no consensus then (and misunderstandings continue to this day) on how far down the class structure the franchise would have reached if the demand for 'Votes for Women' had been won. What was clear was that merely extending the existing property qualification to women would necessarily include fewer women than the 60% of men who qualified because most tenancies (and few people owned their homes at this time) were held by men, unless a woman was widowed or single. During the suffrage campaign, there was fierce debate on the numbers and class of the women who would get the vote if 'Votes for Women' was conceded.[45] This was a significant detail of the British experience, of which many European and American audiences were unaware.

Competing narratives of Finnish women's enfranchisement

Dora Montefiore was not the only person who brought the Finnish suffrage story to a British audience. Baroness Alexandra Gripenberg (Finnish novelist and long-time women's rights advocate) published her account of 'The great victory in Finland' in *The Englishwoman's Review* before Montefiore's trip to Finland.[46] Gripenberg, whom Montefiore was to meet in Finland, stressed how important the strategy of demanding universal suffrage had been to the women's success, both in terms of getting male support and of ensuring that women were included in any reform. However, she placed relatively little stress on the role of the labour movement in women's victory.[47] This is unsurprising when one knows, as many British suffragists did not, that although Gripenberg was a feminist, she was also a conservative nationalist with a strong antipathy to the Left. There were competing stories to tell of Finnish women's enfranchisement and Finns could be as partisan as anyone else in the lessons they drew from this historic episode.

Within Britain's combative suffrage politics, Montefiore defended her analysis of Finnish women's enfranchisement against those who she claimed 'Misrepresented Finnish women' (the title of a piece in *Justice*).[48] She took the *Justice* columnist 'Jill' to task for suggesting erroneously that Alexandra Gripenberg was the leader of the Finnish women MPs. Underlining her

[45] See K. Hunt, 'Class and adult suffrage in Britain during the Great War' in *The British Women's Suffrage Campaign: National and International Perspectives*, ed. J. Purvis and J. Hannam (London, 2021), pp. 136–54.

[46] *The Englishwoman's Review*, 16 July 1906. Gripenberg subsequently published further reports 'From Finland', *The Englishwoman's Review*, 15 Apr. 1907; 15 July 1907.

[47] A. Gripenberg, quoted in *Women, the Family and Freedom: the Debate in Documents*, Vol. 2, 1880–1950, ed. S. G. Bell and K. Offen (Stanford, Calif., 1983), pp. 229–30.

[48] D. B. Montefiore, 'Misrepresented Finnish women', *Justice*, 13 July 1907, p. 8.

own claims to authority on this matter, Montefiore argued, 'unless one has been in Finland, or in touch with Finnish thought, it is difficult to realize how acute are the differences between the various parties'.[49] She not only termed Gripenberg 'the friend and defender of the odious Bobrikoff' (governor general of Finland from 1898 to 1904), but also reported that from her own experience of the recent IWSA congress in Copenhagen, 'the Radical women and Alexandra Gripenberg were not even on bowing terms, so much did the former resent the attitude of the Baroness towards the late oppressor of their country'.[50] In a recent study, Tiina Kinnunen has shown how Gripenberg was both a suffragist and an anti-socialist and nationalist.[51] Her wider politics were therefore in tension with Montefiore's, who became increasingly radical over the years. Although international networks were crucial to both women, the fact that their paths crossed through their participation in the same events and organizations did not mean that they agreed with one another. Indeed, Montefiore increasingly positioned herself in opposition to Gripenberg's politics, particularly in terms of her suffragism.

Montefiore's reading of the achievement of full women's suffrage in Finland made clear whose political actions and friendship she valued among the Finnish women she had met in 1906. In criticizing how the *Labour Leader* had represented Miina Sillanpää (giving her a husband she did not have as well as misspelling her name), Montefiore not only described her as 'my friend' but went on to provide a warm and politically engaged portrait of the woman who was to become Finland's first woman minister.[52] She described how despite being sent into service as a child, Sillanpää had managed to educate herself and then to organize other domestic servants. She had started a newspaper for those in domestic service and eventually founded a modest laundry where unemployed servants could find work. It was at the laundry, Montefiore said, that 'I first found her, a grave, thoughtful and sympathetic woman, between 35 and 40 years of age. We met as often as we could afterwards, for she had much to ask, and I had much to learn.' The key for Montefiore was that the domestic servants'

[49] D. B. Montefiore, 'Misrepresented Finnish women', *Justice*, 13 July 1907, p. 8.

[50] Bobrikoff was appointed by Tsar Nicholas as governor general of Finland in 1898. He was responsible for the russification of the Grand Duchy, becoming a figure of hate. He was assassinated in 1904.

[51] T. Kinnunen, 'The national and international in making a feminist: the case of Alexandra Gripenberg', *Women's History Review*, xxv (2016), 652–70.

[52] Miina Sillanpää was first elected as a Social Democrat to the Finnish parliament in 1907, becoming the country's first woman minister in 1926.

organization 'struck the final "coup" in the general strike that gave Finland her new constitution'.[53]

Montefiore urged socialist women to listen to the voice of the ordinary enfranchised women of Finland rather than to Baroness Gripenberg. She was particularly critical of what she saw as Gripenberg's patronising dismissal of Finland's Social Democratic women MPs as 'uneducated women, tailors, factory workers, and domestic servants, who are not qualified to carry out the higher tasks of a representative assembly'.[54] She challenged Gripenberg and those who shared the Baroness's views: 'The words "laundresses and factory workers," which are used by middle class women as terms of contempt, do not frighten us; we recognize in them units of the great mass of the insurgent people, demanding the same access to the means of life as the privileged few now possess.'[55] In contrast, Montefiore's version of Finnish enfranchisement brought to the fore working-class women such as Miina Sillanpää.

Dora Montefiore had a story she wanted to tell about the lessons to be drawn from Finnish women's success, but she had to find audiences who wanted to hear it. In Britain, she was disappointed that her own party, the SDF, gave her little space to speak or write about her Finnish trip. This was probably because of her reputation as a suffragette. In the immediate aftermath of her Finnish trip this would have played better with parts of the ILP than with the SDF. Certainly, ILP branches seem to have been more eager to hear of her Finnish experiences.[56] In international meetings the situation was rather different. At the first International Socialist Women's Congress held in Stuttgart in August 1907, Montefiore represented the Adult Suffrage Society (ASS). Part of the British delegation (mainly from the ILP) challenged her credentials as they claimed the ASS was not a socialist organization. Their agenda was clear, as these women were limited suffragists who were taking the opportunity to challenge a suffrage position with which they disagreed. According to the socialist newspaper *Clarion*, Clara Zetkin (the leader of German socialist women) made from the chair 'a passionate declaration that the Adult Suffrage Society was in a perfect accord with the spirit of the Congress and that it was also engaged in a

[53] D. B. Montefiore, 'Misrepresented Finnish women', *Justice*, 13 July 1907, p. 8. For servants and British suffrage, see L. Schwartz, *Feminism and the Servant Problem: Class and Domestic Labour in the Women's Suffrage Movement* (Cambridge, 2019).

[54] D. B. Montefiore, 'To the women of the people', *Justice*, 31 Oct. 1908, p. 7.

[55] D. B. Montefiore, 'To the women of the people', *Justice*, 31 Oct. 1908, p. 7.

[56] For example, Ealing ILP, 'Independent Labour Party: Mrs Dora Montefiore at Ealing', *Ealing Gazette*, 4 May 1907, p. 2.

fierce fight against the reactionary bourgeois "feminists"'.[57] Within the Socialist International and in many of its affiliated socialist parties, Zetkin's was a familiar distinction. This was between, on the one hand, middle-class suffragists, whose focus was principally on ending the sex disqualification of women from citizenship for the benefit of their own class, and, on the other, those campaigning for adult suffrage, who were said to be the only suffragists who were determined to include all working-class women in any franchise reforms.

Having had her credentials to attend the Congress confirmed, Montefiore was present to hear Hilja Pärssinen, one of Finland's women MPs, get 'the biggest clap of all from the Congress delegates'.[58] The Congress as a whole supported the kind of suffrage that had led to Pärssinen's election: adult suffrage. As the *Clarion* reported, most speakers from across the globe 'delivered their speeches with such dramatic force as to make the very floor tremble'. They argued, 'We believe in Adult Suffrage, in the class war. We want no sentiment, but citizenship. The proletariat will never be satisfied with a limited measure. It isn't Socialism.' However, there was not complete unanimity. In an amendment to the Congress's resolution advocating full adult suffrage, some of the English delegates made their case for limited women's suffrage. Dora Montefiore was among those speaking against this amendment.[59] Within the international socialist women's movement Montefiore's espousal of adult suffrage and her particular reading of the Finnish case were not exceptional. However, the politics of suffrage within Britain was rather different.

In 1907, the Congress of the Second International came out firmly for adult suffrage, repudiating limited women's suffrage 'as an adulteration of, and caricature upon, the principle of political equality of the female sex'. Instead it called for 'womanhood suffrage' and sought to sever any links between socialists and what they termed bourgeois women suffragists.[60] At the end of that year the SDF, now renamed the Social Democratic Party, produced its *Manifesto on the Question of Universal Adult Suffrage.* It drew on the example of Finland in the same way that Montefiore had done. It was argued that when adult suffrage, 'this democratic reform', had been passed in Finland it had been the result of Social Democratic and Radical agitation. The Finnish experience was contrasted with the confusion within

[57] 'The Women's Socialist Conference', *Clarion*, 23 Aug. 1907, p. 5.

[58] 'The Women's Socialist Conference', *Clarion*, 23 Aug. 1907, p. 5.

[59] 'The Women's Socialist Conference', *Clarion*, 23 Aug. 1907, p. 5.

[60] 'Congress proceedings', *Justice*, 31 Aug. 1907, p. 7. For the effect of the Second International's suffrage resolution on the SDF, see Hunt, *Equivocal Feminists*, pp. 170–80.

the English campaign caused by 'a worn-out middle-class theory of a "property qualification"' which had led to:

> the anomalous position of working women agitating, suffering and going to prison for the sake of an electoral reform, which, if carried, would not only fail to enfranchise them politically, but would, through giving further representation to propertied interests, rivet still faster the chains of their political, economic and social thraldom.[61]

These were the themes that Montefiore would continue to emphasize as she deployed the example of Finland in the ever-more-divided suffrage politics of Britain.

Putting the Finnish example to work in the polarized suffrage politics of Britain

Montefiore chose particular moments to use the Finnish example to make her suffrage point over the next few years. By early 1907, she had broken with the WSPU and was an unequivocal adult suffragist. Increasingly the key issue for her was class. From 1908, she argued that socialist women must sever all connections with the leading women's suffrage organizations on both sides of the militant divide because when they demanded 'Votes for Women' they actually only meant 'Votes for Women Householders'.[62] Exposing the limitations of what she and others termed the 'Limited' demand became increasingly important to her and more urgent as the women's suffrage campaign polarized between a demand which would enfranchise all women, as in Finland, or a demand that would only give the vote to some women.

By the beginning of 1909, Finnish women – including that unique phenomenon, the woman MP – were being invited to speak to suffrage meetings in Britain. Each group seemed to favour a particular woman whose narrative of her countrywomen's enfranchisement was in tune with its particular position on women's suffrage. Aino Malmberg and Dr Thekla Hultin MP spoke for the Women's Freedom League (WFL), while Annie Furuhjelm addressed NUWSS meetings when she was in London attending the IWSA congress.[63] The Finnish story told by the speakers chosen by the

61 'Manifesto on the question of universal adult suffrage', *Justice*, 14 Dec. 1907, p. 7.

62 D. B. Montefiore, 'To the women of the people', *Justice*, 31 Oct. 1908, p. 7.

63 'Programme of forthcoming events', *Women's Franchise*, 31 Dec. 1908, p. 324; 'Two more delegates', *Common Cause*, 22 Apr. 1909, p. 25. Annie Furuhjelm was a feminist activist and journalist who became a vice president of the IWSA in 1909 and was an MP in Finland from 1913 to 1929 as a representative of the Swedish People's Party of Finland, a liberal party that

WFL tended to emphasize the importance of men and women working together, arguing against the notion of a sex war.[64] Malmberg was a Finnish writer living in London whom Montefiore claimed to be 'an excellent comrade of ours', as she had already spoken on behalf of the ASS in 1908.[65] On that occasion, Malmberg told the story of how socialist men and women standing together in a well-organized general strike had wrested adult suffrage from the Tsar. By 1909, Malmberg's emphasis was more on Russia's threat to Finland's liberty and the determination of women to fight to defend their freedoms 'because they are all full citizens, and have tasted the joy of freedom and of the power to make their own laws and administer their own affairs'.[66] On hearing Malmberg speak, Montefiore, now honorary secretary of the ASS, commented, 'Let us take example by the Finns, and learn solidarity in the struggle for the political weapon for every adult man and woman.'[67]

Later in 1909, Montefiore reported to her readers in *Justice* that Aino Malmberg was staying at her house, where she had been writing a pamphlet for the WFL, to be entitled *How Finnish Women Gained Universal Adult Suffrage*. Montefiore claimed the WFL had removed all references to the role of the Finnish Social Democrats in the successful agitation for votes for all women and men. This was without the permission of the author, who was deeply troubled by this 'mangled pamphlet', which was an 'impeachment of her intellectual integrity'. Montefiore observed that 'The history of gaining Universal Adult Suffrage in Finland *cannot be faithfully written* without referring to the fact that the agitation of the Socialists was one of the factors in obtaining this political reform.'[68] Montefiore went on to challenge the behaviour of the leading WFL members Charlotte Despard and Teresa Billington-Grieg, who she claimed had authorized this anti-socialist 'bowdlerising' of the pamphlet despite being members of

spoke for the interests of the minority Swedish-speaking population. Thekla Hultin was Finland's first female PhD, a feminist and journalist and an MP from 1908 to 1924, initially for the Young Finnish Party (liberal and nationalist).

64 'Progress of women: women politicians in Finland', *Votes for Women*, 14 Jan. 1909, p. 261.

65 D. B. Montefiore, 'Two Finnish women who speak for adult suffrage', *Justice*, 16 Jan. 1909, p. 5.

66 D. B. Montefiore, 'Two Finnish women who speak for adult suffrage', *Justice*, 16 Jan. 1909, p. 5.

67 D. B. Montefiore, 'Two Finnish women who speak for adult suffrage', *Justice*, 16 Jan. 1909, p. 5.

68 D. B. Montefiore, 'A challenge to Mrs Despard and Mrs Billington-Greig', *Justice*, 15 May 1909, p. 7. Italics in the original.

socialist organizations. Underlining this dispute between limited and adult suffragists, when Malmberg's pamphlet was eventually advertised in the WFL's paper *The Vote*, its title was *Women's Suffrage in Finland*.[69]

At the same time Montefiore stressed that Finnish women MPs endorsed her own emphasis on the role of socialists in the achievement of adult suffrage. Some were more than willing to confirm Montefiore's reading of Finnish women's enfranchisement. Hilja Pärssinen MP sent a telegram of congratulation from the women of Finland to the Adult Suffrage demonstration held in London in April 1909. Moreover, Pärssinen emphasized that there were real tensions between women MPs in Finland; class rather than sex was the basis for solidarity. She reported that 'the class struggle between the Social Democratic women and the reactionary women is being carried on as fiercely in the Finnish Diet as it is in the political organizations'.[70] Montefiore added, 'One point in her letter seems almost incredible, that women who already possess full political rights should be working for *restricted* municipal rights for women, but Parsinen assures me in her letter that an attempt is being made to grant municipal rights to women on a property basis only.'[71]

Montefiore used this point not only as ammunition in the war of attrition between adult and limited suffragists in Britain, but also more particularly against a rival socialist organization, the ILP. She challenged a paragraph in a recent edition of its newspaper, *Labour Leader*, which had welcomed the election of 'twenty-five lady members' to the Finnish Diet. For Montefiore this language revealed the underlying politics: 'The point for us Socialists to record is surely not how many "lady members" there were or are in a National Parliament, but how many Socialist women members have been elected, and to point out that the fight between the class interests of women Socialists and of all middle-class women is as keen inside Parliament as outside.'[72]

The framing of what exactly Finnish women had achieved and what had assured their victory mattered. The WSPU echoed its own domestic demand by saying that what had been achieved in Finland was that women had 'been granted the right to vote on the same terms as men'.[73] And of course they had, but in the form of adult suffrage rather than the limited

69 *The Vote*, 18 Nov. 1909, p. iv.

70 D. B. Montefiore, 'News from Social-Democratic women in Finland', *Justice*, 15 May 1909, p. 7.

71 D. B. Montefiore, 'News from Social-Democratic women in Finland', *Justice*, 15 May 1909, p. 7.

72 'Female suffrage in Finland', *Labour Leader*, 30 Apr. 1909; D. B. Montefiore, 'News from Social-Democratic women in Finland', *Justice*, 15 May 1909, p. 7.

73 S. Pankhurst, 'History of the suffrage movement', *Votes for Women*, 23 July 1909, p. 967.

property-based franchise. Now the Finnish example was as likely to be deployed in the suffrage press against anti-suffragists as in debates between different kinds of suffragists.[74] However, in 1910, the Russian Empire removed the legislative powers from the Finnish Diet as part of the re-imposition of its Russification programme on the Grand Duchy of Finland. Unsurprisingly, this coloured the debate on what the example of Finland could teach suffragists elsewhere.

New voices and new emphases

Increasingly, when it came to Finnish suffrage, the voice that was heard most loudly in the British suffrage press and beyond was not Dora Montefiore's but that of Aino Malmberg.[75] She was a Finnish woman, exiled in London because of her opposition to Russian oppression, who had been speaking at WFL and ILP meetings across the country from 1909.[76] She was a lecturer and author before her work for progressive causes drove her from Finland, spending time in both Britain and the United States and unable to return home until the Russian Revolution in 1917 freed Finland from Tsarist control. Her role as the British voice of Finnish women was reinforced in 1911, when she was a founding member of the Anglo-Finnish Society.[77] She became joint honorary secretary with Rosalind Travers (who was soon to marry Montefiore's former comrade, the leader of the BSP, H. M. Hyndman), whose book *Letters from Finland* (1910) was much advertised in the suffrage press. Now the issue for Malmberg was more about defending the rights won by Finnish women than using their achievement to bolster the claim that adult suffrage was an achievable demand.

The lessons drawn in the suffrage press and beyond were changing. In the years preceding the First World War, writers most often emphasized that admitting women to the Finnish parliament had not favoured any one political party, had not led to women voters acting as one, had not disrupted the home, had not unsexed Finnish women (whether as voters

[74] One Finnish woman MP argued that a consequence of enfranchisement was that 'there is no cleavage politically along sex lines' – a classic anti-suffragist claim ('The outlook', *Votes for Women*, 14 Jan. 1909, p. 257) – while a visit to Finland in 1910 produced the admission from an anti-suffragist MP that 'none of the disasters anticipated had occurred' (J. Clayton, 'In Finland with the British press', *Votes for Women*, 7 Oct. 1910, p. 7).

[75] For a profile of Malmberg with picture, see *Hull Daily Mail*, 9 Feb. 1912, p. 3.

[76] For example, 'Branch notes', *Women's Franchise*, 28 Jan. 1909, p. 373; 'Notices', *Aberdeen Press & Journal*, 18 Mar. 1911, p. 1.

[77] For the early years of the Anglo-Finnish Society, see <https://www.anglofinnishsociety.org.uk/officers-council/history-anglo-finnish-society> [accessed 13 Feb. 2020].

or MPs) or disturbed the business of the Diet itself.[78] These were all fears stoked by anti-suffragists in Britain and elsewhere. The Finnish example was now cited to make the case for the difference that women voters and legislators made to Finland.[79]

This contrasted with the issue that Montefiore still felt was most important: how best to organize to achieve a fully democratic franchise. In 1911, she was addressing Australian audiences as an experienced international adult suffragist who denounced the limited suffrage demand of 'Votes for Women' as 'disingenuous': 'Beneath the suffragette skirt peeps the cloven hoof of extension of political power to property and privilege.'[80] She now characterized the British women's suffrage movement as 'a desperate and spasmodic effort of entrenched capitalism to keep back the rising waves of democracy and of democratic demand'.[81] It was her judgement that:

> If ... the WSPU had followed the lead laid down by us adult suffragists, they certainly would not have had such vast sums of money at their command for pageants, but they would have had the backing of organised Labour, which is the only backing that counts nowadays.[82]

This, of course, was the kind of strategy which had led to the achievement of full adult suffrage in Finland.

However, the context for domestic suffrage politics was changing with the failure of the Conciliation bills, the formalizing of the Labour/suffrage alliance and the intensification of suffragette militancy. There was also the increasingly long shadow cast by Russia over Finland's sovereignty and democracy. Although Britain's progressive press (suffragist, socialist and labour) continued to cover Finland, it was much more often in terms of the country's liberty rather than its particular franchise.[83]

[78] 'The experience of Finland', *Votes for Women*, 5 Jan. 1912, p. 219; 'International suffrage fair', *The Vote*, 16 Nov. 1912, p. 40; 'Women legislators vindicated', *The Vote*, 14 Feb. 1913, p. 258; 'Finland', *Common Cause*, 12 Sept. 1913, p. 386.

[79] For example, 'Women's influence in legislation in Finland', *The Vote*, 28 Dec. 1912, p. 146.

[80] D. B. Montefiore, 'Scrutator and suffragettes: Mrs Montefiore's view', *The Socialist* [Australia], 10 Mar. 1911.

[81] D. B. Montefiore, '"Merely Mary Ann"', *Maoriland Worker*, 11 Aug. 1911, p. 17.

[82] D. B. Montefiore, 'The British suffragettes', *Maoriland Worker*, 29 Sept. 1911, p. 16.

[83] For example, 'Foreign news', *Common Cause*, 20 Oct. 1910, p. 445; 'Caxton Hall "at home"', *The Vote*, 4 Mar. 1911, p. 226; 'News for socialists', *Labour Leader*, 17 Nov. 1911, p. 132.

By 1913, *The Vote*, referring to recent discussion on women's suffrage in Finland in various mainstream journals such as *The Englishwoman* and *The Review of Reviews*, concluded:

> We have always maintained that the enfranchisement of women will not bring the millennium, but Finland's amazing progress is a practical object-lesson of the value of co-operation of men and women in service to the community to which our legislators here are so persistently blind.[84]

Generally, the language of class and of adult suffrage was much less apparent in discussions of Finland in progressive journals. Of all the suffrage organizations it was the WFL that, despite its continuing commitment to limited women's suffrage within Britain, gave space to reports on Finland in which the achievement of adult suffrage was named and acknowledged. Personal connections with Finnish women, particularly MPs like Thekla Hultin and Annie Furuhjelm, were reinforced by the fact that both women spoke at WFL meetings when visiting Britain and their words were reported in *The Vote*. In contrast, *Justice*'s report of the success of women in the 1913 Finnish general election concluded with the words, 'Class tells!'[85] Its focus was on the fact that the number of socialist women MPs outnumbered all those representing non-socialist parties. But they were not complacent; women were only 14% of the socialist MPs, despite constituting 20% of the party membership. It was also suggested that 'a permanent feature even under adult suffrage' was a 'greater apathy of women to political questions'.[86] This was not the kind of comment that Montefiore was ever likely to make. She had been a dissident member of what was now the British Socialist Party (BSP) partly because of its ambivalence on the Woman Question. By the time of this report, Montefiore was still a socialist and suffragist, but was no longer a party member, having resigned from the BSP at the end of 1912.

Common Cause's report on the same Finnish election results celebrated the numbers of women elected, but had nothing to say about class.[87] However, its report of the visit to England of the Finnish MP Hilja Pärssinen included her description of parliamentary work.

> [W]e have already done a great deal of work in bringing women's questions before the Assembly. We want to endow motherhood, to improve the condition of illegitimate children ... Also we want better factory laws to prevent

[84] 'Women legislators vindicated', *The Vote*, 14 Feb. 1913, p. 258.

[85] 'Finland', *Justice*, 6 Sept. 1913, p. 6.

[86] 'Finland', *Justice*, 6 Sept. 1913, p. 6.

[87] 'Finland', *Common Cause*, 12 Sept. 1913, p. 386.

> night-work and to protect expectant and nursing mothers. The bourgeoisie classes in Parliament will not have such laws, but we are educating the women workers to demand them.[88]

Pärssinen's analysis was even more explicit in her journalism in *Justice*, where she pointed out the strict separation between her Finnish socialist women's organization and 'any bourgeois Women's Society'. In parliament, 'the Social-Democratic women are not satisfied with the mere vote, but attach special importance to the representation in Parliament by women, and especially working women, those being most fitted to stand for their interests'.[89] Montefiore would have concurred with this view.

Conclusion

Dora Montefiore was less involved in domestic politics in the years immediately before the First World War, as from 1910 to 1914 she made a series of extensive extra-European trips to the United States, Australia and South Africa. As she encountered new audiences it was as a propagandist who shared the lessons she drew from her political travels. In Australia, readers of *The Socialist* were told:

> She has travelled and spoken in almost every European country and in America. The majority of the leaders are her personal friends, and she knows firsthand the special problems of the workers in each land.[90]

Her priorities changed in these years as she focused on what she saw as the more urgent intertwined challenges of militarism and imperialism, but she never eschewed adult suffragism. She founded a short-lived journal called *Adult Suffrage*, inauspiciously launched in July 1914.[91] Nor did the war silence her. In November 1915, she again called on suffragists to reframe their demand.

> It is no longer, in the Twentieth Century, property that must be enfranchised, but the individual human being. Men demanded, and they are about to receive representation as human beings who pay taxes, and take their share in the defence of the State. Will women continue to ask for less?[92]

[88] 'Finland', *Common Cause*, 12 Dec. 1913, p. 665.

[89] H. Pärssinen, 'Our socialist sisters in Finland', *Justice*, 27 Dec. 1913, p. 3.

[90] M. Lloyd, 'Mrs Dora B. Montefiore: an appreciation', *The Socialist*, 24 Mar. 1911.

[91] For the announcement of the first number of the bi-weekly *Adult Suffragist*, see *Daily Herald*, 1 July 1914, p. 3.

[92] D. B. Montefiore, 'Wanted a re-statement of suffrage demand', *The Vote*, 19 Nov. 1915, p. 825. For the revival in adult suffrage and Montefiore's role in it, see Hunt, 'Class and adult suffrage in the Great War'.

Once more she used the Finnish example to support her case. She called for the dropping of the old formulas of property qualifications and instead, 'like the women of Finland did when they won their enfranchisement, demand the vote for every woman and every man … If ever clear thinking, decided action and solidarity among organized women were needed, it is now.'[93]

In the years after her visit to Finland in 1906, Dora Montefiore had deployed her experiences, analysis and personal networks within her political work: in lectures, journalism and within a range of British and transnational socialist and suffragist organizations. Travel and the resulting experience gave authority to the political arguments she wished to make. This was particularly the case when the position she took was outside the mainstream or challenged dominant thinking. It was certainly significant that Montefiore was one of the few foreign witnesses to this key moment in Finnish history and in the global struggle for women's citizenship. It also mattered that she met, and then continued to network with, some of the key women who had helped to make Finland the first European country to enfranchise women. What she saw and heard in Finland reinforced her commitment to the goal of full adult suffrage. However, in the tempestuous debates on the franchise in Britain, which centred on determining the most effective strategy to achieve women's enfranchisement, the demand for adult suffrage was often regarded as hopelessly utopian. The Finnish experience, as presented by Montefiore, seemed to show that it was an achievable demand. Her continuing mobilization of the Finnish story domestically and internationally had a power for each new audience precisely because it was based on her experiences. It was only by going to Finland, the sole British suffragist to do so at the time, and by persistently reinforcing the relationships established there with Finnish women like Sillanpää, that Montefiore was able to make her distinct contribution to suffrage politics in Britain and beyond.

Montefiore's political practice continued to involve learning lessons from abroad, deploying these domestically and in subsequent travels to give the authority of experience to a set of arguments which some in her audiences would have found challenging. Few suffrage audiences wanted to hear a message which stressed class so emphatically by challenging a property-based franchise and lauding the power of the organized working class to achieve full adult suffrage. Similarly, the labour movement was not always keen to be reminded that organized women workers, including servants,

93 D. B. Montefiore, 'Wanted a re-statement of suffrage demand', *The Vote*, 19 Nov. 1915, p. 825.

could have a decisive role in achieving political goals. Dora Montefiore was determined that, as an internationalist, the politics she made and in which she took part should not be parochial. This was a political practice premised on making connections – and her trip to Finland was one example of how she made this work.

12. Emotions and empire in suffrage and anti-suffrage politics: Britain, Ireland and Australia in the early twentieth century

Sharon Crozier-De Rosa

Introduction

In December 1916, *The Irish Citizen* (hereafter the *Citizen*), paper of the militant feminist organization the Irish Women's Franchise League (IWFL), reported that it seemed that long-active British suffragists might finally be making some progress. British authorities, it said, had announced that they would be establishing an Electoral Reform Conference. An integral part of this process was scrutinizing the franchise systems of countries which had already granted the female franchise. These countries included the dominions of New Zealand and Australia, which had granted women the right to vote in 1893 and 1902 respectively.[1] In countering anti-suffrage arguments about the potentially devastating impact of the woman vote, many suffragists drew on examples of states which had granted the franchise and yet continued to operate successfully.[2] Irish suffragists were no exception.[3]

[1] However, in contrast to New Zealand, only white women were enfranchised in Australia. For a detailed account of the Australian campaign for the vote, see A. Oldfield, *Woman Suffrage in Australia: A Gift or a Struggle?* (Cambridge, 1992).

[2] Finland was one such example (for more details on Finland, see Karen Hunt's chapter in this volume). However, anti-suffragists tended to find reasons for undermining such exemplary models. For example, the British *Anti-Suffrage Review* cited Australia and Finland – early proponents of the woman vote – as sites where 'the birth-rate is almost the lowest in the civilised world'. Women had the vote and so they were distracted from performing their primary roles of child-bearing and child-rearing. See *The Anti-Suffrage Review*, 31 June 1911, p. 111.

[3] There are too many examples to cite but see, for example, *The Irish Citizen*, 17 Oct. 1914, p. 169 (Australia) and 1 May 1915, p. 388 (New Zealand).

'Emotions and empire in suffrage and anti-suffrage politics', in *The politics of women's suffrage: local, national and international dimensions,* ed. A. Hughes-Johnson and L. Jenkins (London, 2021), pp. 309–330.

However, the *Citizen* also used these exemplary models with a more pointed purpose. In 1916, as the anti-colonial nationalist campaign heated up and more of the activists associated with the paper adopted a radical republican stance (promoting separatism over the attainment of an Irish Home Rule parliament), the *Citizen* deployed such examples to attack the imperial centre. It claimed that Australian and New Zealand suffrage developments demonstrated that the normal hierarchical workings of empire were disrupted because the British imperial centre was being compelled to learn from the experiences of those at the far reaches of its vast empire. In observing this reversal of what had, until relatively recently, been a longstanding protocol – one which dictated that the superior metropolitan centre would lead the inferior colonial peripheries in matters of political importance – the *Citizen* issued the mock-celebratory directive: 'Bravo John Bull; Wake up and get a hustle on! Is the colony to be the father of the Homeland?'[4] It was in Irish women's interests that 'John Bull' would get a move on because, as British subjects, they were appealing for a vote in the British Parliament.

Not surprisingly, given the mix of political aspirations in evidence across the UK in the early twentieth century – from socialism to feminism to Unionism to radical republicanism – emotions were running high. Frustration, indignation and anger were often elicited as activists' demands were denied or delayed. Yet, as prevalent as spontaneous outbursts of political emotions were, emotions were also strategically cultivated by those on all sides of politics. The IWFL's mock directive to 'John Bull' to 'get a move on' was certainly evidence of the deliberate deployment of emotional tactics to achieve political ends. As a minority faction of the joint Irish and British suffrage movement – one which supported militant methods over more mainstream constitutional tactics and increasingly championed radical republican ideals over the more popular Home Rule nationalism – the IWFL set out to shame or embarrass the British imperial centre. It did so by drawing attention to an apparent juxtaposition: the progressive gender politics of a seemingly inferior colonial outpost in the face of the purportedly archaic gender attitudes of the supposedly superior imperial metropole.

This chapter asserts that suffragism was characterized by political emotions, spontaneous and cultivated. Local, national and transnational concerns and priorities intervened in the workings of suffrage politics across the Empire to create a highly volatile emotional milieu. Suffragists, whatever their region or national allegiance, were compelled to reference

4 *The Irish Citizen*, Dec. 1916, p. 237.

this complex interweaving of emotions. Not only that, but participants in suffrage debates – whether proponents or opponents – also learnt to develop emotional strategies which then capitalized on the emotional politics of nation and empire. Yet, historians have been slow to centre their investigations on this emotional dimension.[5] Indeed, many have been reluctant to focus on the highly influential role that emotions have played in political machinations more generally. There are understandable reasons for this, including a traditional conviction that politics have been no place for emotions and historiographical concerns about appropriate methodology and source material.[6] However, this chapter will argue that even in the face of these apprehensions, the realm of emotions provides lucrative ground for building on existing suffrage histories to produce new analyses of the relations between different groups of suffragists, between suffragists and their opponents and between political activists and the general public. It allows us to understand the degree to which different groups of women viewed emotions as integral, even pivotal, components of their activist toolkits.

The field of emotions history also opens up exciting new avenues for historians of empire relations. Exploring the emotional dimensions of suffragism as they connect and disconnect disparate sites along the British imperial spectrum promises new insights into the transnational and transcolonial nature of empire relations, and into the bonds existing and concerns shared across nation-states and between colonial sites. Discrete political communities' attitudes towards democratic reform were not formed in isolation. Rather, they were formulated in response to developments taking place elsewhere. They were also constructed amid a backdrop of shifting international relations. This was certainly so for those nations that made up the British Empire. Suffrage debates – conducted in and across these sites of empire – are revealing of the making and remaking of empire relations at a crucial time in the development of that vast entity. This chapter will trace the circulating emotions of suffrage politics to uncover not only the pivotal role of emotions in the political life of early twentieth-century women, but also the changing relationship between subjects in the imperial centre and those in the peripheries of empire.

[5] For an extensive discussion of emotions in suffrage politics, see S. Crozier-De Rosa, *Shame and the Anti-Feminist Backlash: Britain, Ireland and Australia, 1890–1920* (New York, 2018).

[6] Discussed in S. Crozier-De Rosa, 'Emotions of protest', in *Sources for the History of Emotions: a Guide*, ed. K. Barclay, S. Crozier-De Rosa and P. Stearns (Abingdon, 2020).

A history of emotions and politics

Historians may have been reluctant to engage with the topic, but scholars like Ute Frevert remind us that the relationship between emotions and politics is not new. From ancient times, practitioners and theoreticians of politics have clearly understood that the two are deeply connected. For example, Aristotle advised orators about how to most effectively use rhetorical devices to move audiences' feelings. This advice, Frevert argues, has been taken up by future generations of influential leaders, from Pericles in ancient Greece to Abraham Lincoln during the American Civil War.[7] However, despite the obvious presence of emotions in politics, sociologists Jeff Goodwin, James M. Jasper and Francesca Polletta argued that there has been some hesitation on the part of academic observers to admit to this presence. Instead, they have managed to 'ignore the swirl of passions all around them in political life'.[8] In accounting for this relative absence, political scientist Carol Johnson cited the perceived gendered nature of emotions generally. Traditionally, emotion was associated with the feminized private sphere of home and family, while emotion's supposed antithesis, reason, was associated with the masculinized public world of business and politics.[9] In many ways this gendered approach to emotion helps us to understand why only a small number of histories of women's movements have focused on emotions.[10] Through eliding the emotional dimensions of these movements, feminist historians have avoided the risk of further associating female politics with the taint of irrationality. This is especially true of the historiography of militant suffragism which, as June Purvis has argued, from as far back as the 1930s has been subject to a masculinist agenda which has seen leaders like Emmeline and Christabel Pankhurst characterized as devious, ridiculous,

[7] U. Frevert, 'Emotional politics', The Netherlands Scientific Council for Government Policy Annual Lecture, presented in The Hague on 24 Jan. 2019 <https://www.wrr.nl/publicaties/publicaties/2019/01/25/lezing-ute-frevert-over-emotional-politics> [accessed 9 Sept. 2019].

[8] J. Goodwin, J. M. Jasper and F. Polletta, 'Introduction: why emotions matter', in *Passionate Politics: Emotions and Social Movements*, ed. J. Goodwin, J. M. Jasper and F. Polletta (Chicago, Ill., 2001), pp. 1–27, at pp. 1–2.

[9] C. Johnson, 'From Obama to Abbott: gender identity and the politics of emotion', *Australian Feminist Studies*, xxviii (2013), 14–29, at p. 15.

[10] Examples of those which do focus on emotions include: V. Taylor and L. J. Rupp, 'Loving internationalism: the emotional culture of transnational women's organisations, 1888–1945', *Mobilisation: An International Journal*, vii (2002), 141–58; C. Florin, 'Heightened feelings! Emotions as "capital" in the Swedish suffrage movement', *Women's History Review*, xviii (2009), 181–201; and Crozier-De Rosa, *Shame and the Anti-Feminist Backlash*.

hysterical and even deranged.[11] The historiography of the militant is a field 'riven with debate and controversy'.[12] Emotions form but one of these.

Even when those writing political histories recognized the role of emotions in politics, their observations were still subject to this supposed dualism between emotion and reason. For instance, as emotions scholars Carol Stearns and Peter Stearns noted, those who began to write crowd histories in the 1960s, like George Rudé and Charles Tilly, made the careful decision to avoid labelling protestors as emotional or unreasonable. Rather, they worked to circumvent accusations that crowds were impulsive, irrational and therefore their goals and grievances irrelevant or illegitimate, by ignoring or relegating the role of emotions in their politics.[13] Over the past two decades, sociologists have increasingly turned their attention to uncovering and extending our understanding of the powerful role that emotions play in politics – emotions as strategically deployed or as experienced and embodied feelings. They have investigated the role of emotions as means of motivating, sustaining or even bringing about the demise of political movements.[14] Over the past few years, historians have begun to build on sociological research – including this rejection of the reason-versus-emotion dualism – to consider the influential and complex role of emotions in past political lives.[15] Through examining emotional circulations between Britain, Ireland and Australia in the first decades of the twentieth century, this chapter will demonstrate how growing interest in the history of emotions can be capitalized on to deepen our understanding of the complex and shifting nexus between emotions, empire and suffrage politics.

[11] Purvis cites numerous examples of male historians perpetuating this trend, including George Dangerfield, David Mitchell and Martin Pugh. See J. Purvis, 'Gendering the historiography of the suffragette movement in Edwardian Britain: some reflections', *Women's History Review*, xxii (2013), 577–90.

[12] Purvis, 'Gendering the historiography of the suffragette movement in Edwardian Britain', p. 577.

[13] P. Stearns and C. Stearns, 'Clarifying the history of emotions and emotional standards', *American Historical Review*, xc (1985), 813–36, at pp. 816–17. References are to: G. F. E. Rudé, *The Crowd in History: A Study of Popular Disturbances in France and England, 1730–1848* (New York, 1964) and C. Tilly, *From Mobilization to Revolution* (Reading, Mass., 1978).

[14] See, for example, J. Jasper, *The Emotions of Protest* (Chicago, Ill., 2018); H. Flam and D. King, 'Introduction', in *Emotions and Social Movements* (London, 2005), pp. 1–18; and D. B. Gould, 'Concluding thoughts', *Contemporary European History*, xxiii (2014), 639–44.

[15] For an introduction to historians analysing emotions in politics, see Crozier-De Rosa, 'Emotions of protest'.

Ireland and the complex dynamics of gender, shame and colonization

The Irish had long occupied an ambivalent position in relation to empire. At least since the 1800 Act of Union, those subscribing to Unionist politics considered Ireland an equal partner in the United Kingdom of Great Britain and Ireland (UK) and therefore an integral part of the imperial centre. Those dedicated to nationalist politics operated along a continuum from Home Rule nationalism to anti-colonial republicanism. Early in the twentieth century, the majority of Irish nationalists, led by the Irish Parliamentary Party, supported the Home Rule campaign, which demanded that parliament be restored to the island which would stay within the UK and the Empire. Increasingly after 1916, a growing but still minority group of nationalists advocated republicanism. They looked on Ireland as England's oldest imperial possession and championed secession from the Union and also from the Empire. The body of republicans swelled after failed British attempts to introduce conscription in 1918. These were led in the main by Sinn Féin, whose aspirations for complete autonomy were clearly present in its title, translated from the Gaelic as 'We, Ourselves'. It was the republican spirit which was to direct the ensuing War of Independence (1919–21) which then led to the bitter Irish Civil War (1922–3). Not surprisingly, divisions within the Irish suffrage movement mirrored those in wider Irish society.[16]

Many in Ireland had been campaigning for the female franchise since the 1870s.[17] The majority of suffragists on the island were devoted to constitutional tactics. However, after the initiation of militant tactics in England by the Women's Social and Political Union (WSPU), a small number of Irish suffragists travelled to England and took part in the militant movement there. Some were imprisoned for doing so.[18] By 1912, a minority branch of the Irish suffrage movement, represented in the main by the IWFL, had deployed militant tactics like throwing stones through the windows of government offices in Ireland itself. They were arrested and

[16] For an in-depth analysis of the varying ideas and allegiances of nationalist women, see S. Pašeta, *Irish Nationalist Women, 1900–1918* (Cambridge, 2013).

[17] Activists such as the Dublin-based Quaker Anna Haslam and Belfast Presbyterian Isabella Tod had been campaigning for the vote in Ireland since the 1870s. See M. Cullen, 'Feminism, citizenship and suffrage: a long dialogue', in *Irish Women and the Vote: Becoming Citizens*, ed. L. Ryan and M. Ward (Dublin, 2007), pp. 1–20, p. 12. See also D. Urquhart, *Women in Ulster Politics 1890–1940* (Dublin, 2000). For more on Irish emancipation campaigns generally, see M. Cullen, 'The potential of gender history', in *Gender and Power in Irish History*, ed. M. Gialanella Valiulis (Dublin, 2009), pp. 18–38.

[18] Women had been arrested and imprisoned in England for suffrage militancy since 1907. For example, in 1910 and then again in 1911, Irish women, including IWFL co-founder Margaret Cousins, were imprisoned in England for participating in protests organized

imprisoned.[19] In 1912, a handful of English militant suffragists also travelled to Ireland to deploy militancy there and were subsequently arrested.[20] That Ireland was home to coordinated acts of feminist militancy in 1912 was not accidental. Rather, it reflected the fact that in that year, negotiations over Irish Home Rule had led the Irish Parliamentary Party, which held the balance of power in the Westminster Parliament, to block the passing of the 1912 Conciliation Bill which would have enfranchised eligible women across the United Kingdom. Understandably, the obstructive role that Irish nationalist politics played in suffrage politics that year angered all of those adversely affected, whether British or Irish.

Across the long-running suffrage campaign, Irish and British suffragists were connected in many ways.[21] Their desire to empower women through granting them a vote in the British Parliament made them part of the same network of suffrage activists. Consequently, British and Irish feminists referenced each other's campaigns, exchanged funding, ideas and approaches and travelled across national spaces. British organizations on both sides of the suffrage debate also established branches in Ireland, with varying degrees of success, including the National Union of Women's Suffrage Societies (NUWSS), the Church League for Women's Suffrage (CLWS), the WSPU and the Anti-Suffrage League (later the National League for Opposing Woman Suffrage (NLOWS)).[22] However, the transnational nature of the

by the WSPU. See W. Murphy, *Political Imprisonment and the Irish, 1912–1921* (Oxford, 2014), p. 14.

[19] The first group of Irish women to be imprisoned in Ireland for their militancy consisted of eight women: Hanna Sheehy Skeffington, Margaret Murphy, Jane Murphy, Marguerite Palmer, Marjorie Hasler, Kathleen Houston, Maud Lloyd and Hilda Webb. They were arrested in Dublin in June 1912 for throwing stones through the windows of government offices. See Murphy, *Political Imprisonment and the Irish, 1912–1921*, p. 14.

[20] In July 1912, in what is now a renowned display of militancy, three English militant suffragists – Mary Leigh, Gladys Evans and Lizzie Baker (Jennie Baines) – travelled to Ireland where they threw a small hatchet at Herbert Asquith, visiting British Prime Minister, and John Redmond, leader of the Irish Parliamentary Party, who were meeting to discuss the issue of Irish Home Rule. Later, they also set fire to Dublin's Theatre Royal, where Asquith was due to speak. See S. Crozier-De Rosa, 'Divided sisterhood? Nationalist feminism and militancy in England and Ireland', *Contemporary British History*, xxxii (2018), 448–69.

[21] I use the term 'British' to reflect the fact that suffragists from the 'four nations' – England, Ireland, Scotland and Wales – participated in the movement for the vote in the same British Parliament. At the same time, I respect Irish nationalist women's demands to be considered Irish, not British.

[22] C. Murphy, *The Women's Suffrage Movement and Irish Society in the Early Twentieth Century* (New York and London, 1989), p. 75. For a history of the Irish suffrage movement, also see R. Cullen Owens, *Smashing Times: A History of the Irish Women's Suffrage Movement, 1889–1922* (Dublin, 1984).

British suffrage movement – with campaigns in England, Ireland, Scotland and Wales – grew increasingly complicated as Irish nationalist aspirations were seen to interfere in suffrage politics. Relations became even more fraught after 1916 when some Irish nationalists, members of the IFWL included, began to espouse republicanism over the goal of Home Rule, and as British resentment of demands for separatism became more manifest.[23] More and more, the emotional politics of imperialism and anti-colonial nationalism characterized how national feminist communities framed their demands and how they conducted their exchanges. For Irish women, the emotion of shame – tied to intersecting histories of gender and colonial oppression – held particular resonance.

Shame played a pivotal role in Irish feminist deliberations. The colonizing process, nationalists argued, had imposed shame on the once proud Irish nation through emasculating its manhood. British colonists had achieved this by constructing the Irish as a childlike Celtic 'race' that was erratic, irrational and emotional.[24] Robbed of his manliness, the Irish man had no rights to national autonomy. The ever-virulent British man dominated over him. Irish feminists cited the fact that Irish men were forced to travel to England to represent their constituents as evidence of their subjugated position. Worse than that, these same men were compounding their shame by 'begging' British men for political concessions, specifically the right to have a home-based parliament.[25] Influenced by a desire to avoid further shaming the Irish man, one group of politically active women – the Inghinidhe na hEireann (Daughters of Ireland), a radical nationalist, pro-militant women's group – made the decision to postpone agitating for the vote until the nation's freedom was won. Members were devoted to the vision of women playing a leading role in a free Irish society but, in the meantime, they prioritized the goal of nationalist independence over suffrage. That way, Irish rather than British men could grant Irish women political power. This, these

[23] For a detailed analysis of the fraught relationship between Irish and English suffragists, see Crozier-De Rosa, 'Divided sisterhood? Nationalist feminism and militancy in England and Ireland'.

[24] Begoňa Aretxaga has argued that this pattern of emasculation was premised on different factors in different colonial sites. For example, whereas in Ireland it took the form of the construction of the colonized as 'childlike', in India native men's treatment of their womenfolk was held up by the imperialists as evidence of their inferior, barbaric status (referring here to practices such as sati or widow-burning). See B. Aretxaga, *Shattering Silence: Women, Nationalism, and Political Subjectivity in Northern Ireland* (Princeton, N.J., 1997). See also R. J. C. Young, *The Idea of English Ethnicity* (Oxford, 2008).

[25] See, for example, *Bean na hÉireann*, May 1909, pp. 13–14.

nationalist feminists said, was the only ethical course of action for any committed female nationalist.[26]

As early as 1909, over a decade before the Irish achieved partial independence, the organization's paper, *Bean na hÉireann* (hereafter the *Bean* and translating from the Gaelic as 'Women of Ireland') – which proclaimed itself 'the first and only Nationalist Woman's paper' – accused Irish suffragists of compounding the shame of colonization by begging the British imperialist for political concessions.[27] It declared that Irish suffragists were entering 'into the supreme folly of recognising the English Parliament and begging for concessions'.[28] In this framing of the debate, Irish suffragists were asking Ireland's enemy – more embarrassingly, they were pleading with it – to grant them a say in the affairs of an enemy parliament: the British Parliament. By appealing to the imperialist for the rights of citizenship, Irish women were guilty of acknowledging the British man's ascendancy over the Irish man. The Irish suffragist, the *Bean* asserted, was a woman who was 'scrambling for her mess of pottage, and willing to join in with her country's conquerors and worst enemies to gain her end, but from the point of view of an Irish Nationalist'.[29]

The paper was adamant that Irish men would give their 'sisters' the vote once they had control of their own country.[30] If women were to receive the vote because they believed it was 'the hall-mark of equality', then it was 'from Irishmen that this must be won'.[31]

> The rights of Irishwomen are in Ireland and must be won in Ireland, not in England or any foreign country. If Irishwomen have time and energy to use,

[26] This position allowed for some ambiguity, however, as individual members decided whether to pledge their allegiance to suffragism as well as nationalism – or they changed their allegiances over time. Margaret Ward captures this sense of ambiguity in her biography of Gonne; Gonne, the inaugural president of the organization, 'was never a suffragist, being far too much of a nationalist ever to consider giving absolute priority to women's demands, but she wanted the franchise for women in a free Ireland and, in the meantime, the suffrage movement was challenging the government and therefore had her full support'. See M. Ward, *Maud Gonne: Ireland's Joan of Arc* (London, 1990), p. 102. Senia Pašeta asserts that, by 1912, Gonne had joined the IWFL, spoken at its meetings and donated money to it. See Pašeta, *Irish Nationalist Women, 1900–1918*, p. 108.

[27] This pioneering claim was made in an editorial by Helena Moloney later in the journal's life. See C. L. Innes, '"A voice in directing the affairs of Ireland": *L'Irlande Libre*, *The Shan Van Vocht* and *Bean na hÉireann*', in *Irish Writing: Exile and Subversion*, ed. P. Hyland and N. Sammells (Basingstoke, 1991), pp. 146–58, p. 146.

[28] *Bean na hÉireann*, May 1909, pp. 13–14.

[29] *Bean na hÉireann*, Dec. 1909, p. 13.

[30] *Bean na hÉireann*, Feb. 1909, p. 1.

[31] *Bean na hÉireann*, Feb. 1909, p. 1.

> and the will to make sacrifices and risk liberty, let it be for a nobler and greater end than the right to send hostages to England.[32]

The campaign for the vote was 'humiliating', the paper asserted, because it contributed to the emasculation of the Irish man.[33] Irish suffragists were cast in the role of collaborators in the shameful practice of modern-day colonization.

Those so-called collaborators – feminist nationalists – who refused to concede and who continued to demand to be able to vote in a British Parliament were likewise compelled to reference the shame of colonization in their campaign. They were obliged to deny accusations that they were complicit in the colonized Irish man's shame. Instead, they constructed themselves as patriotic women devoted to using their considerable passion and energies to fight for the political power that would enable them to join with their brothers in the struggle for independence. Again, the goals were the same – national autonomy and women's rights – but the order of priority was reversed. This time, the woman vote was the first goal and with that power Irish men and women could achieve national independence.

Despite their ultimate shared vision of Irish women taking a leading hand in directing the affairs of a free Irish nation, Irish feminist nationalists too resorted to the politics of shame. They countered the *Bean*'s accusations by claiming that it was not they who were acting shamefully. Rather, it was the women behind the *Bean* who were guilty of slavishly obeying Irish men's directives to abandon their feminist aspirations in favour of those of the male-led nationalist campaign. As prominent feminist nationalist Meg Connery put it in 1914 in the pages of the militant suffrage IWFL paper the *Citizen*, women who called themselves suffragists – Unionist and nationalist – while attaching themselves to men's political parties were 'acting slavishly whether they realize it or not'.[34] They were, she said, guilty of displaying an 'anxiety to efface themselves and their sex in the interests of men, which they falsely believe to be the interests of the Nation'. In doing so, they were complicit with men in the act of 'forgetting that a Nation consists of men and women'.[35] It was not only men but also women who were tainted with shame under colonization and, as this case now proved, under anti-colonialism too.

The feminist nationalist Hanna Sheehy Skeffington argued that this gender amnesia had allowed all Irish women – whether nationalist feminist

[32] *Bean na hÉireann*, Feb. 1909, p. 1.

[33] *Bean na hÉireann*, Apr. 1909, p. 15.

[34] *The Irish Citizen*, 8 Aug. 1914, p. 90.

[35] *The Irish Citizen*, 8 Aug. 1914, p. 90.

or feminist nationalist or indeed Unionist – to be reduced to a shameful position in modern Irish society. 'It is barren comfort for us Irishwomen', she wrote, 'to know that in ancient Ireland women occupied a prouder, freer position than they now hold even in the most advanced modern states, that all professions, including that of arms, were freely open to their ambitions'.[36] Memories of past equality did not provide a healing balm or proffer a workable solution for Ireland's current state of gender inequality. What was needed were politically enfranchised women who could stand alongside Irish men and together present a formidable force which would demand Irish freedom. That way, the shame of colonization – for Irish men and Irish women – would be eradicated.

Suffragists like Connery and Sheehy Skeffington walked a thin line between upholding the exclusiveness of the nationalist context in which the Irish suffrage movement was unfolding and promoting a transnational argument that women should have the right to pursue the vote whatever the peculiar circumstances of their country. Their main argument was that all women, regardless of nationality, needed the vote to make real political change and to achieve equal citizenship with men. However, their arguments grew increasingly nationalistic when they perceived their autonomy – as Irish suffragists within an intersecting British and Irish suffrage movement – to be under threat. In 1914, at the outset of the First World War, the *Citizen* responded to directives from the pro-war WSPU leader Christabel Pankhurst that the war should be supported above all else by reasserting that Pankhurst had no authority in Ireland. 'Ireland is not England', the paper stated. '*The Irish Citizen* has always recognised the existence of the Irish Sea.'[37]

Whatever their position on the national question, when articulating their aspirations and defending their strategies, Irish feminists were required to reference the emotional politics of that national question, especially the country's understanding of the fraught relationship between gender, shame and colonization. As the nationalist movement gathered momentum, especially after the failed nationalist uprising of Easter 1916, other emotional politics came to the fore. In their changing relationship with British suffragists, for example, pride in national allegiance began to trump the wellbeing derived from transnational feminist solidarity. Emotional bonds

[36] *Bean na hÉireann*, Nov. 1909, pp. 5–6.

[37] *The Irish Citizen*, 10 Oct. 1914, p. 166. The *Citizen* was also referring back to the previously mentioned incident in 1912 when the WSPU had carried out militancy in Ireland without the permission of Irish suffragists or without considering the volatility of the nationalist situation there. For an extended discussion of the fallout of this incident, see Crozier-De Rosa, 'Divided sisterhood?'.

were continually being made and remade in the face of shifting gendered and nationalist alliances.

Australian women voters, colonial anxiety and national pride

Across the far reaches of the Empire, in Australia, patriotic white women took a different view of nationalist Irish women's increasingly belligerent attitude to the British. Their ardent response is revealing of the specific nature of the anxieties and indignations affecting a remote group of settler-colonists. In 1919, for example, women of the conservative Australian Women's National League (AWNL) writing for their paper, *Woman*, reflected on how the Irish had rejected British attempts to introduce conscripted service for the First World War and had instead instigated a War of Independence. Adopting a tone of impatient indignation, *Woman* accused the Irish of being petulant children (reminding us here of the earlier-mentioned trope of the childlike Celt). The paper went on to claim: 'all the world knows that Ireland is to-day the most prosperous corner of the Empire, and her people the most pampered children of that Empire's great world-wide family'.[38] As for evidence of this, one only had to look at the fact that of all the 'four nations' claiming privileged membership of that cherished entity, the UK, only the Irish remained un-conscripted.

Doubtless, conservative Australian women's indignation arose from the hurt they felt at accusations emanating from the British centre that they – as one of the Empire's only group of women voters – were responsible for treachery towards the Empire because they were responsible for the defeat of two Australian conscription referenda during the First World War.[39] In 1916, Australia introduced a referendum for compulsory overseas military service. Australian women, as enfranchised citizens, would have the chance to vote directly on whether to force men to enlist for the war. This was an extraordinary responsibility. Accordingly, the eyes of the Empire were fixed on them. As the Melbourne newspaper the *Argus* pointed out at the time, women's citizenship was on trial.[40]

Australian women passionately subscribed to both sides of the conscription debate. A minority of pacifists in Australia, most famously represented by Victorian feminist Vida Goldstein and her Women's Peace Army (formed in 1915), opposed conscription. A more significant number of pro-war women, like the loyal women of the AWNL, fervently supported

[38] *Woman*, 1 Dec. 1919, p. 392.

[39] *The Anti-Suffrage Review*, Jan. 1917, p. 3.

[40] *Argus*, 4 Dec. 1917, p. 6. Cited in B. Ziino, 'Great War, total war', in *Making Australian History: Perspectives on the Past Since 1788*, ed. D. Gare and D. Ritter (Melbourne, 2008), pp. 335–44, p. 342.

it. The result of the referendum, however, was not good for those who were keen to demonstrate their loyalty to the Empire. Conducted amid a backdrop of passionate, heated debate and 'raw emotional violence', the 1916 pro-conscription campaign was defeated.[41]

As mentioned earlier, suffragists globally held up societies like Australia and New Zealand as examples of the successful integration of newly enfranchised women voters. Conversely, anti-suffragists scrutinized the actions of newly minted women voters to look for ways in which these women could be held up as warnings to those countries considering enfranchising their own female population. Therefore, whereas suffrage papers can be mined for their positive representation of the Australian woman voter, anti-suffrage papers, like the official organ of the British NLOWS, *The Anti-Suffrage Review* (the *Review*), are valuable for how they capitalized on emotional politics to problematize her. For example, British anti-suffragists seized on the opportunity to blame Australian women voters for the defeat of the conscription referendum. Quoting the Sydney correspondent for the *Times*, the *Review* maintained that the failure of the referendum was due to 'the emotionalism of the women electors, who thought they would be condemning men to death if they voted "Yes" '.[42] The paper continued:

> Their action has dumbfounded some most ardent supporters of Woman Suffrage, because there is irrefragable evidence that they permitted their emotions to guide their pencils in the booths, and reason and patriotism appealed to them in vain. In the supreme trial of citizenship most women 'shirked their duty'.[43]

A second referendum was organized for 1917. The campaign leading up to that event was more emotional and violent than the first, coloured as it was by even more grief, suspicion, bitterness, hysteria and paranoia. That referendum failed too.

Doubtless, British anti-suffragists found it opportunistic to point the finger at what they said was feminine emotionalism. Such sentimental weakness as that displayed by female pacifists had no place in wartime imperial politics when millions of men's lives were at risk; therefore, women had no business having the vote. However, by laying the blame at the feet of all Australian women, they rendered invisible the fierce loyalty and patriotic

[41] J. Beaumont, *Broken Nation: Australians and the Great War* (Sydney, 2013), p. 242.

[42] *The Anti-Suffrage Review*, Jan. 1917, p. 3. The *Review* is the organ of the National League for Opposing Woman Suffrage (NLOWS). For more on the NLOWS, see J. Bush, 'National League for Opposing Woman Suffrage (*act.* 1910–1918)', *Oxford Dictionary of National Biography* <https://doi.org/10.1093/ref:odnb/92492> [accessed 27 Dec. 2019].

[43] *The Anti-Suffrage Review*, Jan. 1917, p. 3.

wartime work of women like those in the AWNL. However they arrived at their conclusion that Australian women had performed a gross dereliction of duty, British anti-suffragists continued to use the example of the defeat of Australia's referenda as evidence of the universal untrustworthiness of women voters.

Loyal Australian women – like the women of the AWNL who had devoted themselves to the task of achieving conscription and who were devastated by the referenda's defeat – emphatically denied that they were guided by emotionalism or that they were responsible for this defeat. Instead, they argued that the stain of empire disloyalty should be attached to 'SOCIALISM, PACIFISM, SINN FEINISM'.[44] The AWNL believed that the Irish represented a significant threat to the integrity of the Empire.[45] The substantial migrant Irish community in Australia, it said, was being led astray by the notorious Irish-born, anti-colonial nationalist, anti-conscriptionist Archbishop of Melbourne, Daniel Mannix.[46] In Ireland itself, the AWNL accused, the Irish were supportive of a violent revolutionary separatist movement. Wherever they were, the Irish component of the Empire was proving treacherous. As such, it provoked feelings of anger, indignation and resentment among these 'loyal' British-Australian women.[47]

Of course, in 1918, at the time that patriotic Australian women were making this claim, a growing number of Irish women were coveting what these antipodean women already had, namely, a parliament at home and voting rights in that parliament. Patriotic women in the far-away Antipodes cherished the sense of connection that the so-called mother country, Britain, and its empire provided.[48] Given this, they did not feel any compulsion to support the political aspirations of women in other colonial sites – including Irish women's nationalist or feminist demands – if they threatened the continuity of the empire which provided this feeling of belonging.

[44] *Woman*, 1 Jan. 1918, p. 373.

[45] For a recent appraisal of Australian attitudes to the Irish diaspora, see E. Malcolm and D. Hall, *A New History of the Irish in Australia* (Sydney, 2018).

[46] J. Griffin, 'Mannix, Daniel (1864–1963)', *Australian Dictionary of Biography* <http://adb.anu.edu.au/biography/mannix-daniel-7478> [accessed 28 Dec. 2019].

[47] Members of the AWNL referred to themselves as 'loyal' because one of their stated objectives was to support loyalty to the throne and Empire. See Australian Women's National League, *History of the Australian Women's National League*, 50th Anniversary Publication (Melbourne, 1954), p. 4.

[48] The politically conservative Australian women whose works I examine referred to England and Britain as the mother country. For more on how they felt connected to the so-called mother country, see chapter 'Shaming British-Australia' in Crozier-De Rosa, *Shame and the Anti-Feminist Backlash*, pp. 107–30.

As white settler-colonists in what was regarded as a remote and hostile Asia-Pacific region, many loyal Australian women considered themselves to be uniquely honoured – and burdened – among all of the Empire's womanhood. They believed that they were endowed with a special racialized mission: to ensure the rejuvenation of the British or Anglo-Saxon 'race' in the supposedly healthier climes and open spaces of the Antipodes. As one of the first groups of Empire womanhood to be enfranchised, Australian women were aware that their vote was a white vote.[49] Believed to belong to a race doomed to extinction, Aboriginal women and men were disenfranchised whether through informal means or formal legislation. They were not to be granted the right to vote until 1962.[50] Not only that, but perceived threats from without (for example, from Japan as Japanese expansionary intentions with regard to places like China, Korea and Russia were imagined as a threat to Australia's borders) as well as those from within (exemplified, for instance, by the presence of cheap Chinese labour in the colonies) combined to create a tense racialized environment. Laws and policies were enacted immediately after federation to ensure racial exclusion.[51]

It was this valued mission, and the seemingly intractable ties it provided to the family of empire, that shaped the emotional politics of 'loyal' Australian women voters. Knowing that the eyes of the world – and certainly those of the mother country – were on them as they performed in their new role of enfranchised citizens intensified Australian women's anxieties. It made them zealous in their determination to prove themselves deserving beneficiaries of the Empire's munificence. 'Shall we not then', the AWNL's *Woman* asked in 1909, 'call to our minds all the proud traditions of our race and stand shoulder to shoulder in the defence of our Empire, determined that not at our door shall lie "the ordering of her disgrace"'.[52]

[49] The Australian settler colonies were some of the first to grant women the right to vote globally and, in the case of the newly federated Australian Commonwealth, one of the first to simultaneously grant women the right to vote and to stand for Parliament (1902).

[50] For a discussion of the exclusion of indigenous subjects and inclusion of white female subjects in the citizenship of the newly federated Australia, see, for example, P. Grimshaw, M. Lake, A. McGrath and M. Quartly, *Creating a Nation, 1788–1900* (Ringwood, Vic., 1994), p. 2.

[51] These included the new commonwealth parliament's 1901 Immigration Restriction Act, which allowed for selective immigration based on language tests and other laws that discriminated against the non-white population already living in Australia by denying them rights to citizenship, welfare benefits, certain occupations and, in some instances, land. See S. Macintyre, *A Concise History of Australia*, Third Edition (Cambridge, 2009), pp. 142–3.

[52] *Woman*, 28 Mar. 1909, p. 426.

As the conscription debacles later demonstrated, supposedly undesirable elements within Australia's borders, like the disruptive Irish, did not make it an easy task to prove the Australian woman's worthiness to those in the metropole. However, it was also the politics of pride – specifically, exuberant displays of national confidence – which created further distrust of the modern Australian woman among some in the imperial centre. For example, in 1917, *Woman* declared of Australia:

> We have a constitution fundamentally more broad-based than its model, the Imperial Parliament. We have transplanted the institutions and the freedom of the Motherland without the sacrifice of the centuries which our forebears had to undergo to secure them for ourselves and future generations. A continent, a magnificent heritage, given us generously to husband, and to till, and wherein to rear if we will, a new and a higher civilisation. Was there ever such generosity on the part of a parent to an offspring? Was there ever such an opportunity afforded to an offspring to make good and to do better than its forebears? Let the character of our people be such as will fit us to occupy it and to lay a just and inalienable claim to its permanent occupancy. This territorial prize is worth all the effort that we as Australians can put forward. Let us prove equal to the task.[53]

Here humble 'truths' mixed with more audacious assertions to create a picture of a grateful 'child' who had outgrown or improved upon a 'parent', albeit it a munificent one.

This growing boldness was confirmed perhaps most famously in 1911 when Australian women marched in the Great Suffrage Procession in London carrying a banner which instructed the imperial centre to: 'Trust the women Mother as I have done'.[54] The very words on this banner revealed a collective belief in the advanced state of Australia's approach to the matter of gender and citizenship.[55] This was very much in line with Australian

[53] *Woman*, 1 June 1917, p. 110.

[54] Many Australian women participated in the British suffrage movement (for example, Vida Goldstein, Dora Montefiore, Nellie Martel, Jessie Street and the more spectacular Muriel Matters). Clare Wright's recent book *You Daughters of Freedom* discusses these women, as well as this 1911 event and banner, in detail. See C. Wright, *You Daughters of Freedom: The Australians Who Won the Vote and Inspired the World* (Melbourne, 2018).

[55] This was a sense of superiority that extended to other facets of society. Activists like Vida Goldstein and Bessie Rischbieth certainly believed that the influence of the woman's vote on issues like prostitution and employment in Australia was far in advance of conditions prevailing in the metropolitan centre. See B. Caine, 'Australian feminism and the British militant suffragettes', paper presented to the Department of the Senate Occasional Lecture Series at Parliament House, Canberra, Australia, 31 Oct. 2003 <https://www.aph.gov.au/binaries/senate/pubs/pops/pop41/caine.pdf> [accessed 21 Jan. 2016].

feminists' imagining of a maternalist welfare state, one which used women's political influence to create a kind of society which focused on the needs of mothers and children and which also drew on women's nurturing capabilities to shape national life for the better.[56] Australian feminists, then, worked to challenge metropolitan assumptions about the superior positioning of women in the imperial centre compared with those in the Empire's outposts, a fact gleefully highlighted by Irish feminist nationalists, as demonstrated by this chapter's opening reference to the *Citizen*'s satirical 'Bravo John Bull' comments.

As historian Barbara Caine has argued, the international woman suffrage movement allowed Antipodean women their first opportunity 'to turn the imperial tables as it were, and to offer their unfortunate British sisters help, guidance and advice'.[57] Such a turning of tables likely gratified political women of a more 'progressive' nature, like suffragist Vida Goldstein, who declared her 'new world' Australian vote to be infinitely more valuable than a restricted 'old world' vote, as reported in *The Anti-Suffrage Review*.[58] Reformers of a similarly progressive nature from countries like Britain and the US certainly looked on political developments emanating from Australia as inspirational.[59] However, more conservative women in Australia, although they took pride in using their privileged position to improve the great British 'race', were much less likely to feel as comfortable as their more progressive sisters in asserting supremacy over the old imperial centre. They were much more anxious to express loyalty and gratitude, and prove their worthiness.[60]

[56] M. Lake, 'Women's changing conception of political power', *Papers on Parliament*, xxix (1997) <https://www.aph.gov.au/About_Parliament/Senate/Research_and_Education/pops/~/link.aspx?_id=D4C36577D9B24C928B424B01279719F7&_z=z> [accessed 29 Sept. 2020].

[57] Caine, 'Australian feminism and the British militant suffragettes'.

[58] For an account of this exchange between Goldstein and a British commentator over the comparative value of the Australian women's and British man's vote, see S. Crozier-De Rosa, 'The national and the transnational in British anti-suffragists' views of Australian women voters', *History Australia*, x (2013), 51–64.

[59] For example, the granting of female suffrage in Australasia was considered a momentous occasion in the United States, prompting well-known figures – such as renowned social reformer Jessie Ackermann, Boston suffragist Maud Park Wood and feminist and prohibitionist Josephine Henry – to consider the potential impact of this development on their own region. See M. Lake, 'State socialism for Australian mothers: Andrew Fisher's radical maternalism in its international and local contexts', *Labour History*, cii (2012), 55–70.

[60] For an extended discussion of loyal Australian women's anxieties, see the chapter 'Shaming British-Australia', in Crozier-De Rosa, *Shame and the Anti-Feminist Backlash*, pp. 107–30.

British anti-suffragists and the embarrassment of colonial naivety

Directives that the British should follow the lead of Australians – whether mock or genuine, emanating from the Irish or the Australians – indicated a belief that political matters in the imperial centre and the colonial peripheries were of equal importance. Across the globe, many reformers reacted positively to Australian social and political reform 'experiments'.[61] As we will see below, British anti-suffragists, however, far from accepting this view, responded indignantly to claims emanating from the colonial peripheries that metropole and peripheries constituted equally important sites of empire. They were also utterly exasperated when they encountered proclamations not only of equality but of colonial superiority as indicated by attempts to get Britain to follow Australia's lead on the matter of democratic reform. Such naïve assertions, coming from the inexperienced colonists, embarrassed those more knowing politicians in the centre of the vast imperial network because they demonstrated the colonists' ignorance of what was certainly accepted wisdom in the metropole, namely that Britain was the essential heart of the Empire. It was the only responsible authority in the Empire. It was Britain's parental beneficence that allowed for the creation of white settler spaces in the Antipodes in the first place and, as its leading and ultimately successful role in the First World War showed, it was Britain's power that held the vast, bountiful but troublesome imperial network together.

Initially, British conservatives set about reminding the young Australian Commonwealth that it may have the freedom to perform social and political experiments, but that this could not be done in the much more serious imperial centre. Mindful not to offend their colonial 'cousins', they did so with emotional restraint.[62] In 1910, for example, the *Review* stated that while not meaning to 'disparage the experiments which have been made by our own Dominions and Colonies', no knowledgeable person would argue that such experiments would 'form any relevant guidance as to what is to take place here'.[63] It clarified that there was 'no real analogy' between granting women the right to vote in places like Utah or Colorado or Australia and

[61] Antoinette Burton, for example, has shown how reformers across a range of fields in Britain sought inspiration from developments and ideas emanating from the 'margins' of empire. See A. Burton, 'Rules of thumb: British history and "imperial culture" in nineteenth and twentieth-century Britain', *Women's History Review*, iii (1994), 483–501, at p. 486.

[62] It should be clarified that, whereas British anti-suffragists referred to Australians as their 'cousins' when denying that colony and metropole were of equal importance, their use of the prefix 'colonial' made it clear that 'cousins' were not equal, indeed that those from the colonies were of lesser importance than those from the centre.

[63] Quoting excerpts from anti-suffrage speeches made in the House of Commons in 1910 in *The Anti-Suffrage Review*, 21 Aug. 1910, pp. 6–13.

New Zealand and thinking about granting women the right to do so in a country like England.[64] The paper reminded its readers that Australia and New Zealand 'have, so far, been happily exempt from the graver problems of Empire'.[65]

Early in 1911, the *Review* reasserted its position by arguing that the Australian woman vote was nothing more than 'an idle compliment Australian men have paid their women'.[66] Not burdened with the onerous task of spreading civilization and modernity, as the British were, Australian men could choose to be so playfully chivalrous.[67] The paper urged readers to remember that Australia managed simply 'its own internal affairs for a sparse population, considerably less than the population of the County of London'. It had 'no questions of peace or war to decide, no India dependent upon it with a population of three hundred millions, entertaining Oriental ideas regarding women'.[68] Within a few months, the *Review*'s tone had become even more embittered: 'Our colonies, with their minor problems, with their remoteness from the complication and danger of the Old World, with their safety under the English flag, and their simpler conditions of life, might try experiments that her children could not ask of England'.[69]

The *Review* then relied on the words of prominent British imperialist and anti-suffragist Violet Markham to drive its point home.[70] Markham declared that granting women the right to vote in Britain – as in places like Australia and New Zealand – could never be in the nation's and the

[64] *The Anti-Suffrage Review*, 16 Mar. 1910, p. 3.

[65] *The Anti-Suffrage Review*, 16 Mar. 1910, p. 3.

[66] *The Anti-Suffrage Review*, 27 Feb. 1911, pp. 25–6. The *Review* made similar claims of New Zealand; Mrs Wentworth Stanley stated that she had lived in Australia and could assure her audience that the women did not work for the vote there. It was simply put in and passed. In New Zealand it was passed after a snap decision and went through by one vote. See *The Anti-Suffrage Review*, 5 May 1913, p. 105.

[67] For more on the interconnections between the British metropole and its empire, including the self-appointed mission of bearers of civilization, see: B. Porter, *The Absent-Minded Imperialists: Empire, Society, and Culture in Britain* (Oxford, 2004); S. Marks, 'History, the nation and empire: sniping from the periphery', *History Workshop Journal*, xxix (1990), 111–19; and K. Kumar, 'Nation and empire: English and British national identity in comparative perspective', *Theory and Society*, xxix (2000), 575–608.

[68] *The Anti-Suffrage Review*, 27 Feb. 1911, pp. 25–6.

[69] *The Anti-Suffrage Review*, 30 May 1911, p. 102.

[70] Markham was not only a committed anti-suffragist at this stage; she was also a dedicated imperialist, as demonstrated, for example, by her commitment to the imperialist organization the Victoria League (1901–present). For more on Markham, see E. Riedi, 'Options for an imperialist woman: the case of Violet Markham, 1899–1914', *Albion*, xxxii (2000), 59–84.

Empire's interests. It would only 'be a weakening and a disturbing element in government and in the exercise of sovereign power'.[71] As 'a woman', she stated, 'I say that it is an intolerable situation for a great nation and a great empire'.[72] The complex logistics of governing the Empire was the crucial factor. Women cannot 'take part in any share of the government of the three hundred and forty millions of coloured people who form the major portion of the population of the empire', she confirmed. All women were politically naïve. How then would they take on the responsibilities of the India Office and share in the government of 'those three hundred millions which people the great Dependency?'[73] There is 'no graver or more difficult problem which lies ahead for the British Empire than the development of the social and political relations of the coloured races under the flag', Markham asserted.[74] The irony here was, of course, that 'race' was used to exemplify British exceptionalism, completely eliding the fact that those women in the Empire who had the power to vote were actually living in settler-colonial states and voting on matters of race and race relations. Still, Markham went on: 'To give political power without full political experience is altogether too great and dangerous an experiment for such an empire as ours, just because we are an empire and not a laboratory for the experiments of cranks and of faddists.'[75] The implication was that cranks and faddists could, and did, experiment in less important sites of empire.

An emotional shift occurred in the pages of the *Review* in the face of repeated and sustained efforts to suggest that Britain follow Antipodean leads, that they mirror the ways of cranks and faddists. The relatively minor irritation of embarrassment evoked by such misguided comparisons gave way to the more pronounced feelings of anger and resentment, especially when it looked like a bill supporting the female franchise was going to be introduced. Similar to the way in which conservative Australian women had depicted the Irish, Australians and New Zealanders were portrayed as the pampered offspring of an overburdened parent. They should not, the *Review* asserted, foolishly ask that those in the mother country allow themselves the same liberties that they afforded themselves.

Through being compelled to reference the Australian woman voter – the very existence of whom was being used by rebellious subjects to undermine the supremacy of the metropolitan centre (as evidenced by Irish feminist

[71] *The Anti-Suffrage Review*, 21 Aug. 1910, pp. 18–19.

[72] *The Anti-Suffrage Review*, 21 Aug. 1910, pp. 18–19.

[73] *The Anti-Suffrage Review*, 21 Aug. 1910, pp. 18–19.

[74] *The Anti-Suffrage Review*, 21 Aug. 1910, pp. 18–19.

[75] *The Anti-Suffrage Review*, 21 Aug. 1910, pp. 18–19.

nationalists) – British conservatives laid bare the emotional and hierarchical politics of empire suffragism. The embarrassing claims of naïve colonial 'cousins' could be tolerated but, once these claims were given enough weight to threaten the hierarchy of relationships which characterized the British Empire, embarrassment turned to anger.

Conclusion

Imperial ties connected women across Britain, Ireland and Australia whether these women wanted them to or not. Whether loyal or disloyal, each group of national womanhood operated within the same imperial framework. Apart from the matter of suffrage, they were affected by similar, if not the same, legislation. They had to frame their aspirations by referencing existing assumptions, for instance, about their country's position on the hierarchical imperial spectrum or about the nature of British or non-British values. Knowledge was shared as ideas and values circulated around the Empire. Therefore, despite the many different circumstances shaping their individual national existences, these separate but linked communities of patriotic womanhood were often compelled to refer to each other when asserting their particular political aspirations.

Casting a discerning eye over the emotional dimensions of interactions between groups of politically active women of different nationalities at a crucial time in the development of the British Empire – as colonies variously morphed into loyal dominions or expressed dangerously revolutionary ideals – is a valuable way of not only understanding the leading role that emotions played in empire suffragism, but also of accessing the nature of shifting relations between sites of empire.

Looking through the lens of the emotions of suffragism, we can ascertain the inescapable impact that narratives about colonial shame had on feminist solidarity in Ireland. Whether they subscribed to the belief that the shamed Irish man's pride could only be restored through abstaining from suffragism or not, Irish feminists were forced to defend themselves from accusations that their feminist actions made them complicit in the ongoing colonizing process. The emotional politics of gender rendered their nationalism uncertain, in others' eyes if not their own, as they were compelled to explain why they were prioritizing their own rights over those of their disempowered nation. Australian women voters, many of whom had not wanted the vote, mediated an emotional terrain that included colonial anxiety and national pride. Their expressions of pride as enfranchised citizens of the Empire, considered by some to be dangerously close to assertions of colonial supremacy, forced British imperialists to reassert the hierarchy of empire. Through these reaffirmations, British anxieties about their place in a modernizing world are revealed. Through the waxing and waning of colonial shame and pride, as well as imperial embarrassment, indignation and anger, we can detect imperial-colonial relations in a state of transition. This heady mixture of emotions was not only instrumental in shaping the nature of empire politics; it also helped to reveal the localized nature of anxieties and aspirations which allows us to delve deeper into core-periphery flows and exchanges, and into the connections and disconnections formed between different groups of national womanhood across British imperial networks.

13. From Votes for Women to world revolution: British and Irish suffragettes and international communism, 1919–39

Maurice J. Casey

Introduction

In a diary entry for 18 August 1930, Charlotte Despard, the veteran suffrage campaigner and one of the founding members of the Women's Freedom League (WFL), recorded that she had met with 'Mrs. Bouvier', whom she described as 'an old friend of the suffrage time'.[1] In the years after the 1918 enactment of partial enfranchisement in Britain and Ireland, former stalwarts of the campaign for the vote regularly crossed paths amid their continued activism. What makes this 1930 reunion of Despard and Mrs Bouvier atypical, however, is where it took place: in Moscow, the crucible of the world revolution. The path that brought these two women together was not only a physical voyage across borders to Soviet Russia but also a shared political journey spanning across decades that began during the suffrage fight. Their involvement in communist networks was shaped by a re-engagement with their ancestral backgrounds, one Irish and the other Russian. In 1921, Eugenie Bouvier, formerly of the Lewisham branch of the Women's Social and Political Union (WSPU) and later the East London Federation of Suffragettes (ELFS), returned to Russia to take part in the construction of socialism in her home country. Meanwhile, Despard, whose family ancestry could be traced to Ireland, moved to Dublin to continue an energetic involvement in Irish republican, feminist and communist circles.

This encounter points to the history which this chapter seeks to narrate: the alternative political pathways outside the Communist Party which shaped how veterans of the suffrage struggle in Britain and Ireland

[1] Diary of a Visit to the USSR, Charlotte Despard, 18 Aug. 1930, Women's Library (hereafter WL), Papers of Charlotte Despard (hereafter CDP), Box FL558.

'From Votes for Women to World Revolution', in *The politics of women's suffrage: local, national and international dimensions,* ed. A. Hughes-Johnson and L. Jenkins (London, 2021), pp. 331–352.

engaged with international communism. Neither Bouvier nor Despard primarily channelled their activism through official Communist Parties.[2] Despard chiefly engaged with the networks of international communism through satellite organizations of Communist Parties that sought to rally sympathizers around causes such as prisoners' rights, famine relief, strike support, opposition to war and defence of the Soviet Union. Her arrival in Moscow was the result of her participation in the Irish section of one such group: the Friends of Soviet Russia. Bouvier's Moscow place of employment reflected her political commitment: the headquarters of the Communist International (Comintern), the organizing body of world Communist Parties. Engagement with Comintern auxiliary organizations and political emigration constituted two important means by which a number of suffrage veterans in Britain and Ireland engaged with international communism. This chapter explores this political activity through women involved in both the Irish and British movement. It examines both well-known figures, such as Despard and Hanna Sheehy Skeffington, alongside more obscure activists, such as Eugenie Bouvier and May O'Callaghan, both of whom were immigrant women active in the British movement. This array of activists is chosen to echo and complement Senia Pašeta's call to acknowledge the deep connection between the Irish and British suffrage movements.[3] This chapter also considers why the Comintern lacked an active policy of engaging with British and Irish feminism.

[2] Bouvier was briefly a member of the Soviet Communist Party but was purged in the Autumn of 1921; see E. Bouvier, Biographical Statement, c. 1921, *Rossiiskii Gosudartsvennyi Arkhiv Sotsial'no-Politischeskoi Istorii* (hereafter RGASPI) 405/65a/4042/1. Despard's biographer noted that she joined the CPGB after its foundation; see M. Mulvihill, *Charlotte Despard: A Biography* (London, 1989), p. 30. If this is the case, her membership may not have lasted long. Her obituary in the CPGB paper notes only that she was a 'good friend' of the Irish Party and makes no mention of her having been an official member of a Communist Party; see 'For two generations she was a rebel', *Daily Worker*, 11 Nov. 1939. Despard was present at the 1933 founding congress of the Communist Party of Ireland as an observer; see S. Byers, *Seán Murray: Marxist-Leninist and Irish Socialist Republican* (Sallins, 2015), p. 63. The text of the speech she delivered at the congress suggests she may have taken up membership at this point, but is not conclusive; see 'Pronounce to world we are communists', *Daily Worker*, 15 June 1933. One CPGB member recalling Despard in 1961 was doubtful that Despard had been a Party member; see Minnie Bowles to Teresa Billington-Greig, 3 Aug. 1961, WL, Teresa Billington Greig Papers, Box FL244, 7/TBG1/71. Finally, I found no file on Despard maintained among the Comintern cadre files held in RGASPI. One would expect to find such a file in the case of a prominent figure like Despard.

[3] S. Pašeta, 'Suffrage and citizenship in Ireland, 1912–18', paper presented at the Institute of Historical Research, University of London, 15 Nov. 2018 <https://humanities-digitallibrary.org/index.php/hdl/catalog/view/paseta/76/211-1> [accessed 31 Oct. 2019], p. 2.

While a growing historiography charts British and Irish women's engagement with liberal internationalism in the interwar period – such as activism through groups including the Women's International League for Peace and Freedom (WILPF) – less has been said about women's involvement with radical, communist-inspired internationalism, particularly in the Irish case.[4] Women within the Communist Party of Great Britain (CPGB) have been examined in studies by Sue Bruley, Karen Hunt and Matthew Worley.[5] Additionally, Kiera Wilkins's recent MA thesis charted the long career of Scottish CPGB member Helen Crawfurd to make the case that historiographical anti-communism and the lack of a transnational framework have obscured Crawfurd's contributions to the movements she participated in.[6] There is no focused study of women within the Communist Party of Ireland during the same period. This is not surprising. A miniscule number of women joined the small Irish communist groups that arose during this period. Although some prominent suffrage campaigners and feminists took up Communist Party membership after the foundation of the CPGB in 1920, notably Crawfurd, Dora Montefiore and Sylvia Pankhurst, the existing literature demonstrates that the experience of Communist Party membership was generally unattractive to veteran feminists.[7] This

[4] For Irish examples, see R. Cullen Owens, *A Social History of Women in Ireland, 1870–1970* (Dublin, 2005), pp. 108–54; M. Ward, 'Nationalism, pacifism, internationalism: Louie Bennett, Hanna Sheehy Skeffington, and the problems of "defining feminism"', in *Gender and Sexuality in Modern Ireland*, ed. A. Bradley and M. Gialanella Valiulis (Amherst, Mass., 1997), pp. 60–84. Elizabeth McKillen's research on the Irish left and the importance of 'Sinn Féinism' for American radicalism, particularly within the labour and women's movement, explores Irish-American internationalist ties; see E. McKillen, 'The Irish Sinn Féin movement and radical labor and feminist dissent in America, 1916–1921', *Labor: Studies in Working-Class History of the Americas*, xvi (2019), 11–37. For a recent account of British women's liberal internationalism with discussion of Ireland, see S. Hellawell, *Feminism, Pacifism and Internationalism: The Women's International League, 1915–1935* (unpublished PhD thesis, University of Northumbria, 2017).

[5] S. Bruley, *Leninism, Stalinism and the Women's Movement in Britain, 1920–1939* (New York and London, 1986); K. Hunt and M. Worley, 'Rethinking British Communist Party women in the 1920s', *Twentieth Century British History*, xv (2004), 1–27. See also J. Hannam and K. Hunt, *Socialist Women: Britain, 1880s to 1920s* (London, 2002), esp. pp. 179–80, 194–5.

[6] K. Wilkins, *Daring and Defiant: Helen Crawfurd (1877–1954), Scottish Suffragette and International Communist* (unpublished MA thesis, Central European University, 2019).

[7] Bruley noted that ten of the women delegates at the first Unity meeting of the CPGB were active in the pre-1918 women's movement; see Bruley, *Leninism, Stalinism*, p. 64, fn 13. For Pankhurst, see, for example, K. Connelly, *Sylvia Pankhurst: Suffragette, Socialist and Scourge of Empire* (London, 2013) and B. Winslow, *Sylvia Pankhurst: Sexual Politics and Political Activism* (London, 1996). Two recent biographical studies of Ellen Wilkinson have also explored her connections to the CPGB; see L. Beers, *Red Ellen: The Life of Ellen*

scholarship also indicates that many women whose political apprenticeship came in the form of Communist Party membership rejected the idea of organizing women separately from men, believing it would divert attention from the class struggle and potentially undermine their sense of being, first and foremost, proletarians just like their male comrades. To only explore the experiences of women who maintained membership of Communist Parties precludes us from understanding how international communism shaped the careers of many other suffrage campaign veterans. Exploring how suffrage veterans navigated revolutionary political pathways beyond Communist Party membership offers further insights into how activist careers were transformed in the aftermath of the campaign for women's suffrage, particularly how existing activist skillsets from the old cause could be transferred into new campaigns.[8]

Engagement with Comintern front organizations

British and Irish women played leading roles in a number of transnational initiatives established by the Comintern. Part bureaucratic apparatus and part revolutionary networking opportunity, the Comintern provided funding and theoretical guidance to the communist parties that emerged across the world. Yet it also played a role in establishing and directing transnational organizations that attracted non-party activists. Engagement with these auxiliary organizations of the Comintern proved a dynamic means for women with suffrage backgrounds to continue their activist careers. Importantly, the majority of British and Irish suffrage veterans who became involved in Comintern initiatives throughout the interwar period appear to have experienced early and ebullient enthusiasm for the Russian Revolution.[9] This enthusiasm was then channelled through the Comintern auxiliary organizations into forms of activism familiar to veterans of the

---

Wilkinson, Socialist, Feminist, Internationalist (Cambridge, Mass., 2017) and M. Perry, *'Red Ellen' Wilkinson: Her Ideas, Movements and World* (Manchester, 2014).

[8] For discussions of the aftermath of the campaign for women's suffrage, particularly how veterans of the campaign attempted to shape emerging historical narratives, see, for example, K. Cowman 'A footnote in history? Mary Gawthorpe, Sylvia Pankhurst, *the Suffragette Movement* and the writing of suffragette history', *Women's History Review*, xiv (2005), 447–66 and L. Jenkins, '"It wasn't like that at all": memory, identity and legacy in Jessie Kenney's *The Flame and the Flood*', *Women's History Review*, xxix (2020), 1034–53.

[9] Of the former suffragettes surveyed in my research, I have found only one exception to this rule. The Anglo-Irish suffragette Katherine Gillett-Gatty (1870–1952), previously of the WSPU and WFL, developed her communist sympathies in the 1930s through antifascist activism and travel in the Soviet Union.

suffrage struggle, such as famine relief efforts, political tourism and anti-imperialist initiatives.

In the aftermath of the Russian Revolution of 1917, socialists across the world, including many with ties to their national suffrage campaigns, became fascinated by developments in Soviet Russia.[10] Despard acts as a useful guide to the world of British and Irish feminist enthusiasm for the Russian Revolution, given that she regularly crossed the Irish Sea during her activist career. She was a vocal supporter of the Russian Revolution with a longstanding interest in the fates and ideals of Russian revolutionaries. When Tsar Nicholas II visited Britain in 1909, Despard recited an account of 'cruel treatment' meted out to Russian comrades fighting Tsarist tyranny to a Finsbury Park crowd.[11] Once the regime was overthrown in 1917, she wrote an open letter addressed to Russian women supporting their liberation.[12] She was also present at the Leeds Conference in June of that year, when British and Irish socialists gathered to welcome the Russian Revolution. Despard was elected at the conference to the 'Council of Workers and Soldiers' Delegates'.[13] In 1921, Despard relocated to Ireland. She later recalled hearing a voice telling her to travel to Ireland during a mass held in Nine Elms that acted as the catalyst for her deeper involvement in Irish politics.[14] She was already enmeshed in these circles through friendships with Irish feminists and a developing attachment to an Irish identity that she fully embraced during the Irish Revolution.[15]

Like Despard, many Irish socialists welcomed the Russian Revolution with enthusiasm during the early years of Soviet power and beyond. The conception that the Irish and Russian Revolutions were part of two distinct but complementary challenges to the international status quo was common within certain Irish radical circles and Irish feminists played a role in promoting this early solidarity with the Soviet cause. An early manifestation of Irish solidarity with the Bolsheviks came in the form of the Dublin-based Russian Revolution and Republic Committee, which included

[10] For American feminist responses, see J. L. Mickenberg, 'Suffragettes and Soviets: American feminists and the spectre of revolutionary Russia', *Journal of American History*, c (2014), 1021–51.

[11] 'The czar's visit', *Justice*, 24 July 1909.

[12] 'To the liberty loving women of Russia', Charlotte Despard, c. 1917, British Library Manuscripts Collection (hereafter BLMC), Samuel Solomonovich Koteliansky Papers, Vol. IX General Correspondence, 57.

[13] Council of Workers' and Soldiers' Delegates, *What Happened at Leeds* (London, 1917), p. 18.

[14] 'How I came to live in Ireland', *An Phoblacht*, 2 July 1932.

[15] Mulvihill, *Despard*, p. 132.

women involved with the Irish Women's Franchise League (IWFL), such as Margaret Connery and Cissie Cahalan.[16] The *Irish Citizen*, the journal of the IWFL, published regular reports on Bolshevik-inspired insurrections across Europe in the years after 1917 and hosted lecturers on revolutionary themes given by figures such as Sylvia Pankhurst and the American suffragist Alice Riggs Hunt.[17] The revolutionary winds from Petrograd also reached Irish activists abroad. Hanna Sheehy Skeffington, among the most prominent and resolute Irish feminists of the early twentieth century, was on a lecturing tour of the United States in 1917 and attended a meeting to welcome the Russian Revolution held in Madison Square Gardens.[18] In 1918, she informed an East Harlem audience that 'the Russians, the Jews and the Irish' were the 'three great revolutionary forces that would, in truth, make the world safe for democracy'.[19] Many of the Irish activists listed as supporters of early Irish-Soviet solidarity initiatives would later reappear on membership lists of Comintern auxiliary organizations.

March 1919 marked a watershed moment in the history of twentieth-century internationalism as revolutionaries gathered for the founding congress of the Comintern. From the early years of its existence, the Comintern directed an array of satellite groups, often referred to as 'front organizations' both by Cold War-era commentators and historians, that sought to rally sympathizers around causes including prisoners' rights, unemployment, hunger relief and anti-colonial campaigns.[20] The anti-communist aura of the term 'front' may suggest a misleading and even paranoid notion of these organizations as the terrifying tentacles of a Bolshevik octopus spreading outward from Moscow. Interrogating the

[16] 'Annual report', *Irish Citizen*, 5 Apr. 1919. Margaret Connery (1879–1956), born in Westport, Co. Mayo, and Cissie Cahalan (1876–1948), born in Cork city, were socialists, feminists and stalwart members of the IWFL.

[17] M. J. Casey, '"The future of feminism"? The Irish Women's Franchise League and the world revolution', *History Ireland: The Irish Revolution, 1919–21, A Global History* (Dublin, 2019), pp. 27–30.

[18] 'Emma Goldman obituary', *Distributive Worker*, Aug. 1940, reproduced in *Hanna Sheehy Skeffington: Suffragette and Sinn Féiner, Her Memoirs and Political Writings*, ed. M. Ward (Dublin, 2017), p. 375.

[19] 'Economic base of revolt in Ireland told', *The Call*, 19 Feb. 1918.

[20] K. Braskén, *The International Workers' Relief, Communism, and Transnational Solidarity: Willi Münzenberg in Weimar Germany* (Basingstoke, 2015), pp. 5–6. For a further discussion of this 'intermediate Empire of the Comintern', see B. H. Bayerlein, 'The "cultural international" as the Comintern's intermediate empire: international mass and sympathizing organisations beyond parties', in *International Communism and Transnational Solidarity: Radical Networks, Mass Movements and Global Politics, 1919–1939*, ed. Holger Weiss (Leiden, 2017), pp. 28–81.

concept of the 'front', Kasper Braskén argues that there is an analytical difference between a group that lured people to communism and one which provided 'already sympathising people the opportunity to engage themselves for the cause in cultural events, celebrations and protest campaigns'.[21] Nevertheless, the term retains its usefulness as a shorthand for non-party groups which acknowledges that their alignment with the Comintern shaped these organizations in important ways. While the Comintern was always connected to these groups through functions such as funding and political guidance, individuals within these organizations had scope for manoeuvre independent of Comintern dictates.[22]

The first such group to channel the energies of British and Irish suffrage veterans was the Workers' International Relief (WIR). Patrizia Dogliani noted that the WIR initially mobilized in a way that mirrored the League of Nations' early activities, continuing the wartime tradition of humanitarian aid.[23] Its earliest campaigns focused on organizing relief for the Russian famine of 1921–2 and alleviating hunger among German workers. The International Women's Secretariat (IWS), the organizing committee for women's propaganda in the Comintern's national sections, appears to have recognized the relevance of relief initiatives for mobilizing women comrades. Hertha Sturm, a German Comintern functionary, wrote to Dora Montefiore in 1922, advising her that a campaign for Russian famine relief was 'absolutely necessary' as a campaign which would 'be a practical way to get your female members together and make them active for a revolutionary task'.[24]

The secretary of the British section of the WIR was Helen Crawfurd, an early member of the CPGB who was appointed to the party's executive committee soon after joining and who had previously been active in the WSPU, the Women's Peace Crusade and the Independent Labour Party.[25]

[21] K. Braskén, *International Workers' Relief*, p. 6.

[22] For a discussion of scholarship on the front groups and the biographical and transnational turns in the historiography, see O. Drachewych, 'The communist transnational? Transnational studies and the history of the Comintern', *History Compass*, xvii (2019), 1–12. Valuable works that reflect this turn include L. Kirschenbaum, *International Communism and the Spanish Civil War: Solidarity and Suspicion* (Cambridge, 2015) and B. Studer, *The Transnational World of the Cominternians* (Basingstoke, 2015).

[23] P. Dogliani, 'The fate of socialist internationalism', in *Internationalisms: A Twentieth-Century History*, ed. G. Sluga and P. Clavin (Cambridge, 2017), p. 56.

[24] H. Sturm to D. Montefiore, 8 Jan. 1922, RGASPI 507/3/12/16-17.

[25] H. Corr, 'Crawfurd [*neé* Jack; *other married name* Anderson], Helen (1877–1954), suffragette and communist', *Oxford Dictionary of National Biography* <https://doi.org/10.1093/ref:odnb/40301> [accessed 10 July 2020].

Alongside Montefiore, she was one of the few suffrage veterans to enter into membership of the CPGB and attain a prominent position within the party in the 1920s. Crawfurd also played a role in assisting Despard, an old comrade from the suffrage struggle, in becoming more closely enmeshed in the networks of international communism. Other names that were listed on the British WIR's executive committee will be familiar to suffrage historians, including those of George Lansbury and Montefiore.[26] Rose Cohen, a young Communist from an East London Jewish background who had once been involved with Pankhurst's East London group, was also involved with the work of the WIR.[27]

The parallels between the WIR's activities and the operational mode of humanitarianism made it a fitting entry-point to the world of international communism for women with backgrounds in organizations such as the WILPF. The Irish section of the WIR, established in 1925, combined the organizational talents and activist histories of Despard and Crawfurd, both of whom were opponents of the war and early members of the WILPF. The Irish committee was tasked with raising funds for the relief of hungry peasants in deprived regions on Ireland's western coastline. Despard, alongside her long-time collaborators Maude Gonne, Sheehy Skeffington and Crawfurd, in addition to the temperamental Irish Labour figure Jim Larkin, helped the effort as prominent and recognizable organizers and supporters.[28] A WIR bulletin described the funds raised for the Irish initiative as poor, citing a 'lack of publicity' as the reason.[29] While the WIR in Ireland was not a resounding success on its own terms, it nonetheless set a precedent; front groups in Ireland with the keen involvement of Despard and her collaborators in Britain would succeed in bringing women activists into a Comintern-inspired initiative.

Both Crawfurd and Despard helped organize another initiative that brought former suffragettes towards open praise of Soviet-style socialism.

[26] The executive committee names are listed on the headed notepaper of the WIR; see, for example, WIR Circular Letter, 27 Feb. 1925, John Johnson Collection, Pollard Box 1, Bodleian Library.

[27] WIR Circular Letter, 27 Feb. 1925, John Johnson Collection, Pollard Box 1, Bodleian Library.

[28] *Workers International Pictorial*, Apr. 1925; 'Russia's gift to Ireland', *Sunday Worker*, 2 Aug. 1925. For further overviews of the WIR and its Irish committee's activities, see A. Grant, 'Workers to the rescue: workers' international relief in Ireland, 1925', *History Ireland*, xix (2011), 38–41 and Wilkins, *Daring and Defiant*, pp. 119–28.

[29] WIR National Conference Report, 19 Apr. 1925, Bodleian Libraries, John Johnson Collection, Pollard Box 4, CPGB Folder.

In 1930, the Irish section of the Friends of Soviet Russia was established, the national branch of an organization that already existed in Britain with Crawfurd as a member.[30] Despard was involved in directing the Irish section.[31] This section attracted a respectable number of prominent women from Irish feminist and republican circles, including Sheehy Skeffington, Gonne, Margaret Connery, Kathleen Lynn, Sidney Gifford and Rosamond Jacob. In a recent article on Harry Kernoff, a Jewish Dubliner and artist who was a member of the society, Elaine Sisson also situated the group within a lively Irish intelligentsia interested in cultural modernism and international artistic currents.[32] From the late 1920s through to the late 1930s, there was a broader publishing phenomenon of Soviet travelogues authored by well-known figures, including accounts by the American writer Theodore Dreiser, the Irish novelist Liam O'Flaherty and the suffragist and journalist Cicely Hamilton.[33] Membership of the 'Friendship' organizations provided an exciting opportunity to undertake the journey made popular in these accounts. Sheehy Skeffington informed her son ahead of her trip that she was 'up to my eyes in Russia, reading up stuff', citing 'women and children, prisons, art, literature, theatre and education' as aspects of Soviet civilization which interested her.[34]

In 1930 and 1931, two delegations departed from Ireland on their way to the Soviet Union. These delegations included veterans of the IWFL such as Connery, who travelled in 1931, and Sheehy Skeffington, who, along with Despard and her old comrade Crawfurd, travelled with the 1930 delegation. Angela Kershaw has noted that, for French feminists, travel to the USSR fulfilled a similar function as travel to international feminist congresses, providing opportunities to conduct feminist research into the condition of women in other countries and provide a means of making important

[30] M. David-Fox, *Showcasing the Great Experiment: Cultural Diplomacy & Western Visitors to the Soviet Union, 1921–1941* (Oxford, 2012), p. 83.

[31] Circular Letter to Friendship Society Members, Charlotte Despard, 4 Apr. 1931, National Library of Ireland (hereafter NLI), Sheehy Skeffington Papers (hereafter SSP), MS 41,178/71.

[32] E. Sisson, 'Designing modernism: Harry Kernoff, Russia, and postindependence Ireland', *Éire-Ireland*, lii (2017), 31–56.

[33] T. Dreiser, *Dreiser Looks at Russia* (New York, 1928); L. O'Flaherty, *I Went to Russia* (London, 1931); C. Hamilton, *Modern Russia as Seen by an Englishwoman* (London, 1934). These are just a few examples of a much wider publishing phenomenon of interwar Soviet travelogues.

[34] Hanna Sheehy-Skeffington to Owen Sheehy-Skeffington, 24 July 1930, NLI, SSP, MS 40,484/5.

contacts.[35] Much the same can be said of the Irish feminist delegates. Despard, for example, spoke with many other foreign delegates during her journey and even addressed a meeting at which Nadezhda Krupskaia, a leading Bolshevik and the widow of Lenin, also spoke.[36] Sheehy Skeffington, meanwhile, conducted research that formed the basis of lectures upon her return.[37] Importantly for those seeking to refute hostile press reports of Bolshevik iniquity, journeys to the USSR converted experience into political propaganda, providing returned delegates with the capability to refute anti-communist reports with the supposedly superior evidence of lived experience.

In addition to political tourism and famine relief, the broad political banners of anti-imperialism and antifascism provided further impetus for the development of groups backed by the Comintern. The League Against Imperialism, a vibrant Comintern-backed organization that attracted a wide swath of progressives, intellectuals and anti-colonial activists, had sections in Britain and Ireland. The Irish section was supported by the likes of Despard and Sheehy Skeffington.[38] British and Irish feminist supporters also joined the Women's World Committee Against War and Fascism, which developed from an August 1934 anti-war conference in Paris. Despard was one of the organization's sponsors and Sylvia Pankhurst was treasurer of its British section.[39] Unable to attend the Paris conference, Despard attended a parallel Sheffield gathering organized by the CPGB, later reporting her experience to a meeting held in Dublin.[40]

Why did these Comintern-linked groups attract certain women activists, particularly women in Ireland? The answer can partly be found by looking to the political space open to them. In the aftermath of enfranchisement and the Irish revolution, the IWFL, which had provided many Irish

[35] A. Kershaw, 'The new Soviet woman and the French debate on gender in the 1920s', in *French Political Travel Writing in the Inter-war Years: Radical Departures*, ed. M. Cornick, M. Hurcombe and A. Kershaw (New York, 2017), p. 126.

[36] Diary of a Visit to the USSR, Charlotte Despard, 1 Sept. 1930, WL, CDP, Box FL558.

[37] For Sheehy Skeffington's lectures on Russia, see Lecture Notes by Hanna Sheehy Skeffington on her Visit to the Soviet Union, c. 1930, NLI, SSP, MS 24,163 (ii).

[38] K. O'Malley, *Ireland, India and Empire: Indo-Irish Radical Connections, 1919–1964* (Manchester, 2008), esp. pp. 32–41; M. Ward, *Hanna Sheehy Skeffington: A Life* (Cork, 1997), p. 295.

[39] J. Liddington, *The Road to Greenham Common: Feminism and Anti-militarism in Britain Since 1820* (New York, 1989), p. 157; Sylvia Pankhurst to the Chairman of the Women's Committee Against War & Fascism, 17 Dec. 1935, BLMC, Estelle Sylvia Pankhurst Papers, Add MS 88925/9/2.

[40] 'War against war and fascism', Report, 17 Sept. 1934, RGASPI 495/89/92/6.

feminists with not only a political cause that transcended national borders but also a social space that welcomed itinerant radicals, fell into abeyance. Groups such as the Irishwomen's International League, the Irish branch of the WILPF, provided some lines of continuity with this transnational mode of feminist activism, but for those like Despard who wanted to explicitly link national and feminist campaigns to an international socialist struggle the Comintern-backed groups often proved more ideologically suitable to their political ideals than organizations such as the WILPF. The Irish branch of the WILPF was continuously fraught by divisions, particularly surrounding the issue of the Irish national question, which republican members considered unresolved.[41] Membership of front groups also required less subordination to a political line than party membership, thus proving attractive to those of a more idiosyncratic radical outlook than orthodox Marxism-Leninism. 'Communist Party member' was an earned identity, one which consumed significant amounts of activist energies through its mandated commitment to study and political discipline. Open party membership could incite persecution, certainly in the Irish Free State, where a continuous red scare ebbed and flowed throughout much of the twentieth century. Sheehy Skeffington suggested in a letter to her son following her 1930 tour through the USSR that it could even be seen as the preserve of a younger activist generation: 'I am not a communist and not likely to be. If I were 21 I might!'[42]

Emigration to Soviet Russia and employment in Comintern institutions

The women who sailed from the London docks towards Leningrad from the late 1920s and into the 1930s to see the great Soviet experiment for themselves were not the first veterans of the suffrage campaign to arrive in the country. Besides those like Montefiore, Crawfurd and Pankhurst who had travelled to Soviet Russia in the early years of the revolutionary state, there were a small number of women with a background in British and Irish suffrage campaigns who travelled to Moscow to work for Comintern institutions. This small wave of women emigrants to the Soviet Union were enticed by a mixture of idealism and employment opportunity. In the case of American women, Julia L. Mickenberg stated that what drew them to the Soviet Union was its embodied promise of 'the good life' and

[41] For an overview of the activities of the Irishwomen's International League, see R. Cullen Owens, *A Social History of Women in Ireland*, pp. 108–54.

[42] Hanna Sheehy Skeffington to Owen Sheehy Skeffington, 10 Sept. 1930, NLI, SSP, MS, 40,484/5.

its inclusion of women's emancipation in that promise.[43] There was also a chance to find meaningful employment in the workers' state. Kevin Morgan and Gidon Cohen have suggested that a number of talented, well-educated women from the male-dominated CPGB may have viewed the new institutions of international communism in Moscow as a less-restrictive world where they could carry out work for the cause.[44] After its foundation, the Comintern required linguistically talented and secretarially trained workers to staff its bureaucratic apparatus. Women activists whose cosmopolitan careers and educations had provided them with a wide roster of languages and whose skills had been applied to the administrative ends of their movement were particularly useful employees for a vast revolutionary organization. Employment as a technical worker in the Comintern thus provided an opportunity for exciting and politically committed work in the revolutionary atmosphere of an experimental society.

Almost all of the suffrage veterans in the Comintern's headquarters were employed in the same section, the Press Bureau, and passed through the same central Moscow office building. An important part of the Comintern apparatus, the Press Bureau was formed shortly after the founding congress of the Comintern in 1919 and tasked with organizing propaganda and publishing documents relating to the Comintern and the Soviet Communist Party in different languages.[45] Each of the suffrage veterans employed in this bureau shared another commonality; they were all past members of Sylvia Pankhurst's ELFS. The socialist and anti-imperialist outlook which characterized this organization doubtlessly shaped these women's ideological development, but it is perhaps just as illuminating to explore how the small number of women who passed from East London through to Moscow maintained similar organizational roles as they transitioned from the suffrage movement to the Comintern.

Among the early women workers employed by the Comintern was the aforementioned Eugenie Bouvier, otherwise known as 'Jeannie' and often referenced in the suffrage press as 'J. A. Bouvier'. Bouvier was born into a wealthy St Petersburg family in 1865 and in 1888 married Paul Emile Bouvier, an Italian-born language teacher, with whom she emigrated to

[43] J. L. Mickenberg, *American Girls in Red Russia: Chasing the Soviet Dream* (Chicago, Ill., 2017), p. 31.

[44] K. Morgan and G. Cohen, 'Rose Cohen', in *Dictionary of Labour Biography*, Vol. XI, ed. K. Gildard, D. Howell and N. Kirk (London, 2003), p. 34.

[45] G. M. Adibekov, E. N. Shkhnazarova and K. P. Shirinya, *Organizatsionnaia Struktura Kominterna, 1919–1943* (Moscow, 1997), pp. 9–10.

England.[46] Remembered in Pankhurst's *The Suffragette Movement* as 'that brave, persistent Russian', Bouvier was among the first militants to take part in window-breaking at Westminster in 1909.[47] Bouvier was also involved with the Men's Political Union for Women's Enfranchisement and was listed as its acting secretary in a 1913 issue of *The Suffragette*.[48] She joined Sylvia Pankhurst's East London Federation in the early years of its operation, following its split from the broader WSPU in 1913. By 1916, she was listed as a committee member of Pankhurst's group, then operating as the Workers' Suffrage Federation (WSF).[49]

As an anti-war socialist, Bouvier welcomed the Russian Revolution of 1917 and addressed public meetings on the Revolution under WSF auspices.[50] Her support for the emancipatory promise of the Bolsheviks did not falter even when her own social class entered the Revolution's crosshairs. The Christian Socialist Conrad Noel recalled Bouvier stating that the Russian authorities ought to have taken away her family's wealth 'years ago, and from all of us who lived on the backs of the people'.[51] When Pankhurst established a pro-Soviet propaganda outfit, the People's Russian Information Bureau, Bouvier joined its team while also helping Bolshevik representatives in Britain with translation work.[52] In 1921, Bouvier travelled from London to continue work as a translator for the Comintern in Soviet Russia.[53] That Bouvier, widowed and approaching retirement age, would swap a comfortable life in Lewisham for impoverished post-Revolutionary Moscow, suggested the importance of political belief in encouraging her return to Russia.

Like many other arrivals at the Comintern, Bouvier was required to submit a biographical statement and questionnaire that charted her social and political background. Interestingly, of all the Comintern personnel files

[46] 'From Russia to Rushey Green and back – Eugenia Bouvier, a Lewisham suffragette', *Running Past* <https://runner500.wordpress.com/2018/02/07/eugenia-bouvier-a-lewisham-suffragette/> [accessed 6 Jan. 2020].

[47] E. S. Pankhurst, *The Suffragette Movement: An Intimate Account of Persons and Ideals* (1931, rpt. London, 1977), p. 523; A. Rosen, *Rise Up Women! The Militant Campaign of the Women's Social and Political Union, 1903–1914* (1974, rpt. Abingdon, 2013), p. 120.

[48] 'Men's Political Union', *The Suffragette*, 23 May 1913.

[49] 'Join the Workers' Suffrage Federation!', *Woman's Dreadnought*, 18 Mar. 1916. The group became known as the Workers' Socialist Federation in 1917.

[50] 'What's on? W.S.F. fixtures outdoor', *Workers' Dreadnought*, 5 May 1917; 'Federation notes', *Workers' Dreadnought*, 28 July 1917.

[51] C. Noel, *Conrad Noel: An Autobiography* (London, 1945), p. 108.

[52] Evgeniia Bouvier, biographical statement, c. 1921, RGASPI 495/65a/4042/1.

[53] 'Moscow at last', *Workers' Dreadnought*, 25 June 1921.

of suffrage veterans examined for this study, Bouvier's provides the only statement that explicitly threads a feminist background through a personal history of socialist activism. Although she referred to herself as an active suffragist socialist in the statement, Bouvier clarified certain moments in her activist history, perhaps to underline her revolutionary credentials to her employer. For example, describing her arrests during the war years, she declared that she had demonstrated against the war 'not from a pacifist, but from a socialist point of view' ('*ne v pasifistskoi a s sotsialisticheskoi tochki zreniia*').[54] An ideology committed to class war was not one which countenanced absolutist pacifism.

Another activist who followed a path from the ELFS suffrage campaign to employment in the Comintern was May O'Callaghan. Born to a middle-class Catholic family in the Irish coastal town of Wexford in 1881, O'Callaghan was the cultured, well-educated and linguistically talented sub-editor of Pankhurst's journal the *Woman's* (later *Workers'*) *Dreadnought* during the war.[55] O'Callaghan was hired by the Comintern in 1924 and employed in the Press Department, eventually becoming head of its English translation section.[56] In the memoir of Joseph Freeman, a leading figure of the interwar American literary left, O'Callaghan appears as 'O.B.', the author's boss in the Comintern who had 'spent a number of years in the suffrage fight under the Pankhursts' before taking up the important and skilled work of Comintern translation.[57] She remained resident in Moscow from 1924 until 1928, after which she returned to London to assist Nellie Cohen, a comrade who had served as Pankhurst's wartime secretary, with her pregnancy. O'Callaghan was never a card-carrying Communist Party member – a fact which allowed her to remain in Moscow for an extended period and immerse herself in emigrant communist life, rather than being recalled home to assist a national Communist Party.

Other women with ties to Pankhurst's ELFS also found employment in Moscow. Rose Cohen and Violet Lansbury, both of whom can be found featured in a photograph of a 1916 pageant organized by the ELFS, found secretarial-style work in Moscow during the 1920s.[58] Both Cohen and Lansbury remained in Soviet Russia for many years. Lansbury returned to

[54] Evgeniia Bouvier, biographical statement, c. 1921, RGASPI 495/65a/4042/1.

[55] Maurice J. Casey, 'O'Callaghan, May', *Dictionary of Irish Biography*, ed. J. McGuire and J. Quinn (Cambridge, 2019) <http://dib.cambridge.org/viewReadPage.do?articleId=a10133> [accessed 10 Jan. 2020].

[56] *Anketa*, May O'Callaghan, 9 July 1924, RGASPI 495/218/31/1.

[57] J. Freeman, *An American Testament: A Narrative of Rebels and Romantics* (London, 1938), p. 433.

[58] The photograph also features two other young East Londoners who would become CPGB members: Rose's sister Nellie and Joan Beauchamp; see R. Taylor, *In Letters of*

London in the late 1930s while in 1937 Cohen was among the many political emigrants in the USSR who lost their lives in the Stalinist Terror.

Ethel 'Molly' Murphy (*neé* Morris), once an organizer for the Sheffield branch of the WSPU, provides another example of a suffrage veteran who emigrated to Moscow. However, Murphy's path is atypical in that the catalyst for her emigration was marital commitment rather than employment prospects. In 1920, Murphy was working as a nurse when she received a visit from J. T. Murphy, a past admirer who had once frequented the WSPU shop where she worked. He outlined the revolutionary activities he had undertaken since they last spoke, then asked her to marry him before he was due to return to Russia.[59] In a memoir first drafted in the early 1960s and published in 1998, Molly stated that she knew little about revolutionary socialism before her reunion with J. T., but believed that 'the same statesmen who had denounced us suffragettes before the war had turned on the Russian Revolution possibly as stupidly as they had turned on our movement and might be just as wrong about the Russian Revolution as they had been about me'.[60] Moved by the stories of famine in the newly established state, Molly agreed to J. T.'s proposal and joined the path towards political emigration through marriage rather than ancestral return or employment opportunity evident in the cases of Bouvier and O'Callaghan.[61] After several weeks on Soviet territory, Molly returned to Britain in 1921 to give birth to a son, Gordon. Molly, along with husband and child, returned to Moscow once more in 1926, remaining in Russia while J. T. worked as the CPGB representative on the Comintern executive.[62] Upon her return from Moscow in 1928, she became involved in CPGB activities in Hackney.[63]

The administrative and linguistic skills that made women such as O'Callaghan and Bouvier valuable to the suffrage movement were the same qualities that made them useful employees in the Comintern apparatus. June Hannam and Karen Hunt have noted that in the early days of British Communism women were likely to attend Comintern congresses as

Gold: The Story of Sylvia Pankhurst and the East London Federation of the Suffragettes in Bow (London, 1993), p. 20.

59 M. Murphy, *Suffragette and Socialist: An Autobiography* (Salford, 1998), pp. 64–7.

60 Murphy, *Suffragette and Socialist*, p. 65. Darlington noted that this autobiography was ghost-written by J. T. Murphy; see R. Darlington, *The Political Trajectory of J. T. Murphy* (Liverpool, 1998), p. xxiii.

61 Murphy, *Suffragette and Socialist*, p. 66.

62 Darlington, *J. T. Murphy*, pp. 87–8, 142, 151–2.

63 Hunt and Worley, 'Rethinking British Communist Party women', p. 7.

technical workers and translators, rather than as fully accredited delegates.[64] While it may have been more prestigious in contemporary terms to arrive as a delegate, technical workers and translators were enormously important for the everyday functioning of the Comintern. They were administrators tasked with the crucial work of guiding the bureaucratic management of worldwide social revolution. The suffrage movement, as Susan Pedersen recently noted, 'needed the fanatics, but it needed editors and accountants and printers and public speakers as well'.[65] This was similarly the case with the international communist movement – and, indeed, all large-scale projects for social transformation.

Tracing how those involved in the technical management of the suffrage struggle transferred their skillset to another movement is a further means by which we can understand post-enfranchisement activist trajectories. Yet, as Mickenberg's work on American women who travelled to Soviet Russia has suggested, a focused biographical case study of women who arrived in Soviet Russia as political emigrants often uncovers certain peculiarities and complexities of their experience.[66] While finding commonalities between women such as Bouvier, O'Callaghan, Cohen, Lansbury and Murphy is useful, it is perhaps just as valuable to consider them as discrete biographical case studies whose motivations for emigration and lives in the Soviet Union were determined by factors such as family attachments, degrees of ideological commitment and linguistic capabilities. In drawing out such specificities, we can write further histories of women's involvement in international communism beyond the relationship between Party women and the Party structure.

The view from the Comintern

Retaining our vantage point from the Comintern headquarters in Moscow, we can ask: did the women's section of the Comintern, headed by Clara Zetkin and tasked with promoting agitation among women in national communist parties, actively engage with feminist movements in Britain and Ireland? The simple answer is no. This should not surprise us. Revolutionaries such as Alexandra Kollontai, often regarded as the leading Bolshevik theorist of women's liberation, consistently warned that a 'bourgeois feminist' programme would mislead the working class into believing that society was divided along lines of gender rather than class. Feminist conscripts into the world of communism were therefore judged

[64] Hannam and Hunt, *Socialist Women*, p. 179.

[65] S. Pedersen, 'A knife to the heart', *London Review of Books*, xl (2018), 10.

[66] Mickenberg, *American Girls in Red Russia.*

more on the basis of what they had done for the workers rather than what they had achieved for women. Likewise, their activism was to proceed on the basis that women would be rallied around the concerns of their class, rather than the specific difficulties they encountered as women confronting a patriarchal society. Communist women's sections could even adopt an oppositional position towards the wider women's movement. A 1928 CPGB women's section report listed tasks such as 'fight against feminism' and 'fight against pacifism'.[67] Similarly, a 1930 meeting of the same section regarding articles for the party press included the suggestion of an article on the role of 'Women's Pacifist Organisation and the necessity for fighting same'.[68] There is little in these files to suggest a conscious campaign to recruit feminists or, indeed, coordinated efforts to make use of those that did come into its grasp.

Yet there was an attempt made by leading women within the international communist movement – such as Kollontai and Clara Zetkin – to establish methods and propaganda that could appeal specifically to women, an attempt which took the institutional form of the IWS. Founded in 1920 on the eve of the Third Comintern Congress, the IWS attempted to organize its work in its early years through a network of women 'correspondents' with two sections, one in Moscow and the other in Berlin.[69] The first woman delegated from Britain to attend an International Communist Women's Conference was Norah Smyth, a close ally of Sylvia Pankhurst and previously a member of the WSPU then later the ELFS, who travelled to Soviet Russia in 1921.[70] Following Pankhurst's expulsion from the CPGB, contact between Britain and the IWS was conducted largely through Montefiore and Crawfurd. From the early liaisons between the IWS and these two veteran feminist correspondents onwards, the tensions and ambiguities of a women's section operating within a movement that denied the relevance of separate women's concerns can be seen. In 1921, a German communist working for the IWS, likely Hertha Sturm, argued in response to Crawfurd and Montefiore's plans for women's circles within the CPGB that it 'contradicts our principles to organize women separately from men'.[71] How could the IWS, an adjunct

[67] 'Statement for Comrade Moirova, made by Phillis Neal', 30 Oct. 1928, RGASPI 507/3/18/204.

[68] 'Minutes of Women's Department Meeting', 20 May 1930, RGASPI 507/3/22/38.

[69] J. J. Marie, 'The women's section of the Comintern, from Lenin to Stalin', in *The Political and Historical Encyclopaedia of Women*, ed. C. Fauré (London, 2003), p. 432.

[70] Letter from 'TW', 31 June 1921, RGASPI 495/198/841/2.

[71] Unnamed German communist to Dora Montefiore and Helen Crawfurd, 8 Jan. 1922, RGASPI 507/3/12/14. Emphasis in original.

organization of the Comintern dedicated to work among women, justify its existence in a movement that refuted sex-based organizing in favour of class unity? This was a tension the IWS proved incapable of resolving. In 1926, the quasi-independent Secretariat was abolished and replaced with a Women's Department directly under the control of the Comintern Executive.

Despite early members of the CPGB recruited from the suffrage movement, particularly its militant strands and the revolutionary confines of East London, the Party largely failed to attract prominent feminist campaigners into its membership. Documents from the 1920s regularly feature Dora Montefiore and Helen Crawfurd, yet also evidence the tensions that impeded their work within the women's section of the CPGB. Montefiore divided working women in Britain into two tendencies, one being those 'who cannot be got at through a pamphlet' and the other being women who 'are quite advanced in their thinking because they have been for years organized inside the Labour Party, the Cooperative of the Railway Women's Guilds or in some of the old Suffrage societies'.[72] Continuing, Montefiore contrasted herself with Crawfurd. She noted that because she had spent more time on the Executive Committee of the CPGB than Crawfurd, she had realized that while most members found women useful at election time and took their subscriptions, 'when it is a question of giving them any control – that is another matter'.[73] Given that Montefiore reported such an atmosphere, it is unsurprising that the front groups could prove better capable of attracting veteran feminist members than the party itself.

Interestingly, the folders reveal that Crawfurd did attempt to create a link between Communist women and feminist activists. In December 1929, Crawfurd wrote a letter asking that her comrades help to fulfil a request made to her by the prominent Scottish feminist Chrystal Macmillan. A month earlier, Macmillan had written to Crawfurd requesting a Russian attendee for a League of Nations conference, noting that: 'You, I know, are in touch with the present regime, and a keen feminist, and one who understands the importance of working on non-party lines where women's questions are concerned.'[74] Forwarding this letter, Crawfurd wrote a request that she wished to be passed on to the Comintern: 'It may seem possibly to some of you a small matter and of little importance to associate with these middle-class women ... Personally I think it would be very valuable

[72] Dora Montefiore to IWS, 30 Apr. 1922, RGASPI 507/3/12/47.

[73] Dora Montefiore to IWS, 30 Apr. 1922, RGASPI 507/3/12/48.

[74] Chrystal Macmillan to Helen Crawfurd, 27 Nov. 1929, RGASPI 507/3/19/264.

and a means of getting information to them' denied by the ordinary press.[75] Crawfurd's suggestion was to arrange for Kollontai, by then a prominent member of the Soviet diplomatic corps, to attend the conference.[76] Suffrage veterans who took up Communist Party membership could retain their connections to the 'diversionary' feminism which they were encouraged to jettison. While Harry Pollitt, a leading figure in the CPGB, recognized Macmillan as a possible 'useful contact', Crawfurd's tone in sending the request – immediately doubtful that her comrades would see the value in the meeting – also reflected the wider failure of either the Comintern or the CPGB to fully exploit its veteran feminist campaigners through encouraging them to engage women beyond the revolutionary fold.[77] Additionally, Macmillan's decision to extend an invitation to Kollontai is itself suggestive, reflecting how a non-radical like Macmillan was nonetheless interested in the perspectives and participation of a revolutionary such as Kollontai.

The names associated with the pre-1918 British women's movements gradually disappear from the letters, branch reports and pamphlets held in the diminishing Comintern Women's Department folders on Britain from the early 1920s to 1939.[78] While this may in part be due to activist exhaustion, an unwillingness to commit to a new cause after decades of struggle or the simple factor of advanced age, there appears to have been a wider failure to attract into the party a younger generation of activists with backgrounds in feminist organizations. One interesting exception to this rule can be found in the Comintern personnel file of the Irish activist Claire Madden. She wrote a biographical statement in 1936 when she was a librarian at Marx House associated with the Holborn branch of the CPGB and the Women's World Committee Against War and Fascism. In the statement, Madden described rebelling against her Unionist father during her childhood and listed her education at Manchester University and associations with the Six Point Group and St Joan's Social and Political Alliances.[79] Her path towards radical politics developed from a determination to join 'some

[75] Helen Crawfurd, likely writing to CPGB Executive or Comintern Women's Department, 29 Dec. 1929, RGASPI 507/3/19/258.

[76] Helen Crawfurd, likely writing to CPGB Executive or Comintern Women's Department, 29 Dec. 1929, RGASPI 507/3/19/259.

[77] Harry Pollitt to Lily Webb, 1 Jan. 1929, RGASPI 507/3/19/266.

[78] The Comintern Women's Department maintained fifteen folders on Britain, ranging in size from roughly fifty pages to several hundred and covering a period from the foundation of the CPGB to the late 1930s; see RGASPI 507/3/11-26. There are two brief folders on Ireland held among the files of the same department; see RGASPI 507/3/83-84.

[79] Kathleen May Claire de la Cherois Madden, biographical statement, 11 July 1936, RGASPI 495/198/424/1-2.

anti-Fascist organisation' after reading about Nazi violence while on holiday in September 1933.[80] Madden noted that she 'thought of [the] Communist Party because [I] believed Mrs. Despard (for whom [I] had great admiration) to be communist'.[81] Madden retained ties to her background in feminist organizations, editing, for example, a 1946 pamphlet titled 'Dorothy Evans and the Six Point Group'.[82] Yet even this political biography of a post-1918 feminist and communist seemingly owed a debt of influence to Despard's own earlier defence of the communist cause.

The CPGB's limited success in drawing prominent women activists into the party such as Crawfurd and Montefiore can be traced to their pre-1918 ties to socialist movements, rather than the Comintern's commitment to developing propaganda aimed at women. This commitment was never viewed as a priority by the Comintern. Indeed, it was rapidly marginalized as a priority over the course of the 1920s and 1930s. As Geoff Eley noted, the CPGB let a valuable chance to build on this relationship between the prewar women's movement and its early membership pass, reflecting both 'the gender blindness of the socialist tradition and the limiting effects of the tightened discipline the Comintern was imposing on national Communisms'.[83] Comintern files hold few surprises for scholars of the British women's movement and its relation to socialism and communism, although they will contain documents of interest to those working on the careers of women such as Montefiore and Crawfurd and insights into the backgrounds of more obscure activists, such as Claire Madden. The files of the Comintern's women's section ultimately provide further evidence for the conclusion that the Communist Parties themselves largely proved a cold house for suffrage veterans.

Conclusion

By the outbreak of the Second World War, international communism no longer channelled the energies of the veterans of the earlier struggle for women's suffrage in Britain and Ireland. This was partly due to the death of Despard at the age of ninety-five in November 1939. Despite her advanced

[80] Kathleen May Claire de la Cherois Madden, biographical statement, 11 July 1936, RGASPI 495/198/424/1-2.

[81] Kathleen May Claire de la Cherois Madden, biographical statement, 11 July 1936, RGASPI 495/198/424/1-2.

[82] *Dorothy Evans and the Six Point Group*, ed. Claire Madden (London, 1946).

[83] G. Eley, 'From welfare politics to welfare states: women and the socialist question', in *Women and Socialism, Socialism and Women: Europe Between the Two World Wars*, ed. H. Gruber and P. M. Graves (Oxford, 1998), p. 524.

age, she had remained an energetic promoter of a politics that crossed the Irish Sea and stood at the intersection of feminism, communism and Irish republicanism. Yet there was also the factor of the Soviet Union's damaged international reputation as a result of the Molotov-Ribbentrop pact, which fundamentally undermined the antifascist credentials that had strengthened and extended international communism's appeal during the 1930s. The show trials of leading Old Bolsheviks also constituted a macabre spectacle and a public component of the Stalinist terror that consumed hundreds of thousands of lives during the late 1930s, including the life of one ELFS veteran, Rose Cohen.[84] Franco's victory in the Spanish Civil War and the collapse of the Spanish Republican government was also a demoralizing experience for the international left. The Comintern had surrendered much of its world revolutionary ambitions by this point while its Women's Department had ceased to operate in any meaningful sense years before. Those who transitioned from suffrage to enfranchisement lived to see one of their political ideals enacted: votes for women. But none would live to see the creation of a worldwide revolutionary socialist society.

Exploring how international communism influenced women who operated beyond the party fold can offer new perspectives on the post-suffrage careers of feminists. Applying this lens in other historiographical contexts may further enhance an argument made here: that front organizations could prove better capable of harnessing the skills and channelling the political principles of veteran feminists than the Communist Parties themselves. Similarly, the Comintern's employment needs could be ably met by women political emigrants with prior experience of a transnational cause that relied on the printed word to spread its message. Moreover, the growing literature on women's internationalism in Britain and Ireland is enriched by a consideration of communism's influence on women campaigners in the interwar period beyond those commonly associated with the political left. Even those activists who were avowedly committed to a non-revolutionary conceptualization of feminism and internationalism operated in a world wherein the Soviet state claimed to have enacted women's liberation and designed tours seeking to prove this assertion. Feminists could reject or accept this claim, but they nonetheless often had to evaluate their strategies in response to it.

Many of the women central to this chapter emerged from two specific militant suffrage organizations: the Dublin membership of the IWFL and Pankhurst's ELFS. This suggests the central importance of a common

[84] For more on Cohen and her fate during the Stalinist terror, see F. Beckett, *Stalin's British Victims* (London, 2004).

social-political world and a shared experience of early enthusiasm for the Russian Revolution in encouraging later engagement with the Soviet experiment, either through involvement with front groups or political emigration. The anti-colonial undercurrent common to the IWFL and the ELFS appears to have been an important shared force channelling women into involvement with the resolutely anti-imperialist Comintern. The women considered herein, whether British women, Irish women or migrant women, often shared a past, ideals and transnational comradeships. The transnational turn in the historiography of interwar radical internationalism has shown that placing activists within such neat categories as 'British' and 'Irish' historical contexts can occlude the ties between activists and the wider networks of radicalism surrounding them. Whether at a public meeting for Irish hunger relief, on a boat bound for Leningrad or sitting in a Moscow office, many of these women could look around and recognize their suffrage comrades alongside them, gathered beneath the broad banner of a new revolutionary cause. Ultimately, the history of feminism and international communism is not just a story of Communist women and Communist Parties. It is a history of two vast movements, the women's movement and the communist movement, and the complex ways in which these two movements influenced, combatted, rejected and accepted one another.

Afterword: a tale of two centennials: suffrage, suffragettes and the limits of political participation in Britain and America*

Nicoletta F. Gullace

Emmeline Pankhurst could hardly have wished for better. Had she been alive to witness the boundless affection for the militant suffragettes one hundred years after the first British women received the vote, she would have discovered a legacy even she could never have imagined. While the suffrage victory was partial, granting female householders over thirty the right to vote, the exclusion of young working-class women was a compromise most suffragists reluctantly accepted.[1] That middle-class women would enjoy many of the same political privileges as middle-class men was a victory, even if not a total one. Though Pankhurst embraced the highly democratic 'soldier's vote', she, like many more moderate suffragists, conceded that propertyless women would have to wait.[2] This omission cost her very little in the adulatory celebrations of the WSPU during Britain's 2018 centenary extravaganza.[3]

Despite euphoria over the 1918 suffrage victory, the years after the partial enfranchisement of women were dispiriting for Pankhurst. Although still revered by her most loyal followers, she found herself under financial constraints, suffering from ill health due to hunger-striking in prison and

* Many thanks to Alexandra Hughes-Johnson, Lyndsey Jenkins and Susan Grayzel for very helpful editorial suggestions on earlier drafts of this essay. All websites re-accessed 11 Nov. 2020 unless otherwise indicated.

[1] L. E. Nym Mayhall, *The Militant Suffrage Movement: Citizenship and Resistance in Britain, 1860–1930* (Oxford, 2003), ch. 7. Female university graduates, Red Cross nurses who had served abroad and female military auxiliaries who had been in war zones were also enfranchised. N. F. Gullace, *"The Blood of Our Sons": Men, Women, and the Renegotiation of British Citizenship during the Great War* (New York, 2002), ch. 8.

[2] Gullace, *Blood of Our Sons*, ch. 8.

[3] L. E. Nym Mayhall, 'Think piece: commemoration and spectacle in the centenary of women's suffrage', *Theory, Culture, and Society*, 16 Oct. 2018 <https://www.theoryculturesociety.org/think-piece-commemoration-and-spectacle-in-the-centenary-of-womens-suffrage/>.

'Afterword: A tale of two centennials', in *The politics of women's suffrage: local, national and international dimensions, ed.* A. Hughes-Johnson and L. Jenkins (London, 2021), pp. 353–374.

burdened with three 'war babies' that she rashly adopted during a moral panic over illegitimacy.[4] More galling, perhaps, her darling Christabel, destined (she believed) to be the first woman in Parliament, lost the 1918 Smethwick election after standing as the 'coupon' candidate for the right-wing Women's Party in this solidly working-class district.[5] Sadly, she herself died in 1928 while campaigning as a Conservative candidate for the constituency of Whitechapel and St George's, less than a month before the Reform Act granting equal suffrage received Royal Assent. Avowedly anti-socialist, hierarchical and wedded to a nationalist agenda, many aspects of Mrs Pankhurst's politics were probably diametrically opposed to those held by the artists, activists and young women bedecked in purple, white and green flooding the streets in gay celebration of the suffragettes during the events of 2018.[6]

Ironically, crowds that heralded Emmeline Pankhurst and the WSPU for their bold and self-immolating campaign worshipped their militancy without very carefully examining their politics. As Laura Mayhall has noted, admiration for suffragette 'spectacle' often overshadowed a realistic sense of the groundwork prepared by the constitutionalist campaign or a true reckoning with the xenophobic thrust of the Pankhursts' movement by the end of the First World War.[7] While several excellent centennial exhibitions acknowledged constitutionalist contributions by Millicent Garrett Fawcett and others, the flamboyance of the militants seemed to capture public imagination, often making them the focus of events undertaken to generate positive public 'impact'.[8] The American women's suffrage centenary would unfold very differently. Occurring only two years later, the US centenary was reduced by COVID-19 lockdowns and overshadowed by renewed attention to the pernicious racial dynamics that tainted the US campaign in its later

[4] J. Purvis, *Emmeline Pankhurst: A Biography* (London, 2002), ch. 21.

[5] N. F. Gullace, 'Christabel Pankhurst and the Smethwick election: right wing feminism, the Great War, and the ideology of consumption', *Women's History Review*, xxiii (2014), 330–46.

[6] M. Pugh, *The Pankhursts* (London, 2001), chs. 14 and 15; V. Thorpe, 'Women of Britain march again to celebrate winning the vote,' *The Guardian*, US edition, 9 Jun. 2018 <https://www.theguardian.com/politics/2018/jun/09/women-processions-uk-cities-right-to-vote-centenary-celebration>.

[7] Nym Mayhall, 'Think piece: commemoration and spectacle'.

[8] 'Millicent Fawcett: statue of Suffragist unveiled', BBC News, 24 Apr. 2018 <https://www.bbc.com/news/uk-politics-43868925>. The discussion of the potential 'public impact' as a factor in receiving government grants for commemorative projects was a theme discussed at 'Women's Suffrage and Beyond: Local, National, and International Contexts', sponsored by Women in the Humanities, Oxford University, 4–5 Oct. 2018.

years – a sad betrayal of the movement's early abolitionist roots.[9] In the wake of the Black Lives Matter movement, it became much more difficult to celebrate a suffrage campaign that would leave many women of colour disenfranchised.[10] While the British women's suffrage centenary marked the 1918 victory as an unequivocal and inspiring triumph, the American centenary shrouded the decades-long campaign for the vote in its manifest failures – failures impossible to ignore during a bitter presidential election marked by pervasive voter suppression.[11]

The Nineteenth Amendment to the US Constitution, ratified on 18 August 1920, stated that 'the right of citizens to vote shall not be denied or abridged by the United States or by any State on account of sex'.[12] Stated in the negative – 'Shall not be denied … on account of …' – rather than in positive language that explicitly granted women the specified right, the law allowed constituencies to find a myriad of other reasons by which to prevent those deemed undesirable from casting a vote. As they had done to African American men, similarly enfranchised in the Fifteenth Amendment (1870), many states erected barriers to voting that ostensibly had nothing to do with race or sex, but which disproportionately disenfranchised the poor, the dispossessed and the formerly enslaved.[13]

The tarnished legacy of the American women's suffrage movement stems, in part, from Elizabeth Cady Stanton and Susan B. Anthony's disparaging

[9] A. Y. Davis, *Women, Race, & Class* (New York, 1983), ch. 1; R. Bleiweis, S. Phadke and J. Frye, '100 years after the 19th Amendment, the fight for women's suffrage continues', Center for American Progress, 18 Aug. 2020 <https://www.americanprogress.org/issues/women/news/2020/08/18/489651/100-years-19th-amendment-fight-womens-suffrage-continues/>.

[10] E. C. Dubois, *Suffrage: Women's Long Battle for the Vote* (New York, 2020), p. 288.

[11] The most common negative response from interviewees participating in Britain's suffrage centenary events was that women had not come far enough since the awarding of the vote. See N. F. Gullace, 'People's suffrage: artists, activists, and public celebration of the Suffrag(ette) Centenary', keynote lecture delivered at Women's Suffrage and Beyond Conference, 4 Oct. 2018; 'Why are Republicans So Afraid of Voters?', *The New York Times*, 1 Nov. 2020 <https://www.nytimes.com/2020/11/01/opinion/us-voting-rights-republicans.html?referringSource=articleShare>.

[12] '19th Amendment to the U.S. Constitution: Women's Right to Vote (1920)', U.S. Government Documents <https://www.ourdocuments.gov/doc.php?flash=false&doc=63> [accessed 29 Nov. 2020]; 'Women's suffrage and the 19th Amendment', U.S. National Archives <https://www.archives.gov/exhibits/featured-documents/amendment-19> [accessed 29 Nov. 2020].

[13] Dubois, *Suffrage*. I am grateful to Ellen Fitzpatrick for sharing insights on the significance of the constitutional language of the suffrage amendments. E. Foner, *The Second Founding: How the Civil War and Reconstruction Remade the Constitution* (New York, 2019).

responses to the proposed enfranchisement of African American men at a time when 'educated' white women were still without the vote.[14] In a bitter split, culminating in 1869, Lucy Stone's American Women's Suffrage Association embraced the extension of political rights to African American men, while suffragists led by Stanton and Anthony regarded the proposed legislation as an affront to white womanhood.[15] Although many American women today revere the 'suffragettes', buying commemorative stamps, downloading a judicial cookbook and heralding suffragists' fight for the vote, for historians, conflicts over the Fifteenth Amendment have often overshadowed the victories of the Nineteenth. Given the wording of legislation that prohibited one form of discrimination while never explicitly excluding another, the Nineteenth Amendment was destined to be as selective and discriminatory as the Fifteenth had been, leaving many Black women barred from the polls.[16] The use of this subtly evasive language was a compromise that all too many white, middle-class suffragists accepted to facilitate passage in the South of a constitutional amendment that might otherwise have failed.[17] Despite the fifty-year gap between these two franchise amendments, the triumph of women's suffrage is thus imbued with the betrayal of freedmen's ability to vote – a breach of faith which has adumbrated a more uncomplicated celebration of what *de facto* became middle-class white women's political enfranchisement.[18]

[14] Dubois, *Suffrage*, ch. 2. Wendell Phillips declared the Fifteenth Amendment to be 'the Negroes Hour', inciting Stanton to write a vitriolic letter to the editor of the *National Slavery Standard* where she decried the primacy of the Black male over the woman's vote. E. C. Stanton, 'The negroes hours', to the editor of the *New York Standard*, 26 Dec. 1865, reproduced in Davis, *Women, Race, & Class.*

[15] Anthony went so far as to tell Douglass in an 1869 debate that, 'if you will not give the whole loaf of justice and suffrage to an entire people, give it to the most intelligent first'. G. Bowers, 'Douglass vs. Anthony: the historical (and contemporary) debate between Black men and white women', TRR: Cultural Criticism Historical Archives, 4 July 2020 [20 May 1869 debate included] <https://therevolutionrelaunch.com/2020/07/04/douglass-vs-anthony-the-historical-and-contemporary-debate-between-black-men-and-white-women/> [accessed 29 Nov. 2020]; Dubois, *Suffrage*, ch. 2.

[16] E. DuBois, M. S. Jones, M. Sinha, B. Wineapple, and moderator L. Tetrault, 'Expanding democracy: the 19th Amendment and voting rights today', John F. Kennedy Presidential Library and Museum Virtual Forum, 28 Oct. 2020 <https://www.jfklibrary.org/events-and-awards/forums/10-28-expanding-democracy-forum-1> [accessed 28 Oct. 2020].

[17] This was the so-called 'southern-strategy'. Dubois, *Suffrage*, pp. 151–154.

[18] During and after the Civil War (1861–5), the federal government, under Reconstruction, passed legislation recognizing African Americans as citizens and awarding Black men the national right to vote in 1870. Because Reconstruction abruptly ended in 1877, Southern states began enacting legislation to disenfranchise Black men.

Long central to the historiography of American women's suffrage, the standoff between white suffragists and the Black male beneficiaries of the Fifteenth Amendment has dominated journalism, documentaries and museum websites, becoming a major focal point of American coverage of the suffrage centennial.[19] The 'marginalization' of Black women suffragists and the clash between the demand for sex equality and the need for racial justice emerged in force as the US debated how to honour the event. The 2019 insertion of a bronze likeness of Black feminist Sojourner Truth into a sculpture of Elizabeth Cady Stanton and Susan B. Anthony planned for Central Park only highlighted the fact that Black feminists had been eschewed in such company and did little to improve the battered reputation of America's women's suffrage movement.[20] While the American public might once have enjoyed an unequivocal celebration of women's rights as much as their British counterparts did, the public discussion of 'systemic racism' in 2020 left Americans much more inclined to accept the critical perspective on the suffrage movement.

Indeed, on both sides of the Atlantic, the crowds of 2020 showed far less interest in reverential celebration, focusing instead on an unseemly past drenched in racism, white supremacy and slavery. Following the murder of George Floyd at the hands of Minneapolis police, British sympathizers, demonstrating solidarity with US Black Lives Matter protests, toppled a statue of philanthropist slave-trader Edward Colston, throwing him into Bristol harbour.[21] More expressions of iconoclasm ensued; activists graffitied

[19] B. Staples, 'How the suffrage movement betrayed Black women', *The New York Times*, 28 July 2018 <https://www.nytimes.com/2018/07/28/opinion/sunday/suffrage-movement-racism-black-women.html>; PBS Teachers Lounge, 'One hundred years ago, all women in the United States were guaranteed the right to vote. FALSE', Unlearning History: The Women's Suffrage Movement, 30 Aug. 2020; United States National Park Service, 'Why the women's rights movement split over the 15th Amendment', Ulysses S. Grant National Historic Site <https://www.nps.gov/articles/000/why-the-women-s-rights-movement-split-over-the-15th-amendment.htm>.

[20] B. Staples, 'A whitewashed monument to women's suffrage: a sculpture that's expected to be unveiled in Central Park next year ignores the important contributions of Black women', *The New York Times*, 14 May 2019 <https://www.nytimes.com/2019/05/14/opinion/central-park-suffrage-monument-racism.html>; N. McGreevy, 'Why the first monument of real women in Central Park matters—and why it's controversial: today, New York City welcomed a public artwork honoring three suffragists: but some scholars argue that the statue obscures more than it celebrates', *Smithsonian Magazine*, 26 Aug. 2020 <https://www.smithsonianmag.com/smart-news/monument-controversy-women-pioneer-central-park-180975662/>.

[21] M. Foster, N. Bashir, R. Picheta and S. Cullinane, 'UK protesters topple statue of slave trader Edward Colston in Bristol', CNN, 8 June 2020 <https://www.cnn.com/2020/06/07/europe/edward-colston-statue-bristol/index.html>.

the words 'Was a Racist' on the base of Winston Churchill's likeness in Parliament Square,[22] protestors defaced statues of compromised dignitaries – echoing the toppling of Confederate monuments in the US – and even the staid administration of Edinburgh University agreed to re-name Hume Tower out of disgust for a passage where the philosopher opined that 'negroes' were 'naturally inferior to whites'.[23] As a number of public institutions reconsidered the conflict between their professed humanitarian values and their financial indebtedness to slavery, many considered sacrificing historic monuments to discredited forefathers as a symbolic (and relatively inexpensive) way to bow to the demands of 'anti-racist' protests and escape embarrassing accusations of hypocrisy.[24]

Compared with the ebullient celebration of the militant suffragettes in 2018, 2020 was not an auspicious moment for a centenary. America's women's suffrage centennial was thus muted, apologetic and often admonitory.[25] If 2018 had been a moment of feminist eruption, achieved in part by the momentum of #MeToo, 2020 was a year when the public scrutinized its painful racial past. The 1619 Project (linking Britain with its erstwhile colony in a bloody economic system founded on slavery), foregrounded the underlying 'erasure' evident in historical memory at the very moment police killings of young African Americans received more attention than ever before. Recognition of endemic inequality and hostility to reverential treatment of a tainted past triggered an international outburst, demanding national histories, foundational myths and public art be scrubbed of the

[22] 'Black Lives Matter protest: why was Churchill's statue defaced?' BBC News, 8 June 2020 <https://www.bbc.com/news/av/uk-england-london-52972531>.

[23] F. Waldmann, 'David Hume was a brilliant philosopher but also a racist involved in slavery', *The Scotsman*, 17 July 2020 <https://www.scotsman.com/news/opinion/columnists/david-hume-was-brilliant-philosopher-also-racist-involved-slavery-dr-felix-waldmann-2915908>.

[24] One of the most highly publicized harbingers of this trend in America was Yale University's renaming of Calhoun College. 'Yale changes Calhoun College's name to honor Grace Murray Hopper', Yale News, 11 Feb. 2017 <https://news.yale.edu/2017/02/11/yale-change-calhoun-college-s-name-honor-grace-murray-hopper-0>. This trend escalated in 2020, most notably with the city of Richmond, Virginia's removal of its Confederate monuments. 'Confederate memorials quietly removed from Virginia Capitol overnight', *The Washington Post*, 24 July 2020 <https://www.washingtonpost.com/local/virginia-politics/confederate-memorials-quietly-removed-from-virginia-capitol-overnight/2020/07/24/8d2a0dee-cced-11ea-bc6a-6841b28d9093_story.html>.

[25] N. Lennard, 'The troubling history — and unfinished work — of the Suffragists: with millions of people disenfranchised along racist lines, this is no time for uncomplicated commemoration', The Intercept, 26 Aug. 2020 <https://theintercept.com/2020/08/26/19th-amendment-womens-suffrage-racism-voting-rights/>.

vestiges of racism.[26] This shift left few historical figures with their reputations unscathed. Emmeline Pankhurst had escaped as the portcullis of historical commemoration slammed shut, but in America her white, middle-class counterparts would be judged for the indignant response of luminaries like Stanton and Anthony to the enfranchisement of male former slaves.[27]

The gyrations of public engagement with history over the past few years have reversed themselves with astonishing rapidity. On one hand, Britain's lugubrious commemoration of the First World War, seemingly impermeable to a more measured historical revisionism, gave way to the joyous finale of the women's suffrage celebration, symbolized by the rebellion of the militant suffragettes.[28] In both cases, the public desired stories of tragedy and triumph, resistant to historical nuance. While academic historians had a major role in consulting on these events, eminent 'talking heads' often found their more circumspect messages swept away by a sensationalistic historical imagination that resonated with a new generation of centenary consumers.[29]

In contrast to 2018, the zealous scrutiny of the past that emerged in 2020 left little room for heroes. The forgiveness once afforded historical figures for antiquated perspectives was no longer gamely bestowed by historians for whom 'the past was a foreign country' – socially, culturally and religiously different from our own and therefore to be judged on its own terms. If the British celebration can be faulted for uncritical pathos and ebullient lionization of flawed and under-analysed figures, the moral condemnation of yesterday's heroes for their failure to meet contemporary ethical standards has left very little to celebrate during the centennial of the Nineteenth Amendment.[30]

[26] N. Hannah-Jones, '1619 Project', *The New York Times*, 14 Aug. 2019 <https://www.nytimes.com/interactive/2019/08/14/magazine/1619-america-slavery.html>.

[27] K. A. Hamlin, 'How racism almost killed women's right to vote: women's suffrage required two constitutional amendments, not one', *The Washington Post*, 4 June 2019 <https://www.washingtonpost.com/outlook/2019/06/04/how-racism-almost-killed-womens-right-vote/>.

[28] 'U.K. women celebrate 100 years of voting rights', *The New York Times*, 10 June 2018 <https://www.nytimes.com/2018/06/10/world/europe/uk-women-suffrage.html>.

[29] For an excellent account of these tendencies in the '14–18 Now' First World War commemoration, see L. Noakes, 'Centenary (United Kingdom)', *International Encyclopedia of the First World War, 1914–1918*, 3 June 2019 <https://encyclopedia.1914–1918-online.net/article/centenary_united_kingdom>.

[30] J. Neuman, 'When white Suffragists campaigned against Black voting rights', blog post, 12 Jan. 2018 <https://www.johannaneuman.com/when-white-suffragists-campaigned-against-black-voting-rights/>.

In the context of such whiplash over the meaning of national histories, it is reassuring to engage with fascinating scholarship that neither praises nor buries the past, but brings to life the suffrage movement through rich, deep and 'thick' historical descriptions and contextualization. Editors Alexandra Hughes-Johnson and Lyndsey Jenkins have arranged a volume that offers both nuance and breadth. If the past is another country, *The Politics of Suffrage* gives us a passport to travel there and provides a Baedeker to the language, culture, fears and passions during incipient moments of emerging feminist activism. This detailed view of the suffrage movement carries us beyond both hagiography and vilification to an embedded understanding of brave and flawed figures contending with the issues of their own time and shaping our own.

Radicalism and respectability

In these chapters, past and present meet. If the celebrants of the 2018 Suffrage Centenary yearned for a relationship with an imagined past – often sartorially assuming the identities of Edwardian rebels through costume, pilgrimage and re-enactment – these chapters remind us that suffragists were viscerally engaged in an imagined future – one where the world would be transformed by the women's vote. These two groups met imperfectly in the more flamboyant expressions of the centenary celebration, necessitating a historicized representation of those who lived before. Eschewing the 'Downtonization' of Edwardian history, *The Politics of Suffrage* takes us from Jennifer Redmond's petitioners of the 1860s to Maurice Casey's surprising revelations about interwar communist allies, Charlotte Despard and Maude Gonne, showing us the range and breadth of a movement far more subtle, persistent and inclusive than the sensationalistic centenary events were able to convey. For all their fun, enthusiasm, pride and noble sentiments, Britain's suffrage centenary had a tendency to mould the past to the wishful thinking of the present. While engaging and informative – particularly about the material culture of the Edwardian years – centenary events often missed the obscurity, tedium and self-effacement in which many suffragists lived and worked.[31]

The chapters in this volume reveal how different that vision of transformation was for feminists, depending upon class, political sympathies, organizational affiliations, geographic situation and time.

[31] C. Hand, 'Suffragette City: an immersive new pop-up comes to Piccadilly Circus', Gasholder, 7 Mar. 2018 <https://www.gasholder.london/2018/03/07/suffragette-city-immersive-new-pop-comes-piccadilly-circus/>.

Rather than embracing the women's suffrage movement as a radical, feel-good campaign, monolithic in its leanings and ambitions, or vilifying the movement itself for the venalities of its leading lights, these chapters illuminate the lesser-known history of the suffrage movement, showing its complexity, enthusiasm and anguish. Extending the meaning of the political, these contributions, as Hughes-Johnson and Jenkins remind us, reveal how suffragists at the local, national and international level worked both within and outside existing structures as they sought to transform women's lived reality and the future through women's citizenship.

Each of the insightful chapters in *The Politics of Suffrage* contends that suffrage was a profoundly political movement and that the ramifications of its politics were prolific, extending into the cultural, social and personal spheres as well. Foundational scholarship on women's suffrage, such as the pioneering work of Sandra Stanley Holton, deftly reveals the way suffragists played the parliamentary game.[32] Holton's work on the Election Fighting Fund and the relationship between constitutionalists and the Labour Party demonstrates the symbiotic union of feminism and socialism in a marriage of convenience, where Labour pledged its commitment to the cause and access to the public sphere, while suffragists provided a broad political network and money to fight contested seats. This emphasis on the legislative and parliamentary history of suffrage is crucial to understanding how suffragists breached the ramparts of the law. By planting their flag, so to speak, in a compromise negotiated towards the end of the First World War, women over thirty gained a beachhead from which later generations would fight for the equal franchise, won ten years later in the 'Flapper vote' of 1928.[33]

While this story is well known, the articles in this volume complicate the political narrative of women's suffrage considerably, revealing the multifaceted suffrage relationship with class identity. As Katherine Connelly shows, adult suffragists insisted on the enfranchisement of working-class women and continued to struggle for equality well after the vote was ostensibly 'won' in 1918. Too many middle-class feminists, however, were willing to compromise on this point. Several chapters deftly explain how the seemingly innocuous embrace of suffrage on 'equal terms with men' in fact abandoned the mobile and propertyless working classes, who had suffered so much for the suffrage campaign. Commensurability between the patronizing attitude of 'Antis', who vowed to minister to the local

32 S. Stanley Holton, *Feminism and Democracy: Women's Suffrage and Reform Politics in Britain 1900–1918* (Cambridge, 1986).

33 C. Law, *Suffrage and Power, The Women's Movement, 1918–1928* (London, 2000).

poor, and the astonishingly similar perspective of 'limited suffragists', who believed votes for women of property would empower them to 'help' their less fortunate sisters, unmasks middle-class moral justification for their periodic abandonment of the political ambitions of the poor. Yet even the imperfect constitutional change enacted in 1918 transformed the electorate in powerful ways.[34]

The Politics of Suffrage picks up where legislative history left off, demonstrating how suffrage politics worked outside the walls of Parliament. From the quotidian drawing rooms of Glaswegian feminists, nervous to publish under their own names, to the international lecture halls where interwar activists spoke to large crowds in America, Finland and Russia, Sarah Pedersen and Karen Hunt reveal how moderates and radicals cross-fertilized the movement in unexpected ways. This range of action, both within and outside of conventional political structures – and taking place over the long expanse of suffrage history – offers crucial perspectives on women whose political tactics ranged from ostentatious respectability to outright rebellion.

This volume reminds us that suffrage unfolded with many contrasts. In girls' high schools, Helen Sunderland demonstrates how pupils enthusiastically debated the pros and cons of women's suffrage, respectably denouncing the militant campaign, while developing their own political perspectives alongside the reticent feminists who judiciously attempted to teach them without unduly influencing their views. These moderate feminists could hardly have contrasted more starkly with the passionate 'birth-strikers', vividly described by Tania Shew, who believed that in refusing to marry, 'know' men or give birth, they would bend patriarchal institutions to their will and win women the vote. While patient middle-class suffragists argued their case quietly in the feminist press, 'sex-strikers' embraced the idea of women's sexual power, exaggerated women's ability to withhold sexual consent and endorsed the transformative possibilities of separatist militancy, which contrasted profoundly with more maternalist, family-oriented claims justifying the need for women's votes.[35] Faith in persuasion was a hallmark of constitutional suffragists, contrasting sharply with the militant stress on 'deeds not words', particularly as more lady-like feminism met with disappointment. In contrast to the popular conviction that women's suffrage was primarily the result of militant radicalism, these

[34] H. L. Smith, *British Women's Suffrage Campaign, 1866–1928* (1998, rpt. London, 2010), ch. 6.

[35] S. Kingsley Kent, *Sex and Suffrage in Britain, 1860–1914* (London, 1990).

chapters show the tremendous range of tactics that expressed feminist aspirations beyond the vote itself.[36]

The varieties of political expression were by no means limited to middle-class feminists. In Canning Town, as Lyndsey Jenkins perceptively shows, working-class women looking for conviviality and a good tea frequented a short-lived but important suffrage club that ended each meeting by singing 'The Red Flag'. Poignantly intertwining the aspirations of feminism with hopes for a socialist society where women could find steady work, common women sought community and a means to create for themselves and their families a better life through the vote. While sharing with Sylvia Pankhurst's East London Federation of Suffragettes a desire for comradeship and a willingness to entertain suffrage militancy, the women of Canning Town were ultimately unable to resolve their fraying relationship with the increasing demands of the WSPU leadership. The East London Federation, as Katherine Connelly powerfully shows, thrived by adopting the settlement ideal and cultivating the aesthetic and personal aspiration of ordinary women. Sylvia's intention to live among the working classes in the East End anchored her locally and freed the East London Federation from the kind of outside patronage that had caused such turmoil in Canning Town.

While working-class women often differed as dramatically in their personal political perspectives as their middle-class counterparts, suffragists of different stripes, as Anna Muggeridge reminds us, found commonality not only in their quest for the vote, but in unifying over social problems. In many cases, women who differed in their party sympathies shared a common interest in infant and maternal welfare, perhaps explaining why such campaigns gained particular prominence after women received the vote. As it became clear that women would not be politically monolithic, campaigns for the common good could knit together diverse groups of women in a common cause.[37] The question of tactics, however, could divide them as well.

In Ireland, feminist Unionists, Home Rulers and nationalists petitioned a Westminster Parliament, the legitimacy of which many did not accept.[38] As Jennifer Redmond reminds us, the radicalism of the Irish militants stood in stark contrast to the parliamentary petitioners of the early suffrage

[36] J. Purvis and S. Stanley Holton (ed.), *Votes for Women* (London, 2000), pp. 1–12; and C. Bolt, 'The ideas of British suffragism', in *Votes for Women*, ed. J. Purvis and S. Stanley Holton (London, 2000), pp. 34–56.

[37] C. Beaumont, *Housewives and Citizens: Domesticity and the Women's Movement in England, 1928–1964* (Manchester, 2013).

[38] S. Pašeta, *Irish Nationalist Women, 1900–1918* (New York, 2013).

movement, careful not to stir disapproval. Instead, these respectable Anglo-Irish women, who favored liberal Home Rule, gently lobbied for the vote – part of the Irish story that has been eclipsed by the more dramatic militant movement that would emerge later on. Sharon Crozier-De Rosa reminds us, however, that imperial suffragists had a complex and fraught relationship with both the metropole and with each other. Racial dynamics and the question of imperial 'responsibility' towards non-European subjects ostensibly incapable of self-government were twisted to justify or negate the argument for women's suffrage. The complexity of suffrage in local, national and imperial contexts perhaps helps explain the splintering of the suffrage movement, as locality, ethnicity and political affiliation all played out in narratives about why women needed the vote.

Indeed, national, regional and local case studies reveal how difficult the cause of the national suffrage movement would have been without the initiative and organizational direction of local women, who faced their own division based on class, faith and political traditions. While paid organizers, versed in local languages and with local connections, could be a help, grassroots initiatives, we learn, were central to sowing suffrage in what Beth Jenkins reminds us had once been thought of as 'rather stony soil'.

Striking in these chapters is the contrast between local and international feminism.[39] If provincial suffragists tended to articulate their political perspective in terms of its ability to address local needs, the internationalists, as Karen Hunt deftly reveals, saw feminist aspirations as part of a global campaign. While Sylvia Pankhurst travelled to America, where she met a diverse group of collaborators who taught her about the cooperative settlement model, Dora Montefiore shuttled back and forth to Finland, the first European country to award women the vote. Like Pankhurst, she became wedded to the vision of adult suffrage, believing passionately in the need for socialist cooperation and oscillating between a desire to 'elevate' the working classes and belief in inter-class comradeship based on full moral equality.

The quest for communion with the working classes, framed in several chapters, reveals an egalitarian desire to overcome the patronizing stance of 'Lady Bountiful' and to engage with the working classes on their own terms. For Sylvia Pankhurst, the settlement ideal inspired her to open a cooperative home where women from all walks of life could live in an environment that promoted peace, beauty and justice. For most middle-class feminists, however, the quest to bring 'salvation' to the working

[39] J. Hannam, K. Holden and M. Auchterlonie, *International Encyclopedia of Women's Suffrage* (Santa Barbara, Calif., 2000), introduction.

class, while avoiding patronage, remained a constant challenge. Sos Eltis brilliantly shows how middle-class suffragists – the so-called 'weakest link' – enjoyed literary depictions of themselves that emphasized their beneficence and solidarity with the working classes, while preserving their elevated status as educated mistresses of the house. In their writings, middle-class feminist authors assumed the language of working-class characters, as they created sympathetic plebian figures who articulated feminist ideals in a common tongue. Women's deftness with the pen, and their use of words to manipulate emotions and sentiment, was also evident as suffragists attempted to shame those metropolitan politicians who refused to follow the lead of white settler colonies, like Australia and New Zealand, which had given women the vote. As Sharon Crozier-De Rosa tellingly shows, both imperial and metropolitan women were adept at manipulating the language and emotions of suffrage for their own ends.

The emphasis on feminism in action and the dedication to aspirations beyond the vote has characterized some of the most important historiography on women and war.[40] It should not surprise us, then, that *The Politics of Suffrage* has used the opportunity of the dual centenaries to enrich the suffrage history of the First World War. Alexandra Hughes-Johnson vividly shows that suffragists neither abandoned the quest for the vote in 1914, nor uniformly turned into patriots or anti-militarist pacifists. The militant Suffragettes of the WSPU and the Independent WSPU, while limited in their tactics by wartime restrictions, nevertheless agitated for the vote, protested against the war and never repudiated militant tactics. While Emmeline and Christabel Pankhurst disowned Sylvia for her anti-war work in the East End, British 'Anti' politicians used identical rhetoric to denounce the enfranchisement of Antipodean women, which they believed had resulted in the defeat of conscription. War made strange bedfellows, nowhere more so than in Ireland, where militant women who sympathized with the Easter Rising, Maurice Casey reminds us, were deeply attracted to the Russian Revolution, becoming part of a feminist wave of political tourism to Russia during and after 1917. While Mrs Pankhurst and Jessie Kenney travelled to Russia to review the Russian Women's Battalion of Death and to convince Russian women to stay in the war, Sylvia Pankhurst, Charlotte Despard and others came to witness the establishment of a just society based on communist principles.[41] That suffragettes turned into both Mosleyites and Marxist-Leninists reveals the radical poles of the suffrage movement and

[40] S. R. Grayzel, *Women's Identities at War: Gender, Motherhood, and Politics in Britain and France during the First World War* (Chapel Hill, N.C., 1999).

[41] Gullace, *Blood of Our Sons*, ch. 6.

demonstrates that feminist engagement with international politics extended well beyond participation in Liberal interwar humanitarianism.[42] Whether working on famine relief, maternal and child welfare or the liberation of the working classes, feminists carried their utopian vision of a just society into the public sphere. Their political aspirations – and the quest for meaningful paid work – dispersed feminists into an international environment that offered new opportunities.[43]

In its political focus, this edited collection reminds us of the many ways in which the politics of women's suffrage can be revealed culturally, socially and interpersonally. As suffragists pieced together inter-class alliances, feminists were often caught between a longed-for vision of an egalitarian future and a longed-for desire to distinguish themselves. For the women of Glasgow, middle-class women writers or the organizers of tea rooms for the poor, their self-fashioning as respectable members of society was key to their claim for citizenship in a society whose parameters and hierarchies they largely accepted. For those looking for a world transformed, rather than simply a world improved, the lure of internationalism would beckon during the interwar period, when more feminist activists than ever before worked in the international sphere. Whether feeding hungry children, resettling refugees or fostering communist transformation, women deployed skills acquired through years of suffrage agitation, and demonstrated a thick-skinned resilience to opposition, ridicule and deprivation as they embraced roles far outside the private sphere.[44]

The adage of second-wave feminism was 'the personal is political', and clearly from this volume we see that the political was also deeply personal. While many extraordinary feminists engaged politically in the national or international arena, other women busied themselves on the local level, often working within existing political structures or formulating new ones to create community, promote ideas of electoral equality and to advocate for policies beneficial to women.[45] Radicalism and respectability remained

[42] J. Gottlieb, *Feminine Fascism: Women in Britain's Fascist Movement, 1923–1945* (London, 2000); E. Ross, 'After the vote: women graduates look for work', paper delivered at Women's Suffrage & Beyond: Local, National, and International Contexts, sponsored by Women in the Humanities, Oxford University, 5 Oct. 2018.

[43] H. McCarthy, '"Shut against the woman and workman alike": democratizing foreign policy between the wars', in *The Aftermath of Suffrage: Women, Gender, and Politics in Britain, 1918–1945*, ed. J. Gottlieb and R. Toye (London, 2013), ch. 8.

[44] B. Cabanas, *The Great War and the Origins of Humanitarianism, 1918–24* (Cambridge, 2014), esp. ch. 5.

[45] K. Hunt and J. Hannam, 'Towards an archaeology of interwar women's politics: the local and the everyday', *The Aftermath of Suffrage: Women, Gender, and Politics in Britain, 1918–1945*, ed. J. Gottlieb and R. Toye (London, 2013), pp. 124–141.

in tension, as different constituents of the women's suffrage movement saw the path to the franchise tied to tactics that either confirmed or destroyed socially accepted views of womanly conduct. Different perspectives could also lead suffragists down very different political paths. Not only did the Pankhurst sisters find each other on the opposite sides of the political centre, but some former militants embraced the radical right, while others committed themselves to international communism from the time of the Russian Revolution until 1939.

Despite the cross-fertilization of the British and American women's suffrage movements, it is not surprising that such an important centennial was celebrated so differently in Britain and the United States. The strong connection between British and American suffragists, who travelled and learnt from one another, spoke in each other's countries and occasionally intermarried, was forged long before women in both nations received the vote in the heady aftermath of the First World War.[46] Yet, the celebration of the two centenaries could not have been more different. Few ordinary Britons could have missed the suffragettes in 2018 or have been unaware of why young women roamed the streets in straw boaters, brandishing signs decrying gender pay-gaps and sexual harassment.[47] In contrast, few Americans probably even realized that a similar milestone had passed in the summer of 2020. Despite museum exhibits, articles, websites and an occasional handful of white-clad women trying to 'get out the vote', it would have been easy to miss an event treated by many American feminists with more embarrassment than joy.[48] At the hundredth anniversary of the ratification of the Nineteenth Amendment on 18 August 2020, the President of the United States was already threatening to contest

[46] S. Stanley Holton, 'From anti-slavery to suffrage militancy: the Bright Circle, Elizabeth Cady Stanton and the British women's movement', in *Suffrage and Beyond: International Feminist Perspectives*, ed. C. Daley and M. Nolan (Auckland, 1994).

[47] 'Suffragettes exhibition in London's Trafalgar Square draws crowds: the Pop-Up Make-A-Stand exhibition features images of 59 key campaigners', *The Guardian*, 6 Feb. 2018 <https://www.theguardian.com/uk-news/2018/feb/06/suffragettes-exhibition-in-londons-trafalgar-square-draws-crowds>; Mark Kerrison/Alamy Live News – Image ID: PoXYCo, Alamy Stock Photos <https://www.alamy.com/london-uk-10th-june-2018-people-dressed-in-suffragette-costume>.

[48] H. Jewel, 'How racism tore apart the early suffrage movement', episode 2 of 'The Fight', *The Lily* and *The Washington Post* <https://www.thelily.com/how-racism-tore-apart-the-early-womens-suffrage-movement/>. Common Core Standards, 'Women's suffrage, racism and intersectionality', ADL Anti-Bias Education Plan <https://www.adl.org/education/educator-resources/lesson-plans/womens-suffrage-racism-and-intersectionality>.

his re-election should he dislike the outcome of the vote.[49] As students, naturalized citizens, former felons and, most of all, African Americans faced the suppression of their votes, the Nineteenth Amendment seemed like just one more flawed attempt to embrace the democratic ideal that Britain so full-throatedly celebrated two years before.[50] A celebration of suffrage is difficult to rejoice in a crumbling democracy. While in retrospect such fears may appear overblown, the half-hearted celebration of women's suffrage in the US grows out of America's unresolved relationship with race and the increasingly apparent electoral legacy of Jim Crow.[51] America's most famous suffragists were complicit in the creation of a constitutional amendment that left states able to exclude not only African Americans, but many other ethnic groups summarily prevented from exercising the vote.[52] Unlike Britain, where the deficiencies of the 1918 Act were resolved domestically, the centenary of the Nineteenth Amendment has taken place at a moment when the promise of universal suffrage seems more elusive than ever.[53]

'I'd rather be a rebel than a slave'

The wound Black feminists experienced at the hands of white suffragists was unexpectedly scratched open during the 2015 premiere of the British

49 E. Lach, 'What happens if Donald Trump fights the election results?' *The New Yorker*, 21 Aug. 2020 <https://www.newyorker.com/news/campaign-chronicles/what-happens-if-donald-trump-fights-the-election-results>.

50 F. Manjoo, '2020 should be the last time we vote like this', *The New York Times*, 4 Nov. 2020 <https://www.nytimes.com/2020/11/04/opinion/election-day-voting.html?referringSource=articleShare>; T. McCoy, 'Election cliffhanger captivates world, prompts fears for fate of U.S. democracy', *The Washington Post*, 5 Nov. 2020 <https://www.washingtonpost.com/world/2020/11/04/world-reaction-us-election-2020/>.

51 Lennard, 'The troubling history'; Foner, *Second Founding*, ch. 4 and epilogue.

52 T. Brown, 'Celebrate Women's suffrage, but don't whitewash the movement's racism', ACLU 100 Years, 24 Aug. 2018 <https://www.aclu.org/blog/womens-rights/celebrate-womens-suffrage-dont-whitewash-movements-racism>.

53 E. Levits, 'Trump's voter-suppression strategy is a crisis (even if it backfires)', *New York Intelligencer*, 29 Oct. 2020 <https://nymag.com/intelligencer/2020/10/historic-voter-turnout-trump-voter-suppression.html>; R. Levinson-King, 'US election 2020: why it can be hard to vote in the US', BBC News, 20 Oct. 2020 <https://www.bbc.com/news/election-us-2020-54240651>; A. Rao, voting rights editor in New York, P. Dillon in Madison, Wisconsin, K. Kelly in Philadelphia and Z. Bennett in Miami Beach, Florida, 'Is America a democracy? If so, why does it deny millions the vote?' *The Guardian*, 7 Nov. 2019 <https://www.theguardian.com/us-news/2019/nov/07/is-america-a-democracy-if-so-why-does-it-deny-millions-the-vote> and 'Why this election calls into question whether America is a democracy', *The Guardian*, 20 Oct. 2020 <https://www.theguardian.com/us-news/2020/oct/30/is-america-a-democracy-us-election-fight-to-vote>.

film *Suffragette*. 'I'd rather be a rebel than a slave', uttered by Mrs Pankhurst at a Women's Rights rally in 1913, caused outrage when it appeared on a tee-shirt worn by Meryl Streep for a *Time Out* cover advertising the film. On Twitter, the photo inspired ire over the apparent racial insensitivity which for some 'carried connotations of the American history of slavery and Confederate rebellion'. Critics of the *Time Out* cover felt that the publicity around the film constituted a 'politics of erasure' which excised 'women of colour' from feminist history.[54] As Twitter user Jamilah Lemieux noted caustically, 'White women have said a lot of terrible things over the course of history, doesn't mean you wear it on a shirt.' *Time Out* responded defensively, noting that the article had been read by at least half a million people in the UK who did not complain. 'The original quote was intended to rouse women to stand up against oppression', noted the editors. '[I]t is a rallying cry and absolutely not intended to criticize those who have no choice but to submit to oppression…'[55]

Despite such complaints, the centenary celebration three years later did little to remedy this omission or to reflect the critical depth of scholarship on issues of race and empire in the British suffrage movement.[56] While women of colour in the Empire may have received the beneficence of white British-born feminists, they enjoyed few of their rights.[57] In keeping with its celebratory ethos, centenary exhibits often acknowledged feminist diversity by focusing on the extraordinary career of such celebrities as Princess Sophia Duleep Singh – militant goddaughter of Queen Victoria, tenant of Hampton Court and feminist tax resister, who in 1913 threw herself in front of Prime Minister Asquith's car while holding a poster reading, 'Give women the vote!' Her sari, on loan from a private collection, was one of the highlights of the British Library suffrage exhibit that year.[58] As Sumita

[54] R. Carroll, 'Suffragette's publicity campaign and the politics of erasure', *The Guardian*, 5 Oct. 2015 <https://www.theguardian.com/film/2015/oct/05/suffragette-film-publicity-campaign-erasure-feminism>; S. Mukherjee, *Indian Suffragettes: Female Identities and Transnational Networks* (Oxford, 2018).

[55] M. Gajanan, 'Meryl Streep and co-stars attract backlash over suffragette t-shirt slogan', *The Guardian*, 5 Oct. 2015 <https://www.theguardian.com/film/2015/oct/05/meryl-streep-backlash-suffragette-t-shirt-slogan>.

[56] I. Fletcher, P. Levine and L. E. Nym Mayhall (ed.), *Women's Suffrage in the British Empire: Citizenship, Nation and Race* (London, 2000); S. Mukherjee, *Indian Suffragettes* (Oxford, 2018).

[57] A. Burton, *Burdens of History: British Feminists, Indian Women, and Imperial Culture, 1865–1915* (Chapel Hill, N.C., 2000).

[58] British Library, 'Suffragette Sophia Duleep Singh', Learning Timelines: Sources from History <https://www.bl.uk/learning/timeline/item124196.html>; B. Alsop, 'Suffrage

Mukherjee has noted, however, the women of the British Empire were involved in a global movement, far more variegated and diverse than the focus on Singh would fully reveal.[59]

Given that both Britain and the United States had fraught relationships with vast non-white populations, why did the failure of many white women suffragists to confront the issue of race play so much larger a role in the US celebration of 2020 that it did in the British suffrage centenary in 2018? In part, this was because, domestically, the British franchise was more clearly fractured by class than by race, and the obvious injustices of the 1918 restrictions were addressed relatively quickly. While the Representation of the People Act of 1918 enfranchised women along explicit lines of class and age, the British rectified this injustice ten years after, awarding the majority of women in the United Kingdom the vote on equal terms with men.[60] Although, as Susan R. Grayzel reminds us in this volume, many women of colour in the British Empire would have to wait for independence to gain the full rights of citizenship, consecutive Reform Acts gradually diminished the difference between domestic electors until the end of plural voting after the Second World War.[61] Neither the 1918 nor the 1928 Reform Acts succeeded in giving women the kind of full equality many suffragists had dreamed of, but they did allow ever broader sectors of the female population to exercise the vote. They also began to roll back restrictive voter registration laws that had vitiated much of the power of British Reform Acts in 1867, 1884 and, for women, in 1918.[62]

America's omissions were not resolved with similar reforms. Despite consecutive constitutional amendments removing electoral disabilities, the US electoral system is plagued with inequalities ranging from hours-long voting lines in inner-cities to inscrutable bureaucratic 'red tape' that constitute, even today, what CNN's John Blake calls 'Jim Crow 2.0'.[63] In a conference on 'Expanding Democracy: The Nineteenth Amendment and Voting Rights Today', held at the Kennedy Library in Boston on 28 October

objects in the British Museum', The British Museum Blog, 23 Feb. 2018 <https://blog.britishmuseum.org/suffrage-objects-in-the-british-museum/>.

59 Mukherjee, *Indian Suffragettes*.

60 J. Alberti, '"A symbol and a key": the suffrage movement in Britain, 1918–1928', in *Votes for Women*, ed. J. Purvis and S. Stanley Holton (London, 2000), pp. 267–290.

61 Plural voting was gradually trimmed and finally abolished in Northern Ireland, its final holdout, in 1968.

62 Gullace, *Blood of our Sons*, pp. 185 and 248.

63 J. Blake, 'Four ways "Jim Crow 2.0" is shaping this presidential election', CNN, 1 Nov. 2020 <https://www.cnn.com/2020/11/01/us/voter-suppression-jim-crow-blake/index.html>.

2020, several of America's leading historians of citizenship inadvertently demonstrated why the constitutional amendment removing disabilities based on sex has not generated the same type of popular enthusiasm the suffrage centennial in Great Britain so manifestly did.[64] Despite the efforts of libraries and museums to honour the women who raised heaven and earth to extend women the vote, the centennial celebration in the US occurred during one of the most blatant moments of voter suppression since the passage of the Voting Rights Act in 1965.[65]

Although both Susan B. Anthony and Sojourner Truth regarded the franchise as implicit in the 'equal protection clause' of the Constitution – each attempting to vote in 1872 – Anthony was arrested for successfully casting a presidential ballot in Rochester, New York, a crime for which she was pardoned by Donald Trump in one of his few acknowledgements of the suffrage centenary.[66] While the Fifteenth Amendment attempted to enfranchise Black men by removing disabilities based on 'race, color, or previous condition of servitude', with the abrupt end of Reconstruction in 1877, courts prioritized the states' right to delimitate who should vote, allowing exclusions on a myriad of other grounds such as poll taxes, literacy tests, grandfather clauses or criminal history.[67] As one African American interviewee recalled of her experiences trying to register to vote in 1940s Georgia, the white men overseeing the voter rolls would 'point to a jar of jelly beans on a nearby table and ask … "How many black jelly beans are in a jar? How many red ones in there?'" With each incorrect answer, she, like many other African Americans, lost the opportunity to register for a ballot.[68] Unlike the right to bear arms, stated unequivocally in the Second Amendment, the removal of disabilities based on race or sex could

[64] Kennedy Library Virtual Forum, 28 Oct. 2020.

[65] American Civil Liberties Union, 'Fighting voter suppression' <https://www.aclu.org/issues/voting-rights/fighting-voter-suppression>; 'Let people vote: our fight for your right to vote during 2020', 14 Oct. 2020 <https://www.aclu.org/news/voting-rights/let-people-vote-our-fight-for-your-right-to-vote-during-2020/>.

[66] DuBois et al., 'Expanding democracy'; White House Press Secretary, 'Statement from the Press Secretary regarding the pardon of Susan B. Anthony', 19 Aug. 2020 <https://www.whitehouse.gov/briefings-statements/statement-press-secretary-regarding-pardon-susan-b-anthony/>; Susan B. Anthony Museum, 'Susan B. Anthony Museum rejects President Trump's pardon of the Suffragist', 20 Aug. 2020 <https://www.npr.org/2020/08/20/904321406/susan-b-anthony-museum-rejects-president-trumps-pardon-of-the-suffragette>; M. Jones, Kennedy Library Virtual Forum, 28 Oct. 2020.

[67] T. Smith, 'Timeline: voter suppression in the US from the Civil War to today', ABC News, 20 Aug. 2020 <https://abcnews.go.com/Politics/timeline-voter-suppression-us-civil-war-today/story?id=72248473>.

[68] Blake, 'Jim Crow 2.0'; Foner, *Second Founding*, ch. 4 and epilogue.

easily – and, the courts opined, legally – be replaced by some other excuse to deny people the vote.

As Ellen Carol DuBois has noted, while the Nineteenth Amendment eliminated sex as a legal disqualification for the vote, it allowed African American, Native American and many immigrant women to be excluded from the franchise, thanks to other bars erected in lieu of an explicit barrier based on sex.[69] Although white women across many western states had been able to vote in presidential elections, thanks to progressive state constitutions, the federal amendment was ratified only when the mother of a young Tennessee politician admonished him to vote accordingly, winning Tennessee by one vote. As enormous as this victory appeared to contemporaries, it only prohibited a sex bar to enfranchisement and never guaranteed an unassailable right to vote on the firmer grounds of US citizenship.[70]

The US women's suffrage centenary, coming on the eve of a highly contentious presidential election, was thus difficult to celebrate unequivocally. Fought in a legal environment where the Civil Rights protections of 1965 had been recently undone by a conservative Supreme Court, the prospects of American democracy had rarely seemed bleaker. As Eric Foner notes, the 1965 Voting Rights Act 'restored the suffrage to millions of black southerners', following a history of targeted voter suppression in the Jim Crow South. Emanating from the Civil Rights-centred jurisprudence of the liberal Warren Court (1953–1969), the Act held states accountable for interference with the voting rights of their Black citizens. In 2013, however, the Supreme Court ruled that such oversight was no longer necessary. In the *Shelby County v. Holder* decision, the court 'invalidated the Voting Rights Act's requirement that certain jurisdictions with long histories of racial discrimination in voting obtain prior federal approval before changing voting rules'.[71] Almost immediately, photo-ID laws sprung up, often biased towards the presumed politics of the holders – in Texas, for example, allowing gun licences, but prohibiting student IDs.[72] In the midst of a tight presidential race, state legislatures, with the help of the courts, allowed Alabama to prohibit curb-side voting for the disabled, upheld Texas's decision to allow only one official ballot drop-box for counties the size of a European country and negated Florida's referendum

[69] DuBois, Kennedy Library Virtual Forum, 28 Oct. 2020.

[70] DuBois, *Suffrage*, p. 276. Radical Republican George W. Julian in 1869 proposed an amendment that would make US citizenship the grounds for enfranchisement, but this failed to gain the necessary traction at the time. The Fourteenth Amendment seemed to carry such a protection already, but it was not interpreted as such by courts.

[71] Foner, *Second Founding*, epilogue.

[72] Kennedy Library Virtual Forum, 28 Oct. 2020.

to allow voting rights to felons who had served their sentences.[73] Indeed, in recent US elections, voters who queued for hours found they had been 'culled' from the rolls, ostensibly because they had not voted recently. This tactic for reducing 'fraud' by eliminating the names of dead or re-districted electors in fact disenfranchised thousands of legitimate voters, falling particularly heavily on the young and minorities, who changed address more frequently.[74]

As record numbers of people signed up for absentee voting due to the COVID-19 pandemic, Donald Trump vociferously questioned the validity of mail-in ballots.[75] During the 2020 presidential election, Democrats and Republicans wrangled over whether ballot envelopes must be notarized, the acceptable post-mark date for mailed ballots and the arrival date by which a ballot could be counted, which varied state by state. To make matters worse, Trump's postal appointee slowed delivery of mail with a series of budget cuts, which stripped the US Post Office of its ability to deliver ballots promptly.[76] Although House Speaker Nancy Pelosi tried to halt the removal of essential postal sorting machinery, millions of mail-in ballots poured into polling centers, causing official tallies to come in late. Donald Trump encouraged armed militias to act as election 'observers' and eventually contested the election, claiming that thousands of ballots had come in late and should be rejected.[77] Amid court rulings that allow states to police their own electoral

[73] A. Liptak, 'Supreme Court bars curbside voting in Alabama', *The New York Times*, 26 Oct. 2020 <https://www.nytimes.com/2020/10/21/us/supreme-court-curbside-voting-alabama.html>; D. Montgomery, 'The Texas Supreme Court upholds the governor's order for a single ballot drop box per county', *The New York Times*, 28 Oct. 2020 <https://www.nytimes.com/2020/10/28/us/elections/the-texas-supreme-court-upholds-the-governors-order-for-a-single-ballot-drop-box-per-county.html>; P. Mazzei, 'Ex-felons in Florida must pay fines before voting, Appeals Court rules', *The New York Times*, 11 Sept. 2020 <https://www.nytimes.com/2020/09/11/us/florida-felon-voting-rights.html>.

[74] M. Wines, 'Culling voter rolls: battling over who even gets to go to the polls', *The New York Times*, 25 Nov. 2017 <https://www.nytimes.com/2017/11/25/us/voter-rolls-registration-culling-election.html>; M. Rourke, 'The messy politics of voter purges', PEW, 25 Oct. 2019 <https://www.pewtrusts.org/en/research-and-analysis/blogs/stateline/2019/10/25/the-messy-politics-of-voter-purges>.

[75] E. Kiely and R. Rieder, 'Trump's repeated false attacks on mail-in ballots', FactCheck.Org: A Project of the Annenberg Public Policy Center, 25 Sept. 2020 <https://www.factcheck.org/2020/09/trumps-repeated-false-attacks-on-mail-in-ballots/>.

[76] E. Larson, 'US ballot delivery delays are not illegal, Postal Service argues', Bloomberg, Oct. 27, 2020 <https://www.aljazeera.com/economy/2020/10/27/bbus-ballot-delivery-delays-arent-illegal-postal-service-argues>.

[77] S. Dewan, 'Armed observers, chants of '4 more years' at polls: is that legal?', *The New York Times*, 30 Oct. 2020 <https://www.nytimes.com/2020/10/30/us/poll-watching-intimidation.html?referringSource=articleShare>.

laws, to practise shameless gerrymandering based on party lines and to make it difficult for minorities to cast their votes, it is perhaps not surprising that the centennial of the Nineteenth Amendment has been a muted affair.[78]

While Emmeline Pankhurst might have been gratified with the encomiums to WSPU radicalism during the height of the centenary, none of the chapters in this impressive volume focus on the militant campaign of Emmeline and Christabel Pankhurst. Instead, the volume avoids both the most sensational and the least progressive manifestations of the British suffrage movement, making room for something more subtle and arguably more meaningful.[79] Despite the tremendous success of the British women's suffrage centenary, by 2020 Americans were largely unable to unequivocally embrace even worthy suffrage efforts. Lacking the flamboyance of the British militants and grappling with the embarrassing implications of white chauvinism in a society revolving on the axis of race, the US failed to launch anything that could be called a celebration. Although female Democrats sported suffragette-inspired white pantsuits and young women in Rochester, New York proclaimed reverence for Susan B. Anthony by placing their 'I voted' stickers on her gravestone on election day, the perceived 'sellout' of African Americans by the suffragists has left a bitter taste.[80] The two suffrage centennials, marking the achievements of a pair of deeply entwined political movements, illustrate the eventual success of one nation to produce a functioning modern democracy, while the other still struggles to do the same. Despite their many shortcomings, the heirs of British suffrage deserved their party; sadly, their American counterparts can only imagine what a celebration of unfettered democracy must be like.

[78] K. Soffen, 'How racial gerrymandering deprives Black people of political power', *The Washington Post*, 9 June 2016 <https://www.washingtonpost.com/news/wonk/wp/2016/06/09/how-a-widespread-practice-to-politically-empower-african-americans-might-actually-harm-them/>; P. Williams, 'Supreme Court allows gerrymandering in North Carolina, Maryland, setting back reform efforts', NBC News, 27 June 2019 <https://www.nbcnews.com/politics/supreme-court/supreme-court-allows-gerrymandering-north-carolina-maryland-n1014656>.

[79] Mayhall, 'Commemoration and spectacle'.

[80] L. Borrelli-Persson, 'For a history-making moment, Kamala Harris wears suffragette white', *Vogue*, 8 Nov. 2020 <https://www.vogue.com/article/for-a-history-making-moment-kamala-harris-wears-suffragette-white-suit>; L. March, 'Visitors flock to Susan B. Anthony's Grave to mark a moment for women', *The New York Times*, 8 Nov. 2020 <https://www.nytimes.com/live/2020/11/07/us/election-results?referringSource=articleShare#visitors-flock-to-susan-b-anthonys-grave-to-mark-a-moment-for-women>.

Index

CPSIA information can be obtained
at www.ICGtesting.com
Printed in the USA
LVHW051320181121
703543LV00002B/5

9 781912 702961